George W. Conklin

Handy Manual of Useful Information and World's Atlas

Vol. 1

George W. Conklin

Handy Manual of Useful Information and World's Atlas
Vol. 1

ISBN/EAN: 9783337371081

Printed in Europe, USA, Canada, Australia, Japan

Cover: Foto ©Lupo / pixelio.de

More available books at **www.hansebooks.com**

CONKLIN'S
HANDY MANUAL

—OF—

USEFUL INFORMATION

AND

WORLD'S ATLAS.

FOR

Mechanics, Merchants, Editors, Lawyers, Printers, Doctors, Farmers, Lumbermen, Bankers, Bookkeepers, Politicians and all classes of workers in every department of human effort; also a compilation of facts for ready reference on 2,000 subjects, being an epitome of matters Historical Statistical, Biographical, Political, Geographical, and of general interest.

A Universal Hand-Book for Ready Reference.

Compiled by PROF. GEO. W. CONKLIN,
Of the Hamilton University.

Copyright, 1888,
By LAIRD & LEE.

CHICAGO, ILL.:
LAIRD & LEE, PUBLISHERS,
LAKESIDE BUILDING.

INDEX.

USEFUL INFORMATION	Index Page	4
MAPS	" "	12
DESCRIPTION OF MAPS, ETC.	" "	13

INDEX TO USEFUL INFORMATION.

PAGE.

A List of the Principal Officers of the U. S. Government and Salaries Paid to Them	15
A Table of Daily Savings at Compound Interest	18
A Woman's Chances to Marry	166
Age and Growth of Trees	60
Air, Composition of	52
Air Line Distances from Washington to Various Parts of the World	22
Alpine Pass—The	50
Alpnach—The Slide of	49
American Coal Fields	209
American Wars	97
Amount of Barbed Wire Required for a Fence	68
Amount of Paint Required for a Given Surface	26
Amount of Oil in Seeds	153
Andersonville Prison	39
Animals—Age of	50
Aqueducts, Famous	53
Armies and Navies of the Principal Nations	141-142-143
Army of the United States	143
Ascents of the Alps	49
Author's Successes	315
Autograph Album Verses	232, 233, 235, 236, 286
Average Rainfall in the United State	67
Average Temperature in the United States	66
Average Weight of Americans	35
Babel—The Tower of	53
Banking Statistics—Aggregate Capital and Deposits	104
" " —Condition of the New York Banks	163
" " —National Banks in the U. S.	102
Barnum's Museums	217
Baseball	217
Baseball Record	259
Battering Rams—Ancient	51
Bell—The Liberty	78
Best Records in Sporting Matters	259, 266
Big Trees	316
Billiards—The Largest Sum Ever Played For	218
Birds—Ranks of Melody In	50
Blondin's Great Feat	217
Board Measurements	246
Books—Number Published	71
Bricks and Brick Layers	51
Bricks in a Cubic Yard—Number of	51
Bricks in a Rod—Number of	51

	PAGE.
Bridge—The Largest	74
Bridges—Notable	38, 39
Brooklyn Suspension Bridge	217
Builders' Estimating Tables	23
Calendar for finding what day any date will fall on	76, 77
California's Big Trees	73
Cannon Balls—Speed of	51
Capacities, Sizes and Weights of Copper	256
Carpenters', Plasterers' and Bricklayers' Work—Estimates	25
Carrying Capacity of Freight Cars	164
Cavern—The Largest	75
Center of Population in the U. S.	92
Certificates of Deposit	174
Charcoal and Charred Timbers	52
Chinese Palace Library	98
Cholera	79, 82
Church Membership	316
Clearing House Clearances	161
Coal and Iron—When First Used	209
Coal Mines—The Deepest	52
Coal Mines—Temperature in	52
Coins—Value of Foreign	227, 228
Coliseum at Rome, The	53
Colors—Symbolic Meaning of	63
Comparative Cost of Freight by Water and Rail	63
Comparative Light Derived From Gas and Oils	52
Composition of Solders	35
Commercial Statistics of New York	160, 164
Commercial Travelers—Tax on	279
Common Carriers	177
Condor—The	51
Contagious Diseases	87, 88
Copyright Laws of the United States	215
Cost of Articles by the Piece from One to One Dozen	226
Cost of Emancipation	68
Cost of Pennsylvania Passenger Railroad Car	63
Cost of Painters' Work	29
Cost of Small Quantities of Hay	153
Cost of Tin Roofing	36, 37
Cotton Crop for Fifty Years	73
Cotton Exchange Transactions	160
Crime—Tendency to Outgrow	230
Currency of the United States	102
Custom House Transactions	161
Derivation of Our Language	316
Desert—The Largest	75
Diameters, Circumference and Areas of Circles	260
Diamond Cutting	150
Dietetic Economies—Practical	59
Digestion—Time Required	89
Dimensions of an Acre	26
Divorces	315

	PAGE.
Divorce Laws of all the States and Territories.............	105
Drafts...	175
Dredging Machines—Capacity of.........................	51
Dry Goods Imports..162,	164
Ducks—Speed Attained by Wild.........................	52
Due Bills...	174
Durability of Different Woods...........................	279
Duties—United States....................................	193
Dynamic Power of Various Foods........................	58
Dynamite—Force Exerted By.............................	230
Empire—The Largest.....................................	217
Engineering Achievements................................ 53,	54
Equestrians—Laws Governing............................	182
Estimates of Materials for Building.......................	29
Excessive Heat in the Past...............................	298
Expectation of Life......................................	307
Facts About the Human Body............................	270
Facts for Housekeepers...................................	76
Facts from the Census...................................	96
Facts Worth Knowing....................................	167
Falls of Montmorenci....................................	50
Falls of Niagara... 50,	56
Falls of Yosemite Valley.................................	50
Falls of Avre in Bavaria.................................	50
Farmers' Statistics.......................................153, 154,	155
Fast Milers of 1887.....................................	151
Fast Passages of Ocean Steamships.......................137, 138,	139
Fastest Railroad Time....................................	18
Fastest Time on Record	218
Fat, Water and Muscle Properties of Food...............	223
Fictitious Names of States...............................	158
Fictitious Names of Cities................................158,	159
Fineness of United States Coins..........................	316
Fire Extinguisher	52
Fires—Great 188, 205,	249
Fisk—Date James Fisk Was Shot........................	188
Flood—Date of the......................................	95
Floor, Wall and Roof Measures...........................	29
Food for Cattle..	153
Foreign Nations and their Rulers..................206, 207,	208
Foreign Coins—Value of.............................227,	228
Forts—the Greatest......................................	74
French Marriages..	109
Friction—The Law of....................................	54
Frost in Siberia..	52
Gas—Pressure of Natural...............................	52
Gestation—Period of in Animals..........................	50
Geological Facts...	55
Gold and Silver Produced in the United States...........229,	230
Gold—Beating...	315
Gold Leaf...	315
Gold—Value of a Ton...................................	157
Governors' Salaries, Terms of Office and State Capitals...156-	157

	PAGE.
Grain Exports from New York	160
Granite Column — The Greatest in History	54
Great Eastern Steamer	74, 111
Greek Phalanx — The Ancient	51
Gun — The Largest in the United States	217
Health Hints	82, 87, 88, 89, 90
Heat and Cold	283, 284
Heat of the Human Body	52
Heart — The Action of the	52
Height of Principal Monuments and Towers	39
Highest Mountains in the World	65
High Bridge and Obelisk in England	205
Historical Events, Principal	112–121
Horses — Durability of	63
Hot Springs — Origin of	52
Hotel Guests	177
Hottest Place on the Globe	53
How Ancient Rome was Supplied with Water	53
How to Raise a Drowned Body	61
How to Get Rid of Rats	61
How to Conduct a Successful Business	209
How to Remove Rust	209
How to Make 32 Kinds of Solder	209
How Sound Travels	212
How to Repair Cracked Bells	212
How to Test the Quality of Steel	212
How to Destroy the Effect of Acid on Clothes	212
How to Wash Silverware	212
How to Cleanse Brushes	213
How to Keep Meat Fresh in Summer	213
How to Write Inscriptions on Metal	213
How to Test the Vitality of Seeds	214
How Confederate Money Dropped in Value	305
How Deep to Plant Corn	69
How Grain Will Shrink	69
How to Build Strong Frames	27
How to Determine Nature of a Suspicious Illness	88
How to Kill Grease Spots Before Painting	26
How to Measure Corn in Crib, Hay in Mow, etc.	69
How to Mix Paints for Tints	282
How to Preserve Eggs	167
How to Tell Any Person's Age	224
Immigration	315
Immigration Statistics from 1820 to 1885	301
Important Events of the Late Civil War	40–47
Imports of Dry Goods at New York	164
Information for Tanners	51
Inns and Innkeepers	176
Interest Laws and Statutes of Limitations in Each State and Territory	191, 192
Interest Tables — 5, 6 and 7 per cent	19, 20, 21

	PAGE.
Iron Furnaces	29
Iron — Statistics	209
Japanese Periodicals	159
Jumbo, the Famous Elephant	217
Lakes — Sizes of	164
Language of Flowers	306
Largest Bell in the World	185
Largest Cities of the Earth	196, 197, 198
Largest Electric Lights	316
Lauterbrunnen	50
Law — Points of	172
Laws Governing Articles Found	135
" " Carriers of Goods	178
" " Certificates of Deposit	174
" " Common Carriers	177
" " Checks	157
" " Drafts	175
" " Due Bills	174
" " Equestrians	182
" " Hotel Guests	177
" " Hotel Keepers	170
" " Landlord and Tenant	183, 184, 185
" " Marriage and Divorce	105
" " Negotiable Instruments	172
" " Passenger Carriers	177
" " Pedestrians	183
" " Promissory Notes	173
" " Sleeping Car Companies	179
" " Sleeping Car Passengers	180
" " The Roads	180
" " Vehicles	181
" " Warehousemen	179
" " Warehouse Receipts	175
Length of Navigation of the Mississippi	305
Library — The Largest	315
Lightning — Distance Reflected	52
Marriage and Divorce Laws in all the States in the Union	105
Marriage in France	109
Mason Work Estimates	28
Maud S. — Price paid by Robert Bonner to W. H. Vanderbilt	218
Measures — Table of	285
Measures of Length	57
" " Land	58
Mercantile Laws	172
Miles of Books	315
Milk — The Demand for	310
Mines in Peru	90
Most Northern Point Reached by Arctic Explorers	223
Molders and Patternmakers' Table	255
Naturalization Laws of the United States	302, 303

	PAGE.
Negotiable Paper and Instruments........................	172
Nervous Deaths	315
News — Derivation of the Word...........................	310
Newspapers...	315
New York State — Soldiers Furnished by..................	218
Notes of Interest...................................217,	218
Notes — Promissory	173
Number of Nails in Carpenter's Work	28
Number of Pounds to Bushel in Various States............	72
Number of Shrubs to an Acre of Ground...................	68
Number of Yards in Miles of Various Nations.............	222
Number of Years Seeds Retain their Vitality	282
Number of Cubic Feet in a Ton of Various Substances.....	56
Occupation of the Inhabitants of the United States.......168,	169
Occupation of Legislators................................	278
Ocean — Greatest Depth of...............................	244
Ocean Steamships....................................136,	140
Oceans—Sizes of	164
Our Ancestors' Illiteracy................................	315
Oxyhydrogun Lime — Distance Perceptible	52
Parliamentary Rules and Usages	9
Passengers Transported	315
Pedestrians..	183
Pension Statistics 146,	147
Periodicals in Japan.....................................	159
Perpetual Snow—Limit of.................................	50
Pile Driving in Sandy Soil...............................	51
Pithy Facts 315,	316
Place of Nativity of Foreign Born Inhabitants of the United States..	205
Poetic Selections —	
Bingen on the Rhine.................................	126
Changes	126
Hereafter	124
Maud Muller..	122
Oh, Why Should the Spirit of Mortal be Proud?........	128
" 'Ostler Joe".......................................	129
The Murderer	133
Twenty Years Ago	134
We Parted in Silence.................................	121
Points of Law	172
Poisons—Antidotes and Treatment.........................	82–86
Political Information :	
A List of the Principal Officers of the U. S. Government, with salaries paid to them...........................	15
Results of the Electoral College Proceedings by States from 1789 to and including 1885	287
Votes by States for President from 1824 to date, showing which party carried the State, and by what majority..	291

	PAGE.
Popular Vote for Presidential Candidates to and including 1885	296
Popular Vote for Presidential Candidates to and including 1885. (Condensed)	16
Appropriations by Congress	299, 300
Pompey's Pillar — The Size of	53
Popular and Electoral Votes for Presidents	16
Population of Every State and Territory	17
Population of the United States	170–171
Population of the Cities of the United States in 1870 and 1880	199–204
Portraits on Bank Notes and Postage Stamps	66
Postage — Rates of	281
Power Required to Start Vessels	51
Press — Statistics of the American	314
Prices of Produce for 29 Years in the Chicago Market.	11, 12, 13, 14
Produce Exchange Transactions	163
Profits of Telegraph Companies	99
Principal of the Public Debt	304
Pulse — The — At Birth	52
Pyramids — Egyptian	53
Pyramids — The Largest	76
Quantity of Bricks Required for a Building	31
Rate of Annual Income on Investments	225
Railroad Accidents in the United States	151
Railroad Bridge at Niagara	150
" Comparative Statistics of in the United States	98
" Earnings, Interest and Dividends of American	97
" Failures in Ten Years	152
" Fastest Time on	280
" Signals	152
Railroad to the Sun	66
Railroads, Cost of in the United States	96
Railroad Mileage of the World	94, 95
Ready Reckoner Table	253
Relative Hardness of Woods	49
Relative Strength of Bodies to Resist Torsion	256
Religion and Religious Statistics	219, 220, 221
River Nile — Interesting Facts About the	53
Rivers — Interesting Matter About	53–54
Rivers — Solid Matter in	52
Rivers — The Longest in the World	155
Road — The Law of the	180
Roman Legion — The	51
Roman Money Mentioned in the New Testament Reduced to American Value	58
Roof Elevations	26
Rowing — The Largest Stake ever Rowed for	218
Rubble Work	28
Rules for Accidents on Water	213
Rules for Spelling	274
Russian Way of Stopping Holes in Ships	61

	PAGE.
Safe Business Rules	276
Salary List of United States Government Employes	15
Salaries of State Officers	439-440
Save a Little	62
Savings Bank Compound Interest	276
Savings Banks	104
Seas — Sizes of	164
Seasoning and Preserving Timber	18
Seed — Quantity Required to Plant an Acre	154, 155
Shingles Required in a Roof	28
Ships — The Largest	218
Silver Mines in Peru	90
Silver Statistics	48, 229
Silver — Weight of a Ton	157
Sizes of Lakes, Seas and Oceans	164
Size and Strength of Cast Iron Columns	252
Sleeping Cars	179
Snow — Limit of Perpetual	50
Soldering Fluid	210
Solomon's Temple — Description of	53
Speed Attained by Birds and Fowls	52
Spelling Rules	274, 275
Sporting Matters — Best Records, etc.	259, 266
Springs in the Ocean	52
Springs in California of Note	52
Standing Army of the United States	143
Steam Heating	209
Steamer Great Eastern	74
Steamer Etruria	137
Steamship Fast Passages	137
" Arrivals from Europe	140
Steamer Savannah	136
Some Good Maxims	166
Stock Brokers' Technicalities	247
Stock Exchange Transactions	162
Strength of Ice	241
Strength of One-Horse Power	298
St. Winfred's Well in England	53
Surveyors' Measurements	58
Table Showing the Average Velocity of Various Bodies	214
Table Showing the Number of Days from any Day in one Month to the Same Day in Another	64
Tables Showing the Requisite Size of Girders and Spans for Warehouses	32-33
Tables for Engineers and Machinists	252
Tanning	51
Telegraph Statistics of the World	99, 100
" " " " United States	100
" " " " Western Union Company	101
Temperature of the Ocean	52
" " Celestial Space	52

	PAGE.
Tempering — The U. S. Government $10,000 Secret	210
Temples Various — Description of	53-54
The Alps	49
The Highest Mountain in the World	50
The Loftiest Inhabited Spot on the Globe	50
Timber for Posts	49
Timber Line on Various Mountains	50
Transmission of Power	51
Trichina — What it is	213
Type — Various Sizes of	51
Theatre—The Largest	74
The Biggest Things	74
The Eleven Great Wonders of America	132
The Fastest Locomotive Ever Built	38
The Largest Telescope	30
The Liberty Bell	78
The Nation's Dead	145
The National Government	15
The Pulse	90
The Use of Capitals	275
The Use of the Steel Square	34
Timber Measurements	243, 245
Time in Which a Sum of Money will Double	22
Time at which Money Doubles at Interest	277
Torpedo Service of the World	314
Trees—The Largest	73, 75
Trinity Church, New York	150
Tunnel—The Largest	75
Useful Information for Architects and Builders	23-35
United States Customs Duties	193-195
United States Customs Articles Free of Duty	195
United States Land Measure and Homestead Laws	70-71
Valuable Suggestions to Clerks and Workingmen	61
Value of Diamonds	31
Value of Different Food for Stock	153
Value of a Ton of Gold or Silver	157
Value of Foreign Coins in United States Money	227-228
Vehicles—Laws Governing	181
Violent Deaths	315
Volcano—The Largest	74
Vote for President in 1884	192
Voters and Voting—Qualifications for in Each State in the Union	189-190
Wages Tables	24-25
War—Men Called by President Lincoln	143
" Colored Troops in the Late Civil	144
" Important Events in the Late Civil	40-47
" The Nation's Dead	145
" The United States Pension Statistics	146
" The Greatest Battles	165
" United States Soldiers in the Late Civil	144

	PAGE.
Wars of the United States	148-150
Warehouse Men	179
Warehouse Receipts	175
Water—Power of	54
Waterfalls—Notable	50
Waterfalls—Height of	188
Wealth of New York City in Real Estate	14
Weather Wisdom	186-188
Wedding Anniversaries	251
Weights and Measures for Cooks	222
Weight of a Cubic Foot of Stone, Metal, Earth, etc.	35
Weight of Cordwood	252
Weight of Iron	254, 257, 258, 267, 268, 269
Weight of Lead Pipe	253
Weight of Various Metals in lbs. per cubic foot	57
Weight of a Cubic Inch " " " " "	57
Weights—Sundry Commercial	57
Weights of Famous Bells	212
Wheat Measurement in Europe	51
Weight of Steel per Foot	267, 268, 269
Weight Required to Tear Asunder Various Articles	245
Weight and Measures—Table	284, 285
Western Union Telegraph Company	101
What a Deed to a Farm Includes	70
What a Horse Can Draw	298
What Royalty Costs England	274
What Smoking Costs	315
What the White House Costs	273
Wire—The Longest Span	74
Yards of Wire to the Bundle	67
You Cannot Count a Trillion	315

INDEX TO ATLAS MAPS.

	PAGE.		PAGE.
Alabama	361	Kentucky	350
Alaska	359	Louisiana	393
Arizona	365	Maine	395
Arkansas	363	Manitoba	341
California	367	Maryland	397
Central America	337	Massachusetts	399
Colorado	371	Mexico	335
Connecticut	369	Michigan	401
Dakota	373	Minnesota	403
Delaware	375	Mississippi	405
Florida	377	Missouri	407
Georgia	379	Montana	409
Idaho	381	Nebraska	411
Illinois	383	Nevada	413
Indiana	385	New Hampshire	347
Indian Territory	387	New Jersey	415
Iowa	389	New Mexico	417
Kansas	391	New York	419

	PAGE.		PAGE.
North America	329	Tennessee	350
North Carolina	353	Texas	429
Ohio	421	Utah	431
Ontario	343	Vermont	347
Oregon	423	Virginia	357
Pennsylvania	425	Washington Territory	433
Quebec	345	West Virginia	357
Rhode Island	427	Wisconsin	435
South America	329	Wyoming	437
South Carolina	352		

INDEX TO ATLAS DESCRIPTIVE MATTER.

	PAGE.		PAGE.
Abyssinia	326	Georgia	378
Afghanistan	322	Guiana	340
Africa	323	Hayti	336
Alabama	360	Illinois	382
Alaska	358	Idaho	380
Algeria	325	India	321
Andes Republics	339	Indiana	384
Antilles, The Great	336	Indian Territory	386
" Lesser	336	Iowa	388
Arabia	322	Jamaica	336
Argentine Republic	340	Japanese Empire, The	320
Arizona	363	Kansas	390
Arkansas	362	Kentucky	349
Asia	318	Louisiana	392
Bahama Islands	336	Madagascar	328
Barbary States, The	325	Maine	394
Beloochistan	322	Manitoba	342
Bokhara	322	Maryland	396
Brazil	339	Massachusetts	398
British Columbia	342	Mexico	334
California	366	Michigan	400
Canada, The Dominion of	342	Minnesota	402
Central Africa	323–327	Mississippi	404
Central America	336	Missouri	406
Ceylon	321	Montana	408
Chili	340	Morocco	325
Chinese Empire, The	320	Nebraska	410
Colorado	370	Nevada	412
Congo Free States, The	327	New Brunswick	344
Connecticut	368	Newfoundland	344
Cuba	336	New Hampshire	346
Dakota	372	New Jersey	414
Delaware	374	New Mexico	416
District of Columbia	438	New York	418
Europe	317	Nile Country, The	326
Farther India	321	North America	328
Florida	376	North Carolina	352

	PAGE.		PAGE.
Nova Scotia	344	Tennessee	351
Ohio	420	Texas	428
Ontario	342	Trancaucasia	320
Oregon	422	Tripoli	326
Palestine	323	Tunis	326
Paraguay	340	Turkey in Asia	322
Pennsylvania	424	United States, The	332
Persia	322	Uruguay	340
Porto Rico	336	Utah	430
Prince Edward Island	344	Venezuela	340
Quebec	344	Vermont	348
Rhode Island	426	Virginia	355
Russian Turkestan	320	Washington, D. C.	438
Sahara	327	Washington Territory	432
Senegambia	328	West Griqualand	327
Siberia	320	West Indies	336
Sierra Leone	328	West Virginia	356
Soudan	327	Wisconsin	434
South America	338	Wyoming	436
South Carolina	354	Zanzibar	327
Southern Africa	324, 327		

BEAR IN MIND

Agents selling this book are making from $5 to $15 per day. We want Agents everywhere. Write to the Publisher for terms to Agents.

Parliamentary Rules and Usages.

Trace each motion to its respective references and you master at a glance the intricacies of Parliamentary usages, comprising some three hundred points of order.

Motion to adjourn......................1 a * B *a* II x
Motion to determine time to which to adjourn ....* a † A *a* II x
Motion to amend......................3 a † A *a* II x
Motion to amend an amendment.........3 a * A *a* II x
Motion to amend the rules.............3 a † A *b* II x
Motion to appeal from Speaker's decision *re* indecorum........................1 a † A *a* II y
Motion to appeal from Speaker's decision generally ....3 a * A *a* II y
Call to order..........................1 a * A *a* III y
Motion to close debate on question.......1 a † A *b* II x
Motion to commit......................3 b † A *a* II x
Motion to extend limits of debate on question................................1 a † A *a* II x
Leave to continue speaking after indecorum.1 a * A *a* II x
Motion that....do lie on the table ....1 a * C *a* II x
Motion to limit debate on question.......1 a † A *b* II x
Objection to consideration of question...1 a * A *b* III y
Motion for the orders of the day........1 a * A *a* III y
Motion to postpone to a definite time....4 a † A *a* II x
Motion to postpone indefinitely..........3 b * A *a* II x
Motion for previous question............1 a * A *b* II x
Questions touching priority of business...1 a † A *a* II x
Questions of privilege..................3 a † A *a* II x
Reading papers........................1 a * A *a* II x
Motion to reconsider a debatable question.3 b * B *a* II x
Motion to reconsider an undebatable question................................1 a * B *a* II z
Motion to refer a question...............3 b † B *a* II x
Motion that committee do not rise.......1 a * B *a* II x
Question whether subject shall be discussed.1 a * A *b* III y
Motion to make subject a special order....3 a † A *b* II x
To substitute in the nature of an amendment................................3 a † A *a* II x
Motion to suspend the rules ....3 a † B *a* II x
Motion to take from the table ....1 a * C *b* II x

To take up a question out of its proper
  order ....1 a * A *b* II x
Motion to withdraw a motion............1 a * A *a* II x
Questions of precedence of questions.....5 6 7 8 9 10 12
Forms in which questions may be
  put. 13 14 15 16 17 18 19

RULES OF PARLIAMENTARY PROCEDURE—
Condensed.

1. Question undebatable; sometimes remarks tacitly allowed.
2. Undebatable if another question is before the assembly.
3. Debatable question.
4. Limited debate only on propriety of postponement.
a. Does not allow reference to main question.
b. Opens the main question to debate.
*. Cannot be amended.
†. May be amended.
A. Can be reconsidered.
B. Cannot be reconsidered.
C. An affirmative vote on this question cannot be reconsidered.
b. Requires two-third vote unless special rules have been enacted.
a. Simple majority suffices to determine the question.
II. Motion must be seconded.
III. Does not require to be seconded.
x. Not in order when another has the floor.
y. Always in order though another may have the floor.
z. May be moved and entered on the record when another has the floor, but the business then before the assembly may not be put aside. The motion must be made by one who voted with the prevailing side, and on the same day the original vote was taken.
5. Fixing the time to which an adjournment may be made; ranks first.
6. To adjourn without limitation; second.
7. Motion for the Orders of the Day; third.
8. Motion that....do lie on the table; fourth.
9. Motion for the previous question; fifth.
10. Motion to postpone definitely; sixth.

12. Motion to commit; seventh.
13. Motion to amend; eighth.
14. Motion to postpone indefinitely; ninth.
15. On motion to strike out the words, " Shall the words stand part of the motion? " unless a majority sustains the words they are struck out.
16. On motion for previous question the form to be observed is, " Shall the main question be now put? " This, if carried, ends debate.
17. On an appeal from the Chair's decision, " Shall the decision he sustained as the ruling of the house? " The Chair is generally sustained.
18. On motion for Orders of the Day, " Will the house now proceed to the Orders of the Day? " This, if carried, supersedes intervening motions.
19. When an objection is raised to considering question, " Shall the question be considered? " objection may be made by any member before debate has commenced, but not subsequently.

[Used by permission from Gaskell's Compendium of Forms Fairbanks & Palmer Publishing Co., publishers.]

Prices of Produce.

RECORD OF THE CHICAGO MARKET FOR 29 YEARS.
No. 2 SPRING WHEAT.

Yrs.	Months the lowest prices were reached.	Range for the entire year.	Months the highest prices were reached.
1858	February	$0 53 a 0 97	August
1859	July and August	50 a 1 15	May
1860	December	66 a 1 13	April
1861	June and July	55 a 1 55	May
1862	January	64 a 92½	August
1863	August	80 a 1 15	October
1864	March	1 07 a 2 26	June
1865	December	85 a 1 25	January
1866	February	78 a 2 03	November
1867	August	55 a 2 85	May
1868	November	1 04½ a 2 20	July
1869	December	76½ a 1 47	August
1870	April	73¾ a 1 31½	July
1871	August	99½ a 1 32	Feb., April and Sept.
1872	November	1 01 a 1 61	August
1873	September	89 a 1 46	July
1874	October	81½ a 1 28	April
1875	February	83¼ a 1 30½	August
1876	July	83 a 1 26¾	December

Yrs.	Months the lowest prices were reached.	Range	Months the highest prices were reached.
1877	August	1 01½ a 1 76½	May
1878	December	77 a 1 14	April
1879	January	81⅝ a 1 32½	December
1880	August	86½ a 1 32	January
1881	January	95⅜ a 1 43¼	October
1882	December	91⅛ a 1 40	April and May
1883	October	90 a 1 13½	June
1884	December	69½ a 96	February
1885	March	73⅜ a 91¾	April
1886	October	7¼ a 85	January

No. 2 Corn.

Yrs.	Months the lowest prices were reached.	Range for the entire year.	Months the highest prices were reached.
1858	May	$0 27 a 66	August
1859	December	42 a 81	October
1860	December	27 a 55	April
1861	Sept. and Oct	20 a 45	May
1862	April	22 a 41	December
1863	January	42 a 98	November
1864	March	76 a 1 40	November
1865	December	38 a 88	January and February
1866	February	33¾ a 1 00	November
1867	March	56¾ a 1 12	October
1868	December	52 a 1 02½	August
1869	January	44 a 97½	August
1870	December	45 a 94½	May
1871	December	39½ a 56½	March and May
1872	October	29½ a 48⅝	May
1873	June	27 a 54¼	December
1874	January	49 a 86	September
1875	December	45½ a 76½	May and July
1876	February	38⅝ a 49	May
1877	March	37⅝ a 58	April
1878	December	29⅞ a 43⅝	March
1879	January	29⅜ a 49	October
1880	April	31½ a 43¾	November
1881	February	35¾ a 76⅜	October
1882	December	49¼ a 81½	July
1883	October	46 a 70	January
1884	December	34½ a 87	September
1885	January	34¼ a 49	April and May
1886	April...?	33 a 43⅝	August

Mess Pork.

Yrs.	Months the lowest prices were reached.	Range for the entire year.	Months the highest prices were reached.
1858	January	$12 00 a 17 50	April
1859	October & November	14 00 a 19 00	May
1860	December	13 00 a 20 00	September & October
1861	December	9 00 a 21 00	April
1862	January	8 00 a 12 25	December

Yrs.	Months the lowest prices were reached.	Range for the entire year.	Months the highest prices were reached.
1863	February	10 00 a18 50	December
1864	January	17 50 a43 00	July and October
1865	March and May	22 50 a38 00	October
1866	December	17 00 a34 00	August
1867	January	18 00 a24 50	September
1868	January	19 62½a30 00	October
1869	January	27 00 a34 00	June and August
1870	December	18 00 a34 50	July
1871	August	12 00 a23 00	January
1872	March	11 05 a16 00	July
1873	November	11 00 a18 00	April and May
1874	Jan., Feb. and March	13 75 a24 75	August
1875	January	17 70 a23 50	October
1876	October	15 20 a22 75	April
1877	December	12 40 a17 95	January
1878	December	6 02½a11 35	January
1879	January	7 27½a13 75	December
1880	April	9 37½a19 00	October
1881	January	12 40 a20 00	September
1882	March	16 00 a24 75	October
1883	Sept. and Oct	10 20 a20 15	May
1884	December	10 55 a19 50	May, June and July
1885	Oct. and Nov	8 00 a13 25	February
1886	May	8 17½a11 70	December

PRIME STEAMED LARD.

Yrs.	Months the lowest prices were reached.	Range for the entire year.	Months the highest prices were reached.
1858	January	$ 8 00 a10 50	May and June
1859	December	9 75 a12 50	October
1860	Jan. and Feb	9 25 a13 00	July, August, September and October
1861	December	6 22½a11 50	April and May
1862	February	5 75 a 9 75	October
1863	January	7 25 a12 00	Nov. and Dec.
1864	March	11 75 a23 50	September
1865	April	16 00 a30 00	September
1866	December	11 25 a23 00	May
1867	January and July	11 25 a13 75	August
1868	January	11 75 a19 50	May and September
1869	Oct. and Nov	16 25 a20 75	February
1870	December	11 00 a17 25	January
1871	Nov. and Dec	8 37½a13 00	February
1872	December	7 00 a11 00	July
1873	November	6 50 a 9 37½	April
1874	January	8 20 a15 50	October
1875	November	11 80 a15 75	April and May
1876	September	9 55 a13 85	March and April
1877	December	7 55 a11 65	January
1878	December	7 32½a 7 80	August
1879	August	5 30 a 7 75	December
1880	June	6 35 a 7 85	November
1881	February	9 20 a13 00	July

1882..March............ ...... 10 05 a 13 10 October
1883..October............... 7 15 a 12 10 May
1884..December............ 6 45 a 10 00 February
1885..November........... 5 85 a 7 10 February and April
1886..October............. 5 62½ a 7 52½ September

The following table shows the receipts of wheat at the points named, from August 1st to December 18th, for two years:

	1886. bu.	1885. bu.
Minneapolis................................	17,882,500	16,072,000
Duluth..	16,569,000	10,395,500
Chicago......................................	10,869,500	7,234,000
Toledo..	8,232,000	5,043,500
Detroit..	5,822,000	5,950,500
St. Louis.....................................	5,406,000	4,845,000
Milwaukee..................................	4,128,000	3,112,000
Kansas City................................	1,933,500	1,555,500
Peoria...	256,000	173,000
Totals................................	71,098,500	54,381,500

WEALTH OF NEW YORK CITY IN REAL ESTATE.

WARDS.	Assessed Valuation, 1885.	Assessed Valuation, 1886.	Increase
I........	$ 76,636,814	$ 80,024,828	$ 388,014
II.......	34,202,140	34,510,945	308,805
III......	38,294,000	38,455,979	161,979
IV......	13,151,809	13,247,303	95,494
V.......	45,539,678	46,693,532	553,854
VI......	23,971,441	24,306,693	335,252
VII.....	16,634,659	16,985,945	351,286
VIII....	38,452,209	39,098,361	646,652
IX......	29,038,766	29,284,610	244,844
X.......	17,497,086	17,916,865	479,780
XI......	16,577,370	16,792,020	214,650
XII.....	121,905,680	133,478,632	11,572,952
XIII....	10,187,345	10,277,415	190,070
XIV....	24,312,215	24,707,219	435,004
XV.....	55,189,266	55,877,776	688,510
XVI....	37,033,514	37,127,804	783,813
XVII...	33,584,931	33,886,593	301,662
XVIII..	77,690,378	78,817,327	437,426
XIX....	198,296,968	205,713,955	7,416,986
XX.....	44,954,495	45,664,676	710,181
XXI....	88,341,311	89,101,173	756,862
XXII...	95,178,889	103,749,757	8,570,868
XXIII..	18,559,059	19,638,126	1,079,067
XXIV..	10,272,115	11,214,370	942,255
Total.	$1,168,443,137	$1,206,112,204	$37,669,267

Salaries of United States Officers, per annum.

PRESIDENT, VICE-PRESIDENT AND CABINET.—President, $50,000; Vice-President, $8,000; Cabinet Officers, $8,000 each.

UNITED STATES SENATORS.—$5,000, with mileage.

CONGRESS.—Members of Congress, $5,000, with mileage.

SUPREME COURT.—Chief Justice, $10,500; Associate Justices $10,000.

CIRCUIT COURTS.—Justices of Circuit Courts, $6,000.

HEADS OF DEPARTMENTS.—Supt. of Bureau of Engraving and Printing, $4,500; Public Printer, $4,500; Supt. of Census, $5,000; Supt. of Naval Observatory, $5,000; Supt. of the Signal Service, $4,000; Director of Geological Surveys, $6,000; Director of the Mint, $4,500; Commissioner of General Land Office, $4,000; Commissioner of Pensions, $3,600; Commissioner of Agriculture. $3,000; Commissioner of Indian Affairs, $3,000; Commissioner of Education, $3,000; Commander of Marine Corps, $3,500; Supt. of Coast and Geodetic Survey, $6,000.

UNITED STATES TREASURY.—Treasurer, $6,000; Register of Treasury, $4,000; Commissioner of Customs, $4,000.

INTERNAL REVENUE AGENCIES.—Supervising Agents, $12 per day; 34 other Agents, per day, $6 to $8.

POST-OFFICE DEPARTMENT, Washington.—Three Assistant Postmaster-Generals, $3,500; Chief Clerk, $2,200.

POSTMASTERS.—Postmasters are divided into four classes. First Class, $3,000 to $4,000, (excepting New York City, which is $8,000); second class, $2,000 to $3,000; third class, $1,000 to $2,000; fourth class less than $1,000. The first three classes are appointed by the President, and confirmed by the Senate; those of fourth class are appointed by the Postmaster-General.

DIPLOMATIC APPOINTMENTS.—Ministers to Germany, Great Britain, France, and Russia, $17,500; Ministers to Brazil, China, Austria-Hungary, Italy, Mexico, Japan, and Spain, $12,000; Ministers to Chili, Peru, and Central Amer., $10,000; Ministers to Argentine Confederation, Hawaiian Islands, Belgium, Hayti, Columbia, Netherlands, Sweden, Turkey, and Venezuela, $7,500; Ministers to Switzerland, Denmark, Paraguay, Bolivia, and Portugal, $5,000; Minister to Liberia, $4,000.

ARMY OFFICERS.—General, $13,500; Lieut.-General, $11,000; Major-General, $7,500; Brigadier-General, $5,500; Colonel, $3,500; Lieutenant-Colonel, $3,000; Major, $2,500; Captain, mounted, $2,000; Captain, not mounted, $1,800; Regimental Adjutant, $1,800; Regimental Quartermaster, $1,800; 1st Lieutenant, mounted, $1,600; 1st Lieutenant, not mounted, $1,500; 2d Lieutenant, mounted, $1,500; 2d Lieutenant, not mounted, $1,400; Chaplain; $1,500.

NAVY OFFICERS.—Admiral, $13,000; Vice-Admiral, $9,000; Rear-Admirals, $6,000; Commodores, $5,000; Captains, $4,500; Commanders, $3,500; Lieut.-Commanders, $2,800; Lieutenants, $2,400; Masters, $1,800; Ensigns, $1,200; Midshipmen, $1,000; Cadet Midshipmen, $500; Mates, $900; Medical and Pay Directors and Medical and Pay Inspectors and Chief Engineers, $4,400; Fleet Surgeons, Fleet Paymasters, and Fleet Engineers, $4,400; Surgeons and Paymasters, $2,800; Chaplains, $2,500.

Popular and Electoral Votes for Presidents.

Year.	CANDIDATES.	PARTY.	Popular Vote.	Elec'l Vote.
1824	Andrew Jackson	Democrat	152,872	99
1824	John Q. Adams	Federal	105,321	84
1824	W. H. Crawford	Republican	44,282	41
1824	Henry Clay	Republican	46,587	37
1828	Andrew Jackson	Democrat	647,231	178
1828	John Q. Adams	Federal	509,097	83
1832	Andrew Jackson	Democrat	687,502	219
1832	Henry Clay	Nat. Republican.	530,189	49
1832	John Floyd	Whig		11
1832	William Wirt	Whig		7
1836	Martin Van Buren	Democrat	761,549	170
1836	W. H. Harrison	Whig		73
1836	Hugh L. White	Whig	736,656	26
1836	Daniel Webster	Whig		14
1836	W. P. Mangum	Whig		11
1840	Martin Van Buren	Democrat	1,128,702	48
1840	W. H. Harrison	Whig	1,275,017	234
1840	J. G. Birney	Liberty	7,059	....
1844	James K. Polk	Democrat	1,337,243	170
1844	Henry Clay	Whig	1,299,068	105
1844	James G. Birney	Liberty	62,300	....
1848	Zachary Taylor	Whig	1,360,101	163
1848	Lewis Cass	Democrat	1,220,544	127
1848	Martin Van Buren	Free Soil	291,263	....
1852	Franklin Pierce	Democrat	1,601,474	254
1852	Winfield Scott	Whig	1,386,578	42
1852	John P. Hale	Free Soil	156,149	....
1856	James Buchanan	Democrat	1,838,169	174
1856	John C. Fremont	Republican	1,341,262	114
1856	Millard Fillmore	American	874,534	8
1860	Abraham Lincoln	Republican	1,866,352	180
1860	Stephen A. Douglas	Democrat	1,375,157	12
1860	John C. Breckenridge	Democrat	845,763	72
1860	John Bell	Union	589,581	39
1864	Abraham Lincoln	Republican	2,216,067	212
1864	Geo. B. McClellan	Democrat	1,808,725	21
1868	U. S. Grant	Republican	3,015,071	214
1868	Horatio Seymour	Democrat	2,709,613	80
1872	U. S. Grant	Republican	3,597,070	286
1872	Horace Greeley	Liberal & Dem	2,834,079	....
1872	Charles O'Conor	Democrat	29,408	....
1872	James Black	Temperance	5,608	....
1876	R. B. Hayes	Republican	4,033,950	185
1876	Samuel J. Tilden	Democrat	4,284,885	184
1876	Peter Cooper	Greenback	81,740	....
1876	G. C. Smith	Prohibition	9,522	....
1876	Scattering		2,636	
1880	James A. Garfield	Republican	4,449,053	214
1880	Winfield S. Hancock	Democrat	4,442,035	155
1880	James B. Weaver	Greenback	307,306	....
1884	Grover Cleveland	Democrat	4,911,017	219
1884	James G Blaine	Republican	4,848,334	182
1884	Benj. F. Butler	Greenback	133,825	....
1884	John P. St. John	Prohibition	151,809	....

Population of Every State and Territory, Etc.

UNITED STATES CENSUS OF 1880.

STATES.	Population.	Area in Sq. Miles.	Electoral Vote.
Alabama	1,262,794	50,722	10
Arkansas	802,564	52,198	7
California	864,686	188,981	8
Colorado	194,649	104,500	3
Connecticut	622,683	4,674	6
Delaware	146,654	2,120	3
Florida	267,351	59,268	4
Georgia	1,539,048	58,000	12
Illinois	3,078,769	55,410	22
Indiana	1,978,362	33,809	15
Iowa	1,624,620	55,045	13
Kansas	995,966	81,313	9
Kentucky	1,648,708	37,600	13
Louisiana	940,103	41,346	8
Maine	648,945	31,776	6
Maryland	934,632	11,184	8
Massachusetts	1,783,012	7,800	14
Michigan	1,636,331	56,451	13
Minnesota	780,806	83,531	7
Mississippi	1,131,592	47,156	9
Missouri	2,168,804	65,350	16
Nebraska	452,433	75,995	5
Nevada	62,265	112,090	3
New Hampshire	346,984	9,280	4
New Jersey	1,130,983	8,320	9
New York	5,083,810	47,000	36
North Carolina	1,400,047	50,704	11
Ohio	3,198,239	39,964	23
Oregon	174,767	95,244	3
Pennsylvania	4,282,786	46,000	30
Rhode Island	276,528	1,306	4
South Carolina	995,622	29,385	9
Tennessee	1,542,463	45,600	12
Texas	1,592,574	237,504	13
Vermont	332,286	10,212	4
Virginia	1,512,806	40,904	12
West Virginia	618,443	23,000	6
Wisconsin	1,315,480	53,924	11
Total of States	49,369,595	2,054,666	401
District of Columbia	177,638	60	
TERRITORIES.			
Arizona	40,441	113,916	
Dakota	135,180	147,490	
Idaho	32,611	90,932	
Montana	39,157	143,776	
New Mexico	118,430	121,201	
Utah	143,906	80,056	
Washington	75,120	69,944	
Wyoming	20,788	93,107	
Total United States	50,152,866	2,915,048	

A Table of Daily Savings at Compound Interest.

Cents a day.	Per Year.	In 10 Years.	Fifty Years
$ .02½	$ 10.00	$ 130	$ 2,900
.05¼	20.00	260	5,800
.11	40.00	520	11,600
.27½	100.00	1,300	29,060
.55	200.00	2,600	58,000
1.10	400.00	5,200	116,000
1.37	500.00	6,500	145,000

Seasoning and Preserving Timber.

For the purpose of seasoning, timber should be piled under shelter, where it may be kept dry, but not exposed to a strong current of air. At the same time there should be a free circulation of air about the timber, with which view slats or blocks of wood should be placed between the pieces that lie over each other, near enough to prevent the timber from bending.

In the sheds, the pieces of timber should be piled in this way, or in square piles, and classed according to age and kind. Each pile should be distinctly marked with the number and kind of pieces, and the age, or the date of receiving them.

The piles should be taken down and made over again at intervals, varying with the length of time which the timber has been cut.

The seasoning of timber requires from two to four years, according to its size.

Gradual drying and seasoning in this manner is considered the most favorable to the durability and strength of timber, but various methods have been prepared for hastening the process. For this purpose, *steaming* and *boiling* timber has been applied with success; *kiln-drying* is serviceable only for boards and pieces of small dimensions, and is apt to cause cracks, and to impair the strength of wood, unless performed very slowly.

Timber of large dimensions is improved by *immersion in water* for some weeks, according to its size, after which, it is less subject to warp and crack in steaming.

Oak timber loses about *one-fifth of its weight* in seasoning, and about *one-third of its weight* in becoming dry.

Fastest Railroad Time.

1 mile—50¼s., 3 miles in 2 m. 36¼s., and 5 miles in 4m. 50s. train which left West Philadelphia for Jersey City (P. R. R.) at 7:35 a. m. (Edward Osmond, engineer) Sept. 4, 1879.

10 miles—8 min., Hamburg to Buffalo, N. Y., Lake Shore and Michigan Southern R. R.; in 9 min., Hudson River road, locomotive and platform car, with steam fire-engine, Peekskill to Sing Sing, N. Y., Feb. 17, 1874.

14 miles—11 min., locomotive Hamilton Davis and six cars, New York Central R. R., 1855.

18 miles—15 min., special train conveying the Duke of Wellington, Paddington to Slough, Eng.

111 miles—98 min., no stop, new Fontaine engine and two coaches, carrying W. H. Vanderbilt and party—Amherstburg to St. Thomas, Canada Southern Railway, May 5, 1881.... 109 min., special train, consisting of locomotive, baggage car, one coach and one Pullman palace-car, Engineer McComber, carrying Bishop of Detroit and a number of the clergy; the time includes 4 min., stoppage at Charing Cross—St. Thomas to Amherstburg Sept. 13, 1877.

FIVE PER CENT. INTEREST TABLE.

DAYS.	$1	$2	$3	$4	$5	$10	$20	$30	$40	$50	$60	$70	$80	$90	$100	$200	$500	$1,000
1	0	0	0	0	0	0	0	0	1	1	1	1	1	1	1	3	7	14
2	0	0	0	0	0	0	1	1	1	1	2	2	2	3	3	6	14	28
3	0	0	0	0	0	0	1	1	1	2	3	3	3	4	4	8	21	42
4	0	0	0	0	0	0	1	1	2	3	3	4	4	5	6	11	28	56
5	0	0	0	0	0	1	1	2	2	3	4	5	6	6	7	14	35	69
6	0	0	0	0	0	1	2	2	3	4	5	6	7	8	8	17	42	83
7	0	0	0	0	0	1	2	3	3	4	6	7	8	9	10	19	49	97
8	0	0	0	0	1	1	2	3	4	5	7	8	9	10	11	22	56	1.11
9	0	0	0	0	1	1	3	4	4	6	7	9	10	11	13	25	63	1.25
10	0	0	0	1	1	1	3	4	5	7	8	10	11	13	14	28	69	1.39
15	0	0	0	1	1	2	4	6	8	10	13	15	17	19	21	42	1.04	2.08
20	0	0	1	1	1	3	6	10	11	14	17	19	22	25	28	56	1.39	2.78
25	0	1	1	1	2	3	7	14	14	17	21	24	28	31	35	69	1.74	3.47
30	0	1	1	2	2	4	8	14	17	23	25	29	33	38	42	83	2.08	4.17
60	1	1	2	3	4	8	18	26	35	44	53	61	70	79	87	1.75	4.38	4.59
90	1	2	3	4	6	13	26	39	52	65	78	91	1.03	1.17	1.29	2.58	6.46	12.92

MONTHS.	$1	$2	$3	$4	$5	$10	$20	$30	$40	$50	$60	$70	$80	$90	$100	$200	$500	$1,000
1	0	1	1	2	2	4	8	13	17	21	25	29	33	38	42	83	2.08	4.17
2	1	2	3	3	4	8	17	25	33	42	50	58	67	75	83	1.67	4.17	8.33
3	1	3	4	5	6	13	25	38	50	63	75	88	1.00	1.13	1.25	2.50	6.25	12.50
4	2	3	5	7	8	17	33	50	67	83	1.00	1.17	1.33	1.50	1.67	3.33	8.33	16.67
5	2	4	6	8	10	21	42	63	83	1.04	1.25	1.46	1.67	1.88	2.08	4.17	10.42	20.83
6	3	5	8	10	13	25	50	75	1.00	1.25	1.50	1.75	2.00	2.25	2.50	5.00	12.50	25.00
7	3	6	9	12	15	29	58	88	1.17	1.46	1.75	2.04	2.33	2.63	2.92	5.93	14.58	29.17
8	4	7	10	13	17	33	67	1.00	1.33	1.67	2.00	2.33	2.67	3.00	3.33	6.67	16.67	33.33
9	4	8	11	15	19	38	75	1.13	1.50	1.88	2.25	2.63	3.00	3.38	3.75	7.50	18.75	37.50
10	5	8	13	17	21	42	83	1.25	1.67	2.08	2.50	2.92	3.33	3.75	4.17	8.33	20.83	41.67
11	5	9	14	18	23	46	92	1.38	1.83	2.29	2.75	3.21	3.67	4.13	4.58	9.17	22.92	45.83
12	5	10	15	20	25	50	1.00	1.50	2.00	2.50	3.00	3.50	4.00	4.50	5.00	10.00	25.00	50.00

SIX PER CENT. INTEREST TABLE.

	$1	$2	$3	$4	$5	$10	$20	$30	$40	$50	$60	$70	$80	$90	$100	$200	$500	$1,000
DAYS																		
1	0	0	0	0	0	0	0	1	1	1	1	1	1	2	2	3	8	17
2	0	0	0	0	0	0	1	1	1	2	2	2	3	3	3	7	17	33
3	0	0	0	0	0	1	1	2	2	2	3	4	4	5	5	10	25	50
4	0	0	0	0	0	1	1	2	3	3	4	5	5	6	7	13	33	67
5	0	0	0	0	0	1	2	3	3	3	5	6	7	8	8	17	42	83
6	0	0	0	0	1	1	2	3	4	5	6	7	8	9	10	20	50	1.00
7	0	0	0	0	1	1	2	3	5	6	7	8	9	11	12	23	58	1.17
8	0	0	0	0	1	1	3	4	5	6	8	9	11	12	13	27	67	1.33
9	0	0	0	1	1	2	3	4	6	7	9	11	12	14	15	30	75	1.50
10	0	0	0	1	1	2	3	5	7	8	10	12	13	15	17	33	83	1.67
15	0	0	1	1	2	3	5	8	10	13	15	18	20	23	25	50	1.25	2.50
20	0	0	1	1	2	3	7	10	13	17	20	23	27	30	33	67	1.67	3.33
25	0	0	1	1	3	4	8	13	17	21	25	29	33	38	42	83	2.08	4.17
30	0	0	1	2	3	5	10	15	20	25	30	35	40	45	50	1.00	2.50	5.00
33	1	1	2	2	3	6	11	17	22	28	33	39	44	50	55	1.10	2.75	5.50
63	1	2	3	4	5	11	21	32	42	53	63	74	84	95	1.05	2.10	5.25	10.50
93	2	3	5	6	8	16	31	47	62	78	93	1.09	1.24	1.40	1.55	3.10	7.75	15.50
MONTHS																		
1	1	1	2	2	3	5	10	15	20	25	30	35	40	45	50	1.00	2.50	5.00
2	1	2	3	4	5	10	20	30	40	50	60	70	80	90	1.00	2.00	5.00	10.00
3	2	3	5	6	8	15	30	45	60	75	90	1.05	1.20	1.35	1.50	3.00	7.50	15.00
4	2	4	6	8	10	20	40	60	80	1.00	1.20	1.40	1.60	1.80	2.00	4.00	10.00	20.00
5	3	5	8	10	13	25	50	75	1.00	1.25	1.50	1.75	2.00	2.25	2.50	5.00	12.50	25.00
6	3	6	9	12	15	30	60	90	1.20	1.50	1.80	2.10	2.40	2.70	3.00	6.00	15.00	30.00
7	4	7	11	14	18	35	70	1.05	1.40	1.75	2.10	2.45	2.80	3.15	3.50	7.00	17.50	35.00
8	4	8	12	16	20	40	80	1.20	1.60	2.00	2.40	2.80	3.20	3.60	4.00	8.00	20.00	40.00
9	5	9	14	18	23	45	90	1.35	1.80	2.25	2.70	3.15	3.60	4.05	4.50	9.00	22.50	45.00
10	5	10	15	20	25	50	1.00	1.50	2.00	2.50	3.00	3.50	4.00	4.50	5.00	10.00	25.00	50.00
11	6	11	17	22	28	55	1.10	1.65	2.20	2.75	3.30	3.85	4.40	4.95	5.50	11.00	27.50	55.00
12	6	12	18	24	30	60	1.20	1.80	2.40	3.00	3.60	4.20	4.80	5.40	6.00	12.00	30.00	60.00

SEVEN PER CENT. INTEREST TABLE.

DAYS	$1	$2	$3	$4	$5	$10	$20	$30	$40	$50	$60	$70	$80	$90	$100	$200	$500	$1,000
1	0	0	0	0	0	0	0	1	1	1	1	1	2	2	2	4	10	19
2	0	0	0	0	0	0	1	1	2	2	2	3	3	4	4	8	19	39
3	0	0	0	0	0	1	1	2	2	3	4	4	5	5	6	12	29	58
4	0	0	0	0	0	1	2	2	3	4	4	5	6	7	8	16	39	78
5	0	0	0	0	0	1	2	3	3	5	6	7	8	9	10	19	49	97
6	0	0	0	0	1	1	2	3	4	6	7	8	9	11	12	23	58	1.17
7	0	0	0	0	1	1	3	4	5	7	8	10	11	12	14	27	68	1.36
8	0	0	0	1	1	2	3	5	6	8	9	11	12	14	16	31	78	1.56
9	0	0	0	1	1	2	4	5	6	9	11	12	14	16	18	35	88	1.75
10	0	0	1	1	1	2	4	6	7	10	12	14	16	18	19	39	97	1.94
15	0	1	1	1	2	3	6	9	12	15	18	20	23	26	29	58	1.46	2.92
20	0	1	1	2	2	4	8	12	16	19	23	27	31	35	39	78	1.94	3.89
25	0	1	1	2	2	5	10	15	19	24	29	34	39	44	49	97	2.43	4.86
30	0	1	2	2	3	6	12	17	23	29	35	41	47	53	58	1.17	2.92	5.83
33	0	1	2	2	3	7	13	20	25	32	39	45	52	58	64	1.29	3.21	6.41
63	1	2	4	5	6	13	24	37	49	61	74	86	98	1.10	1.23	2.45	6.12	12.25
93	2	4	5	7	9	19	36	55	72	91	1.09	1.27	1.45	1.63	1.81	3.62	9.04	18.08

MONTHS	$1	$2	$3	$4	$5	$10	$20	$30	$40	$50	$60	$70	$80	$90	$100	$200	$500	$1,000
1	1	1	2	2	3	6	12	18	23	29	35	41	47	53	58	1.17	2.92	5.83
2	1	2	4	5	6	12	23	35	47	58	70	82	93	1.05	1.17	2.33	5.83	11.67
3	2	4	5	7	9	18	35	53	70	88	1.05	1.23	1.40	1.58	1.75	3.50	8.75	17.50
4	2	5	7	9	12	23	47	70	93	1.17	1.40	1.63	1.87	2.10	2.33	4.67	11.67	23.33
5	3	6	9	12	15	29	58	88	1.17	1.46	1.75	2.04	2.33	2.63	2.92	5.83	14.58	29.17
6	4	7	11	14	18	35	70	1.05	1.40	1.75	2.10	2.45	2.80	3.15	3.50	7.00	17.50	35.00
7	4	8	12	16	20	41	82	1.23	1.63	2.04	2.45	2.86	3.27	3.68	4.08	8.17	20.42	40.83
8	5	9	14	19	23	47	93	1.40	1.87	2.33	2.80	3.27	3.73	4.20	4.67	9.33	23.33	46.67
9	5	10	16	21	26	53	1.05	1.58	2.10	2.63	3.15	3.68	4.20	4.73	5.25	10.50	26.25	52.50
10	6	12	18	23	29	58	1.17	1.75	2.33	2.92	3.50	4.08	4.67	5.25	5.83	11.67	29.17	58.33
11	6	13	19	26	32	64	1.28	1.93	2.57	3.21	3.85	4.49	5.13	5.78	6.42	12.83	32.08	64.17
12	7	14	21	28	35	70	1.40	2.10	2.80	3.50	4.20	4.90	5.60	6.30	7.00	14.00	35.00	70.00

Time in Which a Sum Will Double.

Rate per cent.	Simple Interest.	Compound Interest.
2	50 years	35 years, 1 day.
2½	40 "	28 " 26 days.
3	33 " 4 months	23 " 164 "
3½	28 " 208 days	20 " 54 "
4	25 "	17 " 246 "
4½	22 " 81 days	15 " 273 "
5	20 "	15 " 75 "
6	16 " 8 months	14 " 327 "
7	14 " 104 days	10 " 89 "
8	12½ "	9 " 2 "
9	11 " 40 days	8 " 16 "
10	10 "	7 " 100 "

Air-Line Distances from Washington to Various Parts of the World.

	Miles.		Miles.
Alexandria, Egypt	5,275	Manilla, Phil. Islands	9,360
Amsterdam, Holland	3,555	Mecca, Arabia	6,598
Athens, Greece	5,005	Muscat, Arabia	7,600
Aukland, N. Z.	8,290	Monrovia, Liberia	3,645
Algiers, Algeria	3,425	Morocco, Morocco	3,305
Berlin, Prussia	3,847	Mourzouk, Fezzan	5,525
Berne, Switzerland	3,730	Mozambique, Moz.	7,348
Brussels, Belgium	3,515	Ottawa, Canada	462
Batavia, Java	11,118	Panama, New Gran.	1,825
Bombay, Hindostan	8,548	Parana, A. C.	4,733
Buenos Ayres, A. C.	5,013	Port au Prince, Hayti	1,425
Bremen, Pr.	3,500	Paris, France	3,485
Constantinople, Turkey	4,880	Pekin, China	8,783
Copenhagen, Denmark	3,895	Quebec, Canada	601
Calcutta, Hindostan	9,348	Quito, Ecuador	2,531
Canton, China	9,000	Rio Janeiro, Brazil	4,280
Cairo, Egypt	5,848	Rome, Italy	4,365
Cape Town, Cape Colony	6,684	St. Petersburg, Russia	4,296
Cape of Good Hope	7,380	Stockholm, Sweden	4,055
Caraccas, Venezuela	1,058	Shanghai, China	8,600
Charlotte Town, P. E. I.	820	Singapore, Malay	11,300
Dublin, Ireland	3,076	St. John's N. F.	1,340
Delhi, Hindostan	8,368	San Demingo, S. D.	4,300
Edinburgh, Scotland	3,275	San Juan, Nicaragua	1,740
Frederickton, N. B.	670	San Salvador, A. C.	1,650
Gibraltar, Spain	3,150	Santiago, Chili	4,970
Glasgow, Scotland	3,215	Spanish Town, Jamaica	1,446
Halifax, N. S.	780	Sidney, C. B. I.	975
Hamburg, Germany	3,570	Sydney, Australia	8,963
Havana, Cuba	1,139	St. Paul de Loanda	5,578
Honolulu, S. I.	4,513	Timbuctoo, Soudan	3,395
Jerusalem, Palestine	5,495	Tripoli, Tripoli	4,425
Jamestown, St. Helena	7,150	Tunis, Tunis	4,240
Lima, Peru	3,515	Toronto, Canada	343
Lisbon, Portugal	3,190	Venice, Italy	3,835
Liverpool, England	3,228	Vienna, Austria	4,115
London, England	3,315	Valparaiso, Chili	4,934
City of Mexico, Mex.	1,867	Vera Cruz, Mexico	1,680
Montevideo, Uruguay	5,003	Warsaw, Poland	4,010
Montreal, Canada	471	Yeddo, Japan	7,630
Madrid, Spain	3,485	Zanzibar, Zanzibar	7,078
Moscow, Russia	4,466		

Builders' Estimating Tables.

Table showing quantity of material in every four lineal feet of exterior wall in a balloon frame building, height of wall being given:

Length of Studs.	Size of Sills.	Size of Studs, Braces, etc.	Quantity of Rough Lumber.	Quantity of Inch Boarding.	Siding in sup. feet.	Tar Paper in sup. feet.
8	6x 6	2x4 studs.	42	36	40	74
10	6x 8	4x4 braces.	52	44	50	80
12	6x10	4x4 plates.	62	53	60	96
14	6x10	1x6 ribbons.	69	62	70	112
16	8x10		82	71	80	128
18	8x10	studs	87	80	90	144
20	8x12	16 inches from	98	88	100	160
22	9x12	centers.	109	97	110	176
24	10x12		119	106	420	192
18	10x10	2x6 studs.	122	80	90	144
20	10x12	6x6 braces.	137	88	100	160
22	10x12	4x6 plates.	145	97	110	176
24	12x12	1x6 ribbons.	162	106	120	192
26	10x14		169	114	130	208
28	10x14	studs 16 inch centers.	176	123	140	224
30	12x14		198	132	150	240

Table showing amount of lumber in rafters, collar-piece and boarding, and number of shingles to four lineal feet of roof, measured from eave to eave over ridge. Rafters 16-inch centers:

Width of House. Feet.	Size of Rafters.	Size of Collar-piece.	Quantity of Lumber in Rafter and Collar-piece.	Quant'y of Board'g Feet.	No. of Shingl's
14	2x4	2x4	39	91	560
16	2x4	2x4	45	70	640
18	2x4	2x4	50	79	720
20	2x4	2x4	56	88	800
22	2x4	2x4	62	97	880
24	2x4	2x4	67	106	960
20	2x6	2x6	84	88	800
22	2x6	2x6	92	97	880
24	2x6	2x6	101	106	960
26	2x6	2x6	109	115	1040
28	2x6	2x6	117	124	1120
30	2x6	2x6	126	133	1200

Wages Table — Yearly, Monthly, Weekly Daily and Hourly.

TEN HOURS TO THE DAY.

Wages Per Year.	Wages Per Month.	Wages Per Week.	Wages Per Day.	Wages Per Year.	Wages Per Month.	Wages Per Week.	Wages Per Day.
$1,000 is	$83 33	$19 23	$2 74	$295 is	$24 58	$5 67	81c.
975	81 25	18 75	2 67	290	24 17	5 58	79
950	79 17	18 27	2 60	285	23 75	5 48	78
925	77 08	17 79	2 53	280	23 33	5 38	77
900	75 00	17 31	2 47	275	22 92	5 29	75
875	72 92	16 83	2 40	270	22 50	5 19	74
850	70 83	16 35	2 33	260	21 67	5 00	71
825	68 75	15 87	2 26	250	20 83	4 81	69
800	66 67	15 38	2 19	240	20 00	4 62	66
775	64 58	14 90	2 12	235	19 58	4 52	64
750	62 50	14 42	2 05	230	19 17	4 42	63
725	60 42	13 94	1 99	225	18 75	4 33	62
700	58 33	13 46	1 92	220	18 33	4 23	60
675	56 25	12 99	1 85	215	17 92	4 13	59
650	54 17	12 50	1 78	210	17 50	4 04	58
625	52 08	12 02	1 71	205	17 08	3 94	56
600	50 00	11 54	1 64	200	16 67	3 85	55
575	47 92	11 06	1 58	195	16 25	3 75	53
550	45 83	10 58	1 51	190	15 83	3 64	52
525	43 75	10 10	1 44	185	15 42	3 56	51
500	41 67	9 62	1 37	180	15 00	3 46	49
475	39 58	9 13	1 30	175	14 58	3 37	48
450	37 50	8 66	1 23	170	14 17	3 27	47
425	35 42	8 17	1 16	165	13 75	3 17	45
400	33 33	7 69	1 10	160	13 33	3 08	44
390	32 50	7 50	1 07	155	12 92	2 98	42
380	31 67	7 31	1 04	150	12 50	2 88	41
375	31 25	7 21	1 03	145	12 08	2 79	40
370	30 83	7 12	1 01	140	11 67	2 69	38
360	30 00	6 92	99	135	11 25	2 60	37
350	29 17	6 73	96	130	10 83	2 50	36
340	28 33	6 54	93	125	10 42	2 40	34
330	27 50	6 35	90	120	10 00	2 31	33
325	27 08	6 25	89	115	9 58	2 21	32
320	26 67	6 15	88	110	9 17	2 11	30
310	25 83	5 96	85	105	8 75	2 02	29
300	25 00	5 77	82	100	8 33	1 92	27

Six Days' Wages.	One Day.	Eight Hours.	Six Hours.	Five Hours.	Four Hours.	Two Hours.	One Hour.
$2	33⅓	26⅔	20	16⅔	13⅓	6⅔	3⅓
3	50	40	30	25	20	10	5
4	66⅔	53⅓	40	33⅓	26⅔	13⅓	6⅔
5	83⅓	66⅔	50	41⅔	33⅓	16⅔	8⅓
6	$1 00	80	60	50	40	20	10
7	1 16⅔	93⅓	70	58⅓	46⅔	23⅓	11⅔
8	1 33⅓	$1 06⅔	80	66⅔	53⅓	26⅔	13⅓
9	1 50	1 20	90	75	60	30	15
10	1 66⅔	1 33⅓	$1 00	83⅓	66⅔	33⅓	16⅔
11	1 83⅓	1 46⅔	1 10	91⅔	73⅓	36⅔	18⅓
12	2 00	1 60	1 20	$1 00	80	40	20
13	2 16⅔	1 73⅓	1 30	1 08⅓	86⅔	43⅓	21⅔
14	2 33⅓	1 86⅔	1 40	1 16⅔	93⅓	46⅔	23⅓
15	2 50	2 00	1 50	1 25	$1 00	50	25
16	2 66⅔	2 13⅓	1 60	1 33⅓	1 06⅔	53⅓	26⅛
17	2 83⅓	2 26⅔	1 70	1 41⅔	1 13⅓	56⅔	28⅓
18	3 00	2 40	1 80	1 50	1 20	60	30
19	3 16⅔	2 53⅓	1 90	1 58⅓	1 26⅔	63⅓	31⅔
20	3 33⅓	2 66⅔	2 00	1 66⅔	1 33⅓	66⅔	33⅓

Carpenters', Plasterers' and Bricklayers' Work.

To find how many square yards in a floor or wall: *multiply the length by the width or height, and divide the product by 9.*

How many square yards in a floor 18 ft. long and 14 ft. wide; and how many yards of carpet ¾ yd. wide, will it take?

To divide by a fraction, multiply the number by the *denominator*, and divide the product by the *numerator.*

To multiply by a fraction, multiply by the *numerator* and divide by the *denominator.*

14×18=252 sq feet.
9)252(28 sq. yds.

28
4

3)112(37⅓ yds. carpet.

Ans. 28 sq. yds.
37⅓ yds. carpet.

Find how many square yards in the four walls and ceiling of a room 18 by 20, 11 ft. high; and the cost of plastering the same at 15 cts. per sq yd

The length of the *four* walls is (twice 20 and twice 18) 76 feet, which multiplied by the height gives the sq. ft. in the walls The length multiplied by the width gives the sq. ft. in the ceiling.

76×11=836 sq. ft. in four walls.
18×20=360 " " " ceiling.

9(1196(133 sq. yds. nearly.
.15

Ans. $19.95 for plastering.

To measure square timbers: *multiply the length, width and thickness together, and divide the product by 12.*
How many square feet in a joist 2 by 8, 18 ft. long?
$$2 \times 8 \times 18 = 288 \div 12 = 24 \text{ ft. Ans}$$
Sill 8 by 8, 22 ft. long? $8 \times 8 \times 22 = 1408 \div 12 = 117\frac{1}{3}$ ft. Ans.

Amount of Paint Required for a Given Surface.

It is impossible to give a rule that will apply in all cases, as the amouut varies with the kind and thickness of the paint, the kind of wood or other material to which it is applied, the age of the surface, etc. The following is an approximate rule: Divide the number of square feet of surface by 200. The result will be the number of gallons of liquid paint required to give two coats; or, divide by 18 and the result will be the number of pounds of pure ground white lead required to give three coats.

How to Kill Grease Spots before Painting.

Wash over smoky or greasy parts with saltpetre, or very thin lime white-wash. If soap-suds are used, they must be washed off thoroughly, as they prevent the paint from drying hard.

Dimensions of One Acre.

A square, whose sides are 12,649 rods, or 69.57 yards or 208.71 feet long, contains one acre. Table of dimensions of rectangle containing one acre:

RODS.

1	× 160	1½ × 106⅔	2	× 80		2½ × 64	
3	× 53⅓	3½ × 45 5-7	4	× 40		4½ × 35 5-9	
5	× 32	5½ × 29 1-11	6	× 26⅔		6½ × 24 8-13	
7	× 22 6-7	7½ × 21⅓	8	× 20		8½ × 18 14-17	
9	× 17 7-9	9½ × 16 16-19	10	× 16		10½ × 15 5-21	
11	× 14 6-11	11½ × 13 21-33	12	× 13½		12½ × 12 4-5	
...	...	...	...	...	12 13-20	× 12 13-20	

Roof Elevations.

By the 'pitch" of a roof is meant the relation which the height of the ridge above the level of the roof-plates bears to the span, or the distance between the studs on which the roof rests.
The length of rafters for the most common pitches can be found as follows from any given span:

If ¼ pitch, multiply span by 559, or 7-12 nearly.
If ⅓ " " " " 6 , or 3-5 "
If ⅜ " " " " 625, or ⅝ "
If ½ " " " " .71 , or 7-10 "
If ⅝ " " " " .8 , or 4-5 "
If full " " " " 1.12, or 1⅛ "

To lengths thus obtained must be added amount of projection of rafters at the eaves.

As rafters must be purchased of even lengths, a few inches more or less on their lengths will make a difference to the pitch so slight that it cannot be detected by the eye.

EXAMPLE.—To determine the length of rafters for a' roof constructed one-half pitch, with a span of 24 feet—$24 \times .71 = 17.04$; or, practically, just 17 feet. A projection of one foot for eaves makes the length to be purchased 18 feet.

How To Build Strong Frames.

Sheathing put on diagonally acts as a brace over the whole surface, and requires no more lumber than if put on horizontally. It is well to run the sheathing from each side up parallel with the rafters, if at the gable ends, and at similar angles at the sides. Roofing boards can be put on in the same manner. Studs can be allowed to project above the plates and the rafters spiked to the sides of studs. Partitions should be braced with waste stuff, and in such ways a building can be strengthened that it can be rolled over and over without coming to pieces, and the extra cost will simply consist in a few hours extra labor.

In some parts of the West, and especially in Nebraska, a framed sill is in use, which combines qualities that will make it of service to builders in many localities. A piece of 2x6 or 2x8 is laid upon the wall, and flush with one side of this a 2-inch piece of the same width as the joists is placed on edge and securely spiked on, thus making the bottom and one side of a trough. These can be fastened before being put in place. The joists are placed with their ends upon the bed of the sill and against the side, and spiked to both. The studs are halved down, in this case 8 inches, and nailed to side of sill and joists. The sides of the sill, running parallel with the joists, are formed by two of the joists themselves, either set flush with the face of the wall and the studs let down back, or set back two inches and the studs let down in front.

When the frame is finished, and before the floor is laid, the wall is built up behind and over the sill; thus holding all in place, guarding against wind, as the wall must be torn up before the building will go; and also, incidentally, against rats and other vermin. It will be found fully as strong and much cheaper than timber.

If posts are used for the foundation, a modification of this arrangement will prove equally serviceable. The principal on which it depends is explained at length farther on. It is well known that a thin piece of timber put on edge, as in joists, etc., will support a much greater weight than if laid on its side. The strength of a piece is in direct proportion to the square of its depth and nearly inversely as its length. Thus it will be found that simply the 2x12, 8 feet long, without considering the support afforded to it by the walls, would have a strength equal to four 2x4s 16 feet long. It might be objected that the joists would not rest on the 2x12, but on the 2x6. This is partly true, but the joists are spiked to the 2x12, and are nailed to the studs, which rest on the sill, thus binding the whole together. Particular care must be taken to spike the 2x12 side of the sill to the 2x4 or 2x6 base at short intervals. All the parts must be well nailed together, and especially the studs to the joists, and the sills to the posts. This form will have abundant strength and stiffness if the posts are not over 8 feet apart. A sill constructed in this way, of these dimensions, contains the same number of feet as a 6x6 sill, but will sustain a weight a third greater than the latter, if the weights are placed at the centers, but as the studs are fastened together by the sheathing, the weight will be partly transferred from the sills to the posts. It can also be made of any lengths that will reach from post to post, and the cost can thus be made less.

Shingles Required in a Roof.

To the square foot it takes 9 if exposed four inches; 8 if exposed 4½ inches, and 7 1-5 if exposed 5 inches to the weather.

Find the number of shingles required to cover a roof 38 ft. long, and the rafters on each side 14 ft. Shingles exposed 4½ inches.
28 × 38 = 1064 (sq. ft.) × 8 = 8512 shingles. Ans.

To find the length of rafters, giving the roof *one-third* pitch: take *three-fifths* of the width of the building. If the building is 30 feet wide, they must be 18 feet long, exclusive of projection.

The following very useful and practical calculations will be found exceedingly handy, as guides to the builder, in making up his figures when he is called upon to estimate for all portions of a job, many of which are not entirely in his own particular line:

MASON WORK — BRICK.

1⅛ barrels lime and ⅝ yard sand will lay 1,000 brick.
One man with 1¼ tenders will lay 1,800 to 2,000 brick per day.

RUBBLE.

1¼ barrels lime and 1 yard of sand will lay 100 feet of stone.
One man will lay 150 feet of stone per day with one tender

CEMENT.

1¼ barrels cement and ¾ yard sand will lay 100 feet rubble stone
Same time as to mason and tender as rubble.

NUMBER OF NAILS REQUIRED IN CARPENTER WORK.

To case and hang one door, 1 lb.
To case and hang one window, ¾ lb.
Base, 100 lineal feet, 1 lb.
To put on rafters, joists, etc., 3 lbs. to 1,000 feet.
To put up studding, same.
To lay a 6-inch pine floor, 15 lbs. to 1,000 feet.

LABOR.

To place joists, etc., on wall, $4 per 1,000.
Put up jambs and case a door, $1.50.
Hanging door and locking, 50c. to 75c.
Fitting sash, 50c. to 75c.
Casing window, stool and apron, $1.00.
Hang outside blinds, 50c.
Hang inside blinds, 75c.; if boxed, $1.00.
Lay pine floor, 6 in., 30c. per square.
Lay pine floor, 4 in., 40c. per square.
Lay walnut floor, 3 in., $1 per square.
Roof and sheathing, 25c. per square.
To lay shingles, per 1,000, 75c. per square.

COST OF PAINTERS' WORK.

1 coat shellac, 50c. per square.
1 coat lead and oil, 75c. per square.
2 coats lead and oil, $1.50 per square.
3 coats lead and oil, $2.50 per square.
Sanding, 1 coat, 75c. per square.
Grain oak, 2 coats, $2.50 per square.
Grain walnut, 2 coats, $3.00 per square.
To set glass, 10 per cent. of cost.
Calcimining, 60c. to 75c. per square.
1 coat varnish, 50c. per square.

Floor, Wall and Roof Measure.

To find the number of square yards in a floor or wall: RULE— Multiply the length by the width or height (in feet) and divide the product by 9; the result will be square yards.

ESTIMATES OF MATERIALS.

3½ barrels of lime will do 100 square yards plastering, two coats.
2   "   "   "   "   100   "   "   "   one coat.
1½ bushels of hair   "   100   "   "   "
1¼ yards good sand   "   100   "   "   "
⅓ barrel of plaster (stucco) will hard-finish 100 square yards plastering.
1 barrel of lime will lay 1,000 bricks. (It takes good lime to do it.)
2 barrels of lime will lay 1 cord rubble stone.
½ barrel of lime will lay 1 perch rubble stone. (Estimating ¼ cord to perch.)
To every barrel of lime estimate about ⅝ yards of good sand for plastering and brick work.

IRON FURNACES.—There are about 690 iron furnaces in the United States. These turned out, in 1882, over 5,000,000 tons of pig iron.

THE LARGEST TELESCOPE in the world is the Lord Rosse, which has an aperture of seventy-two inches. The largest in this country is at San Jose, Cal., having an aperture of twenty-eight inches.

Useful Information for Architects and Builders.

NUMBER OF NAILS AND TACKS PER POUND.

NAILS. Size.				No. per lb.		TACKS. Length.		No. per lb.
6 penny,	fence	2	in	80	nails	1 oz....	$\frac{1}{3}$ inch	16,000
8 "	"	$2\frac{1}{2}$	"	50	"	$1\frac{1}{4}$ "	....3-16 "	10,666
10 "	"	3	"	34	"	2 "	....$\frac{1}{4}$ "	 8,000
12 "	"	$3\frac{1}{4}$	"	39	"	$2\frac{1}{2}$ "	....5-16 "	 6,400
3 "	fine	$1\frac{1}{3}$	"	760	"	3 "	....$\frac{3}{8}$ "	 5,333
3 "		$1\frac{1}{4}$	"	480	"	4 "	....7-16 "	 4,000
4 "		$1\frac{1}{2}$	"	300	"	6 "	....9-16 "	 2,666
5 "		$1\frac{3}{4}$	"	200	"	8 "	....$\frac{5}{8}$ "	 2,000
6 "		2	"	160	"	10 "	....11-16 "	 1,600
7 "		$2\frac{1}{4}$	"	128	"	12 "	....$\frac{3}{4}$ "	 1,333
8 "		$2\frac{1}{2}$	"	92	"	14 "	....13-16 "	 1,143
9 "		$2\frac{3}{4}$	"	72	"	16 "	....$\frac{7}{8}$ "	 1,000
10 "		3	"	60	"	18 "	....15-16 "	 888
12 "		$3\frac{1}{4}$	"	44	"	20 "	....1 "	 800
16 "		$3\frac{1}{2}$	"	32	"	22 "	....1 1-16 "	 727
20 "		4	"	24	"	24 "	....$1\frac{1}{8}$ "	 666
30 "		$4\frac{1}{4}$	"	18	"			
40 "		5	"	14	"			
50 "		$5\frac{1}{2}$	"	12	"			

1,000 shingles, laid 4 inches to the weather, will cover 100 square feet of surface, and 5 lbs. of shingle nails will fasten them on.

One-fifth more siding and flooring is needed than the number of square feet of surface to be covered, because of the lap in the siding and matching.

1,000 laths will cover 70 yards of surface, and 11 lbs. of lathe nails will nail them on; 8 bushels of good lime, 16 bushels of sand, and 1 bushel of hair, will make enough good mortar to plaster 100 square yards.

A cord of stone, 3 bushels of lime, and a cubic yard of sand, will lay 100 cubic feet of wall.

Five courses of brick will lay 1 foot in height on a chimney; 16 bricks in a course will make a flue 4 ins. wide and 12 ins. long, and 8 bricks in a course will make a flue 8 ins. wide and 16 ins. long.

Cement 1 bush. and sand 2 bush. will cover $3\frac{1}{2}$ sq. yds. 1 inch thick, $4\frac{1}{2}$ sq. yds. $\frac{3}{4}$ inch thick, and $6\frac{3}{4}$ sq. yds. $\frac{1}{2}$ inch thick; 1 bush. cement and 1 of sand will cover $2\frac{1}{4}$ sq. yds. 1 in. thick, 3 square yards $\frac{3}{4}$ inch thick, and $4\frac{1}{2}$ square yards $\frac{1}{2}$ inch thick.

Quantity of Bricks Required to Construct a Building.

Superficial Feet of Wall.	Number of Bricks to Thickness of					
	4 inch.	8 inch.	12 inch	16 inch	20 inch	24 inch
1	7	15	22	29	37	45
2	15	30	45	60	75	90
3	23	45	68	90	113	135
4	30	60	90	120	150	180
5	38	75	113	150	188	225
6	45	90	135	180	225	270
7	53	105	158	210	263	315
8	60	120	180	240	300	360
9	68	135	203	270	338	405
10	75	150	225	300	375	450
20	150	300	450	600	750	900
30	225	450	675	900	1,125	1,350
40	300	600	900	1,200	1,500	1,800
50	375	750	1,125	1,500	1,875	2,250
60	450	900	1,350	1,800	2,250	2,700
70	525	1,050	1,575	2,100	2,625	3,150
80	600	1,200	1,800	2,400	3,000	3,600
90	675	1,350	2,025	2,700	3,375	4,050
100	750	1,500	2,250	3,000	3,750	4,500
200	1,500	3,000	4,500	6,000	7,500	9,000
300	2,250	4,500	6,750	9,000	11,250	13,500
400	3,000	6,000	9,000	12,000	15,000	18,000

VALUE OF DIAMONDS.

Diamonds averaging one-half carat each, $60 per carat.
Diamonds averaging three-quarters carat each, $80 per carat.
Diamonds averaging one carat each, $100 per carat.
Diamonds averaging one and one-quarter carats each, $110 per carat.
Diamonds averaging one and one-half carats each, $120 per carat.
Diamonds averaging one and three-quarters carats each, $145 per carat.
Diamonds averaging two carats each, $175 per carat.

In other words, the value of the gem increases in the geometrical ratio of its weight. Four diamonds weighing together two carats are worth $120; but one diamond weighing just as much is worth $350. Stones weighing over two carats are about the same price per carat as two-carat stones· they should be dearer, but they are not, simply because the demand for them is limited. If the demand for diamonds were as imperative as the demand for flour or beef, the geometrical ratio would again come into play, and five-carat stones would be valued in the thousands.

TABLE showing the requisite sizes of girders and joists for warehouses, the span and distance apart being given:

Distance apart.	SPAN OF GIRDERS.				Joists.	REMARKS.
	6 Feet.	8 Feet.	10 Feet.	12 Feet.		
Feet.	Inches.	Inches.	Inches.	Inches.	Inches.	Girders to have a bearing at each end and joists six inches.
10	8x12	12x13	12x16	14x18	2½x10	
12	9x12	12x14	12x18	16x18	3 x10	
14	10x12	12x15	14x18	....	3 x12	

TABLE showing quantity of lumber in every four lineal feet of partition, studs being placed 16 centers, waste included:

Height of partition. Feet.	Quantity of Studs 2x4 Feet.	If 2x6. Feet.
8	20	30
9	23	34
10	26	38
11	29	42
12	32	46
13	35	51
14	38	55
15	41	59
16	44	64

TABLE as before, adapted for churches, public halls, etc.

Distance apart.	SPAN OF GIRDERS.				Joists.	REMARKS.
Feet.	6 Feet. Inches.	8 Feet. Inches.	10 Ft. Inches.	12 Ft. Inches.	Inches.	
12	6x10	8x12	12x14	12x16	2 x 8	
13	6x11	9x12	11x15	12x17	2 x 9	
14	6x12	10x12	12x15	11x18	2 x 9	
15	7x12	11x12	11x16	12x16	2 x10	
16	8x12	12x12	12x16	13x18	2 x10	Bearings of girders and joists as above.
17	8x12	9x14	12x17	14x18	2 x12	
18	9x12	10x14	11x18	......	2 x12	
19	9x12	11x14	12x18	......	2½x12	
20	10x12	12x14	13x18	......	2½x12	Both tables are calculated for yellow pine.
21	10x12	11x15	14x18	......	2½x12	
22	11x12	12x15	......	......	3 x12	
23	11x12	11x16	......	......	3 x12	
24	10x12	12x16	......	......	3 x13	
25	10x13	12x17	......	......	3 x13	
26	10x14	12x18	......	......	3 x14	
27	10x14	12x18	......	......	3 x14	

The Use of the Steel Square.

The standard steel square has a blade 24 inches long and 2 inches wide, and a tongue from 14 to 18 inches long and 1½ inches wide. The blade is exactly at right angles with the tongue, and the angle formed by them an exact right angle, or square corner. A proper square should have the ordinary divisions of inches, half inches, quarters and eighths, and often sixteenths and thirty-seconds. Another portion of the square is divided into twelfths of an inch; this portion is simply a scale of 12 feet to an inch, used for any purpose, as measuring scale drawings, etc The diagonal scale on the tongue near the blade, often found on squares, is thus termed from its diagonal lines However, the proper term is centesimal scale, for the reason that by it a unit may be divided into 100 equal parts, and therefore any number to the 100th part of a unit may be expressed. In this scale A B is one inch; then, if it be required to take off 73-100 inches, set one foot of the compasses in the third parallel under 1 at E, extend the other foot to the seventh diagonal in that parallel at G, and the distance between E G is that required, for E F is one inch and F G 73 parts of an inch.

Upon one side of the blade of the square, running parallel with the length, will be found nine lines, divided at intervals of one inch into sections or spaces by cross lines This is the plank, board and scantling measure. On each side of the cross lines referred to are figures, sometimes on one side of the cross line and often spread over the line, thus, 1 | 4—9 | — We will suppose we have a board 12 feet long and 6 inches wide. Looking on the outer edge of the blade we find 12; between the fifth and sixth lines, under 12, will be found 12 again; this is the length of the board. Now follow the space along toward the tongue till we come to the cross line under 6 (on the edge of the blade), this being the width of the board; in this space will be found the figure 6 again, which is the answer in board measure, viz., six feet

On some squares will be found on one side of the blade 9 lines, and crossing these lines diagonally to the right are rows of figures, as seven 1s, seven 2s, seven 3s, etc. This is another style of board measure and gives the feet in a board according to its length and width.

In the center of the tongue will generally be found two parallel lines, half an inch apart, with figures between them; this is termed the Brace Rule. Near the extreme end of the tongue will be found 24-24 and to the right of these 33.95. The 24-24 indicate the two sides of a right-angle-triangle, while the length of the brace is indicated by 33.95. This will explain the use of any of the figures in the brace rule. On the opposite side of the tongue from the brace rule will generally be found the octagon scale, situated between two central parallel lines This space is divided into intervals and numbered thus; 10, 20, 30, 40. 50, 60. Suppose it becomes necessary to describe an octagon ten inches square; draw a square ten inches each way and bisect the square with a horizontal and perpendicular center line. To find the length of the octagon line, place one point of the compasses on any of the main divisions of the scale and the other leg or point on the tenth subdivision. This length being measured off on each side of center lines, touching the line of the octagon, will give the points from which to draw the octagonal lines. The size of the octagon must equal the number of spaces taken off from the tongue by the compasses.

Weight of a Cubic Foot of Earth, Stone, Metal, &c.

Article.	Lbs.	Article.	Lbs.
Alcohol	49	Lead, cast	709
Ash Wood	53	Lead, rolled	711
Bay Wood	51	Milk	64
Brass, gun metal	543	Maple	47
Brandy	58	Mortar	110
Beer	65	Mud	102
Blood	66	Marble, Italian	169
Brick, common	102	Marble, Vermont	165
Cork	15	Mahogany	66
Cedar	35	Oak, Canadian	54
Copper, cast	547	Oak, live, seasoned	67
Copper, plates	543	Oak, white, dry	54
Clay	120	Oil, linseed	59
Coal, Lehigh	56	Pine, yellow	34
Coal, Lackawanna	50	Pine, white	34
Cider	64	Pine, red	37
Chestnut	38	Pine, well seasoned	30
Ebony	83	Platina	1,219
Earth, loose	94	Red Hickory	52
Glass, Window	165	Silver	625¾
Gold	1,203⅔	Steel, plates	487¾
Hickory, pig nut	49	Steel, soft	489
Hickory, shell-bark	43	Stone, common, about	158
Hay, bale	9	Sand, wet, about	128
Hay, pressed	25	Spruce	31
Honey	90	Tin	455
Iron, cast	450	Tar	63
Iron, plates	481	Vinegar	67
Iron, wrought bars	486	Water, salt	64
Ice	57½	Water, rain	62
Lignum Vitæ Wood	83	Willow	36
Logwood	57	Zinc, cast	428

Composition of Solders.

Fine Solder is an alloy of two parts of Block Tin and one part of Lead. Glazing Solder is equal parts of Block Tin and Lead. Plumbing Solder, one part Block Tin, two parts Lead.

AVERAGE WEIGHT of an American man is 141½ pounds; of a woman, 124½ pounds.

Cost of Tin Roofing per Square and per Square Foot.

The following table shows the cost per square and per square foot of tin roofing, laid with 14x20 tin, with tin at any price from $4 to $10 per box. The first column contains the price per box of tin; the second column shows the cost of tin per square (100 square feet) of surface, and the third column shows the cost of tin per square foot of surface:

FLAT SEAM ROOFING -- COST WITH 14x20 TIN.

Price of Tin per box.	Cost per square of flat roof 14x20 Tin.	Cost per sq. foot.	Price of Tin per box.	Cost per square of flat roof 14x20 Tin.	Cost per sq. foot.
$4.25	$2.21	.0221	$8.25	$4.29	.0420
4.50	2.34	.0234	8.50	4.42	.0442
4.75	2.47	.0247	8.75	4.55	.0455
5.00	2.60	.0260	9.00	4.68	.0468
5.25	2.73	.0273	9.25	4.81	.0481
5.50	2.86	.0286	9.50	4.94	.0494
5.75	2.99	.0299	9.75	5.07	.0507
6.00	3.12	.0312	10.00	5.20	.0520
6.25	3.25	.0325	10.25	5.33	.0533
6.50	3.38	.0338	10.50	5.46	.0546
6.75	3.51	.0351	10.75	5.59	.0559
7.00	3.64	.0364	11.00	5.72	.0572
7.25	3.77	.0377	11.25	5.85	.0585
7.50	3.90	.0390	11.50	5.98	.0598
7.75	4.03	.0403	11.75	6.11	.0611
8.00	4.16	.0416	12.00	6.24	.0624

STANDING SEAM ROOFING -- COST WITH 14x20 TIN.

Price of Tin per box.	Cost per Square of stand'g seam roof with 14x20 Tin.	Cost per sq. foot	Price of Tin per box.	Cost per square of stand'g seam roof with 14x20 Tin.	Cost per sq. foot
$4.25	$2.37	.0237	$7.25	$4.03	.0403
4.50	2.51	.0251	7.50	4.17	.0417
4.75	2.65	.0265	7.75	4.31	.0431
5.00	2.79	.0279	8.00	4.45	.0445
5.25	2.93	.0293	8.25	4.59	.0459
5.50	3.06	.0306	8.50	4.73	.0473
5.75	3.20	.0320	8.75	4.87	.0487
6.00	3.34	.0334	9.00	5.01	.0501
6.25	3.48	.0348	9.25	5.15	.0515
6.50	3.62	.0362	9.50	5.29	.0529
6.75	3.76	.0376	9.75	5.43	.0543
7.00	3.90	.0390	10.00	5.57	.0557

Cost of Tin Roofing per Square—continued.

FLAT SEAM ROOFING—COST WITH 20x28 TIN.

Price of Tin per box.	Cost per square of flat roof 20x28 Tin.	Cost per sq. foot.	Price of Tin per box.	Cost per square of flat roof 20x28 Tin.	Cost per sq. foot.
$8.00	$2.01	.0201	$16.00	$4.01	.0401
8.50	2.13	.0213	16.50	4.13	.0413
9.00	2.26	.0226	17.00	4.26	.0426
9.50	2.38	.0238	17.50	4.38	.0438
10.00	2.51	.0251	18.00	4.51	.0451
10.50	2.63	.0263	18.50	4.63	.0463
11.00	2.76	.0276	19.00	4.76	.0476
11.50	2.88	.0288	19.50	4.88	.0488
12.00	3.00	.0300	20.00	5.01	.0501
12.50	3.13	.0313	20.50	5.13	.0513
13.00	3.25	.0325	21.00	5.26	.0526
13.50	3.38	.0338	21.50	5.38	.0538
14.00	3.50	.0350	22.00	5.51	.0551
14.50	3.63	.0363	22.50	5.63	.0563
15.00	3.75	.0375	23.00	5.76	.0576
15.50	3.88	.0388			

STANDING SEAM ROOFING—COST WITH 20x28 TIN.

Price of Tin per box.	Cost per square of standi'g seam roof with 20x28 Tin.	Cost per sq. foot.	Price of Tin per box.	Cost per square of standi'g seam roof with 20x28 Tin.	Cost per sq. foot.
$8.00	$2.15	.0215	$16.50	$4.42	.0442
8.50	2.28	.0228	17.00	4.56	.0456
9.00	2.41	.0241	17.50	4.69	.0469
9.50	2.55	.0255	18.00	4.82	.0482
10.00	2.68	.0268	18.50	4.96	.0496
10.50	2.82	.0282	19.00	5.09	.0509
11.00	2.95	.0295	19.50	5.23	.0523
11.50	3.09	.0309	20.00	5.36	.0536
12.00	3.21	.0321	20.50	5.49	.0549
12.50	3.35	.0335	21.00	5.63	.0563
13.00	3.48	.0348	21.50	5.76	.0576
13.50	3.62	.0362	22.00	5.90	.0590
14.00	3.75	.0375	22.50	6.03	.0603
14.50	3.89	.0389	23.00	6.17	.0617
15.00	4.02	.0402	23.50	6.30	.0630
15.50	4.15	.0415	24.00	6.43	.0643
16.00	4.29	.0429			

The Fastest Locomotive Ever Built.

The largest and fastest passenger engine ever built was by the Rhode Island Locomotive Works, for the New York, Providence and Boston Railroad Company The main driving wheels are six feet in diameter and set but seven feet six inches apart. This arrangement makes her run easily on curves. The cylinders are eighteen inches in diameter, with twenty-four-inch stroke. The boiler is fifty-four inches in diameter at the smoke-stack, with a wagon top. It extends to the very end of the cab, and necessitates the elevation of the engineer's seat to a height far above the fire-door. The fire required three tons of coal before the engine pulled out of the round-house to make her trips. and four tons will be carried on the tender. The tank of the latter will hold 4,000 gallons of water, and the total weight of the engine proper is 93,000 to 95,000 pounds. The weight on the driving wheel will be 66,000 pounds, or 4,800 more than the Connecticut

She looks to be enormously high as she sets up well in the air, and her short smoke-stack adds to her apparent height. Every thing about her is steel. There is not a particle of brass or bright work about her. She will make the run from Providence to Groton, Conn., a distance of 62.5 miles, including a dead stop at Mystic drawbridge, as required by the statutes of Connecticut, in just 62.5 minutes, pulling at the same time eight cars four of which are Pullmans.

Notable Bridges of the World.

Sublician bridge, at Rome, oldest wooden bridge; seventh century. Twice rebuilt, but ruins only remain.

The bridge at Burton, over the Trent; once the longest bridge in England; 1,545 feet.

The old London bridge was the first stone bridge. Commenced in 1176, completed in 1209.

The bridge of the Holy Trinity, Florence, built in 1569; marble; 322 feet long

The Bridge of Sighs, at Venice, over which condemned prisoners passed to execution, was built in 1589.

The Rialto, at Venice, a single marble arch, built from designs of Michael Angelo, 98½ feet long; completed 1591.

Coalbrookdale bridge, England, was the first cast-iron bridge. Built over the Severn in 1779.

New London bridge, granite, from designs by L. Rennier. Commenced in 1824, completed in about seven years; cost $7,291,000.

The Britannia bridge, over the Menai Strait, Wales, 103 feet above high water. Wrought iron, 1,511 feet long, finished in 1850. Cost, $3,008,000.

The Niagara Suspension bridge was built by Roebling, in 1852-55. Cost, $400,000; 245 feet above water, 1,268 feet long, estimated 1,200 tons.

Havre de Grace, over the Susquehanna, 3,271 feet long.

Brooklyn Bridge was commenced under the direction of J.

Roebling in 1870, an completed in about thirteen years; 3,475 feet long, 135 feet high. Cost nearly $15,000,000.

The Canti-Lever bridge, 1884, over the Niagara, steel. Length 910 feet; total weight, 3,000 tons; cost was $222,000.

Rush street bridge, Chicago, Ill., 1884, cost $132,000; the largest general traffic drawbridge in the world. Will accommodate four teams abreast, and its foot passages are seven feet wide in the clear. Swung by steam power and lighted by electric light.

    Cincinnati, over Ohio river (suspension), 2,220 feet long.
    Trajans, over Danube river (stone), 4,770 feet long.
    Highbridge, Harlem (stone), 1,460 feet long.
    Victoria, Montreal (tubular), 9,144 feet long.
    Louisville, over Ohio river (truss), 5,218 feet long.
    St. Louis, over the Mississippi (steel), 2,045 feet long.

Height of Principal Monuments and Towers.

Places.	Names.	Feet.
Egypt	Pyramid of Cheops	486
Belgium	Antwerp Cathedral	476
France	Strasburg Cathedral	474
Egypt	Pyramid of Cephrenes	456
Rome	St. Peter's Church	448
Germany	St. Martin's Church at Landshut	411
England	St. Paul's Church, London	365
England	Salisbury Cathedral	400
Italy	Cathedral at Florence	386
Lombardy	Cathedral at Cremona	397
Germany	Church at Fribourg	386
Spain	Cathedral of Seville	360
Lombardy	Cathedral of Milan	355
Holland	Cathedral of Utrecht	356
Egypt	Pyramid of Sakkarah	356
Bavaria	Cathedral of Notre Dame, Munich	348
Venice	St. Mark's Church	328
Italy	Assinelli Tower, Bologna	272
New York	Trinity Church	284
Hindostan	Column at Delhi	262
China	Porcelain Tower, Nankin	260
Paris	Church of Notre Dame	224
Massachusetts	Bunker Hill Monument	221
Italy	Leaning Tower of Pisa	179
Baltimore	Washington Monument	175
Paris	Monument, Place Vendome	153
Italy	Trajan's Pillar, Rome	151
Paris	Obelisk of Luxor	110

ANDERSONVILLE. — The total number of deaths in Andersonville prison was 12,462, about one-third of which took place in the stockade and two-thirds in the hospital. The greatest number imprisoned at any one time was 33,006. Number of escapes, 328.

Important Events of the Late Civil War.
A CORRECT AND CONCISE ACCOUNT OF THE VICTORIES AND DEFEATS AND IMPORTANT BATTLES.

NOVEMBER, 1860.

10th—Bill to equip and raise 10,000 volunteers introduced in South Carolina Legislature.

18th—Georgia Legislature voted $1,000,000 to arm the State.

20th-23d—Specie payment suspended by banks in Richmond, Baltimore, Washington, Philadelphia and Trenton, also generally through the South.

DECEMBER, 1860.

3d—A John Brown anniversary meeting in Boston broken up by riot.

10th—Louisiana Legislature voted $500,000 to arm the State.

24th—Election in Alabama—60,000 majority for secession.

27th—Troops ordered out in Charleston

JANUARY, 1861.

5th—Steamer Star of the West sailed from N. Y with supplies and reinforcements for Fort Sumter, arrived off Charleston on 9th, was fired upon and driven back to sea; returned to N. Y. on 12th with two shot holes in her hull.

7th—Senator Toombs, of Georgia, made a secession speech in U. S. Senate.

18th—Virginia Legislature appropriated $1,000,000 for the defense of the State.

21st—Jefferson Davis withdrew from U. S. Senate.

31st—U. S. mint at New Orleans seized by State authorities.

FEBRUARY, 1861.

9th—Jefferson Davis elected President of C. S. A.

9th—U. S. $25,000,000 loan bill signed by the President.

MARCH, 1861.

4th—Abraham Lincoln inaugurated President.

26th—Sam Houston, Governor of Texas, deposed for refusal to take an oath of allegiance to the C. S. A.

MAY, 1861.

2d—N. Y. 69th Regiment arrived in Washington.

5th—General Butler took possession of Relay House.

11th—Charleston blockade established.

17th—C. S. Congress authorized issue of $50,000,000 8 % 20-year bonds.

29th—President Davis reached Richmond.

31st—Cavalry skirmish at Fairfax C. H., Va.

JUNE, 1861.

2d—Battle of Phillippo, Va.; Confederates routed.
10th—Battle of Big Bethel, Va.; Union forces repulsed.
11th—Col. Wallace routed Confederate force of 800 at Romney, Va.
14th—Confederates evacuated and burned Harper's Ferry, Va.
18th—Battle of Booneville, Mo.; Confederates routed by Gen. Lyon.
23d—Forty-eight B. & O. R. R. locomotives, valued at $400,000, destroyed by Confederates.
29th—General Council of War held at Washington.

JULY, 1861.

5th—President Lincoln called for 400,000 men and $400,000,000 to put down the rebellion.
5th—Battle of Carthage, Mo.
10th—Battle of Laurel Hill.
11th—Battle at Rich Mountain.
18th—First Battle of Bull Run.
21st—Second Battle of Bull Run. Conflict lasted ten hours, when panic seized Union forces and they fled in disorder to Washington. The loss was:
Confederate, 630 killed; 2,235 wounded;   150 missing—3,015.
Union,   481   "   1,011   "   1,216   "   —2,698.
The number engaged were: Union 40,000 vs. Confederate 47,000, which were reinforced during the battle by 20,000 or 25,000.

AUGUST, 1861.

2d—Battle of Dug Spring, Mo.
4th—Battle of Athens, Mo.
7th—Hampton, Va., burned by Confederates.
8th—Battle of Lovettsville, Va.; Confederates routed.
10th—Battle of Wilson Creek, Mo. Union force, 5,200; Confederate force, 15,000. After six hours fighting, Confederates repulsed.
14th—Martial law declared in St. Louis.
15th—President Davis ordered all Northern men to leave the Confederacy within forty days.
20th—Skirmish of Hawk's Nest, Va.; 4,000 Confederates attacked 11th Ohio Regt.; driven back with 50 killed.
28th—Bombardment and capture of Forts Clark and Hatteras. Confederate loss, 765 prisoners and 1,000 stand of arms.
29th—Lexington, Mo., attacked.

SEPTEMBER, 1861.

6th—Paducah, Ky., occupied by United States forces.
10th—Battle of Carnifex Ferry, Va.
18th—Banks at New Orleans suspended specie payment.
20th—Col. Mulligan surrendered at Lexington, Mo., with 2,500 men, to the Confederates.
24th—Romney, Va., stormed and captured by United States troops.

OCTOBER, 1861.

3d—Battle at Greenbrier, Va.
7th—Gen. W. T. Sherman relieved.
16th—Battle near Pilot Knob, Mo.
21st—Battle of Balls Bluff.
21st—Battle of Wild Cat, Ky.
28th—Battle of Cromwell, Ky.

NOVEMBER, 1861.

1st—Winfield Scott, Commander of the United States army, retired, and Maj.-Gen. Geo. B. McClellan was appointed in his place.
7th—Great naval fight off Hilton Head.
8th—Battle of Belmont, Mo.
11th—Battle of Piketon, Ky.
19th—English packet Trent boarded by Capt. Wilkes, and Mason and Slidell captured. On the 24th inst. they were placed in Fort Warren, Boston Harbor, from which they were released on January 1, 1862, on a demand of the British government.

DECEMBER, 1861.

2d—Naval engagement at Newport News.
9th—Congress passed bill authorizing exchange of prisoners.
10th—Shelling of Free Stone Point by Union gunboats.
20th—Battle of Drainsville, Mo.
30th—Banks of New York, Philadelphia, Albany and Boston suspended specie payment.

JANUARY, 1862.

2d—Battle on Point Royal Island, S. C.
10th—Battle of Middle Creek, Ky.
19th—Battle of Mill Spring, Ky. Confederate loss, 192 killed, 68 wounded, 89 prisoners; Union loss, 39 killed, 207 wounded.

FEBRUARY, 1862.

6th—Fort Henry captured by Union soldiers.
7th and 8th—Battle of Roanoke Island. Union loss, 50 killed, 222 wounded; Confederate loss, 13 killed, 39 wounded, 2,527 prisoners.
13th—Battle of Fort Donelson, which was kept up incessantly till the 16th, when the fort was surrendered to the Union forces. Union loss, 446 killed, 1,735 wounded, 150 prisoners; Confederate loss, 237 killed, 1,007 wounded, 13,300 prisoners.
21st—Battle near Fort Craig, N. M. Union loss, 162 killed, 40 wounded.

MARCH, 1862.

6th to 8th—Battle of Pea Ridge, Arkansas. Union loss, 203 killed, 972 wounded, 176 missing; Confederate loss, 1,100 killed, 2,400 wounded, 1,600 prisoners.
9th—First encounter of iron clad vessels, "Monitor" and "Merrimac," in which the Merrimac was defeated.
10th—Manassas, Va., evacuated by rebels.

14th—Battle of Newbern, N. C.
23d—Battle of Winchester, Va.
28th—Battle of Valles Ranch, N. M.
31st—B. & O. R. R. reopened, after having been closed nearly a year.

APRIL, 1862.

6th and 7th—Battle of Pittsburg Landing. Union loss: 1,735 killed, 7,822 wounded, 4,044 missing. Over 3,000 Confederates were buried on the field.
7th—Island No. 10, Mississippi River, surrendered after a 23 days' bombardment. Confederate loss: 125 guns, 13 steamers, 10,000 small arms, 2,000 horses, 1,000 wagons, and over 6,000 prisoners.
9th—" Shiloh," the famous battle, fought.
11th—Pulaski surrendered after a thirty-hour bombardment
16th—Battle of Lee's Mills.
19th—Battle of Camden, North Carolina.
26th—Commodore Farragut demanded the surrender of New Orleans.

MAY, 1862.

1st—New Orleans captured by Union forces.
5th—Battle of Williamsburg, Virginia.
8th—Battle of West Point, Virginia.
10th—Surrender of Norfolk, Virginia.
10th—General Butler captured $800,000 in gold at New Orleans.
23d—Battle of Front Royal, Virginia.
25th—Battle of Winchester, Virginia.
27th—Battle of Corinth.
31st—Battle of Fair Oaks, Virginia.
31st—Battle of Seven Pines, Virginia.

JUNE, 1862.

4th—Battle of Tranter's Creek, North Carolina.
6th—Great gun-boat fight before Memphis, at the close of which Memphis surrendered unconditionally.
8th—Battle of Cross Keys, Virginia.
9th—Battle of Pt. Republic, Virginia.
26th—Battle at Mechanicsville, Virginia.
27th—Bombardment of Vicksburg, Mississippi.
30th—Battle of White Oak Swamp.

JULY, 1862.

1st—Battle of Malvern Hill, the last of the seven days' fight before Richmond. Total Union loss was 15,224, of which 1,565 were killed.
1st—President Lincoln called for 600,000 men.
5th—Bombardment of Vicksburg.
17th—Postage stamps made a legal tender.
20th—Morgan's Guerillas overtaken and scattered.

AUGUST, 1862.

4th—President Lincoln ordered 300,000 men to be drafted
5th—Battle of Baton Rouge, Louisiana.
5th—Attack on Fort Donelson, Tennessee.
9th—Battle of Cedar Mountain.
21st—Five Confederate regiments crossed the Rappahannock and almost walked into the masked batteries of General Sigel, which opened fire on them with grape and canister, mowing them down by scores, 700 being killed and 2,000 captured.

AUGUST, 1862.

28th—Battle near Centreville, Mo.
28th—Union forces evacuated Fredricksburg, Va.
29th—Battle at Groveton, near Bull Run, Va.
30th—Groveton battle renewed. Gen. Pope defeated.
30th—Battle near Richmond, Ky. Union forces defeated; 200 killed, 700 wounded and 2,000 prisoners taken.

SEPTEMBER, 1862.

1st—Battle near Chantilly, Va.
1st—Battle at Briton's Lane, Tenn.
12th—Harper's Ferry invested by Confederates.
14th—Battle of South Mountain, Md. Union loss, 2,325.
15th—Harper's Ferry surrendered; 11,500 Federals surrendered.
17th—Battle of Antietam. Each army numbered about 100,000—Union loss, 12,469; Confederate loss, 25,542.
17th—Munfordsville, Ky., surrendered to the Confederates; 4,600 Unionists captured.
20th—Battle of Inka, Miss
22d—Emancipation proclamation issued.

OCTOBER, 1862.

3d and 4th—Battle of Corinth, Miss. Union loss, 2,359; Confederate loss, 9,363.
8th and 9th—Battle of Perryville, Mo.
15th—Heavy fight between Lexington and Richmond, Ky.
18th—Morgan, the raider, dashed into Lexington and captured 125 prisoners
22d—Battle of Maysville, Ark.

NOVEMBER, 1862.

1s   Artillery fight at Philmont, Va.
3d—Reconnoisance at the base of Blue Ridge Mountain—Confederates literally driven into the river and drowned by scores.
4th—Galveston, Tex., surrendered.
16th—Capt. Dahlgren, with 54 men, dashed into Fredricksburg, Va., and routed 500 Confederates.
21st—Gen. Sumner demanded the surrender of Fredricksburg, Va.
27th—Battle near Frankfort, Va.
28th—Battle of Cane Hill, Ark.

DECEMBER, 1862.

4th—Winchester, Va., captured by Union soldiers.
5th—Battle near Coffeeville, Miss.
7th—Battle of Prairie Grove, Ark.
11th—Fredricksburg, Va., shelled by Federalists
12th—Fredricksburg captured.
13th—Battle of Fredricksburg, Va.
29th—Gen. Sherman repulsed by the Confederates.
31st—Battle of Murfreesboro.

JANUARY, 1863.

1st—Battle of Galveston.
1st—Battle of Murfreesboro renewed, with fearful results to the Federals. Union loss was 1,500 killed, 6,000 wounded and 4,000 prisoners taken.
7th—Battle of Springfield, Mo

MARCH, 1863.

21st—Battle of Cottage Grove, Tenn.
28th—Battle of Somerville, Ky.

MAY, 1863.

2d—Battles of Fort Gibson, Miss., and Chancelorville, Va.
12th—Battle of Raymond, Miss.
16th—Battle of Champion Hill, Miss
17th—Battle of Big Black River, Miss.
19th—Repulse of the first Vicksburg assault.

JUNE, 1863.

15th—Battle of Winchester, Va.
25th—Chambersburg, Pa , captured by Confederates.
30th—Battle of Hanover Junction, Va.

JULY, 1863.

2d—Battle of Gettysburg.
4th—Gen. Grant captured Vicksburg.
9th—Surrender of Point Hudson.
10th—Repulse of the assault on Fort Wagner
13th—Commencement of the New York draft riots

AUGUST, 1863.

20th—Lawrence, Kansas, was burned.

OCTOBER, 1863

17th—President Lincoln called 300,000 more men.

NOVEMBER, 1863.

15th—Battle of Campbell's Station.
24th—Battles of Lookout Mountain and Missionary Ridge were fought at Chattanooga, Tenn.

MARCH, 1864.

17th—General Grant assumed command of all the armies of the United States.

MAY, 1864.

4th—The army of the Potomac crossed the Rapidan, and encamped in the "Wilderness."
5th and 6th—Battles of the Wilderness, Virginia.
6th—General Sherman began his Atlanta campaign.
9th—Battle of Spottsylvania, Virginia.
14th—Battle of Recasa, Georgia.
25th—Battle of New Hope Church Station, Georgia
26th—The Confederates were repulsed in an attack on City Point, Virginia

JUNE, 1864.

1st—Battle of Cold Harbor, Virginia.
3d—A battle was fought near Cold Harbor, Virginia.
16th—Federals were defeated in an attack on Petersburg, Va.
19th—The investment of Petersburg, Virginia, was begun
19th—The Alabama was sunk off Cherbourg, France, by the Kearsarge
21st and 22d—The Federals were repulsed in attacks upon the Weldon railroad, Virginia
27th—Battle of Kenesaw Mountain
28th—The Confederates moved on Washington by way of the Shenandoah Valley, Virginia

JULY, 1864.

9th—Battle of Monocacy River, Maryland.
20th—Battle of Peach Tree Creek, Georgia.
22d—Battle of Decatur, Georgia.
30th—Another unsuccessful assault was made by the Federals upon Petersburg, Virginia

AUGUST, 1864

6th—Fort Gaines, in Mobile Bay, surrendered to Admiral Farragut.
21st—The Weldon railroad captured.
31st—The battle of Jonesborough.

SEPTEMBER, 1864.

2d—The Federals entered Atlanta.
19th—The battle of Winchester, Virginia.
22d—The battle of Fisher's Creek, Virginia.
30th—Battle at Peebles' Farm, Virginia.

OCTOBER, 1864.

2d—Battle of Holston River, Virginia.
6th—Battle of Allatoona Pass, Georgia.
19th—Battle of Cedar Creek, Virginia.
27th—The Federals were repulsed at Hatcher's Run, Virginia.

NOVEMBER, 1864.

16th—General Sherman began his march to the sea.

DECEMBER, 1864.

13th—Fort McAllister was captured by the Federals.
15th—The battle of Nashville, Tennessee.

25th—The Federals were repulsed in an attack upon Fort Fisher, North Carolina.

JANUARY, 1865

15th—Fort Fisher, N. C., was captured by the Federals.

FEBRUARY, 1865.

5th—The Federals were repulsed at Hatcher's Run, Virginia.

MARCH, 1865.

16th—Battle of Averysborough, North Carolina
18th—Battle of Bentonville, North Carolina
25th—Fort Steadman, near Petersburg, was captured by the Confederates, and recaptured by the Federals
31st—The battle of Five Forks, Virginia

APRIL, 1865.

2d—Richmond was evacuated by the Confederates
9te—Lee surrendered with 26,115 men.
6th—Battle of Farmville, Virginia.
9th—General Lee with his army surrender to General Grant at Appomattox Court House, Virginia.
13th—Mobile surrendered to a combined army and naval attack.
14th—The flag General Anderson had lowered at Fort Sumter was restored to its position.
14th—President Lincoln was assassinated at Washington. He was shot in the back of the head at Ford's Theater by Wilkes Booth, and died next morning.
15th—Andrew Johnson, Vice-President, took the oath of office as President.
25th—Wilkes Booth shot in a barn in Virginia and died in wenty-four hours
26th—General Johnson surrendered to General Sherman in North Carolina.

MAY, 1865.

5th—Galveston, Texas, surrendered to the Federals.
10th—Jeff. Davis captured in Georgia.
13th—A skirmish took place near Brazos, in Eastern Texas.
26th—The Confederates in Texas, under General Kirby Smith, surrendered.
The armies of the East and West were disbanded and returned home, after a review at Washington.

JUNE, 1865.

6th—An order was issued for the release of all prisoners of war in the depots of the North.

JULY, 1865.

7th—Mrs. Surratt, Harold, Payne and Azertoth hanged at Washington for conspiracy in the murder of Lincoln.

DECEMBER, 1865.

18th—Secretary Seward officially declared slavery abolished.

THE SILVER QUESTION.

In all civilized countries either gold or silver has been adopted as the standard of monetary value. The following is a list of the most important countries in the world, divided into three groups, those using (1) a gold standard, (2) a silver standard, (3) a double or variable standard. Of these last it may be said that the term "variable" is preferable to that of "double," inasmuch as the double standard never exists at one and the same time, gold or silver becoming alternately the standard, as the state of the exchanges makes the one or the other the more desirable as the practical medium of exchange.

Gold Standard.	Silver Standard.	Double or Variable Standard.
Australia.	Austria.	Argentine Republic.
Brazil.	Bolivia.	Belgium.
British Colonies in Africa.	China.	Chili.
British N. America.	Cochin China.	Cuba.
Denmark.	Colombia.	France.
Egypt.	Ecuador.	Greece.
German Empire.	E. Indian Isles.	Hayti.
Great Britain and Ireland.	Hungary.	Italy.
Liberia.	India.	Netherlands.
New Zealand.	Japan.	Roumania.
Norway.	Mexico.	Spain.
Portugal.	Peru.	Switzerland.
Sweden.	Russia.	Venezuela.
Turkey.	Tripoli.	United States.

RELATIVE HARDNESS OF WOODS.—Taking shell bark hickory as the highest standard of our forest trees, and calling that 100, other trees will compare with it for hardness as follows;

Shell bark Hickory	100	Yellow Oak	60
Pignut Hickory	96	Hard Maple	56
White Oak	84	White Elm	58
White Ash	77	Red Cedar	56
Dogwood	75	Wild Cherry	55
Scrub Oak	73	Yellow Pine	54
White Hazel	72	Chestnut	52
Apple Tree	70	Yellow Poplar	51
Red Oak	69	Butternut	43
White Beech	65	White Birch	43
Black Walnut	65	White Pine	30
Black Birch	62		

Timber intended for posts, is rendered almost proof against rot by thorough seasoning, charring, and immersion in hot coal tar.

The slide of Alpnach, extending from Mount Pilatus to Lake Lucerne, a distance of 3 miles, is composed of 25,000 trees, stripped of their bark, and laid at an inclination of 10 to 18 degrees. Trees placed in the slide rush from the mountain into the lake in 6 minutes.

The Alps comprise about 180 mountains, from 4,000 to 15,732 feet high, the latter being the height of Mont Blanc, the highest spot in Europe. The summit is a sharp ridge, like the roof of a house, consisting of nearly vertical granite rocks. The ascent requires 2 days, 6 or 8 guides are required, and each guide is paid 100 francs ($20.00). It was ascended by 2 natives, Jacques Belmat and Dr. Packard, Aug. 8, 1786, at 6 a. m. They staid up 30 minutes, with the thermometer at 14 degrees below the freezing point. The provisions froze in their pockets; their faces were frost-bitten, lips swollen, and their sight much weakened, but they soon recovered on their descent. De Saussure records in his ascent August 2, 1760, that the color of the sky was deep blue; the stars were visible in the shade; the barometer sunk to 16.08 inches (being 27.08 in Geneva); the thermometer was 26½ degrees, in the sun 29 degrees (being 87 degrees at Geneva). The thin air works the blood into a high fever, you feel as if you hardly touched the ground, and you scarcely make yourself heard. A French woman, Mademoiselle d'Angeville, ascended in September, 1840, being dragged up the last 1,200 feet by guides, and crying out: "If I die, carry me to the top." When there, she made them lift her up, that she might boast she had been higher than any man in Europe. The ascent of these awful solitudes is most perilous, owing to the narrow paths, tremendous ravines, icy barriers, precipices, etc. In many places every step has to be cut in the ice, the party being tied to each other by ropes, so that if one slips he may be held up by the rest, and silence is enforced, lest the noise of talking should dislodge the avalanches of the Aiguille du Midi. The view from the mountain is inexpressibly grand. On the Alps, the limit of the vine is an elevation of 1,600 feet;

below 1,000 feet, figs, oranges and olives are produced. The limit of the oak is 3,800 ft., of the chestnut 2,800 ft., of the pine 6,500 ft., of heaths and furze to 8,700 and 9,700 ft.; and perpetual snow exists at an elevation of 8,200 feet.

On the Andes, in lat. 2 degrees, the limit of perpetual snow is 14,760 ft.; in Mexico, lat. 19 degrees, the limit is 13,800 ft.; on the peak of Teneriffe, 11,454 ft.; on Mount Etna, 9,000 ft.; on the Caucasus, 9,900 ft.; the Pyrenees, 8,400 ft.; in Lapland, 3,100 ft.; in Iceland, 2.890 ft. The walnut ceases to grow at an elevation of 3,600 ft.; the yellow pine at 6,200 ft.; the Ash at 4,800 ft., and the Fir at 6,700 ft. The loftiest inhabited spot on the globe is the Port House of Ancomarca, on the Andes, in Peru, 16,000 feet above the level of the sea. The 14th peak of the Himalayas, in Asia, 25,659 feet high, is the loftiest mountain in the world.

Lauterbrunnen is a deep part of an Alpine pass, where the sun hardly shines in winter. It abounds with falls, the most remarkable of which is the Staubbach, which falls over the Balm precipice in a drizzling spray from a height of 925 feet; best viewed in the morning sun or by moonlight. In general, it is like a gauze veil, with rainbows dancing up and down it, and when clouds hide the top of the mountain, it seems as poured out of the sky.

In Canada, the falls of Montmorenci are 250 feet high, the falls of Niagara (the Horse Shoe Falls) are 158 feet high and 2,000 feet wide, the American Falls are 164 feet high and 900 feet wide, The Yosemite Valley Falls are 2,600 feet high, and the Ribbon Falls of the Yosemite are 3,300 feet high. The water-fall of the Arve, in Bavaria, is 2,000 feet.

THE PERIODS OF GESTATION are the same in the horse and ass, or 11 months each, camel 12 months, elephant 2 years, lion 5 months, buffalo 12 months, in the human female 9 months, cow 9 months, sheep 5 months, dog 9 weeks, cat 8 weeks, sow 16 weeks, she wolf from 90 to 95 days. The goose sits 30 days, swans 42, hens 21, ducks 30, peahens and turkeys 28, canaries 14, pigeons 14, parrots 40.

AGES OF ANIMALS, &c.— Elephant 100 years and upward, Rhinoceros 20, Camel 100, Lion 25 to 70, Tigers, Leopards, Jaguars and Hyenas (in confinement) about 25 years, Beaver 50 years, Deer 20, Wolf 20, Fox 14 to 16, Llamas 15, Chamois 25, Monkeys and Baboons 16 to 18 years, Hare 8, Squirrel 7, Rabbit 7, Swine 25, Stag under 50, Horse 30, Ass 30, Sheep under 10, Cow 20, Ox 30, Swans, Parrots and Ravens 200, Eagle 100, Geese 80, Hens and Pigeons 10 to 16, Hawks 36 to 40, Cranes 24, Blackbird 10 to 12, Peacock 20, Pelican 40 to 50, Thrush 8 to 10, Wren 2 to 3, Nightingale 15, Blackcap 15, Linnet 14 to 23, Goldfinch 20 to 24, Redbreast 10 to 12, Skylark 10 to 30, Titlark 5 to 6, Chaffinch 20 to 24, Starling 10 to 12, Carp 70 to 150, Pike 30 to 40, Salmon 16, Codfish 14 to 17, Eel 10, Crocodile 100, Tortoise 100 to 200, Whale estimated 1,000, Queen Bees live 4 years, Drones 4 months, Working Bees 6 months.

The melody of singing birds ranks as follows: The nightingale first, then the linnet, titlark, sky lark and wood lark. The mocking bird has the greatest powers of imitation, the robin and goldfinch are superior in vigorous notes.

The condor of Peru has spread wings 40 feet, feathers 20 feet, quills 8 inches round.

In England, a quarter of wheat, comprising 8 bushels, yield 14 bushels 2½ pecks, divided into seven distinct kinds of flour, as follows: Fine flour, 5 bushels 3 pecks; bran, 3 bushels; twenty-penny, 3 bushels; seconds, 2 pecks; pollard, 2 bushels; fine middlings, 1 peck; coarse ditto, 1 peck.

The ancient Greek phalanx comprised 8,000 men, forming a square battalion, with spears crossing each other, and shields united.

The Roman legion was composed of 6,000 men, comprising 10 cohorts of 600 men each, with 300 horsemen.

The ancient battering ram was of massive timber, 60 to 100 feet long, fitted with an iron head. It was erected under shelter to protect the 60 or 100 men required to work it. The largest was equal in force to a 36-lb. shot from a cannon.

PILE DRIVING ON SANDY SOILS.—The greatest force will not effect a penetration exceeding 15 feet.

VARIOUS SIZES OF TYPE.—It requires 205 lines of Diamond type to make 12 inches, of Pearl 178, of Ruby 166, of Nonpareil 143, of Minion 128, of Brevier 112½, of Bourgeois 102½, of Long Primer 89, of Small Pica 83, of Pica 71½, of English 64.

Wire ropes for the transmission of power vary in size from ⅜ to ⅞ inch diam. for from 3 to 300 horse power; to promote flexibility, the rope, made of iron, steel, or copper wire, as may be preferred, is provided with a core of hemp, and the speed is 1 mile per minute, more or less, as desired. The rope should run on a well-balanced, grooved, cast iron wheel, of from 4 to 15 feet diam., according as the transmitted power ranges from 3 to 300 horse; the groove should be well cushioned with soft material, as leather or rubber, for the formation of a durable bed for the rope. With good care the rope will last from 3 to 5 years.

Cannon balls go furthest at an elevation of 30 degrees, and less as the balls are less; the range is furthest when fired from west to east in the direction of the earth's motion, which for the diurnal rotation on its axis, is at the rate of 1,037 miles per hour, and in its orbit, 66,092 miles.

The air's resistance is such, that a cannon ball of 3 lbs. weight, diameter, 2.78 ins. moving with a velocity of 1,800 ft. per second, is resisted by a force equal to 156 lbs.

Brick-layers ascend ladders with loads of 90 lbs., 1 foot per second. There are 484 bricks in a cubic yard, and 4,356 in a rod.

A power of 250 tons is necessary to start a vessel weighing 3,000 tons over greased slides on a marine railway, when in motion, 150 tons only is required.

A modern dredging machine, 123 ft. long, beam 26 ft., breadth over all, 11 ft., will raise 180 tons of mud and clay per hour, 11 feet from water-line.

In tanning, 4 lbs. of oak bark make 1 lb. of leather.

Flame is quenched in air containing 3 per cent. of carbonic acid; the same percentage is fatal to animal life.

100 parts of oak make nearly 23 of charcoal; beech 21, deal 19, apple 23.7, elm 23, ash 25, birch 24, maple 22.8, willow 18, popular 20, red pine 22.10, white pine 23. The charcoal used in gunpowder is made from willow, alder, and a few other woods. The charred timber found in the ruins of Herculaneum has undergone no change in 1,800 years.

Four volumes of nitrogen, and one of oxygen compose atmospheric air in all localities on the globe.

Air extracted from pure water, under an air pump, contains 34.8 per cent. of oxygen. Fish breathe this air, respiring about 35 times per minute. The oxyhydrogen lime light may be seen from mountains at the distance of 200 miles round.

Lightning is reflected 150 to 200 miles.

1,000 cubic feet of 13 candle gas is equivalent to over 7 gals. of sperm oil, 52.9 lbs. of tallow candles, and over 44 lbs. of sperm candles.

The time occupied by gas in traveling from a gas well (in Pennsylvania) through 32 miles of pipe was 22 minutes, pressure at the well was 55 lbs. per inch, pressure at discharge 49 lbs.

The flight of wild ducks is estimated at 90 miles per hour, that of the swift at 200 miles, carrier pigeons 38 miles, swallows 60 miles, migratory birds have crossed the Mediterranean at a speed of 120 miles per hour.

At birth, the beats of the pulse are from 165 to 104, and the inspirations of breath from 70 to 23. From 15 to 20, the pulsations are from 90 to 57, the inspirations, from 24 to 16; from 29 to 50, the pulsations are 112 to 56, the inspirations, 23 to 11. In usual states it is 4 to 1. The action of the heart distributes 2 ozs. of blood from 70 to 80 times in a minute.

The mean heat of the human body is 98 degs. and of the skin 90 degs. Tea and coffee are usually drank at 110 degs.

The deepest coal mine in England is at Killingworth, near Newcastle, and the mean annual temperature at 400 yards below the surface is 77 degrees, and at 300 yards 70 degrees, while at the surface it is but 48 degrees, being 1 degree of increase for every 15 yards. This explains the origin of hot springs, for at 3,300 yards the heat would be equal to boiling water, taking 20 yards to a degree. The heat of the Bath waters is 116 degrees, hence they would appear to rise 1,320 yards.

Peron relates that at the depth of 2,144 feet in the sea the thermometer falls to 45 degrees, when it is 86 degrees at the surface.

Swemberg and Fourier calculate the temperature of the celestial spaces at 50 degrees centigrade below freezing.

In Northern Siberia the ground is frozen permanently to the depth of 660 feet, and only thaws to the extent of 3 or 4 feet in summer. Below 660 feet internal heat begins.

River water contains about 30 grs. of solid matter in every cubic foot. Fresh water springs of great size abound under the sea. Perhaps the most remarkable springs exist in California, where they are noted for producing sulphuric acid, ink, and other remarkable products.

St. Winifred's Well, in England, evolves 120 tons of water per minute, furnishing abundant water power to drive 11 mills within little more than a mile.

The Nile has a fall of 6 ins. in 1,000 miles. The rise of the river commences in June, continuing until the middle of August, attaining an elevation of from 24 to 26 feet, and flowing the valley of Egypt 12 miles wide. In 1829 it rose to 26 cubits, by which 30,000 persons were drowned. It is a terrible climate to live in, owing to the festering heat and detestable exhalations from the mud, etc., left on the retiring of the Nile, which adds about 4 inches to the soil in a century, and encroaches on the sea 16 feet every year. Bricks have been found at the depth of 60 feet, showing the vast antiquity of the country. In productiveness of soil it is excelled by no other in the world.

Belzoni considered the tract between the first and second cataract of the Nile as the hottest on the globe, owing to there being no rain. The natives do not credit the phenomenon of water falling from above. Hence it is that all monuments are so nicely preserved. Buckingham found a building left unfinished about 4,000 years ago, and the chalk marks on the stones were still perfect.

Pompey's Pillar is 92 feet high, and 27½ round at the base.

The French removed a red granite column 95 feet high, weighing 210 tons, from Thebes, and carried it to Paris. The display of costly architectural ruins at Thebes is one of the most astonishing to be seen anywhere in the world. The ruins and costly buildings in old Eastern countries, are so vast in their proportions and so many in number that it would require volumes to describe them.

Babel, now called Birs Nimroud, built at Babylon by Belus, was used as an observatory and as a temple of the Sun. It was composed of 8 square towers, one over the other, in all 670 feet high, and the same dimensions on each side on the ground.

The Coliseum at Rome, built by Vespasian for 100,000 spectators, was in its longest diameter 615.5 feet, and in the shortest 510. embraced 5½ acres, and was 120 feet high.

Eight aqueducts supplied ancient Rome with water, delivering 40 millions of cubic feet daily. That of Claudia was 47 miles long and 100 feet high, so as to furnish the hills. Martia was 41 miles, of which 37 were on 7,000 aches 70 feet high. These vast erections would never have been built had the Romans known that water always rises to its own level.

The Temple of Diana, at Ephesus, was 425 feet long and 225 feet broad, with 127 columns, 60 feet high, to support the roof. It was 220 years in building.

Solomon's Temple, built B. C. 1014, was 60 cubits or 107 feet in length, the breadth 20 cubits or 36 feet, and the height 30 cubits or 54 feet. The porch was 36 feet long and 18 feet wide.

The largest one of the Egyptian pyramids is 543 feet high, 693 feet on the sides, and its base covers 11 acres. The layers of stones are 208 in number. Many stones are over 30 feet long, 4 broad and 3 thick.

The Temple of Ypsambul, in Nubia, is enormously massive and cut out of the solid rock. Belzoni found in it 4 immense figures, 65 feet high, 25 feet over the shoulders, with a face of 7 feet and the ears over 3 feet.

Sesostris erected in the temple in Memphis immense statues of himself and his wife, 50 feet high, and of his children, 28 feet.

In the Temple of the Sun, at Baalbec, are stones more than 60 feet long, 24 feet thick and 16 broad, each embracing 23,000 cubic feet, cut, squared, sculptured and transported from neighboring quarries. Six enormous columns are each 72 feet high, composed of 3 stones 7 feet in diameter. Sesostris is credited with having transported from the mountains of Arabia a rock 32 feet wide and 240 feet long.

The engineering appliances used by the ancients in the movement of these immense masses are but imperfectly understood at the present day.

During modern times, a block of granite weighing 1,217 tons, now used as the pedestal of the equestrian statue of Peter the Great, at St. Petersburg, was transported 4 miles by land over a railway and 13 miles in a vast caisson by water. The railway consisted of two lines of timber furnished with hard metal grooves; between these grooves were placed spheres of hard brass about 6 inches in diameter. On these spheres the frame with its massive load was easily moved by 60 men, working at capstans with treble purchase blocks.

In 1716 Swedenborg contrived to transport (on rolling machines of his own invention) over valleys and mountains, 2 galleys, 5 large boats and 1 sloop, from Stromstadt to Iderfjol (which divides Sweden from Norway on the South), a distance of 14 miles, by which means Charles XII. was able to carry on his plans, and under cover of the galleys and boats to transport on pontoons his heavy artillery to the very walls of Frederickshall.

As an exponent of the laws of friction, it may be stated that a square stone weighing 1,080 lbs. which required a force of 758 lbs. to drag it along the floor of a quarry, roughly chiseled, required only a force of 22 lbs. to move it when mounted on a platform and rollers over a plank floor.

Water is the absolute master, former and secondary agent of the power of motion in everything terrestrial. It is the irresistible power which elaborates everything, and the waters contain more organized beings than the land.

Rivers hold in suspension 100th of their volume (more or less) of mud, so that if 36 cubic miles of water (the estimated quantity) flow daily into the sea, 0.36 cubic miles of soil are daily displaced. The Rhine carries to the sea every day 145,980 cubic feet of mud. The Po carries out the land 228 feet per annum, consequently Adria which 2,500 years ago was on the sea, is now over 20 miles from it.

The enormous amount of alluvium deposited by the Mississippi is almost incalculable, and constantly renders necessary extensive engineering operations in order to remove the impediments to navigation.

The Geological Society of London has a slab 2 ft. square in which is embedded 250 fishes. Fossil sea turtles have shells 8 ft. long. There are beds of sea shells 2,000 ft. high on Mount Etna, and strata of gray clay, filled with shells, much higher. Shells and organic remains abound in Chili, from 9 to 1,400 ft. above the sea level. Workmen near Eureka, Nevada, while blasting in the solid rock, 40 ft. below the surface, found imbedded in a piece of it a petrified wasp's nest, the texture of which, though turned to stone, was plainly visible. On breaking it open, some cells, larva, and two perfectly formed wasps were found, also petrified. The rock is of a granite sandstone of sedimentary formation. The Atlantosaurus, an enormous monster from Colorado, is, per Prof. Marsh, the largest land animal as yet discovered. It was some 50 or 60 ft. in length, and, when erect, at least 30 ft. high. It doubtless browsed upon the foliage of the mountain forests, portions of which are preserved with its remains.

The islands of the Icy Sea, per Pallas, are full of elephants and rhinoceros' bones, and the islands opposite the Lena are almost composed of them and fossil wood. A mammoth, a carnivorous animal, much larger than an elephant, was found in Siberia in the ice, perfect in its eyes, flesh, hair, skin, etc., with long mane and tail of stout, black bristles; many others, together with elephants, have been found in Siberia and Hudson's Bay, a positive proof that the temperature of the Tropics existed at one time in these ragions. The bones of the Mastodon of North America, as arranged in Peale's Museum, form a skeleton 18 ft. long, 11 ft. 5 ins. high, with tusks, 10 ft. 7 ins. The Iguamadon, an enormous herbivorous reptile, discovered by Mantell, is 70 ft. long, the body is 4 ft. 9 ins. in diam., with a horn of bone, and a tail 52½ ft. The bones of the Mammoth are quite numerous in the United States; the molar tooth weighs 8 lbs., and the joint of the bone of the leg is a foot in diam.

During the glacial period, in which the climate of Greenland extended as far south as New York, the world was covered with immense moving masses of ice, which in their progress from north to south moved rocks hundreds of miles and remodelled the topography of various countries. The effects of these glacial movements were the pulverization of the various rocks, thus forming sand from sandstone, calcareous soil from limestone, and clay from granite and gneiss, transforming barren rock into fertile soil.

The alluvial deposits contain remains which indicate a vast antiquity. The skeleton of a whale was dug up in the vicinity of Niagara a few years ago, a sure indication that that region formed at one time the bed of an ocean. All the land about the Clyde rests upon the beds of shells, bones of stags, elephants, etc., and at Yealm Bridge, and Ketley, near Plymouth, there are caves containing bones of rhinoceroses, elephants, hyenas, bears, foxes, wolves, dogs, horses, oxen, sheep, etc. Agassiz describes 300 new species of fossil fish found in England, of which 50 exists in London clay. A bed of oyster shells 9 miles long and 18 feet thick exists in the interior of Norfolk; a pair of stags' horns have been found on the shores of the Mersey, near Liverpool, at 30 feet, and pieces of timber at 40 feet. Palms and cocoa nuts have been found imbedded in the London clay, clearly indicating the existence at one time of a tropical climate in what is now the temperate zone. An old Roman port off Romney marsh is now several miles out at sea, and proofs are abundant that Great Britain was at one time united to the continent.

No doubt exists that the Falls of Niagara were at one time precipitated into an ocean over Queenston Heights, and Sir Charles Lyell computes that a period of at least 30,000 to 35,000 years have elapsed while the falls have been cutting their way through seven miles of rock to their present position; the retrograde movement is still going on, slowly but surely, every day.

A volcano now extinct, near Mount D'Orr in the interior of France, emitted a flow of lava at a comparatively recent period, which filled up the channel of a river in its course. The water rose, passing over the impediment in its course, and has up to this time cut a channel 50 feet deep through the lava bed. From the remains of an old Roman bridge known to have been constructed about 2,000 years ago, it appears that the erosion of the water into the lava has been considerably less than six inches during that period, which would indicate that it has required over 200,000 years to cut the channel to its present depth of 50 feet.

Myriads of ages have elapsed while the rushing waters have been cutting out those tremendous ravines in the hard rock, known as the Canyons of Mexico, Texas, Colorado, and the Rocky Mountains. The great Canyon of the Colorado river is 298 miles long and the sides rise perpendicularly above the water to a height of 5,000 or 6,000 feet.

On Oak Orchard creek and the Genesee river, between Rochester and Lake Ontario, are enormous chasms, worn by the water, 7 miles long. On the Genesee, south of Rochester, a cut exists from Mount Morris to Portage, sometimes 400 feet deep. In the Rocky Mountains, near the source of the Missouri river, there is a gorge 6 miles long and 1,200 feet deep. In the Mississippi, at St. Anthony's Falls, the river has eroded a passage through limestone rock 7 miles long, to which distance the cataract has receded. In the passage of the Connecticut river at Brattleboro and Bellows Falls, it can be proved that the river was once at least 700 feet above its present level.

NUMBER OF CUBIC FEET IN A TON (AVOIRDUPOIS) OF DIFFERENT MATERIALS.—Cast Iron 4.98, Wrought Iron 4.59, Bar Iron 4.69, Steel (soft) 4.57, Steel (hard) 4.59, Copper (sheet) 4.62, Copper (cast) 4.04, Brass 4.17, Lead 3.15, Tin (cast) 4.91, Zinc (cast) 4.98, Granite 13.514, Marble 13.343, Paving Stone 14.83, Millstone 14.42, Grindstone 17, Common Stone 14.22, Fire Brick 16.284, Brick (mean) 21.961, Anthracite Coal 21.?84 and 24.958, Cannel Coal 23,609, Cotton Bale (mean) 154.48, Pressed (ditto) from 89.6 to 1.14, Hay (bale) 23.517, Bale (mean) 154.48, Hay (pressed) 89.6, Clay 158.69, Common Soil 16.335, Mud 21.987, Loose Sand 23.893, Earth with Gravel 16,742, India Rubber 39.69, Plaster of Paris 21.3, Glass 12.44, Ice 38.58, Chalk (British) 17.92, Tallow 38, Oil 39, Fresh Water 35.84, Salt Water 34.931.

Weight of Various Materials in Lbs. (Avoirdupois) per Cubic Foot.—Pure Gold 1,203.6, Standard Gold 1,102.9, Hammered Gold 1,210.11, Pure Silver 654.6, Hammered Silver 656.9, Standard Silver 658.4, Cast Brass 524,8, Brass Wire 534, Bismuth (Cast) 613.9, Antimony 418.9, Bronze 513.4, Cobalt (Cast) 488.2, Copper (Cast) 459.3, Copper (Sheet) 557.2, Copper (Wire) 554.9, Wrought Iron 486.75, Iron Plates 481.5, Cast Iron 450.4, Gun Metal 543.75, Cast Lead 709.5, Rolled do. 711.75, Red Lead 558.75, Tin 455.7, Platinum (Pure) 1,218, Hammered do. 1,271, Mercury 60 deg., Fluid 848, Mercury (Solid) 977, Nickel (Cast) 487.9, Steel (Plates) 480.75, Steel (Soft) 489.6, Type Metal 653.1, Zinc (Cast) 439, Granite 165.75, Millstone 155.3, Marble (Mean, of nineteen kinds) 180, Grindstones 133.9, Firebrick 137.5, Tile 114.44, Brick (Mean) 102, Clay 102, Limestone (Mean, of seven sorts) 184.1, Loose Earth or Sand 95, Coarse Sand 112.5, Ordinary Soil 124, Mud 102, Clay and Stones 160, Slate 167 to 181.25, Plaster Paris 73.5, Plumbago 131.35, Anthracite Coal from 89.75 to 102.5, Cannel Coal from 77.33 to 82.33, Charcoal from Hard Wood 18.5, ditto from Soft Wood 18, Port Wine 62.31, Fresh Water 62.5, Sea Water 64.3, Dead Sea Water 77.5, Vinegar 67.5, Alum 107.10, Asbestos (Starry) 192.1, Ice at 32 degs. 57.5, Sulphur 127.1, Peat 375 to 83.1, Marl (Mean) 109.33, Hydraulic Lime 171.60, Quartz 166.25, Rock Crystal 170.94, Salt (Common) 133.12, Lard 59.20, Whale Oil 57.70, Olive Oil 57.19.

Weight of a Cubic Inch of Various Metals in Pounds.— Hammered Gold .701 lbs., Cast do (pure) .698, 20 Carats Fine do. .567, Hammered Silver .382, Pure do. .378, Cast Steel .287, Cast Iron .263, Sheet Iron .279, Rolled Platinum .797, Wire do .762, Hammered do .735, Sheet Copper .323, Sheet Brass .304, Lead .410, Cast Tin .264, Cast Zinc .245.

Sundry Commercial Weights.—A ton of wood is 2 stones of 14 lbs. each. A pack of wool is 240 lbs. A sack of wool is 22 stones of 14 lbs., or 308 lbs. In Scotland, it is 24 of 16 lbs. A keel of 8 Newcastle chaldrons is 15½ London chaldrons. 56 or 60 lbs. is a truss of hay, 40 lbs. a truss of straw; 36 trusses a load. A bushel of rock salt is 65 lbs., of crushed salt 56 lbs., of foreign salt, 84 lbs. A tierce of beef, in Ireland, is 304 lbs., and of pork 320 lbs. A fodder of lead is 19½ cwt. in London and 21 cwt. in the North. A man's load is 5 bushels, a market load 40 (or 5 quarters). A last is 10 quarters of corn, or 2 cart loads, 12 sacks of wool, 24 barrels of gunpowder, 12 barrels of ashes, herring, soap, &c., and 18 barrels of salt. A hundred of of salt 126 barrels.

Sundry Measures of Length.—The hair's breadth is the smallest, of which 48 are an inch. Four barley-corns laid breadthways are ¾ of an inch, called a digit, and 3 barley-corns lengthways are an inch. An inch is divided into 12 lines and by mechanics into 8ths. A nail used in cloth measure is 2¼ ins. or the 16th of a yard. A palm is 3 ins, and a span 9 ins. An English Statute mile is 1,760 yds. or 5,280 ft., an Irish mile 2,240 yds., a Scotch mile 1,984 yds., 80 Scotch miles being equivalent to 91 English, and 11 Irish to 14 English.

Roman money mentioned in the New Testament reduced to English and American standard:

	£	s.	d.	far.		$	cts.
A Mite...............	0	0	0	0.75	......	0	00.343
A Farthing, about....	0	0	0	1.50	......	0	00.687
A Penny, or Denarius	0	0	7	2.	......	0	13.75
A Pound, or Mina....	3	2	6	0.	......	13	75.

NOTE. — The above determinations of Scripture measures, weights, &c., are principally by the Rt. Rev. Richard, Bishop of Peterborough.

GUNTER'S CHAIN, LAND MEASUREMENT, &C.—7.92 inches constitute 1 link; 100 links 1 chain, 4 rods or poles, or 66 feet, and 80 chains 1 mile. A square chain is 16 square poles, and 10 square chains are 1 acre. Four roods are an acre, each containing 1,210 square yards, or 34,785 yards, or 94 yards 28 inches each side.

Forty poles of 30.25 square yards each is a rood, and a pole is 5½ yards each way.

An acre is 4,840 square yards, or 69 yards 1 foot 8½ inches each way; and 2 acres, or 9,680 square yds. are 98 yds. 1 ft. 2 ins. each way; and 3 acres are 120½ yards each way. A square mile, or a U. S. section of land, is 640 acres, being 1,060 yards each way; half a mile, or 880 yds. each way, is 160 acres; a quarter of a mile, or 440 yds. each way, is a park or farm of 40 acres; and a furlong, or 220 yds. each way, is 10 acres.

Any length or breadth in yards which multiplied make 4,840 is an acre; any which makes 12.10 is a rood, and 30.25 is a pole.

An English acre is a square of nearly 70 yds. each way; a Scotch of 77½ yds., and an Irish of 88½ yds.

DYNAMIC POWER OF VARIOUS KINDS OF FOOD.—One lb. of oatmeal will furnish as much power as 2 lbs. of bread and more than 3 lbs. of lean veal. One lb. butter gives a working force equal to that of 9 lbs. of potatoes, 12 lbs. of milk and more than 5 lbs. of lean beef. One lb. of lump sugar is equal in force to 2 lbs. of ham, or 8 lbs. of cabbage. The habitual use of spirituous liquors is inimical to health, and inevitably tends to shorten life. A mechanic or laboring man of average size requires, according to Moleschott, 23 ozs. of dry, solid matter daily, one-fifth nitrogenous. Food, as usually prepared, contains 50 per cent. of water, which would increase the quantity to 46 ozs., or 3 lbs. 14 ozs., with at least an equal weight of water in addition daily. The same authority indicates as healthy proportions, of albuminous matter 4.587 ozs., fatty matter 2.964, carbo-hydrate 14.250, salts 1.058, total 22.859 ozs., for daily use. This quantity of food will vary greatly in the requirements of individuals engaged in sedentary employments, or of persons with weak constitutions or impaired digestion, as also whether employed in the open air or within doors, much also depending on the temperature. Preference should be given to the food which most readily yields the materials required by nature in the formation of the human frame. Beef contains about 4 lbs. of such minerals in every 100 lbs. Dried extract of beef contains 21 lbs. in each 100 lbs. Bread made from unbolted wheat flour is also very rich in such elements, much more so than superfine flour hence the common use of Graham bread for dyspepsia and other ailments. The analysis of Liebig, Johnston, and others give in 100 parts, the following proportions of nutritious elements, viz.: Indian corn 12.30, barley 14.00, wheat 14.06, oats 19.91. A fish diet is well adapted to sustain intellectual, or brain labor. What is required may be best known from the fact that a human body weighing 154 lbs. contains, on a rough estimate, of water 14 gals. (consisting of oxygen 111 lbs., of hydrogen 14 lbs.), carbon 21 lbs., nitrogen 3 lbs., 8 ozs., calcium 2 lbs., sodium 2¼ ozs., phosphorus 1¾ lbs., potassium ½ oz., sulphur 2 ozs. 219 grs., fluorine 2 ozs., chlorine 2 oz. 47 grs., iron 100 grs., magnesium 12 grs., silicon 2 grs. After death, the human body is by gradual decay slowly resolved into these its component parts, which elements are again used in the complex and wonderful laboratory of nature, to vivify the countless forms of vegetable life. These in their turn fulfill their appointed law by yielding up their substance for the formation of other bodies. What a suggestive comment on mortal ambition to witness the present inhabitants of Egypt engaged in what they consider the lucrative commerce of quarrying out the bones of the ancient inhabitants from the catacombs where they have been entombed for thousands of years and transporting them by the ship-load to England in order to fertilize the crops which are destined to assist in forming the bone and sinew of the British nation!

PRACTICAL DIETETIC ECONOMIES.—The following table, compiled from various authorities, is eminently and practically useful, presenting as it does at a glance the available percentage of nutritive elements contained in the leading staples used as human food.

Raw Cucumbers	2	Raw Beef	26
" Melons	3	" Grapes	27
Boiled Turnips	4½	" Plums	29
Milk	7	Broiled Mutton	30
Cabbage	7½	Oatmeal Porridge	75
Currants	10	Rye Bread	79
Whipped Eggs	13	Boiled Beans	87
Beets	14	Boiled Rice	88
Apples	16	Barley Bread	88
Peaches	20	Wheat Bread	90
Boiled Codfish	21	Baked Corn Bread	91
Broiled Venison	22	Boiled Barley	92
Potatoes	22½	Butter	92
Fried Veal	24	Boiled Peas	93
Roast Pork	24	Raw Oils	95
Roast Poultry	26		

The figures present a diversity, but the general results are fixed and invariable, presenting to the economist the relative amount of nutriment supplied by each kind of food. It will be seen that the most wholesome and nutritious articles, as oatmeal, flour, peas, beans, rice, crushed wheat, corn bread, etc., are vastly superior to beef in supplying effective ability to labor, besides being obtainable at about one-third the price of the latter. It will be seen that the nutriment supplied by beef is 26 per cent., while the cereals yield from 75 to 95 per cent.; while there is no room for dispute as to the comparative healthiness of the different kinds of diet. The bounding circulation, good digestion and mental activity enjoyed by day, together with the sound sleep accorded by night, to the man who prefers plain to luxurious living, and vegetable to animal food, are certainly well worth striving for. If a fair percentage of wholesome ripe fruit be used with the above noted diet, its value and the enjoyment of using it will be greatly enhanced. After all that can be said, pro and con, touching a vegetable diet, certain are we that the average man who limits himself to a well-selected regimen of vegetable food will, accidents aside, go through life with a clear mind in a healthy body, will sleep sounder, and come nearer the alloted age of three-score and ten, have a better digestion, and have fewer headaches than the man who indulges in roast beef with the usual variations.

AGE AND GROWTH OF TREES.—An oak tree in 3 years grows 2 ft. 10½ ins. A larch 3 ft. 7½ ins., at 70 years it is full grown, and a tree of 79 years was 102 ft. high and 12 ft. girth, containing 253 cubic ft. Another of 80 years was 90 ft. and 17 ft. and 300 cubic feet. An elm tree in 3 years grows 8 ft. 3 in. A beech, 1 ft. 8 in. A poplar, 6 ft. A willow, 9 ft. 3 in. An elm is full grown in 150 years and it lives 500 or 600. Ash is full grown in 100 and oak in 200. The mahogany is full grown in 200 years to a vast size. A Polish oak 40 ft. round had 600 circles. An oak in Dorsetshire in 1755 was 68 ft. round, 2 near Cranborne Lodge are 38 ft. and 36 ft. There are yews from 10 to 20 ft. diam., whose age is from 1,000 to 2,000 years. A lime in the Crisons is 51 ft. round and about 600 years old. An elm in the Pays de Vaud is 18 ft. diam. and 360 years old. The African baobab is the patriarch of living organizations, one specimen by its circles is estimated at 5,700 years old by Adamson and Humboldt. The trunk is but 12 or 15 ft. to the branches, and often 75 ft. round. A cypress in Mexico is 120 ft. round and is estimated by De Candolle to be older than Adamson's baobab. The cypress of Montezuma is 41 feet round. Strabo wrote of a cypress in Persia as being 2,500 years old. The largest tree in Mexico is 127 ft. round and 120 high, with branches of 30 ft. A chestnut tree on Mount Etna is 196 ft. round close to the ground and 5 of its branches resemble great trees. De Candolle says there are oaks in France 1,500 years old. The Wallace oak near Paisley is nearly 800 years old. The yew trees at Fountain's Abbey are about 1,200 years old. That at Crowhurst, 1,500. That at Fortingal, above 2,000. That at Braburn, 2,500 to 3,000. Ivys reach 500 or 600 years. The larch the same. The lime 600 or 700 years. The trunk of a walnut tree 12 ft. in diam., hollowed out, and furnished as a sitting-room, was imported from America and exhibited in London. The trunk was 80 ft. high, without a branch, and the entire height 150 ft., the bark 12 ins. thick and the branches from 3 to 4 ft. in diam. The California pine is from 150 to 200 ft. high and from 20 to 60 ft. in diam. The forests in watered, tropical countries are formed of trees from 100 to 200 ft. high, which grow to the water's edge of rivers, presenting a solid and impenetrable barrier of trunks 10 or 12 ft. in diam. The dragon tree is in girth from 40 to 100 ft. and 50 or 60 feet high, and a misosa in South America is described whose head is 600 ft. round.

The duration of well seasoned wood, when kept dry, is very great, as beams still exist which are known to be nearly 1,100 years old. Piles driven by the Romans, and used in the formation of bridges prior to the Christian era, have been examined of late, and found to be perfectly sound after an immersion of nearly 2,000 years.

RUSSIAN WAY OF STOPPING HOLES IN SHIPS.—In that country there has lately been invented and successfully applied, a ready means for stopping holes made in ships by collision or otherwise. It consists of a plaster made of two rectangular sheets of canvas sewed together, bordered with a rope, and containing a waterproof material. A sounding-line has to be passed under the keel, and brought up on the other side, then the plaster can be lowered to the hole and made fast. Several cases are cited in which this invention has been employed with advantage, and a large number of Russian ships are now furnished with such plasters. It is proposed that men be specially trained and ready for the maneuvring of the apparatus.

HOW TO RAISE THE BODY OF A DROWNED PERSON.—In a recent failure to recover the body of a drowned person in New Jersey, a French-Canadian undertook the job, and proceeded as follows: Having supplied himself with some glass gallon-jars and a quantity of unslaked lime he went in a boat to the place where the man was seen to go down. One of the jars was filled half full of lime, then filled up with water and tightly corked. It was then dropped into the water and soon after exploded at the bottom of the river with a loud report. After the third trial, each time at a different place, the body rose to the surface and was secured.

HOW TO GET RID OF RATS.—Get a piece of lead pipe and use it as a funnel to introduce about 1½ ozs. of sulphide of potassium into any outside holes tenanted by rats, not to be used in dwellings. To get rid of mice use tartar emetic mingled with any favorite food, they will eat, sicken, and take their leave.

VALUABLE SUGGESTIONS TO CLERKS AND WORKINGMEN.—Never consider time wasted that is spent in learning rudiments. In acquiring a knowledge of any art or handicraft the greatest difficulty is experienced at the beginning, because our work then possesses little or nothing of interest. Our first lessons in drawing or music, or with tools, are very simple; indeed so simple are they that we are disposed to undervalue their importance. The temptation is to skip a few pages and begin further on in the book. But such a course is fatal to success. To learn principles thoroughly is to succeed. Be content to learn one thing at a time, whether it be to push a plane square and true, or draw a straight line. Whatever you learn, learn it absolutely, without possible question. This will enable you to advance steadily, step by step, year after year, and some day you will wonder why you have been enabled to distance the geniuses who once seemed so far in advance of you.

Set your heart upon what you have in hand. Valuable knowledge is acquired only by intense devotion. You must give your entire mind to whatever you undertake, otherwise you fail, or succeed indifferently, which is but little better than failure.

Learn, therefore, to estimate properly the value of what is called leisure time. There is entirely too much of this in the world. Do not mistake our meaning. Rest is necessary and play is well in its place, but young men who hope to do something in life must not expect to play one-third of their time.

While you resolve to acquire a thorough knowledge of your art, be equally as anxious to know something beyond it. A craftsman ought to be ashamed of himself who knows nothing but the use of his tools. Having the time to acquire it, be careful to properly estimate the value of knowledge. Remember of what use it will be to you in ten thousand instances as you go along in life, and be as conscientious in learning rudiments here as elsewhere. Learn to spell correctly, to write a good plain hand, and to punctuate your sentences.

Do not dress beyond your means; never spend your last dollar, unless for food to keep yourself or some one else from starving. You will always feel better to keep a little money in your pocket. At the earliest possible opportunity save up a few dollars and place the amount in a savings bank. It will serve as a magnet to attract other money that might be foolishly spent.

Just as soon as you can command the means, buy a piece of ground. Do not wait until you have saved enough to pay all down, but begin by paying one-third or one-quarter. Do not be afraid to go in debt for land, for it increases in value.

SAVE A LITTLE.—Every man who is obliged to work for his living should make a point to lay up a little money for that "rainy day" which we are all liable to encounter when least expected. The best way to do this is to open an account with a savings bank. Accumulated money is always safe; it is always ready to use when needed. Scrape together five dollars, make your deposit, receive your bank book, and then resolve to deposit a given sum, small though it be, once a month, or once a week, according to circumstances. Nobody knows without trying it, how easy a thing it is to save money when an account with a bank has been opened. With such an account a man feels a desire to enlarge his deposit. It gives him lessons in frugality and economy, weans him from habits of extravagance, and is the very best guard in the world against intemperance, dissipation and vice. Refer to page 277 for a table showing the time required by money to double itself when loaned at interest.

SYMBOLIC MEANING OF COLORS.—White was the emblem of light, religious purity, innocence, faith, joy and life. In the judge, it indicates integrity; in the sick, humility; in the woman, chastity.

Red, the ruby, signifies fire, divine love, heat of the creative power, and royalty. White and red roses express love and wisdom. The red color of the blood has its origin in the action of the heart, which corresponds to, or symbolizes love. In a bad sense, red corresponds to the infernal love of evil, hatred, etc.

Blue, or the sapphire, expresses heaven, the firmament, truth from a celestial origin, constancy and fidelity.

Yellow, or gold, is the symbol of the sun, of the goodness of God, of marriage and faithfulness. In a bad sense yellow signifies inconstancy, jealousy and deceit.

Green, the emerald, is the color of the spring, of hope, particularly of the hope of immortality and of victory, as the color of the laurel and palm.

Violet, the amethyst, signifies love and truth, or passion and suffering. Purple and scarlet signify things good and true from a celestial origin.

Black corresponds to despair, darkness, earthliness, mourning, negation, wickedness and death.

DURABILITY OF A HORSE.—A horse will travel 400 yards in $4\frac{1}{2}$ minutes at a walk, 400 yds. in 2 minutes at a trot, and 400 yds. in 1 minute at a gallop. The usual work of a horse is taken at 22,500 lbs. raised 1 foot per minute, for 8 hours per day. A horse will carry 250 lbs. 25 miles per day of 8 hours. An average draught-horse will draw 1,600 lbs. 23 miles per day on a level road, weight of wagon included. The average weight of a horse is 1,000 lbs.; his strength is equal to that of 5 men. In a horse mill moving at 3 feet per second, track 25 feet diameter, he exerts with the machine the power of $4\frac{1}{2}$ horses. The greatest amount a horse can pull in a horizontal line is 900 lbs.; but he can only do this momentarily, in continued exertion, probably half of this is the limit. He attains his growth in 5 years, will live 25, average 16 years. A horse will live 25 days on water, without solid food, 17 days without eating or drinking, but only 5 days on solid food, without drinking.

A cart drawn by horses over an ordinary road will travel 1.1 miles per hour of trip. A 4-horse team will haul from 25 to 36 cubic feet of lime stone at each load. The time expended in loading, unloading, etc., including delays, averages 35 minutes per trip. The cost of loading and unloading a cart, using a horse cram at the quarry, and unloading by hand, when labor is $1.25 per day, and a horse 75 cents, is 25 cents per perch=24.75 cubic feet. The work done by an animal is greatest when the velocity with which he moves is $\frac{1}{8}$ of the greatest with which he can move when not impeded, and the force then exerted .45 of the utmost force the animal can exert at a dead pull.

COMPARATIVE COST OF FREIGHT BY WATER AND RAIL.—It has been proved by actual test that a single tow-boat can transport at one trip from the Ohio to New Orleans 29,000 tons of coal, loaded in barges. Estimating in this way the boat and its tow, worked by a few men, carries as much freight to its destination as 3,000 cars and 100 locomotives, manned by 600 men, could transport.

COST OF A PENNSYLVANIA RAILROAD PASSENGER CAR.—Detailed cost of constructing one first-class Standard Passenger Car, at the Altoona shops of the Pennsylvania R. R., the total cost being $4,423.75. The principal items are as follows:

Labor	$1,263 94	1 Air Brake, complete	131 79
Proportion of Fuel and Stores	28 61	57 Sash Balances	44 61
2,480 feet Poplar	86 80	61 Lights Glasses	65 83
3,434 feet Ash	127 08	2 Stoves	77 56
1,100 feet Pine	20 90	25 Sets Seat Fixtures	50 50
2,350 feet Yellow Pine	70 50	3 Bronze Lamps	13 50
500 feet Oak	10 00	2 Bronze Door Locks	15 20
450 feet Hickory	13 50	Butts and Hinges	15 58
700 feet Mich. Pine	49 00	13 Basket Racks	77 35
400 feet Cherry	16 00	12 Sash Levers	42 00
439 feet Maple veneer	24 14	61 Bronze Window Lifts	24 40
4 pairs Wheels and Axles	332 85	61 Window Fasteners	16 47
2 pairs Passenger Car Trucks	533 62	238 Sheets Tin	41 44
13 gallons Varnish	52 34	273 lbs. Galvanized Iron	25 31
45 lbs. Glue	14 33	96 yards Scarlet Plush	228 87
2,925 lbs. Iron	87 75	44 yards Green Plush	109 99
792 lbs. Castings	16 99	61 yards Sheeting	10 30
Screws	51 88	243 lbs. Hair	72 95
Gas Regulator and Guage	25 25	12 Springs	22 96
2 Two-Light Chandeliers	50 72	12 Spiral Elliptic Springs	20 29
2 Gas Tanks	84 00	1 Head Lining	80 63
		2 packets Gold Leaf	14 58
		Various small items	261 44
			$4,423.75

TABLE, SHOWING THE NUMBER OF DAYS FROM ANY DAY IN ONE MONTH TO THE SAME DAY IN ANOTHER.

From \ To	Jan.	Feb.	Mar.	April	May	June	July	Aug.	Sept.	Oct.	Nov.	Dec.
January	365	31	59	90	120	151	181	212	243	273	304	334
February	334	365	28	59	89	120	150	181	212	242	273	303
March	306	337	365	31	61	92	122	153	184	214	245	275
April	275	306	334	365	30	61	91	122	153	183	214	244
May	245	276	304	335	365	31	61	92	123	153	184	214
June	214	245	273	304	334	365	30	61	92	122	153	183
July	184	215	243	274	304	335	365	31	62	92	123	153
August	153	184	212	243	273	304	334	365	31	61	92	122
September	122	153	181	212	242	273	303	334	365	30	61	91
October	92	123	151	182	212	243	273	304	335	365	31	61
November	61	92	120	151	181	212	242	273	304	334	365	30
December	31	62	90	121	151	182	212	243	274	304	335	365

EXPLANATION.—To find the number of days from January 20 to Dec. 20, follow the horizontal line opposite January until you reach the column headed by December, when you will find 334, representing the required number of days, and so on with the other months. During leap year, if February enters into the calculation, add one day to the result.

Highest and Greatest Mountains in the World.

Name.	Country	Feet High.	Miles
Mt. Everest (Himalayas)	Thibet	29,002	5¾
Sorato, the highest in America	Bolivia	21,284	4
Illimani	Bolivia	21,145	4
Chimborazo	Ecuador	21,422	4⅔
Hindoo-Koosh	Afghanistan	20,600	3¾
Demavend, highest of Elburz Mts	Persia	20,000	3¾
Cotopaxi, highest volcano in the world	Ecuador	19,496	3¾
Antisana	Ecuador	19,150	3½
St. Elias, highest in North America	Alaska	17,850	3⅓
Popocatapetl, volcano	Mexico	17,540	3⅓
Mt. Roa, highest in Oceanica	Hawaii	16,000	3
Mt. Brown, highest peak of R'ky Mts	Brit. America	15,900	3
Mont Blanc, highest in Europe, Alps	Savoy	15,732	3
Mt. Rosa, next highest peak of Alps	Savoy	15,150	2⅞
Limit of perpetual show at the	Equator	15,207	2⅞
Pichinca	Ecuador	15,924	3
Mt. Whitney	California	14,887	2¾
Mt. Fairweather	Alaska	14,500	2¾
Mt. Shasta	California	14,442	2¾
Mt. Ranier	Wash. Territ'y	14,444	2¾
Long's Peak, Rocky Mountains	Colorado	14,271	2⅔
Mt. Ararat	Armenia	14,320	2⅓
Pike's Peak	Colorado	14,216	2⅓
Mt. Ophir	Sumatra	13,800	2⅝
Fremont's Peak, Rocky Mountains	Wyoming	13,570	2⅝
Mt. St. Helens	Wash Territ'y	13,400	2½
Peak of Teneriffe	Canaries	12,182	2⅛
Miltzin, highest of Atlas Mountains	Morocco	11,500	2
Mt. Hood	Oregon	11,225	2
Mt. Lebanon	Syria	10,533	2
Mt. Perda, highest of Pyrenees	France	10,950	2
Mt. Ætna, volcano	Sicily	10,835	2
Monte Corno, highest of Appenines	Naples	9,523	1¾
Sneehattan, highest Dovrefield Mts	Norway	8,115	1½
Pindus, highest in	Greece	7,677	1½
Mount Sinai	Arabia	6,541	1¼
Black Mountain, highest in	N. Carolina	6,760	1¼
Mt. Washington, highest White Mts	N Hampshire	6,285	1¼
Mt. Marcy, highest in	New York	5,402	1
Mt Hecla, volcano	Iceland	5,104	1
Ben Nevis, highest in Great Britain	Scotland	4,406	⅞
Mansfield, highest of Green Mountains	Vermont	4,280	¾
Peaks of Otter	Virginia	4,260	¾
Mt. Vesuvius	Naples	4,253	¾
Round Top, highest of Catskill Mts	New York	3,804	¾

ONE HORSE POWER is the strength necessary to lift 33,000 pounds one foot per minute

Portraits on Bank Notes and Postage Stamps.

On United States notes—$1, Washington; $2, Jefferson; $5, Jackson; $10, Webster; $20, Hamilton; $50, Franklin; $100, Lincoln; $500, General Mansfield; $1,000, DeWitt Clinton; $5,000, Madison; $10,000, Jackson. On silver certificates—$10, Robert Morris; $20, Commodore Decatur; $50, Edward Everett; $100, James Monroe; $500, Charles Sumner, and $1,000, W. L. Marcy. On gold notes—$20, Garfield; $50, Silas Wright; $100, Thomas H. Benton; $500, A. Lincoln; $1,000, Alexander Hamilton; $5,000, James Madison; $10,000, Andrew Jackson.

Those which appear upon postage stamps are: On 10-cent stamp, the head of Jefferson, from life-size statue by Powers; 6-cent, Lincoln, from bust by Volk; 5-cent, Garfield; 4-cent, Jackson; 2-cent, Washington, after Houdon's bust; 1-cent, Franklin, from profile bust by Rubicht.

Average Temperature in United States.

City	Temp	City	Temp
Tucson, Arizona	69	Salt Lake City, Utah	52
Jacksonville, Florida	69	Romney, West Virginia	52
New Orleans, Louisiana	69	Indianapolis, Indiana	51
Austin, Texas	67	Leavenworth, Kansas	51
Mobile, Alabama	66	Santa Fe, New Mexico Ter	51
Jackson, Mississippi	64	Sterlacoom, W. Ter	51
Little Rock, Arkansas	63	Hartford, Connecticut	50
Columbia, S. Carolina	62	Springfield, Illinois	50
Ft. Gibson, Indian Ter	60	Camp Scott, Nevada	50
Raleigh, N Carolina	59	Des Moines, Iowa	49
Atlanta, Georgia	58	Omaha, Nebraska	49
Nashville, Tennessee	58	Denver, Colorado	48
Richmond, Virginia	57	Boston, Massachusetts	48
Louisville, Kentucky	56	Albany, New York	48
San Francisco, California	55	Providence, Rhode Island	48
Washington, D. C	55	Detroit, Michigan	47
St. Louis, Missouri	55	Ft. Randall, Dakota Ter	47
Baltimore, Maryland	54	Sitka, Alaska	46
Harrisburg, Pennsylvania	54	Concord, New Hampshire	46
Wilmington, Delaware	53	Augusta, Maine	45
Trenton, New Jersey	53	Madison, Wisconsin	45
Columbus, Ohio	53	Helena, Montana Ter	43
Portland, Oregon	53	Montpelier, Vermont	43
Ft. Boise, Idaho	52	St. Paul, Minnesota	42

If a railway were built to the sun, and trains upon it were run at the rate of thirty miles an hour, day and night without a stop, it would require 350 years to make the journey from the earth to the sun.

Average Rainfall in the United States.

PLACE.	Inches.	PLACE.	Inches.
Ft. Garland, Colorado	6	Ft. Smith, Arkansas	40
Ft. Bridger, Utah Ter.	6	Providence, Rhode Island	41
Ft. Bliss, Texas	9	New Bedford, Mass.	41
Ft. Colville, Wash. Ter.	9	Baltimore, Maryland	41
San Diego, California	9	Muscatine, Iowa	42
Ft. Craig, New Mexico Ter.	11	St. Louis, Missouri	43
Ft. Defiance, Arizona	14	Marietta, Ohio	43
Ft. Randall, Dakota Ter.	16	Richmond, Indiana	43
Ft. Marcy, New Mexico Ter.	16	Gaston, N. Carolina	43
Ft. Massachusetts, Colorado	17	New York City, N. Y.	43
Sacramento, California	21	Charleston, S. Carolina	43
Dallas, Oregon	21	Philadelphia, Pennsylvania	44
San Francisco, California	21	New Haven, Connecticut	44
Mackinac, Michigan	23	Cincinnati, Ohio	44
Salt Lake City, Utah Ter.	23	Brunswick, Maine	44
Ft. Snelling, Minnesota	25	Boston, Massachusetts	44
Ft. Kearney	25	Newark, New Jersey	44
Penn Yan, New York	28	Memphis, Tennessee	45
Milwaukee, Wisconsin	30	Fortress Monroe, Virginia	47
Detroit, Michigan	30	Springdale, Kentucky	48
Ft. Leavenworth, Kansas	31	Savannah, Georgia	48
Ft. Brown, Texas	33	New Orleans, Louisiana	51
Buffalo, New York	33	Natchez, Mississippi	53
Burlington, Vermont	34	Huntsville, Alabama	54
Peoria, Illinois	35	Washington, Arkansas	54
Key West, Florida	36	Ft. Myers, Florida	56
Ft. Gibson, Indian Ter.	36	Ft. Tonson, Indian Ter.	57
White Sulphur Springs, Va.	37	Meadow Valley, California	57
Washington, D. C.	37	Baton Rouge, Louisiana	60
Pittsburgh, Pennsylvania	37	Mt. Vernon, Alabama	66
Cleveland, Ohio	37	Ft. Haskin, Oregon	66
Ft Vancouver	38	Sitka, Alaska	83
Hanover, New Hampshire	40	Neah Bay, Wash. Ter.	123

Yards of Wire per Bundle.

Wires all weigh 63 lbs. to the bundle

Wire Gauge.	Yards in Bundle.	Wire Gauge.	Yards in Bundle.
No. 0	71	No. 11	529
" 1	91	" 12	700
" 2	105	" 13	893
" 3	121	" 14	1142
" 4	143	" 15	1468
" 5	170	" 16	1954
" 6	203	" 17	2540
" 7	239	" 18	3150
" 8	286	" 19	4085
" 9	342	" 20	4912
" 10	420		

Amount of Barbed Wire Required for Fences.

Estimated number of pounds of barbed wire required to fence space or distances mentioned, with one, two or three lines of wire, based upon each pound of wire measuring one rod (16½ feet).

	1 Line.	2 Lines.	3 Lines
1 square acre	50⅔ lbs.	101⅓ lbs.	152 lbs.
1 side of a square acre	12⅔ lbs	25⅓ lbs.	38 lbs.
1 square half-acre	36 lbs.	72 lbs.	108 lbs.
1 square mile	1280 lbs.	2560 lbs.	3840 lbs.
1 side of a square mile	320 lbs.	640 lbs.	960 lbs.
1 rod in length	1 lb.	2 lbs.	3 lbs.
100 rods in length	100 lbs.	200 lbs	300 lbs.
100 feet in length	6 1-16 lbs.	12⅛ lbs.	18 3-16 lbs

Number of Shrubs or Plants for an Acre of Ground.

Dist. apart	No. of Plants.	Dist. apart.	No of Plants.
3 inches by 3 inches	696,960	6 feet by 6 feet	1,210
4 inches by 4 inches	392,040	6½ feet by 6½ feet	1,031
6 inches by 6 inches	174,240	7 feet by 7 feet	881
9 inches by 9 inches	77,440	8 feet by 8 feet	680
1 foot by 1 foot	43,560	9 feet by 9 feet	537
1½ feet by 1½ feet	19,360	10 feet by 10 feet	435
2 feet by 1 foot	21,780	11 feet by 11 feet	360
2 feet by 2 feet	10,890	12 feet by 12 feet	302
2½ feet by 2½ feet	6,960	13 feet by 13 feet	257
3 feet by 1 foot	14,520	14 feet by 14 feet	222
3 feet by 2 feet	7,260	15 feet by 15 feet	193
3 feet by 3 feet	4,840	16 feet by 16 feet	170
3½ feet by 3½ feet	3,555	16½ feet by 16½ feet	160
4 feet by 1 foot	10,890	17 feet by 17 feet	150
4 feet by 2 feet	5,445	18 feet by 18 feet	134
4 feet by 3 feet	3,630	19 feet by 16 feet	120
4 feet by 4 feet	2,722	20 feet by 20 feet	108
4½ feet by 4½ feet	2,151	25 feet by 25 feet	69
5 feet by 1 foot	8,712	30 feet by 30 feet	48
5 feet by 2 feet	4,356	33 feet by 33 feet	40
5 feet by 3 feet	2,904	40 feet by 40 feet	27
5 feet by 4 feet	2,178	50 feet by 50 feet	17
5 feet by 5 feet	1,742	60 feet by 60 feet	12
5½ feet by 5½ feet	1,417	66 feet by 66 feet	10

COST OF EMANCIPATION.—If the total cost of the Civil War be divided among the slaves set free, emancipation cost about $700 per slave.

How Deep in the Ground to Plant Corn.

The following is the result of an experiment with Indian Corn. That which was planted at the depth of

⅞ inch, sprout appeared in.............................. 8 days
1 inch, sprout appeared in............................... 8½ days
1½ inch, sprout appeared in............................. 9½ days
2 inches, sprout appeared in............................ 10 days
2½ inches, sprout appeared in........................... 11½ days
3 inches, sprout appeared in............................ 12 days
3½ inches, sprout appeared in........................... 13 days
4 inches, sprout appeared in............................ 13½ days

The more shallow the seed was covered with earth, the more rapidly the sprout made its appearance, and the stronger afterwards was the stalk. The deeper the seed lay, the longer it remained before it came to the surface. Four inches was too deep for the maize, and also too deep for smaller kernels.

How to Measure Corn in Crib, Hay in a Mow, etc.

This rule will apply to a crib of any kind. Two cubic feet of sound, dry corn in the ear will make a bushel shelled. To get the quantity of shelled corn in a crib of corn in the ear, measure the length, breadth and height of the crib, inside of the rail; multiply the length by the breadth and the product by the height; then divide the product by two, and you have the number of bushels in the crib.

To find the number of bushels of apples, potatoes, etc., in a bin, multiply the length, breadth and thickness together, and this product by 8, and point off one figure in the product for decimals.

To find the amount of hay in a mow, allow 512 cubic feet for a ton, and it will come out very near correct.

How Grain will Shrink.

Farmers rarely gain by keeping their grain after it is fit for market, when the shrinkage is taken into account. Wheat, from the time it is threshed, will shrink two quarts to the bushel or six per cent. in six months, in the most favorable circumstances. Hence, it follows that ninety-four cents a bushel for wheat when first threshed in August, is as good, taking into account the shrinkage alone, as one dollar in the following February.

Corn shrinks much more from the time it is first husked. One hundred bushels of ears, as they come from the field in November, will be reduced to not far from eighty. So that forty cents a bushel for corn in the ear, as it comes from the field, is as good as fifty in March, shrinkage only being taken into the account.

In the case of potatoes — taking those that rot and are otherwise lost — together with the shrinkage, there is but little doubt that between October and June, the loss to the owner who holds them is not less than thirty-three per cent.

This estimate is taken on the basis of interest at 7 per cent., and takes no account of loss by vermin.

What a Deed to a Farm in many States Includes.

Everyone knows it conveys all the fences standing on the farm, but all might not think it also included the fencing-stuff, posts, rails, etc., which had once been used in the fence, but had been taken down and piled up for future use again in the same place. But new fencing material, just bought, and never attached to the soil, would not pass. So piles of hop poles stored away, if once used on the land and intended to be again so used, have been considered a part of it, but loose boards or scaffold poles merely laid across the beams of the barn, and never fastened to it, would not be, and the seller of the farm might take them away. Standing trees, of course, also pass as part of the land; so do trees blown down or cut down, and still left in the woods where they fell, but not if cut, and corded up for sale; the wood has then become personal property.

If there be any manure in the barnyard, or in the compost heap on the field, ready for immediate use, the buyer ordinarily, in the absence of any contrary agreement, takes that also as belonging to the farm, though it might not be so, if the owner had previously sold it to some other party, and had collected it together in a heap by itself, for such an act might be a technical severance from the oil, and so convert real into personal estate; and even a lessee of a farm could not take away the manure made on the place while he was in occupation. Growing crops also pass by the deed of a farm, unless they are expressly reserved; and when it is not intended to convey those, it should be so stated in the deed itself; a mere oral agreement to that effect would not be, in most States, valid in law. Another mode is to stipulate that possession is not to be given until some future day, in which case the crops or manures may be removed before that time.

As to the buildings on the farm, though generally mentioned in the deed, it is not absolutely necessary they should be. A deed of land ordinarily carries all the buildings on it, belonging to the grantor, whether mentioned or not; and this rule includes the lumber and timber of any old building which has been taken down or blown down, and packed away for future use on farm.

United States Land Measure and Homestead Law.

A township is 36 sections, each a mile square. A section is 640 acres. A quarter section, half a mile square, is 160 acres. An eighth section, half a mile long, north and south, and a quarter of a mile wide, is 80 acres. A sixteenth section, a quarter of a mile square, is 40 acres

The sections are all numbered 1 to 36, commencing at northeast corner, thus:

6	5	4	3	2	NW NE / SW SE
7	8	9	10	11	12
18	17	16	15	14	13
19	20	21	22	23	24
30	29	28	27	26	25
31	32	33	34	35	36

The sections are all divided in quarters, which are named by the cardinal points, as in section 1. The quarters are divided in the same way. The description of a forty-acre lot would read: The south half of the west half of the south-west quarter of section 1 in township 24, north of range 7 west, or as the case might be; and sometimes will fall short, and sometimes overrun the number of acres it is supposed to contain.

HOMESTEAD PRIVILEGE.—The laws give to every citizen, and to those who have declared their intention to become citizens, the right to a homestead on SURVEYED lands, to the extent of one-quarter section, or 160 acres, or a half-quarter section, or 80 acres; the former in cases in the class of lower priced lands held by law at $1.25 per acre, the latter of high priced lands held at $2.50 per acre, when disposed of to cash buyers. The pre-emption privilege is restricted to heads of families, widows, or single persons over the age of twenty-one.

Every soldier and officer in the army, and every seaman, marine and officer of the navy, during the recent rebellion, may enter 160 acres from either class, and length of time served in the army or navy deducted from the time required to perfect title.

BOOKS PUBLISHED.—There are published daily, throughut the world, about 100 new books, or 30,000 a year.

Number of Pounds to the Bushel, legal weight, in Different States.

States	Buckwh't	Corn on the Cob	Shelled Corn	Corn Meal	Onions	Sweet Potatoes	Potatoes	Turnips	Peas	Beans	Barley	Wheat	Oats	Rye	Dried Apples	Flax Seed	Clover Seed	Blue Gr'ss Seed	Anthrac'te Coal	Timothy Seed
Arkansas	52	70	56	50	57	50	60	..	46	60	48	60	32	56	24	56	60	14	80	45
California	40	..	52	..	..	..	60	..	..	..	50	60	32	54	..	..	..	..	..	..
Connecticut	48	..	56	..	..	..	60	..	..	..	48	60	32	56	..	56	..	14	..	45
Georgia	52	70	56	48	57	55	60	55	..	..	47	60	32	56	24	56	60	14	80	45
Illinois	52	70	56	48	57	55	60	50	60	60	48	60	32	56	24	54	60	14	80	45
Indiana	50	68	56	50	48	46	60	55	..	..	48	60	32	56	25	56	60	14	..	45
Iowa	52	70	56	..	57	..	60	..	..	..	48	60	32	56	24	..	..	14	80	45
Kansas	50	70	56	50	57	50	60	60	60	60	48	60	30	56	24	56	60	14	80	45
Kentucky	55	70	56	50	52	55	60	55	60	64	47	60	32	56	28	55	64	14	..	44
Maine	48	..	56	..	52	..	60	..	..	..	48	60	32	50	22	55	60	..	..	..
Massachusetts	48	..	56	..	54	..	60	..	..	..	48	60	32	56	..	56	..	..	..	..
Michigan	48	70	56	50	57	56	60	58	..	60	48	60	32	56	28	56	60	..	..	45
Minnesota	42	..	56	..	..	54	60	..	..	62	43	60	30	50	25	55	64	14	..	..
Missouri	52	..	56	..	..	..	60	..	..	..	48	60	32	56	..	..	60	..	..	..
New Hampshire	..	..	56	50	57	..	60	..	60	60	48	60	32	56	22	56	..	..	..	..
New Jersey	50	..	56	..	..	..	60	..	60	60	48	60	32	56	..	..	..	..	..	45
New York	48	..	56	46	50	54	56	..	60	60	48	60	32	56	..	..	..	..	..	..
North Carolina	50	..	54	..	..	..	60	..	50	..	47	60	32	56	..	56	60	..	..	45
Ohio	50	..	56	50	50	50	60	..	60	62	48	60	32	56	22	55	64	14	..	..
Pennsylvania	48	..	56	..	50	..	56	..	..	..	48	60	32	56	..	..	62	..	..	..
Rhode Island	..	..	56	..	..	..	..	..	..	..	48	60	33	56	..	44	..	..	..	..
South Carolina	56	70	56	50	57	50	60	..	60	60	48	60	32	56	26	..	60	..	..	45
Tennessee	56	72	56	56	52	50	60	60	60	60	48	60	32	56	26	56	60	14	80	45
Vermont	46	..	52	50	57	56	60	55	..	..	48	60	32	56	28	..	..	..	80	45
Virginia	52	70	56	50	56	..	60	..	..	..	48	60	32	56	28	56	60	14	..	45
Wisconsin	50	70	56	..	50	..	60	42	..	..	48	60	32	56	..	56	60	..	..	45

COTTON CROP OF THE UNITED STATES FOR A HALF CENTURY.

Year.	Bales.	Year.	Bales.
1829	870,415	1857	2,939,519
1830	976,845	1858	3,113,962
1831	1,038,848	1859	3,851,481
1832	987,487	1860	4,669,770
1833	1,070,438	1861	3,656,006
1834	1,205,324	1862 to 1865	No record
1835	1,254,328		
1836	1,360,752		
1837	1,422,930	1866	2,193,987
1838	1,801,497	1867	2,019,774
1839	1,360,532	1868	2,593,993
1840	1,177,835	1869	2,439,039
1841	1,634,945	1870	3,154,946
1842	1,683,574	1871	4,352,317
1843	2,378,875	1872	2,974,351
1844	2,030,409	1873	3,930,508
1845	2,394,503	1874	4,170,388
1846	2,100,537	1875	3,832,991
1847	2,778,651	1876	4,669,288
1848	2,347,634	1877	4,485,423
1849	2,728,596	1878	4,811,265
1850	2,096,706	1879	5,073,531
1851	2,355,257	1880	5,757,397
1852	2,015,029	1881	6,589,329
1853	3,262,882	1882	5,435,845
1854	2,930,027	1883	6,992,234
1855	2,847,339	1884	5,714,052
1856	3,527,845	1885	6,474,000

The returns are for the years ending September 1. The report from 1829 to 1884, inclusive, is from the *Commercial and Financial Chronicle*, and the estimate for 1885 is from *Bradstreet's*. The average net weight per bale is 440 pounds.

The big trees (redwoods) of Calaveras County, Cal., are 92 in number, ten being thirty feet in diameter. They range in height from 150 to 237 feet, and in age from 1,000 to 3,500 years.

THE BIGGEST THINGS.

Interesting Facts Useful When You Get Into an Argument.

The largest theater in the world is the new Opera-house in Paris. It covers nearly three acres of ground; its cubic mass is 4,287,000 feet; it cost about 100,000,000 francs. The largest suspension bridge is the one between New York City and Brooklyn; the length of the main span is 1,595 feet 6 inches; the entire length of the bridge is 5,980 feet. The loftiest active volcano is Popocatapetl — " smoking mountain "— thirty-five miles southwest of Puebla, Mexico; it is 17,748 feet above the sea level, and has a crater three miles in circumference, and 1,000 feet deep. The longest span of wire in the world is used for a telegraph in India over the River Kistnah. It is more than 6,000 feet in length, and is 1,200 feet high. The largest ship in the world is the Great Eastern. She is 680 feet long, 83 feet broad, and 60 feet deep, being 28,627 tons burden, 18,915 gross, and 13,334 net register.

The greatest fortress, from a strategical point of view, is the famous stronghold of Gibraltar. It occupies a rocky peninsula jutting out into the sea, about three miles long and three-quarters of a mile wide. One central rock rises to a hight of 1,435 feet above the sea level. Its northern face is almost perpendicular, while its east side is full of tremendous precipices. On the south it terminates in what is called Europa Point. The west side is less steep than the east, and between its base and the sea is the narrow, almost level span on which the town of Gibraltar is built. The fortress is considered impregnable to military assault. The regular garrison in time of peace numbers about 7,000.

The biggest cavern is the Mammoth Cave, in Edmonson County, Kentucky. It is near Green River, about six miles from Cave City, and twenty-eight from Bowling Green. The cave consists of a succession of irregular chambers, some of which are large, situated on different levels. Some of these are traversed by the navigable branches of the subterranean Echo River. Blind fish are found in its waters.

The longest tunnel in the world is that of the St. Gothard, on the line of railroad between Lucerne and Milan. The summit of the tunnel is 900 feet below the surface at Andermatt, and 6,600 feet beneath the peak of Kastlehorn, of the St. Gothard group. The tunnel is 26½ feet wide, and is 18 feet 10 inches from the floor to the crown of the arched roof. It is 9½ miles long.

The biggest trees in the world are the mammoth trees of California. One of a grove in Tulare County, according to measurements made by members of the State Geological Survey, was shown to be 276 feet in height, 108 feet in circumference at base, and 76 feet at a point 12 feet above ground. Some of the trees are 376 feet high, and 34 feet in diameter. Some of the largest that have been felled indicate an age of from 2,000 to 2,500 years.

The largest library is the Bibliotheque National, in Paris, founded by Louis XIV. It contains 1,400,000 volumes, 300,000 pamphlets. 175,000 manuscripts, 300,000 maps and charts, and 150,000 coins and medals. The collection of engravings exceeds 1,300,000, contained in some 10,000 volumes. The portraits number about 100,000.

The largest desert is that of Sahara, a vast region of Northern Africa, extending from the Atlantic Ocean on the west to the valley of the Nile on the east. The length from east to west is about 3,000 miles, its average breadth about 900 miles, its area about 2,000,000 square miles. Rain falls in torrents in the Sahara at intervals of five, ten and twenty years. In summer the heat during the day is excessive, but the nights are often cold.

A CALENDAR FOR ASCERTAINING ANY DAY OF THE WEEK FOR ANY GIVEN TIME WITHIN THE PRESENT CENTURY.

Years 1801 to 1900.

Years	Jan.	Feb.	Mar.	Apr.	May	June	July	Aug.	Sept.	Oct.	Nov.	Dec.
1801 1807 1818 1829 1835 1846 1857 1863 1874 1885 1891	4	7	7	3	5	1	3	6	2	4	7	2
1802 1813 1819 1830 1841 1847 1858 1869 1875 1886 1897	5	1	1	4	6	2	4	7	3	5	1	3
1803 1814 1825 1831 1842 1853 1859 1870 1881 1887 1898	6	2	2	5	7	3	5	1	4	6	2	4
1805 1811 1822 1833 1839 1850 1861 1867 1878 1889 1895	2	5	5	1	3	6	1	4	7	2	5	7
1806 1817 1823 1834 1845 1851 1862 1871 1879 1890	3	6	6	2	4	7	2	5	1	3	6	1
1809 1815 1826 1837 1843 1854 1865 1882 .... 1893 1899	7	3	3	6	1	4	6	2	5	7	3	5
1810 1821 1827 1838 1849 1855 1866 1877 1883 1894 1900	1	4	4	7	2	5	7	3	6	1	4	6

LEAP YEARS.

Years	Jan.	Feb.	Mar.	Apr.	May	June	July	Aug.	Sept.	Oct.	Nov.	Dec.
1804 1832 1860 1888	7	3 (29)	4	7	2	5	7	3	6	1	4	6
1808 1836 1864 1892	5	1	2	5	7	3	5	1	4	6	2	4
1812 1840 1868 1896	3	6	7	3	5	1	3	6	2	4	7	2
1816 1844 1872	1	4	5	1	3	6	1	4	7	2	5	7
1820 1848 1876	6	2	3	6	1	4	6	2	5	7	3	5
1824 1852 1880	4	7	1	4	6	2	4	7	3	5	1	3
1828 1856 1884	2	5	6	2	4	7	2	5	1	3	6	1

NOTE.—To ascertain any day of the week in any year of the present century, first look in the table of years for the year required, and under the months are figures which refer to the corresponding figures at the head of the columns of days below. *For Example:* To know what day of the week May 4 will be on in the year 1872, in the table of years look for 1872, and in a parallel line, under May, is figure 3, which directs to column 3, in which it will be seen that May 4 falls on Saturday.

1	2	3	4	5	6	7
Monday....1	Tuesday....1	Wednesday..1	Thursday....1	Friday....1	Saturday....1	*Sunday*....1
Tuesday....2	Wednesday..2	Thursday....2	Friday....2	Saturday....2	*Sunday*....2	Monday....2
Wednesday..3	Thursday....3	Friday....3	Saturday....3	*Sunday*....3	Monday....3	Tuesday....3
Thursday....4	Friday....4	Saturday....4	*Sunday*....4	Monday....4	Tuesday....4	Wednesday..4
Friday....5	Saturday....5	*Sunday*....5	Monday....5	Tuesday....5	Wednesday..5	Thursday....5
Saturday....6	*Sunday*....6	Monday....6	Tuesday....6	Wednesday..6	Thursday....6	Friday....6
Sunday....7	Monday....7	Tuesday....7	Wednesday..7	Thursday....7	Friday....7	Saturday....7
Monday....8	Tuesday....8	Wednesday..8	Thursday....8	Friday....8	Saturday....8	*Sunday*....8
Tuesday....9	Wednesday..9	Thursday....9	Friday....9	Saturday....9	*Sunday*....9	Monday....9
Wednesday.10	Thursday.10	Friday....10	Saturday.10	*Sunday*...10	Monday....10	Tuesday....10
Thursday...11	Friday....11	Saturday.11	*Sunday*...11	Monday....11	Tuesday....11	Wednesday.11
Friday....12	Saturday.12	*Sunday*...12	Monday....12	Tuesday....12	Wednesday.12	Thursday....12
Saturday.13	*Sunday*...13	Monday....13	Tuesday....13	Wednesday.13	Thursday....13	Friday....13
Sunday....14	Monday....14	Tuesday....14	Wednesday.14	Thursday....14	Friday....14	Saturday....14
Monday....15	Tuesday....15	Wednesday.15	Thursday....15	Friday....15	Saturday....15	*Sunday*....15
Tuesday....16	Wednesday.16	Thursday....16	Friday....16	Saturday....16	*Sunday*....16	Monday....16
Wednesday.17	Thursday....17	Friday....17	Saturday....17	*Sunday*....17	Monday....17	Tuesday....17
Thursday...18	Friday....18	Saturday....18	*Sunday*....18	Monday....18	Tuesday....18	Wednesday.18
Friday....19	Saturday....19	*Sunday*....19	Monday....19	Tuesday....19	Wednesday.19	Thursday....19
Saturday.20	*Sunday*....20	Monday....20	Tuesday....20	Wednesday.20	Thursday....20	Friday....20
Sunday....21	Monday....21	Tuesday....21	Wednesday.21	Thursday....21	Friday....21	Saturday....21
Monday....22	Tuesday....22	Wednesday.22	Thursday....22	Friday....22	Saturday....22	*Sunday*....22
Tuesday....23	Wednesday.23	Thursday....23	Friday....23	Saturday....23	*Sunday*....23	Monday....23
Wednesday.24	Thursday....24	Friday....24	Saturday....24	*Sunday*....24	Monday....24	Tuesday....24
Thursday...25	Friday....25	Saturday....25	*Sunday*....25	Monday....25	Tuesday....25	Wednesday.25
Friday....26	Saturday....26	*Sunday*....26	Monday....26	Tuesday....26	Wednesday.26	Thursday....26
Saturday.27	*Sunday*....27	Monday....27	Tuesday....27	Wednesday.27	Thursday....27	Friday....27
Sunday....28	Monday....28	Tuesday....28	Wednesday.28	Thursday....28	Friday....28	Saturday....28
Monday....29	Tuesday....29	Wednesday.29	Thursday....29	Friday....29	Saturday....29	*Sunday*....29
Tuesday....30	Wednesday.30	Thursday....30	Friday....30	Saturday....30	*Sunday*....30	Monday....30
Wednesday.31	Thursday....31	Friday....31	Saturday....31	*Sunday*....31	Monday....31	Tuesday....31

THE LIBERTY BELL.

The Philadelphia *News* gives some interesting particulars of the history of the Independence Bell:

The order for the bell was given in 1751. The State House of Pennsylvania, in Philadelphia, work on which had been suspended for a number of years, was then approaching completion. The lower floors were already occupied by the Supreme Court in the chamber, while in the other assembled the Freemen of the Province of Pennsylvania, then consisting of one body. A committee was appointed by the Freemen, with Peter Norris as chairman, and empowered to have a new bell cast for the building. The commission for the bell was in the sam year awarded to Robert Charles, of London, the specification being that the bell should weigh about 2,000 pounds and cost £100 sterling. It was to be made by the best workmen, to be examined carefully before being shipped, and to contain, in well-shaped letters around it, the inscription: "By order of the Province of Pennsylvania, for the State House in the City of Philadelphia, 1752." An order was given to place underneath this the fatal and prophetic words from Leviticus xxv. 10: "Proclaim liberty throughout the land and to all the inhabitants thereof."

The reason for the selection of this text has been a subject of much conjecture, but the true reason is apparent when the full text is read. It is as follows: "And ye shall hallow the fiftieth year and proclaim liberty throughout the land and to all the inhabitants thereof." In selecting the text the good Quakers had in memory the arrival of William Penn and their forefathers more than half a century before.

In August, 1752, the bell arrived, but though in apparent good order, it was cracked by a stroke of the clapper while being tested. It could not be sent back, as the captain of the vessel who had brought it ovei could not take it on board. Two skillful men undertook to recast the bell, which, on being opened, revealed a bell which pleased very much. But it was also found to be defective. The original bell was considered too high, and a quantity of copper was added to the composition, but too much copper was added. There were a great many witticisms on account of the second failure, and the ingenious workmen undertook to recast the bell, which they successfully did, and it was placed in condition in June, 1753.

On Monday, the 8th of July (not the 4th), at noon, true to its motto, it rang out the memorable message of " Liberty throughout the land and to all the inhabitants thereof."

For fifty years the bell continued to be rung on every festival and anniversary until it eventually cracked.

An ineffectual attempt was made to cause it to continue serviceable by enlarging the cause of its dissonance and chipping the edges. It was removed from its position in the tower to a lower story, and only used on occasions of public sorrow, such as the death of ex-Presidents and statesmen. Subsequently it was placed on the original timbers in the vestibule of the State House, and in 1873 it was suspended in a prominent position immediately beneath where a larger bell presented to the city in 1866 now proclaims the passing hours.

CHOLERA.

CHOLERA.— Known in its native country, India, under the names Morshi, Mordeshi and Visuchika; first appeared in Europe in 1831; was first introduced into Canada and the United States in 1832, spread as an epidemic, and lasted in some localities until 1835.

Second European epidemic began in 1847; reached New York and New Orleans in December, 1848; Canada in April, 1849; continuing epidemically in the United States until 1852; almost died out in Europe at the close of 1850, but broke out afresh in 1852, and was again imported into this country in 1853, not entirely disappearing until 1855.

Third epidemic in Europe began in 1865; cases at Ward's Island, New York, in November, but the contagion not fairly introduced into the United States until the spring of 1866; died out here in 1867, and in most European countries in 1869-70; a fresh outbreak there in 1871 reached this country again in February, 1873, when it spread from New Orleans and involved nineteen States in eight months.

Fourth epidemic followed a violent outbreak in Egypt in 1883 (the "Damietta outbreak"); cases at Marseilles in October, but existence concealed; declared epidemic at Toulon in June, 1884; spread throughout Southern France, thence into Italy; existence suspected in Spain, but denied during the winter of 1884-85, but during the spring and summer of 1885 it invaded nearly all parts of the kingdom, causing over one hundred thousand deaths; attacked Italy again during the autumn, and at the close of 1885 was reported in Venice, Trieste and in the province of Brittany. Cases were reported in various other parts of Europe, but no spread resulted, except in the countries named. So far as known, only one infected vessel arrived in this country; deaths from cholera had occurred during the voyage, but the vessel was properly cared for on her arrival in New York Bay, latter part of September, 1885.

The first European epidemic lasted *seven* years—from 1831 to 1837, inclusive—dying out during cold weather, and reappearing in spring in previously infected localities, and thence spreading to localities which had previously escaped; in many instances more severely scourging localities in the second or subsequent years than during the first visitation. The second epidemic lasted *seventeen* years—1847 to 1863—with a remarkable intermission in 1851-52, and numerous fluctuations of intensity, the severest in 1849-50 and in 1853-55. The third lasted *ten* years—1865 to 1874—with a remission in 1869-70, and a fresh outbreak in 1871. In all of them the disease was brought to the United States within two years after it had become epidemic in countries in close commercial relation with this conntry, and in each epidemic there were several distinct importations of the contagion.

DEDUCTION—*That whenever, and as long as Asiatic*

cholera exists on the European continent, this country is in danger of a cholera epidemic.

Three things are necessary for a cholera epidemic:

'First, the cholera poison; second, filthy local conditions of air, soil and water; third, individual predisposition. If, by quarantine, the poison can be kept out of the country, the other two factors might be disregarded. But since the most rigidly enforced quarantines have heretofore failed to prevent the introduction of the poison, it is essential that such measures of local and individual sanitation be enforced as will secure cleanliness of person, of habitation and of surroundings—of air, water and soil. Certain of these conditions the individual can only indirectly control, but for his own immediate environment, his dwelling and premises and his personal hygiene, he is himself responsible. And these conditions have much to do with determining the individual predisposition.

Cholera is most surely guarded against by keeping the body clean and well nourished, and the mind equable and contented; underfeeding, anxiety, overwork, exposure to extremes of temperature, intemperance in eating or drinking—all tend to reduce the resistance of the system to the influence of any morbid poison, and more especially that of cholera.

If cholera should, unfortunately, make its appearance, the following most important precaution should be observed:

No diarrhea, or even lax condition of the bowels, should be disregarded while there is a single case of cholera in the country. An attack of cholera is usually preceded by a loose, painless diarrhea, although less frequently one may pass from apparently perfect health after a single dejection into the state of cholera collapse. But, as a rule, there is the premonitory stage above indicated, and which may last from one to five days. Such attacks, if promptly and properly treated, may almost invariably be cured, but if neglected, may develop into malignant cholera.

꙳ TREATMENT.—First, absolute rest; second, a teaspoonful of the following mixture every two hours until the diarrhea is checked:

CHOLERA MIXTURE.

Aromatic sulphuric acid........One ounce.
Paregoric......................Three ounces.

DOSE.— One teaspoonful in four tablespoonfuls o water.

This is the simplest and most generally useful combination, and should be kept ready for use in the house, office, store and workshop during a cholera season.

A good doctor should be called, but the above treatment is to be followed until the doctor arrives. Meantime take no food or stimulants of any kind, but allay thirst with ice.

PREVENTIVE.— In addition to ordinary prudence in diet and drink, especial care should be taken as to the quality of drinking-water used. If not known to be absolutely pure, add a teaspoonful of aromatic sulphuric acid (elixir of vitriol) to one quart of water. Epidemics of cholera have been arrested, when every other means failed, by using water thus acidulated. It may be flavored with lemons and sweetened.

There is good reason for believing that the cholera poison is absolutely destroyed by mineral acids. It would be well, therefore, to confine the drink exclusively to this mineral-acid lemonade so long as there is any danger of cholera. No other single precaution is of so much importance as this.

POISONS—ANTIDOTES AND TREATMENT.

Immediately on discovering that poison has been swallowed, send for a physician with all possible haste. Until his arrival, the treatment should either be with a view to removing the poison by an emetic or neutralizing its effects by an antidote.

EMETICS. — Ground mustard, a tablespoonful in a tumbler of warm water, is an emetic usually quickly procured. Give the patient one-fourth of it at once, and follow with a cup of warm water. Repeat the dose every minute or two until vomiting takes place. Give tepid water freely. Mustard has a special value in most cases where an emetic is needed, as it is also stimulating in its effects.

Common salt is also used as an emetic, a teacup of water with as much salt as the water will dissolve being given every few moments until vomiting occurs.

Tickling the throat with a feather, or with the finger, is a valuable aid to the action of an emetic.

After vomiting takes place, the white of eggs in warm water, warm milk, gum-arabic water, or flour and water, may be given to further cleanse the stomach and to soothe the irritated mucous membrane.

The following table gives the common poisons and suggestions as to the treatment for each, and, together with the above, may be of assistance until the arrival of a physician:

ACIDS—MINERAL.—Chalk, magnesia (plaster off wall), solution of cooking soda, or saleratus; then barley-water, linseed-tea, or olive-oil.
ACONITE.—Emetics, stimulants external and internal
ANTIMONY.—Strong tea in large quantities.
AQUA FORTIS.—Same as *Acids, Mineral.*
ARSENIC.—Give milk in large quantities, or the white of eggs, or flour and water. Follow with stimulants.
ATROPIA.—Same as *Belladonna.*
ARGENTI NIT.—Large teaspoonful of salt in cup of water; repeat in ten minutes; then give castor-oil and linseed-tea or barley-water.
BAD FISH OR OTHER FOOD.—Emetics; then a large dose of castor-oil with some warm spice. Mustard-plaster to pit of stomach if necessary.
BED-BUG POISON.—Same as *Corrosive Sublimate.*
BLUE VITRIOL.—Same as *Cupri Sulph.* and *Copper*.
CANNABIS INDICA.—Hot brandy and water, lemon juice, vegetable acids, vinegar; allow patient to sleep; blister to nape of neck.
CANTHARIDES. - Emetics, followed by barley-water, flaxseed-tea, or other soothing drinks.
CARBOLIC ACID. -Castor or olive-oil.
CAUSTIC POTASH.—Same as *Potash.*
CAUSTIC SODA.—Same as *Potash.*
CHLORINE WATER.—Albumen (white of egg), milk, flour.

CHLOROFORM.—Fresh air; incline the body so as to get the head as low as possible;. pull the tongue forward; dash cold water on the chest at intervals and excite respiration by any other means.

CHLORIDE OF TIN.—Milk in large quantities with magnesia, chalk or whiting in it; raw eggs beaten up with water or milk.

CHLORAL HYDRATE.—Same as *Chloroform*.

CHLORIDE OF ZINC.—Milk with white of eggs in it. Large Doses.

COBALT.—Same as *Arsenic*.

COLCHICUM.—Emetics; then barley water, linseed-tea, etc. If stupor (*coma*) be present, give brandy, coffee, ammonia.

CONIUM.—Emetics, followed by stimulants externally and internally.

COPPER.—Milk and whites of eggs; large quantities; then strong tea. Don't give vinegar.

COPPERAS.—Emetics. Mucilaginous drinks.

CORROSIVE SUBLIMATE.—White of eggs in a little water. Repeat dose at intervals of two or three minutes until patient vomits. Use milk or flour and water if you can't get eggs.

CROTON OIL.—Emetics; then flaxseed-tea, gum-arabic water, slippery elm, etc.

CUPRI SULPH.—Whites of eggs. Same as *Copper*.

CYANIDE OF POTASSIUM.—Same as *Prussic Acid*.

DIGITALIS.—Emetics. Keep the patient lying down. Stimulants externally and internally.

FOWLER'S SOLUTION.—Same as *Arsenic*.

HASCHISCH.—Same as *Cannabis Indica*.

HEMLOCK.—Same as *Conium*.

HENBANE.—Same as *Hyoscyamus*.

HYDROCYANIC ACID.—Fresh air and artificial respiration, with dashes of cold water.

HYOSCYAMUS.—Emetics; lemon-juice stimulants external and internal.

INDELIBLE INK.—Same as *Argenti Nit*.

INDIAN HEMP.—Same as *Cannabis Indica*.

IODINE.—Emetics; starch or flour in water; barley water or other demulcent drinks.

IVY POISONING.—Apply soft-soap freely to affected parts; or bathe the poisoned skin frequently with weak tincture of belladonna.

LAUDANUM.—Same as *Opium*.

LEAD.—Two ounces of Epsom salts in a pint of water; wineglassful every ten minutes until it operates freely. Afterward milk.

LEAD SALTS.—Same as *Lead*.

LEAD WATER.—Same as *Lead*.

LOBELIA.—Stimulants externally and internally.

LUNAR CAUSTIC.—Same as *Argenti Nit*.

LYE.—Same as *Potash*.

MERCURY.—Same as *Corrosive Sublimate*.

MINERAL ACID.—Same as *Acids, Mineral*.

MORPHIA.—Same as *Opium*.

MURIATIC ACID.—Same as *Acids, Mineral*.

NITRATE OF SILVER.—Same as *Argenti Nit*.

NITRE.—Same as *Saltpetre*.

NITRIC ACID.—Same as *Acids, Mineral*.

NUX VOMICA.—Emetics, artificial respiration, linseed-tea or barley-water; to an adult 30 drops laudanum to relieve the spasms.

OIL OF BITTER ALMONDS.—Same as *Prussic Acid*.

OIL OF VITRIOL.—Same as *Acids, Mineral*.

OPIUM.—Emetics (10 grains of sulphate of copper if possible); after vomiting, which must be induced quickly, give plenty of strong coffee with brandy, put mustard plasters around calves of legs; keep patient aroused by walking around, dashing cold water in face, heating soles of feet, or whipping body with towls wrung out in cold water. If the patient is allowed to go to sleep before the effect of the opium has passed off, death will result.

OXALIC ACID.—Same as *Acids, Mineral*.

PAREGORIC.—Same as *Opium*.

PARIS GREEN.—Same as *Arsenic*.

PHOSPHORUS.—Emetics, large quantities of tepid water, with magnesia, chalk, whiting, or even flour stirred in it.

POTASH.—Vinegar and water, oranges, lemons, sour

beer, cider, or sour fruit; then give oil—linseed or olive.

PRUSSIC ACID.—Sal-volatile and water; apply smelling-salts to nostrils; dash cold water in face; stimulants.

RATSBANE.—Same as *Arsenic*.

RED PRECIPITATE.—Same as *Corrosive Sublimate*

RED LEAD.—Same as *Lead*.

"ROUGH ON RATS."—Same as *Arsenic*.

SALTPETRE.—Flour and water in large doses; linseed or sweet oil.

SALTS OF TIN.—Milk in large quantities.

SILVER, NITRATE OF.— Same as *Argenti Nit.*

SPANISH FLY.—Same as *Cantharides*.

SPIRITS OF SALTS.—Same as *Acids, Mineral.*

STRAMONIUM.—Same as *Belladonna*.

STRYCHNINE.—Same as *Nux Vomica*.

SUGAR OF LEAD.—Same as *Lead Salts*.

SULPHURIC ACID.—Same as *Acids, Mineral.*

SULPHATE OF ZINC.—Same as *Zinc Salts*.

TARTAR EMETIC.—Same as *Antimony*.

TARTARIZED ANTIMONY.—Same as *Antimony*.

TOBACCO.—Emetics; stimulants external and internal.

VERDIGRIS.—Same as *Copper*.

VERMILION.—Same as *Corrosive Sublimate*.

VOLATILE ALKALI.—Same as *Potash*.

WHITE PRECIPITATE.—Same as *Arsenic*.

WHITE VITRIOL.—Same as *Zinc Salts*.

ZINC SALTS.—Give milk with whites of eggs freely; afterward warm barley-water or linseed-tea.

Fortress Monroe is the largest single fortification in the world. It has already cost the Government over $3,000,000. The water battery is considered one of the finest military works in the world.

Leon P. Fredemeyer is credited with having trundled a wheelbarrow from San Francisco, Cal., to New York in 7 months and 16 days. He arrived in New York July 4, 1879.

CONTAGIOUS AND ERUPTIVE DISEASES.

It will often relieve a mother's anxiety to know how long after a child has been exposed to a contagious disease that there is danger the disease has been contracted. The following table gives the *period of incubation* — or anxious period — and other information concerning the more important diseases.

Disease.	Symptoms usually appear.	Anxious period ranges from	Patient is infectious.
Chicken-Pox	On 14th day	10–18 days.	Until all scabs have fallen off.
Diphtheria	" 2d day	2–5 days.	14 days after disappearance of membrane
Measles	" 14th day	10–14 days.	*Until scaling and cough have ceased.
Mumps	" 19th day	16–24 days.	14 days from commencement.
Rotheln	" 14th day	12–20 days.	10–14 days from commencement.
Scarlet Fever	" 4th day	1–7 days.	Until all scaling has ceased.
Small-Pox	" 12th day	1–14 days.	Until all scabs have fallen off.
Typhoid Fever	" 21st day	1–28 days.	Until diarrhea ceases.
Whooping-Cough	" 14th day	7–14 days.	†Six weeks from beginning to whoop.

* In measles the patient is infectious three days before the eruption appears.
† In whooping-cough the patient is infectious during the primary cough, which may be three weeks before the whooping begins.

The following points may help to determine the nature of a suspicious illness:

Rash or Eruption.	Appearance.	Disease.	Duration in days.	Remarks.
Small rose pimples changing to vesicles.	2d day of fever or after 24 hours' illness.	CHICKEN-POX.	6–7	Scabs form about 4th day of fever.
Diffuse redness and swelling.	2d or 3d day of illness.	ERYSIPELAS.		
Small red dots like flea-bites.	4th day of fever or after 72 hours' illness.	MEASLES.	6–10	Rash fades on 7th day.
Bright scarlet, diffused.	2d day of fever or after 24 hours' illness.	SCARLET FEVER.	8–19	Rash fades on 5th day.
Small red pimples changing to vesicles, then pustules.	3d day of fever or after 48 hours' illness.	SMALL-POX.	14–21	Scabs form 9th or 10th day, fall off about 14th.
Rose colored spots, scattered.	7th to 14th day.	TYPHOID FEVER.	22–30	Accompanied by diarrhea.

DIGESTION.

Average time required for the digestion of various articles of food:

	Hours.	Min.
Apples, sweet (boiled)	2	30
Barley (boiled)	2	
Beans, Lima (boiled)	2	30
Beef (roasted)	3	
Beef (fried)	4	
Beef, salt (boiled)	2	45
Bread	3	30
Butter	3	30
Cheese	3	30
Chicken (fricasseed)	2	40
Custard (baked)	2	45
Duck (roasted)	4	
Eggs (raw)	2	
Eggs (soft-boiled)	3	
Eggs (hard-boiled)	3	30
Eggs (fried)	3	30
Fish, various kinds (raw, boiled, fried)	2	44
Fowl (roast)	4	
Hashed meat and vegetables (warm)	2	30
Lamb (boiled)	2	30
Milk (raw)	2	15
Milk (boiled)	2	
Mutton (boiled)	3	
Mutton (roast)	3	15
Oysters (roast)	3	15
Oysters (stewed)	3	30
Pigs' feet, soused (boiled)	1	
Potatoes (baked)	2	30
Pork, salt (stewed)	3	
Pork (roast)	3	15
Rice (boiled)	1	
Sago (boiled)	1	45
Soup, barley	1	30
Soup, chicken, etc. (average)	3	15
Tripe, soused (boiled)	1	
Turkey (roast)	2	30
Veal (boiled)	4	
Veal (fried)	4	30

THE PULSE.

The natural rate of the pulse varies at different ages as follows:

	Beats per Minute.
At birth	130—140
One year	115—130
Two years	100—115
Three years	95—105
Four to seven years	85— 95
Seven to fourteen years	80— 90
Fourteen to twenty-one years	75— 85
Twenty-one to sixty years	70— 75
Old age	75— 85

Discovery of Silver, and History of the Miues of Peru.

The existence of silver at Cerro de Pasco was discovered by chance in the year 1630. An Indian, tending his sheep, was the individual destined to bring to light the source of such vast amounts of silver as were afterwards extracted from these deposits. One night, while this shepherd was resting with his flocks at Santa Rosa, he built a fire to protect himself from the severe cold. Next morning he saw with astonishment that the stones on which his fagots had burned were melted and showed thin lines of silver. He hastened to the town and communicated the fact of his discovery to a Spanish merchant of the place. He lost no time in taking possession of the mine, after the manner of a squatter, and naming it after Santa Rosa, of Lima, set to working it, deriving therefrom a very large fortune.

On the news of this discovery reaching Lima, a great tide of emigration set out for the new mines; among the progressive miners who caught the contagion was Don Martin Retuerto, who settled upon Yauricocha as his place of labor, and here he opened the first adit leading into the side of the great hill. This mine was actively worked up to the year 1740, over a century, and then the descendants of Retuerto sold it to the family of Don

Jose Maiz. There seemed to be a fatality in this. No sooner had the mine changed owners than it was flooded, and the new possessors were obliged to toil incessantly for twenty years before the ore was again reached. Immense amounts of silver were being taken from the district, but as greater depths were made the inundations occurred with more frequency, and stoppages ensued.

Meantime an intelligent and enterprising miner conceived the idea of draining the submerged shafts by employing steam power, and in 1815 entered upon a contract to bring the pumping machinery from England. This was done after overcoming the greatest difficulty in transporting the machines from the coast to the interior, and in July, 1816, the pumping engines were placed in position and commenced work in a satisfactory manner. In order to render the transportation of this machinery possible over the narrow paths of the Cordillera, where all burdens are carried by pack-mules and llamas, it all had to be constructed in pieces, no one of which should weigh over 150 pounds.

Up to this time the silver produced by the mines was obtained from the oxidized ore; but so soon as the pumping engines were employed and the shafts sunken to a much greater depth, ore of a highly superior character was found in which were virgin silver, rosicler, and sulphates of silver. Everything progressed favorably until 1828, when the pumping apparatus was paralyzed by the explosion of the boilers; the drained mines were again inundated, the machinery disappeared under the waters, and of a necessity work was stopped in the greater number of the mines.

The decadence of the Cerro de Pasco mines dates from 1828, when the original pumping apparatus was destroyed and the shafts inundated. The mines are still filled with water, and the incalculable wealth contained in their veins and pockets is awaiting the advent of energy and intelligence for its liberation. Up to 1828, from the time of the discovery of silver on a considerable scale at the Cerro de Pasco, it is estimated by careful computers that $400,000,000 of the precious metal were extracted from these deposits.

CENTER OF POPULATION IN THE UNITED STATES.

POSITION OF CENTER OF POPULATION.

Date.	N. Lat.			W. Long.			Approximate location by important towns.	Westward movement during preceding decade.
	°	′	″	°	′	″		Miles.
1790	39	16	30	76	11	12	23 miles east of Baltimore, Md.	....
1800	39	16	06	76	56	30	18 miles west of Baltimore, Md.	41
1810	39	11	30	77	37	12	40 miles N. W. by west of Washington, D. C.	36
1820	39	05	42	78	33	00	16 miles north of Woodstock, Va.	50
1830	38	57	54	79	16	54	19 miles W. S. W. of Moorefield, West Va.	39
1840	39	02	00	80	18	00	16 miles south of Clarksburg, West Va.	55
1850	38	59	00	81	19	00	23 miles S. E. of Parkersburg, West Va.	55
1860	39	00	24	82	48	48	20 miles south of Chillicothe, Ohio.	81
1870	39	12	00	83	35	42	48 miles E. by N. of Cincinnati, Ohio.	42
1880	39	04	08	84	39	40	8 miles W. by S. of Cincinnati, Ohio, and 1½ miles S. E. of Taylorville, Ky.	58
							Total............	457

The center of population in 1880 was in the State of Kentucky, one mile from the south bank of the Ohio River, one and a half miles from the village of Taylorsville, Ky., and eight miles west by south from the heart of the city of Cincinnati.

A noteworthy feature of the movement of the center of population westward since 1790 is the closeness with which it has clung to the parallel of 39° North Latitude.

Legal Holidays in the Various States.

JANUARY 1. NEW YEAR'S DAY: in Alabama, California, Colorado, Connecticut, Florida, Georgia, Illinois, Indiana, Iowa, Kansas, Louisiana, Maine, Michigan, Minnesota, Mississippi, Missouri, Nebraska, Nevada, New Jersey, New York, Ohio, Pennsylvania, South Carolina, Tennessee, Texas, Vermont, Virginia, West Virginia, and Wisconsin.

JANUARY 8. ANNIVERSARY OF THE BATTLE OF NEW ORLEANS: in Louisiana.

FEBRUARY 22. WASHINGTON'S BIRTHDAY: in California, Colorado, Connecticut, Florida, Georgia, Kentucky, Louisiana, Maine, Maryland, Massachusetts, Michigan, Minnesota, Missouri, Nebraska, Nevada, New Hampshire, New Jersey, New York, Ohio, Pennsylvania, Rhode Island, South Carolina, Texas, Virginia, West Virginia, and Wisconsin.

MARCH 2. ANNIVERSARY OF TEXAN INDEPENDENCE: in Texas.

MARCH 4. FIREMAN'S ANNIVERSARY: in New Orleans, La.

MARDI-GRAS: in Louisiana, and the cities of Mobile, Montgomery and Selma, Ala.

APRIL 21. ANNIVERSARY OF THE BATTLE OF SAN JACINTO: in Texas.

GOOD FRIDAY: in Louisiana, Maryland, Minnesota, and Pennsylvania.

APRIL 26. MEMORIAL DAY: in Georgia.

MAY 30. DECORATION DAY: in California, Colorado, Connecticut, Iowa, Massachussetts, New Hampshire, New Jersey, New York, Pennsylvania, Rhode Island, Vermont.

JULY 4. INDEPENDENCE DAY: in all the States.

GENERAL ELECTION DAY: in California, Florida, Maryland, Missouri, New Jersey, New York, South Carolina, Texas and Wisconsin.

THANKSGIVING DAY: in all the States.

DECEMBER 25. CHRISTMAS DAY: in all the States.

Sundays and Fast Days (whenever appointed) are legal holidays in all the States.

RAILROAD MILEAGE OF THE WORLD.

(Compiled from the latest Official Reports.)

COUNTRIES.	Year.	Miles of Line.
Algeria	1884	993
Argentine Republic	1884	3,151
Austria-Hungary	1884	12,820
Belgium	1883	2,700
Bolivia	1883	28
Brazil	1884	5,000
Bulgaria	1884	140
Canada	1884	9,065
Cape of Good Hope	1884	1,213
Chili	1883	1,378
China	1883	40
Colombia	1883	140
Costa Rica	1884	99
Cuba	1883	1,087
Denmark	1884	1,106
Dutch East Indies	1882	442
Ecuador	1884	76
Egypt	1884	1,276
France	1884	17,000
Germany	1884	22,617
Great Britain and Ireland	1884	18,681
Greece	1883	107
Guatemala	1883	26
Hawaii	1884	32
Honduras	1883	29
India, British	1884	10,832
Italy	1883	5,651
Japan	1884	236
Luxemburg	1883	226
Mexico	1885	3,620
Netherlands	1884	1,320
New South Wales	1884	1,320

RAILROAD MILEAGE OF THE WORLD.
(*Continued.*)

COUNTRIES.	Year.	Miles of Line.
New Zealand	1884	1,486
Nicaragua	1882	33
Norway	1885	971
Paraguay	1885	45
Peru	1883	2,030
Portugal	1884	950
Queensland	1884	1,038
Roumania	1884	850
Russia	1883	15,274
San Salvador	1883	33
Servia	1884	208
South Australia	1884	991
Spain	1885	6,904
Sweden	1884	4,000
Switzerland	1883	1,810
Tasmania	1884	167
Tunis	1883	200
Turkey	1882	1,076
United States	1885	125,152
Uruguay	1885	271
Victoria	1884	1,562
Western Australia	1884	55
Total mileage		287,557

The Date of the Flood.

The Vulgate and Hebrew gives the time and date .... 1,654 B. C.
The Samaritan Pentateuch .... 1,307 "
The Greeks .... 2,262 "

RAILROAD STATISTICS.

MILEAGE, CAPITAL, DEBT AND COST OF RAILROADS IN THE UNITED STATES.

STATES.	Miles of Line.	Miles of Line Worked	Capital Stock.	Funded Debt.	Total Investment.	Cost of Railroad and Equipment.
New England....	6,405	6,407	$ 104,597,904	$ 136,696,843	$ 356,898,480	$ 334,124,293
Middle States....	18,256	17,520	1,050,207,585	980,215,773	2,120,295,426	1,685,141,937
Southern States....	19,826	17,025	405,339,989	470,622,988	908,448,926	839,308,967
Western States....	72,704	66,122	1,795,111,437	1,836,286,254	3,732,799,948	3,520,173,233
Pacific States....	7,691	6,098	307,359,771	236,293,914	557,956,274	545,716,014
Total U. S., January, 1885..	125,152	113,173	$3,762,616,686	$3,669,115,772	$7,676,399,054	$6,924,554,444

The above table and the two following ones are compiled from Poor's Manual of the Railroads of the United States for 1885.

Facts From the Census.

Number of families in the United States....	9,945,916
Number of dwellings in the United States....	8,955,842
Number of acres to a family....	186.62
Number of persons to a square mile....	17.29
Number of persons to a dwelling....	5.60
Number of persons to a family....	5.04
Number of families to a square mile....	3.43
Number of dwellings to a square mile....	3.02

EARNINGS AND INTEREST AND DIVIDEND PAYMENTS OF RAILROADS IN THE UNITED STATES.

STATES.	GROSS EARNINGS.			Net Earnings.	Interest paid on Bonds.	Dividend paid on Stock.
	From Passengers.	From Freight.	From all Sources.			
New England...	$25,678,097	$ 29,450,680	$ 58,558,913	$ 16,513,814	$ 7,204,380	$ 9,117,661
Middle States...	54,581,157	151,123,136	222,307,819	77,150,187	50,536,215	37,216,495
Southern States...	21,213,506	43,678,825	69,857,988	23,831,483	18,971,461	3,241,356
Western States...	93,983,421	257,768,506	377,964,310	135,716,991	80,994,343	39,319,133
Pacific States...	11,334,520	20,848,763	34,617,578	13,801,436	9,579,740	4,309,190
Total U. S., January, 1885..	$206,790,701	$502,869,910	$763,306,608	$266,513,911	$167,286,139	$93,203,835

AMERICAN WARS.

Algerine War............................	1815
American Revolution...................	1775
Barbary War............................	1803
Dutch War.............................	1673
Queen Anne's War.....................	1744
King William's War....................	1689
Indian War.............................	1790
King Philip's War......................	1675
First Seminole War....................	1817
Second Seminole War..................	1835
Tecumseh War.........................	1804
War of 1812...........................	1812
The Southern Rebellion................	1861
Mexican War..........................	1846
French and Indian War................	1754

COMPARATIVE STATISTICS OF RAILROADS IN THE UNITED STATES, 1879–1885.

Year Ending.	Capital Stock.	Miles Line Worked.	Funded Debt.	Gross Earnings.	Net Earnings.	Interest Paid.	Dividends Paid.
1879.....	$2,395,657,293	79,009	$2,319,489,172	$525,620,577	$216,544,999	$112,237,515	$ 61,681,470
1880.....	2,708,673,375	82,146	2,530,874,943	613,733,610	255,557,555	107,866,328	77,115,371
1881.....	3,177,375,179	92,971	2,878,423,606	701,780,982	272,506,787	128,587,302	93,344,199
1882.....	3,511,935,824	104,971	3,235,543,323	770,209,899	280,316,696	154,295,380	102,031,534
1883.....	3,708,060,583	110,414	3,500,879,914	823,772,924	293,367,285	173,139,064	102,052,584
1884.....	3,762,616,686	115,672	3,669,115,772	770,684,908	268,106,258	176,694,302	93,203,85?

In the seventh century the imperial palace of China had 80,000 volumes in it. In the fifteenth century 2,000 royal commissioners condensed the vast mass of Chinese learning and literature into 23,000 volumes of manuscript, but it still remains unprinted. In 1726 another condensation was attempted, which was published in 5,000 volumes. A complete copy of this very comprehensive and valuable work has been secured for the British Museum, whose own amazing catalogue scarcely eclipses that of the imperial library published at the close of the eighteenth century, and enumerating upward of 173,000 volumes on all branches of literature, without including works of fiction, dramas, or any books relating to the Taoust or Buddhist religions. It is, however, necessary to add that the majority of these books are little more than mere, commentaries, by intellectual pigmies of modern days, on the writings of men possessed of a far wider range of thought and freer imagination than these their cramped descendants.

Telegraphs of the United States.

LINES.	Miles of Wire.	Miles of Poles.	No. of Offices.	No. of Employes.
Western Union............	462,285	147,500	14,184	23,254
Baltimore and Ohio......	54,900	7,848	1,290	1,995
United Lines.............	22,727	3,058	472	930
Postal Telegraph.........	7,641	2,112	183	1,158
Southern	5,242	1,627	51	172
U. S. Government.......	3,000	3,000	55	90
Deseret	1,092	963	56	57
Smaller Lines............	81,552	49,656	4,373	6,756
Total................	638,439	215,764	20,664	34,422

Telegraph Statistics of the World.

COUNTRIES.	Year.	Miles of Lines.	Miles of Wires.	No. of Messages.
Algeria....................	1882	3,645	8,678	....
Austria-Hungary	1883	32,684	95,188	9,974,993
Bavaria	1883	5,215	22,848	....
Belgium...................	1884	3,713	16,830	7,039,368
Bolivia	1881	182	364	....
Brazil.....................	1883	4,888	8,533	338,053
Bulgaria	1883	1,325	1,975	311,185
Canada	1883	23,330	....	....
Cape of Good Hope.......	1883	4,031	....	679,588
Chili	1884	6,840	13,680	....
China.....................	1885	3,089	5,482	....
Columbia..................	1883	2,357	4,714	....
Costa Rica	1883	450	726	....
Cuba......................	1882	2,835	5,987	....
Denmark..................	1882	2,283	6,316	1,216,307
Dutch East Indies.........	1882	3,682	....	412,837
Egypt	1885	3,222	5,283	....
France....................	1883	46,932	145,282	26,174,567
Germany..................	1883	47,637	170,960	18,377,626
Great Britain and Ireland..	1884	27,604	140,498	31,843,120
Greece....................	1883	3,720	3,890	....
Guatemala	1884	2,880	....	223,994
Hawaii....................	1884	175	350	....
Honduras..................	1884	1,800	....	107,730
India, British.............	1883	21,740	62,830	1,799,179

TELEGRAPH STATISTICS, ETC.—(Continued).

Countries.	Year.	Miles of Lines.	Miles of Wires.	No. of Messages.
Italy	1883	17,258	....	6,454,942
Japan	1883	4,733	12,470	2,784,287
Luxemburg	1883	196	372	....
Mexico	1884	19,000	58,800	....
Montenegro	1884	280	....	....
Netherlands	1884	2,660	15,714	3,228,442
New South Wales	1883	10,000	17,272	2,107,288
New Zealand	1884	4,074	10,037	1,299,400
Nicaragua	1882	800	....	....
Norway	1884	5,629	10,075	912,634
Orange Free State	1883	276	352	....
Paraguay	1883	45	90	....
Persia	1880	3,647	5,947	500,000
Peru	1878	550	1,183	....
Portugal	1883	2,920	7,084	1,122,548
Queensland	1883	6,614	10,617	917,605
Roumania	1883	3,000	6,240	1,244,435
Russia	1883	65,726	148,532	10,222,664
San Salvador	1883	750	1,000	....
Servia	1882	1,405	2,035	....
South Australia	1883	5,278	8,824	....
Spain	1883	10,733	26,160	3,019,831
Sweden	1884	5,347	12,945	1,209,088
Switzerland	1884	4,270	10,346	2,977,649
Tasmania	1884	1,273	1,543	235,697
Transvaal	1884	110	165	....
Tunis	1884	2,500	....	....
Turkey	1884	14,617	26,060	1,259,133
United States	1885	215,764	638,439	70,000,000
Uruguay	1883	1,405	....	....
Victoria	1884	3,600	7,271	1,474,971
Western Australia	1883	2,359	....	....
Total miles		673,168		

One dollar loaned for 100 years at the following rates of interest compounded will amount to the figures set opposite the per cent. at the end of that time:

3 per cent ....$	19.25
6 " "	340.00
8 " "	2,203.00
10 " "	13,809.00
12 " "	85,075.00
18 " "	15,145,007.00
24 " "	2,551,799,404.00

The moral is—*lend instead of borrow.*

THE WESTERN UNION TELEGRAPH COMPANY.

Statement Exhibiting, the Mileage of Lines Operated, Number of Offices, Number of Messages Sent, Receipts, Expenses and Profits for Each Year Since 1866.

YEARS.	Miles of Poles and Cables.	Miles of Wire.	Offices.	Messages.	Receipts.	Expenses.	Profits.
1866	37,380	75,686	2,250	5,879,282	$6,468,925	$3,944,006	$2,624,920
1867	46,270	85,291	2,565	6,404,595	7,004,560	4,362,849	2,641,711
1868	50,183	97,594	3,219	7,934,933	7,316,918	4,568,117	2,748,801
1869	52,099	104,584	3,607	9,157,646	7,138,738	4,910,772	2,227,966
1870	54,109	112,191	3,972	10,646,077	7,637,449	5,104,787	2,532,662
1871	56,032	121,151	4,606	12,444,499	8,457,096	5,666,863	2,790,233
1872	62,033	137,190	5,237	14,456,832	9,333,019	6,575,056	2,757,963
1873	65,757	154,472	5,740	16,329,256	9,262,654	6,755,734	2,506,920
1874	71,585	175,735	6,188	17,153,710	9,564,575	6,335,415	3,229,158
1875	72,833	179,496	6,365	18,729,567	10,034,984	6,635,474	3,399,510
1876	73,532	183,832	7,072	21,158,941	9,812,353	6,672,223	3,140,128
1877	76,955	194,323	7,500	23,918,894	9,861,355	6,309,813	3,551,543
1878	81,002	206,202	8,014	25,070,106	10,960,640	6,160,200	4,800,440
1879	82,987	211,566	8,534	29,215,509	12,782,895	6,948,957	5,833,938
1880	85,645	233,534	9,077	32,500,000	14,393,544	8,485,264	5,908,280
1881	110,340	327,171	10,837	38,842,247	17,114,166	9,996,096	7,118,070
1882	131,060	374,368	12,068	41,181,177	19,454,903	11,794,553	7,660,350
1883	144,294	432,726	12,917	42,076,226	19,632,940	13,022,504	6,610,436
1884	145,037	450,571	13,761	42,096,583	17,706,834	12,005,910	5,700,924
1885	147,500	462,283	14,184				

BANKING STATISTICS.

THE NATIONAL BANKS OF THE UNITED STATES.

Year Ending Sept. 1.	No. of Banks.	Capital.	Surplus.	Total Dividends.	Total Net Earnings.	Ratio of Dividends to Capital.	Ratio of Dividends to Capital and Surplus.	Ratio of Earnings to Capital and Surplus.
1870	1,061	$425,317,104	$91,630,620	$42,559,438	$55,810,819	10.12	8.35	10.96
1871	1,693	445,999,264	98,286,591	44,330,429	54,558,473	10.14	8.31	10.23
1872	1,852	465,676,023	105,181,942	46,687,115	58,075,430	10.19	8.33	10.36
1873	1,955	488,109,951	118,113,848	49,649,090	65,048,478	10.31	8.30	10.87
1874	1,971	489,938,284	128,364,039	48,459,305	59,580,931	9.90	7.87	9.68
1875	2,047	497,864,833	134,123,649	49,068,601	57,936,224	9.89	7.81	9.22
1876	2,081	500,432,271	132,251,078	47,375,410	43,638,152	9.42	7.45	6.87
1877	2,072	486,324,090	124,349,254	42,921,085	34,866,990	8.93	7.09	5.62
1878	2,047	470,231,896	118,687,134	36,941,613	30,605,589	7.80	6.21	5.14
1879	2,045	455,132,056	115,149,351	34,942,921	31,551,860	7.60	6.07	5.49
1880	2,072	454,215,062	120,145,659	36,411,473	45,186,034	8.02	6.35	7.88
1881	2,100	458,934,485	126,238,394	38,377,485	53,622,563	8.38	6.59	9.20
1882	2,197	473,947,715	133,579,931	40,791,928	53,321,234	8.73	6.81	8.88
1883	2,350	494,640,140	141,232,187	40,678,678	54,007,148	8.30	6.50	8.60
1884	2,582	518,605,725	147,721,475	41,254,473	52,362,783	8.00	6.20	8.00
1885	2,665	524,599,602	146,903,495	40,656,121	43,625,497	7.80	6.00	6.50

In the following table are given the amounts and kinds of the outstanding currency of the United States and of the national banks on January 1, of each year, from 1866 to 1885, and on November 1, 1885, to which is prefixed the amount on August 31, 1865, when the public debt reached its maximum.

Days.	United States Issues.				Notes of National Banks, including Gold Notes.	Aggregate.	Currency Price of $100 Gold.	Gold Price of $100 Currency.
	Legal-tender Notes.	Old Demand Notes.	Fractional Currency.					
Aug. 31, 1865.	$432,553,912	$402,965	$26,344,742		$176,213,955	$635,515,574	$144 25	$69 32
Jan. 1, 1866.	425,839,319	392,670	26,000,420		236,636,098	688,867,007	144 50	69 20
Jan. 1, 1867.	380,276,160	221,632	28,732,812		298,588,419	767,819,023	133 00	75 18
Jan. 1, 1868.	336,000,000	159,127	31,597,583		299,846,206	687,602,916	133 25	75 04
Jan. 1, 1869.	356,000,000	128,098	34,215,715		299,747,569	690,091,382	135 00	74 07
Jan. 1, 1870.	356,000,000	113,098	39,762,664		299,629,322	695,505,084	120 00	83 33
Jan. 1, 1871.	356,000,000	107,086	39,995,089		306,307,672	702,403,847	110 75	90 29
Jan. 1, 1872.	357,500,000	92,801	40,767,877		328,465,431	726,826,109	109 50	91 32
Jan. 1, 1873.	358,557,907	84,387	45,722,061		344,582,812	748,947,167	112 00	89 28
Jan. 1, 1874.	378,401,702	79,637	48,544,792		350,848,336	777,874,367	110 25	90 70
Jan. 1, 1875.	382,000,000	72,317	46,390,598		354,128,250	782,591,165	112 50	88 89
Jan. 1, 1876.	371,827,220	69,642	44,147,072		346,479,756	762,523,690	112 75	88 69
Jan. 1, 1877.	366,055,084	65,462	26,348,206		321,595,606	714,064,358	107 00	93 46
Jan. 1, 1878.	349,943,776	63,532	17,764,109		321,672,505	689,443,922	102 87	97 21
Jan. 1, 1879.	346,681,016	62,035	16,108,159		323,791,674	686,642,884	100 00	100 00
Jan. 1, 1880.	346,681,016	61,350	15,674,304		342,387,336	704,804,006	100 00	100 00
Jan. 1, 1881.	346,681,016	60,745	15,523,464		344,355,203	706,620,428	100 00	100 00
Jan. 1, 1882.	346,681,016	59,920	15,451,861		362,421,988	724,614,785	100 00	100 00
Jan. 1, 1883.	346,681,016	59,295	15,398,008		361,882,791	724,021,110	100 00	100 00
Jan. 1, 1884.	346,681,016	58,680	15,365,362		349,949,352	612,054,410	100 00	100 00
Jan. 1, 1885.	346,681,016	58,240	15,347,277		329,158,623	691,245,156	100 00	100 00
Nov. 1, 1885.	346,681,016	57,825	15,337,096		*315,847,168	677,923,105	100 00	100 00

* Includes $384,269 notes of gold banks and $568,081 mutilated currency in transit.

AGGREGATE BANKING CAPITAL AND DEPOSITS IN THE UNITED STATES, 1876-1882.

The following report by the Comptroller of the Currency shows the aggregate amount of capital and deposits of all the banking institutions of the United States for a series of years. The law repealing the tax on capital and deposits of State banks and private bankers went into effect November 30, 1882, and the Comptroller therefore has no data for continuing the table beyond that date.

Years.	National Banks.			State Banks, Private Bankers, etc.			Savings Banks with Capital.			Savings Banks without Capital.		Total.		
	No.	Capital.	Deposits.	No.	Capital.	Deposits.	No.	Capital.	Deposits.	No.	Deposits.	No.	Capital.	Deposits.
		Mills.	Mills.		Mills.	Mills.		Mills.	Mills.		Mills.		Mills.	Mills.
1876	2,091	500	713	3,803	214	480	26	5	37	691	844	6,611	710	2,075
1877	2,078	481	768	3,709	218	470	26	4	38	676	843	6,579	704	2,120
1878	2,006	470	677	3,799	202	413	23	3	26	668	803	6,450	675	1,920
1879	2,048	455	713	3,639	197	397	29	4	36	644	747	6,360	656	1,893
1880	2,076	455	900	3,798	190	501	29	4	34	629	783	6,532	650	2,219
1881	2,115	460	1,039	4,016	206	627	36	4	37	629	862	6,796	670	2,667
1882	2,239	477	1,131	4,403	231	747	38	3	41	622	929	7,302	712	2,850
1882*	2,308	484	1,119	4,473	228	779	42	4	43	625	960	7,448	717	2,902

* In the last table of the series the returns are given for the six months ending May 31, 1882, and also for the six months ending November 30, of the same year.

In 1885 there were 646 savings banks in the United States, having deposits of $1,095,172,147; surplus, $88,647,315; undivided profits, $13,106,319; other liabilities, $6,099,877.

Marriage and Divorce Laws of all the States and Territories.

Marriage, Licenses.—Required in all the States and Territories except Dakota, Montana, New Mexico, New Jersey, and New York. In Maryland legal marriage can be had only by an ordained minister.

Marriage, Prohibition of.—Marriage between whites and persons of negro descent are prohibited and punishable in California, Colorado, Delaware, Georgia, Florida, Kentucky, Maryland, Mississippi, Missouri, Nebraska, North Carolina, Oregon, South Carolina, Tenńessee, Texas, Virginia, and West Virginia.

Marriages between whites and Indians are prohibited in Arizona and North Carolina.

Marriages between whites and Chinese are prohibited in Arizona.

The marriage of first cousins is forbidden in Arkansas, Dakota, Indiana, Kansas, Montana, Nevada, New Mexico, Ohio, Washington Territory, and Wyoming, and in some of them is declared incestuous and void.

Marriage, Age to Contract.—In New Jersey and Ohio males under twenty-one years and females under eighteen years of age must obtain the consent of parents or guardians. In Massachusetts a marriage between a male over fourteen and a female over twelve is legal, even without the consent of parents.

Marriage, Presumption of.—In Missouri it has been held that where parties cohabit and represent themselves as husband and wife, a marriage is presumed, and when parties capable of contracting agree, in express terms, with each other, to be husband and wife, and cohabit as such, the marriage is valid, without any further ceremony being performed. In California marriage is declared a civil contract; consent, followed by a mutual assumption of marital rights and obligations, is sufficient.

Divorce, Previous Residence Required.—Dakota, ninety days; Arizona, Idaho, Nebraska, Nevada, and Wyoming, six months; Colorado, Illinois, Iowa, Kansas, Kentucky, Maine, Mississippi, Minnesota, Montana, New Hampshire, Ohio, Oregon, Pennsylvania, Rhode Island, Vermont (both parties, as husband and wife), West Virginia, and Wisconsin, one year; Florida, Indiana, Maryland, North Carolina, and Tennessee, two years; Connecticut, Massachusetts, and New Jersey (for desertion), three years.

Divorce, Causes for.—The violation of the marriage vow is cause for absolute divorce in all the States, excepting South Carolina, which has no divorce law.

Willful desertion, one year, in Arizona, Arkansas, Colorado, Dakota, Florida, Idaho, Kansas, Kentucky, Montana, Nevada, Rhode Island, Utah, Wisconsin and Wyoming.

Willful desertion, two years, in Alabama, Illinois, Indiana, Iowa, Michigan, Mississippi, Nebraska, Pennsylvania, Tennessee.

Willful desertion, three years, in Connecticut, Delaware, Georgia, Maine, Maryland, Massachusetts, Minnesota, New Hampshire, New Jersey, Ohio, Oregon, Vermont, and West Virginia.

Willful desertion, five years, in Virginia.

Habitual drunkenness, in all the States, *except* Louisiana, Maryland, New Jersey, New York, North Carolina, Pennsylvania, South Carolina, Texas, Vermont, Virginia, and West Virginia.

"Imprisonment for felony" or "conviction of felony," in all the States, *except* Florida, Louisiana, Maine, Maryland, Nevada, New Jersey, New York, North Carolina, Rhode Island, South Carolina, and Wisconsin.

"Cruel and abusive treatment," "intolerable cruelty," "extreme cruelty," or "inhuman treatment," in all the States, *except* Florida, Kentucky, Louisiana, Maryland, Michigan, New York, North Carolina, Pennsylvania, South Carolina, Tennessee, and West Virginia.

"Failure to provide, one year, in California, Nevada,

and Wyoming; two years in Indiana and Idaho; three years in Massachusetts; no time specified in Maine, Nebraska, Rhode Island, and Vermont. "Gross neglect of duty," in Kansas; willful neglect for three years, in Delaware.

Fraud and fraudulent contract, in Connecticut, Georgia, Idaho, Kansas, Ohio, and Pennsylvania.

Absence without being heard of, in New Hampshire; absence two years, in Tennessee; seven years, in Connecticut and Vermont; absence, without reasonable cause, one year, in Missouri: separation five years, in Kentucky; voluntary separation, five years, in Wisconsin.

Ungovernable temper, in Kentucky; "habitual indulgence in violent and ungovernable temper," in Florida; "such indignities as make life intolerable," in Missouri and Wyoming; "indignities as render life burdensome," in Oregon and Pennsylvania.

Other causes in different States are as follows: "Husband notoriously immoral before marriage, unknown to wife," in West Virginia; "fugitive from justice," in Virginia; "gross misbehavior or wickedness," in Rhode Island; "attempt on life," in Illinois; "refusal of wife to move into the State," in Tennessee; "mental incapacity at time of marriage," in Georgia; "three years with any religious society that believes the marriage relation unlawful," in Massachusetts; "joining any religious sect that believes marriage unlawful, and refusing to cohabit six months," in New Hampshire; "parties cannot live in peace and union," in Utah; "settled aversion, which tends to permanently destroy all peace and happiness," in Kentucky.

In Georgia an absolute divorce is granted only after the concurrent verdict of two juries, at different terms of the court. In New York absolute divorce is granted for but one cause, adultery. In South Carolina there is no divorce law.

All of the causes above enumerated are for absolute or full divorce.

Divorce, Remarriage.—There are no restrictions upon remarriage, by divorced persons, in Connecticut, Kentucky, Illinois, and Minnesota. Either party may remarry, but defendant must wait two years, and obtain permission from the court, in Massachusetts. The decree of the court may restrain the guilty party from remarrying in Virginia. Parties cannot remarry until after two years, except by permission of the court, in Maine. In the State of New York the plaintiff may remarry, but the defendant cannot do so during the plaintiff's lifetime, unless the decree be modified or proof that five years have elapsed, and that complainant has married again, and defendant's conduct has been uniformly good. Any violation of this is punished as bigamy, even though the other party has been married.

The courts of every State, and particularly of New York, are very jealous of their jurisdiction, and generally refuse to recognize as valid a divorce against one of the citizens of the State by the court of another State, unless both parties to the suit were subject at the time to the jurisdiction of the court granting the divorce.

. Kansas courts grant divorces for the reason that the applicant's husband or wife has obtained a divorce in another State, and the applicant has been forbidden to remarry. If a wife in New York obtains a divorce from her husband, and he is forbidden to remarry, he may go to Kanaas and obtain a divorce on that ground. If his wife contests the case, or can be served with the papers in Kansas, so that she is brought under the jurisdiction of the Kansas court, the courts of New York must recognize the divorce as valid, and cannot punish the husband for remarrying in New York.

New York permits polygamy and polyandry in certain cases. Desertion for five years, without knowledge that the deserter is living, permits the one deserted to marry again; and the second marriage is valid, though the deserter returns. The second marriage may be declared void, but only from the date of the decree, by a court of competent jurisdiction, upon proper petition; but if no such petition is made, and all parties are satisfied, one husband may live in lawful wedlock with two or more wives, or one wife with two or more husbands. The children will inherit, and both wives will be entitled to dower.

Marriages in the United States Between its Citizens and Those of the French Republic.

FROM A REPORT BY THOMAS WILSON, CONSUL AT NICE, FRANCE.

I desire to call the attention of the Department to this subject, in the hope that some mode may be found to prevent citizens of the United States marrying French citizens from being unwittingly entrapped (that is the right word) into making a marriage which is good enough in the United States, or where made, but is a mock marriage in France.

It seems to me this matter calls for the intervention of the Government, for a Government can have no higher duty to its citizens than to throw such protection around them as that they may not be thus entrapped, or if they will marry, that it will not be done in the belief that the marriage, because valid according to the laws of his or her own country, the United States, where it is performed, is therefore valid in France, the country of which the other party is a citizen. That these things occur, and are productive of great misery to American citizens who are in a condition least able to bear it, is, alas, too manifest in the number of American (and English) women who are in France, the cast-off and discharged wives of Frenchmen. I do but state a fact well known to everybody, except apparently to those girls (and their parents or guardians) who are about to marry Frenchmen, and the minister of the gospel authorized to marry them.

I regard it as useless to attempt to make any treaty or other arrangement with the French Government by which all marriages made in the United States, even though in strict accordance with its laws, shall here be recognized as legal.

The customs and law of France and its conservatism concerning the *etat civil* of its citizens, the necessity for publicity of the marriage, and the opportunity required to prevent it if illegal, together with the recognized authority of the parent over the family, are too strong to be overborne and set aside, in order to do justice to those foreigners who may have put their foot in it by marrying French citizens in another country.

Another reason exists why no such arrangement can ever be made with France. Frenchmen (as well as some others) are shocked at the rapidity and flippancy, not to mention the clandestinity, with which marriages are not infrequently contracted in the United States. They do not believe they are or ought to be valid.

A clandestine acquaintance or courtship, ending in a runaway match, inaugurated with a ladder and a lantern, a midnight flight, a hurried marriage *en dishabille*, and a furious father arriving a few minutes too late—to call this a valid marriage may do in the United States, but to ask the law of France to do so would be to ask impossibilities. It would be regarded as but a youthful escapade, not a serious matter, one to be overlooked and excused, and his family would justify and protect him, when, after having sown his wild oats, gotten tired of eating husks in a foreign land, he returns to his home to take his proper place among them.

The objects of the institution of marriage are so different in the two countries that their different customs cannot be reconciled.

In France the patriarchal theory prevails to a great extent, and the family more than the individual is the unit. Family councils are recognized by law, which have and exercise as complete jurisdiction over the movements and fate of individuals as ever did a court of chancery. Accordingly the prime object of marriage, after French ideas and customs, is the foundation of a family. The happiness of the contracting parties, or their love for each other, is a secondary consideration. The arrangements of a marriage are made and its suitability decreed by the heads of the two respective families.

In the United States the man and woman to be married are considered as the parties most interested, and so they make the arrangements. In France the parents consider themselves most interested, and so they make the arrangements. This is the custom of the country and every one yields to it. A Frenchwoman, with a husband and a child, separated from each other and both sick, would leave her husband and fly to her child. The husband and wife in their relation to each other are regarded, in public estimation, as only secondary and incidental to the primary and main object, the family.

In France men over twenty-five years of age and women over twenty-one may marry without the consent of their parents, but it can only be after making three *actes respecteuse;* that is, petitions in formal and respectful language, addressed to the parents, soliciting their consent, with an interval of one month between each.

The same trouble exists in France as respects marriages made in England; and the English Government has taken some steps to protect its subjects by first providing for a certificate of the French consul, as agreed on between the two Governments, and notified to the consuls by circular from the French Government, of December 23, 1884, that the formalities of the French law have been complied with by the French citizen; and, second, warning all registrars throughout the Kingdom not to celebrate any marriage to which a French citizen is a party without the production of this certificate.

The Steamer Great Eastern.

The construction commenced May 1, 1854, and the work of launching her, which lasted from November 3, 1857, to January 31, 1858, cost £60,000, hydraulic pressure being employed. Her extreme length is 680 feet, breadth 82½ feet, and including paddle-boxes, 118 feet; height, 58 feet, or 70 feet to top of bulwarks. She has eight engines, capable in actual work of 11,000 horse-power, and has besides 20 auxiliary engines. She was sold in 1864 for £25,000, and was employed on several occasions with success as a cable-laying vessel. The Great Eastern was sold at public auction October 28, 1885, for $126,000.

A List of 365 Principal Historical Events from 1492 to Date.

JANUARY.

1. New Year's Day.
2. Quakers free slaves, 1788.
3. Battle of Princeton, 1777.
4. National Fast, 1861.
5. Richmond burned, 1781.
6. Santa Anna president, 1853.
7. Millard Fillmore born, 1800.
8. Mississippi seceded, 1861.
9. New York founded, 1614.
10. Battle Middle Creek, Ky., 1862.
11. Arkansas Post surrendered, 1863.
12. Vicksburg fortified, 1861.
13. Gen. Taylor ordered to Mexico, 1846.
14. Peace declared, 1783.
15. Edward Everett died, 1865.
16. Napier appointed envoy to United States, 1857.
17. Benjamin Franklin born, 1706.
18. Georgia seceded, 1861.
19. Battle Mill Spring, Ky., 1862.
20. Independence United States recognized, 1783.
21. Fremont born, 1813.
22. Battle Frenchtown, 1813.
23. Battle Encarnacion, Mex., 1847.
24. President Johnson's imp. trial, 1868.
25. Louisiana seceded, 1861.
26. Michigan admitted, 1837.
27. Audubon died, 1851.
28. William H. Prescott died, 1859.
29. Kansas admitted, 1861.
30. N. P. Banks born, 1816.
31. Str. Metropolis lost, 1878.

FEBRUARY.

1. Texas seceded, 1861.
2. Peace with Mexico, 1848.
3. Horace Greeley born, 1811.
4. Confederate Congress met, 1861.
5. Hatcher's Run, Va., 1865.
6. Fort Henry captured, 1862.
7. U. S. Bank suspends, 1841.
8. Jeff Davis elected President, 1861.
9. Bishop Waugh died, 1858.
10. Treaty of Paris, 1763.
11. Charleston evacuated, 1865.
12. A. Lincoln born, 1809.
13. Fernando Wood died, 1881.
14. St. Valentine's Day.
15. Bishop Vightman died, 1882.
16. Fort Donelson surrendered, 1862.
17. Columbia, S. C., burned, 1865.
18. Jeff Davis inaugurated, 1861.
19. First National Thanksgiving, 1795
20. Battle Olistee, Fla., 1864.
21. Battle Valverde, N. M., 1861.
22. Washington born, 1732.
23. Nashville taken, 1862.
24. Peacock captured, 1813.
25. Battle Trenton, 1776.
26. Gen. Sickles acquitted, 1859.
27. Longfellow born, 1807.
28. Black Warrior seized, 1854.

MARCH.

1. Nebraska admitted, 1867.
2. Missouri admitted, 1821.
3. Florida admitted, 1845.
4. Vermont admitted, 1791.
5. Boston massacre, 1770.
6. Battle Pea Ridge, 1862.
7. Bible Society founded, 1804.
8. Wesley started for America, 1738.
9. Monitor destroys Merrimac, 1862.
10. McClellan crossed Potomac, 1862.
11. Benjamin West died, 1820.

12 Chicago flood, 1849.
13 Pocahontas died, 1617.
14 Jackson born, 1767.
15 Battle Guilford C. H., 1781.
16 Expunging Res. ad., 1837.
17 St. Patrick's Day.
18 Calhoun born, 1782.
19 Patent of Conn. issued, 1631.
20 Uncle Tom's Cabin pub., 1852.
21 Nevada admitted, 1864.
22 Stamp Act passed, 1765.
23 Battle Winchester, 1862.
24 Longfellow died, 1882.
25 Port Bill passed, 1774.
26 Gov. Winthrop died, 1640.
27 Vera Cruz taken, 1847.
28 Essex captured, 1814.
29 J. J. Astor died, 1848.
30 Crimean war ends, 1856.
31 Calhoun died, 1850.

APRIL.
1 Battle Five Forks, 1865.
2 Jefferson born, 1743.
3 Richmond captured, 1865.
4 President Harrison died, 1841.
5 Yorktown besieged, 1862.
6 Washington elected, 1789.
7 Channing born, 1780.
8 Louisiana admitted, 1812.
9 Lee's surrender, 1865.
10 Modoc massacre, 1873.
11 Mobile evacuated, 1865.
12 Henry Clay born, 1777.
13 Fall of Sumter, 1862.
14 Lincoln shot, 1865.
15 First call for troops, 1861.
16 Slavery abolished D. C., 1862.
17 Benjamin Franklin died, 1790.
18 Battle Cerro Gordo, 1847.
19 Battle Lexington, 1775.
20 Plymouth, N. C., captured, 1864.
21 Norfolk Navy Yard captured, 1861.

22 Buchanan born, 1791.
23 Stephen A. Douglas born, 1831.
24 First newspaper published in America, 1704
25 Bishop Ames died, 1879.
26 Johnston surrendered, 1865.
27 U. S. Grant born, 1822.
28 Maryland admiited, 1788.
29 Bishop Morris born, 1794.
30 Washington inaugurated, 1789.

MAY.

1 Seige of Fort Meigs, 1813.
2 Battle of Chancellorville, 1863.
3 Columbus discovered Jamaica, 1494
4 Yorktown evacuated, 1862.
5 Battle of Williamsburg, 1862.
6 Tennessee seceded, 1861.
7 Arkansas seceded, 1861.
8 Battle of Palo Alto, 1846.
9 Battle Resaca de la Palma, 1846.
10 Jeff Davis captured, 1865.
11 Minnesota admitted, 1858.
12 Crown Point captured, 1775.
13 Jamestown, Va., settled, 1607.
14 Battle Jackson, Miss., 1863.
15 Battle Resaca, Ga., 1864.
16 W. H. Seward born, 1801.
17 Great fire, St. Louis, 1849.
18 Matamoras captured, 1846.
19 Hawthorne died, 1864.
20 Lafayette died, 1834.
21 North Carolina seceded, 1861.
22 Assault on Vicksburg, 1863.
23 South Carolina admitted, 1778
24 Brooklyn bridge opened, 1883.
25 Philadelphia Convention met, **1748.**
26 Pequod massacre, 1637.
27 Fort Erie evacuated, 1813.
28 Noah Webster died, 1843.
29 Rhode Island admitted, 1790.
30 Congress met in Washington, 1808.
31 Battle Seven Pines. 1862.

JUNE.

1. Kentucky admitted, 1792.
2. Battle Cold Harbor, Va., 1864.
3. Battle Phillippi, Va., 1861.
4. Fort Pillow captured, 1862.
5. Battle Piedmont, Va., 1864.
6. Memphis taken, 1862.
7. United States Bank founded, 1791.
8. Jamestown, Va., abandoned, 1610.
9. Georgia chartered, 1732.
10. Battle Big Bethel, 1861.
11. Sherman arrives Kenesaw, 1864.
12. Bryant died, 1878.
13. Fugitive slave bill repealed, 1864.
14. Tax on tea ordered, 1767.
15. Arkansas admitted, 1836.
16. Battle Bunker Hill, 1775.
17. Charleston, Mass., burned, 1775.
18. War declared Great Britian, 1812.
19. Alabama sunk by Kearsage, 1864.
20. United States Flag adopted, 1777.
21. New Hampshire admitted, 1788.
22. Battle Craney Id., 1813.
23. Battle Springfield, N. J., 1780.
24. Labrador discovered, 1497.
25. Gen. Custer killed, 1876.
26. Seven days' fight, Virginia, 1862.
27. Vera Cruz surrendered, 1847.
28. Battle of Charleston, 1776.
29. Henry Clay died, 1852.
30. Guiteau hanged, 1882.

JULY.

1. Battle Gettysburg begun, 1863.
2. President Garfield shot, 1881.
3. Massacre of Wyoming, 1778.
4. Independence Day.
5. British captured Ticonderoga, 1777.
6. Battle Carthage, Mo., 1861.
7. Mrs. Surratt hanged, 1865.
8. Abercrombie defeated, 1758.
9. Braddock's defeat, 1755.

10 Columbus born, 1447.
11 J. Q. Adams born, 1767.
12 Hull invades Canada, 1812.
13 Draft riots, New York, 1863.
14 Second Chicago fire, 1874.
15 Stony Point captured, 1779.
16 Battle Point au Play, 1814.
17 Fort Mackinaw captured, 1812.
18 Assaults on Fort Wagner, 1863.
19 Great fire in New York, 1845.
20 Confederate Congress met, 1861.
21 First Battle Bull Run, 1861.
22 McPherson killed, 1864.
23 Battle Caloosahatchie, 1839.
24 Van Buren died, 1862.
25 Battle Lundy's Lane, 1814.
26 Louis Phillippe died, 1850.
27 John Morgan captured, 1863.
28 Fighting ends at Atlanta, 1864.
29 Confederate soldiers paroled, 1865.
30 Chambersburg burned, 1864.
31 Battle Montmorenci, 1759.

AUGUST.

1 Columbus discovered mainland, 1498.
2 Battle Sandusky, 1813.
3 Columbus left Spain, 1492.
4 Iowa adopted Constitution, 1846.
5 Mobile forts attacked, 1864.
6 Ram Tennessee captured, 1864.
7 Great fire New York, 1778.
8 Battle of Mackinaw, 1814.
9 Battle of Cedar Mt., Va., 1862.
10 Missouri admitted, 1821.
11 Davis Straits discovered, 1585.
12 New York rioters convicted, 1863.
13 Fort Erie bombarded, 1814.
14 Oswego taken, 1756.
15 Lafayette revisits United States, 1824.
16 Hull's surrender, 1812.
17 N. E. Courant established, 1721.
18 Battle Fishing Creek, 1780.

19 Guerriere captured, 1812.
20 Battle Contreras, 1847.
21 Lawrence, Kas., burned, 1863.
22 Yacht America wins, 1851.
23 New Mexico annexed, 1846.
24 Washington taken, 1814.
25 British army in Chesapeake, **1777**.
26 Stamp Act riot, 1768.
27 Battle Long Island, 1776.
28 First cable message, 1858.
29 Capture of Hatteras, 1861.
30 William Penn died, 1718.
31 Battle Jonesboro, Ga., 1864.

SEPTEMBER.

1 Lopez garroted, 1851.
2 Atlanta evacuated, 1864.
3 Treaty of Paris, 1783.
4 Gen. Morgan killed, 1864.
5 Continental Congress met, **1774**.
6 May Flower sailed, 1620.
7 Brazil declared independent, **1822**.
8 Montreal surrendered, 1760.
9 California admitted, 1850.
10 Hudson River discovered, **1609**.
11 Battle Brandywine, 1777.
12 Battle Chapultepec, 1847.
13 Battle Quebec, 1759.
14 Fulton's steamboat starts, 1807.
15 Fenimore Cooper born, 1789.
16 Battle Harlem Plains, 1776.
17 Battle Antietam, 1862.
18 Surrender of Quebec, 1759.
19 Battle Saratoga, 1777.
20 Capture of Lexington, Mo., **1861**.
21 Andre captured, 1780.
22 Battle Fisher's Hill, Va., 1864.
23 Serapis captured, 1779.
24 Montery surrendered, 1846.
25 Battle Montreal, 1775.
26 Philadelphia captured by British, **1777**.
27 Steamer Artic lost, 1854.

28 Fort Harrison, Va., captured, 1864.
29 Draft in New York, 1862.
30 Peace treaty with France, 1800.

OCTOBER.

1 British troops arrived Boston, 1768.
2 Andre executed, 1780.
3 Blackhawk died, 1838.
4 Battle Corinth, 1862.
5 Tecumseh killed, 1813.
6 Peace proclaimed, 1783.
7 E. A. Poe died, 1849.
8 Battle Perryville, Ky., 1862.
9 Great Chicago fire, 1871.
10 B. West born, 1738.
11 Prince of Wales arrived in New York, 1860.
12 R. E. Lee died, 1870.
13 Battle of Queenstown, 1812.
14 William Penn born, 1644.
15 Chippewa Plains, 1814.
16 First newspaper in New York, 1725.
17 Burgoyne surrendered, 1777.
18 Sloop Frolic captured, 1812.
19 Surrender of Cornwallis, 1781.
20 Steamer Florida captured, 1864.
21 Battle Ball's Bluff, 1861.
22 Battle Fort Mercer, 1777.
23 Battle St. Regis, 1812.
24 Daniel Webster died, 1852.
25 Macedonian captured, 1812.
26 Fight of Chatauqua, 1813.
27 Ram Albemarle destroyed, 1864.
28 Harvard College founded, 1636.
29 Battle White Plains, 1776.
30 Old John St. Church died, 1768.
31 Nevada admitted, 1864.

NOVEMBER.

1 Battle French Creek, 1813.
2 Erie Canal finished, 1825.
3 Bryant born, 1794.
4 Declaration of rights by Congress, 1774.
5 Grant's second election, 1872.

6 Lincoln elected, 1860.
7 Battle of Tippecanoe, 1811.
8 Mason and Slidell seized, 1861.
9 May Flower arrived Cape Cod, 1620.
10 Dutch seized rule New York, 1674.
11 Battle Shrysler's Field, 1813.
12 Conscription declared unconstitutional, 1863.
13 Montreal captured, 1775.
14 Sherman marched to sea, 1864.
15 Great fire in New York, 1835.
16 Fort Washington captured, 1776.
17 Jeff Davis threatens reprisal, 1862.
18 Battle Fish Dam, S. C., 1780.
19 Garfield born, 1831.
20 Battle Belle Isle, 1759.
21 North Carolina admitted, 1789.
22 Bishop Wiley died, 1884.
23 Bragg defeated, 1863.
24 Battle Lookout Mountain, 1863.
25 Evacuation New York, 1783.
26 Battle Mission Ridge, 1863.
27 Hoosac Tunnel opened, 1873.
28 Irving died, 1859.
29 Wendell Phillips born, 1811.
30 Revolutionary War ends, 1782.

DECEMBER.

1 Statute Washington unveiled, 1811.
2 John Brown executed, 1859.
3 Illinois admitted, 1818.
4 Alabama admitted, 1818.
5 Van Buren born, 1782.
6 Carver landed New England, 1620.
7 Delaware admitted, 1787.
8 Washington crossing Delaware, 1776.
9 Buffalo burned, 1813.
10 Mississippi admitted, 1817.
11 Pilgrims landed, 1620.
12 Pennsylvania admitted, 1787.
13 Battle Fredericksburg, Va., 1862.
14 Washington died, 1799.
15 Hartford convention, 1814.

16 Boston Tea Party, 1773.
17 General Bolivar died, 1830.
18 New Jersey admitted, 1787.
19 Massacre Narragansetts, 1675.
20 South Carolina seceded, 1860.
21 Savannah captured, 1864.
22 Embargo on American ships, 1807.
23 Washington resigned commission, 1783.
24 Fort Fisher stormed, 1864.
25 Christmas.
26 Major Anderson occupied Sumter, 1860.
27 Battle Chickasaw Bayou, 1862.
28 Iowa admitted, 1846.
29 Texas admitted, 1845.
30 New Mexico purchased, 1853.
31 Monitor founded, 1862.

WE PARTED IN SILENCE

BY MRS. CRAWFORD.

We parted in silence, we parted by night,
  On the banks of that lonely river;
Where the fragrant limes their boughs unite
  We met — and we parted forever!
The night-bird sung, and the stars above
  Told many a touching story
Of friends long passed to the kingdom of love,
  Where the soul wears its mantle of glory.

We parted in silence,— our cheeks were wet
  With the tears that were past controlling;
We vowed we would never, no, never forget,
  And those vows, at the time, were consoling;
But those lips that echoed the sounds of mine
  Are as cold as that lonely river;
And that eye, that beautiful spirit's shrine,
  Has shrouded its fires forever.

And now, on the midnight sky I look,
  And my heart grows full of weeping;
Each star is to me a sealed book,
  Some tale of that loved one keeping.
We parted in silence, we parted in tears,
  On the banks of that lonely river;
But the odor and bloom of those bygone years
  Shall hang o'er its waters forever.

MAUD MULLER.

BY JOHN G. WHITTIER.

Maud Muller, on a summer's day,
Raked the meadow, sweet with hay.

Beneath her torn hat glowed the wealth
Of simple beauty and rustic health.

Singing, she wrought, and her merry glee
The mock-bird echoed from his tree.

But, when she glanced to the far-off town,
White from its hill-slope looking down,

The sweet song died, and a vague unrest
And a nameless longing filled her breast —

A wish, that she hardly dared to own,
For something better than she had known.

The Judge rode slowly down the lane,
Smoothing his horse's chestnut mane.

He drew his bridle in the shade
Of the apple-trees to greet the maid.

She stooped where the cool spring bubbles up
And filled for him her small tin cup.

And blushed as she gave it, looking down
On her feet so bare, and her tattered gown.

"Thanks!" said the Judge, "a sweeter draught
From a fairer hand was never quaffed."

He spoke of the grass and flowers and trees,
Of the singing birds and the humming bees;

Then talked of the haying, and wondered whether
The cloud in the west would bring foul weather.

And Maud forgot her brier-torn gown,
And her graceful ankles bare and brown,

And listened, while a pleased surprise
Looked from her long-lashed, hazel eyes.

At last, like one who for delay
Seeks a vain excuse, he rode away.

Maud Muller looked and sighed: "Ah me!
That I the Judge's bride might be!

"He would dress me up in silks so fine,
And praise and toast me at his wine.

"My father would wear a broadcloth coat;
My brother should sail a painted boat.

"I'd dress my mother so grand and gay;
And the baby should have a new toy each day.

"And I'd feed the hungry and clothe the poor,
And all should bless me who left our door."

The Judge looked back as he climbed the hill,
And saw Maud Muller standing still:

"A form more fair, a face more sweet,
Ne'er hath it been my lot to meet.

"And her modest answer and graceful air
Show her wise and good as she is fair.

"Would she were mine, and I to-day,
Like her, a harvester of hay.

"No doubtful balance of rights and wrongs,
No weary lawyers with endless tongues,

"But low of cattle, and song of birds,
And health, and quiet, and loving words."

But he thought of his sister, proud and cold,
And his mother, vain of her rank and gold.

So, closing his heart, the Judge rode on,
And Maud was left in the field alone.

But the lawyers smiled that afternoon,
When he hummed in court an old love tune.

And the young girl mused beside the well,
Till the rain on the unraked clover fell.

He wedded a wife of richest dower,
Who lived for fashion, as he for power.

Yet oft, in his marble hearth's white glow,
He watched a picture come and go;

And sweet Maud Muller's hazel eyes
Looked out in their innocent surprise.

Oft, when the wine in his glass was red,
He longed for the wayside well instead.

And closed his eyes on his garnished rooms,
To dream of meadows and clover-blooms;

And the proud man sighed with a secret pain,
"Ah, that I were free again!

"Free as when I rode that day
Where the barefoot maiden raked the hay."

She wedded a man unlearned and poor,
And many children played round her door.

But care and sorrow, and child-birth pain,
Left their traces on heart and brain.

And oft, when the summer sun shone hot
On the new-mown hay in the meadow lot,
And she heard the little spring brook fall
Over the roadside, through the wall.

THE OLD OAKEN BUCKET.

BY SAMUEL WOODWORTH.

How dear to this heart are the scenes of my childhood,
  When fond recollection presents them to view!
The orchard, the meadow, the deep-tangled wildwood,
  And every loved spot which my infancy knew!
The wide-spreading pond, and the mill that stood by it;
  The bridge, and the rock where the cataract fell;
The cot of my father, the dairy-house nigh it,
  And e'en the rude bucket that hung in the well:
The old oaken bucket, the iron-bound bucket,
  The moss-covered bucket which hung in the well.

That moss-covered vessel I hailed as a treasure;
  For often at noon, when I returned from the field,
I found it the source of an exquisite pleasure,
  The purest and sweetest that nature can yield.
How ardent I seized it with hands that were glowing,
  And quick to the white-pebbled bottom it fell!
Then soon, with the emblem of truth overflowing,
  And dripping with coolness, it rose from the well;
The old oaken bucket, the iron-bound bucket,
  The moss-covered bucket, arose from the well.

How sweet from the green, mossy brim to receive it,
  As, poised on the curb, it inclined to my lips!
Not a full, blushing goblet could tempt me to leave it,
  The brightest that beauty or revelry sips.
And now far removed from the loved habitation,
  The tear of regret will intrusively swell,
As fancy reverts to my father's plantation.
  And sighs for the bucket that hangs in the well:
The old oaken bucket, the iron-bound bucket,
  The moss-covered bucket that hangs in the well.

HEREAFTER.

O land beyond the setting sun!
  O realm more fair than poet's dream!
How clear thy silvery streamlets run,
  How bright thy golden glories gleam!

Earth holds no counterpart of thine,
  The dark-browed Orient, jewel-crowned,
Pales, as she bows before thy shrine,
  Shrouded in mystery so profound.

The dazzling North, the stately West,
  Whose rivers flow from mount to sea;
The South, flower-wreathed in languid rest,
  What are they all compared with thee?

All lands, all realms beneath yon dome,
  Where God's own hand hath hung the stars,
To thee with humblest homage come,
  O world beyond the crystal bars!

Thou blest hereafter! Mortal tongue
  Hath striven in vain thy speech to learn,
And fancy wanders, lost among
  The flowery paths for which we yearn.

But well we know, that fair and bright,
  Far beyond human ken or dream,
Too glorious for our feeble sight,
  Thy skies of cloudless azure beam.

We know thy happy valleys lie
  In green repose, supremely blest;
We know against thy sapphire sky
  Thy mountain peaks sublimely rest.

And sometimes even now we catch
  Faint gleamings from the far-off shore,
And still with eager eyes we watch
  For one sweet sign or token more.

For oh, the deeply loved are there!
  The brave, the fair, the good, the wise,
Who pined for thy serener air,
  Nor shunned thy solemn mysteries.

There are the hopes that, one by one,
  Died even as we gave them birth;
The dreams that passed ere well begun,
  Too dear, too beautiful for earth.

The aspirations, strong of wing,
  Aiming at heights we could not reach;
The songs we tried in vain to sing;
  Thoughts too vast for human speech;

Thou hast them all, Hereafter! Thou
  Shalt keep them safely till that hour
When, with God's seal on heart and brow,
  We claim them in immortal power!

CHANGES.

Whom first we love, you know, we seldom wed.
  Time rules us all. And life, indeed, is not
The thing we planned it out, ere hope was dead;
  And then, we women cannot choose our lot.

Much must be borne which it is hard to bear;
  Much given away which it were sweet to keep.
God help us all! who need, indeed, His care;
  And yet, I know, the Shepherd loves His sheep.

My little boy begins to babble now,
  Upon my knee, his earliest infant prayer;
He has his father's eager eyes, I know;
  And, they say too, his mother's sunny hair.

But when he sleeps, and smiles upon my knee,
  And I can feel his light breath come and go,
I think of one (Heaven help and pity me!)
  Who loved me, and whom I loved, long ago.

Who might have been   * * . *   ah! what, I dare not think!
  We are all changed. God judges for us best.
God help us do our duty, and not shrink,
  And trust in Heaven humbly for the rest.

But blame us women not, if some appear
  Too cold at times; and some too gay and light.
Some griefs gnaw deep. Some woes are hard to bear.
  Who knows the past, and who can judge us right?

Ah! were we judged by what we might have been,
  And not by what we are — too apt to fall!
My little child — he sleeps and smiles between
  These thoughts and me. In Heaven we shall know all.

BINGEN ON THE RHINE.

BY CAROLINE E. NORTON.

A Soldier of the Legion lay dying in Algiers:
There was lack of woman's nursing, there was dearth of woman's tears;
But a comrade stood beside him, while his life-blood ebbed away,
And bent with pitying glances, to hear what he might say.
The dying soldier faltered, as he took that comrade's hand,
And he said, "I never more shall see my own, my native land:
Take a message and a token to some distant friends of mine;
For I was born at Bingen — at Bingen on the Rhine!

"Tell my brothers and companions, when they meet and crowd around,
To hear my mournful story, in the pleasant vineyard ground,
That we fought the battle bravely; and when the day was done,
Full many a corpse lay ghastly pale beneath the setting sun.
And midst the dead and dying were some grown old in war,
The death-wounds on their gallant breasts the last of many scars;
But some were young, and suddenly beheld life's morn decline;
And one had come from Bingen — fair Bingen on the Rhine!

"Tell my mother that her other sons shall comfort her old age,
For I was still a truant bird that thought his home a cage;
For my father was a soldier, and even as a child
My heart leaped forth to hear him tell of struggles fierce and wild;
And when he died, and left us to divide his scanty hoard,
I let them take whate'er they would — but kept my father's sword;
And with boyish love I hung it, where the bright light used to shine
On the cottage wall at Bingen — calm Bingen on the Rhine!

"Tell my sister not to weep for me, and sob with drooping head,
When the troops come marching home again, with glad and gallant tread;
But to look upon them proudly, with a calm and steadfast eye,
For her brother was a soldier, too, and not afraid to die;
And if a comrade seek her love, I ask her in my name
To listen to him kindly, without regret or shame;
And to hang the old sword in its place, my father's sword and mine,
For the honor of old Bingen — dear Bingen on the Rhine!

"There's another, not a sister; in the happy days gone by
You'd have known her by the merriment that sparkled in her eye;
Too innocent for coquetry, too fond for idle scorning;
O friend! I fear the lightest heart makes sometimes heaviest mourning.
Tell her the last night of my life (for ere this moon be risen,
My body will be out of pain, my soul be out of prison)
I dreamed I stood with her, and saw the yellow sunlight shine
On the vine-clad hills of Bingen — fair Bingen on the Rhine!

"I saw the blue Rhine sweep along; I heard, or seemed to hear,
The German songs we used to sing, in chorus sweet and clear;
And down the pleasant river, and up the slanting hill,
The echoing chorus sounded, through the evening calm and still;
And her glad blue eyes were on me, as we passed, with friendly talk,
Down many a path beloved of yore, and well-remembered walk;
And her little hand lay lightly, confidingly in mine:
But we'll meet no more at Bingen — loved Bingen on the Rhine!"

His voice grew faint and hoarse — his grasp was childish weak;
His eyes put on a dying look — he sighed, and ceased to speak;
His comrade bent to lift him, but the spark of life had fled:
The soldier of the Legion in a foreign land was dead!

And the soft moon rose up slowly, and calmly she looked down
On the red sand of the battle-field, with bloody corpses strown.
Yes, calmly on that dreadful scene her pale light seemed to shine,
As it shown on distant Bingen — fair Bingen on the Rhine!

Oh, Why Should the Spirit of Mortal be Proud?

BY WILLIAM KNOX.

Oh, why should the spirit of mortal be proud?
Like a swift-fleeting meteor, a fast-flying cloud,
A flash of the lightning, a break of the wave,
Man passes from life to his rest in the grave.

The leaves of the oak and the willow shall fade,
Be scattered around and together be laid;
And the young and the old, and the low and the high,
Shall molder to dust, and together shall lie.

The infant a mother attended and loved,
The mother that infant's affection who proved;
The husband that mother and infant who blessed,
Each, all, are away to their dwellings of rest.

The maid on whose cheek, on whose brow, in whose eye,
Shone beauty and pleasure — her triumphs are by;
And the memory of those who loved her and praised,
Are alike from the minds of the living erased.

The hand of the king that the sceptre hath borne,
The brow of the priest that the mitre hath worn,
The eye of the sage and the heart of the brave,
Are hidden and lost in the depth of the grave.

The peasant, whose lot was to sow and to reap;
The herdsman, who climbed with his goats up the steep;
The beggar, who wandered in search of his bread,
Have faded away like the grass that we tread.

The saint who enjoyed the communion of Heaven,
The sinner who dared to remain unforgiven,
The wise and the foolish, the guilty and just,
Have quietly mingled their bones in the dust.

So the multitude goes, like the flowers or the weed
That withers away to let others succeed;
So the multitude comes, even those we behold,
To repeat every tale that has often been told.

For we are the same our fathers have been;
We see the same sights our fathers have seen,—
We drink the same stream and view the same sun,
And run the same course our fathers have run.

The thoughts we are thinking our fathers would think,
From the death we are shrinking our fathers would shrink,
To the life we are clinging they also would cling;
But it speeds for us all, like a bird on the wing.

They loved, but the story we cannot unfold;
They scorned, but the heart of the haughty is cold;
They grieved, but no wail from their slumbers will come;
They joyed, but the tongue of their gladness is dumb.

They died, aye! they died; and we things that are now,
Who walk on the turf that lies over their brow,
Who make in their dwellings a transient abode,
Meet the things that they met on their pilgrimage road.

Yea! hope and despondency, pleasure and pain,
We mingle together in sunshine and rain;
And the smiles and the tears, the song and the dirge
Still follow each other, like surge upon surge.

'Tis the wink of an eye, 'tis the draught of a breath;
From the blossom of health to the paleness of death,
From the gilded saloon to the bier and the shroud,—
Oh, why should the spirit of mortal be proud?

"'OSTLER JOE."

As recited and made famous by Mrs. James Brown Potter, at Washington, D. C.

"'OSTLER JOE."

I stood at eve, as the sun went down, by a grave where a woman lies,
Who lured men's souls to the shores of sin with the light of her wanton eyes;
Who sang the song that the siren sang on the treacherous Lurley height,
Whose face was as fair as a summer day and whose heart was as black as night.

Yet a blossom I fain would pluck to-day from the garden above her dust —
Not the languorous lily of soulless sin, nor the blood-red rose of lust.
But a sweet white blossom of holy love that grew in the one green spot
In the arid desert of Phryne's life where all was parched and hot.

In the summer, when the meadows were aglow with blue and red,
Joe, the 'ostler of the Magpie, and fair Annie Smith were wed.
Plump was Annie, plump and pretty, with a cheek as white as snow;
He was anything but handsome, was the Magpie's 'Ostler Joe.

But he won the winsome lassie. They'd a cottage and a cow,
And her matronhood sat lightly on the village beauty's brow,
Sped the months and came a baby — such a blue-eyed baby boy!
Joe was working in the stables when they told him of his joy.

He was rubbing down the horses, and he gave them then and there
All a special feed of clover, just in honor of the heir.
It had been his great ambition, and he told the horses so,
That the Fates would send a baby who might bear the name of Joe.

Little Joe the child was christened, and, like babies, grew apace;
He'd his mother's eyes of azure, and his father's honest face.
Swift the happy years went over, years of blue and cloudless sky,
Love was lord of that small cottage, and the tempest passed them by.

Passed them by for years, then swiftly burst in fury o'er their home.
Down the lane by Annie's cottage chanced a gentleman to roam;
Thrice he came and saw her sitting by the window with her child,
And he nodded to the baby, and the baby laughed and smiled.

So at last it grew to know him — little Joe was nearly four;
He would call the "pretty gemplin" as he passed the open door;
And one day he ran and caught him, and in child's play pulled him in;
And the baby Joe had prayed for brought about the mother's sin.

'Twas the same old wretched story that for ages bards have sung,
'Twas a woman weak and wanton and a villain's tempting tongue;
'Twas a picture deftly painted for a silly creature's eyes
Of the Babylonian wonders and the joy that in them lies.

Annie listened and was tempted; she was tempted and she fell,
As the angels fell from heaven to the blackest depth of hell;
She was promised wealth and splendor, and a life of guilty sloth,
Yellow gold for child and husband, and the woman left them both.

Home one eve came Joe the 'Ostler with a cheery cry of "Wife!"—
Finding that which blurred forever all the story of his life.
She had left a silly letter — through the cruel scrawl he spelt;
Then he sought the lonely bedroom, joined his hands and knelt.

"Now, O Lord, O God, forgive her, for she ain't to blame," he cried;
"For I owt t' a seen her trouble, and 'a gone away and died.
Why, a wench like her — God bless her! — 'twasn't likely as he'd rest
With her bonny head forever on a 'ostler's ragged vest.

"It was kind o' her to bear me all this long and happy time;
So, for my sake please to bless her, though you count her deed a crime.
If so be I don't pray proper, Lord, forgive me; for you see,
I can talk all right to 'osses, but I'm nervous like with Thee."

Never a line came to the cottage from the woman who had flown.
Joe, the baby, died that winter, and the man was left alone.
Ne'er a bitter word he uttered, but in silence kissed the rod,
Saving what he told the horses, saving what he told his God.

Far away in mighty London rose the woman into fame,
For her beauty won men's homage, and she prospered in her shame;
Quick from lord to lord she flitted, higher still each prize she won,
And her rival paled beside her as the stars beside the sun.

Next she made the stage her market, and she dragged Art's temple down
To the level of a show-place for the outcasts of the town.
And the kisses she had given to poor 'Ostler Joe for nought
With their gold and costly jewels rich and titled lovers bought.

Went the years with flying footsteps while the star was at its height;
Then the darkness came on swiftly, and the gloaming turned to night.
Shattered strength and faded beauty tore the laurels from her brow;
Of the thousands who had worshiped never one came near her now.

Broken down in health and fortune, men forgot her very name,
'Till the news that she was dying woke the echoes of her fame;
And the papers in their gossip mentioned how an "actress" lay
Sick to death i humble lodgings, growing weaker every day.

One there was who read the story in a far-off country place,
And that night the dying woman woke and looked upon his face;
Once again the strong arms clasped her that had clasped her long ago,
And the weary head lay pillowed on the breast of 'Ostler Joe.

All the past had he forgotten, all the sorrow and the shame;
He had found her sick and lonely, and his wife he now could claim.
Since the grand folks who had known her one and all had slunk away,
He could clasp his long-lost darling, and no man could say him nay.

In his arms death found her laying, in his arms her spirit fled;
And his tears came down in torrents as he knelt beside her dead.
Never once his love had faltered through her base, unhallowed life;
And the stone above her ashes bears the honored name of wife.

That's the blossom I fain would pluck to-day from the garden above her dust;
Not the languorous lily of soulless sin or the blood-red rose of lust;
But a sweet, white blossom of holy love that grew in th' one green spot
In the arid desert of Phryne's life where all was parched and hot.

GEORGE R. SIMS.

The Eleven Great Wonders in America.

Croton Aqueduct, in New York City.

City Park, Philadelphia, Pennsylvania. The largest park in the world.

Lake Superior. The largest lake in the world.

Mammoth Cave, in Kentucky.

Niagara Falls. A sheet of water three-quarters of a mile wide, with a fall of 175 feet.

Natural Bridge, over Cedar Creek, in Virginia.

New State Capitol, at Albany, N. Y.

New York and Brooklyn Bridge.

The Central Park, in New York City.

Washington Monument, Washington, D. C., 555 feet high.

Yosemite Valley, California; 57 miles from Coulterville. A valley from 8 to 10 miles long, and about one mile wide. Has very steep slopes about 3,500 feet high; has a perpendicular precipice 3,089 feet high; a rock almost perpendicular, 3,270 feet high; and waterfalls from 700 to 1,000.

THE MURDERER.

[An Unpublished Poem by Edgar Allen Poe.]

Ye glittering stars! how fair ye shine to-night,
And O, thou beauteous moon! thy fairy light
Is peeping thro' those iron bars so near me.
How silent is the night — how clear and bright!
I nothing hear, nor aught there is to hear me
Shunned by all, as if the world did fear me;
Alone in chains! Ah, me! the cursed spell
That brought me here. Heaven could not cheer me
Within these walls — within this dark, cold cell,
This gloomy, dreary, solitary hell.

And thou, so slow, O Time! so passing slow;
Keeping my soul in bondage, in this woe
So torturing — this uncontrollable pain;
Was I to blame? I was, they say. Then so
Be it. Will this deep sanguinary stain
Of my dark crime forever haunt my brain?
Must I live here and never, never hear
The sweetness of a friendly voice again?
Must I this torture feel year after year?
Live, die in hell, and Paradise so near?

Am I dead to Thee, O Christ? Thou who sought
The prisoner in his lonely cell; taught
Him to feel the enchantment of Thy love —
Am I dead to Thee? Canst Thou not be brought
By prayer from Thy celestial throne above
Into this darkened cell? Dost Thou, too, reprove
My soul? Thou, too, doom it to endless misery?
Am I so hardened that I can not move
The divine, forgiving love in Thee?
Canst Thou be Christ and have no love for me?

What! lost am I? Ne'er will I feel the bliss
Of heaven? Ne'er feel the joys above this
World of sin? What! never? Is my destiny
Hell? Into that dark, fathomless abyss
Of sin and crime? 'Into that misery
Eternal? Into that unquenchable sea
Of fire? Is there my future — is it there?
Ah! it comes before my eyes. See! see! Ye
Infernal fiends! why come ye here. How dare
Ye come? Away! mock me not with your stare!

Away, ye fiends! Why at me now? Am I
Not hardened yet? Am I not fit for hell? Why
Test me again? O, horrors, hear the groans
Of tortured victims! Ah! see them lie
Bleeding and in chains! Hear the mocking moans
Of the madden'd demons, in deep, wild tones!

See them hurl their victims into the hot mire!
Now see the devils dance! What! Are they stones?
Have they no hearts, no love, no kind desire?
Fearfully reveling 'midst Jehovah's fire!

Cries, cries! horrible cries assail my ears!
I see her! My murdered victim now appears
Before me! Hear her pleading for mercy;
Ah! see her stare, with eyes swollen with tears;
Horrors! see her white arms outstretched to me,
Begging for life! O woe! O misery!
Take me, demons! take me out of this cell;
Satan, I'm thine! Hear, hear, I call on thee;
Torture me — rack me with the pains of hell;
Do what thou wilt, but break this madd'ning spell.

Listen! What's that? My soul, they come, they come!
The demons come to take thee to thy home!
See, see! No, no! O, heavens! What brought this
Pale skeleton here? Speak! speak! What! dumb?
And hast thou naught to say? What is thy office?
Away, fiend! What! move not for me! What is
Thy want? Speak, devil, speak! Come, come, unsheath
Thy tongue. Com'st thou from the dark abyss
Of sin? Hold, hold! I know thee — my breath!
Ha! ha! I know thee now — 'tis Death! 'tis Death!

Twenty Years Ago.

I've wandered to the village, Tom; I've sat beneath the tree,
Upon the school-house play-ground, that sheltered you and me;
But none were left to greet me, Tom, and few were left to know,
Who played with us upon the green, some twenty years ago.

The grass is just as green, Tom; barefooted boys at play
Were sporting, just as we did then, with spirits just as gay.
But the "master" sleeps upon the hill, which, coated o'er with snow,
Afforded us a sliding-place, some twenty years ago.

The old school-house is altered now; the benches are replaced
By new ones, very like the same our penknives once defaced;
But the same old bricks are in the wall, the bell swings to and fro
Its music's just the same, dear Tom, 'twas twenty years ago.

The boys were playing some old game, beneath that same old tree;
I have forgot the name just now—you've played the same with me,
On that same spot; 'twas played with knives, by throwing so and so;
The loser had a task to do—there, twenty years ago.

The river's running just as still; the willows on its side
Are larger than they were, Tom; the stream appears less wide;

But the grape-vine swing is ruined now, where once we played the beau,
And swung our sweethearts—pretty girls—just twenty years ago.

The spring that bubbled 'neath the hill, close by the spreading beach,
Is very low—'twas then so high that we could scarcely reach;
And kneeling down to get a drink, dear Tom, I started so,
To see how sadly I am changed, since twenty years ago.

Near by that spring, upon an elm, you know I cut your name,
Your sweetheart's just beneath it, Tom, and you did mine the same.
Some heartless wretch has peeled the bark, 'twas dying sure but slow,
Just as SHE died, whose name you cut some twenty years ago.

My lids have long been dry, Tom, but tears came to my eyes;
I thought of her I loved so well, those early broken ties;
I visited the old church-yard, and took some flowers to strow
Upon the graves of those we loved, some twenty years ago.

Some are in the church-yard laid, some sleep beneath the sea;
But few are left of our own old class, excepting you and me;
And when our time shall come, Tom, and we are called to go,
I hope they'll lay us where we played, just twenty years ago.

The Law of Finding.

The law of finding is that the finder has a clear title against everyone but the owner. The proprietor of a hotel or a shop has no right to demand the property or premises. Such proprietor may make regulations in regard to lost property which will bind their employes, but they cannot bind the public. The law of finding was declared by the King's bench over 100 years ago, in a case in which the facts were these:

A person found a wallet containing a sum of money on a shop floor. He handed the wallet and contents to the shopkeeper to be returned to the owner. After three years, during which the owner did not call for his property, the finder demanded the wallet and the money from the shopkeeper. The latter refused to deliver them up on the ground that they were found on the premises. The former then sued the shopkeeper, and it was held as above set forth, that against all the world but the owner the title of the finder is perfect. And the finder has been held to stand in the place of the owner, so that he was permitted to prevail in an action against a person who found an article which the plaintiff had originally found, but subsequently lost. The police have no special rights in regard to articles lost, unless those rights are conferred by statute. Receivers of articles found are trustees for the owner or finder. They have no power in the absence of special statute to keep an article against the finder, any more than the finder has to retain an article against the owner.

Steamer "Savannah," the First that Crossed the Atlantic.

The Times (of London, England), in the issue of May 18, 1819, thus announced the expected event:

"GREAT EXPERIMENT.—A new steam-vessel of 300 tons has been built at New York for the express purpose of carrying passengers across the Atlantic. She is to come to Liverpool direct."

This steamer, named the Savannah, the first that crossed the Atlantic, was built at New York by Francis Ficket. Her engines were made by Stephen Vail, of Morristown. She was launched on the 22d of August, 1818. She could carry only seventy-five tons of coal and twenty-five cords of wood. Commanded by Captain Moses Rogers, of New London, Conn., the Savannah sailed from Savannah, Ga., on the 25th of May, 1819, bound for St. Petersburg via Liverpool. She reached the latter port on the 20th of June, having used steam eighteen days out of the twenty-six

STEAMER ETRURIA.

This steamer made the fastest time of any ocean steamer. She left Queenstown, Sunday, August 16, 1885, arrived at New York, Saturday, August 22, at 3:35 p. m., making the passage in 6 days, 5 hours and 44 minutes. Her first day's running, counting from 2:26 p. m. on Sunday until the following noon, was 424 knots, followed by 464, 450, 465, 464, 464 and 70, from noon to 3:35 p. m. on Saturday. The distance which she traveled shows that the Etruria maintained the unexampled speed of 21½ miles per hour continuous steaming for the entire voyage. The best single day's run was made by the Etruria on her second westward voyage, on which occasion she steamed 481 nautical miles, which is equal to 557 statute miles, and required a speed of more than 23 miles per hour to accomplish.

She is 520 feet long, 57 feet beam, and 41 feet deep to upper deck (to promenade deck, 49 feet), 8,000 tons, and 14,500 horse-power, built of steel throughout, and is not classed in any of the books, as her construction far exceeds the requirements of the book surveyors. She is divided into ten water-tight compartments, most of the bulkheads being carried to the upper deck, and has three steel masts, is bark-rigged, and can spread a large area of canvas when required.

The Etruria leaves port with 3,000 tons of coal, and will burn, on an average, 320 tons every 24 hours.

Fast Passages of Ocean Steamships.

Queenstown to New York — 6d. 5h., 44 meantime, Etruria, Cunard line; sailed 2:26 p. m., August 16, arrived 3:25 p. m., August 22, 1885. Distance covered, 2,801 knots, or about 3,250 statute miles. Computed from Roche's Point to bar off Sandy Hook, adding 4h. 35m. for difference in time. *Fastest passage.*

—6d. 15h. 41m., America, National line; sailed 1:50 p. m., May 29, arrived 10:15 p. m., June 4, 1884. Computed from Fastnet to Sandy Hook, adding 4h. 22m.

—6d. 21h. 38m., Alaska, Guion line; sailed 12:10 p. m., September 16, arrived 5:26 a. m., 23, 1883. Computed from Fastnet to Sandy Hook, adding 4h. 22m.

—7d. 10h. 53m., Britannic, White Star line; sailed 4:35 p. m., August 10, arrived 11:06 p. m., 17, 1877. Computed from Fastnet to Sandy Hook, adding 4h, 22m.

—7d. 14h. 12m., City of Berlin, Inman line; sailed 7 p. m., October 5, arrived 4:50 a. m., 13, 1877. Computed from Roche's Point to Sandy Hook, adding 4h. 22m.

New York to Queenstown—6d. 6h. 41m., actual time, Oregon, Cunard line; sailed 7:44 a. m., December 17, arrived 7 p. m., 23, 1884. Computed from bar off Sandy Hook to Roche's Point, deducting 4h. 35m. for difference.

—6d. 14h. 18m., America, National line; sailed 9:11 a. m., June 11, arrived 4:25 a. m., June 18, 1884. Computed from Sandy Hook to Fastnet, deducting 4h. 22m.

—6d. 18h. 37m., Alaska, Guion line; sailed 6:21 p. m., September 12, arrived 5:20 p. m., 19, 1882. Computed from Sandy Hook to Fastnet, deducting 4h. 22m.

—7d. 12h. 17m., Britannic, White Star line; sailed 12:22 p. m., October 11, arrived 5:01 a. m., October 19, 1884. Time computed from Sandy Hook to Fastnet, deducting 4h. 22m.

—7d. 15 h. 48m., City of Berlin, Inman line; sailed 9 a. m., October 2, arrived 5:10 a. m., 10, 1875. Computed from Sandy Hook to Roche's Point, deducting 4h. 22m.

—New York to Southampton, Eng.— 7d. 16h. 28m.,

actual time, Eider, North German Lloyd line; sailed 8:32 a. m., June 25, arrived 6 a. m., July 3, 1884. Computed from Sandy Hook to the Needles, deducting 5h. for difference. *Fastest passage.*

Southampton to New York — 7d. 18h. 10m., Eider, N. G. L. line; sailed 7 p. m., April 7, arrived 8:10 a. m., 25, 1884. Computed from the Needles to Sandy Hook, adding 5h.

New York to Havana, Cuba — 3d. 9h. 33m., Newport, N. Y. & C. M. line; sailed 4:55 p. m., May 20, arrived 1:45 a. m. 24, 1882. Computed from Sandy Hook to Harbor, adding 33m. for difference in time.

Havana to New York — 2d. 23h. 45m., City of Puebla, N. Y. H. & M. line; sailed 6:58 p. m., June 30 arrived 7:16 p. m., July 3, 1883. Computed from' Morro Castle to Sandy Hook, deducting 33m. for difference in time. *Fastest passage.*

——3d. 56m., Newport, N. Y. & C. M. line; sailed 5:55 p. m., July 23, arrived 7:24 p. m., July 26, 1884. Computed from Harbor to Sandy Hook, deducting 33m.

Galveston, Texas, to New York — 5d. 12h. 10m., Alamo; sailed 9 a. m., June 25, arrived 3 a. m., July 1, 1884, exclusive of over 6h. detention at Key West, Fla. Computed from Galveston bar to Sandy Hook bar, allowing 65m. for difference in time.

——New York to Galveston, Texas — 5d. 20h. 15m., Alamo; sailed 4:30 p. m., August 9, arrived 10 p, m., 15, 1884, exclusive of 8h. detention at Key West. An unauthenticated despatch says the Alamo made the run in 5d. 18h. 30m., arriving December 25, 1885.

Aspinwall to New York — 6d. 5h. 30m., Henry Chauncey; sailed 5:55 a. m., November 13, arrived 11:25 p. m., November 19, 1865. Computed from pier to pier.

New York to Nassua, N. P. — 3d. 1h. 45m., Cienfuegos; sailed 4:45 p. m., February 14, arrived at anchorage 6:30 p. m., February 17, 1883. No time allowance; 75th meridian standard.

Sydney, Aus., to San Francisco, Cal.—22d. 19h., Zealandia; arrived February 22, 1885.
Yokohama, Japan, to San Francisco, Cal.—13d. 21h. 43m., Steamer Arabic; arrived October 21, 1882.

STEAMSHIP PASSENGER ARRIVALS FROM EUROPE.

The following table shows the number of steerage passengers landed at Castle Garden during the year 1885; also cabin passengers landed at the Port of New York and the number carried by each line:

Steamship Line.	Where from.	Steerage	Cabin.
North German Lloyd	Bremen	68,395	8,858
Hamburg-American	Hamburg	38,943	3,109
White Star	Liverpool	24,123	5,633
Inman	Liverpool	21,185	5,300
Red Star	Antwerp	21,112	2,714
Cunard	Liverpool	16,556	12,026
General Transatlantic	Havre	11,551	3,559
Carr Line	Hamburg	11,137	....
Anchor Line	Glasgow	11,032	3,088
Liverpool & Gt. West.	Liverpool	10,258	3,216
State Line	Glasgow	8,046	2,020
National	Liverpool	6,702	323
Thingvalia	Copenhagen	5,860	645
Anchor Line	Liverpool	4,035	2,378
Netherlands	Rotterdam	3,822	575
Fabre Line	Mediterranean	3,680	44
Stettin Lloyd	Stettin	3,212	67
Anchor Line	Mediterranean	3,146	11
I. & V. Florio	Mediterranean	2,790	166
Netherlands	Amsterdam	2,723	279
Bordeaux Line	Bordeaux	1,157	177
National	London	473	8
Monarch Line	London	393	825
Great Western	Bristol	187	35
Miscellaneous	....	652	84
Total		281,170	55,160

Armies and Navies of the Principal Nations.

Austria-Hungary.—Regular army, 1876, 296,158; war-footing, 1,043,351. Navy, 68 vessels, of which 12 were iron-clads; officers and men, 6,274.

Belgium.—The army, is composed of 3,214 officers, 40,590 soldiers on pay, and 62,534 without pay; total on war-footing, 103,124.

Brazil.—Regular army, 17,751; war-footing, 32,000. Navy, 11 iron-clads, 45 other vessels, and 9 for port service; men, over 6,000.

Chili.—Regular army, 3,316; war-footing, over 28,000. Navy, 10 vessels, including two iron-clads.

China.—Regular army, about 700,000; war-footing, 1,260,000. Navy, 38 vessels.

Denmark.—Regular army, 35,657; reserves, 13,279. Navy, 27 steamers, of which 7 were armor-clad.

Egypt.—Regular army, about 63,000; war-footing, 128,090. Navy, 14 vessels.

France.—By a law which went into force June 1, 1873, every Frenchman capable of bearing arms is made liable to twenty years' military service, viz.: four in the standing army, five in the reserve of the standing army, five in the territorial army, and six in the reserve of the territorial army. This gives France a force of about 500,000 in time of peace, and 1,750,000 on a war-footing. Navy, 1878, 222 vessels, of which 19 were first-rate iron-clads; sailors and marines, about 65,000.

Germany.—Regular army, 418,842; war-footing, 1,315,634. Navy, 70 vessels, including 17 iron-clads; men, about 8,000.

Great Britain.—In the British army the term of service is twelve years, after which a soldier can serve for nine years more. The strength of the regular army is 272,602, distributed as follows: 178,641 in Great Britain, 31,311 in the colonies, and 62,650 in India. Territorial army, including yeomanry, militia and volunteers, 304,202. Imperial army of natives in India, 127,170. Navy, 64 iron-clads, about 360 steamers and 125 sailing vessels. Of this number 261 are manned by 46,590 seamen and 14,000 marines. Navy, reserved, 21,420.

Italy.—Standing army, 659,615 (but the strength of the regular army is given as about 20,000 only); provisional militia, 260,325; officers of reserve, 2,167; territorial militia, 290,518 — total, 1,212,620. Other figures place the army on a war-footing at less than 900,000. Navy, 66 vessels, of which 18 a reiron-clads; men, about 12,000.

Japan.—Regular army, 31,680; war-footing, 46,350. Navy, 16 steam vessels, including three iron-clads; men, about 4,000.

Mexico.—Regular army, about 22,000.

Netherlands.—Regular army in Europe, 62,900; war-footing, 160,000. East Indian army, 39,413. Navy, 99 steamers and 16 sailing vessels.

Norway.—Regular army, about 13,000. Navy, 119 vessels, manned by about 4,300 men.

Persia. Army, peace-footing, usually about 25,000; war-footing, about 100,000.

Peru.—Regular army, about 13,000. Navy, 18 vessels.

Portugal.—Regular army, 35,496; war-footing, about 75,000. Navy, 22 steamers and 12 sailing vessels.

Roumania.—Regular army, 17,169; war-footing, 42,449. Territorial army, 54,473.

Russia.—The nominal strength of the army is 768,467; war-footing, 1,213,259. Other figures estimate the war-footing at nearly 1,700,000. Navy, 221 vessels, of which 27 are armor-clad; men, about 30,000.

Spain.—According to a new plan of the Minister of War, the army is to consist of 100,000 men, but in 1878 it was about 300,000. Navy, 123 vessels, including six iron-clads.

Sweden.—Regular army, 36,495; war-footing, 156,970. Navy, 42 steamers and 97 other vessels.

Switzerland.—In the Federal army consisted of 119,982 in the Bundesanug, and 91,728 in the landwehr.

Turkey.—Army on peace-footing, about 150,000; war-footing, estimated, 611,100. Navy, 20 iron-clads and 70 steamers, manned by 30,000 sailors and 4,000 marines.

United States.—Regular army, according to the official returns for 1879, 2,127 officers, 24,262 men, and 385 officers retired. Recent estimates place the war-forces of the United States, viz.: the militia and the regular army, at over 3,750,000. Navy, 142 ships, of which only 93 are effective; officers. 2,380; men, 7,850.

Men Called by President Lincoln During the Late War.

The total number called for, under all calls made by the President, from April 15, 1861, to April 14, 1865, was 2,759,049.

Their terms of service under the calls were from three months to three years.

United States Soldiers in the Late Civil War.

	Aggregate.
New York	455,568
Pennsylvania	366,326
Ohio	317,133
Illinois	258,217
Indiana	195,147
Massachusetts	151,785
Missouri	107,773
Wisconsin	96,118
Michigan	90,119
New Jersey	79,511
Kentucky	78,540
Iowa	75,860
Maine	71,745
Connecticut	52,270
Maryland	49,730
Vermont	35,256
New Hampshire	34,605
West Virginia	30,003
Minnesota	25,034
Rhode Island	23,711
Kansas	20,097
District of Columbia	16,872
Delaware	13,651
Total	2,653,062

Colored Troops in U. S. Army During the War.

Louisiana	24,052
Kentucky	23,703
Tennessee	20,133
Mississippi	17,869
Maryland	8,718
Pennsylvania	8,612
Missouri	8,344
Virginia	5,723
Arkansas	5,526
South Carolina	5,462
Ohio	5,092
North Carolina	5,035
Alabama	4,969
New York	4,125
Massachusetts	3,966
Georgia	3,486
District of Columbia	3,269
Kansas	2,080
Rhode Island	1,837
Illinois	1,811
Connecticut	1,764
Indiana	1,597
Michigan	1,387
New Jersey	1,185
Florida	1,044
Delaware	954
At large	733
Iowa	440
West Virginia	196
Wisconsin	155
New Hampshire	125
Vermont	120
Maine	104
Minnesota	104
Colorado Territory	95
Texas	47
Officers	7,122
Not accounted for	5,083
Total	**186,017**

The Nation's Dead.

A recent report shows that the nation's dead are buried in seventy-nine national cemeteries, of which twelve are in the Northern States. Among the principal ones in the North are Cyprus Hill, Brooklyn, N. Y., with its 3,786 dead; Finn's Point, N. J., which contains the remains of 2,644 unknown dead; Gettysburg, Pa., with its 1,967 known and 1,608 unknown dead; Mound City, Ill., with 2,505 known and 2,721 unknown graves; Philadelphia, with 1,909 dead, and Woodlawn, Elmira, N. Y., with its 3,090 dead. In the South, near the scenes of terrible conflicts, are located the largest depositories of the nation's heroic dead:

Arlington, Va., 16,264, of whom 4,349 are unknown.
Beaufort, S. C., 9,241, of whom 4,493 are unknown.
Chalmette, La., 12,511, of whom 5,674 are unknown.
Chattanooga, Tenn., 12,962, of whom 4,963 are unknown.
Fredericksburg, Va., 15,257, of whom 12,770 are unknown.
Jefferson Barracks, Mo., 11,490, of whom 2,906 are unknown.
Little Rock, Ark., 5,602, of whom 2,337 are unknown.
City Point, Va., 5,122, of whom 1,374 are unknown.
Marietta, Ga., 10,151, of whom 2,963 are unknown.
Memphis, Tenn., 13,997, of whom 8,817 are unknown.
Nashville, Tenn., 16,526, of whom 4,701 are unknown.
Poplar Grove, Va, 6,199, of whom 4,001 are unknown.
Richmond, Va., 6,542, of whom 5,700 are unknown.
Salisbury, N. C., 12,126, of whom 12,032 are unknown.
Stone River, Tenn., 5,602, of whom 288 are unknown.
Vicksburg, Miss., 16,600, of whom 12,704 are unknown.
Antietam, Va., 4,671, of whom 1,818 are unknown.
Winchester, Va., 4,559, of whom 2,365 are unknown.

In all, the remains of 300,000 men who fought for the Stars and Stripes find guarded graves in our national cemeteries. Two cemeteries are mainly devoted to the brave men who perished in the loathsome prisons of the same name — Andersonville, Ga., which contains 13,714 graves, and Salisbury, with its 12,126 dead, of whom 12,032 are unknown.

UNITED STATES PENSION STATISTICS.
NUMBER OF PENSION CLAIMS, PENSIONERS AND DISBURSEMENTS, 1861-1885.

Fiscal Year ending June 30.	Army and Navy. Claims Allowed.		Total No. of Applications Filed.	Total No. of Claims Allowed.
	Invalids.	Widows, Etc.		
1861............	....	....	....	....
1862............	413	49	2,437	462
1863............	4,121	3,763	49,332	7,884
1864............	17,041	22,446	53,599	39,487
1865............	15,212	24,959	72,684	40,171
1866............	22,883	27,294	65,256	50,177
1867............	16,598	19,893	36,753	36,482
1868............	9,460	19,461	20,768	28,921
1869............	7,292	15,904	26,066	23,196
1870............	5,721	12,500	24,851	18,221
1871............	7,934	8,399	43,969	16,562
1872............	6,468	7,244	26,391	34,333
1873............	6,551	4,073	18,303	16,052
1874............	5,937	3,152	16,734	10,462
1875............	5,760	4,736	18,704	11,152
1876............	5,360	4,376	23,523	9,977
1877............	7,282	3,861	22,715	11,326
1878............	7,414	3,550	44,587	11,962
1879............	7,242	3,379	57,118	31,346
1880............	10,176	4,455	141,466	19,545
1881............	21,394	3,920	31,116	27,394
1882............	22,946	3,999	40,939	27.664
1883............	32,014	5,303	48,776	38,162
1884............	27,414	6,366	41,785	34,192
1885............	27,580	7,743	40,918	35,767
Total	300,204	220,825	968,840	580,897

NOTE.—In the number of pensioners on the roll under the heads of "Invalids" and "Widows," etc., are included survivors and widows of the war of 1812, respectively, commencing with the year 1871.

U. S. PENSION STATISTICS—(Continued).

Fiscal Year ending June 30.	Number of Pensioners on the Roll and the Amount Paid for Pensions, with Cost of Disbursements.			
	Invalids.	Widows, Etc.	Total.	Disbursements.
1861	4,337	4,299	8,636	$1,072,462
1862	4,341	3,818	8,159	790,385
1863	7,821	6,970	14,791	1,025,140
1864	23,479	27,656	51,135	4,564,617
1865	35,880	50,106	85,986	8,525,153
1866	55,652	71,070	126,722	13,459,996
1867	69,565	83,678	153,183	18,619,916
1868	75,957	93,686	169,643	24,010,982
1869	82,859	105,104	187,963	28,422,884
1870	87,521	111,165	198,686	27,780,812
1871	93,394	114,101	207,495	33,077,384
1872	113,954	118,275	232,229	30,169,341
1873	119,500	118,911	238,411	29,185,290
1874	121,628	114,613	236,241	30,593,750
1875	122,989	111,832	234,821	29,683,117
1876	124,239	107,898	232,137	28,351,600
1877	128,723	103,381	222,104	28,580,157
1878	131,649	92,349	223,998	26,844,415
1879	138,615	104,140	242,755	33,780,526
1880	145,410	105,392	250,802	57,240,540
1881	164,110	104,720	268,830	50,626,539
1882	182,633	103,064	285,697	54,296,281
1883	206,042	97.616	303,638	60,431,973
1884	225,470	97,286	322,756	57,273,537
1885	247,146	97,979	345,125	65,693,707
Total				$744,040,541

The number of pensions allowed by the United States to soldiers who served in wars previous to the civil war of 1861-65 and to their widows have been as follows: War of the Revolution, 62,069; war of 1812 with Great Britain, 67,048; war with Mexico, 7,619: Indian and all other wars, 1,389; Navy, 3,563.

Wars of the United States.

STATEMENT OF THE NUMBER OF UNITED STATES TROOPS ENGAGED

WARS.	DATE. From—	DATE. To—	TROOPS ENGAGED. Regulars.	TROOPS ENGAGED. Militia and Volunteers.	Total.
War of the Revolution	April 19, 1775	April 11, 1783	130,711	58,750	....
Estimated additional				105,330	309,791
Northwestern Indian wars	Sept. 19, 1790	Aug. 3, 1795	....	....	8,983
War with France	July 9, 1798	Sept. 30, 1800	....	....	*4,593
War with Tripoli	June 10, 1801	June 4, 1805	....	....	*3,339
Northwestern Indian war; General Harrison	Sept. 11, 1811	Nov. 11, 1811	250	660	910
Creek Indian war	July 27, 1813	Aug. 9, 1814	600	13,181	13,781
War of 1812 with Great Britain	June 18, 1812	Feb. 17, 1815	85,000	471,622	576,622
Seminole Indian war	Nov. 20, 1817	Oct. 21, 1818	1,000	6,911	7,911
Black Hawk Indian war	April 21, 1831	Sept. 31, 1832	1,339	5,126	6,465
Cherokee disturbance or removal	1836	1837	....	9,494	9,494

148

WARS OF THE UNITED STATES—CONTINUED.

WARS.	DATE.		TROOPS ENGAGED.		
	From—	To—	Regulars.	Militia and Volunteers.	Total.
Creek Indian war or disturbance	May 5, 1836	Sept. 30, 1837	935	12,483	13,483
Florida Indian war	Dec. 23, 1835	Aug. 14, 1843	11,169	29,953	41,000
Aroostook disturbance	1838	1839	....	1,500	1,500
War with Mexico	April 24, 1846	July 4, 1848	30,954	73,776	112,230
Apache, Navajo, and Utah war	1849	1855	1,500	1,061	2,561
Comanche Indian war	1854	1854	....	503	503
Seminole Indian war	1856	1858	....	2,687	2,687
Civil war	1861	1865	....	....	2,859,132

*Naval forces engaged. The number of troops on the Confederate side during the Civil War was about 600,000.

, The number of casualties in the volunteer and regular armies of the United States, during the war of 1861–65, was reported by the Provost-Marshal General in 1866:

WARS OF THE UNITED STATES—Continued.

Killed in battle, 61,362; died of wounds, 34,727; died of disease, 183,287; total died, 279,376; total deserted, 199,105.

Number of soldiers in the Confederate service, who died of wounds or disease (partial statement), 133,821. Deserted (partial statement), 104,428.

Number of United States troops captured during the war, 212,608; Confederate troops captured, 476,169.

Number of United States troops paroled on the field, 16,431; Confederate troops paroled on the field, 248,599.

Number of United States troops who died while prisoners, 29,725; Confederate troops who died while prisoners, 26,774.

The casualties on the American side in the last war with Great Britain, 1812-15, were: Killed, 1,877; wounded, 3,737; total, 5,614.

The casualties on the American side in the war with Mexico, 1846-48, were: Killed, 1,049; died of wounds, 904; wounded, 3,420.

The estimated cost to the United States of the Revolutionary War was $135,193,703; of the war of 1812 with Great Britain, $107,159,003; of the Mexican War, $100,000,000; of the Civil War (including all expenses growing out of the war), $6,189,929,909.

The height of the railway bridge at Niagara river, above the river, is 250 feet.

The largest diamond-cutting house is the Amsterdam, where they employ 400 men. The famous Kohinoor diamond was cut there. The cutters make from $7 to $12 and even $14 a day.

Trinity Church, New York, is 283 feet in height.

The Fast-Milers of 1887.

Name.	Age.	Sire.	Wt. Carried.	Course.	Date.	Time.
Stuyvesant	3	Glengarry	111½	Sheepshead	Sept. 7	1.40
Burch	a	Enquirer	112½	Sheepshead	July 2	1.40¼
Stuyvesant	3	Glengarry	110	Sheepshead	June 28	1.40½
Jackabin	3	Jils Johnson	103	Chicago	June 25	1.40½
Eolian	4	Eolus	111¾	Sheepshead	Sept. 1	1.40¾
Troubadour	5	Lisbon	115	Sheepshead	June 30	1.41
Orvid	3	Glengarry	101½	Sheepshead	July 2	1.41
Aurelia	3	Algerine	100	Chicago	July 9	1.41
Aurelia	3	Algerine	90	San Francisco	Apl. 16	1.41¼
Touche Pas	3	Spendthrift	97	Sheepshead	Sept. 3	1.41¼
Eolian	4	Eolus	120	Sheepshead	Sept.16	1.41¼
Pink Cottage	a	Buckden	105	Buffalo	July 15	1.41½
Hanover	3	Hindoo	118	Sheepshead	June 21	1.41¾
Hanover	3	Hindoo	112	Washington	Oct. 31	1.41¾
Jackabin	3	Jils Johnson	111¼	Chicago	July 16	1.41¾
Valuable	3	Ten Broeck	105	Lexington	Oct. 21	1.41¾
Flageoletta	3	Raydon d'Or	100	Sheepshead	Sept.17	1.41¾
Jackabin	3	Jils Johnson	118	Chicago	July 2	1.42
Kenny	3	Duke of Montrose	113	San Francisco	Nov. 5	1.42
Repetta	a	Reform	107	Buffalo	July 13	1.42
Redstone	5	Wanderer	100	Sheepshead	Sept. 8	1.42
Governor	4	Glengarry	90	Nashville	Nov. 2	1.42
Rosalind	3	Billet	98	Chicago	July 1	1.42¼
Poteen	3	Powhattan	109	Nashville	Nov. 3	1.42¼
Ten Strike	6	Ten Broeck	105	Brooklyn	May 26	1.42¼
Aurelia	3	Algerine	90	San Francisco	Apl. 23	1.42¼
Buckstone	a	Stonehenge	107	Brooklyn	May 14	1.42¼
Hindoo Rose	3	Hindoo	92	Chicago	Aug. 20	1.42¼
Queen Bess	3	Hyder Ali	93	Sheepshead	Sept. 8	1.42¼
Redstone	5	Wanderer	100	Sheepshead	Sept. 8	1.42¼
Sam Bennett	6	Rebel	108	Chicago	Sept.12	1.42¼
Phil Lee	4	Glen Athol	102	Brooklyn	Sept.21	1.42¼
Troubadour	5	Lisbon	122	Brooklyn	May 27	1.42½
Snowdrop	2	Joe Hooker		Sacramento	Sept.19	1.42½
Binette	6	Billet	112	Sacramento	May 4	1.42½
Telie Doe	5	Gt. Tom	112	Washington	Nov. 5	1.42½
Gold Flea	4	Longfellow	108	Chicago	July 12	1.42½
Font	3	Fonso	105	St. Louis	June 10	1.42½

Railroad Failures in Ten Years.
SOLD UNDER FORECLOSURE.

Years.	No. Roads.	Mileage.	Capital Stock and Bonded Debt.
1876	30	3,840	$217,848,000
1877	54	3,875	198,984,000
1878	48	3,906	311,631,000
1879	65	4,909	243,288,000
1880	31	3,775	263,882,000
1881	29	2,617	127,923,000
1882	16	867	65,426,000
1883	18	1,354	47,100,000
1884	15	710	23,504,000
1885	22	3,156	278,494,000
Total for ten years	328	29,009	$1,778,080,000

RAILWAY SIGNALS.

One whistle signifies " down brakes."
Two whistles signify " off brakes."
Three whistles signify " back up."
Continued whistles signify " danger."
Rapid short whistles " a cattle alarm."

A sweeping parting of the hands on a level with the eyes, signifies " go ahead."

Downward motion of the hands with extended arms, signifies " stop."

Beckoning motion of one hand, signifies " back."

Red flag waved up the track, signifies " danger."

Red flag stuck up by the roadside, signifies " danger ahead."

Red flag carried on a locomotive, signifies " an engine following."

Red flag hoisted at a station is a signal to " stop."

Lanterns at night raised and lowered vertically, is a signal " to start."

Lanterns swung at right angles across the track, means " stop."

Lanterns swung in a circle, signifies " back the train."

COST OF SMALL QUANTITIES OF HAY.

Price per Ton.	25 lbs. worth.	40 lbs. worth.	100 lbs. worth.	200 lbs. worth.	300 lbs. worth.
$ 4 00	5 cts.	10 cts.	20 cts.	$ 40	$ 60
5 00	6 "	12 "	25 "	50	75
6 00	7½ "	15 "	30 "	60	90
7 00	8½ "	17 "	35 "	70	1 05
8 00	10 "	20 "	40 "	80	1 20
9 00	11 "	22 "	45 "	90	1 35
10 00	12½ "	25 "	50 "	1 00	1 50
11 00	13½ "	27 "	55 "	1 19	1 65
12 00	15 "	30 "	60 "	1 20	1 80
13 00	16 "	32 "	65 "	1 30	1 95
14 00	17½ "	35 "	70 "	1 40	2 10
15 00	18½ "	37 "	75 "	1 50	2 25

AMOUNT OF OIL IN SEEDS.

Kind of Seed.	Per cent. Oil.	Kind of Seed.	Per cent. Oil.
Bitter Almond	55	Oats	6½
Barley	2½	Rapeseed	55
Clover hay	5	Sweet Almond	47
Hemp seed	19	Turnip seed	45
Indian corn	7	White mustard	37
Linseed	17	Wheat bran	4
Meadow hay	3½	Wheat-straw	3
Oat-straw	4	Wheat flour	3

RELATIVE VALUE OF DIFFERENT FOODS FOR STOCK.

One hundred pounds of good hay for stock are equal to:

Articles.	Pounds.	Articles.	Pounds.
Beans	28	Oats	59
Beets	669	Oil-cake, linseed	43
Clover, red, green	373	Peas, dry	37½
Carrots	371	Potatoes	350
Corn	62	Rye-straw	429
Clover, red, dry	88	Rye	53½
Lucerne	89	Turnips	469
Mangolds	368½	Wheat	44½
Oat-straw	317		

Quantity of Seed Required to Plant an Acre.

16 quarts Asparagus in 12 inch drills.
20 " Beans, pole, Lima, 4 by 4 feet.
10 " Beans, Carolina, prolific, etc., 4 by 3 feet.
10 " Corn, sugar.
8 " Corn, field.
3 " Cucumber, in hills.
20 " Flax, broadcast.
6 " Grass, timothy with clover.
10 " Grass, timothy without clover.
25 " Grass, orchard.
20 " Grass, red top or heads.
28 " Grass, blue.
20 " Grass, rye.
2 " Pumpkin, in hills 8 by 8 feet.
8,000 Asparagus plants, 4 by 1½ feet.
25,000 Celery plants, 4 by ½ feet.
17,500 Pepper plants, 2½ by 1 foot.
3,800 Tomato plants.
2½ bushels Barley.
1½ " Beans, bush, in drills 2½ feet.
2 " Peas, in drills, short varieties.
1 to 1½ " Peas, in drills, tall varieties.
3 " Peas, broadcast.
8 " Potatoes.
1¾ " Rye, broadcast.
1½ " Rye, drilled.
1¼ " Wheat, in drills.
2 " Wheat, broadcast.
12 ounces Cabbage, outside, for transplanting.
4 " Cabbage, sown in frames.
8 " Celery, seed.
3 " Tomatoes, in frames.
8 " Tomatoes, seed in hills 3 by 3 feet.
9 pounds Beets and mangold, drills, 2½ feet.
12 " Broom corn in drills.
4 " Carrot, in drills, 2½ feet.
13 " Clover, white Dutch.
10 " Clover, Lucerne.
6 " Clover, Alsike.
12 " Clover, large red with timothy.
16 " Clover, large red without timothy.

25 " Corn, salad, drill 10 inches.
3 " Lettuce, in rows 2½ feet.
35 " Lawn grass.
3 " Melons, water, in hills 8 by 8 feet.
2 " Melons, citrons, in hills 4 by 4 feet.
50 " Onions, in beds for sets.
7 " Onions, in rows for large bulbs.
5 " Parsnip, in drills 2½ feet.
4 " Parsley, in drills 2 feet.
10 " Radish, in drills 2 feet.
3 " Squash, bush, in hills 4 by 4 feet.
3 " Turnips, in drills 2 feet.
3 " Turnips, broadcast.

The Longest Rivers in the World

Miles.
  233—Thames.
  300—Kenebec.
  350—Hudson.
  400—Delaware.
  450—Connecticut.
  500—James.
  500—Potomac.
  500—Susquehanna.
  600—Alabama.
  600—Cumberland.
  700—Red River of the **North.**
  800—Tennessee.
  900—Kansas.
  950—Rhine.
  950—Ohio.
  _,000—Yellowstone.
  1,100—Colorada, in **California.**
  1,200—Red River.
  1,200—Nebraska.
  1,200—Columbia.
  1,300—San Francisco.
  1,600—Danube.
  1,800—Rio Grande.
  2,000—Volga.
  2,000—Arkansas.

2,000—Madeira.
2,200—St. Lawrence.
2,500—Obe.
2,600—Niger, or Jobila.
2,600—Lena.
2,800—Mississippi, proper.
4,100—Missouri, to the sea, forming longest in the world.
2,900—Missouri, to its junction with the Mississippi.
3,600—Amazon.
3,000—Nile.

GOVERNORS' SALARIES, TERMS OF OFFICE AND STATE CAPITALS.

Terms of Office.	States and Territories.	Capitals.	Yearly Salaries.
One year	Massachusetts	Boston	$ 4,000
One year	Rhode Island	Newport	1,000
Two years	Alabama	Montgomery	3,000
Two years	Arkansas	Little Rock	3,000
Two years	Colorado	Denver	5,000
Two years	Connecticut	Hartford	2,000
Two years	Georgia	Atlanta	3,000
Two years	Iowa	Des Moines	3,000
Two years	Kansas	Topeka	3,000
Two years	Maine	Augusta	2,000
Two years	Michigan	Lansing	1,000
Two years	Minnesota	St. Paul	3,300
Two years	Nebraska	Lincoln	2,500
Two years	New Hampshire	Concord	1,000
Two years	Ohio	Columbus	4,000
Two years	South Carolina	Columbia	3,500
Two years	Tennessee	Nashville	4,000
Two years	Texas	Austin	4,000
Two years	Vermont	Montpelier	1,000
Two years	Wisconsin	Madison	5,000
Three years	New Jersey	Trenton	5,000
Three years	New York	Albany	10,000
Four years	Arizona Territory	Prescott	2,600
Four years	California	Sacramento	6,000
Four years	Dakota Territory	Yankton	2,600
Four years	Delaware	Dover	2,000

Four years..	Florida............	Tallahassee...	3,500
Four years..	Idaho Territory..	Boise City....	2,600
Four years..	Illinois............	Springfield...	6,000
Four years..	Indiana............	Indianapolis..	5,000
Four years..	Indian Territory.	Tahlequah...	2,600
Four years..	Kentucky........	Frankfort....	5,000
Four years..	Louisiana........	Baton Rouge..	4,000
Four years..	Maryland.........	Annapolis....	4,500
Four years..	Mississippi.......	Jackson.......	4,000
Four years..	Missouri..........	Jefferson City.	5,000
Four years..	Montana Ter....	Helena........	2,600
Four years..	Nevada...........	Carson City...	5,000
Four years..	New Mexico Ter.	Santa Fe.....	2,600
Four years..	North Carolina...	Raleigh.......	3,000
Four years..	Oregon...........	Salem.........	1,500
Four years..	Pennsylvania.....	Harrisburg....	10,000
Four years..	Utah Territory..	Salt Lake City	2,600
Four years..	Virginia..........	Richmond....	5,000
Four years..	Washington Ter.	Olympia......	2,600
Four years..	West Virginia...	Wheeling.....	2,700
Four years..	Wyoming Ter.....	Cheyenne....	2,600

VALUE OF A TON OF GOLD OR SILVER.

A ton of pure gold is worth $602,799.21.
$1,000,000 gold coin weighs 3,685.8 pounds.
A ton of silver is worth $37,704.84.
$1,000,000 silver coin weighs 58,929.9 pounds.

CURIOSITIES OF THE BIBLE.

The Bible contains 3,566,480 letters, 773,746 words, 31,173 verses, 1,189 chapters and 66 books. The word AND occurs 46,277 times. The word LORD occurs 1,855 times. The word REVEREND occurs but once, which is in the 9th verse of the 111th Psalm. The middle verse is the 8th verse of the 118th Psalm. The 21st verse of the 7th chapter of Ezra contains all the letters of the alphabet, except the letter J. The longest verse is the 9th verse of the 8th chapter of Esther. The shortest verse is the 35th verse of the 11th chapter of St. John. There are no words or names of more than six syllables.

FICTITIOUS NAMES OF STATES

Wisconsin—Badger State.
Massachusetts—Bay State.
Mississippi—Bayou State.
Arkansas—Bear State.
Louisiana—Creole State.
Delaware—Diamond State.
New York—Empire State.
New York—Excelsior State.
Connecticut—Freestone State.
New Hampshire—Granite State.
Vermont—Green-Mountain State.
Iowa—Hawkeye State.
Indiana—Hoosier State.
Pennsylvania—Keystone State.
Michigan—Lake State.
Texas—Lone-Star State.
Maine—Lumber State.
Virginia—Mother of Presidents.
Virginia—Mother of States.
Connecticut—Nutmeg State.
Massachussetts—Old Colony.
Virginia—Old Dominion.
North Carolina—Old North State.
South Carolina—Palmetto State.
Florida—Peninsular State.
Maine—Pine-Tree State.
Illinois—Prairie State.
North Carolina—Turpentine State.

FICTITIOUS NAMES OF CITIES

Hannibal, Missouri—Bluff City.
Philadelphia—City of Brotherly Love.
Brooklyn, N. Y.—City of Churches.

New Haven, Conn.—City of Elms.
Washington—City of Magnificent Distances.
Boston, Mass.—City of Notions.
Nashville, Tenn.—City of Rocks.
Lowell, Mass.—City of Spindles.
Detroit—City of the Straits.
New Orleans—Crescent City.
New York—Empire City.
Louisville, Ky.—Falls City.
Rochester, N. Y.—Flour City.
Springfield, Ill.—Flower City.
Cleveland, Ohio—Forest City.
Portland, Me.—Forest City.
Chicago, Ill.—Garden City.
Keokuk, Iowa—Gate City.
New York—Gotham.
Boston, Mass.—Hub of the Universe.
Pittsburg, Pa.—Iron City.
Baltimore—Monumental City.
St. Louis, Mo.—Mound City.
Philadelphia, Pa.—Quaker City.
Cincinnati, Ohio—Queen City.
Buffalo, N. Y.—Queen City of the Lakes.
Indianapolis, Ind.—Railroad City.
Pittsburg—Smoky City.

Periodicals in Japan.

There are some 130 periodicals issued weekly, semi-monthly, or monthly, on religion, government regulations, politics, laws, army and navy, agriculture, trade and commerce, shipping and navigation, literature, education, science, fine arts, medicines, etc., in Japan.

It is a peculiarity of the Japanese daily newspapers that in each of them the editorial article is made about the same length every day. In some papers it covers a column and a half, while in others it is longer. One editorial is published in each number, and it is only in very rare cases that two or more editorials are printed.

Commercial Statistics of the City of New York.

COTTON EXCHANGE TRANSACTIONS.

MONTH.	FUTURE SALES.		HIGHEST AND LOWEST PRICE.	
	1884. Bales.	1885. Bales.	1884. Cents.	1885. Cents.
January	2,091,900	2,619,400	11.29 a 9.69	11.37 a 9.52
February	1,313,500	2,042,300	11.40 a 9.80	11.54 a 9.61
March	1,783,100	2,885,400	11.46 a 9.93	11.55 a 9.73
April	3,475,400	1,848,000	12.00 a 10.05	11.60 a 9.83
May	1,587,300	1,840,000	12.06 a 10.13	11.70 a 9.93
June	2,075,100	1,858,000	12.14 a 10.57	11.80 a 10.02
July	1,524,000	1,722,600	12.14 a 10.57	11.88 a 10.11
August	1,316,500	828,200	12.25 a 10.66	11.94 a 9.81
September	1,530,200	2,088,900	11.12 a 9.82	11.57 a 9.68
October	2,477,200	2,070,900	11.30 a 9.69	11.30 a 9.46
November	2,012,700	2,119,400	11.15 a 9.59	11.10 a 9.39
December	2,895,700	2,618,700	11.25 a 9.61	11.15 a 9.43

GRAIN EXPORT FROM THE PORT OF NEW YORK.

NATIONALITY.	Bushels.	No. of Vessels.
American	none.	none.
Austrian	624,324	20
British	20,374,334	690
Belgian	4,518,177	73
Brazilian	8,125	1
Danish	1,134,022	30
Dutch	1,461,728	41
French	1,404,855	41
German	4,904,792	204
Italian	1,280,301	45
Norwegian	69,310	4
Portuguese	450,628	21
Spanish	835,691	20
Swedish	32,907	1
Totals	47,103,264	1,191

Commercial Statistics, Etc.—Continued.

CUSTOM HOUSE TRANSACTIONS.

1885.	Imports.	Foreign Exports.	Domestic Exports.
January..	$28,461,271	$1,199,012	$31,480,982
February.	28,847,070	802,969	22,903,198
March ...	35,646,728	894,739	25,277,817
April....	32,259,481	928,313	26,060,326
May......	28,101,855	854,049	27,487,435
June.....	30,973,698	939,953	27,594,945
July.....	33,370,601	769,731	25,792,822
August ..	34,990,145	766,661	26,355,140
Septemb'r	32,930,402	600,625	27,548,584
October .	34,404,319	869,893	27,291,289
November	32,037,924	600,615	24,362,286
December	34,000,000	600,000	25,000,000
Total..	$386,084,494	$9,819,568	$317,154,796

The total receipts for customs for 1885 were $128,292,-636.80; in 1884 they amounted to $132,416,696.94; showing, therefore, a falling off for the year 1885.

CLEARING HOUSE TRANSACTIONS.

1885.	Exchanges.	Balances.
January........	$2,185,377,595.52	$123,227,916.54
February.....	1,900,176,637.44	90,550,296.16
March...	2,012,757,921.16	98,136,918.79
April.........	1,867,988,743.35	105,431,162.32
May..........	1,997,837,280.91	106,158,666.84
June	1,922,335,680.53	108,187,995.69
July..........	2,376,114,984.64	114,525,111.11
August........	2,041,097,444.16	97,918,800.35
September.....	2,101,128,912.62	102,619,902.29
October.......	3,189,746,197.10	136,009,947.30
November.....	3,318,946,571.72	120,799,054.50
December.....	3,238,393,366.88	152,901,882.68
Total.......	$28,152,201,336.02	$1,356,470,654.57

The Clearing House has now a membership of 64.

Commercial Statistics, Etc.—Continued.

IMPORTS OF FOREIGN DRY GOODS AT NEW YORK.

Year.	Value.	Year.	Value.
1850	$60,106,375	1868	80,905,834
1851	62,846,731	1869	94,725,417
1852	64,654,154	1870	109,498,523
1853	93,704,211	1871	132,480,777
1854	80,842,936	1872	136,831,612
1855	64,974,062	1873	114,160,465
1856	93,362,893	1874	106,520,453
1857	90,534,129	1875	99,816,025
1858	60,154,509	1876	86,716,163
1859	113,152,624	1877	$77,756,778
1860	103,927,100	1878	74,863,197
1861	43,636,689	1879	91,549,600
1862	56,121,227	1880	119,844,120
1863	67,274,547	1881	111,537,020
1864	71,589,752	1882	132,262,730
1865	91,965,138	1883	121,508,817
1866	126,221,855	1884	113,906,176
1867	86,263,643	1885	100,542,360

STOCK EXCHANGE TRANSACTIONS.

1885.	No. of Shares of Stock.	Government Bonds.	State & R. R. Bonds.
January	6,957,971	$1,573,500	$31,990,300
February	7,081,480	928,000	36,119,000
March	6,708,015	657,000	28,249,400
April	4,594,046	903,800	24,537,300
May	5,174,715	1,915,200	39,500,050
June	4,508,444	2,912,200	48,054,500
July	8,019,782	1,236,900	74,565,000
August	6,887,444	1,062,000	56,284,689
September	5,846,679	1,069,500	48,993,100
October	12,681,182	1,275,000	108,426,850
November	13,508,025	707,000	90,156,803
December	11,206,594	1,339,100	75,895,050
Total, 1885	$93,184,478	†$15,570,200	†$662,772,042
" 1884	95,052,052	14,879,700	508,815,800

*Estimated two days. †Less one day.

Commercial Statistics, Etc.—Continued.

CONDITION OF THE NEW YORK BANKS.

	1882. Dec. 30.	1883. Dec. 29.	1884. Dec. 27.	1885. Dec. 26.
Loans	$311,071,200	$327,535,700	$295,874,200	$336,938,300
Specie	57,627,100	60,468,100	88,170,500	90,988,200
Legal tenders	18,664,200	26,479,100	36,592,300	27,212,700
Reserve held	76,291,300	86,947,200	124,762,800	118,200,900
Legal reserve	72,915,900	80,198,250	83,818,025	93,488,250
Surplus reserve	3,375,400	6,748,950	40,944,775	24,712,650
Deposits	291,663,600	320,793,000	335,272,100	373,953,000
Circulation	17,625,500	15,456,800	11,618,600	9,924,400

PRODUCE EXCHANGE TRANSACTIONS.

SALES MADE AT THE "CALLS."

1885.	Wheat, bush.	Corn, bush.	Oats, bush.	Lard, tcs.	Margins.
January	10,024,000	4,480,000	565,000	17,250	$2,664,160
February	3,408,000	3,280,000	120,000	9,600	1,243,610
March	3,664,000	2,312,000	250,000	11,750	1,534,645
April	5,736,000	2,536,000	145,000	5,750	3,609,420
May	4,752,000	2,592,000	395,000	5,500	1,943,930
June	4,840,000	1,256,000	225,000	5,750	1,231,145
July	3,424,000	824,000	270,000	4,000	1,346,450
August	4,200,000	1,096,000	660,000	8,500	2,911,900
September	4,088,000	696,000	475,000	11,250	2,023,590
October	4,272,000	1,240,000	427,000	10,750	2,284,505
November	7,112,000	2,048,000	315,000	4,500	2,292,505
December	4,944,000	1,968,000	280,000	6,000	2,500,000
Total	56,464,000	24,328,000	4,127,000	100,500	25,582,860

Commercial Statistics, Etc.—Continued.

IMPORTS OF DRY GOODS AT NEW YORK FOR THREE YEARS.

	1883.	1884.	1885.
Manufactures of wool	$31,462,217	$28,862,874	$25,970,061
Manufactures of cotton	25,918,700	22,842,717	21,022,164
Manufactures of silk	36,841,942	35,069,781	28,974,925
Manufactures of flax	17,115,046	15,868,015	4,897,591
Miscellaneous dry goods	10,120,912	10,462,789	9,677,619
Total imports	$121,508,817	$113,906,176	$100,542,360

Size of Lakes, Seas and Oceans.

LAKES.	Miles Long.	Miles Wide.	SEAS.	Miles Long.
Cayuga	36	4	Aral	250
George	36	3	Baltic	600
Constance	45	10	Black	932
Geneva	50	10	Caribbean	1,800
Lake of the Woods	70	25	China	1,700
Champlain	123	12	Caspian	640
Ladoga	125	75	Japan	1,000
Maracaybo	150	60	Mediterranean	2,000
Great Bear	150	40	Okhotsk	600
Ontario	180	40	Red	1,400
Athabasca	200	20	White	450
Winnipeg	240	40	OCEANS.	Miles Square.
Huron	250	90		
Erie	270	50	Arctic	5,000,000
Great Slave	300	45	Southern	10,000,000
Michigan	330	60	Indian	20,000,000
Baikal	360	35	Atlantic	40,000,000
Superior	380	120	Pacific	80,000,000

Carrying Capacity of a Ten Ton Freight Car.

Flour ... 90 barrels.	Butter ... 20,000 pounds.
Lime ... 70 "	Lumber ... 6,000 feet.
Salt ... 70 "	Wheat ... 340 bushels.
Whisky ... 60 "	Barley ... 300 "
Flour ... 200 sacks.	Apples ... 370 "
Eggs ... 130 to 160 barrels.	Corn ... 400 "
Wood ... 6 cords.	Potatoes ... 430 "
Sheep ... 80 to 100 head.	Bran ... 1,000 "
Hogs ... 50 to 60 "	Oats ... 680 "
Cattle ... 18 to 20 "	Flax Seed ... 360 "

The Greatest Battles in History.

The Battle of Actium, B. C. 31, in which the combined fleets of Antony and Cleopatra were defeated by Octavius, and imperialism established in the person of Octavius.

The Battle of Arbela, B. C. 331, in which the Persians, under Tarius, were defeated by the Macedonians and Greeks under Alexander the Great.

The Battle of Marathon, B. C. 490, in which the Athenians, under Mietiades, defeated the Persians, under Datis.

The Battle of Syracuse, B. C. 413, in which the Athenians were defeated by the Syracusans and their allies.

The Battle of Metaurus, B. C. 207, in which the Carthagenians, under Hasdrubul, were defeated by the Romans, under the Consuls, Caius, Claudius, Nero and Marcus Livius.

The Battle of Philippi, B. C. 42, in which Brutus and Cassius were defeated by Octavius and Antony. The fate of the Republic was decided.

The Battle of Blenheim, A. D. 1704, in which the French and Bavarians, under Marshal Tallard, were defeated by the English and their allies, under Marlborough.

The Battle of Chalons, A. D. 451, in which the Huns, under Attila, called the "Scourge of God," were defeated by the confederate armies of Romans and Visigoths.

Battle of Hastings, A. D. 1066, in which Harold, commanding the English army, was defeated by William the Conquerer of Normandy.

The Battle of Lutzen, 1632, which decided the religious liberties of Germany. Gustavus Adolphus was killed.

The Battle of Pultowa, A. D. 1709, in which Charles XII. of Sweden, was defeated by the Russians, under Peter the Great.

The Battle of Tours, A. D. 732, in which the Saracens were defeated by Charles Martel. Christendom was rescued from Islam.

On the 21st of October, 1805, the Great Naval Battle

of Trafalgar was fought. The English defeated the French and destroyed the hopes of Napoleon as to a successful invasion of England.

The Battle of Valmy, A. D. 1792, in which an invading army of Prussians, Austrians and Hessians, under the command of the Duke of Brunswick, were defeated by the French, under Dumouriez.

The Battle of Waterloo, 1815, in which the French, under Napoleon, were defeated by the allied armies of Russia, Austria, Prussia and England, under the Duke of Wellington.

A Woman's Chance to Marry.

¼ of 1 per cent., from 50 to 56 years of age.
⅜ of 1 per cent., from 45 to 50 years of age.
2½ per cent., from 40 to 45 years of age.
3¾ per cent., from 35 to 40 years of age.
15½ per cent., from 30 to 35 years of age.
18 per cent., from 25 to 30 years of age.
52 per cent., from 20 to 25 years of age.
14½ per cent., from 15 to 20 years of age.

SOME GOOD MAXIMS.

There is nothing better in heaven than religion.

Our actions of to-day are the thoughts of yesterday.

A truthful woman is the greatest adornment of a home.

If you live in impure thoughts you will be impure in your lives.

Profanity is more or less a profession of your loyalty to the devil.

Nobody ever went to sleep indifferent to religion and waked up in heaven.

A child is loved by God because it has no opinions and wants to learn something.

Don't get into anybody's way with your naturalness, but try to be yourself wherever you go.

Run into heaven barefooted and bareheaded rather tn miss it on account of anything in the world.

How to Preserve Eggs.

To each pailful of water, add two pints of fresh slacked lime and one pint of common salt; mix well. Fill your barrel half full with this fluid, put your eggs down in it any time after June, and they will keep two years if desired.

Facts Worth Knowing.

There are 2,754 languages.
America was discovered in 1492.
A square mile contains 640 acres.
Envelopes were first used in 1839.
Telescopes were invented in 1590.
A barrel of rice weighs 600 pounds.
A barrel of flour weighs 196 pounds.
A barrel of pork weighs 200 pounds.
A firkin of butter weighs 56 pounds.
The first steel pen was made in 1830.
A span is ten and seven-eighth inches.
A hand (horse measure) is four inches.
Watches were first constructed in 1476.
The first iron steamship was built in 1830.
The first lucifer match was made in 1829.
Gold was discovered in California in 1848.
The first horse railroad was built in 1826-7.
The average human life is thirty-one years.
Coaches were first used in England in 1569.
Modern needles first came into use in 1545.
Space has a temperature of 200 degrees below zero.
Kerosene was first used for lighting purposes in 1826.
The first newspaper was published in England in 1588.
The first newspaper advertisement appeared in 1652.
Robert Bonner refused $100,000.00 for the famous trotter Maud S
Until 1776 cotton-spinning was performed by the hand-spinning wheel.
Measure 209 feet on each side and you will have a square acre within an inch.
The first sewing machine was patented by Elias Howe, Jr., in 1846.
The first steam engine on this continent was brought from England in 1753.
The first knives were used in England, and the first wheeled carriages in France in 1559.
The national colors of the United States were adopted by Congress in 1777
The cost of coal burned by an ocean steamer on a trip will average $13,000.
The sun is 92,500,000 miles from the earth The latter receives only one two-billionth of the solar heat.
The nearest fixed star is 16,000,000,000 miles distant, and takes three years for light to reach the earth.

Occupation of the Inhabitants of the United States.

(Census of 1880.)

STATES AND TERRITORIES.	Total Population, 10 years and over.	All kinds of occupations.	Agriculture.	Professional and Personal Services.	Trade and Transportation.	Manufacturing, Mechanical Trades and Mining.
Alabama..................	851,780	492,790	380,630	72,211	16,953	22,996
Arizona..................	32,922	22,271	3,435	8,210	3,251	7,374
Arkansas................	531,876	260,692	216,655	23,466	9,233	11,338
California................	681,062	376,505	79,396	121,435	57,392	118,282
Colorado................	158,220	101,251	13,539	24,813	15,491	47,408
Connecticut.............	497,393	241,333	44,026	51,296	29,920	116,091
Dakota..................	99,849	57,844	28,508	14,016	6,219	9,101
Delaware................	110,856	54,580	17,849	17,016	4,967	14,148
District of Columbia.....	136,907	66,624	1,464	39,975	9,848	15,337
Florida..................	184,650	91,536	58,731	17,923	6,446	8,436
Georgia.................	1,043,840	597,862	432,204	104,269	25,222	36,197
Idaho...................	25,005	15,578	3,858	3,861	1,327	6,532
Illinois..................	2,269,315	999,780	436,371	229,467	128,372	205,570
Indiana.................	1,468,095	635,080	331,240	137,281	56,432	110,127
Iowa....................	1,181,641	528,302	303,557	103,932	50,872	69,941
Kansas..................	704,297	322,285	206,080	53,507	26,379	36,319
Kentucky...............	1,163,498	519,854	320,571	104,239	33,563	61,481
Louisiana...............	649,070	363,228	205,306	98,111	29,130	30,681
Maine..................	519,669	331,993	82,130	47,411	29,790	72,662
Maryland...............	695,364	324,432	90,927	98,934	49,234	85,337
Massachusetts..........	1,432,183	720,774	64,973	170,160	115,376	370,265

168

Michigan	1,236,686	569,204	240,319	143,249	54,000	130,91...
Minnesota	559,977	255,125	131,535	59,452	24,349	39,78...
Mississippi	753,693	415,506	339,938	49,448	12,975	13,145
Missouri	1,557,631	692,959	355,297	148,588	79,300	109,774
Montana	31,989	22,255	4,513	6,954	2,766	8,022
Nebraska	318,271	152,614	90,507	28,746	15,106	18,255
Nevada	50,666	32,233	4,180	10,373	4,449	18,231
New Hampshire	286,188	142,468	44,490	28,206	11,735	58,037
New Jersey	865,591	396,879	59,214	10,722	66,382	160,561
New Mexico	87,966	40,822	14,139	19,042	3,264	4,377
New York	3,981,428	1,884,645	377,460	537,897	339,419	629,869
North Carolina	959,951	480,187	360,937	69,321	15,966	33,963
Ohio	2,399,367	994,475	397,495	259,371	104,315	242,294
Oregon	130,565	67,343	27,091	16,645	6,149	17,458
Pennsylvania	3,203,215	1,456,067	301,112	446,713	179,965	528,277
Rhode Island	220,461	116,979	10,945	24,657	15,217	66,160
South Carolina	667,456	392,102	294,602	64,246	13,556	19,698
Tennessee	1,062,130	447,970	294,153	94,107	23,628	36,082
Texas	1,064,196	522,133	359,317	97,561	34,909	30,346
Utah	97,194	40,055	14,550	11,144	4,149	10,212
Vermont	264,052	118,584	55,251	28,174	8,945	26,214
Virginia	1,059,034	494,240	254,099	146,664	30,418	63,059
Washington Territory	55,720	30,122	12,781	6,640	3,405	7,296
West Virginia	428,587	176,199	107,578	31,680	10,653	26,288
Wisconsin	965,712	417,455	195,901	97,494	37,550	86,510
Wyoming	16,479	8,884	1,639	4,011	1,545	1,689
Total, 1880	36,761,607	17,392,099	7,670,463	4,074,238	1,810,256	3,837,112
Total, 1870	28,228,945	12,505,923	5,922,471	2,684,793	1,191,238	2,707,421

Population of the United States.
(Census of 1880.)

States and Territories	Total Population 1880.	Population by Races.					Voting Population. Males of 21 years and over.			
		White, 1880.	Colored, 1880.	Chinese, 1880.*	Ind'ns civ. or taxed, 1880.		White.			Colored.†
						Native.	Foreign Born.	Total.	
Alabama	1,262,505	662,185	600,103	4	213	136,058	5,403	141,461	118,423
Arizona	40,440	35,160	155	1,632	3,493	9,790	8,256	18,046	2,352
Arkansas	802,525	591,531	210,666	133	195	129,675	6,475	136,150	46,827
California	864,694	767,181	6,018	75,218	16,277	165,209	127,374	262,583	66,809
Colorado	194,327	191,126	2,435	612	154	65,215	26,873	92,088	1,520
Connecticut	622,700	610,769	11,547	129	255	116,747	55,012	173,756	3,532
Dakota	135,177	133,147	401	238	1,391	5,476	25,486	50,962	641
Delaware	146,608	120,160	26,442	11	5	27,447	4,455	31,902	6,396
District of Columbia	177,624	118,006	59,596	17	5	23,764	8,191	31,955	13,918
Florida	269,493	143,605	126,690	18	180	30,351	3,859	34,210	27,489
Georgia	1,542,180	816,906	725,133	17	124	172,044	5,923	177,967	143,471
Idaho	32,610	29,013	53	3,379	165	7,331	4,338	11,669	3,126
Illinois	3,077,871	3,031,151	46,368	212	140	505,272	277,889	783,161	13,686
Indiana	1,978,301	1,958,798	39,228	29	246	414,252	73,446	487,698	10,739
Iowa	1,624,615	1,614,600	9,516	33	466	287,590	126,103	413,633	3,025
Kansas	996,096	952,555	43,107	19	815	201,354	53,595	254,949	10,765
Kentucky	1,648,690	1,377,179	271,451	10	50	287,362	30,217	317,578	58,642

Louisiana	939,946	454,954	483,655	489	848	81,777	27,033	108,810	107,977
Maine	648,936	646,852	1,451	8	625	164,173	22,486	186,659	664
Maryland	934,943	724,693	210,230	5	15	144,586	38,936	183,522	48,584
Massachusetts	1,783,085	1,763,782	18,697	237	369	326,002	170,690	496,692	5,956
Michigan	1,636,937	1,614,560	15,100	28	7,249	285,469	176,088	461,557	6,130
Minnesota	780,773	776,884	1,564	25	2,300	88,622	123,777	212,399	1,086
Mississippi	1,131,597	479,398	650,291	51	1,857	102,580	5,674	108,254	130,278
Missouri	2,168,380	2,022,826	145,350	91	113	396,322	111,843	508,165	33,641
Montana	39,159	35,385	346	1,765	1,663	12,162	7,474	19,636	1,908
Nebraska	452,402	449,764	2,385	18	235	83,334	44,864	128,198	844
Nevada	62,266	53,556	488	5,419	2,803	11,442	14,191	25,633	5,622
New Hampshire	346,991	346,229	685	14	63	88,790	16,111	104,901	237
New Jersey	1,131,116	1,092,017	38,853	172	74	190,656	99,309	289,965	10,670
New Mexico	119,565	108,721	1,015	57	9,772	26,423	4,558	30,981	3,095
New York	5,082,871	5,016,022	65,104	926	819	852,094	536,598	1,388,692	20,059
North Carolina	1,399,750	867,242	531,277	1	1,230	187,637	2,095	189,732	105,018
Ohio	3,198,062	3,117,920	79,900	112	130	613,485	191,386	804,871	21,706
Oregon	174,768	163,075	487	9,512	1,694	38,006	13,630	51,636	7,993
Pennsylvania	4,282,891	4,197,016	85,535	156	184	797,532	272,860	1,070,592	23,892
Rhode Island	276,531	269,939	6,488	27	77	47,904	27,108	75,012	1,886
South Carolina	995,577	391,105	604,332	9	131	82,910	3,990	86,900	118,883
Tennessee	1,542,359	1,138,831	403,151	25	352	240,939	9,116	250,055	80,250
Texas	1,591,749	1,197,237	393,384	136	992	246,018	55,719	301,737	78,639
Utah	143,963	142,423	232	501	307	13,795	18,283	32,078	695
Vermont	332,286	331,218	1,057	......	11	77,774	17,533	95,307	314
Virginia	1,512,565	880,858	631,616	6	85	198,277	7,971	206,248	128,257
Washington Territory	75,116	67,199	325	3,187	4,405	15,858	8,393	24,251	3,419
West Virginia	618,457	592,537	25,886	5	29	123,569	9,208	132,777	6,384
Wisconsin	1,315,497	1,309,618	2,702	16	3,161	149,463	189,469	338,932	1,550
Wyoming	20,789	19,437	298	914	140	6,042	3,199	9,241	939
Total United States	50,155,783	43,402,970	6,580,793	105,613	66,407	8,270,518	3,072,487	11,242,005	1,487,344

NOTES TO TABLE ON PRECEDING PAGES.

*Includes 148 Japanese.

†Colored includes also Indians taxed (or civilized), Chinese and Japanese. In California most of the population classified as colored are Chinese, and are not voters.

NOTE.—Alaska and the Indian Territory are not included in the above, not having been organized when the census of 1880 was taken. The population of Alaska (1880) was 30,178, mostly natives. The population of the Indian Territory was estimated at 70,000. Indians not taxed are excluded by law from the census. The estimated number in 1881 was about 245,000, excluding Alaska. The whole population of the United States in 1880 was estimated by Spofford at 50,500,000. The estimated population of the United States at the beginning of 1886 is 57,500,000.

The total male population of the United States in 1880 was 25,518,820; female, 24,636,963. The total native population was 43,475,840; foreign born, 6,679,943.

POINTS OF LAW.

(*By a Supreme Court Lawyer.*)

The advice on matters in the following pages has been acquired at a great expense, and is absolutely correct. It can be relied upon as such.

Lawyers fees can be saved and much annoyance and expense avoided by acting on the advice given here.*

NEGOTIABLE INSTRUMENTS.

Introduction.—The laws governing mercantile transactions, and particularly such as relate to negotiable instruments, are, in the main, of very ancient origin, and are derived for the most part from the well established usages of merchants, which have been adopted, sanctioned and confirmed by the courts, and in many instances

---

*Copyright 1887—All rights reserved

redeclared by statute. These usages and customs constitute what is called, in the language of the books, the law-merchant.

Promissory Notes.—A note of hand, as it is called, is a written promise to pay to a person certain, his order, or bearer, at a specified time, a given sum of money. To render it negotiable, that is, so that it may be transferred by indorsement or delivery, it must be payable to "order" or "bearer," and unless these words appear it will not be negotiable. Further, the promise must be absolute and uncoupled with any condition, and the time of payment must be certain and not dependent upon any contingency, Again, the promise must be for a definite sum and must be payable in money. These are all of the essence of negotiability. Failing in any of the foregoing particulars, the note may still be good as a contract, but it will not be a negotiable instrument.

It may be written upon anything capable of receiving written characters, in any language susceptible of translation, and with any substance that will leave a permanent mark; hence a note written in pencil is just as valid as one written with ink. It need not be dated, for delivery gives it effect, although a date is customary and proper, and when no time is specified it is payable on demand. It need not be signed at the bottom, provided the name of the maker elsewhere appears and was written with intent to bind, as: "I, John Smith, promise," etc., but the better way is to subscribe the note.

The payee must be named or designated, unless the note is drawn to bearer, and if drawn to the maker's own order possesses no validity until he has indorsed it. A note payable to bearer is transferable by simple delivery and passes from hand to hand without anything further, and the same is true of a note payable to the payee's order after he has indorsed it. In such a case any holder may write over such indorsement an order to pay to himself. But if indorsed in full, that is to pay to some person certain, it can only be transferred by the subsequent indorsement of such designated person.

It is customary to write notes for "value received," but this is not necessary, for a negotiable note imports a consideration, and, except as between the parties, want of consideration cannot be shown if the note was negotiated in good faith and before maturity, while as between the parties consideration may always be disproved, even though expressed. The better practice, however, is to write them as expressing consideration.

One who places his name on the back of a note as an indorser thereby enters into an undertaking with his assignee, as well as others into whose hands the note may come, that he will pay it if the maker does not; but he may protect himself against the claims of subsequent indorsers by making his indorsement "without recourse." On the other hand, a party, by simply receiving and passing a note while under a blank indorsement, and without putting his name to it, assumes no responsibility in relation to it.

The holder or indorsee of a note has a right of action against every one whose name appears on the same, whether as maker or indorser, but it is his duty to present the note promptly at maturity and demand payment; if payment is refused, he should immediately notify the indorsers, and a failure so to do will, in most cases, discharge the indorser from liability. He should further use all reasonable means to compel payment by the maker before resorting to the indorsers, and the law only excuses him from this duty where at the time of maturity the maker is hopelessly insolvent and a suit against him would be unavailing.

Prior to maturity, any person who takes a note without notice of any defect, and pays therefor a valuable consideration, will be protected against any equities existing in favor of the maker; but one who takes it as a mere volunteer, paying no value therefor, or one who receives it after it has become due, even though in good faith, and for value, will take it subject to all its infirmities, and any defense that would have been availing as against the payee may be interposed as to them.

Due Bills are not distinguishable in general effect from promissory notes, and are governed by the same rules and assignable in the same manner.

Certificates of Deposit are, in effect, promissory notes, and subject to the same rules and principles applicable to that class of paper.

Warehouse Receipts are not technically negotiable, but stand in the place of the property itself; the delivery of the receipts has the same effect, in transferring the title to the property, as the delivery of the property itself. They are, however, frequently declared negotiable paper by statute.

Drafts.—The draft, or bill of exchange, is the oldest form of negotiable paper, and is said to have existed as early as the first century. Drafts are governed by the same general rules as notes, and all the remarks of the foregoing paragraphs concerning negotiability are equally applicable here.

It is the duty of the holder of a bill to present it for acceptance without delay, and if it is payable at sight, or at a certain time after sight, no right of action will accrue against any person until it has been so presented. If it be not accepted, when properly presented, or, if accepted, be not paid when due, the further duty devolves on the holder to have it regularly protested by a notary public. This is essential, however, only in case of foreign bills, and is not required for inland exchange or notes. Simple notice in the latter case is sufficient.

Checks.—A check on bank is a species of bill of exchange, but is governed by somewhat different rules from the ordinary bill. It need not be presented for acceptance, for a bank is bound to pay at any time if it have funds of the drawer on deposit; nor is it material that the holder delay presentment for payment. A check should, however, be presented immediately; this the drawer has a right to expect, and the delay is at the holder's risk, for if the bank fails in the meantime, the loss falls on him, if the drawer had funds on deposit sufficient to have paid the check had it been timely presented.

Certifying a check practically amounts to an acceptance and binds the bank as an acceptor.

Checks should be drawn to order to guard against loss and theft, and at the same time it acts as a receipt of the payee. A check is not a payment until it has been cashed. In paying a forged check the loss falls on the bank, which is bound to know the signature of its own depositors, and, in like manner, if the check has been fraudulently raised, the drawer is chargeable only with the original amount.

INNS AND INN-KEEPERS.

An Inn is a public house for the lodging and entertainment of travelers for compensation, and the person who conducts such house is called an inn-keeper. To enable him to obtain his compensation the law invests an inn-keeper with peculiar privileges, giving him a lien upon the personal property brought into the inn by the guest, and on the other hand holds him to a strict degree of responsibility to the guest if the goods are lost or stolen.

The essential character of an inn is, that it is open for all who may desire to visit it ; hence, a mere private boarding-house, or lodging-house, cannot, in any proper sense, be regarded as an inn; nor will a coffee-house or restaurant come within the term. A person who entertains travelers occasionally, although he may receive compensation, is not an inn-keeper, nor liable as such, provided he does not hold himself out in that character.

An Inn-keeper is bound to receive all travelers and wayfaring persons who may apply to him, and to provide entertainment for them, if he can accommodate them, unless they are drunk, or disorderly, or afflicted with contagious diseases. If a person be disorderly he may not only refuse to receive him, but even after he has received him may eject him from the house.

He is further bound to exercise a high degree of care over the person and property of his guests, and is held to a strict responsibility for all loss or damage which may occur through his negligence. This responsibility extends not only to his own acts, and the acts of his servants, but also to the acts of his other guests. The liability of an inn-keeper commences from the time the goods are brought into the inn or delivered to any of the inn-keeper's servants; and a delivery into the personal custody of the inn-keeper is not necessary in order to make him responsible. He is not liable for what are termed the acts of God, or the public enemy; nor for property destroyed without his negligence by accidental fire; and, generally, the inn-keeper will be exonorated if the negligence of the guest occasion the loss in such a way that the loss would not have happened if the guest had used the ordinary care that a prudent man may be reasonably expected to have taken under the circumstances.

The strict liability of an inn-keeper has been much modified by statute, particularly in regard to money and valuables, and where the inn-keeper provides, in the office or some other convenient place in the hotel, an iron safe for the keeping of money,. jewels, etc., and notifies his guests of that fact, and the guest neglects to avail himself of the opportunity thus afforded, the inn-keeper will not be liable for the losses sustained by the guest by theft or otherwise.

A guest, in the restricted and legal sense of that term, is the only person who is entitled to the privileges of protection, and to entitle him to this he must have the character of a traveler, a mere sojourner or temporary lodger, in distinction from one who engages for a fixed period, and at a certain agreed rate; but if a party is in fact a wayfarer, and his visit is only transient, it matters not how long he remains, provided he retains this character Thus, regular boarders by the week or month are not guests, nor are they entitled to the privileges of guests; and on the other hand, in the absence of an enabling statute, the landlord is not, as to them, an inn-keeper, and as such entitled to a lien on their effects for his compensation.

COMMON CARRIERS.

Generally.—A common carrier is one who undertakes for hire to transport the persons or goods of such as choose to employ him, from one point to another, and who does this as a business. The law compels him to take the goods or persons of all who may apply and to make due transport of them; it gives him a lien on such goods or on the baggage of passengers for his compensation, but at the same time holds him liable for all loss or injury, even though occurring without any fault or neglect on his part. Included under this head are dray and truckmen, hackmen, stage coach, railway and steamboat companies, and indeed all who hold themselves out as transporters, either of persons or goods, whether by land or water.

•*Carriers of Passengers.*—A carrier of passengers is bound to receive all who apply; to treat all alike; to provide proper carriages and not to overload them; to stop at proper intervals for rest or food; to carry his passengers over the whole route contracted for, and to exercise the utmost care in protecting them from peril while on the journey. Failing in any of these particulars he is responsible, not only to the extent of the actual damage caused thereby, but frequently for pain and injury to the feelings.

In the sale of a ticket for transportation the foregoing is the implied agreement on the part of the carrier, and the passenger on the other hand accepts such ticket and contracts for passage subject to the reasonable regulations of the company.

A carrier of passengers is liable for any loss or damage to the baggage of his passengers, but only to the extent of what may reasonably and naturally be carried as baggage. This would not include large sums of money, nor merchandise, and, as a rule, damages in this respect are limited to such articles of necessity and personal convenience as are usually carried by travelers. Nor will the carrier be liable for any baggage not delivered to him or his servants; and hence, if the passenger keeps his baggage about his person, or in his own hands, or within his sight and immediate control, he assumes the risk of loss, and the carrier will not be held liable unless himself in fault.

Carriers of Goods.—A common carrier is an insurer of the safe transportation and delivery of all property intrusted to him for carriage, except as against such losses as are caused by the immediate act of God or the public enemy, and this liability continues until the goods have arrived at their destination and for a reasonable time after they are unloaded. But after safe delivery in the freight depot of the carrier and a reasonable time has elapsed for their removal, and particularly if notice of their arrival has been given to the consignee, the liability of the carrier as such ceases, and he will hold the property as a warehouseman only. In this latter event he will be bound to no more than ordinary care.

The acts of God are held to extend only to such inevitable accidents as occur without the intervention of man's agency. Hence, the carrier is not responsible for losses occurring from natural causes, such as frost, fermentation, evaporation or natural decay of perishable articles, nor for the natural and necessary wear in the course of transportation, provided he exercises all reasonable care to have the loss or deterioration as little as practicable.

Carriers, both by land and water, are bound to take the goods of all who offer, and if they refuse, without just excuse, are liable to an action; yet they may restrict their business within such limits as they may deem expedient, and are not bound to accept goods out of the usual line of their business. They may also qualify their responsibility by notice brought to the knowledge of the shipper and assented to by him, but cannot even then excuse gross negligence on their part.

Warehousemen are persons who receive goods and merchandise to be stored for hire, and is the character sustained by a carrier after the goods have reached their destination. A warehouseman is bound to use ordinary care in preserving such goods and merchandise, and his neglect so to do will render him liable for any damage that may accrue. His liability commences as soon as the goods arrive at the warehouse.

Sleeping Cars.—Though sleeping cars are, comparatively, a modern invention, their wide use and general adoption by the public has already created quite a voluminous mass of law upon the subject, and the rights, both of the companies and the public, have become tolerably well defined. The service of the railway companies and of the sleeping car companies, though rendered in connection, are entirely separate and distinct. The business of the former is to furnish transportation, of the latter to provide accommodations that travelers may sleep, and in so doing they deal only with persons who are provided with tickets entitling them to transportation by the railway company over whose lines they operate.

The sleeping car companies are not common carriers, like the railway companies, nor are they subject to the duties or responsibilities of carriers, nor can they be considered as inn-keepers, though performing many of their offices. They are not, therefore, insurers of the safety of all property taken into the car by one who has purchased the use of a berth. They are, however, bound to afford protection to a sleeping passenger, and to exercise a reasonable care that he does not suffer loss. The faithful performance of this undertaking is the limit of their duty in this respect. They must keep a watch during the night to see that no unauthorized persons intrude themselves into the car, and take reasonable care to prevent thefts by the occupants; failing in this, they are liable for neglect.

The measure of their liability is limited to the value of such articles as are usually and ordinarily carried for comfort and convenience: the small articles usually carried in the hand, the clothing and personal ornaments of the passenger, and a reasonable sum of money for traveling expenses.

The nature of the employment of the sleeping car companies is public, and in this respect is the same as a common carrier or inn-keeper. They must treat all persons with fairness, and without unjust discrimination. Where there are berths not engaged, it is their duty to furnish them to unobjectionable applicants on tender of the customary price.

The passenger, when he is assigned a berth, impliedly agrees to conduct himself in a quiet and orderly manner, to take good care of the berth while in his possession, and surrender the same at the end of his journey in as good condition as when assigned to him, necessary wear excepted. The company, on the other hand, impliedly agrees that it will use ordinary and proper means to preserve order in the car during the journey, and especially during the sleeping hours; that it will furnish such conveniences as are necessary to the health and comfort of the passenger and permit him to quietly and peaceably occupy the berth engaged by him during the journey.

THE LAW OF THE ROAD.

General Principles.—To prevent collisions, and to secure the safety and convenience of travelers meeting and passing each other upon the highway, a code of rules has been adopted which constitutes what is called the law of the road. These rules, originally established by custom, have, in many instances, been re-enacted and declared by statute, and are of general and uniform observance in all parts of the United States. In general, they apply to private ways, as well as public roads, and, indeed, extend to all places appropriated, either by law or in fact, for the purposes of travel.

The fundamental rule, applicable alike to all who use a traveled way, is, that every person must exercise reasonable care, adapted to the place and circumstances, to prevent collision and avoid accidents, and to this all other rules are subsidiary. No one will be entitled to redress for an injury sustained on the highway where his own negligence contributed to such injury, nor will the fact that a fellow-traveler fails to observe the law in the use of the road absolve another who is in the right from the duty of exercising ordinary care to avoid injury to himself or to prevent injury to the party who is in the wrong. At the same time, a person lawfully using a public highway has a right to assume that a fellow-traveler will observe the law and exercise ordinary care and prudence, and to govern his own conduct in determining his use of the road accordingly. This assumption he may rely on, not to justify carelessness on his own part, but to warrant him in pursuing his business in a convenient manner.

Vehicles.—It is a primary rule that vehicles meeting on a highway must bear or keep to the right. This, however, applies only to passing vehicles, for a person having before him the entire road free from carriages or other obstructions, and having no notice of any carriage behind him, is at liberty to travel upon any part of the way as suits his convenience or pleasure, and no blame can be imputed to him. But while a traveler may well occupy any part of the road if no other is using any portion of it, he must, upon all occasions of the meeting of another, reasonably turn to the right; and in all cases of a crowded condition of a thoroughfare must keep to the right of the center or traveled part of the way. A driver may, indeed, pass on the left side of the road, or across it, for the purpose of stopping at a house, a store, or other object on that side; but he must not interfere or obstruct another lawfully passing on that side; and if he does, he acts at his peril, and must answer for the consequences of his violation of duty. In such case he must pass before or wait until the person on that side of the way has passed on

Where two drivers are moving in the same direction, the one in advance is entitled to the road, provided he does not obstruct it, and is not bound to turn out for the other if there is room for the latter to pass on either side; if, however, there is not sufficient room to pass, the foremost traveler should yield an equal share of the road, on request made, if that is practicable. If it is not practicable, then they must defer passing until they reach more favorable grounds. If the leading traveler then refuses to comply with the request to permit the other to pass him, he will be answerable for such refusal. Ordinarily, when a driver attempts to pass another on a public road, he does so at his peril, and will be held responsible for all damages which he causes to the one whom he attempts to pass, and whose right to the proper use of the road is as great as his, unless the latter is guilty of such recklessness, or even gross carelessness, as would bring disaster upon himself.

The rule requiring persons meeting upon the highway to keep to the right is not imperative, however, and where a driver cannot safely turn to the right on meeting another vehicle, the law will absolve him from negligence in not attempting impossibilities; but where it is not practicable to pass to the right, either of the travelers should stop a reasonable time until the other passes; nor will the rule apply in the winter season, when the depth of snow renders it difficult or impossible to ascertain where the center of the road is. In such cases the center of the road is the beaten or traveled track, without reference to the worked part of the road. Again, the rule does not apply when one vehicle is passing along one street and another is passing into said street from a cross street.

A traveler is bound to keep his harness and carriage in good condition, and is liable for any damage that may result from a failure to do so; he must not drive at an immoderate rate of speed, and must yield the road to a heavier or loaded vehicle.

Equestrians are not governed by the same stringent rules that apply to drivers of vehicles, and usually all that is required of them is to exercise prudent care under the existing circumstances. They need not turn out in any particular direction or meeting another horseman or a vehicle, but in crowded thoroughfares must keep to the proper side in passing, and must yield the traveled part of the road to a wagon.

Pedestrians have a right to use the carriage-way as well as the sidewalk, and drivers must exercise reasonable care to avoid injuring them, but a foot-passenger in crossing the street of a city has no prior right of way over a passing vehicle; both are bound to act with prudence to avoid an accident, and it is as much the duty of the pedestrian to look out for passing vehicles as it is for the driver to see that he does not run over any one; nor does the rule requiring vehicles to keep to the right apply to carriages and foot-passengers, for, as regards a foot-passenger, a carriage may go on either side.

LANDLORD AND TENANT.

The relation of landlord and tenant exists by virtue of a contract for the use or occupation of lands or tenements, either for a definite period, for life, or at will. It is usually created by express contract, but its existence will be implied by law whenever there is an ownership of land on the one hand and an occupation of it by permission on the other. In every such case it will be presumed that the occupant intends to compensate the owner for such use. While the relation may be inferred from a variety of circumstances, the most obvious acknowledgment is the payment of rent. If a tenant under an express contract hold over after the termination of his term, the landlord may consider him as a tenant, and, indeed, is so understood, unless he takes some steps to eject him. If the landlord receives rent from him, or by any other act admits the tenancy, a new leasing begins, and can only be terminated by a proper notice to quit.

The rights and obligations of the parties are usually considered as having commenced from the date of the lease, if there be one, and no other time has been designated as the commencement of the tenancy, or, if there be no date from the delivery of the papers, and if there be no writings, from the time the tenant entered into possession.

The Landlord is bound to protect the possession of

his tenant, and to defend him against every one asserting a paramount right. Nor can the landlord do any act himself calculated to disturb the enjoyment of the tenant. He must, unless otherwise agreed, pay all taxes and assessments on the property, and all other charges of his own creation; and if the tenant, in order to protect himself in the enjoyment of the land, is compelled to make a payment which should have been made by the landlord, he may call upon his landlord to reimburse him, or deduct the amount from the rent.

The landlord has no right of possession during the continuance of the lease, nor indeed any substantial rights in the property further than such as may be necessary to protect his reversionary interests. He may go upon the premises peaceably and during reasonable hours, for the purpose of viewing same and ascertaining whether any waste or injury has been committed, and may make such repairs as are necessary to prevent waste; but he is under no obligation to make any repairs, nor does he guarantee that the premises are reasonably fit for the purposes for which they were taken. Nor can the tenant make any repairs at the expense of the landlord in the absence of a special agreement.

The tenant is entitled to all the rights incident to possession, and to the use of all the privileges appendant to the land, and, on the other hand, is personally liable for any misuse of same, or any nuisance or obstruction he may erect. He must use the premises in such a manner that no substantial injury shall be done them, and that they may revert to the landlord at the end of the term unimpaired by any negligent or willful conduct on his part. He must keep the premises in fair repair at his own expense, but is not bound to rebuild structures which have accidentally become ruinous during his occupation; nor is he answerable for incidental wear and tear, nor accidental fire, or flood.

He must further punctually pay the rent reserved, or if none have been specifically reserved, then such reasonable compensation as the premises are fairly worth. In the absence of special agreement he must pay only for the time he has had the beneficial enjoyment, but if he has agreed to pay for an entire term, as a rule nothing short of an eviction will excuse him from such payment. If he is evicted by a third person, or if the landlord annoys him by the erection of a nuisance, or renders the premises untenantable, or makes his occupation so uncomfortable as to justify his removal, he will be discharged from the payment of rent.

The rights and liabilities of the relation are not confined to the immediate parties, but attach to all persons to whom the estate is transferred, or who may succeed to the possession of the premises. A landlord may not violate his tenant's rights by a sale of the property, nor can the tenant avoid his responsibiiity by assigning his term. The purchaser of the property becomes, in one case, the landlord, with all his rights and remedies, while in the other the assignee of the tenant assumes all the responsibilities of the latter, but the original lessee is not thereby discharged from his obligations.

The tenancy may be terminatea in a variety of ways. If for a definite time, or conditioned on the happening of a certain event, it expires by its own limitation, and usually, when depending upon the express conditions of a lease, no notice to quit is necessary. If from year to year, or at will, a notice is always necessary. This must be in writing, and explicitly require the tenant to surrender up the premises. It must be served upon the tenant and afford the statutory notice in regard to time. A breach of any of the covenants of the lease will forfeit the tenant's rights, and when a tenancy has been terminated, by whatever cause, the landlord's right to re-enter becomes absolute.

The largest bell in the world is the great bell of Moscow, at the foot of the Kremlin. Its circumference at the bottom is nearly 68 feet, and its height more than 21 feet. In its stoutest part it is 23 inches thick, and its weight has been computed to be 443,772 lbs. It has never been hung, and was probably cast on the spot where it now stands. A piece of the bell is broken off. The fracture is supposed to have been occasioned by water having been thrown upon it when heated by the building erected over it being on fire.

WEATHER WISDOM.

HERSCHEL'S WEATHER TABLE.

FOR FORETELLING THE WEATHER, THROUGHOUT ALL THE LUNATIONS OF EACH YEAR, FOREVER

This table, and the accompanying remarks, are the result of many years' actual observation, the whole being constructed on a due consideration of the attraction of the Sun and Moon, in their several positions respecting the Earth, and will, by simple inspection, show the observer what kind of weather will most probably follow the entrance of the Moon into any of its quarters, and that so near the truth as to seldom or never be found to fail.

If New Moon, First Quarter, Full Moon or Last Quarter happens	In Summer.	In Winter.
Between midnight and 2 o'clock	Fair	Frost unless wind Southwest.
" 2 and 4 morning	Cold and showers	Snow and stormy.
" 4 and 6 "	Rain	Rain.
" 6 and 8 "	Wind and rain	Stormy.
" 8 and 10 "	Changeable	Cold rain if wind W., snow if E.
" 10 and 12 "	Frequent showers	Cold and high wind.
" 12 and 2 afternoon	Very rainy	Snow or rain.
" 2 and 4 "	Changeable	Fair and mild.
" 4 and 6 "	Fair	Fair.
" 6 and 8 "	Fair if wind N. W.	Fair and frosty if wind N. or N. E.
" 8 and 10 "	Rainy if S. or S. W.	Rain or snow if South or S. W.
" 10 and midnight	Fair	Fair and frosty.

SUNSET COLORS.—A gray, lowering sunset, or one where the sky is green or yellowish green, indicates rain. A red sunrise, with clouds lowering later in the morning, also indicates rain.

HALO (SUN DOGS).—By halo we mean the large circles, or parts of circles, about the sun or moon. A halo occurring after fine weather indicates a storm.

CORONA.—By this term we mean the small colored circles frequently seen around the sun or moon. A corona growing smaller indicates rain; growing larger, fair weather.

RAINBOWS.—A morning rainbow is regarded as a sign of rain; an evening rainbow of fair weather.

SKY COLOR.—A deep blue color of the sky, even when seen through clouds, indicates fair weather; a growing whiteness, an approaching storm.

FOG.—Fogs indicate settled weather. A morning fog usually breaks away before noon.

VISIBILITY.—Unusual clearness of the atmosphere, unusual brightness or twinkling of the stars, indicate rain.

CLOUDS.—In observing clouds, we observe their kinds, motions and outlines. The clouds frequently called "mare's tails" we term Cirri. They are marked by their light texture, fibrous and sundered as in the "mare's tail," or interlacing as in the far-spreading white cloud, which produces the halo. Small, regularly formed groups of these clouds are frequently seen in fair and settled weather. The Cirri are also the clouds on the forepart of the storm. In this case they are usually more abundant, their outline is very ragged, and they generally blend into a white, far-reaching cloud-bank. The cloud well known as "cotton bales," or "thunder heads," we term cumulus. When they appear during the heat of the day and pass away in the evening, continued fair weather may be expected. When they increase with rapidity, sink into the lower part of the atmosphere, and remain as the evening approaches, rain is at hand. If loose patches appear thrown out from their surfaces, showers may be expected. The clouds usually seen after nightfall, lying in one horizontal plane, and not of great extent, are attendant on fine weather. Small, black, inky clouds and dark scud indicate rain.

BAROMETER.— In using the barometer, we should notice whether it be greatly above or below the mean height and the rapidity of its rise or fall. If it be higher and steady, continued fair, though not cloudless weather may be expected. If it be lower and falling, rain, or at least damp, cloudy weather, is at hand. A rapid rise or fall (greater than 0.01 inch per hour) indicates continued unsettled weather and much wind.

FROST.— The first frost and last frost are usually preceded by a temperature very much above the mean.

HEIGHTS OF WATERFALLS.

	FEET.
Cerosola Cascade, Alps, Switzerland	2,400
Falls of Arve, Savoy	1,100
Falls of St. Anthony, Upper Mississippi	60
Falls of Terni, near Rome	300
Fryer's, near Lochness, Scotland	200
Genesee Falls, Rochester, N. Y.	96
Lanterbaum, Lake Theen, Switzerland	900
Lidford Cascade, Devonshire, England	100
Missouri Falls, North America	90
Natchikin Falls, Kamschatka	300
Niagara Falls, North America	164
Mont Morency Falls, Canada, Quebec	250
Nile Cataracts, Upper Egypt	40
Passaic Falls, New Jersey	71
Tivoli Cascade, near Rome	40
Waterfall Mountain Cascade, South Africa	85

Great fire at Washington, broke out December 15, 1883. Great fire in New York occurred in December, 1885. Over 500 buildings and $20,000,000 worth of property was destroyed. The second great fire occurred on September 6, 1839. Over $10,000,000 worth of property was destroyed. Great fire at Chicago, Ill., was in October, 1871.

⁕ James Fisk was shot in the Grand Central Hotel on Broadway, N. Y., on January 6, 1872.

QUALIFICATIONS FOR VOTING IN EACH STATE OF THE UNION.

STATES.	Voters must be males, 21 years old, and	Previous residence required.		
		State.	County.	Precinct.
Alabama	Citizens or have declared intentions	1 year	3 months	1 month
Arkansas	Citizens or have declared intentions	1 year	6 months	1 month
California	Actual citizens	1 year	90 days	30 days
Colorado	Citizens or have declared intentions	6 months		
Connecticut	Actual citizens	1 year	6 months	6 months
Delaware	Actual county tax-payers	1 year	1 month	
Florida	United States citizens or have declared intentions	1 year	6 months	
Georgia	Actual citizens	1 year	6 months	
Illinois	Actual citizens	1 year	90 days	30 days
Indiana	Citizens or have declared intentions	6 months	60 days	30 days
Iowa	Actual citizens	6 months	60 days	
Kansas	Citizens or have declared intentions	6 months		30 days
Kentucky	Free white male citizens	2 years	2 years	60 days
Louisiana	Citizens or have declared intentions	1 year	6 months	30 days
Maine	Actual citizens	3 months		
Maryland	Actual citizens	1 year	6 months	
Massachusetts	Citizens	1 year		6 months
Michigan	Citizens or have declared intentions	3 months		10 days
Minnesota	Citizens or have declared intentions	4 months		10 days
Mississippi	Actual citizens	6 months	1 month	
Missouri	Citizens or have declared intentions	1 year	60 days	
Nebraska	Citizens or have declared intentions	6 months		
Nevada	Citizens or have declared intentions	6 months	30 days	

QUALIFICATIONS FOR VOTING, ETC.—(Continued).

STATES.	Voters must be males, 21 years old, and	Previous residence required.		
		State.	County.	Precinct.
New Hampshire	Actual citizens			Town 6 m.
New Jersey	Actual citizens	1 year	5 months	
New York	Actual citizens	1 year	4 months	30 days
North Carolina	Actual citizens	12 months	90 days	
Ohio	Actual citizens	1 year		
Oregon	Citizens or have declared intentions	6 months		
Pennsylvania	Actual citizens	1 year		2 months
Rhode Island	Actual tax-paying citizens	1 year		Town 6 m.
South Carolina	Actual citizens	1 year	60 days	
Tennessee	Actual citizens	12 months	6 months	6 months.
Texas	Citizens or have declared intentions	1 year		
Vermont	Actual citizens	1 year		Town 3 m
Virginia	Actual citizens	12 months		
West Virginia	Actual citizens	1 year	60 days	
Wisconsin	Citizens or have declared intentions	1 year		

Women are entitled to full suffrage in Utah, Washington, and Wyoming Territories. They can vote at school elections in Massachussets and a few other States.

REGISTRATION.—In California, Connecticut, Illinois, Iowa, Maine, Massachusetts, Michigan, Minnesota, Nebraska, New Hampshire, Rhode Island, Vermont, Virginia and Wisconsin registration is required by law. In Colorado, Florida, Maryland, Mississippi, Nevada, North Carolina, Pennsylvania and South Carolina registration is a constitutional requirement. In Kansas and Missouri registration is required in cities only, in Ohio in the cities of Cincinnati and Cleveland only, and in New York and New Jersey in cities of 10,000 inhabitants and upward. In Alabama, Delaware, Georgia, Indiana, Kentucky, Louisiana and Tennessee no registration is required; and in Arkansas, Texas and West Virginia it is prohibited by the State Constitution.

INTEREST LAWS AND STATUTES OF LIMITATIONS.

STATES AND TERRITORIES.	INTEREST LAWS.		STATUTES OF LIMITATIONS.		
	Legal Rate.	Rate Allowed by Contract.	Judgments, Years.	Notes, Years.	Open Accounts, Years.
	per ct	*per ct*			
Alabama	8	8	20	6	3
Arkansas	6	10	10	5	3
Arizona	10	Any rate.	2	3	2
California	7	Any rate.	5	4	2
Colorado	10	Any rate.	6	6	6
Connecticut	6	6	17	17	6
Dakota	7	12	20	6	6
Delaware	6	6	21	6	3
District of Columbia	6	10	12	3	3
Florida	8	Any rate.	20	5	3
Georgia	7	8	7	7	4
Idaho	10	18	6	5	4
Illinois	6	8	7	10	5
Indiana	6	8	20	10	6
Iowa	6	10	20	10	5
Kansas	7	12	5	5	3
Kentucky	6	10	15	15	2
Louisiana	5	8	10	5	3
Maine	6	Any rate.	20	6	6
Maryland	6	6	12	3	3
Massachusetts	6	Any rate.	20	6	6
Michigan	7	10	6	6	2
Minnesota	7	10	10	6	6
Mississippi	6	10	7	6	3
Missouri	6	10	5	10	5
Montana	10	Any rate.	6	6	2
Nebraska	7	10	5	5	5
Nevada	10	Any rate.	6	6	4
New Hampshire	6	6	20	6	6
New Jersey	6	6	20	6	6
New Mexico	6	12	15	6	4
New York*	6	6	20	6	6
North Carolina	6	8	10	3	3
Ohio	6	8	5	15	6
Oregon	8	10	10	6	1
Pennsylvania	6	6	5	6	6
Rhode Island	6	Any rate.	20	6	6

INTEREST LAWS, Etc.—(Continued).

STATES AND TERRITORIES.	INTEREST LAWS.		STATUTES OF LIMITATIONS.		
	Legal Rate.	Rate Allowed by Contract.	Judgments, Years.	Notes, Years.	Open Accounts, Years.
	per ct	*per ct.*			
South Carolina......	7	Any rate.	10	6	6
Tennessee	6	10	10	6	6
Texas...............	8	12	15	4	2
Utah................	10	Any rate.	5	4	2
Vermont.............	6	6	8	6	6
Virginia.............	6	8	10	5	2
Washington Ter.....	10	Any rate.	6	6	3
West Virginia.......	6	6	10	10	3
Wisconsin	7	10	20	6	6
Wyoming	12	Any rate.	5	5	4

*New York has by a recent law legalized any rate of interest on call loans of $5,000 or upwards, on collateral security.

ANALYSIS OF THE VOTE FOR PRESIDENT IN 1884.

The following is an analysis of the popular vote for President in 1884:

Northern Democratic vote..................3,194,832
Southern Democratic vote..................1,716,143
Northern Republican vote..................3,589,056
Southern Republican vote..................1,255,966
Republican vote in Republican States........2,599,331
Republican vote in Democratic States........2,246,091
Democratic vote in Democratic States........2,719,098
Democratic vote in Republican States........2,191,777
St. John vote in Republican States..........   99.261
St. John vote in Democratic States..........   52,548
Butler vote in Republican States............   93,327
Butler vote in Democratic States............   40,500

UNITED STATES CUSTOMS DUTIES.
(ABRIDGED.)

Animals for breeding purposes	free on Consular certificate.
" otherwise	20 per cent.
Ale, Porter, and Beer, in bottles	35 cts per gallon
" " " in casks	20 cts per gallon
Books, charts, new	25 per cent
" " for Colleges, Libraries, or printed more than 20 years, or in use abroad more than 1 year and not for sale	free
Boots, Shoes, Leather	35 per cent
Bronze, manufactures of	45 per cent
Carpets, Audersson, Axminster, and all woven whole for room	45 cts per sq yd and 30 per cent
" Brussels, Tapestry, printed on the warp, or otherwise	30 cts per sq yd and 30 per cent
" Brussels, wrought by the Jacquard machine	44 cts per sq yd and 35 per cent
" Saxony, Wilton & Tornay Velvet, wrought by the Jacquard machine	45 cts per sq yd and 30 per cent
" Treble Ingrain, three ply, and Worsted China Venetian	12 cts per sq yd and 30 per cent
" Velvet, Patent or Tapestry, printed on the warp or otherwise	25 cts per sq yd and 30 per cent
Carriages	35 per cent
China—Porcelain and Parian Ware, plain	55 per cent
" Gilded, ornamented or decorated	60 per cent
Cigars, Cheroots, and Cigarettes	$2.50 per lb and 25 per cent
Clocks	35 per cent
Clothing, wholly or in part of wool	40 cts per lb and 35 per cent
" Linen	40 per cent
" Silk component	50 per cent
" All other descriptions	35 per cent
Coal and Coke, bituminous	75 cts per ton
Coral, cut or manufactured	25 per cent
Cutlery, Table, etc	35 per cent
" Pen, Jack and Pocket Knives	50 per cent
Diamonds and other precious stones, set	25 per cent
" Unset	10 per cent
Effects, personal, old	free on oath
Engravings	25 per cent
Furniture	35 per cent

Furs, manufactured	20 per cent
Gilt and plated ware, etc.	35 per cent
Glass ware	45 per cent
Gloves, Kid	50 per cent
Gold and silver ware, etc.	45 per cent
Guns	25 per cent
Hats (ladies'), chip, straw, or other vegetable substance, hair, whalebone	20 per cent
" Trimmed with silk and artificial flowers exceeding the value of the hat	50 per cent
" With feathers and artificial flowers	50 per cent
Hay	$2 per ton
Household effects, in use abroad one year and not for sale	free
Instruments, professional, in use	free
Iron, Pig and Scrap	$6.72 per ton
Jewelry—Gold, Silver or imitation	25 per cent
" Jet and Imitation of	25 per cent
Laces, Silk	50 per cent
" Silk and Cotton	50 per cent
" Thread	35 per cent
Leather, manufactures of	35 per cent
Linen—Table, Toweling, etc.	30 per cent
" " " "	35 per cent
Machinery, brass or iron	45 per cent
" Copper or Steel	45 per cent
Musical Instruments	25 per cent
Oils—Animal	25 per cent
" Castor	80 cts per gallon
" Olive	25 per cent
Paintings	30 per cent
" if work of an American artist	free
" Frames for ditto	35 per cent
Photographs	25 per cent
Pipes—Meerschaum, Wood, and of all other material, except common clay	70 per cent
Prints or Engravings	25 per cent
Rubber Boots, Shoes, and other articles wholly of rubber (not fabrics)	25 per cent
" Braces, Suspenders, Webbing, etc., unless in part silk	30 per cent
" Silk, Cotton, Worsted or Leather.	50 per cent
Saddles and Harness	35 per cent
Shawls—Silk	50 per cent
" Camel's Hair or other wool	35 cts per lb and 40 per cent
Silk—Dress and Piece	50 per cent
Smokers' Articles	70 per cent
Snuff	50 cts per lb
Soap—Castile	20 cts per lb
" Fancy, Perfumed, Toilet, and Windsor	15 cts per lb

Statuary, Marble	50 per cent
Stereoscopic Views, on glass or paper	40 and 25 per cent respectively
Spirits—Brandy, Whisky, Gin, etc.	$2 per proof gallon
Umbrellas—Silk or Alpaca	50 per cent
Velvet—Silk	50 per cent
" Cotton or mostly cotton	40 per cent
Watches	25 per cent
Wines—All *still* Wines, such as Sherry, Claret, or Hock, in casks	50 cts per gallon
Ditto, in bottles of 1 pint and less	$1.60 per case
Ditto, in bottles of over 1 pint and less than 1 quart	1.60 per doz
All Champagnes and Sparkling Wines in bottles of ½ pints or less	1.75 per doz
Ditto, in bottles of over ½ pint and not more than 1 pint	$3.50 per doz
Ditto, in bottles of over 1 pint and not more than one quart	7.00 per doz
Ditto, in bottles of over 1 quart (extra)	2.25 per gallon

and 3 cts per bottle.

ARTICLES FREE OF DUTY.

Actors' costumes and effects intended for personal use.
Animals for breeding purposes.
Antiquities not for sale.
Articles and tools of trade.
Art works of American artists.
Bed feathers.
Birds, land and water fowl.
Books printed over twenty years.
Coal—anthracite.
Cocoa.
Coffee.
Collections of antiquities, etc., for use in colleges, museums, incorporated societies, etc.
Diamonds, rough.
Effects of American citizens dying abroad, if accompanied by Consular certificate.
Engravings (engraved over 20 years).
Farina.
Fertilizers.
Fruits and nuts.
Furs, undressed.
Hides, raw.
Household effects in use abroad over one year and not for sale.

India rubber.
Mineral waters, natural.
Mother of pearl, unmanufactured.
Natural history specimens (not for sale).
Newspapers.
Periodicals.
Personal effects when old and in use over one year.
Plants, trees and shrubs.
Rags, other than wool.
Rubber—crude.
Scientific instruments.
Skins—raw.
Tapioca.
Tea.
United States manufactures forwarded to foreign countries and returned.
Wax, Vegetable and Mineral.

Largest Cities of the Earth.
POPULATION ACCORDING TO LATEST CENSUS.

London, England	3,832,441
Paris, France	2,269,023
Canton, China (est.)	1,500,000
New York, United States	1,206,577
Berlin, Prussia	1,122,330
Vienna, Austria	1,103,857
Tschantshau-fu, China (est.)	1,000,000
Singau-fu, China (est.)	1,000,000
Siangtau, China (est.)	1,000,000
Tientsing, China (est.)	950,000
St. Petersburg, Russia	927,467
Philadelphia, United States	847,170
Tschingtu-fu, China (est.)	800,000
Moscow, Russia	748,000
Calcutta, India	683,329
Bombay, India	644,405
Constantinople, Turkey (est.)	600,000
Bangkok, India (est.)	600,000
Tschungking-fu, China (est.)	600,000

Hankow, China (est.)	600,000
Foochow, China (est.)	600,000
Tokio, Japan	594,283
Brooklyn, United States	566,689
Glasgow, Scotland	555,289
Liverpool, England	552,423
Chicago, United States	503,185
Sutchau, China (est.)	500,000
Schaohing, China (est.)	500,000
Peking, China (est.)	500,000
Naples, Italy	494,314
Nangkin, China (est.)	450,000
Birmingham, England	400,757
Hangtseheu-fu, China, (est.)	400,000
Fatschau, China (est.)	400,000
Madrid, Spain	397,690
Madras, India	397,552
Manchester, England	393,676
Boston, United States	390,406
Warsaw, Poland	383,973
Brussels, Belgium	377,084
Lyons, France	376,613
Buda-Pesth, Hungary	365,051
Marseilles, France	360,099
Jangtschau, China	360,000
St. Louis, United States	350,518
Baltimore, United States	332,313
Amsterdam, Holland	328,047
Cairo, Egypt	327,462
Milan, Italy	321,839
Leeds, England	309,126
Rome, Italy	300,467
Hamburg, Germany	289,849
Lucknow, India	284,779
Sheffield, England	284,410
Osaka, Japan	284,105
Breslau, Prussia	279,212
Shanghai, China	278,000
Rio de Janeiro, Brazil	274,972
Copenhagen, Denmark	273,727
Cincinnati, United States	255,809
Turin, Italy	252,832

Melbourne, Australia	252,000
Weihein, China (est.)	250,000
Taijuen-fu, China (est.)	250,000
Leinkhong, China (est.)	250,000
Dublin, Ireland	249,486
Barcelona, Spain	249,106
Lisbon, Portugal	246,343
Palermo, Italy	244,991
Mexico, Mexico	236,500
Taiwau-fu, China (est.)	235,000
San Francisco, United States	233,959
Munich, Bavaria	230,023
Tengtschau-fu, China (est.)	230,000
Kioto, Japan	229,810
Edinburgh, Scotland	228,075
Bordeaux, France	221,305
Bucharest, Roumania	221,000
Dresden, Saxony	220,818
New Orleans, United States	216,690
Belfast, Ireland	207,671
Bristol, England	206,503
Kagoshima, Japan (est.)	200,000
Hyderabad, India (est.)	200,000
Gwelior, India (est.)	200,000
Tsinau-fu, China (est.)	200,000
Jongping, China (est.)	200,000
Hutscheu, China (est.)	200,000
Teheran, Persia (est.)	200,000
Odessa, Russia	193,513
Sydney, Australia	187,381
Nottingham, England	186,656
Bradford, England	183,032
Genoa, Italy	179,515
Lisle, France	178,144
Buenos Ayres, Argentine Republic	177,787
Stockholm, Sweden	176,745
Salford, England	176,233

Population of Cities in the United States.

In response to a personal letter sent to the mayor of each of the following cities, their estimate of the present population is under the heading 1887. Where no 1887 estimate is given, no replies were received, and it is therefore to be supposed no change of any importance has taken place.

	1887.	1880.	1870.
New York City ...	1,500,000	1,206,299	942,292
Philadelphia, Pa ..	1,125,000	847,170	674,022
Brooklyn, N. Y. ...	750,000	566,663	396,099
Chicago, Ill	750,000	503,185	293,977
Boston, Mass.	362,000	362,839	250,526
St. Louis, Mo	450,000	350,518	310,864
Baltimore, Md.	460,000	332,313	267,354
Cincinnati, Ohio ...	300,000	255,139	216,239
San Francisco, Cal .	310,000	233,959	149,473
New Orleans, La ...	....	216,090	191,418
Cleveland, Ohio. ...	230,000	160,146	72,829
Pittsburgh, Pa.	....	156,389	86,076
Buffalo, N. Y.	240,000	155,134	117,714
Washington, D. C..	203,459	147,293	109,199
Newark, N. J.	160,000	136,508	105,059
Louisville, Ky	185,000	123,758	100,752
Jersey City, N. J ...	....	120,722	82,546
Detroit, Mich.	220,000	116,340	79,577
Milwaukee, Wis. ...	175,677	115,587	71,440
Providence, R. I ...	122,050	104,857	68,904
Albany, N. Y.	105,000	90,758	69,422
Rochester, N. Y. ..	125,000	89,366	62,386
Allegheny, Pa.	....	78,682	53,180
Indianapolis, Ind ..	90,000	75,056	48,244
Richmond, Va.	80,000	63,600	51,038
New Haven, Conn .	80,000	62,882	50,840
Lowell, Mass	70,000	59,475	40,928
Worcester, Mass. ..	68,389	58,291	41,105
Troy, N. Y.	65,000	56,747	46,464
Kansas City, Mo. ..	80,000	55,785	32,260
Cambridge, Mass. ..	62,000	52,669	39,634
Syracuse, N. Y.	80,000	51,792	43,051
Columbus, Ohio. ...	74,215	51,617	31,274
Paterson, N. J.	62,000	51,031	33,579
Toledo, Ohio.	73,500	50,137	31,584

Charleston, S. C.		49,984	48,956
Fall River, Mass		48,961	26,766
Minneapolis, Minn		46,887	13,066
Scranton, Pa.	86,666	45,850	35,092
Nashville, Tenn		43,350	25,865
Reading, Pa.	56,300	43,278	33,930
Wilmington, Del.	56,000	42,478	30,841
Hartford, Conn		42,015	37,180
Camden, N. J.		41,659	20,045
St. Paul, Minn.	145,000	41,473	20,030
Lawrence, Mass.		39,151	28,921
Dayton, Ohio.		38,678	30,473
Lynn, Mass.		38,274	28,233
Atlanta, Ga	60,846	37,409	27,789
Denver, Col	70,000	35,629	4,759
Oakland, Cal.	45,000	34,555	10,500
Utica, N. Y.		33,914	28,804
Portland, Me.	40,000	33,810	31,413
Memphis, Tenn.	75,000	33,592	40,226
Springfield, Mass.	40,000	33,340	26,703
Manchester, N. H.	40,000	32,630	23,536
St. Joseph, Mo.		32,431	10,565
Grand Rapids, Mich.		32,016	16,507
Hoboken, N. J.		30,999	20,297
Harrisburg, Pa.	40,000	30,762	23,104
Wheeling, W. Va.		30,737	19,280
Savannah, Ga.	45,492	30,709	28,235
Omaha, Neb.	85,000	30,518	16,083
Trenton, N. J.	47,000	29,910	22,874
Covington, Ky.	40,000	29,720	24,505
Evanston, Ind.		29,280	21,830
Peoria, Ill.	45,000	29,259	22,849
Mobile, Ala		29,132	32,034
Elizabeth, N. J.		28,289	20,832
Erie, Pa		27,737	19,646
Bridgeport, Conn	42,000	27,643	18,969
Salem, Mass.	28,500	27,563	24,117
Quincy, Ill		27,268	24,052
Fort Wayne, Ind.		26,888	17,718
New Bedford, Mass	35,000	26,845	21,320
Terre Haute, Ind		26,042	16,103
Lancaster, Pa©	30,000	25,769	20,233

Somerville, Mass.	32,000	24,933	14,685
Davenport, Iowa	26,000	24,831	20,038
Wilkesbarre, Pa	40,000	23,339	10,174
Des Moines, Iowa	35,000	22,408	12,025
Dubuque, Iowa		22,254	18,434
Galveston, Tex	40,000	22,248	13,818
Norfolk, Va		21,966	19,229
Auburn, N. Y	26,000	21,924	17,225
Holyoke, Mass		21,915	10,733
Augusta, Ga		21,891	15,389
Chelsea, Mass	28,000	21,782	18,547
Petersburg, Va	23,000	21,656	18,950
Sacramento, Cal		21,420	16,283
Taunton, Mass		21,213	18,629
Oswego, N. Y		21,116	20,910
Salt Lake, Utah		20,768	12,854
Springfield, Ohio	33,481	20,730	12,652
Bay City, Mich	32,000	20,693	7,004
San Antonio, Tex	42,500	20,550	12,256
Elmira, N. Y		20,541	15,863
Newport, Ky	20,400	20,430	15,087
Poughkeepsie, N. Y		20,207	20,080
Springfield, Ill	28,584	19,743	17,364
Altoona, Pa		19,710	10,610
Burlington, Iowa	27,000	19,450	14,930
Cohoes, N. Y	25,000	19,416	15,357
Gloucester, Mass	22,000	19,329	15,389
Lewiston, Me		19,083	13,600
Pawtucket, R. I		19,030	6,619
East Saginaw, Mich	16,000	19,016	11,350
Williamsport, Pa		18,934	16,030
Yonkers, N. Y		18,892	12,733
Haverhill, Mass	25,000	18,472	13,052
Zanesville, Ohio		18,113	10,011
Newburgh, N. Y	21,500	18,049	17,014
Council Bluffs, Iowa	27,000	18,063	10,020
Allentown, Pa		18,063	13,884
Waterbury, Conn	35,000	17,806	10,826
Portland, Oregon		17,577	8,293
Wilmington, N. C	20,000	17,350	13,446
Binghamton, N. Y	23,500	17,317	12,692
Bloomington, Ill		17,180	14,590

New Brunswick, N. J	25,000	17,166	15,058
Newton, Mass		16,995	12,825
Bangor, Me		16,856	18,289
Montgomery, Ala		16,713	10,588
Lexington, Kansas		16,656	14,801
Leavenworth, Kansas	29,150	16,546	17,873
Houston, Tex		16,513	9,382
Akron, Ohio		16,512	10,066
New Albany, Ind		16,423	14,396
Jackson, Mich		16,105	11,447
Woonsocket, R. I	20,000	16,059	11,527
Racine, Wis		16,031	9,880
Lynchburg, Va	22,240	15,959	6,825
Sandusky, Ohio		15,838	13,000
Oshkosh, Wis	25,000	15,748	12,663
Newport, R. I	19,560	15,693	12,251
Topeka, Kan	30,000	15,452	5,790
Youngstown, Ohio		15,435	8,075
Norwich, Conn		15,112	16,653
Atchison, Kan	21,000	15,105	7,054
Chester, Pa		14,997	9,485
La Fayette, Ind	25,000	14,860	13,506
La Crosse, Wis	31,000	14,505	7,785
Norwalk, Conn		13,956	12,119
York, Pa	20,000	13,940	11,003
Concord, N. H		13,843	12,241
Lincoln, R. I		13,765	7,889
Alexandria, Va	15,000	13,659	13,570
Schenectady, N. Y	18,000	13,655	11,026
Brockton, Mass		13,608	8,007
Newburyport, Mass		13,538	12,595
Lockport, N. Y	18,000	13,522	12,426
Nashua, N. H	16,000	13,397	10,543
Pittsfield, Mass		13,364	11,112
South Bend, Ind	22,000	13,280	7,206
Pottsville, Pa		13,253	12,384
Orange, N. J	16,000	13,207	9,348
Little Rock, Ark	29,000	13,138	12,380
Rockford, Ill	20,000	13,129	11,049
Fond du Lac, Wis	16,000	13,094	12,764
Norristown, Pa	17,000	13,063	10,753
Chattanooga, Tenn	36,000	12,892	6,093

Macon, Ga	35,000	12,749	10,810
Richmond, Ind	17,000	12,742	9,445
Biddeford, Me	14,000	12,651	10,282
Georgetown, D. C		12,578	11,384
San Jose, Cal	20,000	12,567	9,089
Fitchburg, Mass	16,500	12,429	11,260
Canton, Ohio		12,258	8,660
Rome, N. Y		12,194	11,000
Northampton, Mass		12,172	10,160
Warwick, R. I		12,164	10,458
Rutland, Vt		12,149	9,834
Hamilton, Ohio	17,000	12,122	11,081
Keokuk, Iowa	18,000	12,117	12,766
Steubenville, Ohio	16,000	12,003	8,107
Malden, Mass	12,017	12,017	7,367
Easton, Pa	13,000	11,924	10,987
Aurora, Ill	20,000	11,873	11,162
Vicksburg, Miss	18,105	11,814	12,443
Waltham, Mass	15,000	11,712	9,065
Dover, N. H		11,687	9,204
Danbury, Conn		11,666	8,753
Rock Island, Ill	13,000	11,659	7,890
Joliet, Ill	18,000	11,657	7,263
Derby, Conn		11,650	8,020
Galesburg, Ill		11,437	10,158
Portsmouth, Va		11,390	10,590
Burlington, Vt		11,365	14,387
Portsmouth, Ohio	12,000	11,321	10,592
Stamford, Conn	11,298	11,297	9,714
Chicopee, Mass	11,528	11,286	9,607
Muskegon, Mich		11,262	6,002
Logansport, Ind	15,283	11,198	8,950
Los Angelos, Cal	55,000	11,183	5,728
Attleborough, Mass		11,111	6,769
Hannibal, Mo	14,000	11,074	10,125
Austin, Tex	24,000	11,013	4,428
Chillicothe, Ohio	12,500	10,938	8,920
Woburn, Mass		10,931	8,560
Jacksonville, Ill		10,929	9,202
Virginia City, Nev		10,917	7,058
Watertown, N. Y	14,000	10,697	9,336
Cumberland, Md	12,000	10,693	8,056

Belleville, Ill.		10,683	8,146
Quincy, Mass.	14,000	10,570	7,442
Weymouth, Mass.		10,570	9,010
New London, Conn.		10,537	9,576
Saginaw, Mich.		10,525	7,460
Ogdensburgh, N. Y.	11,659	10,341	10,076
Madison, Wis.	13,500	10,324	9,176
Stockton, Cal.	16,000	10,282	10,066
Winona, Minn.		10,208	7,192
Shenandoah, Pa.		10,147	2,951
Marlborough, Mass.		10,127	8,474
Columbus, Ga.		10,123	7,401
Eau Claire, Wis.		10,119	2,293
Cedar Rapids, Iowa	20,000	10,104	5,940
Columbia, S. C.	15,000	10,036	9,298
Key West, Fla.		9,890	5,016
Mansfield, Ohio.		9,859	8,029
Knoxville, Tenn.		9,693	8,682
Portsmouth, N. H.		9,690	9,211
Newark, Ohio	14,000	9,600	6,698
Sedalia, Mo.		9,561	4,560
Auburn, Me.		9,555	6,169
Decatur, Ill.		9,547	7,161
Amsterdam, N. Y.		9,466	5,426
Jeffersonville, Ind.		9,357	7,254
Jamestown, N. Y.		9,357	5,336
Milford, Mass.		9,310	9,890
Raleigh, N. C.	14,000	9,265	7,790
East St. Louis, Ill.		9,185	5,644
Ithaca, N. Y.		9,105	8,462
Stillwater, Minn.	17,343	9,055	4,124
Clinton, Iowa.		9,052	6,129
Titusville, Pa.	10,000	9,046	8,039
Peabody, Mass.		9,028	7,343
Janesville, Wis.		9,019	8,798
Cairo, Ill.		9,011	6,267
Ottumwa, Iowa.		9,004	5,214
Alton, Ill.	14,000	8,975	8,665
Madison, Ind.		8,945	10,709

Places of Nativity of the Foreign-Born Inhabitants of the United States.

(Census of 1880.)

Germany	1,966,742	Russia	35,722
Ireland	1,854,571	Belgium	15,535
British America	717,084	Luxemburg	12,836
England	662,676	Hungary	11,526
Sweden	194,337	West Indies	9,484
Norway	181,729	Portugal	8,138
Scotland	170,136	Cuba	6,917
France	106,971	Spain	5,121
China	104,467	Australia	4,906
Switzerland	88,621	South America	4,566
Bohemia	85,361	India	1,707
Wales	83,302	Turkey	1,205
Mexico	68,399	Sandwich Islands	1,147
Denmark	64,196	Greece	776
Holland	58,090	Central America	707
Poland	48,557	Japan	401
Italy	44,230	Malta	305
Austria	39,663	Greenland	129

The great fire in London commenced on September 2, 1866, burned three days and three nights, destroyed eighty-nine churches, including St. Paul, the City Gates, the Royal Exchange, Custom House, Guildhall, and 13,200 houses, laying waste 400 streets.

The High Bridge and Obelisk which spans the river Witham, at Lincoln, England, was erected in 1763, occupies the site of the ancient chapel of St. Thomas the Martyr, in which the corporation founded a chantry in the reign of Edward I., probably that the priests might pray for the redemption of souls of ancient officials; for, as the reader will by this time know, they were no small sinners, whatever may be said of their reformed successors of the nineteenth century. In 1863 it underwent great alterations, and a fountain was erected and opened on the Prince of Wales' wedding-day, and called the "Albert Fountain," by Charles Doughty, Esq., Mayor.

Foreign Nations and their Rulers.

WITH POPULATION, AREA IN SQUARE MILES, CAPITAL, FORMS OF GOVERNMENT, RULERS, ETC.

Countries.	Population.	Sq. Miles.	Capitals.	Form of Government.	Present Head.	Title.	Accessor.	Present Age.
China	371,180,000	4,419,150	Peking	Abs. Desp.	Kuang Su	Emp.	1875	15
British Empire	315,885,000	8,991,254	London	Lim. Mon.	Victoria	Queen	1837	67
Russian Empire	202,683,124	8,459,229	St. Petersburg	Abs. Mon.	Alexander III	Emp.	1881	42
France and Colonies	63,672,048	970,477	Paris	Republic.	F. P. Jules Grevy	Pres.	1879	74
United States	*57,500,000	3,602,990	Washington	Republic.	Grover Cleveland	Pres.	1885	50
German Empire	45,234,061	208,683	Berlin	Lim. Mon.	William	Emp.	1861	90
Austro-Hung. Empire	39,206,052	261,591	Vienna	Lim. Mon.	Francis Joseph I	Emp.	1848	57
Japan	36,700,118	147,669	Tokio	Lim. Mon.	Mutsuhito	Emp.	1867	35
Holland and Colonies	33,042,238	778,187	The Hague	Lim. Mon.	William III	King.	1849	70
Turkish Empire	32,000,000	1,731,280	Constantin'ple	Abs. Mon.	Abdul Hamid II	Sultan	1876	39
Italy	28,459,451	111,410	Rome	Lim. Mon.	Humbert	King.	1878	43
Spain and Colonies	24,872,621	361,953	Madrid	Lim. Mon.	Marie Mercedes	Queen	1885	6
Sokoto	12,600,000	178,000	Sokoto	Abs. Desp.		Sultan		
Corea	10,519,000	91,430	Suel	Abs. Desp.				
Brazil	10,200,000	3,219,000	Rio de Janeiro	Lim. Mon.	Pedro II	Emp.	1831	62
Mexico	10,007,000	751,177	Mexico	Republic.	Porfrio Diaz	Pres.	1884	
Congo State	8,000,000	802		Fr. State.	Leopold	Sovereign	1876	51
Persia	7,653,600	636,000	Teheran	Abs. Desp.	Nasser ed Deen	Shah	1848	58

FOREIGN NATIONS AND THEIR RULERS, ETC.—(CONTINUED).

COUNTRIES.	Population.	Sq. Miles.	Capitals.	Form of Government.	Present Head.	Title.	Accessor.	Present Age.
Portugal and Colonies.	7,249,050	240,691	Lisbon	Lim. Mon	Louis	King	1861	49
Egypt †	6,806,381	494,000	Cairo	Abs. Mon	Mohammed Teyfik	Khedive	1879	34
Sweden and Norway	6,554,448	295,714	Stockholm	Lim. Mon	Oscar II	King	1872	58
Morocco	6,500,000	314,000	Fez	Abs. Desp	Mulai Hassan	Sultan	1873	..
Belgium	5,720,807	11,373	Brussels	Lim. Mon	Leopold II	King	1865	51
Siam	5,700,000	280,550	Bangkok	Abs. Desp	Khulalonkorn I	King	1868	34
Roumania †	5,376,000	46,314	Bucharest	Lim. Mon	Charles I	Prince	1866	48
Colombia	4,000,000	331,420	Bogato	Republic	Rafael Nunez	Pres	1884	..
Afghanistan	4,000,000	279,000	Cabul	Abs. Desp	Abdur'hm'n Kahn	Amir	1880	..
Argentine Republic	3,026,000	109,513	Buenos Ayres	Republic	Julio A. Roca	Pres	1880	..
Madagascar	3,000,000	228,570	Antananarivo	Abs. Desp	Ranavalo III	Queen	1883	..
Abyssinia	3,000,000	129,000		Abs. Desp	Johannes II	Sultan	1872	..
Saxony †	2,972,805	5,789	Dresden	Lim. Mon	Albert	King	1873	59
Peru	2,970,000	805,040	Lima	Republic		Pres	1885	..
Switzerland	2,846,102	15,981	Berne	Republic	Adolph Duecher	Pres	1885	..
Bolivia	2,325,000	481,600	La Paz	Republic	Narciso Campero	Pres	1880	..
Bokhara	2,130,000	92,300	Samarcand	Abs. Desp		Khan	1885	..
Venezuela	2,121,988	566,159	Caracas	Republic	Joaquin Crespo	Pres	1884	..
Chili	2,115,340	307,525	Santiago	Republic	Dom. Santa Maria	Pres	1881	..
Denmark	2,045,179	14,842	Copenhagen	Lim. Mon	Christian IX	King	1863	69
Bulgaria †	2,000,000	24,700	Sofia	Lim. Mon	Alexander	Prince	1879	29
Greece	1,979,453	24,977	Athens	Lim. Mon	George I	King	1864	41

FOREIGN NATIONS AND THEIR RULERS, Etc.—(Concluded).

Countries.	Population.	Sq. Miles.	Capitals.	Form of Government.	Present Head.	Title.	Accessor.	Present Age.
Wurtemburg †	1,971,118	7,531	Stuttgart	Lim. Mon	Charles	King	1864	64
Servia	1,820,000	18,757	Belgrave	Lim. Mon	Milan	King	1868	33
Oman	1,600,000	81,000	Muscat	Abs. Mon	Seyyed Torrkee	Sultan	1871	
Guatemala	1,278,311	46,774	N'w Guat'mala	Republic	M. L. Barillas	Pres	1885	
Ecuador	1,146,000	248,312	Quito	Republic	J. M. P. Caamano	Pres	1883	
Tripoli †	1,010,000	399,000	Tripoli	Abs. Mon	Ahmed Rassim	Gov. Gen.	1881	
Transvaal	800,000	110,193	Pretoria	Republic	Kruger	Pres	1883	
Salvador	554,000	*7,228	San Salvador	Republic	Fr. Menendez	Pres	1885	
Uruguay	520,536	72,112	Montevideo	Republic	Maximo Santos	Pres	1882	
Paraguay	476,000	92,000	Asuncion	Republic	Gen. Caballero	Pres	1880	
Honduras	458,000	42,658	Tegucigalpa	Republic	Louiz Bogran	Pres	1883	
Nicaragua	400,000	51,660	Managua	Republic	Aden Cardenas	Pres	1883	
Dominica	300,000	20,596	San Domingo	Republic	Gen. Bellini	Pres	1884	
Montenegro	245,380	3,486	Cetigno	Abs. Mon	Nicholas	Prince	1860	46
Costa Rica	180,000	19,985	Jan Jose	Republic	Bernado Soto	Pres	1885	
Orange Free State	133,518	41,484	Bloemfontein	Republic	I. H. Brand	Pres		64
Hayti	93,000	49,830	Port-au-Prince	Republic	Gen. Salomon	Pres	1879	
Hawaii	66,097	6,587	Honolulu	Lim. Mon	David Kalakaua	King	1874	51

* Estimated population, 1886. † Also enumerated with the Turkish Empire. ‡ Also enumerated with the German Empire.

How to Conduct a Successful Business.—That short credit and small profits forms the golden rule for success in trade may be seen from the following table, exhibiting the amounts realized for $100 at various percentages during various periods.

	Am't at 3 pr. ct.	Am't at 5 pr. ct.	Am't at 8 pr. ct.	Am't at 10 pr. ct.
If turned over every 3 months,	$326.20	$703.99	$2,172.45	$4,525.92
" " " 6 "	180.61	265.32	466.09	672.75
" " " 8 "	155.79	207.89	317.21	417.72
" " " 12 "	134.39	162.88	215.89	250.37
" " " 2 years,	115.92	127.62	146.93	161.05
" " " 5 "	106.09	110.25	116.64	121.00

Concerning Coal and Iron.—First notice of stone coal is B. C. 371.
The coal fields of England were the first practically developed.
First record of stone coal used in England was A. D. 820.
Records of regular mining in England first made in 1180.
Coal first used in London in 1240.
First tax laid on coal in England in 1379.
Tax was repealed in 1831, having been taxed 400 years.
First patent for making iron with pit coal was granted to Simeon Sturtevant, in 1612, but was not successful.
Iron first made in a blast furnace with pit coal with success by a Mr. Darby, of Colebrook Dale, England, in 1713.

On Coal, Steam Heating, Etc.—In 1747 iron was made in England with pit coal, suitable for the manufacture of cannon. In 1788 the production of iron with pit coal in England was 48,300 tons; with charcoal, 13,000 tons. In 1864 the production of iron in Great Britain was 5,000,000 tons. Wooden rails in mines were used in 1777. Cast-iron rails in mines were used in 1790. Wrought-iron rails in mines were used in 1815. Coal gas first made use of practically in 1798.

American Coal Fields.—First coal fields worked in America were the bituminous fields at Richmond, Va., discovered in 1750. This coal was used at Westham, on the James river, to make shot and shell during the War of Independence. The first use of anthracite coal was in 1768-69. First used for smithing purposes in 1790. First used to burn in a common grate in 1808. First successful use of anthracite coal for the smelting of iron was in 1839, at the Pioneer Furnace, at Pottsville, Pa. It had been tried on the Lehigh in 1826, but was unsuccessful. The great shaft of the Philadelphia and Reading Iron Company has been sunk to a depth of 1,569 feet from the surface to the great mammoth coal vein which attains a thickness of 25 feet, in that distance passing through no less than 15 coal seams, of which 6 are workable and have an average thickness together of 64 feet. Even then there are a number of coal seams underlying these.

How to Remove Rust.—If you immerse the articles in kerosene oil and let them remain for some time, the rust will become so much loosened as to come off very easy.

How to Make 32 Kinds of Solder.—1. Plumbers' solder.—Lead 2 parts, tin 1 part. 2. Tinmen's solder.—Lead 1 part, tin

1 part. 3. Zinc solder.—Tin 1 part, lead 1 to 2 parts. 4. Pewter solder. Lead 1 part, bismuth 1 to 2 parts. 5. Spelter solder.—Equal parts copper and zinc. 6. Pewterers' soft solder.—Bismuth 2, lead 4, tin 3 parts. 7. Another.—Bismuth 1, lead 1, tin 2 parts. 8. Another pewter solder.—Tin 2 parts, lead 1 part. 9. Glazier's solder.—Tin 3 parts, lead 1 part. 10. Solder for copper.—Copper 10 parts, zinc 9 parts. 11. Yellow solder for brass or copper.—Copper 32 lbs., zinc 29 lbs., tin 1 lb. 12. Brass solder.—Copper 61.25 parts, zinc 38.75 parts. 13. Brass solder, yellow and easily fusible.—Copper 45, zinc 55 parts. 14. Brass solder, white.—Copper 57.41 parts, tin 14.60 parts, zinc 27.99 parts. 15. Another solder for copper.—Tin 2 parts, lead 1 part. When the copper is thick heat it by a naked fire, if thin use a tinned copper tool. Use muriate or chloride of zinc as a flux. The same solder will do for iron, cast iron, or steel; if the pieces are thick, heat by a naked fire or immerse in the solder. 16. Black solder.—Copper 2, zinc 3, tin 2 parts. 17. Another.—Sheet brass 20 lbs., tin 6 lbs., zinc 1 lb. 18. Cold brazing without fire or lamp.—Fluoric acid 1 oz., oxy muriatic acid 1 oz., mix in a lead bottle. Put a chalk mark each side where you want to braze. This mixture will keep about 6 months in one bottle. 19. Cold soldering without fire or lamp.—Bismuth ¼ oz., quicksilver ¼ oz., block tin filings 1 oz., spirits salts 1 oz., all mixed together. 20. To solder iron to steel or either to brass.—Tin 3 parts, copper 39½ parts, zinc 7½ parts. When applied in a molten state it will firmly unite metals first named to each other. 21. Plumbers' solder.—Bismuth 1, lead 5, tin 3 parts, is a first-class composition. 22. White solder for raised Britannia ware.—Tin 100 lbs., hardening 8 lbs., antimony 8 lbs. 23. Hardening for Britannia.—(To be mixed separately from the other ingredients). Copper 2 lbs., tin 1 lb. 24. Best soft solder for cast Britannia ware.—Tin 8 lbs., lead 5 lbs. 25. Bismuth solder.—Tin 1, lead 3, bismuth 3 parts. 26. Solder for brass that will stand hammering.—Brass 78.26 parts, zinc 17.41 parts, silver 4.33 parts, add a little chloride of potassium to your borax for a flux. 27. Solder for steel joints.—Silver 19 parts, copper 1 part, brass 2 parts. Melt all together. 28. Hard solder.—Copper 2 parts, zinc 1 part. Melt together. 29. Solder for brass.—Copper 3 parts, zinc 1 part, with borax. 30. Solder for copper.—Brass 6 parts, zinc 1 part, tin 1 part, melt all together well and pour out to cool. 31. Solder for platina.—Gold with borax. 32. Solder for iron.—The best solder for iron is good tough brass with a little borax.

N. B.—In soldering, the surfaces to be joined are made perfectly clean and smooth, and then covered with sal. ammoniac, resin or other flux, the solder is then applied, being melted on and smoothed over by a tinned soldering iron.

SOLDERING FLUID.—Take 2 oz. muriatic acid, add zinc till bubbles cease to rise, add ½ teaspoonful of sal-ammoniac.

THE UNITED STATES GOVERNMENT TEMPERING SECRET.—The following process and mixtures, patented by Garman and Siegfried, and owned by the Steel Refining and Tempering Co., of Boston, Mass., cost the U. S. Government $10,000 for the right o using in their shops, and is said to impart extraordinary hardness and durability to the poorest kinds of steel. Siegfried's specification reads as follows: "I first heat the steel to a cherry red in a clean smith's fire, and then cover the steel with chloride of sodium (common salt), purifying the fire also by throwing in salt. I work the steel in this condition, and while subjected to this treatment, until it is brought into nearly its finished form. I then substitute for the salt a compound composed of the following ingredients, and in about the following proportions: One part by weight of each of the following substances; chloride of sodium (salt), sulphate of copper, sal-ammoniac, and sal-soda, together with ½ part by weight of pure nitrate of potassa (saltpetre), said ingredients being pulverized and mixed; I alternately heat the steel and treat it by covering with this mixture and hammering it until it is thoroughly refined and brought into its finished form. I then return it to the fire and heat it slowly to a cherry red, and then plunge it into a bath composed of the following ingredients, in substantially the following proportions for the required quantity: of rain water, 1 gal.; alum, sal-soda, sulphate of copper, of each 1½ ozs.; of nitrate of potassa (saltpetre), 1 oz., and of chloride of sodium (salt), 6 ozs. These quantities and proportions are stated as being what I regard as practically the best, but it is manifest that they may be slightly changed without departing from the principles of my invention."

How to Petrify Wood.—Gum salt, rock alum, white vinegar, chalk and pebbles powder, of each an equal quantity. Mix well together. If, after the ebullition is over, you throw into this liquid any wood or porus substance, it will petrify it.

How to Construct an Æolian Harp.—Make a box with the top, bottom and sides of thin wood, and the ends 1½ inch beech, form it the same length as the width of the window in which it is to be placed. The box should be 3 or 4 inches deep, and 6 or 7 inches wide. In the top of the box, which acts as a sounding board, make 3 circular holes about two inches in diameter, and an equal distance apart. Glue across the sounding board, about 2½ inches from each end, 2 pieces of hard wood ¼ inch thick and ½ inch high, to serve as bridges. You must now procure from any musical instrument maker twelve steel pegs, similiar to those of a piano-forte, and 12 small brass pins. Insert them in the following manner into the beech; first commence with a brass pin, then insert a steel peg, and so on, placing them alternately ½ in. apart to the number of twelve. Now for the other end, which you must commence with a steel peg, exactly opposite the brass pin at the other end, then a brass pin, and so on, alternately, to the number of 12; by this arrangement you have a steel peg and a brass pin always opposite each other, which is done so that the pressure of the strings on the instrument shall be uniform. Now string the instrument with 12 first violin strings, making a loop at one end of each string, which put over the brass pins, and wind the other ends round the opposite steel pegs. Tune them in unison, but do not draw them tight. To increase the current of air, a thin board may be placed about two inches above the strings, supported at each end by 2 pieces of wood. Place the instrument in a partly opened window, and to increase the draft open the opposite door.

How Sound Travels.—In dry air at 82 deg. 1,142 ft. per second, or about 775 miles per hour; in water, 4,900 ft. per second; in iron, 17,500 ft.; in copper, 10,378 feet; and in wood from 12 to 16,000 ft. per second. In water, a bell heard at 45,000 ft., could be heard in the air out of the water but 656 ft. In a balloon the barking of dogs can be heard on the ground at an elevation of 4 miles. Divers on the wreck of the Hussar frigate, 100 ft. under water, at Hell Gate, near New York, heard the paddle wheels of distant steamers hours before they hove in sight. The report of a rifle on a still day may be heard at 5,300 yds.; a military band at 5,200 yds. The fire of the English on landing in Egypt was distinctly heard 130 miles. Dr. Jamieson says he heard, during calm weather, every word of a sermon at a distance of 2 miles.

Weights of Famous Bells.—The bell of Notre Dame, Montreal, Que., weighs 28,560 lbs.; that of the City Hall, New York, 22,300 lbs.; of St. Paul's, London, 11,470; "Big Ben," Westminster, 30,350; "Great Tom," of Oxford, 18,000; St. Peter's, Rome, 18,607; Rouen, France, 40,000; St. Ivan's, Moscow, 127,830; one unhung at Moscow, 440,000, and one in China weighs 120,000 lbs.

How to Repair Cracked Bells.—The discordant tones of a cracked bell being due to the jarring of the rugged, uneven edges of the crack against each other, the best remedy that can be applied is to cut a thin slit with a toothless saw driven at a very high velocity, say 3 or 4,000 revolutions per minute, in such a manner as to cut away the opposing edges of the fracture wherever they come in contact. This will restore the original tone of the bell.

How to Test Quality of Steel.—Good tool steel, with a white heat, will fall to pieces; with bright red heat will crumble under the hammer; with middling heat may be drawn to a needle-point.

To test hardening qualities, draw under a low heat to a gradually tapered square point and plunge into cold water; if broken point will scratch glass, the quality is good.

To test tenacity, a hardened piece will be driven into cast-iron by a hardened hammer—if poor, will be crumbled. Excellence will be in proportion to tenacity in hard state. Soft steel of good quality gives a curved line fracture and uniform gray texture. Tool steel should be dull silver color, uniform, entirely free from sparkling qualities.

Aquafortis, applied to the surface of steel, produces a black spot; on iron the metal remains clean. The slightest vein of iron or steel can be readily detected by this method.

How to Destroy the Effects of Acid on Clothes.—Dampen as soon as possible, after exposure to the acid, with spirits ammonia. It will destroy the effect immediately.

How to Wash Silverware.—Never use a particle of soap on your silverware, as it dulls the lustre, giving the article more the appearance of pewter than silver. When it wants cleaning, rub it with a piece of soft leather and prepared chalk, the latter made into a kind of paste with pure water, for the reason that water not pure might contain gritty particles.

How to Cleanse Brushes.—The best method of cleansing watchmakers' and jewelers' brushes is to wash them out in a strong soda water. When the backs are wood, you must favor that part as much as possible; for being glued, the water may injure them.

How to Keep Fresh Meat a Week or Two in Summer.—Farmers or others living at a distance from butchers can keep fresh meat very nicely for a week or two, by putting it into sour milk, or buttermilk, placing it in a cool cellar. The bone or fat need not be removed. Rinse well when used.

How to Write Inscriptions on Metals.—Take ½ lb. of nitric acid and 1 oz. of muriatic acid. Mix, shake well together, and it is ready for use. Cover the place you wish to mark with melted beeswax; when cold, write your inscription plainly in the wax clear to the metal with a sharp instrument; then apply the mixed acids with a feather, carefully filling each letter. Let it remain from 1 to 10 minutes, according to appearance desired; then throw on water, which stops the process and removes the wax.

Rules for Accidents on Water.—When upset in a boat or thrown into the water and unable to swim, draw the breath in well; keep the mouth tight shut; do not struggle and throw the arms up, but yield quietly to the water; hold the head well up, and stretch out the hands only below the water; to throw the hands or feet up will pitch the body below the water, hands or feet up will pitch the body head down, and cause the whole person to go immediately under water. Keep the head above, and everything else under water.

Every one should learn to swim; no animal, aquatic, fowl, or reptile, requires to be taught this, for they do it naturally. Few persons exist who have not some time or other seen a bullfrog perform his masterly movements in the water, and it would detract from no one's dignity to take a few lessons from him. In learning, the beginner might sustain himself by a plank, a block of wood, an attachment composed of cork, an inflated bladder, a flying kite, or a stout cord attached to a long rod held by an assistant on the land. Learn to swim, cost what it will.

Trichina is the term applied to a minute, slender and transparent worm, scarcely 1-20th of an inch in length, which has recently been discovered to exist naturally in the muscles of swine, and is frequently transferred to the human stomach when pork is used as food. Enough of these filthy parasites have been detected in half a pound of pork to engender 30,000,000 more, the females being very prolific, each giving birth to from 60 to 100 young, and dying soon after. The young thread-like worm at first ranges freely through the stomach and intestines, remaining for a short time within the lining membrane of the intestines, causing irritation, diarrhea, and sometimes death, if present in sufficient numbers. As they become stronger, they begin to penetrate the walls of the intestines in order to effect a lodgment in the voluntary muscles, causing intense muscular pain and severe enduring cramps, and sometimes tetanic symptoms. After 4 weeks migration they encyst themselves permanently on the muscular fibre, and begin to secrete a delicate sac which gradually becomes calcareous. In this torpid state they remain during the person's lifetime.

THE VITALITY OF SEEDS may be tested by placing almost any of the larger seeds or grains on a hot pan or griddle; when the vitality is perfect the grain will pop, or crack open with more or less noise. When the vitality is defective, or lost, it remains immovable in the vessel. A botanist's recipe for improving and fertilizing all kinds of seed, consists in the preparation of a solution of lime, nitre, and pigeon's dung in water, and therein steeping the seed. Tested on wheat, the produce of some of these grains was reported at 60, 70 and 80 stems, many of the ears 5 inches long, and 50 corns each, and none less than 40. The same botanist produced 500 plants from 1 grain, and 576,840 grains, weighing 47 lbs. Grains of wheat in different countries yield from 6, 10, 16, and even 30 to 1: Cape wheat 80 to 1. Barley yields from 50 to 120. Oats increase from 100 to 1,000. Wheat and millet seed germinate in one day, barley in 7, cabbage in 10, almond and chestnut and peaches require 12 months, and roses and filbert 24. A field of wheat buried under an avalanche for 25 years, proceeded on its growth, etc., as soon as the snow had melted. A bulbous root found in the hand of a mummy, above 2,000 years old, lately produced a plant. Potatoes planted below 3 feet do not vegetate; at ½ foot they grow quickest, and at 2 are retarded 2 or 3 months.

COMPARATIVE VALUE OF FOOD FOR HORSES.—100 lbs. of good hay is equivalent in value to 59 lbs. of oats, 57 lbs. of corn, 275 of carrots, 54 lbs. of rye or barley, 105 lbs. of wheat bran, 400 lbs. of green clover, 275 lbs. of green corn, 374 lbs. of wheat straw, 442 lbs. of rye straw, 400 lbs. of dried corn stalks, 45 lbs. of wheat, 59 lbs. of corn, 62 lbs. of sun-flower seeds, 69 lbs. of linseed cake, 195 lbs. of oat straw, 105 lbs. of wheat bran; 1 lb. of oil cake is equal to 14 lbs. cabbage.

TABLE SHOWING THE AVERAGE VELOCITIES OF VARIOUS BODIES.

	Per hour.	Per sec.
A man walks	3 miles, or	4 feet.
Slow rivers flow	3 " or	4 "
Rapid rivers flow	7 " or	10 "
A horse trots	7 " or	10 "
A moderate wind blows	7 " or	10 "
Sailing vessels run	10 " or	14 "
Steamboats run	18 " or	26 "
A horse runs	20 " or	29 "
A storm moves	36 " or	52 "
A hurricane moves	80 " or	117 "
Sound moves	743 " or	1142 "
A rifle ball moves	1000 " or	1466 "
Light moves		192,000 miles.
Electricity moves		288,000 miles.

COPYRIGHT LAWS OF THE UNITED STATES.

Any citizen of the United States, or resident therein, who is the author, inventor, designer, or proprietor of any book, map, chart, dramatic or musical composition, engraving, cut, print, or photograph or negative thereof, or of a painting, drawing, chromo, statue, statuary, and of models or designs intended to be perfected as works of the fine arts, and the executors, administrators or assigns of any such person, may secure to himself the sole liberty of printing, publishing, completing, copying, executing and vending the same, and, if a dramatic composition, of publicly performing or representing it, or causing it to be performed or represented by others.

Every applicant for a copyright must state distinctly the name and residence of the claimant, and whether right is claimed as author, designer, or proprietor. No affidavit or formal application is required.

A printed copy of the title of the book, map, chart, dramatic or musical composition, engraving, cut, print or photograph, or a description of the painting, drawing, chromo, statue, statuary, or model or design for a work of the fine arts, for which copyright is desired, must be sent by mail or otherwise, prepaid, addressed: "Librarian of Congress, Washington, D. C." This must be done before publication of the book or other article.

A fee of 50 cents, for recording the title of each book or other article, must be inclosed with the title as above, and 50 cents in addition (or one dollar in all) for each certificate of copyright under seal of the Librarian of Congress, which will be transmitted by early mail.

Within ten days after publication of each book or other article, two complete copies must be sent prepaid, or under free labels, furnished by the Librarian, to perfect the copyright, with the address, "Librarian of Congress, Washington, D. C."

Without the deposit of copies above required the copyright is void, and a penalty of $25 is incurred.

No copyright is valid unless notice is given by inserting in every copy published:

"*Entered according to act of Congress, in the year* ——, *by* ——, *in the office of the Librarian of Congress at Washington,*" or, at the option of the person entering the copyright, the words: "*Copyright, 18*—, *by* ——."

The law imposes a penalty of $100 upon any person who has not obtained a copyright who shall insert the notice, "*Entered according to act of Congress,*" or "*Copyright,*" or words of the same import, in or upon any book or other article.

Each copyright secures the exclusive right of publishing the book or article copyrighted for the term of twenty-eight years. Six months before the end of that time, the author or designer, or his widow or children, may secure a renewal for the further term of fourteen years, making forty-two years in all.

Any copyright is assignable in law by an instrument of writing, but such assignment must be recorded in the office of the Librarian of Congress within sixty days from its date. The fee for this record and certificate is one dollar.

Any author may reserve the right to translate or to dramatize his own work. In this case notice should be given by printing the words "Right of Translation Reserved," or "All Rights Reserved," below the notice of copyright entry, and notifying the Librarian of Congress of such reservation, to be entered upon the record.

In the case of books published in more than one volume, or of periodicals published in numbers, or of engravings, photographs, or other articles published with variations, a copyright is to be entered for each volume or part of a book, or number of a periodical, or variety, as to style, title, or inscription, of any other article.

Copyrights cannot be granted upon trade-marks, nor upon labels intended to be used with any article of manufacture. If protection for such prints or labels is desired, application must be made to the Patent Office, where they are registered at a fee of $6 for labels, and $25 for trade-marks.

NOTES OF INTEREST.

Barnum's Museum, at the corner of Broadway and Ann street, was destroyed by fire, July 13, 1865. Barnum's second museum, Broadway and Spring street, was destroyed by fire, March 13, 1868.

Baseball.— The distance from the home plate to the pitcher's position is 50 feet, so that must be the distance the ball is pitched. The distance from the home plate to the first base is 90 feet, and 127 feet 4 inches to second base.

Blondin walked a tight rope over the Falls of Niagara, June 30, 1859.

Brooklyn Bridge was first proposed by Col. Julius W. Adams in 1865. The act of incorporation was passed in 1866. Survey began by John Roebling in 1869. Construction began January 2, 1870. The first rope thrown across the river August 14, 1866.

The largest empire in the world is that of Great Britain, comprising 8,557,658 square miles— more than a sixth part of the land of the globe, and embracing under its rule nearly a sixth part of the population of the world.

The largest gun in the United States, mounted, is the 20-inch Rodman smooth-bore at Fort Hamilton, N. Y. H. Its dimensions are as follows: Extreme length, 243.5 inches; maximum diameter, 64 inches; minimum diameter, 34 inches; length of bore in calibers, 10.50 inches. The service charge is 200 pounds of powder, and the weight of the projectile is 1,000 pounds. There is also a 12¼-inch rifle (wrought-iron lined) at Sandy Hook. Weight, 89,350 pounds; extreme length, 262.8 inches; maximum diameter, 55 inches; minimum diameter, 27.55 inches; length of bore in calibers, 18.53. This gun is used for experimental purposes, principally in testing powder. Charges from 70 to 200 pounds are used. Weight of projectile, from 700 to 800 pounds.

Jumbo, the famous elephant, was bought from a wandering band of Arabs — according to Sir Samuel Baker — when four years of age. Then was brought to the Jardin des Plantes, Paris from there he was transferred to the London Zoological Gardens, in 1866, and remained there until purchased by Barnum, Bailey & Hutchinson, in 1882. Was killed by a locomotive at Ontario, Canada, in 1885.

Maud S. was sold to Robert Bonner for $40,000, by William H. Vanderbilt, 1885.

New York, during the Rebellion, furnished more soldiers than any other State. The following is the number of men furnished by the six States that furnished the largest quota: First, New York State, 445,568; Pennsylvania, 366,326; Ohio, 317,133; Illinois, 258,217; Indiana, 195,147; Massachusetts, 151,785.

The largest stake ever rowed for was $6,000, in the four-oared race for the championship between the Samuel Collyer and the Floyd T. Field, at Poughkeepsie, N. Y., July 18, 1865, and won by the Samuel Collyer. The crew of the latter were Denny Leary and the Biglin brothers, while Stevens, Wooden, Burger and Benway rowed the Floyd T. Field.

The greatest billiard match ever played in America was 2,000 points up, four caroms, for $10,000, between Phelan and Sweereiter, at Detroit, Mich., on April 12, 1859. Phelan was the winner, scoring 2,001 points to his opponent's 1,994.

The fastest time made by a steamer from New York to New Orleans was made by the Louisiana. On March 7, 1885, at 4:45 p. m. she left Pier 9, passing Sandy Hook at 5:50, and arrived at New Orleans, La., on March 13, 1885, at 2 p. m. She made the trip from wharf to wharf in 5 days, 9 hours and 15 minutes, and from bar to bar in a little less than five days. This is a little faster than the former rapid passage of this steamer, and is the quickest ever made between New York and New Orleans.

The Great Republic is the largest wooden sailing vessel ever built in this country. The largest iron sailing vessel ever built in this country was the Clarence S. Bennett. built by Henry W. Gorringe.

RELIGIOUS STATISTICS.
NUMBERS IN THE WORLD ACCORDING TO CREED.

CREED.	No. of Followers.	CREED.	No. of Followers.
Christianity	338,000,000	Confucianism	80,000,000
Buddhism	340,000,000	Sintoism	14,000,000
Mohammedanism	219,000,000	Judaism	7,000,000
Brahmanism	175,000,000		

CHRISTIAN DIVISIONS.

COUNTRIES.	Whole Population	Roman Catholics.	Protestants.	Eastern Churches.
America	84,500,000	47,300,000	30,000,000	....
Europe	301,800,000	147,300,000	71,500,000	69,300,000
Asia	798,000,000	4,900,000	1,800,000	8,500,000
Africa	203,300,000	1,100,000	1,200,000	3,200,000
Australia, Polynesia	4,400,000	400,000	1,500,000	....
Total	1,392,000,000	201,000,000	106,000,000	81,000,000

The estimates in the two preceding tables are from Schem's "Statistics of the World."

RELIGIOUS DENOMINATIONS IN THE UNITED STATES.

Denominations.	Churches.	Ministers.	Members.
Adventist, Second........	800	600	70,000
Adventist, Seventh-Day....	640	144	15,570
Baptist..................	26,060	16,596	2,296,327
Baptist, Anti-Mission......	900	400	40,000
Baptist, Free-Will.........	1,432	1,213	78,012
Baptist, Seventh-Day......	94	110	8,539
Baptist, Six-Principle......	20	12	2,000
Christian (Disciples of Christ)................	5,100	3,782	591,821
Congregational..........	3,804	3,713	381,697
Dunkards (The Brethren)..	250	200	100,000
Episcopal, Protestant......	3,013	3,725	398,990
Episcopal, Reformed......		100	9,448
Evangelical Association....	1,576	1,545	117,027
Friends..................	392	200	60,000
Jews....................	269	202	13,683
Lutheran................	5,553	3,132	950,868
Monnonite	300	350	50,000
Methodist, Episcopal......	17,935	24,658	1,724,420
Methodist, Episcopal (South)		11,703	860,687
Methodist, Episcopal African................		1,738	387,576
Methodist, Episcopal African Zion..............		1,800	300,000
Methodist, Episcopal Colored...................		638	112,938
Methodist, Free..........		260	12,318
Methodist, Congregational.		225	13,750
Methodist, Primitive......		52	3,369
Methodist, Protestant......		1,385	135,000
Methodist, Welsh Calvinistic	1,134	600	118,979
Methodist, Wesleyan......		400	17,087
Moravian	84	94	9,491
Mormon	654	3,906	110,377

RELIGIOUS DENOMINATIONS—(Continued).

Denominations.	Churches.	Ministers.	Members.
New Jerusalem (Swedenborgian)	93	89	3,994
Presbyterian	5,858	5,218	600,695
Presbyterian (South)	2,010	1,081	123,806
Presbyterian, Cumberland	2,457	1,386	111,863
Presbyterian, Reformed	167	143	17,273
Presbyterian, United	826	719	84,573
Reformed Church (late Dutch)	509	545	80,167
Reformed Church (late German)	1,405	748	155,857
Roman Catholic	6,241	6,546	*
Shaker	18	68	2,400
Unitarian, Congregational	335	394	17,960
United Brethern in Christ	4,524	2,196	157,835
Universalist	956	729	27,429
Winebrennerians (Church of God)	400	350	30,000

*According to Roman Catholic publications there are 6,883,954 adherents of that faith in the United States, though church-membership is not reported.

ENGLISH-SPEAKING RELIGIOUS COMMUNITIES OF THE WORLD.

Episcopalians	21,100,000
Methodists of all descriptions	15,800,000
Roman Catholics	14,340,000
Presbyterians of all descriptions	10,500,000
Baptists of all descriptions	8,180,000
Congregationalists	6,000,000
Unitarians	1,000,000
Free Thought	1,100,000
Minor Religious Sects	2,000,000
Of no particular religion	9,000,000
English-speaking population	89,020,000

Weights and Measures for Cooks, etc.

1 pound of wheat flour is equal to .... 1 quart
1 pound and 2 ounces of Indian meal make .... 1 quart
1 pound of soft butter is equal to .... 1 quart
1 pound and 2 ounces of best brown sugar make. ...... 1 quart
1 pound and 1 ounce of powdered white sugar make...... 1 quart
1 pound of broken loaf sugar is equal to.................... 1 quart
4 large tablespoonfuls make.. ½ gill
1 common-sized tumbler holds .... ½ pint
1 common-sized wine-glass is equal to. .... ½ gill
1 tea-cup holds.. 1 gill
1 large wine-glass holds .... 2 ounces
1 tablespoonful is equal to .... ½ ounce

Number of Yards in Miles of Different Nations.

	YARDS.
Swedish	11,704
Hanover	11,559
Oldenburg	10,820
Hesse	10,547
Bohemian	10,187
Luthenian	9,784
Saxon	9,905
Swiss	9,166
Hungarian	9,113
Prussian	8,498
Danish	8,244
Hamburg	8,244
German Geographical	8,100
Polish	8,100
Arabian	2,148
Brebant	6,082
Burgundy	6,183
Chinese Ills.	628
Dutch	6,395
United States	1,760
English Geographical	2,025
Flemish	6,869
French	4,860
Irish	3,338
Italian	2,025
Persian paisang	6,086
Portuguese	6,760
Roman	2,035
Russian	1,167
Scotch	1,984
Silesian	7,083
Spanish	7,416
Turkey	1,821

Fat, Water and Muscle Properties of Food.

100 parts.	Water.	Muscle.	Fat.
Cucumbers	97.0	1.5	1.0
Turnips	94.4	1.1	4.0
Cabbage	90.0	4.0	5.0
Milk — cows	86.0	5.0	8.0
Apples	84.0	5.0	10.0
Eggs, yolk of	79.0	15.0	27.0
Potatoes	75.2	1.4	22.5
Veal	68.5	10.1	16.5
Eggs, white of	53.0	17.0	.0
Lamb	50.5	11.0	35.0
Beef	50.0	15.0	30.0
Chicken	46.0	18.0	32.0
Mutton	44.0	12.5	40.0
Pork	38.5	10.0	50.0
Beans	14.8	24.0	57.7
Buckwheat	14.2	8.6	75.4
Barley	14.0	15.0	68.8
Corn	14.0	12.0	73.0
Peas	14.0	23.4	60.0
Wheat	14.0	14.6	69.4
Oats	13.6	17.0	66.4
Rice	13.5	6.5	79.5
Cheese	10.0	65.0	19.0
Butter			100.0

Most Northern Point Reached by Arctic Explorers.

Year.	Explorers.	No. Latitude.		
1607	Hudson	80d	23m	00s
1773	Phipps (Lord Musgrove)	80d	48m	00s
1806	Scoresby	81d	12m	42s
1827	Parry	82d	45m	30s
1874	Meyer (on land)	82d	09m	00s
1875	Markham (Nare's expedition)	83d	20m	26s
1876	Payer	83d	07m	00s
1884	Lockwood (Greely's party)	83d	24m	00s

The distance from the farthest point of polar discovery to the pole itself is 460 miles. But this polar radius, though only 460 miles in extent, is covered by ice gorges and precipices of incredible difficulty; and frost is so severe that no instrument of human invention can measure its intensity, and it blisters the skin like extreme heat.

The greatest progress that has ever been made across these wildernesses of storm, of fury and desolation, was at the rate of six miles a day, the explorers often resting as many days as they had before traveled miles in a single day.

There is a good deal of amusement in the following magical table of figures. It will enable you to tell how old the young ladies are. Just hand this table to a young lady, and request her to tell you in which column or columns her age is contained, and add together the figures at the top of the columns in which her age is found, and you have the great secret. Thus, suppose her age to be 17, you will find that number in the first and fifth columns; add the first figures of these two columns.

Here is the magic table:

1	2	4	8	16	32
3	3	5	9	17	33
5	6	6	10	18	34
7	7	7	11	19	35
9	10	12	12	20	36
11	11	13	13	21	37
13	14	14	14	22	38
15	15	15	15	23	39
17	18	20	24	24	40
19	19	21	25	25	41
21	22	22	26	26	42
23	23	23	27	27	43
25	26	28	28	28	44
27	27	29	29	29	45
29	30	30	30	30	46
31	31	31	31	31	47
33	34	36	40	48	48
35	35	37	41	49	49
37	38	38	42	50	50
39	39	39	43	51	51
41	42	44	44	52	52
43	43	45	45	53	53
45	46	46	46	54	54
47	47	47	47	55	55
49	50	52	56	56	56
51	51	53	57	57	57
53	54	54	58	58	58
55	55	55	59	59	59
57	58	60	60	60	60
59	59	61	61	61	61
61	62	62	62	62	62
63	63	63	63	63	63

ANOTHER METHOD.—Girls of a marriageable age do not like to tell how old they are, but you can find out by following the subjoined instructions, the young lady doing the figuring. Tell her to put down the number of the month in which she was born; then to multiply it by two; then to add five; then to multiply it by 50; then to add her age; then to subtract 365; then to add 115; then tell her to tell you the amount she has left. The two figures to the right will denote her age, and the remainder the month of her birth. For example, the amount is 822, she is twenty-two years old, and was born in the eighth month (August). Try it.

Rate of Annual Income on Investments,
PAR VALUE BEING $100, BEARING INTEREST AT

Price Paid.	Five Per cent.	Six Per cent.	Seven Per cent.	Eight Per cent.	Ten Per cent.
$50	10.00	12.00	14.00	16.00	20.00
55	9.09	10.90	12.72	14.55	18.18
60	8.33	10.00	11.66	13.33	16.66
65	7.69	9.23	10.76	12.30	15.38
70	7.14	8.57	10.00	11.42	14.28
75	6.66	8.00	9.33	10.66	13.35
80	6.25	7.50	8.75	10.00	12.50
82½	6.06	7.27	8.48	9.69	11.12
85	5.88	7.05	8.23	9.41	11.76
87½	5.71	6.85	8.00	9.14	11.42
90	5.55	6.66	7.77	8.88	11.11
92½	5.40	6.48	7.56	8.64	10.80
95	5.26	6.31	7.36	8.42	10.52
96	5.20	6.25	7.29	8.33	10.41
97	5.15	6.18	7.21	8.24	10.30
97½	5.12	6.15	7.17	8.20	10.25
98	5.10	6.12	7.14	8.16	10.20
99	5.05	6.06	7.07	8.08	10.10
100	5.00	6.00	7.00	8.00	10.00
101	4.95	5.94	6.93	7.92	9.90
102	4.90	5.88	6.86	7.84	9.80
103	4.85	5.82	6.79	7.76	9.70
104	4.80	5.76	6.73	7.69	9.61
105	4.76	5.71	6.66	7.61	9.52
110	4.54	5.45	6.36	7.27	9.09
115	4.34	5.21	6.08	6.95	8.69
120	4.16	5.00	5.83	6.66	8.33
125	4.00	4.90	5.60	6.40	8.00
130	3.84	4.61	5.38	6.15	7.69
135	3.70	4.44	5.18	5.92	7.40
140	3.57	4.28	5.00	5.71	7.14
145	3.44	4.13	4.82	5.51	6.89
150	3.33	4.00	4.66	5.33	6.66
160	3.20	3.75	4.40	5.00	6.40

Greatest Tunnels in the World.

Mount St. Gothard, 49,170 feet long (the longest in the world); Mount Cenis, 40,620 feet long; Hoosac, 23,700 feet long; Thames, 1,680 feet long; Harecastle, 8,778 feet long; Kilsby, 6,210 feet long; Baltimore, 32,400 feet long.

PLAYING-CARDS. — In 1882 there were manufactured, in German~ ~~~, 4,500,000 packs of playing-cards.

Cost of Articles by the Piece, from 1 to 1 Dozen.

12 cost	$1 00	$1 25	$1 50	$1 75	$2 00	$2 25	$2 50
11 cost	92	1 15	1 38	1 60	1 83	2 06	2 29
10 cost	83	1 04	1 25	1 46	1 67	1 88	2 08
9 cost	75	94	1 13	1 29	1 50	1 69	1 88
8 cost	67	83	1 00	1 17	1 33	1 50	1 67
7 cost	58	73	88	1 02	1 17	1 31	1 46
6 cost	50	63	75	88	1 00	1 13	1 25
5 cost	42	52	63	73	83	94	1 04
4 cost	33	42	50	56	67	75	83
3 cost	25	31	38	44	50	56	63
2 cost	17	21	25	29	33	38	42
1 cost	8⅓	10½	12½	14⅝	16⅔	18¾	21⅛

12 cost	$2 75	$3 00	$3 25	$3 50	$3 75	$4 00	$4 25
11 cost	2 52	2 75	2 98	3 21	3 44	3 67	3 89
10 cost	2 29	2 50	2 73	2 92	3 13	3 33	3 54
9 cost	2 06	2 25	2 44	2 63	2 81	3 00	3 19
8 cost	1 83	2 00	2 17	2 33	2 56	2 67	2 83
7 cost	1 60	1 75	1 90	2 04	2 19	2 33	2 48
6 cost	1 38	1 50	1 63	1 75	1 88	2 00	2 13
5 cost	1 15	1 25	1 36	1 46	1 56	1 67	1 77
4 cost	92	1 00	1 09	1 17	1 25	1 33	1 42
3 cost	69	75	82	88	94	1 00	1 06
2 cost	46	50	55	58	63	67	71
1 cost	23	25	28	29¼	31¼	33⅓	35½

12 cost	$4 50	$4 75	$5 00	$5 25	$5 50	$5 75	$6 00
11 cost	4 13	4 23	4 58	4 81	5 04	5 27	5 50
10 cost	3 75	3 96	4 17	4 38	4 58	4 79	5 00
9 cost	3 38	3 56	3 75	3 94	4 13	4 31	4 50
8 cost	3 00	3 17	3 33	3 50	3 67	3 83	4 00
7 cost	2 63	2 77	2 92	3 06	3 21	3 35	3 50
6 cost	2 25	2 34	2 50	2 63	2 75	2 87	3 00
5 cost	1 88	1 98	2 08	2 19	2 29	2 40	2 50
4 cost	1 50	1 58	1 67	1 75	1 83	1 92	2 00
3 cost	1 13	1 19	1 25	1 31	1 38	1 44	1 50
2 cost	75	79	83	88	92	96	1 00
1 cost	37½	39⅝	41⅔	43¾	46	48	50

12 cost	$6 25	$6 50	$6 75	$7 00	$7 25	$7 50	$7 76
11 cost	5 73	5 96	6 19	6 42	6 65	6 88	7 11
10 cost	5 25	5 42	5 63	5 83	6 04	6 25	6 46
9 cost	4 69	4 88	5 06	5 25	5 44	5 63	5 81
8 cost	4 17	4 33	4 50	4 67	4 93	5 00	5 17
7 cost	3 65	3 79	3 94	4 08	4 23	4 38	4 52
6 cost	3 13	3 25	3 38	3 50	3 63	3 75	3 88
5 cost	2 60	2 71	2 81	2 92	3 02	3 13	3 23
4 cost	2 08	2 17	2 25	2 33	2 42	2 50	2 58
3 cost	1 56	1 63	1 69	1 75	1 81	1 88	1 94
2 cost	1 94	1 08	1 13	1 17	1 21	1 25	1 29
1 cost	52⅛	54¼	56¼	58⅓	60½	62½	64⅝

Value of Foreign Coins in United States Money.

Country.	Monetary Unit.	Standard.	Values in U. S. Money.	Standard Coin.
Argentine Repub.	Peso	Gold and silver.	$ 96.5	1-20, 1-10, 1-5, 1-2 and 1 peso, 1-2 argentine and argentine.
Austria	Florin	Silver	37.1	
Belgium	Franc	Gold and silver.	19.3	5, 10 and 20 francs.
Bolivia	Boliviano	Silver	75.1	Boliviano.
Brazil	Milreis of 1,000 reis	Gold	54.6	
Canada	Dollar	Gold	1 00	
Chili	Peso	Gold and silver.	91.2	Condor, doubloon and escudo.
Cuba	Peso	Gold and silver.	93.2	1-16, 1-8, 1-4, 1-2 and 1 doubloon.
Denmark	Crown	Gold	26.8	10 and 20 crowns.
Ecuador	Peso	Silver	75.1	Peso.
Egypt	Piaster	Gold	04.9	5, 10, 25, 50 and 100 piasters.
France	Franc	Gold and silver.	19.3	5, 10 and 20 francs.
German Empire	Mark	Gold	23.8	5, 10 and 20 marks.
Great Britain	Pound sterling	Gold	4 86.6½	1-2 sovereign and sovereign.
Greece	Drachma	Gold and silver.	19.3	5, 10, 20, 50 and 100 drachmas.
Hayti	Gourde	Gold and silver.	96.5	1, 2, 5 and 10 gourdes.
India	Rupee of 16 annas	Silver	35.7	
Italy	Lira	Gold and silver.	19.3	5, 10, 20, 50 and 100 lire.
Japan	Yen	Silver	81.9	1, 2, 5, 10 and 20 yen, gold, and silver yen.
Liberia	Dollar	Gold	1 00	
Mexico	Dollar	Silver	81.6	Peso or dollar, 5, 10, 25 and 50 centavo.

VALUE OF FOREIGN COINS IN UNITED STATES MONEY—(Continued).

Country.	Monetary Unit.	Standard.	Value in U. S. Money.	Standard Coin.
Netherlands	Florin	Gold and silver	40.2	10 and 20 crowns.
Norway	Crown	Gold	26.8	Sol.
Peru	Sol	Silver	75.1	Sol.
Portugal	Milreis of 1,000 reis	Gold	1 08	2, 5 and 10 milreis.
Russia	Rouble of 100 copecks	Silver	60.1	1-4, 1-2 and 1 rouble.
Spain	Peseta of 100 centimes	Gold and silver	19.3	5, 10, 20, 50 and 100 pesetas.
Sweden	Crown	Gold	26.8	10 and 20 crowns.
Switzerland	Franc	Gold and silver	19.3	5, 10 and 20 francs.
Tripoli	Mahbub of 20 piasters	Silver	67.7	
Turkey	Piaster	Gold	04.4	25, 50, 100, 250 and 500 piasters.
U. S. Colombia	Peso	Silver	75.1	Peso.
Venezuela	Bolivar	Gold and silver	19.3	5, 10, 20, 50 and 100 bolivar.

TREASURY DEPARTMENT, WASHINGTON, D. C.,
January 1, 1886.

The foregoing estimation, made by the Director of the Mint, of the value of the foreign coins above mentioned, I hereby proclaim to be the values of such coins expressed in the money of account of the United States, and to be taken in estimating the values of all foreign merchandise, made out in any of said currencies, imported on or after January 1, 1886.

DANIEL MANNING,
Secretary of the Treasury.

Gold and Silver Produced in the United States.

The following estimate of the gold and silver produced in the United States, since the discovery of gold in California, is compiled from the official reports of the Director of the United States Mint:

Year.	Gold.	Silver.	Total.
1849	$40,000,000	$50,000	$40,050,000
1850	50,000,000	50,000	50,050,000
1851	55,000,000	50,000	55,050,000
1852	60,000,000	50,000	60,050,000
1853	65,000,000	50,000	65,050,000
1854	60,000,000	50,000	60,050,000
1855	55,000,000	50,000	55,050,000
1856	55,000,000	50,000	55,050,000
1857	55,000,000	50,000	55,050,000
1858	50,000,000	500,000	50,500,000
1859	50,000,000	100,000	50,100,000
1860	46,000,000	150,000	46,150,000
1861	43,000,000	2,000,000	45,000,000
1862	39,200,000	4,500,000	43,700,000
1863	40,000,000	8,500,000	48,500,000
1864	46,100,000	11,000,000	57,100,000
1865	53,225,000	11,250,000	64,475,000
1866	53,500,000	10,000,000	63,500,000
1867	51,725,000	13,500,000	65,225,000
1868	48,000,000	12,000,000	60,000,000
1869	49,500,000	12,000,000	61,500,000
1870	50,000,000	16,000,000	66,000,000
1871	43,500,000	23,000,000	66,500,000
1872	36,000,000	28,750,000	64,750,000
1873	36,000,000	35,750,000	71,750,000
1874	33,490,902	37,324,594	70,815,496
1875	33,467,856	31,727,560	65,195,416
1876	39,429,166	38,783,016	78,712,182
1877	46,897,390	39,793,573	86,690,963

GOLD AND SILVER PRODUCED IN THE UNITED STATES—(Continued).

Year.	Gold.	Silver.	Total
1878	51,206,360	45,281,385	96,487,745
1879	38,899,858	40,812,132	79,711,990
1880	36,000,000	38,450,000	74,450,000
1881	34,700,000	43,000,000	77,700,000
1882	32,500,000	46,800,000	79,300,000
1883	30,000,000	46,200,000	76,200,000
1884	30,800,000	48,800,000	79,600,000

Total Gold, $1,638,541,532. Silver, $645,972,290. Grand total, $2,296,508,702.

Force Exerted by Dynamite.

Nitro-glycerine and dynamite do not, when exploded, exert as much force as is popularly believed. To speak precisely, the power developed by the explosion of a ton of dynamite is equal to 45,675 foot-tons. One ton of nitro-glycerine similarly exploded will exert a power of 54,452 foot-tons; and one ton of blasting gelatine, similarly exploded, 71,050 foot-tons. These figures, although large, are not enormous, and need not excite terror. Seventy-one thousand tons of ordinary building stone, if arranged in the form of a cube, would measure only ninety feet on the side, and if it were possible to concentrate the whole force of a ton of blasting gelatine at the moment of explosion on such a mass, the only effect would be to lift it to a height of a foot. The foregoing figures are derived from experiments made at Ardeer with an instrument that gives accurate results in measuring the force of explosives.

It would seem that with age people outgrow the tendency to commit crime. Of 18,000 prisoners in New York State 10,000 of them are not more than 30 years of age, while probably 8,000 are under 25 years.

Lumber and Log Measurement at Sight.

Showing net proceeds (fractions of feet omitted) of logs in 1 inch boards, deducting saw kerf and slabs. If the required dimension is not in the table, unite two or three suitable numbers together. The length will be found in the left hand column and the diameter in inches on the head of the other columns.

Length, Feet.	Diam. 10	Diam. 11	Diam. 12	Diam. 13	Diam. 14	Diam. 15	Diam. 16	Diam. 17	Diam. 18
10	23	31	40	50	62	75	90	105	122
11	25	34	44	55	69	83	99	116	135
12	27	37	48	61	75	91	108	126	147
13	29	40	52	66	81	98	117	137	159
14	32	43	56	71	88	106	126	148	171
15	34	46	60	76	94	113	135	158	184
16	36	49	64	81	100	121	144	169	196
17	38	52	68	86	106	128	153	179	208
18	41	55	72	91	112	136	162	190	220
19	43	58	76	96	119	143	171	201	232
20	46	61	80	101	125	151	180	211	244
21	48	64	84	106	131	158	189	222	257
22	50	67	88	111	137	166	198	232	269
23	52	70	92	116	144	174	207	243	281
24	54	74	96	122	150	181	216	254	294
25	56	77	100	127	156	189	225	264	308
26	59	80	104	132	163	196	234	274	318
27	61	83	108	137	169	204	243	285	330
28	63	86	112	142	175	212	252	296	342
29	65	89	116	147	182	219	261	306	355
30	68	92	120	152	188	226	270	316	368
31	70	95	124	157	193	234	279	327	380
32	72	98	128	162	200	242	288	338	392
33	74	101	132	169	206	249	297	348	404
34	77	104	136	172	212	256	306	358	416
35	79	107	140	177	219	265	315	369	428
36	81	110	144	182	224	272	324	380	440

LUMBER AND LOG MEASUREMENT—(Cont'ed)

Length, Feet.	Diam. 19	Diam. 20	Diam. 21	Diam. 22	Diam. 23	Diam. 24	Diam. 25	Diam. 26	Diam. 27
10	140	160	180	202	225	250	275	302	330
11	154	176	198	223	248	275	302	333	363
12	169	192	217	243	271	300	331	363	397
13	183	208	235	263	293	325	358	393	430
14	197	224	253	283	313	350	386	433	463
15	211	240	271	303	336	375	413	453	496
16	225	256	289	324	359	400	441	484	530
17	239	272	307	344	383	425	468	514	563
18	253	288	325	364	406	450	496	544	596
19	267	304	343	384	429	475	523	574	630
20	280	320	361	404	452	500	550	605	661
21	293	336	379	425	473	525	579	635	693
22	309	352	397	445	496	550	605	665	726
23	323	368	415	465	519	575	632	695	760
24	338	384	433	486	541	600	662	726	794
25	351	400	451	506	562	625	689	756	827
26	366	416	370	526	586	650	716	786	860
27	380	432	488	546	606	675	744	826	893
28	394	448	506	566	626	700	772	866	926
29	408	464	524	586	649	725	799	886	959
30	422	480	542	606	672	750	826	906	992
31	436	496	560	627	695	775	854	937	1026
32	450	512	578	648	718	800	882	968	1060
33	464	528	596	668	742	825	909	998	1093
34	478	544	614	688	766	850	936	1028	1126
35	492	560	632	708	789	875	964	1058	1159
36	506	576	650	728	812	900	992	1088	1192

Whate'er her rank, whate'er her lot,
  Where'er her influence ranges,
The art to bless is ne'er forgot,
  The will to comfort never changes.

There are two souls whose equal flow
  In gentle streams so calmly run
That when they part — they part! ah, no!
  They cannot part; their souls are one.

LUMBER AND LOG MEASUREMENT—(Cont'ed).

Length, Feet.	Diam. 28	Diam. 29	Diam. 30	Diam. 31	Diam. 32	Diam. 33	Diam. 34	Diam. 35	Diam. 36
10	360	391	422	456	490	526	562	601	640
11	396	430	465	502	539	578	619	661	704
12	432	469	507	547	588	631	675	721	768
13	468	508	549	592	627	684	731	781	832
14	504	547	561	638	686	736	781	841	896
15	540	586	633	683	735	789	844	901	960
16	576	625	676	729	784	842	900	961	1024
17	612	664	718	774	833	895	956	1021	1088
18	648	703	761	820	882	946	1012	1081	1152
19	684	742	803	865	931	999	1069	1141	1216
20	720	782	845	912	980	1052	1125	1202	1280
21	756	820	887	957	1029	1103	1181	1261	1344
22	792	860	930	1004	1078	1156	1238	1322	1408
23	828	898	972	1049	1127	1209	1295	1381	1472
24	864	938	1014	1094	1176	1262	1350	1442	1536
25	900	977	1056	1139	1225	1315	1406	1501	1600
26	936	1016	1098	1184	1274	1368	1462	1562	1664
27	972	1055	1140	1230	1323	1420	1518	1622	1728
28	1008	1094	1182	1276	1372	1472	1574	1682	1792
29	1044	1133	1224	1321	1421	1525	1631	1742	1856
30	1080	1172	1266	1366	1470	1578	1688	1802	1920
31	1116	1211	1309	1412	1519	1631	1744	1862	1984
32	1152	1250	1352	1458	1568	1684	1800	1922	2048
33	1188	1289	1394	1503	1617	1737	1856	1982	2112
34	1224	1328	1436	1548	1666	1790	1912	2042	2176
35	1260	1367	1479	1594	1715	1841	1968	2102	2240
36	1296	1406	1522	1640	1764	1892	2024	2162	2304

Save thy toiling, spare thy treasure,
All I ask is friendship's pleasure;
Let the shining orb lie darkling,
Bring no gem in lustre sparkling.
  Gifts and gold are naught to me;
  I would only look on thee!

LUMBER MEASUREMENT TABLE.

Square timber and scantling brought down to 1 inch board measure. *Example:* To find the number of feet in a beam 6x10 and 24 feet in length, consult the table, and opposite 24 and under 6x10 you will find 120, the correct number of feet.

Feet.	DIMENSIONS EACH WAY IN INCHES.								
	2x4	2x5	2x6	2x7	2x8	3x3	3x4	3x5	3x6
6	4.	5.	6.	7.	8.	5.6	6.	7.6	9.
7	4.8	5.10	7.	8.2	9.4	5.3	7.	8.9	10.6
8	5.4	6.8	8	9.4	10.8	6.	8.	10.	12.
9	6.	7.6	9.	10.6	12.	6.9	9.	11.3	13.6
10	6.8	8.4	10.	11.8	13.5	7.6	10.	12.6	15.
11	7.4	9.2	11.	12.10	14.8	8.3	11.	13.9	16.6
12	8.	10.	12.	14.	16.	9.	12.	15.	18.
13	8.8	10.10	13	15.2	17.4	9.9	13.	16.3	19.6
14	9.4	11.8	14.	16.4	18.8	10.6	14.	17.6	21.
15	10.	12.6	15.	17.6	20.	11.3	15.	18.9	22.6
16	10.8	13.4	16.	18.8	21.4	12.	16.	20.	24.
17	11.4	14.2	17.	19.10	22.8	12.9	17.	21.3	25.6
18	12.	15.	18.	21.	24.	13.6	18.	22.6	27.
19	12.8	15.10	19.	22.2	25.4	14.3	19.	23.9	28.6
20	13.4	16.8	20.	23.4	26.8	15.	20.	25.	30.
21	14.	17.6	21.	24.6	28.	15.9	21.	26.3	31.6
22	14.8	18.4	22.	25.8	29.4	16.6	22.	27.6	33.
23	15.4	19.2	23.	26.10	30.8	17.3	23.	28.9	34.6
24	16.	20.	24.	28.	32.	18.	24.	30.	36.
25	16.8	20.10	25.	29.2	33.4	18.9	25.	31.3	37.6
30	20.	25.	30.	35.	40.	22.6	30.	37.6	45.
34	22.8	28.4	34.	39.3	45.4	25.6	34.	42.6	51.
40	26.8	33.4	40.	46.8	53.4	30.	40.	50.	60.
42	28.	35.	42.	49.	56.	31.6	42.	52.6	63.
44	29.4	36.8	44.	51.4	58.1	33.	44.	55.	66.

LUMBER MEASUREMENT TABLE—(Continued).

Feet.	DIMENSIONS EACH WAY IN INCHES.								
	3x7	3x8	4x4	4x5	4x6	4x7	4x8	4x9	5x5
6....	10.6	12.	8.	10.	12.	14.	16.	18.	12.6
7....	12.3	14.	9.4	11.8	14.	16.4	18.8	21.	14.7
8....	14.	16.	10.	13.4	16.	18.8	21.4	24.	16.8
9....	15.9	18	12.	15.	18.	21.	24.	27.	18.9
10....	17.6	20.	13.4	16.8	20.	23.4	26.8	30.	20.10
11....	19.3	22.	14.8	18.4	22.	25.8	29.4	33.	22.11
12....	21.	24.	16.	20.	24.	28.	32.	36.	25.
13....	22.9	26.	17.4	21.8	26.	30.4	34.8	39.	27.1
14....	24.6	28.	18.8	23.4	28.	32.8	37.4	42.	29.2
15....	26.3	30.	20.0	25.	30	35.	40	45.	31.3
16....	28.	32.	21.4	26.8	32.	37.4	42.8	48.	33.4
17....	29.9	34.	22.8	28.4	34.	39.8	45.4	51.	35.5
18....	31.6	36.	24.	30.	36.	42.	48.	54.	37.6
19....	33.3	38.	24.4	31.8	38.	44.4	50.8	57.	39.7
20....	35.	40.	26.8	33.4	40.	46.8	53.4	60.	41.8
21....	36.9	42.	28.	35.	42.	49.	56.	63.	43.9
22....	38.6	44.	29.4	36.8	44.	51.4	58.8	66.	45.10
23....	40.3	46.	30.8	38.4	46.	53.8	61.4	69.	47.11
24...	42.	48.	32.	40.	48.	56.	64.	72.	50.
25....	43.9	50.	33.4	41.8	50.	58.4	66.8	75.	52.1
30....	52.6	60.	40.	50.	60.	70.	80.	90.	62.6
34....	59.6	68.	45.4	58.8	68.	79.4	90.8	102.	70.10
40....	70.	80.	53.	66.8	80.	93.4	106.8	120.	83.4
42....	73.6	84.	56.	70.	84.	98.	112.	126.	87.6
44....	77.	88.	58.8	73.6	88.	102.8	117.4	132.	90.8

There's one little tune you can play,
  That I fancy all others above.
You learned it of "Cupid" one day;
  It begins with and ends with "I love."

Deem it not an idle thing
  A pleasant word to speak;
The face you wear, the thoughts you bring
  A heart may heal or break.

LUMBER MEASUREMENT TABLE—(Continued).

Feet.	DIMENSIONS EACH WAY IN INCHES.							
	5x6	5x7	5x8	6x6	6x7	6x8	6x9	6x10
6	15.	17.6	20.	18.	21.	24.	27.	30.
7	17.6	20.5	23.4	21.	24.6	28.	31.6	35.
8	20.	23.4	26.8	24.	28.	32.	36.	40.
9	22.6	26.3	30.	27.	31.6	36.	40.6	45.
10	25.	29.2	33.4	30.	35.	40.	45.	50.
11	27.6	32.1	36.8	33.	38.6	44.	49.6	55.
12	30.	35.	40.	36.	42.	48.	54.	60.
13	32.6	37.11	43.4	39.	45.6	52.	58.6	65.
14	35.	40.10	46.8	42.	49.	56.	63.	70.
15	37.6	43.9	50.	45.	52.6	60.	67.6	75.
16	40.	46.8	53.4	48.	56.	64.	72.	80.
17	42.6	49.7	56.8	51.	59.6	68.	76.6	85.
18	45.	52.6	60.	54.	63.	72.	81.	90.
19	47.6	55.5	63.4	57.	66.6	76.	85.6	95.
20	50.	58.4	66.8	60.	70.	80.	90.	100.
21	52.6	61.3	70.	63.	73.6	84.	94.6	105.
22	55.	64.2	73.4	66.	77.	88.	99.	110.
23	57.6	67.1	76.8	69.	80.6	92	103.6	115.
24	60.	70.	80.	72.	84.	96.	108.	120.
25	62.6	72.11	83.4	75.	87.6	100.	112.6	125.
30	75.	87.6	100.	90.	105.	120.	135.	150.
34	85.	99.2	113.4	102.	119.	136.	153.	170.
40	100.	116.8	133.4	120.	140.	160.	180.	200.
42	105.	122.6	140.	126.	147.	168.	189.	210.
44	110.	128.4	146.8	132.	154.	176.	198.	220.

Oh, dearest of my heart,
Of life itself you form a part.
I think, I dream, I pray for thee,
Just as I hope you do for me.

LUMBER MEASUREMENT AT SIGHT.

ONE INCH BOARD MEASURE.

For Plank, double or treble the product, as may be required. If a board or plank is longer or wider than the dimensions here given, add two suitable numbers together. The left-hand column contains the length in feet; the width in inches heads each column.

FEET LONG.	6 in W		7 in W		8 in W		9 in W		10 in W		11 in W		12 in W	
	ft.	in.	ft.	in.	ft.	in.	ft.	in.	ft.	in.	ft.	in.	ft.	in.
8...	4	0	4	8	5	4	6	0	6	8	7	4	8	0
9...	4	6	5	3	6	0	6	9	7	6	8	3	9	0
10...	5	0	5	10	6	8	7	6	8	4	9	2	10	0
11...	5	6	6	5	7	4	8	3	9	2	10	1	11	0
12...	6	0	7	0	8	0	9	0	10	0	11	0	12	0
13...	6	6	7	7	8	8	9	9	10	10	11	11	13	0
14...	7	0	8	2	9	4	10	6	11	8	12	10	14	0
15...	7	6	8	9	10	0	11	3	12	6	13	9	15	0
16...	8	0	9	4	10	8	12	0	13	4	14	8	16	0
17...	8	6	9	11	11	4	12	9	14	2	15	7	17	0
18...	9	0	10	6	12	0	13	6	15	0	16	6	18	0
19...	9	6	11	1	12	8	14	3	15	10	17	5	19	0
20...	10	0	11	8	13	4	15	0	16	8	18	4	20	0
21...	10	6	12	3	14	0	15	9	17	6	19	3	21	0
22...	11	0	12	10	14	8	16	6	18	4	20	2	22	0
23...	11	6	13	5	15	4	17	3	19	2	21	1	23	0
24...	12	0	14	0	16	0	18	0	20	0	22	0	24	0
25...	12	6	14	7	16	8	18	9	20	10	22	11	25	0
26...	13	0	15	2	17	4	19	6	21	8	23	10	26	0
27...	13	6	15	9	18	0	20	3	22	6	24	9	27	0
28...	14	0	16	4	18	8	21	0	23	4	25	8	28	0
29...	14	6	16	11	19	4	21	9	24	2	26	7	29	0
30...	15	0	17	6	20	0	22	6	25	0	27	6	30	0
31...	15	6	18	1	20	8	23	3	25	10	28	5	31	0
32...	16	0	18	8	21	4	24	0	26	8	29	4	32	0
33...	16	6	19	3	22	0	24	9	27	6	30	3	33	0
34...	17	0	19	10	22	8	25	6	28	4	31	2	34	0
35...	17	6	20	5	23	4	26	3	29	2	32	1	35	0
36...	18	0	21	0	24	0	27	0	30	0	33	0	36	0

LUMBER MEASUREMENT AT SIGHT.
(Continued.)

Feet Long.	13 in W		14 in W		15 in W		16 in W		17 in W		18 in W		19 in W	
	ft.	in.	ft.	in.	ft.	in.	ft.	in.	ft.	in.	ft.	in.	ft.	in.
8...	8	8	9	4	10	0	10	8	11	4	12	0	12	8
9...	9	9	10	6	11	3	12	0	12	9	13	6	14	3
10...	10	10	11	8	12	6	13	4	14	2	15	0	15	10
11...	11	11	12	10	13	9	14	8	15	7	16	6	17	5
12...	13	0	14	0	15	0	16	0	17	0	18	0	19	0
13...	14	1	15	2	16	3	17	4	18	5	19	6	20	7
14...	15	2	16	4	17	6	18	8	19	10	21	0	22	2
15...	16	3	17	6	18	9	20	0	21	3	22	6	23	9
16...	17	4	18	8	20	0	21	4	22	8	24	0	25	4
17...	18	5	19	10	21	3	22	8	24	1	25	6	26	11
18...	19	6	21	0	22	6	24	0	25	6	27	0	28	6
19...	20	7	22	2	23	9	25	4	26	11	28	6	30	1
20...	21	8	23	4	25	0	26	8	28	4	30	0	31	8
21...	22	9	24	6	26	3	28	0	29	9	31	6	33	3
22...	23	10	25	8	27	6	29	4	31	2	33	0	34	10
23...	24	11	26	10	28	9	30	8	32	7	34	6	36	5
24...	26	0	28	0	30	0	32	0	34	0	36	0	38	0
25...	27	1	29	2	31	3	33	4	35	5	37	6	39	7
26...	28	2	30	4	32	6	34	8	36	10	39	0	41	2
27...	29	3	31	6	33	9	36	0	38	3	40	6	42	9
28...	30	4	32	8	35	0	37	4	39	8	42	0	44	4
29...	31	5	33	10	36	3	38	8	41	1	43	6	45	11
30...	32	6	35	0	37	6	40	0	42	6	45	0	47	6
31...	33	7	36	2	38	9	41	6	44	0	46	6	49	0
32...	34	8	37	4	40	0	42	6	45	6	48	0	50	6
33...	35	9	38	6	41	3	44	0	46	6	49	6	52	0
34...	36	10	39	8	42	6	45	6	48	0	51	0	54	0
35...	37	11	40	10	43	9	46	6	49	6	52	6	55	6
36...	39	0	42	0	45	0	48	0	51	0	54	0	57	0

LUMBER MEASUREMENT AT SIGHT.
(Continued.)

FEET LONG.	20 in W		21 in W		22 in W		23 in W		24 in W		25 in W	
	ft.	in.	ft.	in.	ft.	in.	ft.	in.	ft.	in.	ft.	in.
8	13	4	14	0	14	8	15	4	16	0	16	8
9	15	0	15	9	16	6	17	3	18	0	18	9
10	16	8	17	6	18	4	19	2	20	0	20	10
11	18	4	19	3	20	2	21	1	22	0	22	11
12	20	0	21	0	22	0	23	0	24	0	25	0
13	21	8	22	9	23	10	24	11	26	0	27	1
14	23	4	24	6	25	8	26	10	28	0	29	2
15	25	0	26	3	27	6	28	9	30	0	31	3
16	26	8	28	0	29	4	30	8	32	0	33	4
17	28	4	29	9	31	2	32	7	34	0	35	5
18	30	0	31	6	33	0	34	6	36	0	37	6
19	31	8	33	3	34	10	36	5	38	0	39	7
20	33	4	35	0	36	8	38	4	40	0	41	8
21	35	0	36	9	38	6	40	3	42	0	43	9
22	36	8	38	6	40	4	42	2	44	0	45	10
23	38	4	40	3	42	2	44	1	46	0	47	11
24	40	0	42	0	44	0	46	0	48	0	50	0
25	41	8	43	9	45	10	47	11	50	0	52	1
26	43	4	45	6	47	8	49	10	52	0	54	2
27	45	0	47	3	49	6	51	9	54	0	56	3
28	46	8	49	0	51	4	53	8	56	0	58	4
29	48	4	50	9	53	2	55	7	58	0	60	5
30	50	0	51	6	55	0	57	6	60	0	62	6
31	51	6	54	0	57	0	59	6	62	0	64	6
32	53	6	56	0	58	6	61	6	64	0	66	6
33	55	0	57	6	60	6	63	0	66	0	68	4
34	56	6	59	6	62	6	65	0	68	0	70	6
35	58	6	61	0	64	0	67	0	70	0	73	0
36	60	0	63	0	66	0	69	0	72	0	75	0

LUMBER MEASUREMENT TABLE.

Square Timber and Scantling—Measurement at Sight.
Dimensions in inches head each column, and the length will be found in the left-hand column. If the required dimensions cannot be found in the table, add two lengths or breadths together, or take part of some length or breadth, as the case may require.

FEET.	DIMENSIONS EACH WAY IN INCHES.								
	6.11	6.12	7.7	7.8	7.9	7.10	7.11	7.12	8.8
6	33.	36.	24. 6	28.	31.6	35.	38. 6	42.	32.
7	38.6	42.	28. 7	32.8	36.9	40.10	41.11	49.	37.4
8	44.	48.	32. 8	37.4	42.	46. 8	55. 4	56.	42.8
9	49.6	54.	36. 9	42.	47.3	52. 6	57. 9	63.	48.
10	55.	60.	40.10	46.8	52.6	58. 4	64. 2	70.	53.4
11	60.6	66.	40.11	51.4	57.9	64. 2	70. 7	77.	58.8
12	66.	72.	49.	56.	63.	70.	77.	84.	64.
13	71.6	78.	53. 1	60.8	68.3	75.10	83. 5	91.	69.4
14	77.	84.	57. 2	65.4	73.6	81. 8	89.10	98.	74.8
15	82.6	90.	61. 3	70.	78.9	87. 6	96. 3	105.	80.
16	88.	96.	64. 4	74.8	84.	93. 4	102. 8	112.	85.4
17	93.6	102.	69. 5	79.4	89.3	99. 2	109. 1	119.	90.8
18	99.	108.	73. 6	84.	94.6	105.	115. 6	126.	96.
19	104.6	114.	77. 7	88.8	99.9	110.10	121.11	133.	101.4
20	110.	120.	81. 8	93.4	105.	116. 8	128. 4	140.	106.8
21	115.6	126.	85. 9	98.	110.3	122. 6	134. 9	147.	112.
22	121.	132.	89.10	102.8	115.6	128. 5	141. 2	154.	117.4
23	126.6	138.	93.11	107.4	120.9	134. 2	147. 7	161.	122.8
24	132.	144.	98.	112.	126.	140.	154.	168.	128.
26	143.	156.	106.2	121.4	136.6	151. 8	166.10	182.	138.8
28	154.	168.	114.4	130.8	147.	163.	179. 8	196.	148.8
30	165.	180.	122.6	140.	157.6	175.	192. 6	210.	160.
32	176.	192.	128.8	149.4	168.	186. 8	205. 4	224.	170.8

LUMBER MEASUREMENT TABLE.
(*Continued.*)

FEET.	DIMENSIONS EACH WAY IN INCHES.							
	8.9	8.10	8.11	8.12	9.9	9.10	9.11	9.12
6........	36.	40.	44.	48.	40.6	45.	49.6	54.
7........	42.	46.8	51.4	56.	47.3	52.6	57.9	63.
8........	48.	53.4	58.8	64.	54.	60.	66.	72.
9........	54.	60.	66.	72.	60.9	67.6	74.3	81.
10........	60.	66.8	73.4	80.	67.6	75.	82.6	90.
11........	66.	73.4	80.8	88.	74.3	82.6	90.9	99.
12........	72.	80.	88.	96.	81.	90.	99.	108.
13........	78.	86.8	95.4	104.	87.9	97.6	107.3	117.
14........	84.	93.4	102.8	112.	94.6	105.	115.6	126.
15........	90.	100.	110.	120.	101.3	112.6	123.9	135.
16........	96.	106.8	117.4	128.	108.	120.	132.	144.
17........	102.	113.4	124.8	136.	114.9	127.6	140.3	153.
18........	108.	120.	132.	144.	121.6	135.	148.6	162.
19........	114.	126.8	139.4	152.	128.3	142.6	156.9	171.
20........	120.	133.4	146.8	160.	135.	150.	165.	180.
21........	126.	140.	154.	168.	141.9	157.6	173.3	189.
22........	132.	146.8	161.4	176.	148.6	165.	181.6	198.
23........	138.	153.4	168.8	184.	155.3	172.6	189.9	207.
24........	144.	160.	176.	192.	162.	180.	198.	216.
26........	156.	173.4	190.8	208.	175.6	195.2	214.6	234.
28........	168.	186.8	205.4	224.	189.	210.	231.	252.
30........	180.	200.	220.	240.	202.6	225.	247.6	270.
32........	192.	213.8	234.8	256.	216.	240.	264.	288.

Strength of Ice of Various Thicknesses.

Ice two inches thick will bear men to walk on.

Ice four inches thick will bear horses and riders.

Ice six inches thick will bear teams with moderate loads.

Ice eight inches thick will bear teams with very heavy loads

Ice ten inches thick will sustain a pressure of 1,000 pounds per square foot.

LUMBER MEASUREMENT TABLE.
(Continued.)

FEET	DIMENSIONS EACH WAY IN INCHES.							
	10.10	10.11	10.12	11.11	11.12	12.12	12.13	12.14
6...	50.	55.	60.	60.6	66.	72.	78.	84.
7...	58.4	64. 2	70.	70.7	77.	84.	91.	98.
8...	66.8	73. 4	80.	80.8	88.	96.	104.	112.
9...	75.	86. 6	90.	90.9	99.	108.	117.	126.
10...	83.4	91. 8	100.	100.10	110.	120.	130.	140.
11...	91.8	100.10	110.	110.11	121.	132.	143.	154.
12...	100.	110.	120.	121.	132.	144.	156.	168.
13...	108.4	119. 2	130.	131.1	143.	156.	169.	182.
14...	116.8	128. 4	140.	141.2	154.	168.	182.	196.
15...	125.	137. 6	150.	151.3	165.	180.	195.	210.
16...	133.4	146. 8	160.	161.4	176.	192.	208.	224.
17...	141.8	155.10	170.	171.5	187.	204.	221.	238.
18...	150.	165.	180.	181.6	198.	216.	234.	252.
19...	158.4	174. 2	190.	191.7	209.	228.	247.	266.
20...	166.8	183. 4	200.	201.8	220.	240.	260.	280.
21...	175.	192. 6	210.	211.9	231.	252.	273.	294.
22...	183.4	201. 8	220.	221.10	242.	264.	286.	308.
23...	191.8	210.10	230.	231.11	253.	276.	299.	322.
24...	200.	220.	240.	242.	264.	288.	312.	336.
26...	216.8	238. 4	260.	262.2	286.	312.	338.	364.
28...	233.8	256. 8	280.	282.4	308.	336.	364.	392.
30...	250.	275. 6	300.	302.6	330.	370.	390.	420.
32...	266.8	293. 4	320.	322.8	352.	384.	416.	448.

The Savannah was the first steam-propelled vessel that crossed the Atlantic. She was American built, 380 tons burden, and in 1819 sailed first to Savannah from New York, thence direct to Liverpool, where she arrived in eighteen days, seven of which she used steam. From Liverpool she proceeded to Copenhagen, and to St. Petersburg.

Timber Measurement Table,

Showing the cubical contents (fractions of feet omitted) of round logs, masts, spars, etc. Length of log is shown in left-hand column. Diameter is shown at the head of column. If, the desired dimensions are not shown, double some numbers.

L. ft.	10	11	12	13	14	15	16	17	18	19
8...	4	5	6	7	8	10	11	12	14	16
9...	5	6	7	8	9	11	12	14	16	18
10...	5	7	8	9	10	12	14	16	18	20
11...	6	7	8	10	12	13	16	17	19	22
12...	6	8	9	11	13	15	17	19	21	24
13...	7	9	10	12	14	16	18	20	23	26
14...	7	9	11	13	15	17	19	22	25	28
15...	8	10	12	14	16	18	21	23	26	30
16...	9	11	12	14	17	20	22	25	28	32
17...	9	11	13	16	18	21	24	27	30	33
18...	10	12	14	16	19	22	25	28	32	35
19...	10	13	15	17	21	23	27	30	33	37
20...	11	13	16	18	21	25	28	31	35	39
21...	11	14	16	19	22	26	29	33	37	41
22...	12	15	17	20	23	27	31	35	39	43
23...	12	16	18	21	24	28	32	36	41	45
24...	13	16	19	22	26	30	34	38	42	47
25...	14	17	20	23	27	31	35	39	44	49
26...	14	17	20	24	28	32	36	41	46	51
27...	15	18	21	25	29	33	38	42	48	53
28...	15	18	22	26	30	35	39	44	49	55
29...	16	19	23	27	31	36	41	45	51	57
30...	16	20	24	28	32	37	42	47	53	59
31...	17	20	24	29	33	38	43	48	55	61
32...	17	21	25	29	34	40	45	50	57	63
33...	18	22	26	30	35	41	46	52	58	65
34...	19	22	27	31	36	42	48	53	60	67
35...	19	23	28	32	37	43	49	55	62	69
36...	20	24	28	33	39	44	50	57	64	71

TIMBER MEASUREMENT TABLE—(Continued).

L. Ft.	20	21	22	23	24	25	26	27	28
8	17	19	21	23	25	27	29	32	34
9	20	22	24	26	28	31	33	36	38
10	22	24	26	29	31	34	37	40	43
11	24	26	29	32	35	37	41	43	47
12	26	29	32	34	38	41	44	47	51
13	28	31	34	37	41	44	48	51	56
14	31	34	37	40	44	48	52	55	60
15	33	36	40	43	47	51	55	59	64
16	35	38	42	46	50	55	59	63	68
17	37	41	45	49	53	58	63	68	73
18	39	43	48	52	57	61	66	72	77
19	41	45	50	55	60	65	70	75	81
20	44	48	53	58	63	68	74	79	85
21	46	50	55	61	66	71	77	83	90
22	48	53	58	64	69	75	81	87	94
23	50	55	61	66	72	78	85	91	98
24	52	58	63	69	75	82	88	95	102
25	54	60	66	72	79	85	92	99	107
26	57	63	69	75	82	89	96	103	111
27	59	65	71	78	85	92	99	107	115
28	61	67	74	81	88	95	103	111	120
29	63	70	77	84	91	99	107	115	124
30	65	72	79	86	94	102	110	119	128
31	68	75	82	89	98	106	114	123	132
32	70	77	85	92	100	109	118	127	137
33	72	79	87	95	104	112	121	130	141
34	74	82	90	98	107	116	125	135	145
35	76	84	93	101	110	119	129	139	149
36	79	86	95	104	113	123	133	143	154

Greatest Known Depth of the Ocean.

The greatest depth which has been ascertained by sounding is 25,720 feet, or 4,620 fathoms. The average depth between 60 degrees north and 60 degrees south is almost three miles.

TIMBER MEASUREMENT TABLE—(Continued).

L. Ft.	29	30	31	32	33	34	35	36	37
8	37	39	42	45	48	50	53	57	60
9	41	44	47	50	53	57	60	64	67
10	46	49	52	56	59	63	67	71	75
11	50	53	57	61	65	69	73	77	82
12	55	58	62	67	71	76	80	85	90
13	60	63	68	72	77	82	87	92	97
14	64	68	73	78	83	88	94	99	105
15	69	73	78	84	89	95	100	106	112
16	73	78	83	89	95	101	107	113	114
17	78	83	89	95	101	107	114	121	127
18	82	88	94	100	106	114	120	128	134
19	87	93	99	106	112	120	127	135	142
20	91	98	105	112	118	126	134	142	149
21	96	103	111	117	124	132	140	149	157
22	101	109	116	123	130	139	147	156	164
23	105	113	121	128	136	145	154	163	172
24	111	118	127	134	143	151	160	170	179
25	116	123	131	139	149	158	167	178	187
26	120	128	137	145	154	164	174	185	194
27	125	133	142	151	160	170	180	192	202
28	129	136	147	156	166	177	187	198	209
29	134	143	153	162	172	183	194	206	217
30	138	148	158	168	177	189	200	213	224
31	143	152	163	173	182	195	207	220	232
32	148	157	169	178	188	202	214	227	239
33	152	162	174	184	194	208	220	234	247
34	157	167	179	190	200	214	227	241	254
35	161	172	182	196	205	220	234	248	261
36	166	177	190	201	212	227	240	255	269

The following shows weight required to tear asunder bars one inch square of the following material:

●Oak, 5⅙ tons; Fir, 5¼ tons; Cast Iron, 7¾ tons; Wrought Iron, 10 tons; Wrought Copper, 15 tons; English Bar Iron, 25 tons; American Iron, 37½ tons; Blistered Steel, 59½ tons.

Logs Reduced to Running Board Measure. Logs Reduced to One Inch Board Measure.

If the log is longer than is contained in the table, take any two lengths.

The first column on the left gives the length of the log in feet, The figures under D denote the diameters of the logs in inches. Fractional parts of inches are not given.

The diameter of timber is usually taken 20 feet from the butt. All logs short of 20 feet, take the diameter at the top or small end.

To find the number of feet of boards which a log will produce when sawed, take the length of feet in the first column on the left hand, and the diameter at the top of the page in inches.

Suppose a log 12 feet long and 24 inches in diameter. In the left hand column is the length, and opposite 12 under 24 is 300, the number of feet of boards in a log of that length and diameter.

Feet Long.	D. 12	D. 13	D. 14	D. 15	D. 16	D. 17	D. 18	D. 19	D. 20	D. 21	D. 22	D. 23	D. 24
10..	54	66	76	93	104	107	137	154	179	194	210	237	256
11..	59	72	83	102	114	131	151	169	196	213	231	261	270
12..	64	78	90	111	124	143	164	184	213	232	252	285	300
13..	69	84	97	120	134	154	177	199	231	251	273	308	327
14..	74	90	104	129	144	166	191	214	249	270	293	332	350
15 :	79	96	111	138	154	177	204	229	266	289	314	355	376
16..	84	102	118	146	164	189	217	244	284	308	335	379	401
17..	89	108	126	155	173	200	231	259	301	327	356	402	426
18..	94	114	133	164	183	212	244	274	319	346	377	426	451
19..	99	121	140	173	193	223	257	289	336	365	398	449	477
20..	104	127	147	182	203	236	271	304	354	384	419	473	501
21..	109	133	154	191	213	247	284	319	371	403	440	497	527
22..	114	139	161	200	223	259	297	334	389	422	461	520	552
23..	119	145	168	209	233	270	311	349	407	441	481	542	568
24..	124	151	176	218	243	282	325	364	424	460	502	568	613
25 ·	129	157	183	227	253	293	337	379	442	479	523	591	628
26..	134	163	190	236	263	305	350	394	459	498	544	615	653
27..	139	169	197	245	273	316	363	409	477	517	565	639	678
28..	144	175	204	254	283	328	376	424	494	536	586	663	703
29..	149	181	211	263	293	339	389	439	512	555	607	687	728
30..	154	187	218	272	303	351	402	454	529	574	628	711	753
31..	159	193	225	281	313	362	415	469	547	593	649	735	778

If we're right we can't be hurt by the truth, and if we ain't right we ought to be hurt righteously.

You show me a man who keeps the Sabbath day holy and I'll show you a man that's a Christian all the week.

LOGS REDUCED TO RUNNING BOARD MEASURE, ETC.—*Continued.*

Feet Long.	D. 25	D. 26	D. 27	D. 28	D. 29	D. 30	D. 31	D. 32	D. 33	D. 34	D. 35	D. 36
10...	283	309	339	359	377	407	440	456	486	496	543	573
11...	311	340	374	396	415	447	484	502	535	546	598	630
12...	340	371	408	432	453	489	528	548	584	596	653	688
13...	369	404	442	469	491	530	572	594	633	646	708	746
14...	397	435	476	505	529	571	618	640	682	696	762	803
15...	426	465	511	541	567	612	662	686	731	746	817	861
16...	455	496	545	578	605	653	706	732	780	796	872	919
17...	483	527	579	614	643	694	751	778	829	846	927	976
18...	512	558	613	650	681	735	795	824	878	896	981	1034
19...	541	590	647	688	719	776	839	870	927	946	1036	1092
20...	569	621	681	724	757	817	884	916	976	996	1091	1148
21...	598	652	716	760	796	859	928	962	1025	1046	1146	1206
22...	627	684	750	796	834	900	972	1008	1074	1096	1200	1264
23...	655	715	784	833	872	941	1017	1054	1123	1146	1255	1318
24...	684	746	818	869	910	982	1061	1100	1172	1196	1310	1376
25...	713	777	853	906	948	1023	1105	1146	1221	2246	1365	1434
26...	742	808	887	942	986	1064	1149	1192	1270	1296	1420	1492
27...	771	839	921	970	1024	1105	1193	1238	1319	1346	1475	1550
28...	800	870	955	1015	1062	1146	1237	1284	1368	1396	1530	1608
29...	829	901	989	1052	1100	1187	1281	1330	1417	1446	1585	1666
30...	858	932	1023	1088	1138	1228	1325	1376	1466	1496	1640	1724
31...	887	963	1057	1125	1176	1269	1369	1422	1515	1546	1695	1782

Stock Brokers' Technicalities.

A BULL is one who operates to depress the value of stocks, that he may buy for a rise.

A BEAR is one who sells stocks for future delivery, which he does not own at the time of sale.

A CORNER is when the Bears cannot buy or borrow the stock to deliver in fulfillment of their contracts.

OVERLOADED is when the Bulls cannot take and pay for the stock they have purchased.

SHORT is when a person or party sells stocks when they have none, and expect to buy or borrow in time to deliver.

LONG is when a person or party has a plentiful supply of stocks.

A POOL or RING is a combination formed to control prices.

A broker is said to CARRY stocks for his customer when he has bought and is holding it for his account.

A WASH is a pretended sale by special agreement between buyer and seller, for the purpose of getting a quotation reported.

A PUT AND CALL is when a person gives so much per cent. for the option of buying or selling so much stock on a certain day, at a price fixed the day the option is given.

Board and Plank Measurement at Sight.

This table gives the Sq. Ft. and In. in Board from 6 to 25 inches wide, and from 8 to 36 feet long. If a board be longer than 36 ft. unite two numbers. Thus, if a board is 40 ft. long and 16 in. wide, add 30 and 10 and you have 53 ft. 4 in. For 2 in. plank double the product.

Feet Long.	6 in. W.		7 in. W.		8 in. W.		9 in. W.		10 in. W.		11 in. W.		12 in. W.		13 in. W.		14 in. W.		15 in. W.	
	ft.	in.	ft.	in.	ft.	in.	ft.	in.	ft.	in.	ft.	in.	ft.	in.	ft.	in.	ft.	in.	ft.	in.
8	4	0	4	8	5	4	6	0	6	8	7	4	8	0	8	8	9	4	10	0
9	4	6	5	3	6	0	6	9	7	6	8	3	9	0	9	9	10	6	11	3
10	5	0	5	10	6	8	7	6	8	4	9	2	10	0	10	10	11	8	12	6
11	5	6	6	5	7	4	8	3	9	2	10	1	11	0	11	11	12	10	12	9
12	6	0	7	0	8	0	9	0	10	0	11	0	12	0	13	0	14	0	15	0
13	6	6	7	7	8	8	9	9	10	10	11	11	13	0	14	1	15	2	16	3
14	7	0	8	2	9	4	10	6	11	8	12	10	14	0	15	2	16	4	17	6
15	7	6	8	9	10	0	11	3	12	6	13	9	15	0	16	3	17	6	18	9
16	8	0	9	4	10	8	12	0	13	4	14	8	16	0	17	4	18	8	20	0
17	8	6	9	11	11	4	12	9	14	2	15	7	17	0	18	5	19	10	21	3
18	9	0	10	6	12	0	13	6	15	0	16	6	18	0	19	6	21	0	22	6
19	9	6	11	1	12	8	14	3	15	10	17	5	19	0	20	7	22	2	23	9
20	10	0	11	8	13	4	15	0	16	8	18	4	20	0	21	8	23	4	25	0
21	10	6	12	3	14	0	15	9	17	6	19	3	21	0	22	9	24	6	26	3
22	11	0	12	10	14	8	16	6	18	4	20	2	22	0	23	10	25	8	27	6
23	11	6	13	5	15	4	17	3	19	2	21	1	23	0	24	11	26	10	28	9
24	12	0	14	0	16	0	18	0	20	0	22	0	24	0	26	0	28	0	30	0
25	12	6	14	7	16	8	18	9	20	10	22	11	25	0	27	1	29	2	31	3
26	13	0	15	2	17	4	19	6	21	8	23	10	26	0	28	2	30	4	32	6
27	13	6	15	9	18	0	20	3	22	6	24	9	27	0	29	3	31	6	33	9
28	14	0	16	4	18	8	21	0	23	4	25	8	28	0	30	4	32	8	35	0
29	14	6	16	11	19	4	21	9	24	2	26	7	29	0	31	5	33	10	36	3
30	15	0	17	6	20	0	22	6	25	0	27	6	30	0	32	6	35	0	37	6
31	15	6	18	1	20	8	23	3	25	10	28	5	31	0	33	7	36	2	38	9
32	16	0	18	8	21	4	24	0	26	8	29	4	32	0	34	8	37	4	40	0
33	16	6	19	3	22	0	24	9	27	6	30	3	33	0	35	9	38	6	41	3
34	17	0	19	10	22	8	25	6	28	4	31	2	34	0	36	10	39	8	42	6
35	17	6	20	5	23	4	26	3	29	2	32	1	35	0	37	11	40	10	43	9
36	18	0	1	0	24	0	27	0	30	0	33	0	36	0	39	0	42	0	45	0

The infidelity that hurts is the infidelity of the man who makes out that he's on God's side, and then won't live up.

Find me a man preparing himself to hear the gospel and I can show you a man that is going to be benefited by the gospel.

BOARD AND PLANK MEASUREMENT.—*Continued.*

Feet Long.	16 in. W.		17 in. W.		18 in. W.		19 in. W.		20 in. W.		21 in. W.		22 in. W.		23 in. W.		24 in. W.		25 in. W.	
	ft.	in.	ft.	in.	ft.	in.	ft.	in.	ft.	in.	ft.	in.	ft.	in.	ft.	in.	ft.	in.	ft.	in.
8	10	8	11	4	12	0	12	8	13	4	14	0	14	8	15	4	16	0	16	8
9	12	0	12	9	13	6	14	3	15	0	15	9	16	6	17	3	18	0	18	9
10	13	4	14	2	15	0	13	10	16	8	17	6	18	4	19	2	20	0	20	10
11	14	8	15	7	16	6	17	5	18	4	19	3	20	2	21	1	22	0	22	11
12	16	0	17	0	18	0	19	0	20	0	21	0	22	0	23	0	24	0	25	0
13	17	4	18	5	19	6	20	7	21	8	22	9	23	10	24	11	26	0	27	1
14	18	8	19	10	21	0	22	2	23	4	24	6	25	8	26	10	28	0	29	2
15	20	0	21	3	22	6	23	9	25	0	26	3	27	6	28	9	30	0	31	3
16	21	4	22	8	24	0	25	4	26	8	28	0	29	4	30	8	32	0	33	4
17	22	8	24	1	25	6	26	11	28	4	29	9	31	2	32	7	34	0	35	5
18	24	0	25	6	27	0	28	6	30	0	31	6	33	0	34	6	36	0	37	6
19	25	4	26	11	28	6	30	1	31	8	33	3	34	10	36	5	38	0	39	7
20	26	8	28	4	30	0	31	8	33	4	35	0	36	8	38	4	40	0	41	8
21	28	0	29	9	31	6	33	3	35	0	36	9	38	6	40	3	42	0	43	9
22	29	4	31	2	33	0	34	10	36	8	38	6	40	4	42	2	44	0	45	10
23	30	8	32	7	34	6	36	5	38	4	40	3	42	2	44	1	46	0	47	11
24	33	0	34	0	36	0	38	0	40	0	42	0	44	0	46	0	48	0	50	0
25	34	4	35	5	37	6	39	7	41	8	43	9	45	10	47	11	50	0	52	1
26	35	8	36	10	39	0	41	2	43	4	45	6	47	8	49	10	52	0	54	2
27	36	0	38	3	40	6	42	9	45	0	47	3	49	6	51	9	54	0	56	3
28	37	4	39	8	42	0	44	4	46	8	49	0	51	4	53	8	56	0	58	4
29	38	8	41	1	43	6	45	11	48	4	50	9	53	2	55	7	58	0	60	5
30	40	0	42	6	45	0	47	6	50	0	51	6	55	0	57	6	60	0	62	6

Famous Destructive Fires.

New York, Dec., 1835 — over five hundred buildings and $20,000,000 worth of property destroyed; Sept. 6, 1839 — $10,000,000 worth of property destroyed. Pittsburg, April 10, 1845 — one thousand buildings burnt; loss, $6,000,000. St. Louis, May 4, 1851 — a large portion of the city burned; loss, $11,000,000. Portland, Me., July 4, 1866 — almost entirely destroyed; loss, $15,000,000. Chicago, Ill., Oct. 8-9, 1871 — over 2,000 acres burnt over; estimated loss, $195,000,000; July 14, 1874, another great fire destroyed $4,000,000 worth of property. Boston, Mass., Nov. 9, 1872 — nearly 450 buildings destroyed; loss, over $73,000,000. St. John, N. B., June 21, 1877 — loss, $12,500,000.

WOOD AND BARK MEASUREMENT AT SIGHT.

The Cord of Wood or Bark is 8 feet long, 4 feet high, and 4 feet wide, as established by law in most of the States and the Dominion of Canada. If the Wood is 8 feet long, double the product. Fractions of feet are omitted in the Table. Price will be found heading the columns, number of feet in the left-hand column.

Ft.	$1 50	$1 75	$2 00	$2 25	$2 50	$2 75	$3 00	$3 25	$3 50
1	01	01	01	02	02	02	02	02	02
2	02	02	03	03	04	04	05	05	05
3	03	04	04	05	06	06	07	07	08
4	05	06	06	07	08	09	09	10	10
5	06	07	08	09	10	11	12	13	13
6	07	08	09	11	12	13	14	15	16
7	08	10	11	12	14	15	16	17	19
8	09	11	12	14	16	18	19	20	21
16	19	22	25	28	31	35	37	40	43
24	28	33	37	42	47	52	56	61	65
32	38	44	50	56	63	69	75	81	87
40	47	55	63	70	78	86	94	1 02	1 09
48	56	66	75	84	94	1 03	1 12	1 22	1 31
56	61	77	88	98	1 09	1 20	1 13	1 42	1 53
64	75	88	1 00	1 13	1 25	1 38	1 50	1 62	1 75
72	84	98	1 13	1 27	1 41	1 55	1 69	1 83	1 96
80	94	1 09	1 25	1 41	1 56	1 72	1 88	2 03	2 18
84	98	1 15	1 31	1 48	1 64	1 81	1 97	2 13	2 29
88	1 03	1 20	1 38	1 55	1 72	1 89	2 06	2 23	2 40
92	1 08	1 26	1 44	1 62	1 80	1 98	2 15	2 33	2 51
96	1 13	1 31	1 50	1 69	1 88	2 06	2 25	2 44	2 62
104	1 22	1 42	1 63	1 83	2 03	2 23	2 44	2 64	2 84
112	1 31	1 53	1 75	1 97	2 19	2 41	2 62	2 84	3 06
120	1 41	1 64	1 88	2 11	2 34	2 58	2 81	3 05	3 28
128	1 50	1 75	2 00	2 25	2 50	2 75	3 00	3 25	3 50

WOOD AND BARK MEASUREMENT AT SIGHT.
(Continued.)

Ft.	$4 00	$4 50	$5 00	$5 50	$6 00	$6 50	$7 00	$7 50	$8 00
1	03	03	03	04	04	05	05	05	06
2	06	07	07	08	09	10	10	11	12
3	09	10	11	12	14	15	16	17	18
4	12	14	15	17	18	20	21	23	25
5	15	17	19	21	23	25	27	29	31
6	18	21	23	25	28	30	32	35	37
7	21	24	27	30	32	35	38	41	43
8	24	28	31	34	37	40	43	46	50
16	49	56	62	68	74	81	87	93	1 00
24	75	84	93	1 03	1 12	1 22	1 31	1 41	1 50
32	1 00	1 12	1 25	1 37	1 50	1 62	1 75	1 87	2 00
40	1 25	1 40	1 56	1 72	1 87	2 03	2 19	2 34	2 50
48	1 50	1 68	1 87	2 06	2 25	2 44	2 62	2 81	3 00
56	1 75	1 96	2 18	2 40	2 62	2 84	3 06	3 28	3 50
64	2 00	2 25	2 50	2 75	3 00	3 25	3 50	3 75	4 00
72	2 25	2 53	2 81	3 09	3 37	3 65	3 93	4 28	4 50
80	2 50	2 81	3 13	3 43	3 74	4 06	4 37	4 68	5 00
84	2 62	2 95	3 28	3 60	3 94	4 26	4 59	4 92	5 25
88	2 75	3 09	3 43	3 78	4 12	4 47	4 81	5 16	5 50
92	2 87	3 23	3 59	3 95	4 30	4 67	5 03	5 40	5 75
96	3 00	3 37	3 75	4 12	4 49	4 87	5 25	5 62	6 00
104	3 25	3 65	4 05	4 47	4 87	5 28	5 69	6 09	6 50
112	3 50	3 93	4 38	4 80	5 24	5 69	6 12	6 56	7 00
120	3 75	4 21	4 68	5 15	5 62	6 09	6 56	7 03	7 50
128	4 00	4 50	5 00	5 50	6 00	6 50	7 00	7 50	8 00

The Wedding Anniversary.

Fifth year......................Wooden Wedding
Tenth year.........................Tin Wedding
Fifteenth year.................Crystal Wedding
Twentieth year..................China Wedding
Twenty-fifth year..............Silver Wedding
Thirtieth year..................Pearl Wedding
Fortieth year....................Ruby Wedding
Fiftieth year..................Golden Wedding
Seventy-fifth year............Diamond Wedding

Table for Engineers and Machinists.

SIZE AND STRENGTH OF CAST IRON COLUMNS. IRON 1 IN. THICK.

Diameter in inches.	Height in Feet. Load in Cwt.										
	4	6	8	10	12	14	16	18	20	22	24
2	72	60	49	40	32	26	22	18	15	13	11
2½	119	105	91	77	65	55	47	40	34	29	25
3	178	143	145	128	111	97	84	73	64	56	49
3½	247	232	214	191	172	156	135	119	106	94	83
4	326	318	288	266	242	220	198	178	160	144	13x
4¼	418	400	379	354	327	301	275	251	229	208	189
5	522	501	479	452	427	394	365	337	310	285	262
6	607	592	573	550	525	497	469	440	413	386	360
7	1032	1013	989	959	924	887	848	808	765	725	686
8	1333	1315	1289	1259	1224	1185	1142	1097	1052	1005	959
9	1716	2697	1672	1640	1603	1561	1515	1461	1461	1364	1311
10	2119	2100	2077	2045	2007	1964	1916	1865	1811	1755	1697
11	2570	2550	2520	2490	2450	2410	2358	2305	2248	2189	2127
12	3050	3040	3020	2970	2930	2900	2830	2780	2730	2670	2600

WEIGHTS OF CORDWOOD.

	Lbs.	Carbon.
One cord of Hickory	4,468	100
" Hard Maple	2,864	58
" Beech	3,234	64
" Ash	3,449	79
" Birch	2,363	49
" Pitch Pine	1,903	43
" Canada Pine	1,870	42
" Yellow Oak	2,920	61
" White Oak	1,870	81
" Lombardy Poplar	1,775	41
" Red Oak	3,255	70

READY RECKONER TABLE.

For computing Wages, Rent, Board, etc. The sum will be found heading the columns, and the days and weeks on the extreme left-hand column. If the desired sum is not in the table, double or treble two or three suitable numbers.

Time.	$2.50	$2.75	$3.00	$3.25	$3.50	$3.75	$4.00	$4.25	$4.50	$4.75
Days 1	.36	.39	.43	.44	.50	.53	.57	.61	.64	.68
Days 2	.72	.78	.86	.93	1.00	1.07	1.14	1.21	1.28	1.36
Days 3	1.08	1.17	1.29	1.39	1.50	1.61	1.71	1.82	1.93	2.03
Days 4	1.44	1.56	1.71	1.86	2.00	2.14	2.28	2.43	2.57	2.71
Days 5	1.80	1.95	2.14	2.32	2.50	2.68	2.86	3.03	3.21	3.39
Days 6	2.15	2.34	2.57	2.78	3.00	3.21	3.43	3.64	3.86	4.07
Weeks 1	2.50	2.75	3.00	3.25	3.50	3.75	4.00	4.25	4.50	4.75
Weeks 2	5.09	5.50	6.00	6.50	7.00	7.50	8.00	8.50	9.00	9.50
Weeks 3	7.50	8.25	9.00	9.75	10.50	11.25	12.00	12.75	13.50	14.25
Weeks 4	10.00	11.00	12.00	13.00	14.00	15.00	16.00	17.00	18.00	19.00
Weeks 5	12.50	13.75	15.00	16.25	17.50	18.75	20.00	21.25	22.50	23.75

Time.	$5.00	$5.25	$5.50	$5.75	$6.00	$6.25	$6.50	$6.75	$7.00	$8.00
Days 1	.71	.75	.79	.82	.86	.89	.93	.96	1.00	1.14
Days 2	1.43	1.50	1.58	1.64	1.72	1.78	1.86	1.92	2.00	2.28
Days 3	2.14	2.25	2.37	2.46	2.23	2.67	2.79	2.88	3.00	3.52
Days 4	2.86	3.00	3.15	3.28	3.44	3.56	3.72	3.84	4.00	4.26
Days 5	3.57	3.75	3.94	4.10	4.30	4.45	4.65	4.80	5.00	5.72
Days 6	4.28	4.50	4.73	4.92	5.16	5.34	5.58	5.76	6.00	6.86
Week 1	5.00	5.25	5.50	5.75	6.00	6.25	6.50	6.75	7.00	8.00
Week 2	10.00	10.50	11.00	11.50	12.00	12.50	13.00	13.50	14.00	16.00
Week 3	15.00	15.75	16.50	17.25	18.00	18.75	19.50	20.25	21.00	24.00
Week 4	20.00	21.00	22.00	23.00	24.00	25.00	26.00	27.00	28.00	32.00
Week 5	25.00	26.25	27.50	28.75	30.00	31.25	32.50	33.50	35.00	40.00

WEIGHT OF LEAD PIPE—DIFFERENT SIZES.

Caliber.	AAA Weight per foot		AA Weight per foot		A Weight per foot		B Weight per foot		C Weight per foot		D Weight per foot		D Light Weight per foot		E Weight per foot		E Light Weight per foot	
In.	lb.	oz.	lb.	oz.	lb.	oz.	lb.	oz.	lb.	oz.	lb.	oz.	lb.	oz.	lb.	oz.	lb.	oz.
3/8	1	8	1	5	1	2	1	0	0	13	0	10	......		0	8	......	
1/2	3	0	2	0	1	12	1	4	1	0	0	13	......		0	11	0	9
5/8	3	8	2	12	2	8	2	0	1	12	1	8	1	4	1	0	1	12
3/4	4	8	3	8	3	0	2	4	2	0	1	12	1	8	1	4	1	0
1	6	0	4	12	4	0	3	4	2	8	2	0	......		1	8	......	
1 1/4	6	12	5	12	4	12	3	12	3	0	2	8	......		2	0	......	
1 1/2	9	0	8	0	6	4	5	0	4	4	3	8	......		3	4	......	
2	10	12	9	0	7	0	6	0	5	4	4	0	......		......		......	

WEIGHT OF IRON PER FOOT.

Round.		Square.		Flat.		Flat.		Flat.	
Size.	Weight.	Size.	Weight.	Size.	Weight.	Size.	Weight.	Size.	Weight.
¼	.163	¼	.208	1 x¼	.833	1¾x½	2.91	4½x¾	11.25
⅜	.368	⅜	.468	1⅛x¼	.937	2 x½	3.33	5 x¾	12.50
½	.654	½	.833	1¼x¼	1.04	2¼x½	3.74	5½x¾	13.75
⅝	1.02	⅝	1.30	1⅜x¼	1.14	2½x½	4.16	6 x¾	15.00
¾	1.47	¾	1.87	1½x¼	1.25	2¾x½	4.58	1 x⅞	2.91
⅞	2.00	⅞	2.55	1¾x¼	1.45	3 x½	5.00	1⅛x⅞	3.28
1	2.61	1	3.33	2 x¼	1.66	3½x½	5.[illegible]	1¼x⅞	3.6
1⅛	3.31	1⅛	4.21	2¼x¼	1.87	4 x½	6.66	1⅜x⅞	4.01
1¼	4.09	1¼	5.20	2½x½	2.08	5 x½	8.33	1½x⅞	4.37
1⅜	4.95	1⅜	6.30	2¾x¼	2.29	6 x½	10.00	1¾x⅞	5.10
1½	5.89	1½	7.50	3 x¼	2.50	1 x⅝	2.08	2 x⅞	5.83
1⅝	6.91	1⅝	8.80	3¼x¼	2.70	1⅛x⅝	2.34	2¼x⅞	6.56
1¾	8.01	1¾	[illegible] 20	3½x¼	2.91	1¼x⅝	2.60	2½x⅞	7.29
1⅞	9.20	[illegible]	11.71	3¾x¼	3.12	1⅜x⅝	2.86	2¾x⅞	8.02
2	10.47	2	13.33	4 x¼	3.33	1½x⅝	3.12	3 x⅞	8.75
2⅛	11.82	2⅛	15.05	4½x¼	3.75	1¾x⅝	3.64	3½x⅞	10.20
2¼	13.25	2¼	16.87	5 x¼	4.17	2 x⅝	4.16	4 x⅞	11.66
2⅜	14.76	2½	20.80	6 x¼	5.00	2¼x⅝	4.68	4½x⅞	13.12
2½	16.36	2¾	25.20	1 x⅜	1.25	2½x⅝	5.20	5 x⅞	14.58
2¾	19.79	3	30.00	1⅛x⅜	1.40	2¾x⅝	5.72	5½x⅞	16.04
3	23.56	3⅛	32.55	1¼x⅜	1.56	3 x⅝	6.25	6 x⅞	17.50
3⅛	25.56	3¼	35.20	1⅜x⅜	1.71	3½x⅝	7.29	1⅛x1	3.75
3¼	27.65	3⅜	37.96	1½x⅜	1.87	4 x⅝	8.33	1¼x1	4.16

3⅜	29.82	3½	40.80	1¾x⅜	2.18	5 x⅝	10.41	1⅜x1	4.5
3½	32.07	3¾	46.87	2 x⅜	2.50	6 x⅝	12.50	1½x1	5.00
3¾	36.81	4	53.33	2¼x⅝	2.81	1 x¾	2.50	1¾x1	5.83
4	41.88	4¼	60.20	2½x⅜	3.12	1⅛x¾	2.81	2 x1	6.66
4⅛	44.54	4½	67.50	2¾x⅜	3.43	1¼x¾	3.12	2¼x1	7.50
4¼	47.28	4¾	75.20	3 x⅜	3.75	1⅜x¾	3.43	2½x1	8.33
4⅜	50.11	5	83.33	3½x⅜	4.37	1½x¾	3.75	2¾x1	9.16
4½	53.01	5¼	93.20	4 x⅜	5.00	1¾x¾	4.37	3 x1	10.00
4¾	59.06	5½	102.20	5 x⅜	6.25	2 x¾	5.00	3½x1	11.66
5	65.45	6	112.20	6 x⅜	[illegible].50	2¼x¾	5.62	4 x1	13.33
5¼	73.02	....	....	1 x½	1.66	2½x¾	6.25	4½x1	15.00
5½	80.03	....	....	1⅛x½	1.87	2¾x¾	6.87	5 x1	16.66
5¾	87.08	....	....	1¼x¼	2.08	3 x¾	8.50	5½x1	18.33
6	95.06	....	....	1⅜x½	2.29	3½x¾	8.75	6 x1	20.00
6½	112.02	....	....	1½x½	2.50	4 x¾	10.00	6½x1	21.66

WEIGHT OF FLAT STEEL PER FOOT.

	1	1⅛	1¼	1⅜	1½	1¾	2	2¼	2½	2¾	3	3¼	3½
¼	.852	.958	1.06	1.17	1.27	1.49	1.70	1.91	2.13	2.34	2.55	2.77	2.97
⅜	1.27	1.43	1.59	1.75	1.91	2.23	2.55	2.87	3.20	3.51	3.83	4.15	4.47
½	1.70	1.91	2.13	2.34	2.55	2.98	3.40	3.83	4.26	4.68	5.11	5.53	5.98
⅝	2.13	2.39	2.66	2.92	3.19	3.72	4.26	4.79	5.32	5.85	6.39	6.92	7.45

MOULDERS AND PATTERN MAKERS' TABLE.

Cast Iron being 1,		Bar Iron being 1,		White Pine being 1,	
Bar Iron equal	1.07	Cast Iron equal	.95	Cast Iron equal	13.
Steel "	1.08	Steel "	1.03	Brass "	12.7
Brass "	1.16	Copper "	1.16	Copper "	33.4
Copper "	1.2[illegible]	Brass "	1.09	Lead "	18.1
Lead "	1.5[illegible]	Lead "	1.48	Zinc "	11.5

RELATIVE STRENGTH OF BODIES TO RESIST TORSION.

LEAD BEING 1.

Tin	1.4	Gun Metal	5.0	English Iron	10.1
Copper	4.3	Cast Iron	9.0	Blistered Steel	16.6
Yellow Brass	4.6	Swedish Iron	9.5	Shear Steel	17.0

CAPACITIES, SIZE AND WEIGHT OF COPPERS.

Depth in Inches.	Gallons.	Weight in pounds.	Depth in inches.	Gallons.	Weight in pounds.	Depth in inches.	Gallons.	Weight in pounds.
9¾	1	1½	24	15	22½	29½	29	43½
12¼	2	3	24½	16	24	30	30	45
14	3	4½	25	17	25½	32	36	54
15½	4	6	25½	18	27	34	43	64½
16½	5	7½	26	19	28½	35	48	72
17½	6	9	26½	20	30	36	53	79½
18½	7	10½	26¾	21	31½	37	58	87
19½	8	12	27	22	33	38	63	74½
20¼	9	13½	27¼	23	34½	39	67	100½
21	10	15	27½	24	36	40	71	106½
21½	11	16½	27¾	25	37½	45	104	156
22	12	18	28	26	39	50	146	219
22½	13	19½	28½	27	40½			
23¼	14	21	29	28	42			

WEIGHT OF SQUARE AND ROUND CAST IRON.

Square per Foot.			Round per Foot.			
Size.	Weight.	Size.	Weight.	Size.	Weight.	
Inches square.	Pounds.	Inches square.	Pounds.	Inches Diam.	Pounds.	
½	.78	4	50.	½	.61	
⅝	1.22	4⅛	53.14	⅝	.95	
¾	1.75	4¼	56.44	¾	1.38	
⅞	2.39	4⅜	59.81	⅞	1.87	
1	3.12	4½	63.28	1	2.45	
1⅛	3.95	4⅝	66.84	1⅛	3.10	
1¼	4.88	4¾	70.50	1¼	3.83	
1⅜	5.90	4⅞	74.26	1⅜	4.64	
1½	7.03	5	78.12	1½	5.52	
1⅝	8.25	5⅛	82.08	1⅝	6.48	
1¾	9.57	5¼	86.13	1¾	7.51	
1⅞	10.93	5⅜	90.28	1⅞	8.62	
2	12.50	5½	94.53	2	9.81	
2⅛	14.11	5⅝	98.87	2⅛	11.08	
2¼	15.81	5¾	103.32	2¼	12.42	
2⅜	17.62	5⅞	107.86	2⅜	13.84	
2½	19.53	6	112.50	2½	15.33	

Size.	Weight.
Inches Diam.	Pounds.
4⅛	41.66
4¼	44.27
4⅜	46.97
4½	49.70
4⅝	52.50
4¾	55.37
4⅞	58.32
5	61.35
5⅛	64.46
5¼	67.64
5⅜	70.09
5½	74.24
5⅝	77.65
5¾	91.14
5⅓	84.71
6	88.35
6¼	95.87

WEIGHT OF SQUARE AND ROUND CAST IRON, Etc.—(Continued).

Square per Foot.			Round per Foot.		
Size. Inches square.	Weight. Pounds.	Size. Inches square.	Weight. Pounds.	Size. Inches Diam.	Weight. Pounds.
2⅝	21.53	6¼	122.08	2⅝	16.91
2¾	23.63	6½	132.03	2¾	18.56
2⅞	25.83	6¾	142.38	2⅞	20.28
3	28.12	7	153.12	3	22.18
3⅛	30.51	7¼	164.25	3⅛	23.96
3¼	33.	7½	175.78	3¼	25.92
3⅜	35.59	7¾	187.68	3⅜	27.95
3½	38.28	8	200.12	3½	30.16
3⅝	41.06	8¼	212.56	3⅝	32.25
3¾	43.94	8½	225.78	3¾	34.51
3⅞	46.92	8¾	239.25	3⅞	36.85
		9	253.12	4	39.27

Size. Inches Diam.	Weight. Pounds.
6½	103.69
6¾	111.82
7	120.26
7¼	129.
7½	138.05
7¾	147.41
8	157.08
8¼	167.05
8½	177.19
8¾	187.91
9	198.79
9¼	210.

SPORTING MATTERS.

Base Ball Record For Eleven Years.

Summary for 1887—National League.

	Played.	Won.	Lost.	Percent.
Detroit	124	79	45	.637
Philadelphia	123	75	48	.609
Chicago	121	71	50	.586
New York	124	68	55	.548
Boston	121	61	60	.504
Pittsburg	125	55	70	.440
Washington	122	46	76	.377
Indianapolis	126	37	89	.293

Winners of the National League Games for Eleven Years.

		Won.	Lost.
1876	Chicago	52	14
1877	Boston	31	17
1878	Boston	41	19
1879	Providence	59	25
1880	Chicago	67	17
1881	Chicago	56	28
1882	Chicago	55	29
1883	Boston	63	35
1884	Providence	84	28
1885	Chicago	87	25
1886	Chicago	90	34
1887	Detroit	79	45

American Association Games for 1887.

	Played.	Won.	Lost.	Percent.
St. Louis	135	95	40	.703
Cincinnati	133	80	53	.601
Baltimore	134	76	58	.567
Louisville	134	75	59	.559
Athletic	133	63	70	.473
Brooklyn	132	59	73	.446
Metropolitan	132	43	89	.325
Cleveland	130	40	90	.307

BEST TURF RECORDS FOR THE SEASON OF 1886.

Trotting mile—Harry Wilkes, 2:14¼, at Cleveland, July 29.
Pacing mile—Little Mac, 2:13¾, Detroit, July 23.
Running mile—Burch, 1:41, at Coney Island, September 11.

BEST TROTTING RECORDS.

One mile—Maud S., Cleveland, Ohio, July 30, 1885, 2:08¾.
Two miles—Fanny Witherspoon, Chicago, Illinois, September 25, 1885, 4:43.
Three miles—Huntress, Prospect Park, Long Island, September 23, 1872, 7:21¼.
Four miles—Trustee, Union Course, Long Island, June 13, 1849, 11:06.
Five miles—Lady Mack, San Francisco, California, April 2, 1874, 13:00.
Ten miles—Controller, San Francisco, California, November 23, 1878, 27:23¼.
Twelve miles—Topgallant, Philadelphia, Pennsylvania, 1830, 38:00.
Fifteen miles—Girder, San Francisco, California, August 6, 1874, 47:20.
Twenty miles—Capt. McGowan, Boston, Massachusetts, October 31, 1865, 58:25.
Fifty miles—Ariel, Albany, New York, 1846, 3:55:40½.
Hundred miles—Conquerer, Long Island, November 12, 1853, 8:55:53.
Fastest by Stallion—Maxy Cobb, 2:13¼, Providence, Rhode Island, September 30, 1884.
Fastest by Mare—Maud S., Cleveland, Ohio, July 30, 1885.
Fastest by Gelding—Jay-Eye-See, 2:10, Philadelphia, August 15, 1884.

Big Winners on the Running Track.

The following is a list of the big winners on the running turf

NAME AND AGE.	Starts.	First.	Second.	Third.	Amount won.
The Bard (3)	17	11	5	..	$41,895
Tremont (2)	13	13	..	..	40,045
Inspector B. (3)	17	9	3	2	38,375
Dew Drop (3)	12	7	4	1	27,785
Miss Woodford (6)	7	6	1	..	21,680
Volante (4)	18	12	4	1	21,535
Ben Ali (3)	12	7	2	2	19,348
King Fox (2)	5	4	1	..	17,948
Barnum (a)	43	24	9	5	17,185
Jim Gray (3)	22	9	4	2	15,625
Hanover (2)	3	3	..	..	14,535
Blue Wing (3)	19	4	7	1	13,470
Connemara (2)	12	8	2	..	13,338
Lucky B. (6)	21	9	3	3	13,070
Firenzi (2)	8	5	2	..	13,015
Silver Cloud (3)	16	2	..	8	12,870
Montana Regent (3)	15	7	4	2	12,455
Millie (3)	23	10	3	6	12,443
Elkwood (3)	23	5	9	4	12,020
Kingston (2)	6	2	4	..	11,500
Grisette (2)	16	6	2	2	11,115
Kaloolah (3)	13	5	2	3	10,320
Jennie T. (2)	11	6	1	2	10,120
Rupert (4)	16	7	5	2	10,093

Speedy Bicycle Records.

These records have been made up to the close of the season of 1886. A bicycle race closed at Minneapolis on December 25, 1886, in which Shock beat all previous records by making 1,405 miles in 142 hours.

Riders who have made a mile on the wheel in

less than three minutes are: N. H. Van Sicklen, Chicago, 2:46 1-2; W. A. Rowe, 2:29 1-2; George M. Hendee, 2:31 1-5; E. P. Burnham, 2:32 1-2; W. A. Rhodes, 2:34 3-5; W. F. Knapp, 2:40; A. B. Rich, 2:40 1-2; Asa Dolph, 2:41; C. L. Kluge, 2:41; F. R. Cook, 2:42 1-5; Cola Stone, 2:44 1-2; W. E. Crist, 2:46 2-5. Among the others who have made a mile within three minutes, but whose exact records are not readily accessible, are: F. F. Ives, Elliott Norton, C. P. Adams, George Weber, L. B. Hamilton, John Brooks, H. S. Kavanaugh, A. L. Jennen, J. W. Lord, Henry Schwartz, C. D. Heath, C. R. Hoag, C. S. Stevens, V. C. Place, and L. A. Howell.

S. G. Whittaker, of Chicago, has made a wonderful record for himself on the wheel this year, and has demonstrated the great possibilities of the bicycle for practical every day use. He holds all the road records from 1 to 300 miles inclusive. He has made a mile in 2:54; 20 miles, 5y:46; 50 miles, 2:56:00; 100 miles, 6:01:00; 200 miles, 15:30:00, and 300 miles, 23:46:00. This riding represents 20 miles at the rate of a mile in a trifle less than three minutes; 50 miles at 3:30; 100 miles at 3:36; 200 miles at 4:39; and 300 miles at 4:45. It is a marvelous exhibition of speed and endurance. F. F. Ives, of Boston, holds the 24-hour road record with 305 miles. An English lad of seventeen rods from Land's End at the north end of Scotland to John o' Groat's at the south tip of England, a distance of 896 miles, in five days and one hour, a feat that has never been equaled.

W. A. Rowe, of Lynn, Mass., holds the racing records from one mile to 22 miles, 150 yards. He has made a mile in 2:29 1-2; 5 miles in 13:10; 20 miles, 58:20 1-2; 22 miles, 150 yards, 1:00:00. In 1880, George Waller, twenty-one years old, covered 1,404 miles in six days, in Agricultural Hall, London, Eng., and 1,404 miles is still the six-day record.

GLASS BALL SHOOTING.

The following are the best records at glass ball shooting: 300 glass balls broken in succession by A. H. Bogardus, at Lincoln, Ill., on July 4, 1877; 500 glass balls broken in 24 minutes and 2 seconds by J. C. Haskell,

Lynn, Mass., May 30, 1881. He shot at 514, thrown from two traps, 14 yards rise, 12 feet apart. 900 glass balls broken by A. H. Bogardus, at Bradford, Pa., November 20, 1879. He shot at 1,000, from three traps, 14 yards apart. 1,000 glass balls were broken in 1 hour, 1 minute, 54 seconds, by A. H. Bogardus, at New York City, December 20, 1879. The two traps were placed 15 yards apart, 15 yards rise, and he loaded his own gun, and changed the barrels at the end of every hundred. 1,500 glass balls in 1 hour, 37 minutes and 20 seconds; 2,000 in 2 hours, 14 minutes, 43 seconds; 3,000 in 3 hours, 34 minutes, 40 seconds; 4,000 in 4 hours, 48 minutes, 43 seconds; 4,500 in 5 hours, 32 minutes, 45 seconds; 5,000 in 6 hours, 22 minutes, 30 seconds; 5,500 in 7 hours, 19 minutes, 2 seconds, out of 5,854 shot at, by A. H. Bogardus, New York City, December 20, 1879. The above records from 1,500 were shot at 15 yards rise, two traps, 12 feet apart. 5,000 out of 6,222 glass balls were broken by Dr. W. E. Carver, at Brooklyn, N. Y., July 13, 1878. He used Winchester rifles and was assisted in loading.

SWIMMING.

80 yards, 53¾ seconds. E. T. Jones, Lambeth Baths, London, England, October 21, 1878.

100 yards, 1:08½. E. T. Jones, two turns, Lambeth Baths, London, England, October 21, 1878.

160 yards, 2:02. W. Beckwith, with three turns, Lambeth Baths, London, England, August 20, 1881.

200 yards, 2:40. W. Beckwith, 9 turns, Lambeth Baths, London, England, December 17, 1883.

220 yards, 2:54¼. J. J. Collier, straightaway, London, July 7, 1883.

300 yards, 4:08. W. Beckwith, 14 turns, Westminster Aquarium, London, England, December 17, 1883.

400 yards, 5:36. J. Finney, 18 turns, Westminster Aquarium, London, England, December 19, 1883.

440 yards, 6:12. J. Finney, 21 turns, Westminster Aquarium, London, England, December 19, 1883.

500 yards, 7:07. J. Finney, 24 turns, Westminster Aquarium, London, England, December 19, 1883.

600 yards, 8:40. J. Finney, Westminster Aquarium, London, England, December 19, 1883.

700 yards, 10:12. J. Finney, Westminster Aquarium, London, England, December 19, 1883.

800 yards, 11:45. W. Beckwith, 39 turns, Westminster Aquarium, London, England, December 19, 1883.

880 yards, 13:46¼. J. J. Collier, open still water, 5 turns, Hollingworth Lake, July 7, 1883.

1,000 yards, 15:08½. W. Beckwith, Lambeth Baths, London, England, September 10, 1881.

1,000 yards, 15:44. J. J. Collier, open still water, Hollingworth Lake, England, August 23, 1884.

1,100 yards, 17:25¼. J. J. Collier, still water, Hollingworth Lake, England, August 23, 1884.

1,320 yards, 21:05½. J. J. Collier, still water, Hollingworth Lake, England, August 23, 1884.

1,540 yards, 24:34. J. J. Collier, still water, Hollingworth Lake, England, August 23, 1884.

1 mile, 28:19¾. J. J. Collier, open still water, Hollingworth Lake, England, August 23, 1884.

3 miles 1,480 yards, 1:44:44. J. Finney, 175 turns, Westminster Aquarium, London, England, December 22, 1883.

5 miles, 1:04:23. C. Whyte, with tide, Thames River, England, July 13, 1870.

20⅜ miles (about) 5:51. F. Cavill, Thames River, England, July 6, 1876.

35 miles (about) 21:45. Captain Matthew Webb, Dover, England to Calais, France, August 24 and 25, 1875.

40 miles (about) 9:57. Captain Matthew Webb, with tide, Thames River, England, July 12, 1878.

74 miles, 84 hours, restricted to 14 hours per day. Captain Matthew Webb, Lambeth Baths, London, England, May 19 to 24, 1879.

74 hours, including 4 minutes rest. Captain Matthew Webb, Scarborough, England, August 9 to 12, 1880.

94 miles 32 laps, 60 hours, restricted to 10 hours per day. W. Beckwith, London, England, June 20 to 25, 1881.

Captain Matthew Webb kept afloat without touching anything 60 consecutive hours. Scarborough, England, June 29 to July 1, 110.

Ernest Von Shoening swam from pier 1, New York

city, to pier at Norton's Point, Coney Island, and returned unassisted; about 20 miles, in 8 hours, 45 minutes, August 22, 1880.

N. T. Collinge swam a half mile every hour for 48 consecutive hours. Rochdale Baths, England, February 15 and 16, 1878.

Best Lady Swimming Records.

1 mile, 35:34. Miss Theresa Johnson, Devonshire Baths, London, England, October 31, 1883.
2 miles, 1:21:27. Miss Laura Seigeman, Hasting's Baths, London, England, September 12, 1879.
3 miles, 2:09:48¼. Miss Laura Seigeman, Hasting's Baths, London, England, September 22, 1879.
5 miles, 1:09. Miss Agnes Beckwith, age 14, with tide, Thames River, England, September 1, 1875.
9 miles, 3½ furlongs, 2:24:30. Miss Emily Parker, age 14, tide water, Thames River, England, September 18, 1875.
10 miles, 2:43. Miss Agnes Beckwith, with tide, Thames River, England, July 5, 1876.
20 miles, 6:25. Miss Agnes Beckwith, without assistance, Thames River, England, July 17, 1878.
31 consecutive hours without assistance, by Miss Edith Johnson, Blackpool Baths, England, May, 1880.
100 hours (not consecutive) out of 137, by Miss Agnes Beckwith, Westminster Aquarium, London, England, September 13 to 18, 1880.

Best Record for Staying Under Water.

4 minutes 2¾ seconds. Peter Johnson, professional, tank, Royal Music Hall, London, England, April 6, 1882.
2 minutes 51¼ seconds. "Lurline, the Water Queen," Oxford Music Hall, London, England, December 29, 1881.

Best Record for Swimming on Back.

100 yards, 1:24. J. M. Taylor, professional, Rochdale Baths, London, England, November 4, 1879.
880 yards, 16:29. Harry Gurr, Serpentine, London, England, June 1, 1865.

Best Plunging Record.

70 feet 1 inch. J. Strickland, professional, measurement taken from edge of diving board, which was five feet above water, City Baths, Melbourne, Australia, March 15, 1880.

70 feet 7 inches. Horace Davenport, amateur, Lambeth Baths, October 2, 1882.

65 feet. T. Ingram, professional, Floating Baths, Charing Cross, London, July 31, 1879.

Best Records for Swimming Under Water.

·13 yards 1 foot. James Finney, professional, Blackpool, England, October 20, 1882.

57 yards 2 feet. J. G. Rushforth, amateur, Rochdale Baths, England, October 13, 1883.

Diameters, Circumferences and Areas of Circles.

Example.—Required the circumference of a circle, loop, or ring, the diameter being 3 ft. 4 in. In the column of circumferences, opposite the indicated diameter, stands 10 ft. 5⅝ in., the circumference required.

Example.—If a wheel is ordered to be made to contain 60 teeth, the pitch of the teeth to be 3⅞ inches, the dimensions of the wheel may be known simply as follows. Multiply the pitch of the tooth by the number of teeth the wheel is to contain, and the product will be the circumference of the wheel, thus—

3⅞ inches pitch of the tooth.
10 × 6 = 60 the number of teeth.

Feet 19 4½ inches, the circumference of the wheel. The diameter answering to this circumference is 6 ft. 2 in.; consequently with one half of this number as a radius, the circumference of the wheel will be described

WEIGHT OF BRASS, COPPER, STEEL, PLATE IRON, WROUGHT IRON PIPE, Etc.

Diameter and Side of Square.	BRASS.		COPPER.	
	Weight of Round.	Weight of Square.	Weight of Round.	Weight of Square.
Inches.	Lbs.	Lbs.	Lbs.	Lbs.
¼	.17	.22	.19	.24
⅜	.39	.50	.42	.54
½	.70	.90	.75	.96
⅝	1.10	1.40	1.17	1.50
¾	1.59	2.02	1.69	2.16
⅞	2.16	2.75	2.31	2.94
1	2.83	3.60	3.02	3.84
1⅛	3.58	4.56	3.82	4.86
1¼	4.42	5.63	4.71	6.
1⅜	5.35	6.81	5.71	7.27
1½	6.36	8.10	6.79	8.65
1⅝	7.47	9.51	7.94	10.15
1¾	8.66	11.03	9.21	11.77
1⅞	9.95	12.66	10.61	13.53
2	11.32	14.41	12.08	15.38
2⅛	12.78	16.27	13.64	17.36
2¼	14.32	18.24	15.29	19.47
2⅜	15.96	20.32	17.03	21.69
2½	17.68	22.53	18.87	24.03
2⅝	19.50	24.83	20.81	26.50
2¾	21.40	27.25	22.84	29.08
2⅞	23.39	29.78	24.92	31.79
3	25.47	32.43	27.13	34.61

WEIGHT OF BRASS, COPPER, STEEL, PLATE IRON, WROUGHT IRON PIPE, Etc.

(Continued).

Diameter and Side of Square.	STEEL.		LEAD.	
	Weight of Round.	Weight of Square.	Weight of Round.	Weight of Square.
Inches.	Lbs.	Lbs.	Lbs.	Lbs.
1/4	.17	.21		
3/8	.38	.48		
1/2	.67	.85		
5/8	1.04	1 33		
3/4	1.50	1.91		
7/8	2.05	2.61		
1	2 67	3 40	3.87	4.95
1 1/8	3.38	4.34	4 90	6.23
1 1/4	4 18	5 32	6 06	7.71
1 3/8	5.06	6.44	7 33	9.33
1 1/2	6.02	7.67	8.72	11 11
1 5/8	7 07	9.	10 24	13.04
1 3/4	8.20	10.14	11 87	15 12
1 7/8	9 41	11 98	13 63	17 36
2	10.71	13 63	15.51	19.75
2 1/8	12 05	15 80	17.51	22.29
2 1/4	13 51	17 20	19 63	25.
2 3/8	15 05	19 17	21 80	27 80
2 1/2	16.68	21.21	24 24	30.86
2 5/8	18.39	23 41	26 72	34.02
2 3/4	20.18	25 70	29 33	37.34
2 7/8	22 06	28 10	32.05	40.81
3	24 23	30 60	34 90	44 14

WEIGHT OF BRASS, COPPER, STEEL, PLATE IRON, WROUGHT IRON PIPE, Etc.

(Continued.)

PLATE IRON		FLAT CAST IRON.		WR'T IRON PIPE.		PLANTING TABLE.	
Thickness in parts of an inch	IRON.	Size.	Weight.	Int. Diam. Inchs.	Weight per Foot.	Feet Distance.	No. of Hills.
		Ins.	Lbs.	⅛	.24	1	43,560
1-16	2.5	¼	9 37	¼	.42	1½	19,369
1-8	5.0	⅜	14 06	⅜	.56	2	10,890
3-16	7.5	½	18 75	½	85	2½	6,969
1-4	10.0	⅝	23 43	¾	1 13	3	4,840
5-16	12.5	¾	28 12	1	1.67	3½	3,556
3-8	15.0	⅞	32 18	1¼	2 26	4	2,722
7-16	17.5	1	37.50	1½	2.69	4½	2,151
1-2	20.0	1⅛	42 18	2	3.66	5	1,742
5-8	25.0	1¼	46 87	2½	5.77	5½	1,449
3-4	30.0	1⅜	51 56	3	7.55	6	1,210
7-8	40.0	1½	56 25	3½	9 05	6½	1,031
1		1⅝	60 93	4	10 73	7	889
		1¾	65 62	4½	12 49	7½	775
		1⅞	70 31	5	14.56	8	680
		2	75.	6	18 76	8½	602
				7	23	9	538
				8	8	9½	482
						10	436
						10½	361
						12	302
						15	193
						18	135
						20	108
						25	69
						30	48

FACTS ABOUT THE HUMAN BODY

The weight of the male infant at birth is 7 lbs. avoirdupois; that of the female is not quite 6½ lbs. The maximum weight (140½ lbs.) of the male is attained at the age of 40; that of the female (nearly 124 lbs.) is not attained until 50; from which ages they decline afterwards; the male to 127¼ lbs., the female to 100 lbs., nearly a stone. The full-grown adult is 20 times as heavy as a new-born infant. In the first year he triples his weight, afterwards the growth proceeds in geometrical progression, so that if 50 infants in their first year weigh 1,000 lbs., they will in the second weigh 1210 lbs.; in the third 1331; in the fourth 1464 lbs.; the term remaining very constant up to the ages of 11–12 in females, and 12–13 in males, where it must be nearly doubled; afterwards it may be continued, and will be found very nearly correct up to the age of 18 or 19, when the growth proceeds very slowly. At an equality of age the male is generally heavier than the female. Towards the age of 12 years only an individual of each sex has the same weight. The male attains the maximum weight at about the age of 40, and he begins to lose it very sensibly towards 60. At 80 he loses about 13.2328 lbs., and the stature is diminished 2.756 inches. Females attain their maximum weight at about 50. The mean weight of a mature man is 104 lbs., and of an average woman 94 lbs. In old age they lose about 12 or 14 lbs. Men weigh most at 40, women at 50, and begin to lose weight at 60. The mean weight of both sexes in old age is that which they had at 19.

When the male and female have assumed their complete development they weigh almost exactly 20 times as much as at birth, while the stature is about 3½ times greater.

Children lose weight during the first three days after birth; at the age of a week they sensibly increase; after one year they triple their weight; then they require six years to double their weight, and 13 to quadruple it

It has been computed that nearly two years sickness is experienced by every person before he is 70 years old, and therefore that 10 days per annum is the average sickness of human life. Till 40 it is but half, and after 50 it rapidly increases. The mixed and fanciful diet of man is considered the cause of numerous diseases from which animals are exempt. Many diseases have abated with changes of diet, and others are virulent in particular countries, arising from peculiarities.

Human Longevity.—Of 100,000 male and female children, in the first month they are reduced to 90,396, or nearly a tenth? In the second, to 87,936. In the third, to 86,175. In the fourth, to 84,720. In the fifth, to 83,571. In the sixth, to 82,526, and by the end of the first year to 77,528, the deaths being 2 to 9. The next four years reduces the 77,528 to 62,448, indicating 37,552 deaths before the completion of the fifth year.

At 25 years the 100,000 are half, or 49,995; at 52, one-third. At 58½ a fourth, or 25,000; at 67, a fifth; at 76, a tenth; at 81, a twentieth, or 5,000; and ten attain 100. Children die in large proportions because their diseases cannot be explained, and because the organs are not habituated to the functions of life. The mean of life varies in different countries from 40 to 45. A generation from father to son is about 30 years; of men in general 5-6ths die before 70, and 15-16ths before 80. After 80 it is rather endurance than enjoyment. The nerves are blunted, the senses fail, the muscles are rigid, the softer tubes become hard, the memory fails, the brain ossifies, the affections are buried, and hope ceases. The 16th die at 80; except a 133d, at 90. The remainder die from inability to live, at or before 100.

About the age of 36 the lean man usually becomes fatter and the fat man leaner. Again, between the years 43 and 50 his appetite fails, his complexion fades, and his tongue is apt to be furred on the least exertion of body or mind. At this period his muscles become flabby, his joints weak; his spirits droop, and his sleep is imperfect and unrefreshing. After suffering under these complaints a year, or perhaps two, he starts afresh with renewed vigor, and goes on to 61 or 62, when a similar change takes place, but with aggravated symptoms. When these grand periods have been successively passed, the gravity of incumbent years is more strongly marked, and he begins to boast of his age.

In Russia, much more than in any other country, instances of longevity are numerous, if true. In the report of the Holy Synod, in 1827, during the year 1825, and only among the Greek religion, 848 men had reached upwards of 100 years of age; 32 had passed their 120th year; 4 from 130 to 135. Out of 606,818 men who died in 1826, 2,765 were above 90; 1432 above 95; and 848 above 100 years of age. Among this last number 88 were above 115; 24 more than 120; 7 above 125; and one 130. Riley asserts that Arabs in the Desert live 200 years.

On the average, men have their first-born at 30 and women at 28. The greatest number of deliveries take place between 25 and 35. The greatest number of deliveries take place in the winter months, and in February, and the smallest in July, *i. e.*, to February, as 4 to 5 in towns and 3 to 4 in the country. The night births are to the day as 5 to 4.

Human Strength.—In Schulze's experiments on human strength, he found that men of five feet, weighing 126 lbs., could lift vertically 156 lbs. 8 inches; 217 lbs. 1.2 inches. Others, 6.1 feet, weighing 183 lbs., 156 lbs. 13 inches, and 217 lbs. 6 inches; others 6 feet 3 inches, weighing 158 lbs., 156 lbs. 16 inches, and 217 lbs. 9 inches. By a great variety of experiments he determined the mean human strength at 30 lbs., with a velocity of 2.5 feet per second; or it is equal to the raising half a hogshead 10 feet in a minute.

A good authority reckoned 1 horse equal to 5 men. Porters carry from 150 to 250 pounds. A man draws horizontally 70 to 80 lbs., and thrusts at the height of his chest 28 or 30 lbs. In hot climates men cannot perform half the continued labor. A man's mean labor is sufficient to raise 10 lbs. 10 feet in a second, for 10 hours per day, or 100 lbs. 1 foot in a second, or 36,000 feet in 10 hours; that is, 100 pounds per day would be 3,600,000 feet in a day, which he calls a dynamic unit. The force of a man in turning a winch is taken at 116 lbs.; or as much as would raise 256 lbs. 3,281 feet in a day; his force in pumping is as 190, or equal to 410 lbs. in 3,281 feet; in ringing, 259, or 572 lbs. in 3,281 feet; and in rowing 273, or 608 lbs. in 3,281 feet. In working a pump, a winch, a bell, and rowing, the effects are as 100, 167, 227 and 248. A man with an augur exerts a force of 100 lbs., with a screw-driver of 84 lbs., with a windlass 60 lbs., a hand-plane 50 lbs., a hand-saw 36 lbs.

What the White House Costs.

Salary of President	$50,000
Additional appropriations are about	75,000
A total of	$125,000

The President has the following corps of assistants:

Private Secretary	$3,250
Assistant Private Secretary	2,250
Stenographer	1,800
Five Messengers, $1,200 each	6,000
Steward	......
Two Doorkeepers, $1,200 each	2,400
Two Ushers, $1,200, $1,400	2,600
Night Usher	1,200
Watchman	900

And a few other minor clerks and telegraph operators.

SUNDRIES.

Incidental expenses	$8,000
White House repairs — Carpets and refurnishing	12,500
Fuel	2,500
Green-house	4,000
Gas, matches and stable	15,000

These amounts, with others of minor importance, consume the entire appropriations.

COST OF ROYALTY IN ENGLAND.

Pounds reduced to dollars.

The Queen — Privy purse	$300,000	
Sundries	1,629,000	
		$1,929,000
Prince of Wales		200,000
Princess		50,000
Prince Albert Victor		50,000
Crown Princess of Russia		40,000
Duke of Edinburgh		125,000
Princess Christian		30,000
Marchioness of Lorne		30,000
Duke of Connaught		125,000
Duke of Albany		125,000
Duke of Cambridge		30,000
Duchess of Mecklenburg-Strelitz		15,000
Duke of Cambridge		60,000
Duchess of Teck		25,000
Total		$2,834,000

Rules for Spelling.

Words ending in *e* drop that letter before the termination *able*, as in move, movable; unless ending in *ce* or *ge*, when it is retained, as in change, changeable, etc.

Words of one syllable, ending in a consonant, with a single vowel before it, double the consonants in derivatives; as, ship, shipping, etc. But if ending in a consonant with a double vowel before it, they do not double the consonant in derivatives; as troop, trooper, etc.

Words of more than one syllable, ending in a consonant preceded by a single vowel, and accented on the last syllable, double that consonant in derivatives; as commit, committed; but except chagrin, chagrined.

All words of one syllable ending in *l*, with a single vowel before it, have double *ll* at the close; as mill, sell

All words of one syllable ending in *l*, with a double vowel before it, have only one *l* at the close; as mail, sail.

The words foretell, distill, instill and fulfill, retain the double *ll* of their primitives. Derivatives of dull, skill, will and full also retain the *ll* when the accent falls on these words; as dullness, skillful, willful, fullness.

Words of more than one syllable ending in *l* have only one *l* at the close; as delightful, faithful; unless the accent falls on the last syllable; as befall, etc.

Words ending in *l*, double the letter in the termination *ly*.

Participles ending in *ing*, from verbs ending in *e*, lose the final *e;* as have, having; make, making, etc.; but verbs ending in *ee* retain both; as see, seeing. The word dye, to color, however, must retain the *e* before *ing*.

All verbs ending in *ly*, and nouns ending in *ment*, retain the *e* final of the primitives; as brave, bravely; refine, refinement; except words ending in *dge;* as acknowledge, acknowledgment.

Nouns ending in *y*, preceded by a vowel, form their plural by adding *s;* as money, moneys; but if *y* is preceded by a consonant, it is changed to *ies* in the plural; as bounty, bounties.

Compound words whose primitives end in *y*, change the *y* into *i;* as beauty, beautiful.

THE USE OF CAPITALS.

1. Every entire sentence should begin with a capital.
2. Proper names, and adjectives derived from these, should begin with a capital.
3. All appellations of the Deity should begin with a capital.
4. Official and honorary titles begin with a capital.
5. Every line of poetry should begin with a capital.
6. Titles of books and the heads of their chapters and divisions are printed in capitals.
7. The pronoun I and the exclamation O are always capitals.
8. The days of the week and the months of the year begin with capitals.
9. Every quotation should begin with a capital letter.
10. Names of religious denominations begin with capitals.
11. In preparing accounts, each item should begin with a capital.
12. Any word of very special importance may begin with a capital.

Savings Bank Compound Interest Table.

Showing the amount of $1, from 1 year to 15 years, with Compound Interest added semi-annually, at different rates.

		Ten Per cent.	Nine Per cent.	Eight Per cent.	Seven Per cent.	Six Per cent.	Five Per cent.	Four Per cent.	Three Per cent.
15	years	$4.32	$3.74	$3.24	$2.80	$2.42	$2.09	$1.80	$1.56
14	"	3.62	3.42	2.99	2.62	2.28	1.99	1.73	1.51
13	"	3.55	3.14	2.77	2.44	2.15	1.90	1.67	1.47
12	"	3.22	2.87	2.56	2.28	2.03	1.80	1.60	1.42
11	"	2.92	2.63	2.36	2.13	1.91	1.72	1.54	1.38
10	"	2.65	2.41	2.19	1.98	1.80	1.63	1.48	1.34
9½	"	2.52	2.30	2.10	1.92	1.75	1.59	1.45	1.32
9	"	2.40	2.20	2.02	1.85	1.70	1.55	1.42	1.30
8½	"	2.29	2.11	1.94	1.79	1.65	1.52	1.39	1.28
8	"	2.18	2.02	1.87	1.73	1.60	1.48	1.37	1.26
7½	"	2.07	1.93	1.80	1.67	1.55	1.44	1.34	1.24
7	"	1.97	1.85	1.73	1.61	1.51	1.41	1.31	1.23
6½	"	1.88	1.77	1.66	1.56	1.46	1.37	1.29	1.21
6	"	1.79	1.69	1.60	1.51	1.42	1.34	1.26	1.19
5½	"	1.71	1.62	1.53	1.45	1.38	1.31	1.24	1.17
5	"	1.62	1.55	1.48	1.41	1.34	1.28	1.21	1.16
4½	"	1.55	1.48	1.42	1.36	1.30	1.24	1.19	1.14
4	"	1.47	1.42	1.36	1.31	1.26	1.21	1.17	1.12
3½	"	1.40	1.36	1.31	1.27	1.22	1.18	1.14	1.10
3	"	1.34	1.30	1.26	1.22	1.19	1.15	1.12	1.09
2¼	"	1.27	1.24	1.21	1.18	1.15	1.13	1.10	1.07
2	"	1.21	1.19	1.16	1.14	1.12	1.10	1.08	1.06
1½	"	1.15	1.14	1.12	1.10	1.09	1.07	1.06	1.04
1	"	1.10	1.09	1.08	1.07	1.06	1.05	1.04	1.03
½	"	1.05	1.04	1.04	1.03	1.03	1.02	1.02	1.01

ONE DOLLAR LOANED 100 YEARS at Compound Interest would amount to the following sum:

24 per cent.....$2,351,799,404.00	10 per cent..........$13,809.00
18 " 15,145,207.00	6 " 340.00
15 " 1,174,405.00	3 " 19.25
12 " 84,675.00	1 " 2.75

Safe Business Rules.

Business men, in business hours, attend only to business matters. Social calls are best adapted to the social circle. Make your business known in few words, without loss of time. Let your dealings with a stranger be most carefully considered, and tried friendship duly appreciated. A mean act will soon recoil, and a man of honor will be esteemed. Leave "tricks of trade" to those whose education was never completed. Treat all with respect, confide in few, wrong no man. Be never afraid to say no, and always prompt to acknowledge and rectify a wrong. Leave nothing for to-morrow that should be done to-day. Because a friend is polite, do not think that his time is valueless. Have a place for every thing, and every thing in its place. To preserve long friendship, keep a short credit; the way to get credit is to be punctual; the way to preserve it is not to use it much. Settle often; have short accounts. Trust no man's appearances; they are often deceptive, and assumed for the purpose of obtaining credit. Rogues generally dress well. The rich are genally plain men. Be well satisfied before you give a credit that those to whom you give it are safe men to be trusted.

Time at which Money Doubles at Interest.

Rate per cent.	Simple Interest.	Compound Interest.
10	10 years.	7 years 100 days.
9	11 years 40 days.	8 years 16 days.
8	12½ years.	9 years 2 days.
7	14 years 104 days.	10 years 89 days.
6	16 years 8 months.	11 years 327 days.
5	20 years.	15 years 75 days.
4½	22 years 81 days.	15 years 273 days.
4	25 years.	17 years 246 days.
3½	28 years 208 days.	20 years 54 days.
3	33 years 4 months.	23 years 164 days.
2½	40 years.	28 years 26 days.
2	50 years.	35 years 1 day.

Legal Brevities.

A note dated on Sunday is void. A note obtained by fraud, or from one intoxicated, is void. If a note be lost or stolen, it does not release the maker, he must pay it. An endorser of a note is exempt from liability, if not served with notice of its dishonor within 24 hours of its non-payment. A note by a minor is void. Notes bear interest only when so stated. Principals are responsible for their agents. Each individual in partnership is responsible for the whole amount of the debts of the firm

Ignorance of the law excuses no one. It is a fraud to conceal a fraud. It is illegal to compound a felony. The law compels no one to do impossibilities. An agreement without consideration is void. Signatures in lead pencil are good in law. A receipt for money is not legally conclusive. The acts of one partner bind all the others. Contracts made on Sunday cannot be enforced. A contract with a minor is void. A contract made with a lunatic is void. Written contracts concerning land must be under seal.

Occupations of Legislators.

OCCUPATIONS.	ENGLISH. New House of Comm'ns.	FRENCH. Chamber of Deputies.	AMERIC'N. Forty-ninth Congress.
Lawyers................	134	133	302
Soldiers................	54	13	..
Merchants.............	42	18	22
Journalists	34	42	10
Bankers...............	25	5	9
Brewers and Distillers..	24	..	..
Shipowners	21	3	..
Railroad Presidents and Agents	..	..	5
Farmers and Planters..	..	..	21
Physicians.............	16	40	8
Manufacturers.........	..	..	18
Professors.............	9	14	..
Engineers.............	6	18	1
Professional Politicans.	..	..	4
Miners................	..	..	2
Clergymen............	2	3	2
Surveyor	..	..	1
Mechanic.............	..	..	1
Builder and Contractor	..	..	1

TAX ON COMMERCIAL TRAVELERS.

The following is a list of places and amount of taxation on commercial travelers: Alabama, $15.50 per year; Arizona, $200 per year; Beaufort, S. C., $10 per visit; Bennettsville, S. C., $1 per visit; Batesburg, S. C., 75 cents per day; Charleston, S. C., $10 per month; Cumberland, Md., $1 per day; Delaware, $25 per year; Deadwood, D. T., $5 per week; Darlington, S. C., $1; East St. Louis, $2 per day; Elkton, Md., per cent. on stock carried; Florida, $25 per year; Hartwell, Ga., $5 per trip; Johnston, S. C., 50 cents per day; Lewistown, Idaho, $5 per trip; Montana, $100 per year for each county; Memphis, Tenn., $10 per week or $25 per month; Mobile, Ala., $3 per day or $7 a week; Natchez, Miss., 25 cents per day; New Orleans, La., $50 per year; Newport, Ky., $1 per month; North Carolina, $100 per year; Nevada, $100 per year; Orangeburg, S. C., $2 per day; St. Matthews, S. C., $1 per day; San Francisco, Cal., $25 per quarter; Texas, $35 a year; Tucson, Arizona, $50 per quarter; Tombstone, Arizona, $10 per day; Virginia, $75 per year; Wilmington, N. C., $3 per day; Washington, D. C., $200 per year; Walhalla, S. C., $1 per day.

Durability of Different Woods.

Experiments have been made by driving sticks, made of different woods, each two feet long and one and one-half inches square, into the ground, only one-half an inch projecting outward. It was found that in five years, all those made of oak, elm, ash, fir, soft mahogany, and nearly every variety of pine, were totally rotten. Larch, hard pine and teak wood were decayed on the outside only; while acacia, with the exception of being also slightly attacked on the exterior, was otherwise sound. Hard mahogany and cedar of Lebanon were in tolerably good condition; but only Virginia cedar was found as good as when put in the ground. This is of some importance to builders, showing what wood should be avoided, and what others used by preference in underground work.

The duration of wood, when kept dry, is very great, as

beams still exist which are known to be nearly 1,100 years old. Piles driven by the Romans prior to the Christian era, have been examined of late, and found to be perfectly sound, after an immersion of nearly 2,000 years.

The wood of some tools will last longer than the metals; as in spades, hoes and plows. In other tools the wood is first gone; as in wagons, wheel-barrows and machines. Such wood should be painted or oiled; the paint not only looks well, but preserves the wood; petroleum oil is as good as any other.

Hard wood stumps decay in five or six years; spruce stumps decay in about the same time; hemlock stumps in eight to nine years; cedar, eight to nine years; pine stumps, never.

Cedar, oak, yellow pine and chestnut are the most durable woods in dry places.

FASTEST RAILROAD TIME.

1 mile—50¼ s., 3 miles in 2m. 36¼ s., and 5 miles in 4m. 50s,; train which left West Philadelphia for Jersey City (P. R. R.) at 7:35 a. m. (Edward Osmond, engineer) September 4, 1879.

10 miles—8 min., Hamburg to Buffalo, N. Y., Lake Shore and Michigan Southern R. R.; in 9 min., Hudson River road, locomotive and platform car, with steam fire-engine, Peekskill to Sing Sing, N, Y., February 17, 1874.

14 miles—11 min., locomotive Hamilton Davis and six cars, New York Central R. R., 1855.

18 miles—15 min., special train conveying the Duke of Wellington, Paddington to Slough, England.

111 miles—98 min., no stop, new Fontaine engine and two coaches, carrying W. H. Vanderbilt and party—Amherstburg to St. Thomas, Canada Southern Railway, May 5, 1881....109 min., special train, consisting of locomotive, baggage-car, one coach and one Pullman palace-car, Engineer McComber, carrying Bishop of Detroit and a number of the clergy; the time includes 4 min. stoppage at Charing Cross—St. Thomas to Amherstburg, September 13, 1877.

RATES OF POSTAGE.

Letters.—Prepaid by stamps, 2 cents each ounce or fraction thereof to all parts of the United States and Canada; forwarded to another postoffice without charge on request of the person addressed; if not called for, returned to the writer free, if indorsed with that request. If the stamp is omitted, the letter is forwarded to the Dead Letter Office, and returned to the writer. For Registering letters the charge is 10 cents additional. Drop 'etters at letter-carrier offices, 2 cents per ounce or fracion thereof; at other offices, 1 cent per ounce or fraction thereof. On insufficiently prepaid matter mailed in Canada, 3 cents per ½ ounce or fraction thereof. Stamped Postal Cards, furnished only by Government, 1 cent each. If anything except a printed address slip is pasted on a Postal Card, or anything but the address written on the face, letter postage is charged. Postage on all newspapers and periodicals sent from newspaper offices to any part of the United States, to regular subscribers, must be paid in advance at the office of mailing.

Second-Class Matter.—Periodicals issued at regular intervals—at least four times a year—and having a regular list of subscribers, with supplement, sample copies, 1 cent a pound; periodicals, other than weekly, if delivered by letter-carrier, 1 cent each; if over 2 ounces, 2 cents each. When sent by other than publishers, for 4 ounces or less, 1 cent.

Third-Class Matter (not exceeding 4 pounds).—Printed matter, books, proof-sheets, corrected or uncorrected, unsealed circulars, inclosed so as to admit of easy inspection without cutting cords or wrapper, 1 cent for each 2 ounces.

Fourth-Class Matter.—Not exceeding 4 pounds, embracing merchandise and samples, excluding liquids, poisons, greasy, inflammable or explosive articles, live animals, insects, etc., 1 cent an ounce. Postage to Canada and British North American States, 2 cents per ounce; must be prepaid; otherwise, 6 cents.

Number of Years Seeds Retain Their Vitality.

Vegetables.	Years.
Artichoke	5 to 6
Asparagus	2 to 3
Beans	2 to 3
Beets	3 to 4
Broccoli	5 to 6
Cucumber	8 to 10
Cauliflower	5 to 6
Cress	3 to 4
Carrots	2 to 3
Celery	2 to 3
Corn (on cob)	2 to 3
Endive	5 to 6
Egg Plant	1 to 2
Leek	2 to 3
Lettuce	3 to 4
Melon	8 to 10
Mustard	3 to 4
Okra	3 to 4
Onion	2 to 3
Pea	5 to 6
Pumpkin	8 to 10
Parsley	2 to 3
Parsnip	2 to 4
Pepper	2 to 3
Rhubarb	3 to 4
Squash	8 to 10
Spinach	3 to 4
Turnip	3 to 6
Tomato	2 to 3

HOW TO MIX PAINTS FOR TINTS.

Red and Black makes.....................Brown
Lake and White makes.....................Rose
White and Brown makes...................Chestnut
White, Blue and Lake makes..................Purple
Blue and Lead Color makes...................Pearl

White and Carmine makes.....................Pink
Indigo and Lamp-Black makes............Silver Gray
White and Lamp-Black makes............Lead Color
Black and Venetian Red makes.............Chocolate
White and Green makes.................Bright Green
Purp e and White makes................French White
Light Green and Black makes.............Dark Green
White and Green makes....................Pea Green
White and Emerald Green makes........Brilliant Green
Red and Yellow makes.......................Orange
White and Yellow makes.................Straw Color
White, Blue and Black makes..............Pearl Gray
White, Lake and Vermillion makes........Flesh Color
Umber, White and Venetian Red makes.........Drab
White, Yellow and Venetian Red makes........Cream
Red, Blue, Black and Red makes................Olive
Yellow, White and a little Venetian Red makes....Buff

DEGREES OF HEAT AND COLD REQUIRED TO FREEZE, MELT AND BOIL THE FOLLOWING SUBSTANCES.

Degrees of Heat ABOVE ZERO at which the following articles Melt.

Cast Iron	3,500
Glass	2,400
Copper	2,160
Gold	1,983
Brass	1,900
Silver	1,850
Antimony	950
Zinc	780
Lead	590
Bismuth	476
Tin	420
Gutta Percha	150
Lard	96
Ice	35

Degrees of Cold ABOVE ZERO at which the following articles Freeze.

Turpentine (Spirits) 15
Strong Wine.................................. 20
Milk........... 29
Water 32

Degrees of Heat ABOVE ZERO at which the following articles Boil.

Blood Heat..................................... 98
Alcohol....................................... 175
Water 210
Petroleum..................................... 305
Linseed Oil................................... 600
Quicksilver................................... 630

Tables of Weights and Measures.
CUBIC MEASURE.

1,728 cubic inches 1 cubic foot, 27 cubic feet 1 cubic yard, 128 cubic feet 1 cord (wood), 40 cubic feet 1 ton (shipping), 2,150.42 cubic inches 1 standard bushel, 268.8 cubic inches 1 standard gallon, 1 cubic foot four-fifths of a bushel.

SURVEYOR'S MEASURE.

7.92 inches 1 link, 25 links 1 rod, 4 rods 1 chain, 10 square chains or 160 square rods 1 acre, 640 acres 1 square mile.

LONG MEASURE—DISTANCE.

3 barleycorns 1 inch, 12 inches 1 foot, 3 feet 1 yard, 5½ yards 1 rod, 40 rods 1 furlong, 8 furlongs 1 mile.

DRY MEASURE.

2 pints make 1 quart, 8 quarts make 1 peck, 4 pecks make 1 bushel, 36 bushels make 1 chaldron.

LIQUID OR WINE MEASURE.

4 gills make 1 pint, 2 pints make 1 quart, 4 quarts make 1 gallon, 31½ gallons make 1 barrel, 2 barrels make 1 hogshead.

APOTHECARIES' WEIGHT.

20 grains make 1 scruple, 3 scruples make 1 drachm, 8 drachms make 1 ounce, 12 ounces make 1 pound.

TROY WEIGHT.

24 grains make 1 pennyweight, 20 pennyweight make 1 ounce. By this weight, gold, silver and jewels only are weighed. The ounce and pound in this are same as in Apothecaries' weight.

AVOIRDUPOIS WEIGHT.

6 drachms make 1 ounce, 16 ounces make 1 pound, 25 pounds make 1 quarter, 4 quarters make 100 weight, 2,000 pounds make 1 ton.

CIRCULAR MEASURE.

60 seconds make 1 minute, 60 minutes make 1 degree, 30 degrees make 1 sign, 90 degrees make 1 quadrant, 4 quadrants or 360 degrees make 1 circle.

TIME MEASURE.

60 seconds make 1 minute, 60 minutes make 1 hour, 24 hours make 1 day, 7 days make 1 week, 4 weeks make 1 lunar month, 28, 29, 30, or 31 days make 1 calendar month (30 days make 1 month in computing interest), 52 weeks and 1 day, or 12 calendar months make 1 year, 365 days, 5 hours, 48 minutes, and 49 seconds make 1 solar year.

SQUARE MEASURE.

144 square inches 1 square foot, 9 square feet 1 square yard, 30¼ square yards 1 square rod, 40 square rods 1 rood, 4 roods 1 acre.

CLOTH MEASURE.

2¼ inches 1 nail, 4 nails 1 quarter, 4 quarters 1 yard.

MISCELLANEOUS.

3 inches 1 palm, 4 inches 1 hand, 6 inches 1 span, 18 inches 1 cubit, 21.8 inches 1 Bible cubit, 2½ feet 1 military pace.

Choice Selections for Autograph Albums.

In leisure moments cast a look
Upon the pages of this book;
When absent friends thy thoughts engage,
Think of the one who fills this page.

Go forth, thou little volume,
  I leave thee to thy fate;
'To love and friendship truly
  Thy leaves I dedicate.

Go, little book, thy destined course pursue,
Collect memorials of the just and true,
And beg of every friend so near
Some token of remembrance dear.

In this fair garden plants shall grow,
And in their freshness bud and blow —
Plants to which love has beauty lent,
And blossoms sweet of sentiment.

What's the use of always fretting
  At the trials we shall find
Ever strewn along our pathway—
  Travel on, and never mind.

When the golden sun is setting,
  And your mind from care is free,
When of others you are thinking,
  Will you sometimes think of me?

I can but add one little pearl
  To all the gems about thee scattered;
And say again, sweet, artless girl,
  That all the poets have not flattered.

Think not, though distant that thou art,
  Thou canst forgotten be;
While memory lives within my heart
  I will remember *thee*.

May happiness ever be thy lot,
  Wherever thou shalt be;
And joy and pleasure light the spot
  That may be home to thee.

POLITICAL INFORMATION.

Result of the Electoral College proceedings by States from 1789 to and including 1885.

1789, WASHINGTON AND ADAMS—Washington had the vote of all the states, viz., New Hampshire, Massachusetts, Connecticut, New Jersey, Pennsylvania, Delaware, Maryland, Virginia, South Carolina and Georgia; total 69 votes.
Adams had all of New Hampshire, Massachusetts, 5 of the 7 of Connecticut, 1 of the 6 of New Jersey, 8 of the 10 of Pennsylvania, 5 of the 10 of Virginia; total 34.

1793, WASHINGTON AND ADAMS—Washington had the votes of all the states, viz.: New Hampshire, New York, New Jersey, Pennsylvania, Delaware, Maryland, Virginia, Kentucky, North Carolina, South Carolina and Georgia; total 132.
Adams carried all these states with the exception of New York, Virginia, Kentucky, North Carolina and Georgia; total 77 votes.

1797, ADAMS AND JEFFERSON—Adams had the votes of New Hampshire, Massachusetts, Rhode Island, Connecticut, Vermont, New York, New Jersey, Delaware, 1 of the 15 of Pennsylvania, 1 of the 20 of Virginia, 1 of the 12 of North Carolina, and 7 of the 11 of Maryland; total 71.
Thomas Jefferson had 14 of the 15 votes of Pennsylvania, 4 of the 11 of Maryland, 20 of the 21 of Virginia, Kentucky, 11 of the 12 of North Carolina, Tennessee, Georgia and South Carolina; total 68.

1801, JEFFERSON AND BURR—Had the votes of the states of New York, 8 of the 15 of Pennsylvania, 5 of the 10 of Maryland, Virginia, Kentucky, 8 of the 12 of North Carolina, Tennessee, South Carolina and Georgia; total 73. House decided Jefferson President, and Burr Vice-President.
ADAMS AND PINCKNEY—Had the votes of states of New Hampshire, Massachusetts, Rhode Island, Connecticut, Vermont, New Jersey, 7 of the 15 of Pennsylvania, Delaware, 5 of the 10 of Maryland, and 4 of the 12 of North Carolina; total 65.

1805, JEFFERSON AND CLINTON—Had the votes of states of New Hampshire, Massachusetts, Rhode Island, Vermont, New York, New Jersey, Pennsylvania, Maryland, Virginia, North Carolina, South Carolina, Georgia, Tennessee, Kentucky and Ohio; total 162.
PINCKNEY AND KING—Had the votes of states of Connecticut, Delaware and 2 of the 11 of Maryland; total 14.

1809, MADISON AND CLINTON—Had the votes of the states of Vermont, New York, New Jersey, Pennsylvania, 9 of the 11 of Maryland, Virginia, 11 of the 14 of North Carolina, South Carolina, Georgia, Kentucky, Tennessee and Ohio; total 122.
PINCKNEY AND KING—Had the votes of the states of New York, Massachusetts, Rhode Island, Connecticut, Delaware, 2 of the 11 of Maryland, and 3 of the 14 of North Carolina; total 47.

1813, MADISON AND GERRY—Carried Vermont, Pennsylvania,

6 of the 11 of Maryland, Virginia, North Carolina, South Carolina, Georgia, Kentucky, Tennessee, Ohio and Louisiana; total 128.

CLINTON AND INGERSOLL—Had the votes of the states of New Hampshire, Massachusetts, Rhode Island, Connecticut, New York, New Jersey, Delaware and 5 of the 11 of Maryland; total 89.

1817, MONROE AND TOMPKINS—Had the votes of the states of New Hampshire, Rhode Island, Vermont, New York, New Jersey, Pennsylvania, Maryland, Virginia, North Carolina, South Carolina, Georgia, Kentucky, Tennessee, Ohio, Louisiana and Indiana; total 183.

KING AND HOWARD—Had the votes of the states of Massachusetts, Connecticut and Delaware; total 34.

1821, MONROE AND TOMPKINS—Had the votes of every state in the Union; total 231.

ADAMS AND STOCKTON—Adams had 1 vote of the 8 of New Hampshire, and Stockton 8 of the 15 of Massachusetts.

1825, ADAMS AND CALHOUN—Had the votes of the states of Maine, New Hampshire, Massachusetts, Rhode Island, Connecticut, Vermont, 26 of the 36 of New York, 1 of the 3 of Delaware, 3 of the 11 of Maryland, 2 of the 5 of Louisiana, and 1 of the 3 of Illinois; total 84 for Adams. Calhoun for Vice-President carried several states that Adams did not carry, and had a total of 182 votes.

CRAWFORD—Had 5 of the 36 votes of New York, 2 of the 3 of Delaware, and 1 of the 11 of Maryland, Virginia and Georgia; total 41.

JACKSON—Had 1 of the 36 votes of New York, New Jersey, Pennsylvania, 7 of the 11 of Maryland, North Carolina, South Carolina, Tennessee, 3 of the 5 of Louisiana, Mississippi, Indiana, Illinois and Alabama; total 99.

CLAY—Had 4 of the 36 votes of New York, Kentucky, Ohio and Missouri; total 37.

No choice by the electoral college, it devolving upon House of Representatives. A choice was reached on first ballot as follows: Adams—Connecticut, Illinois, Kentucky, Louisiana, Maine, Maryland, Massachusetts, Missouri, New Hampshire, New York, Ohio, Rhode Island and Vermont; 13 states. Jackson—Alabama, Indiana, Missouri, New Jersey, Pennsylvania, South Carolina and Tennessee; 7 states. Crawford—Delaware, Georgia, North Carolina and Virginia; 4 states.

1829—JACKSON AND CALHOUN—Had 1 of the votes of the 9 of Maine, 20 of the 36 of New York, Pennsylvania, 5 of the 11 of Maryland, Virginia, North Carolina, South Carolina, Georgia, Kentucky, Tennessee, Ohio, Indiana, Mississippi, Illinois, Alabama and Missouri; total 178.

ADAMS AND RUSH—Had 8 of the 9 votes of Maine, New Hampshire, Massachusetts, Rhode Island, Connecticut, Vermont, 16 of the 36 of New York, New Jersey, Delaware, and 6 of the 11 of Maryland; total 83.

1833, JACKSON AND VAN BUREN—Had the votes of Maine, New Hampshire, New York, New Jersey, Pennsylvania, 3 of the 8 of Maryland, Virginia, North Carolina, Georgia, Tennessee,

Ohio, Louisiana, Mississippi, Indiana, Illinois, Alabama and Missouri; total 219.

CLAY AND SERGEANT—Had the votes of the states of Massachusetts, Rhode Island, Connecticut, Delaware, 5 of the 8 of Maryland, and Kentucky; total 49.

1837, VAN BUREN AND JOHNSON—Had the votes of the states of Maine, New Hampshire, Rhode Island, Connecticut, New York, Pennsylvania, Virginia, North Carolina, Louisiana, Mississippi, Illinois, Alabama, Missouri, Arkansas and Michigan; total 170.

HARRISON AND GRANGER—Had the votes of the states of Vermont, New Jersey, Delaware, Maryland, Kentucky, Ohio and Indiana; total 73.

1841, HARRISON AND TYLER—Had the votes of the states of Maine, Massachusetts, Rhode Island, Connecticut, Vermont, New York, New Jersey, Pennsylvania, Delaware, Maryland, North Carolina, Georgia, Kentucky, Tennessee, Ohio, Louisiana, Mississippi, Indiana and Michigan; total 234.

VAN BUREN—Had the votes of the states of New Hampshire, Virginia, South Carolina, Illinois, Alabama, Missouri and Arkansas; total 60.

1845, POLK AND DALLAS—Had the votes of the states of Maine, New Hampshire, New York, Pennsylvania, Virginia, South Carolina, Georgia, Louisiana, Mississippi, Indiana, Illinois, Alabama, Missouri, Arkansas and Michigan; total 170.

CLAY AND FRELINGHUYSEN—Had the votes of the states of Rhode Island, Connecticut, Vermont, New Jersey, Delaware, Maryland, North Carolina, Kentucky, Tennessee and Ohio; total 105.

1849, TAYLOR AND FILLMORE—Had the votes of the states of Massachusetts, Rhode Island, Connecticut, Vermont, New York, New Jersey, Pennsylvania, Delaware, Maryland, North Carolina, Georgia, Kentucky, Tennessee, Louisiana and Florida; total 163.

CASS AND BUTLER—Had the votes of the states of Maine, New Hampshire, Virginia, South Carolina, Ohio, Mississippi, Indiana, Illinois, Alabama, Missouri, Arkansas, Michigan, Texas, Iowa and Wisconsin; total 127.

1853, PIERCE AND KING—Had the votes of the states of Maine, New Hampshire, Rhode Island, Connecticut, New York, New Jersey, Pennsylvania, Delaware, Maryland, Virginia, North Carolina, South Carolina, Georgia, Ohio, Louisiana, Mississippi, Indiana, Illinois, Alabama, Missouri, Arkansas, Michigan, Florida, Texas, Iowa, Wisconsin and California; total 254.

SCOTT AND GRAHAM—Had the votes of the states of Massachusetts, Vermont, Kentucky and Tennessee; total 42.

1857, BUCHANAN AND BRECKINRIDGE—Had the votes of the states of New Jersey, Pennsylvania, Delaware, Virginia, North Carolina, South Carolina, Georgia, Kentucky, Tennessee, Louisiana, Mississippi, Indiana, Illinois, Alabama, Missouri, Arkansas, Florida, Texas and California; total 174.

FREMONT AND DAYTON—Had the votes of the states of Maine, New Hampshire, Massachusetts, Rhode Island, Connecticut,

Vermont, New York, Ohio, Michigan, Iowa and Wisconsin; total 114.

FILLMORE AND DONELSON—Had the votes of the state of Maryland; total 8.

1861, LINCOLN AND HAMLIN—Had the votes of the states of Maine, New Hampshire, Massachusetts, Rhode Island, Connecticut, Vermont, New York, 4 of the 7 of New Jersey, Pennsylvania, Ohio, Indiana, Illinois, Michigan, Iowa, Wisconsin, California, Minnesota and Oregon; total 180.

BRECKINRIDGE AND LANE—Had the votes of the states of Delaware, Maryland, North Carolina, South Carolina, Georgia, Louisiana, Mississippi, Alabama, Arkansas, Florida and Texas; total 72.

DOUGLAS AND JOHNSON—Had the votes of the states of Missouri, and 3 of the 7 of New Jersey; total 12.

BELL AND EVERETT—Had the votes of the states of Virginia, Kentucky and Tennessee; total 39.

1865, LINCOLN AND JOHNSON—Had the votes of the states of Maine, New Hampshire, Massachusetts, Rhode Island, Connecticut, Vermont, New York, Pennsylvania, Maryland, Ohio, Indiana, Illinois, Missouri, Michigan, Wisconsin, Iowa, California, Minnesota, Oregon, Kansas, West Virginia and Nebraska; total 212.

McCLELLAN AND PENDLETON—Had the votes of the states of New Jersey, Delaware and Kentucky; total 21.

Eleven states did not vote, viz.: Alabama, Arkansas, Florida, Georgia, Louisiana, Mississippi, North Carolina, South Carolina, Tennessee, Texas and Virginia.

1869, GRANT AND COLFAX—Had the votes of the states of Maine, New Hampshire, Vermont, Massachusetts, Rhode Island, Connecticut, Pennsylvania, North Carolina, South Carolina, Alabama, Ohio, Tennessee, Indiana, Illinois, Missouri, Arkansas, Michigan, Florida, Iowa, Wisconsin, California, Minnesota, Kansas, West Virginia, Nevada and Nebraska; total 214.

SEYMOUR AND BLAIR—Had the votes of the states of New York, New Jersey, Delaware, Maryland, Georgia, Louisiana, Kentucky and Oregon; total 80.

Three states did not vote, viz.: Mississippi, Texas and Virginia.

1873, GRANT AND WILSON—Had the votes of the states of Maine, New Hampshire, Vermont, Massachusetts, Rhode Island, Connecticut, New York, New Jersey, Pennsylvania, Delaware, Virginia, North Carolina, South Carolina, Alabama, Ohio, Indiana, Illinois, Mississippi, Michigan, Florida, Iowa, Wisconsin, California, Minnesota, Oregon, Kansas, West Virginia, Nebraska and Nevada; total 286.

GREELEY AND BROWN—Had the votes of the states of Maryland, Georgia, Kentucky, Tennessee, Missouri and Texas; total 63.

Three electoral votes of Georgia cast for Greeley, and the votes of Arkansas, 6, and Louisiana, 8, cast for Grant, were rejected.

1877, HAYES AND WHEELER—Had the votes of the states of

Maine, New Hampshire, Vermont, Massachusetts, Rhode Island, Pennsylvania, South Carolina, Ohio, Louisiana, Illinois, Michigan, Florida, Iowa, Wisconsin, California, Minnesota, Oregon, Kansas, Nevada, Nebraska and Colorado; total 185.

TILDEN AND HENDRICKS—Had the votes of the states of Connecticut, New York, New Jersey, Delaware, Maryland, Virginia, North Carolina, Georgia, Alabama, Kentucky, Tennessee, Indiana, Missouri, Arkansas, Mississippi, Texas and West Virginia; total 184.

1881, GARFIELD AND ARTHUR—Had the votes of the states of Maine, New Hampshire, Vermont, Massachusetts, Rhode Island, Connecticut, New York, Pennsylvania, Ohio, Indiana, Illinois, Michigan, Iowa, Wisconsin, 1 of the 6 of California, Minnesota, Oregon, Kansas, Nebraska and Colorado; total 214.

HANCOCK AND ENGLISH—Had the votes of the states of New Jersey, Delaware, Maryland, Virginia, North Carolina, South Carolina, Georgia, Alabama, Louisiana, Kentucky, Tennessee, Missouri, Arkansas, Mississippi, Florida, Texas, 5 of the 6 of California, West Virginia and Nebraska; total 155.

1885, CLEVELAND AND HENDRICKS—Had the votes of the states of Alabama, Arkansas, Connecticut, Delaware, Florida, Georgia, Indiana, Kentucky, Louisiana, Maryland, Mississippi, Missouri, New Jersey, New York, North Carolina, South Carolina, Tennessee, Texas, Virginia, West Virginia; total 203.

BLAINE AND LOGAN—Had the votes of the states of California, Colorado, Illinois, Iowa, Kansas, Maine, Massachusetts, Michigan, Minnesota, Nebraska, Nevada, New Hampshire, Ohio, Oregon, Pennsylvania, Rhode Island, Vermont, Wisconsin; total 166.

VOTE BY STATES.

Showing vote for electors in each State from 1824 to and including 1885. Prior to 1824 legislatures chose electors. In South Carolina this rule was followed up to 1868, and in Colorado in 1876.

ALABAMA—1824, Dem. majority 5,280; 1828, Dem. majority, 15,200; 1836, Dem. majority 3,431; 1840, Dem. majority 5,520; 1844, Dem. majority 11,656; 1848, Dem. majority 881; 1852, Dem. majority 11,843; 1856, Dem. majority 18,187; 1860, Dem. majority 7,355; 1868, Rep. majority 4,278; 1872, Rep. majority 10,828; 1876, Dem. majority 33,772; 1880, Dem. majority 29,867; 1884, Dem. plurality 33,529.

ARKANSAS—1836, Dem. majority 1,162; 1840, Dem. majority 889; 1844, Dem. majority 4,042; 1848, Dem. majority 1,712; 1852, Dem. majority 4,769; 1856, Dem. majority 11,123; 1860, Dem. majority 3,411; 1868, Rep. majority 3,034; 1872, Rep. majority 3,446; 1876, Dem. majority 19,113; 1880, Dem. majority 14,749; 1884, Dem. plurality 22,208.

CALIFORNIA—1852, Dem. majority 5,119; 1856, Dem. plurality 17,200; 1870, Rep. plurality 657; 1864, Rep. majority 18,293; 1868, Rep. majority 506; 1872, Rep. majority 12,234; 1876, Rep. majority 2,738; 1880, Dem. plurality 78; 1884, Rep. plurality 13,128.

COLORADO—1880, Rep. majority 1,368.

CONNECTICUT—1824, Loose Constructionist (Rep.) majority 5,609; 1828, Loose Constructionist (Rep.) majority 9,381; 1832, Loose Constructionist (Rep.) majority 6,486; 1836, Dem. majority 768; 1840, Whig (Rep.) majority 6,131; 1844, Whig (Rep.) majority 1,048; 1848, Whig (Rep.) plurality 3,268; 1852, Dem. plurality 2,892; 1856, Rep. majority 5,105; 1860, Rep. majority 10,238; 1864, Rep. majority 2,406; 1868, Rep. majority 3,043; 1872, Rep. majority 4,348; 1876, Dem majority 1,712; 1880, Rep. majority 1,788; 1884, Dem. plurality 1,274.

DELAWARE—1828, Loose Constructionist (Rep.) majority 420; 1832, Loose Constructionist (Rep.) majority 166; 1836, Whig (Rep.) majority 583; 1840, Whig (Rep.) majority 1,083; 1844, Whig (Rep.) majority 282; 1848, Whig (Rep.) majority 443; 1852, Dem. plurality 25; 1856, Dem. majority 1,521; 1860, Dem. plurality 3,483; 1864, Dem. majority 612; 1868, Dem. majority 3,357; 1872, Rep. majority 422; 1876, Dem. majority 2,629; 1880, Dem. majority 1,023; 1884, Dem. plurality 423.

FLORIDA—1848, Whig (Rep.) majority 1,269; 1852, Dem. majority 1,443; 1856, Dem majority 1,525; 1860, Dem. majority 2,739; 1872, Rep. majority 2,336; 1876, Rep. majority 926; 1880, Dem. majority 4,310; 1884, Dem. plurality 3,738.

GEORGIA—1836, Whig (Rep.) majority 2,804; 1840, Whig (Rep.) majority 8,328; 1844, Dem majority 2,071; 1848, Whig (Rep) majority 2,742: 1852, Dem majority 18,045; 1856, Dem. majority 14,350; 1860, Dem plurality 9,003; 1868, Dem majority 45,588; 1872, Dem majority 9,806; 1876, Dem majority 79,642; 1880, Dem majority 4,199; 1884, Dem plurality 46,961.

ILLINOIS—1824, Dem plurality 359; 1828, Dem majority 5,182; 1832, Dem majority 8,718; 1836, Dem majority 3,114; 1840, Dem majority 1,790; 1844, Dem majority 8,822; 1848, Dem plurality 3,253; 1852, Dem majority 5,697; 1856, Dem plurality 9,159; 1860, Rep majority 5,629; 1864, Rep majority 30,766; 1868, Rep majority 51,160; 1872, Rep majority 53,948; 1876, Rep majority 1,971; 1880, Rep majority 14,358; 1884, Rep plurality 25,122.

INDIANA—1824, Dem plurality 2,028; 1828, Dem majority 5,185; 1832, Dem majority 16,080; 1836, Whig (Rep) majority 8,801; 1840, Whig (Rep) majority 13,607; 1844, Dem majority 208; 1848, Dem plurality 4,838; 1852, Dem majority 7,510; 1856, Dem majority 1,909; 1860, Rep majority 5,923; 1864, Rep majority 20,189; 1868, Rep majority 9,568; 1872, Rep majority 21,098; 1876, Dem plurality 5,515; 1880, Rep plurality 6,641; 1884, Dem plurality 6,527.

IOWA—1848, Dem plurality 1,009; 1852, Dem majority 303; 1856, Rep plurality 7,784; 1860, Rep majority 12,487; 1864, Rep majority 39,479; 1868, Rep majority 46,359; 1872, Rep majority 58,149; 1876, Rep majority 50,191; 1880, Rep majority 45,732; 1884, Rep plurality 19,796.

KANSAS—1864, Rep majority 12,750; 1868, Rep majority

17,058; 1872, Rep majority 33,482; 1876, Rep majority 32,511; 1880, Rep majority 42,021; 1884, Rep plurality 64,274.

KENTUCKY—1824, Loose Constructionist (Rep) majority 10,329; 1828, Dem majority 7,912; 1832, Loose Constructionist (Rep) majority 7,149; 1836, Whig (Rep) majority 5,520; 1840, Whig (Rep) majority 25,873; 1844, Whig (Rep) majority 9,267; 1848, Whig (Rep) majority 17,421; 1852, Whig (Rep) majority 2,997; 1856; Dem majority 6,912; 1860, Constitutional Union plurality 12,915; 1864, Dem majority 36,515; 1868, Dem majority 76,324; 1872, Dem majority 8,855; 1876, Dem majority 59,772; 1880, Dem majority 31,951; 1884, Dem plurality 34,839.

LOUISIANA—1828, Dem. majority 508; 1832, Dem. majority 1,521; 1836, Dem. majority 270; 1840, Whig (Rep.) majority 3,680; 1844, Dem. majority 699; 1848, Whig (Rep.) majority 2,847; 1852, Dem. majority 1,392; 1856, Dem. majority 1,455; 1860, Dem. plurality 2,477; 1868, Dem. majority 46,962; 1872, Rep. majority 14,634; 1876, Rep. majority 4,499; 1880, Dem. majority 33,419; 1884, Dem. plurality 16,250.

MAINE—1824, Loose Constructionist (Rep.) majority 4,540; 1828, Loose Constructionist (Rep.) majority 6,848; 1840, Whig (Rep.) majority 217; 1844, Dem. majority 6,505; 1848, Dem. plurality 4,755; 1852, Dem. majority 1,036; 1856, Rep. majority 24,974; 1860, Rep. majority 27,704; 1864, Rep. majority 17,592; 1868, Rep. majority 28,033; 1872, Rep. majority 32,355; 1876, Rep. majority 15,814; 1880, Rep. majority 4,460; 1884, Rep. plurality 20,069.

MARYLAND—1824, Loose Constructionist (Rep.) plurality 109; 1828, Loose Constructionist (Rep.) majority 1,181; 1832, Loose Constructionist (Rep.) majority 4; 1836, Whig (Rep.) majority 3,685; 1840, Whig (Rep.) majority 4,776; 1844, Whig (Rep.) majority 3,308; 1848, Whig (Rep.) majority 3,049; 1852, Dem. majority 4,900; 1856, Know-Nothing majority 8,064; 1860, Dem. plurality 722; 1864, Rep. majority 7,414; 1868, Dem. majority 31,919; 1872, Dem. majority 908; 1876, Dem. majority 19,756; 1880, Dem. majority 15,191; 1884, Dem. plurality 11,305.

MASSACHUSETTS—1824, Loose Constructionist (Rep.) majority 24,071; 1828, Loose Constructionist (Rep.) majority 22,817; 1832, Loose Constructionist (Rep.) majority 18,458; 1836, Whig (Rep.) majority 7,592; 1840, Whig (Rep.) majority 19,305; 1844, Whig (Rep.) majority 2,712; 1848, Whig (Rep.) plurality 23,014; 1852, Whig (Rep.) plurality 8,114; 1856, Rep. majority 49,324; 1860, Rep. majority 43,981; 1864, Rep. majority 77,997; 1858, Rep. majority 77,069; 1872, Rep. majority 74,212; 1876, Rep. majority 40,423; 1880, Rep. majority 49,097; 1884, Rep. plurality 24,372.

MICHIGAN—1836, Dem. majority 3,360; 1840, Whig (Rep.) majority 1,514; 1844, Dem. plurality 3,423; 1848, Dem. plurality 6,747; 1852, Dem. majority 746; 1856, Rep. majority 17,966; 1860, Rep. majority 22,213; 1864, Rep. majority 16,017; 1868, Rep. majority 31,481; 1872, Rep. majority 55,968; 1876, Rep.

majority 15,542; 1880, Rep. majority 19,095; 1884, Rep. plurality 3,308.

MINNESOTA—1860, Rep. majority 9,339; 1864, Rep. majority 7,685; 1868, Rep. majority 15,470; 1872, Rep. majority 20,694; 1876, Rep. majority 21,780; 1880, Rep. majority 40,588; 1884, Rep. plurality 38,738.

MISSISSIPPI—1824, Dem. majority 1,421; 1828, Dem. majority 5,182; 1832, Dem majority 5,919; 1836, Dem majority 291; 1840, Whig (Rep) majority 2,523; 1844, Dem majority 5,920; 1848, Dem majority 615; 1852, Dem majority 9,328; 1856, Dem majority 11,251; 1860, Dem majority 12,474; 1872, Rep majority 34,887; 1876, Dem majority 59,568; 1880, Dem majority 35,099; 1884, Dem plurality 33,001.

MISSOURI—1824, Loose Constructionist (Rep) majority 103; 1828, Dem majority 4,810; 1832, Dem majority 5,192; 1836, Dem majority 2,658; 1840, Dem majority 6,788; 1844, Dem majority 10,118; 1848, Dem majority 7,406; 1852, Dem majority 8,369; 1856, Dem majority 9,640; 1860, Dem plurality 429; 1864, Rep majority 41,072; 1868, Rep majority 21,232; 1872, Dem majority 29,809; 1876, Dem majority 54,389; 1880, Dem majority 19,997; 1884, Dem plurality 33,059.

NEBRASKA—1868, Rep majority 4,290; 1872, Rep majority 10,517; 1876, Rep majority 10,326; 1880, Rep majority 22,603; 1884, Rep plurality 22,512.

NEVADA—1864, Rep majority 3,232; 1868, Rep majority 1,262; 1882, Rep majority 2,177; 1876, Rep majority 1,075; 1880, Dem majority 879; 1884, Rep plurality 1,615.

NEW HAMPSHIRE—1824, Loose Constructionist (Rep) majority 3,464; 1828, Loose Constructionist (Rep) majority 3,384; 1832, Dem majority 6,476; 1836, Dem plurality 12,494; 1840, Dem majority 6,386; 1844, Dem majority 5,133; 1848, Dem majority 5,422; 1852, Dem majority 7,155; 1856, Rep majority 5,134; 1860, Rep majority 9,085; 1864, Rep majority 3,529; 1868, Rep majority 6,967; 1872, Rep majority 5,444; 1876, Rep majority 2,954; 1880, Rep majority 3,530; 1884, Rep plurality 4,059.

NEW JERSEY—1824, Dem majority 679; 1820, Loose Constructionist (Rep) majority 1,808; 1832, Dem majority 463; 1836, Whig (Rep) majority 545; 1840, Whig (Rep) majority 2,248; 1844, Whig (Rep) majority 692; 1848, Whig (Rep) majority 2,285; 1852, Dem majority 5,399; 1856, Dem plurality 18,605; 1860, Dem majority 4,477; 1864, Dem majority 7,301; 1868, Dem majority 2,870; 1872, Rep majority 14,570; 1876, Dem majority 11,690; 1880, Dem plurality 2,010; 1884, Dem plurality 4,412.

NEW YORK—1828, Dem majority 4,350; 1832, Dem majority 13,601; 1836, Dem majority 28,272; 1840, Whig (Rep) majority 10,500; 1844, Dem plurality 5,106; 1848, Whig (Rep) majority 98,093; 1852, Dem majority 1,872; 1856, Rep plurality 80,129; 1860, Rep majority 50,136; 1864, Rep majority 6,749; 1868, Dem majority 10,000; 1872, Rep majority 51,800; 1876, Dem majority 26,568; 1880, Rep majority 8,660; 1884, Dem plurality 1,148.

NORTH CAROLINA—1824, Dem majority 4,794; 1828, Dem majorlty 23,939; 1832, Dem majority 20,299; 1836, Dem majority

3,284; 1840, Whig (Rep) majority 12,158; 1844, Whig (Rep) majority 3,945; 1848, Whig (Rep) majority 8,681; 1852, Dem majority 627; 1856, Dem majority 11,360; 1860, Dem majority 648; 1868, Rep. majority 12,168; 1872, Rep majority 24,675; 1876, Dem majority 17,010; 1880, Dem. majority 8,326; 1884, Dem plurality 17,884.

OHIO—1824, Loose Constructionist (Rep) plurality 798; 1828, Dem majority 4,201; 1832, Dem majority 4,707; 1836, Whig (Rep) majority 8,457; 1840, Whig (Rep) majority 22,472; 1844, Whig (Rep) plurality 5,940; 1848, Dem plurality 16,415; 1852, Dem plurality 16,694; 1856, Rep plurality 16,623; 1860, Rep majority 20,779; 1864, Rep majority 59,586; 1868, Rep majority 41,617; 1872, Rep majority 34,268; 1876, Rep majority 2,747; 1880, Rep majority 27,771; 1884, Rep plurality 31,802.

OREGON—1860, Rep plurality 1,318; 1864, Rep majority 1,431; 1868, Dem majority 164; 1872, Rep majority 3,517; 1876, Rep majority 547; 1880, Rep majority 422; 1884, Rep plurality 2,256.

PENNSYLVANIA—1824, Dem majority 24,845; 1828, Dem majority 50,804; 1832, Dem majority 34,267; 1836, Dem majority 4,364; 1840, Whig (Rep) majority 2; 1844, Dem. majority 3,194; 1848, Whig (Rep) majority 3,074; 1852, Dem majority 10,869; 1856, Dem majority 1,025; 1860, Rep majority 59,618; 1864, Rep majority 20,075; 1868, Rep majority 28,898; 1872, Rep majority 135,918; 1876, Rep majority 9,375; 1880, Rep majority 16,608; 1884, Rep plurality 81,019.

RHODE ISLAND—1824, Loose Constructionist (Rep) majority 1,945; 1828, Loose Constructionist (Rep) majority 1,933; 1832, Loose Constructionist (Rep) majority 684; 1836, Dem majority 254; 1840, Whig (Rep) majority 1,935; 1844, Whig (Rep) majority 2,348; 1848, Whig (Rep) majority 2,403; 1852, Dem majority 465; 1856, Rep majority 3,112; 1860, Rep majority 4,537; 1864, Rep. majority 5,222; 1868, Rep majority 6,445; 1872, Rep majority 8,336; 1876, Rep majority 4,947; 1880, Rep majority 7,180; 1884, Rep plurality 6,639.

SOUTH CAROLINA—1868, Rep majority 17,064; 1872, Rep majority 49,400; 1876, Rep majority 964; 1880, Dem majority 54,241; 1884, Dem plurality 48,112.

TENNESSEE—1824, Dem majority 19,669; 1828, Dem majority 41,850; 1832, Dem majority 27,304; 1836, Whig (Rep) majority 9,842; 1840, Whig (Rep) majority 12,102; 1844, Whig (Rep) majority 113; 1848, Whig (Rep) majority 6,286; 1852, Whig (Rep) majority 1,880; 1856, Dem majority 7,460; 1860, Constitutipnal Union plurality 4,565; 1868, Rep majority 30,499; 1882, Dem majority 8,736; 1876, Dem majority 43,600; 1880, Dem majority 14,598; 1884, Dem plurality 8,275.

TEXAS—1848, Dem majority 6,150; 1852, Dem majority 8,557; 1856, Dem majority 15,530; 1860, Dem majority 32,110; 1872, Dem majority 16,595; 1876, Dem majority 59,955; 1880, Dem majority 70,878; 1884, Dem plurality 132,168.

VERMONT—1828, Loose Constructionist (Rep) majority 16,579; 1832, Loose Constructionist (Rep) majority 3,282; 1836, Whig (Rep) majority 6,954; 1840, Whig (Rep) majority 14,117; 1844, Whig (Rep) majority 4,775; 1848, Whig (Rep) plurality 9,285; 1852, Whig (Rep) majority 508; 1856, Rep majority 28,447; 1860, Rep majority 24,772; 1864, Rep majority 29,098; 1868, Rep majority 32,122; 1872, Rep majority 29,961; 1876, Rep majority 23,838; 1880, Rep majority 26,036; 1884, Rep plurality 22,183.

VIRGINIA—1824, Dem majority 2,023; 1828, Dem majority 14,651; 1832, Dem majority 22,158; 1836, Dem majority 6,893; 1840, Dem majority 1,392; 1844, Dem majority 5,893; 1848, Dem majority 1,453; 1852, Dem majority 15,286; 1856, Dem majority 29,105; 1860, Constitutional Union plurality 358; 1872, Rep majority 1,772; 1876, Dem majority 44,112; 1880, Regular Dem majority 12,810; Dem plurality 6,315.

WEST VIRGINIA—1864, Rep majority 12,714; 1868, Rep majority 8,869; 1872, Rep majority 2,264; 1876, Dem majority 12,384; 1880, Dem majority 2,069; 1884, Dem plurality 4,221.

WISCONSIN—1848, Dem plurality 1,254; 1852, Dem majority 2,604; 1856, Rep majority 12,668; 1860, Rep majority 20,040; 1864, Rep majority 17,574; 1868, Rep majority 24,150; 1872, Rep majority 17,686; 1876, Rep majority 5,205; 1880, Rep majority 21,783; 1884, Rep. plurality 14,693.

POPULAR VOTE.

For Presidential candidates from 1824 to and including 1885. Prior to 1824 electors were chosen by the legislatures of the different states.

1824, J. Q. ADAMS—Had 105,321 to 155,872 for Jackson, 44,282 for Crawford, and 46,587 for Clay. Jackson over Adams, 50,551. Adams less than combined vote of others, 140,869. Of the whole vote Adams had 29.92 per cent., Jackson 44.27. Clay 13.23, Crawford 13.23. Adams elected by House of Representatives.

1828, JACKSON—Had 647,231 to 509,097 for Adams. Jackson's majority, 138,134. Of the whole vote Jackson had 55.97 per cent., Adams 44.03.

1832, JACKSON—Had 687,502 to 530,189 for Clay, and 33,108 for Floyd and Wirt combined. Jackson's majority, 124,205. Of the whole vote Jackson had 54.96 per cent., Clay 42.39, and the others combined 2.65.

1836, VAN BUREN—Had 761,549 to 736,656, the combined vote for Harrison, White, Webster and Maguin. Van Buren's majority, 24,893. Of the whole vote Van Buren had 50.83 per cent., and the others combined 49.17.

1840, HARRISON—Had 1,275,017 to 1,128,702 for Van Buren, and 7,059 for Birney. Harrison's majority, 139,256. Of the whole vote Harrison had 52.89 per cent., Van Buren 46.82, and Birney .29.

1844, POLK — Had 1,337,243 to 1,299,068 for Clay, and 62,300 for Birney. Polk over Clay, 38,175. Polk less than others combined, 24,125. Of the whole vote Polk had 49.55 per cent., Clay 48.14, and Birney 2.21.

1848, TAYLOR — Had 1,360,101 to 1,220,544 for Cass, and 291,263 for Van Buren. Taylor over Cass, 139,557. Taylor less than others combined, 151,706. Of the whole vote Taylor had 47.36 per cent., Cass 42.50, and Van Buren 10.14.

1852, PIERCE — Had 1,601,474 to 1,386,578 for Scott, and 156,149 for Hale. Pierce over all, 58,747. Of the whole vote Pierce had 50.90 per cent., Scott 44.10, and Hale 4.97.

1856, BUCHANAN — Had 1,838,169 to 1,341,264 for Fremont, and 874,534 for Fillmore. Buchanan over Fremont 496,905. Buchanan less than combined vote of others, 377,629. Of the whole vote Buchanan had 45.34 per cent., Fremont 33.09, and Fillmore 21.57.

1860, LINCOLN — Had 1,866,352 to 1,375,157 for Douglas, 845,763 for Breckinridge, and 589,581 for Bell. Lincoln over Breckinridge, 491,195. Lincoln less than Douglas and Breckinridge combined, 354,568. Lincoln less than combined vote of all others, 944,149. Of the whole vote Lincoln had 39.91 per cent., Douglas 29.40, Breckinridge 18.08, and Bell 12.61.

1864, LINCOLN — Had 2,216,067 to 1,808,725 for McClellan. (Eleven states not voting, viz.: Alabama, Arkansas, Florida, Georgia, Louisiana, Mississippi, North Carolina, South Carolina, Tennessee, Texas and Virginia.) Lincoln's majority, 408,342. Of the whole vote Lincoln had 55.06 per cent., and McClellan 44.94.

1868, GRANT — Had 3,015,071 to 2,709,613 for Seymour. (Three states not voting, viz.: Mississippi, Texas and Virginia.) Grant's majority, 305,458. Of the whole vote Grant had 52.67 per cent., and McClellan 47.33.

1872, GRANT — Had 3,597,070 to 2,834,079 for Greeley, 29,408 for O'Connor, and 5,608 for Black. Grant's majority, 729,975. Of the whole vote Grant had 55.63 per cent., Greeley 43.83, O'Connor .15, Black .09.

1876, HAYES — Had 4,033,950 to 4,284,885 for Tilden, 81,740 for Cooper, 9,522 for Smith, and 2,636 scattering. Tilden's majority over Hayes, 250,935. Tilden's majority of the entire vote cast, 157,037. Hayes less than the combined vote of others, 344,833. Of the whole vote cast Hayes had 47.95 per cent., Tilden 50.94 per cent., Cooper .97 per cent., Smith .11 per cent., scattering .03.

1880, GARFIELD — Had 4,449,053 to 4,442,035 for Hancock, 307,306 for Weaver, and 12,576 scattering. Garfield over Hancock, 7,018. Garfield less than the combined vote for others, 313,864. Of the popular vote Garfield had 48.26 per cent., Hancock 48.25, Weaver 3.33, scattering .13.

1884, CLEVELAND — Had 4,913,248 to 4,848,150 for Blaine, 151,062 for St. John, 133,728 for Butler. Cleveland over Blaine, 65,098. Cleveland less than entire vote of opponents, 219,712.

SUMMARY—Of the Presidents, Adams, Federalist; Polk, Democrat; Taylor, Whig; Buchanan, Democrat; Lincoln, Republican; Garfield, Republican, and Cleveland, Democrat, did not, when elected, receive a majority of the popular vote. The highest percentage of popular vote received by any President was 55.97 for Jackson, Democrat, in 1828, and the lowest 39.91 for Lincoln, Republican, in 1860; Hayes, Republican, next lowest, with 47.95. Hayes, with the exception of John Quincy Adams, who was chosen by House of Representatives, was the only President ever elected who did not have a majority over his principal competitor, and Tilden the only defeated candidate who had a majority over the President-elect, and a majority of all the votes cast.

WHAT A HORSE CAN DRAW—On metal rails a horse can draw:
One and two-thirds times as much as on asphalt pavement.
Three and one-third times as much as on good Belgian blocks.
Five times as much as on ordinary Belgian blocks.
Seven times as much as on good cobble-stone.
Thirteen times as much as on ordinary cobble-stone.
Twenty times as much as on an earth road.
Forty times as much as on sand.

A modern compilation of engineering maxims states that a horse can drag, as compared with what he can carry on his back, in the following proportions: On the worst earthen road, three times more; on a good macadamized road, nine; on plank, twenty-five; on a stone trackway, thirty-three, and on a good railway, fifty-four times as much.

EXCESSIVE HEAT IN THE PAST.—In 1303 and 1304 the Rhine, Loire, and Seine ran dry. The heat in several French provinces during the summer of 1705 was equal to that of a glass furnace. Meat could be cooked by merely exposing it to the sun. Not a soul dare venture out between noon and 4 p. m. In 1718 many shops had to close. The theaters never opened their doors for three months. Not a drop of water fell during six months. In 1773 the thermometer rose to 118 degrees. In 1778 the heat of Bologna was so great that a great number of people were stifled. There was not sufficient air for the breath, and people had to take refuge under the ground. In July, 1793, the heat again became intolerable. Vegetables were burned up, and fruit dried on the trees. The furniture and wood-work in dwelling-houses cracked and split up; meat went bad in an hour.

LIST OF APPROPRIATIONS BY CONGRESS, 1873-1886.

The following have been the annual appropriations made by the United States Congress for the expenses of the Government for each fiscal year ending June 30, from 1873 to 1886, inclusive:

	1873.	1874.	1875.	1876.	1877.	1878.	1879.
Deficiencies	$6,596,677	$11,143,240	$4,053,812	$2,387,372	$834,696	$2,547,186	$15,213,259
Legislative, Executive & Judicial	18,624,973	18,170,441	20,758,255	16,038,699	16,057,021	15,756,774	15,868,694
Sundry Civil	20,134,669	32,173,258	26,924,747	29,459,853	15,895,065	17,079,256	24,968,590
Support of the Army	28,683,615	31,796,009	27,788,500	27,933,830	27,621,868	None.	51,279,679
Naval Service	18,231,086	22,275,708	20,813,947	17,001,307	12,741,791	13,589,933	14,153,432
Indian Service	6,196,363	5,505,219	5,538,275	5,425,627	4,567,018	4,827,666	4,734,876
Rivers & Harbors	5,588,000	7,352,900	5,228,000	6,648,518	5,015,000	None.	8,322,700
Forts and Fortifications	2,037,000	1,899,000	904,000	850,000	315,000	275,000	275,000
Military Academy	326,101	344,318	339,835	364,740	290,065	286,604	292,804
Post-Office Dept.	6,425,970	6,496,602	7,175,542	8,376,205	5,927,498	2,939,725	4,222,275
Pensions	30,480,000	30,480,000	29,980,000	30,000,000	29,533,500	28,533,000	29,371,574
Consular and Diplomatic	1,268,819	1,311,359	3,404,804	1,374,985	1,188,797	1,146,748	1,087,535
Miscellaneous	9,623,477	3,342,648	2,108,041	1,853,805	4,134,692	1,425,092	2,226,390
Totals	154,216,751	172,290,701	155,017,758	147,714,941	124,122,011	88,356,983	172,016,809

LIST OF APPROPRIATIONS BY CONGRESS—CONTINUED.

	1880.	1881.	1882. ¶	1883.	1884.	1885.	1886.
Deficiencies	$ 4,633,824	$ 6,118,085	$ 5,110,862	$ 9,853,869	$ 2,832,680	$ 4,385,836	$ 3,332,717
Legislative, Executive & Judicial	16,136,230	16,532,009	17,797,398	29,322,908	20,763,843	21,556,902	21,495,661
Sundry Civil	19,724,869	22,503,508	22,011,223	25,425,479	23,713,404	22,346,750	25,961,904
Support of the Army	26,797,300	26,425,800	26,687,800	27,032,099	24,681,250	24,454,450	24,014,052
Naval Service	14,028,469	14,405,798	14,566,038	14,903,559	15,954,247	8,931,856	21,280,767
Indian Service	4,713,479	4,657,263	4,587,869	5,219,604	5,388,656	5,933,151	5,773,329
Rivers & Harbors	9,577,495	8,976,500	11,451,300	18,988,875	None.	14,940,300	None.
Forts and Fortifications	275,000	550,000	575,000	375,000	670,000	700,000	735,000
Military Acad'my	319,547	316,234	322,435	335,557	318,657	314,563	309,902
Post-Office Dept.	5,872,376	3,883,420	1,152,258	1,902,178	Indefinite.	Indefinite.	Indefinite.
Pensions	56,233,200	41,644,000	68,282,307	116,000,000	86,575,000	20,810,000	60,000,000
Consular & Diplomatic	1,097,735	1,180,335	1,191,435	1,256,655	1,296,255	1,225,140	1,242,925
Agricult'r'l D'pt*	....	253,300	335,500	427,280	405,640	480,190	580,790
Dis. of Col'mbia†	....	3,425,247	3,379,571	3,496,050	3,505,495	3,594,256	3,622,683
Miscellaneous	2,995,124	4,959,332	1,128,006	5,888,994	1,806,439	7,800,004	2,268,383
Totals	162,404,648	155,830,841	179,579,000	251,428,117	187,911,566	137,451,398	170,608,114

*Previous to 1881 appopriations for the agricultural department were included in the legislative, executive and judicial appropriations. † Previous to 1881 appropriations for the District of Columbia were included in the sundry civil expenses appropriations.

IMMIGRANTS INTO THE UNITED STATES
1820–1885.

Year.	Total Immigrants.	Year.	Total Immigrants.
1820	8,385	1854	427,833
1821	7,127	1855	200,877
1822	6,911	1856	195,857
1823	6,354	1857	246,945
1824	7,912	1858	119,501
1825	10,199	1859	118,616
1826	10,837	1860	150,237
1827	18,875	1861	89,724
1828	28,382	1862	89,007
1829	22,520	1863	174,524
1830	23,322	1864	193,195
1831	22,633	1865	247,453
1832	60,482	1866	167,757
1833	58,610	Fiscal Year ending June 30	
1834	65,365	1867	298,967
1835	43,374	1868	282,189
1836	76,242	1869	352,768
1837	79,340	1870	387,203
1838	38,914	1871	321,350
1839	68,069	1872	404,806
1840	84,066	1873	459,803
1841	80,289	1874	313,339
1842	104,565	1875	227,468
1843	52,496	1876	169,986
1844	78,615	1877	111,857
1845	114,371	1878	138,469
1846	154,416	1879	177,826
1847	234,968	1880	457,257
1848	226,527	1881	669,431
1849	297,024	1882	788,992
1850	369,980	1883	603,322
1851	379,466	1884	518,592
1852	371,603	1885	395,346
1853	368,645	Total	13,114,441

NATURALIZATION LAWS OF THE UNITED STATES.

The conditions under and the manner in which an alien may be admitted to become a citizen of the United States are prescribed by Sections 2165-74 of the Revised Statutes of the United States.

DECLARATION OF INTENTION.

The alien must declare upon oath, before a circuit or district court of the United States, or a district or supreme court of the Territories, or a court of record of any of the States having common law jurisdiction, and a seal and clerk, two years at least prior to his admission, that it is, *bona fide*, his intention to become a citizen of the United States, and to renounce forever all allegiance and fidelity to any foreign prince or State, and particularly to the one of which he may be at the time a citizen or subject.

OATH ON APPLICATION FOR ADMISSION.

He must, at the time of his application to be admitted, declare on oath, before some one of the courts above specified, "that he will support the Constitution of the United States, and that he absolutely and entirely renounces and abjures all allegiance and fidelity to every foreign prince, potentate, State or sovereignty, and particularly, by name, to the prince, potentate, State or sovereignty of which he was before a citizen or subject," which proceedings must be recorded by the clerk of the court.

CONDITIONS FOR CITIZENSHIP.

If it shall appear to the satisfaction of the court to which the alien has applied that he has resided continuously within the United States for at least five years, and within the State or Territory where such court is at the time held one year at least; and that during that time "he has behaved as a man of good moral character, attached to the principles of the Constitution of the United States, and well disposed to the good order and happiness of the same," he will be admitted to citizenship.

TITLES OF NOBILITY.

If the applicant has borne any hereditary title or order

of nobility, he must make an express renunciation of the same at the time of his application.

SOLDIERS.

Any alien of the age of twenty-one years and upward, who has been in the armies of the United States and has been honorably discharged therefrom, may become a citizen on his petition, without any previous declaration of intention, provided that he has resided in the United States at least one year previous to his application, and is of good moral character.

MINORS.

Any alien under the age of twenty-one years who has resided in the United States three years next preceding his arriving at that age, and who has continued to reside therein to the time he may make application to be admitted a citizen thereof, may, after he arrives at the age of twenty-one years, and after he has resided five years within the United States, including the three years of his minority, be admitted a citizen; but he must make a declaration on oath and prove to the satisfaction of the court that for two years next preceding it has been his *bona-fide* intention to become a citizen.

CHILDREN OF NATURALIZED CITIZENS.

The children of persons who have been duly naturalized, being under the age of twenty-one years at the time of the naturalization of their parents, shall, if dwelling in the United States, be considered as citizens thereof.

CITIZENS' CHILDREN WHO ARE BORN ABROAD.

The children of persons who now are or have been citizens of the United States are, though born out of the limits and jurisdiction of the United States, considered as citizens thereof.

PROTECTION ABROAD TO NATURALIZED CITIZENS.

Section 2000 of the Revised Statutes of the United States declares that "all naturalized citizens of the United States while in foreign countries are entitled to and shall receive from this Government the same protection of persons and property which is accorded to native-born citizens."

PRINCIPAL OF THE PUBLIC DEBT.

Statement of Outstanding Principal of the Public Debt of the United States on January 1 of each year from 1791 to 1842, inclusive, and on July 1 of each year from 1843 to 1885, inclusive.

Jan. 1.		Jan. 1.		Jan. 1.		July 1.	
1791	$75,463,476.52	1815	$99,833,660.15	1839	$3,573,343.82	1862	$524,176,412.13
1792	77,227,924.66	1816	127,334,933.74	1840	5,250,875.54	1863	1,119,772,138.63
1793	80,352,634.04	1817	123,491,965.16	1841	13,594,480.73	1864	1,815,784,370.57
1794	78,427,404.77	1818	103,466,633.83	1842	20,601,226.28	1865	2,680,647,869.74
1795	80,747,587.39	1819	95,529,648.28	July 1.		1866	2,773,236,173.69
1796	83,762,172.07	1820	91,015,566.15	1843	32,742,922.00	1867	2,678,126,103.87
1797	82,064,479.33	1821	89,987,427.66	1844	23,461,652.50	1868	2,611,687,851.19
1798	79,228,529.12	1822	93,546,676.98	1845	15,925,303.01	1869	2,588,452,213.94
1799	78,408,669.77	1823	90,875,877.28	1846	15,550,202.97	1870	2,480,672,427.81
1800	82,976,294.35	1824	90,269,777.77	1847	38,826,534.77	1871	2,353,211,332.32
1801	83,038,050.80	1825	83,788,432.71	1848	47,044,862.23	1872	2,253,251,328.78
1802	86,712,632.25	1826	81,054,059.99	1849	63,061,858.69	1873	2,234,482,993.20
1803	77,054,686.30	1827	73,987,357.20	1850	63,452,773.55	1874	2,251,690,468.43
1804	86,427,120.88	1828	67,475,043.87	1851	68,304,796.02	1875	2,232,284,531.95
1805	82,312,150.50	1829	58,421,413.67	1852	66,199,341.71	1876	2,180,395,067.15
1806	75,723,270.66	1830	48,565,406.50	1853	59,803,117.70	1877	2,205,301,392.10
1807	69,218,398.64	1831	39,123,191.68	1854	42,242,222.42	1878	2,256,203,892.53
1808	65,196,317.97	1832	24,322,235.18	1855	35,586,858.56	1879	2,245,495,072.04
1809	57,023,192.09	1833	7,001,698.83	1856	31,972,537.90	1880	2,120,415,370.63
1810	53,173,217.52	1834	4,769,082.08	1857	28,699,831.85	1881	2,069,013,569.58
1811	48,005,587.76	1835	37,513.05	1858	44,911,881.03	1882	1,918,312,994.03
1812	45,209,737.90	1836	336,957.83	1859	58,496,837.88	1883	1,884,171,728.07
1813	55,962,827.57	1837	3,308,124.07	1860	64,842,287.88	1884	1,830,528,923.57
1814	81,487,846.24	1838	10,434,221.14	1861	90,580,873.72	1885	1,876,424,275.14
						Dec. 1, 1886	1,715,507,80.00

How the price of Southern Confederate Money Dropped.

When the first issue of the Confederate money was scattered among the people, it commanded a slight premium. It then scaled down as follows: June, 1861, 90c.; December 1, 1861, 80c.; December 15, 1861, 75c.; February 1, 1862, 60c.; February 1, 1863, 20c.; June, 1863, 8c.; January, 1864, 2c.; November, 1864, 4½c.; January, 1865, 2½c., April 1, 1865, 1½c. After that date, it took from $800 to $1,000 in Confederate money to buy a one-dollar greenback.

Length of Navigation of the Mississippi River.

The length of navigation of the Mississippi river itself for ordinary large steamboats is about 2,161 miles, but small steamers can ascend about 650 miles further. The following are its principal navigable tributaries, with the miles open to navigation.

	Miles.		Miles.
Minnesota	295	Wisconsin	160
Chippewa	90	Rock	64
Iowa	80	Illinois	350
Missouri	2,900	Yellowstone	474
Big Horn	50	Ohio	950
Allegheny	325	Monongahela	110
Muskingum	94	Kenawha	94
Kentucky	105	Green	200
Wabash	365	Cumberland	600
Tennessee	270	Clinch	50
Osage	302	St. Francis	180
White	779	Black	147
Little White	48	Arkansas	884
Big Hatchie	75	Issaquena	161
Sunflower	271	Yazoo	228
Tallahatchie	175	Big Black	35
Red	986	Cane	54
Cypress	44	Ouachita	384
Black	61	Bœuf	55
Bartholomew	100	Tensas	112
Macon	60	Teche	91
Atchafalya	218	D'Arbonne	50
Lafourche	168		

The other navigable tributaries have less than fifty miles each of navigation. The total miles of navigation of these fifty-five streams is about 16,500 miles, or about two-thirds the distance around the world. The Mississippi and its tributaries may be estimated to possess 15,550 miles navigable to steamboats, and 20,221 miles navigable to barges.

Language of Flowers.

FLOWERS.	SENTIMENTS.
Acacia	Concealed love.
Almond	Hope.
Apple-Blossom	Preference.
Arbutus, Trailing	Welcome.
Bell Flower	Gratitude.
Box	Constancy.
Calla Lily	Feminine beauty.
Cedar	I live for thee.
China Aster	I will think of it.
Chrysanthemum, Rose	I love.
Clover, Red	Industry.
Corn	Riches.
Cowslip, American	You are my divinity.
Daffodil	Chivalry.
Dahlia	Forever thine.
Daisy, Garden	I partake your sentiments.
Daisy, White	Innocence.
Daisy, Wild	I will think of it.
Elm, American	Patriotism.
Forget-me-not	True love.
Fuschia, Scarlet	Taste.
Geranium, Apple	Present preference.
Geranium, Ivy	Your hand for the next dance.
Geranium, Rose	Preference.
Gillyflower	Lasting beauty.
Golden Rod	Encouragement.
Hawthorn	Hope.
Heliotrope, Peruvian	I love you; Devotion.
Honeysuckle	Bond of love.
Horse-Chestnut	Luxury.
Hyacinth	Jealousy.
Mint	Virtue.
Morning Glory	Coquetry.
Myrtle	Love.
Oats	Music.
Orange	Generosity.
Pansy	Think of me.
Pink	Pure affection.
Pink, Red	Pure, ardent love.
Rose, Moss	Superior merit.
Rose, Tea	Always lovely.
Rose, White	I am worthy of you.
Snowball	Winter.
Tuberose	Dangerous pleasures.
Verbena	Sensibility.
Violet, Blue	Love.
Violet, White	Modesty.

Glass windows were first introduced into England in the eighth century.

EXPECTATION OF LIFE.

The mortality tables governing life insurance, and in use in the United States, have been the "Combined Experience or Actuaries' Table," based on the experience of seventeen English life insurance companies, deduced from 32,537 policies, and the "American Experience Table," arranged by Mr. Sheppard Homans in 1868, from the experience of the Mutual Life Insurance Company of New York, and other companies. These not being a fair expression of the mortality of American assured lives, the American Chamber of Life Insurance, in 1873, began the collection of statistics of mortality experience. After ten years the work was completed, and it embraces the experience of thirty life insurance companies, covering over a million policies. The following table was made from it, and shows, on the average, the number of additional years any person may expect to live, at a given age:

AGE.	EXPECTATION OF LIFE. YEARS.	
	Males.	Females.
10	49.99	48.05
11	49.32	47.21
12	48.64	46.40
13	47.95	45.64
14	47.26	44.91
15	46.57	44.19
16	45.88	43.48
17	45.18	42.79
18	44.48	42.12
19	43.78	41.46
20	43.07	40.82
21	42.36	40.19
22	41.65	39.56
23	40.93	38.96
24	40.21	38.38

EXPECTATION OF LIFE.—CONTINUED.

Age.	Expectation of Life. Years.	
	Males.	Females.
25	39.49	37.80
26	38.77	37.23
27	38.04	36.66
28	37.31	36.08
29	36.58	35.49
30	35.85	34.89
31	35.12	34.29
32	34.38	33.69
33	33.65	33.06
34	32.91	32.42
35	32.17	31.78
36	31.43	31.13
37	30.70	30.47
38	29.96	29.81
39	29.22	29.16
40	28.48	28.48
41	27.75	27.82
42	27.01	27.15
43	26.28	26.45
44	25.55	25.74
45	24.82	25.02
46	24.09	24.30
47	23.38	23.57
48	22.66	22.83
49	21.95	22.08
50	21.24	21.33
51	20.54	20.59
52	19.84	19.87
53	19.15	19.15
54	18.47	18.44
55	17.80	17.73
56	17.13	17.03
57	16.47	16.35

EXPECTATION OF LIFE.—Continued.

Age.	Expectation of Life. Years.	
	Males.	Females.
58	15.83	15.67
59	15.19	15.02
60	14.56	14.37
61	13.94	13.73
62	13.34	13.10
63	12.74	12.49
64	12.16	11.90
65	11.60	11.31
66	11.04	10.74
67	10.50	10.19
68	9.97	9.65
69	9.46	9.13
70	8.97	8.12
71	8.49	8.63
72	8.02	7.25
73	7.57	7.70
74	7.14	6.36
75	6.72	6.94
76	6.32	5.53
77	5.93	5.15
78	5.57	5.88
79	5.21	4.42
80	4.87	4.19
81	4.55	4.87
82	4.24	3.58
83	3.95	3.39
84	3.67	3.03
85	3.40	3.88
86	3.14	2.64
87	2.89	2.42
88	2.64	2.22
89	2.39	2.0'
90	2.17	2.85

EXPECTATION OF LIFE.—Continued.

AGE.	EXPECTATION OF LIFE. YEARS.	
	Male.	Female.
91	1.98	1.79
92	1.81	1.53
93	1.64	1.49
94	1.49	1.36
95	1.34	1.24
96	1.18	1.23
97	1.03	1.09
98	.83	.93
99	.50	.50

The word "news" was not, as many suppose, derived from the adjective new, but from the fact that many years ago it was customary to put at the head of the periodical publications of the day the initial letters of the compass, thus:

$$\begin{matrix} & N & \\ W- & | & -E \\ & S & \end{matrix}$$

Signifying that the matter contained therein was from the four quarters of the globe. From the letters came the word "news."

To supply the demand for milk and its products in this country 15,000,000 cows are required. To furnish food for them the cultivation of over 60,000,000 acres of land is required. In caring for the cows and their milk 700,000 men find employment and 1,000,000 horses are needed. Cows and horses consume annually 30,000,000 tons of hay, 90,000,000 bushels of cornmeal and the same amount of oatmeal, 275,000,000 of oats, 2,000,000 bushels of bran, and 30,000,000 bushels of corn, to say nothing of the brewery grains and questionable feed of various kinds that is used all over the country. It costs $400,000,000 to feed these cows and horses.

LIFE INSURANCE STATISTICS.

CONDITION OF COMPANIES JANUARY 1, 1885, AND BUSINESS THE YEAR PRECEDING.

No. of Com's.	Assets.	Premiums Received.	Total Income.	Payments to Policyholders (Losses, Dividends, Surrenders, etc.)	Total Expenditures.	New Policies Issued.*		Policies in Force.	
						No.	Amount.	No.	Amount.
47	$519,674,563	$75,603,966	$101,924,731	$61,216,639	$81,811,206	983,023	$428,703,280	1,895,412	$2,093,492,289

CONDITION OF ASSESSMENT COMPANIES.†

No. of Companies.	Assets.	Assessments collected.	Total Income.	Payments to Policyholders.	Total Expenditures.	Membership.		Insurance in Force.	
						Admitted during year	Died	No. of Members	Amount
430	$3,557,052	$23,856,945	No report.	$22,932,056	$26,489,108	313,321	9,563	1,655,975	$3,785,163,363

*Including industrial policies. †According to the report made at the annual meeting of Mutual Benefit Life Associations, at Boston, August 25, 1885.

Life Insurance Statistics—Continued.

INCOME AND DISBURSEMENTS FOR A QUARTER CENTURY.

The following table shows the receipts and disbursements of the "old line" life insurance companies reporting to the New York Insurance Department for 25 years.

Year ending Dec. 31.	No. of Companies.	Total Income.	Total Payments for Losses, Endowments, and Annuities.	Total Payments for Lapsed, Surrendered and Purchased Policies.	Total Dividends to Policy-holders.
1860	17	$5,998,144	$1,360,000	$243,954	$497,848
1861	17	6,202,416	1,474,005	665,341	637,522
1862	18	7,440,491	1,705,610	468,235	627,574
1863	22	10,624,986	2,305,892	361,830	1,031,939
1864	27	16,163,138	3,136,659	407,754	1,036,912
1865	30	24,887,020	4,125,442	691,382	1,475,212
1866	39	40,375,666	6,428,472	1,226,856	2,532,477
1867	43	56,481,997	8,253,003	2,067,782	6,183,624
1868	55	77,382,158	11,058,686	3,762,735	11,707,663
1869	70	98,507,319	15,692,831	5,148,900	15,733,862
1870	71	105,026,148	19,522,712	9,616,988	15,809,557
1871	68	113,490,562	28,773,041	13,263,390	14,624,608
1872	59	117,306,029	25,672,380	13,922,009	20,077,999
1873	56	118,396,502	27,232,435	16,669,594	22,938,235
1874	50	115,732,714	25,797,860	22,453,955	16,617,018
1875	45	108,645,084	27,174,631	20,414,574	17,900,605
1876	38	96,358,583	25,567,850	21,354,376	16,187,128
1877	34	86,162,144	26,103,386	19,152,318	15,397,370
1878	34	80,462,999	29,153,226	17,095,994	14,637,449
1879	34	77,700,403	31,684,522	12,207,823	13,479,613
1880	34	77,403,445	30,032,174	9,923,026	13,171,992
1881	30	79,820,513	31,068,144	8,497,354	12,579,151
1882	30	85,070,134	29,826,874	9,255,077	13,555,105
1883	29	92,562,763	33,894,306	8,837,857	13,417,464
1884	29	96,974,376	35,602,544	9,503,530	13,043,498
Total	25 yrs	$1,795,266,734	$482,646,585	$227,212,634	$274,901,425

Life Insurance Statistics—Continued.

INCOME, Etc.—(Continued.)

Year Ending Dec. 31.	No. of Companies.	Total Payments to Policy-holders.	Taxes, Commissions, and other Expenses.	Total Disbursements.
1860	17	$2,101,802	$744,801	$2,908,936
1861	17	2,776,858	792,100	3,638,481
1862	18	2,801,419	871,867	3,759,153
1863	22	3,699,661	1,935,011	5,764,243
1864	27	4,581,325	2,299,142	7,021,649
1865	30	6,292,036	4,025,619	10,595,355
1866	39	10,187,805	6,770,335	17,176,660
1867	43	16,504,409	9,480,443	26,325,215
1868	55	26,529,084	13,789,689	40,959,021
1869	70	36,575,593	17,278,478	54,471,576
1870	71	44,949,257	18,340,431	63,876,840
1871	68	56,661,039	20,247	77,536,280
1872	59	59,672,388	18,006,001	78,207,257
1873	56	66,840,264	17,208,206	84,501,446
1874	50	64,868,833	15,986,881	81,232,333
1875	45	65,489,810	14,128,594	79,982,466
1876	38	63,109,354	13,174,419	76,618,183
1877	34	60,652,974	15,327,565	74,337,324
1878	34	60,886,669	10,992,051	72,128,070
1879	34	57,371,958	11,208,133	68,858,363
1880	34	53,127,192	12,851,312	66,317,859
1881	30	52,144,649	13,089,414	65,484,687
1882	30	52,637,056	13,338,788	66,242,344
1883	29	56,149,627	15,295,264	71,743,588
1884	29	58,149,572	18,153,435	76,632,098
Total	25 yrs.	$984,760,644	$283,340,546	$1,276,319,231

Total assets of the 29 companies last reported, $491,487,719; surplus as to policy-holders, $81,811,191.

The velocity of sound depends on the elasticity and density of the medium; the elasticity acts like a spring between the molecules of the medium; the greater the density the slower the motion, because there are more molecules to be set in motion and hence more time is required. Warm air is rarer than cold air, hence sound travels more rapidly in warm air than in cold air. At the freezing point sound waves travel 1,090 feet per second. A change of 1 degree varies the velocity about 1 foot per second.

STATISTICS OF THE AMERICAN PRESS.

YEAR.	ALL CLASSES.		DAILIES.		WEEKLIES.		ALL OTHERS.	
	Number.	Circulation.	Number.	Circulation.	Number.	Circulation.	Number.	Circulat'n
1850	2,536	5,142,177	254	758,454	1,902	2,944,629	370	1,439,094
1860	4,051	13,663,409	387	1,478,435	3,173	7,581,930	491	4,603,044
1870	5,871	20,842,475	574	2,601,547	4,295	10,594,643	1,002	7,646,285
1880	11,403	31,177,924	980	3,637,424	8,718	19,459,107	1,705	8,081,393

THE TORPEDO SERVICE OF THE WORLD.

The Secretary of the Navy has published the following table to illustrate the importance attached elsewhere than in the United States to the torpedo boat as a branch of naval warfare. The table gives a list of these boats possessed and in process of construction by other countries. *The United States has* NONE.

NATION.	In service 1884	Ord'red for 1885	REMARKS.
England	128	55	Does not include those in colonies.
Germany	11	61	Fleet to be increased to 150 of first-class.
France	82	77	Fleet to number 283 in all.
Russia	131	14	Fleet to number 180 in all.
Austria	14	2	Fleet to number 70 in all.
Denmark	12	..	To build 21 more.
Greece	37	..	
Italy	53	18	To build 100 more.
China	5	10	One of these is to be 764 feet long.
Japan	..	..	The largest boat under construction, 166 feet long, is now building for Japan by Yarrow & Co. Others are building in Germany.

PITHY FACTS.

NEWSPAPERS.—The number of daily newspapers in the United States is over 1,300, with an aggregate circulation of 4,800,000.

NERVOUS DEATHS.—About eleven per cent. of the deaths in the United States are the result of some form of nervous disease; a cause which does not find mention in mortality statistics of other countries.

VIOLENT DEATHS.—Out of a thousand deaths, forty-one are violent in the United States, and sixteen throughout Europe. The lowest number is seven, in Russia, and the greatest European is thirty-eight in Switzerland.

THE LARGEST LIBRARY in the world is the Imperial at Paris, which contains over 2,000,000 volumes.

MILES OF BOOKS.—In the library at the British Museum there are over thirty-two miles of shelves filled with books.

DIVORCES.—The number of divorces per 1,000 marriages is 4 in London, 10 in Berlin, 15 in Munich, 23 in Vienna, 25 in Paris, 73 in Boston, and 223 in San Francisco.

OUR ANCESTORS' ILLITERACY.—Out of the twenty-six Barons who signed the Magna Charta, only three could write their names. The remainder made their mark.

YOU CANNOT COUNT A TRILLION.—It is impossible to count a trillion. Had Adam counted continuously from his creation to the present day, he would not have reached that number, for it would take him over 9,512 years. At the rate of 200 a minute, there could be counted 12,000 an hour, 288,000 a day, and 105,120,000 a year.

WHAT SMOKING COSTS.—The expense of smoking three five-cent cigars a day, principal and interest, for ten years, is $745,74; for twenty-five years, $3,110.74. The expense of three ten-cent cigars, at the end of ten years, is $1,471.56; for twenty-five years, $6,382.47. At the end of fifty years, it is $54,162.14.

IMMIGRATION.—The total number of immigrants to the United States, from 1821 to the close of 1883, was 12,337,100.

COLD can be beaten 1,200 times thinner than printing paper. One ounce will cover 146 square feet. A cubic inch, at $18 per ounce, is worth $210.

PASSENGERS TRANSPORTED.—Steamers between Europe and America carry about 70,000 passengers per month. Railways throughout the world transport about 145,000,000 passengers per month.

AUTHORS' SUCCESS.—It is said that Judge Tourgee received over $70,000 for his Fool's Errand. Disraeli, $5,000 for his Endymion; Moore, $15,500 for his Lalla Rookh, and Victor Hugo $12,000 for Ernani.

LARGEST ELECTRIC LIGHTS. — The rapidity with which modern improvements are adopted, is shown by the fact that in 1883 the largest electric light in the world was at the Sidney Lighthouse, Australia, which has a power of 180,000 candles, and that the fourth largest is at San Jose, Cal , 24,000 candle power (the light at Paris, in Palais d' Industrie, equal to 150,000 candle power, and the Marseilles light of 40,000 candles, being greater). The Sidney light is visible fifty miles; that of San Jose sheds light two miles around.

DERIVATION OF OUR LANGUAGE. — Over three-eighths of the words in the English language are derived from the Latin, over one-fourth from the French, about one-tenth from the Saxon, and a little less from the Greek. The indebtedness to other languages is small.

CHURCH MEMBERSHIP. — The Baptist Church has the largest membership in the United States of any Evangelical denomination, having about 2,250,000 members. The Methodist has about 1,700,000; Lutheran, 950,000; Presbyterian, 600,000; Christian, 591,000; Congregational, 385,000; Protestant-Episcopal, 345,000; Universalist, 27,000; Unitarian, 18,000, and Roman Catholic (claim adherents), 6,800,000.

THE ATTENDANCE at the International Exhibition at New York, in 1853, was 600,000; Paris, 1855, 4,533,469; London, 1862, 6,211,100; Paris, 1867, 9,300,000; Vienna, 1873, 7,254,867; Philadelphia, 1876, 10,200,000; Paris, 1878, 16,100,000.

BIG TREES. — Of ninety-two redwood trees in Calaveras Grove, Cal., ten are over thirty feet in diameter, and eighty-two have a diameter of from fifteen to thirty feet. Their ages are estimated at from 1,000 to 3,500 years. Their height ranges from 150 to 237 feet.

FINENESS OF UNITED STATES COIN. — The gold coins are nine-tenths fine; the silver coins, nine-tenths fine; the copper-nickel coins, such as the 5-cent piece and 3-cent piece, are one-fourth nickel and three-fourths copper; the bronze coins are 95 per cent. copper and 5 per cent. tin and zinc. The alloy in the gold coins is silver and copper; in the silver coins, copper.

BEAR IN MIND

We want agents for this book. For terms to agents, address

EUROPE.

Europe is a peninsula, projecting from Asia. It is situated in the same latitude as the United States and the Dominion of Canada.

The extreme length of Europe from northeast to southwest is about 3,500 miles. The population is about six times that of the United States.

Its water boundary, if a continuous line, would reach four-fifths of the way around the world.

The British Isles are separated from the continent by the North Sea, which has an average depth of about 600 feet. There is much evidence to show that they were formerly a part of the mainland.

In relative extent of coast Europe surpasses all other countries. It is partly to the great number of indentations of the coast that Europe owes its commercial supremacy.

The islands of Europe constitute about one-twentieth of its area.

The greater part of the continent is low and level. Russia and all the territory bordering on the North and Baltic seas constitute a vast plain, called Low Europe. The basin of the Caspian Sea and much of the Netherlands are below the sea-level.

A high plateau, extending along the southern part of the continent, is known as High Europe. This plateau is surrounded by the irregular and broken mountain ranges which constitute the Alpine System, the main axis of the continent.

The Alps are the highest range. The other principal ranges are the Pyrenees, Apennines, Balkan, Carpathian and Caucasus mountains.

The Alps have long been celebrated for the number and extent of their glaciers, among which are the sources of the Rhine, Rhone, Po and several tributaries of the Danube.

The chief lake region of Europe is in Northwestern Russia. Lake Ladoga is the largest lake.

The lakes in Switzerland, especially Geneva and Constance, are celebrated for their beautiful scenery. There are many salt lakes in Russia, most of which are situated in the basin of the Caspian Sea.

Most of the rivers of Western Europe are connected with one another by canals, and are navigable.

CLIMATE.—Europe enjoys a more equable climate than any other country situated in corresponding latitudes. Its mildness is due, chiefly, to the southwesterly winds, which are warmed by the water of the Gulf Stream.

Rain is most abundant on the western coasts.

The tundras, or frozen marshes of the Arctic Slope, are covered with mosses and willows. South of this region is a belt of dense forest, chiefly of pine, oak, elm and ash.

Grains, hemp, flax and tobacco are cultivated in the central regions. The cultivation of the grape, olive, orange, lemon, fig, mulberry and cotton is confined, chiefly, to the Mediterranean Coast.

Most of the wild animals have disappeared. The reindeer, white bear and other animals valuable for their furs are, however, found in the more thinly settled regions; the wolf and wild boar are common in the forests, and the chamois and ibex inhabit the Alpine heights.

Water-fowl are numerous. The sardine, herring, pilchard, anchovy and other fish suitable for food abound in the surrounding waters.

MINERALS.—Coal, iron and copper are very widely distributed. Silver, zinc and lead are plentiful in the central highlands. Quicksilver, niter, sulphur and salt in volcanic regions. Coral of great beauty and value is obtained in the Mediterranean Sea.

PEOPLE.—The inhabitants of Europe, numbering about 330,000,-000, belong to the Caucasian and Mongolian races.

ASIA.

Asia, the largest country in the world, occupies the eastern part of the Eastern Continent.

It contains about one-third of the land surface of the earth—is twice as large as North America, and nearly five times the size of the United States. Its greatest length is 7,500 miles, nearly one-third the circumference of the earth.

The islands of Asia are a partly submerged mountain chain. All of them volcanic.

The northwestern Asia is a continuous plain; the southeastern, an elevated plateau traversed by high mountains. The line of greatest length is also the line which separates the highlands from the lowlands. From the Hindoo Koosh, the mountain ranges of Asia radiate toward the east.

The Himalaya Mountains are the highest in the world. The summit of Mt. Everest is over 29,000 feet above the sea-level, being more than 6,000 feet higher than the highest peak of the American continent.

The Caspian Sea and the Sea of Aral are thought to have been formerly arms of the ocean. Both are salt lakes. The former is below the sea-level.

Lake Baikal is the largest body of fresh water in Asia and is about as large as Lake Erie.

The rivers of Asia, though of great length, are distinguished by narrow valleys, rather than large basins. Most of them rise in the central highlands, from which they radiate in three directions, —north, east, and south, and mingle their waters with those of three oceans

The Yang-tse and Hoang rivers are subject to great changes, brought about by the shifting of their channels. In 1851, the Hoang Ho burst through its banks and poured its waters into the Gulf of Pecheelee, and within two years its lower course had so changed that the mouth of the river had shifted 250 miles from its former position.

Central Hindoostan is often called the Plateau of the Deccan.

The Obi is the only river navigable to any considerable distance.

The river valleys and the plains which are well watered are extremely fertile. The high, central region and the western plateaus are dry, sandy, and barren.

Every degree of temperature and moisture may be found in Asia, from that of the frozen tundras of Siberia, to that of the hot, pestilential jungles of India. The deserts of Arabia, Persia, Turkestan and Gobi receive little or no rain, while the southern slope of the Himalaya is annually inundated.

Siberia is swept by icy winds from the Arctic Ocean; Arabia, by the hot and fatal simoom. India is traversed by winds which scorch the entire surface for half the year, and flood it with rain the remaining part.

Destructive cyclones often visit the coast, frequently piling up the waters of the Bay of Bengal until the lowlands of the Ganges are submerged.

Southern Asia is covered with a dense tropical vegetation. The palm, bamboo, and banyan tree are abundant Rice, cotton, sugar-cane, flax, jute, hemp, poppy, and the spices, are the principal plants cultivated in the plains and valleys of Southern Asia.

Central Asia produces the plants which thrive best in the temperate zones. Vast forests of pine, larch, teak, maple and birch are on the upland terraces of Siberia. The chief cultivated plants of Central, Eastern and Southeastern Asia are wheat, tea and rice.

Western Asia produces the famous Mocha coffee, tobacco, the fig, date and olive.

Nearly all the domestic animals of the earth are found in Asia, and most of them are native to it. The camel and elephant are used as beasts of burden.

Southern Asia abounds in fierce animals and dangerous reptiles. The largest animals are the elephant, rhinoceros, tapir, lion, tiger, hyena, and jackal. The reptiles include the crocodile, python and cobra de capello. Monkeys and beautiful birds are numerous.

In the colder regions the bear, wolf, fox, buffalo and several species of wild cattle are common. Also many kinds of deer.

Gold and platinum are widely diffused throughout the Ural Mountains and the central plateaus.

Silver is mined in Siberia. Copper and iron are abundant and widely distributed.

Tin is abundant in the Malay Peninsula and the Island of Banca, near Sumatra.

Petroleum is found in the basin of the Caspian Sea.

Asia has always been famous for precious stones. Most of the large and valuable diamonds, sapphires, rubies, and emeralds are from the mines of India.

The finest pearls are obtained in the Persian Gulf and in the water along the coasts of Ceylon.

Asia is probably the birthplace of the human race. The strongest evidences of history and science point to the highlands of Asia as the birthplace of man. Somewhere in the valleys of Persia, the old name of which was Arya, there lived a people who built houses, cultivated the soil and had forms of government.

They believed in an Omipotent Being and also a spirit of evil. Fully one-half the inhabitants of the earth live in China and India.

Siberia, Russian Turkestan and Trancaucasia are subject to Russia, whose capital is St. Petersburgh.

Siberia may be divided into three belts; agricultural and grazing land in the South; forests in the middle; and frozen marshes in the North.

Gold, silver, copper and other metals are mined in the mountains; and numerous wild animals are hunted for their furs.

Trade is carried on by means of caravans and camel trains. In summer boats navigate the rivers, and in winter sledges are drawn on the ice and snow by dogs, horses and reindeer.

The chief cities are Tiflis in Transcaucasia, west of the Caspian Sea; Tashkend, in Russian Turkestan; Omsk, in Western Siberia; and Irkootsk, in Eastern Siberia. Yakootsk, on the Lena River is said to be the coldest city in the world.

The Chinese Empire is larger by one-half than the United States and contains about six times as many inhabitants.

China contains the greater part of the population. The land is fertile and well cultivated, agriculture being the chief occupation of the people. Rivers and canals are numerous; much traveling is done in boats. Thousands of the inhabitants of China have their houses and gardens on rafts and boats which float on the rivers. These people live by gardening and fishing. In their floating houses their children are born, are married and die. A young child falling overboard there is kept from drowning by means of an empty gourd which its mother had tied between its shoulders.

The food of the Chinese consists, principally, of rice and fish.

The leading exports from China are tea, silk, porcelain and pottery.

Its trade is carried on, mainly, with Great Britain, Australia and the United States, by means of ships, and with Russia by means of caravans.

Many of the inhabitants of the other divisions of the empire are wandering tribes, whose occupation is the raising of horses, sheep and goats.

Pekin, the capital of the Chinese Empire, is noted for its surrounding walls, magnificent gates and heathen temples. Its houses are only one or two stories high. Its population is greater than that of New York City.

Thibet is situated on a high plateau, surrounded by the highest mountains in the world.

Corea is a kingdom. It was, until recently, under the control of the Chinese government.

The Empire of Japan consists of islands, which contain mountains, streams, forests, and a well cultivated soil. Japan contains beautiful lakes, rivers, water-falls, trees, and flowers of great variety; bears, deer, wolves, and foxes; pheasants and other birds. The celebrated mountain in Japan is Fujiyama, whose summit is covered with snow nearly all the year. In summer bands of pilgrims dressed in white travel to its summit to worship idols there.

The principal occupations of the Japanese are agriculture, manufacturing and mining.

Its exports comprise tea, rice, silks, porcelain, fans and lacquered ware.

Tokio, the capital, is the residence of the emperor, called the mikado. Its chief port is Yokahama.

India is larger than all the Pacific States and Territories, and contains about four times as many inhabitants as the United States.

The Empire of India is ruled by the Governor-General, who is appointed by Victoria, Queen of Great Britain and Ireland and Empress of India. Next to the Chinese Empire it is the most populous in the world. India was settled by the Aryans, about 1400 B. C. They were Brahmins, but unlike the Brahmins of the present time in their religious teaching and practices. Their language was the Sanskrit. The people are divided into castes. They believe in the transmigration of souls. Gautama or Buddha, about 500 B. C., introduced a form of religion which, after a long struggle with Brahmanism, was overcome in India and transplanted in China, where it has degenerated into a debasing form of idolatry. Queen Elizabeth chartered the East India Company in 1600 A. D. The vast empire, which had grown by its conquests, was transferred to the British Crown in 1858.

Nearly the whole of India is subject to Great Britain, either absolutely or as tributary states.

India is remarkable for its high, snow-covered peaks, hot climate and large population.

Its low plains in the north are the most fertile in the world. The west and south contain desert tracts.

Agriculture and stock-raising are the principal industries.

The exports are cotton, opium, rice, wheat and jute. Cattle, camels, buffalos, sheep and goats are numerous. The inhabitants subsist, principally, upon rice, fish and tea.

Calcutta is the capital and the largest city in India, and the most important city in Asia. Bombay, on the western coast, and Madras, on the eastern, are important cities.

Ceylon is a mountainous island, belonging to Great Britain. It is famous for coffee and spices. Pearl oysters abound on the southern coast, and the fishery is often very profitable.

Farther India or Indo-China, forming the southeastern peninsula of Asia, comprises the kingdoms of Burmah, Siam and Anam, Lower Cochin China, Cambodia and the Malay Peninsula.

This division of Asia is remarkable for its long mountain ranges and fertile valleys, its hot, moist climate, and its dense forests and jungles.

It contains large, savage animals, and many tribes of people scarcely removed from barbarism.

The chief occupation of the inhabitants is the cultivation of rice, which is their principal article of food.

Bangkok, the capital of Siam, is the largest city in Farther India. It contains royal palaces and many pagodas. These are surrounded by bamboo houses built on piles.

Mandalay is the capital of Burmah.

Saigon is a sea-port of French Cochin China.

Singapore, on the Island of Singapore, is a sea-port belonging to Great Britain.

Persia, Afghanistan, Beloochistan and Bokhara are remarkable for their desert tracts, forest-covered mountains and fertile river valleys.

The principal products are grain, fruits, sugar, indigo and dates.

Many of the inhabitants own large flocks of goats and sheep, while others are engaged in the manufacture of silk goods, shawls, rugs and perfumery, or in the caravan trade. There are, also, many roving, warlike tribes. Nearly all are Mohammedans.

Persia is remarkable for extensive salt deserts. Near the Caspian Sea, however, vegetation is luxuriant. Here, as in other Mohammedan countries, education is confined to learning portions of the Koran and scraps of poetry. The Persians are a slow, easy-going people, hospitable, generous, but procrastinating.

These countries are important because of their situation between Russia and the Indian Ocean. Afghanistan has been called the "gateway to India."

Teheran, the capital of Persia, and Tabriz, are the chief cities.

Cabul, Herat and Candahar are the principal cities in Afghanistan.

Arabia is chiefly a hot, desert plateau, with oases of different sizes, in which dates, grapes, tamarinds and other fruits grow.

It has no general government, the inhabitants being ruled by sheiks or chiefs. The rulers are called Sultans.

Arabia is celebrated for fine dromedaries and horses, and excellent coffee.

Muscat, the capital of Oman, is the largest city in Arabia, and the chief sea-port.

Aden is a fortified sea-port belonging to Great Britain.

Mecca, the birthplace of Mohammed, is visited by many Mohammedan pilgrims every year. It is said to be the hottest city in the world.

Turkey in Asia is a part of the Ottoman, or Turkish Empire, whose capital is Constantinople.

Its northern part is remarkable for forests, mountains and fertile valleys. Its eastern part for the fertile plains of the Tigris and Euphrates, and its southern for a desert region.

Tropical fruits, cotton, grain and tobacco grow abundantly.

The people are chiefly Turks and Arabs, professing the Mohammedan religion.

Smyrna, an important commercial port and steamer station, is the largest city.

Damascus is the oldest city in the world. It contains grand old mosques, and is the center of the caravan trade. Its manufactures comprise saddles and silk goods.

Palestine, or the Holy Land, is mentioned in Scripture as the Promised Land of the Ancient Hebrews, and the birthplace of Christianity. It contains the cities of Jerusalem and Bethlehem, the Valley of the Jordan, the Dead Sea and the Sea of Galilee.

AFRICA.

Africa, the south-western continent of the Old World, is the only country stretching entirely across the Torrid Zone.

It is a peninsula, joined to Asia by the Isthmus of Suez. The ship-canal, constructed across the isthmus, makes it, artificially, an island. The shortest distance across the Isthmus of Suez is about seventy-two miles; the line of the canal is one hundred miles. The average height of the isthmus above sea-level is scarcely ten feet.

The Suez Canal was completed in 1869. It has a depth of twenty-four feet, and a clear channel seventy-two feet in width. By connecting the Red sea with the Mediterranean, this canal furnishes a shorter route between European ports and India, than that around the Cape of Good Hope. It extends from Port Said, on the Mediterranean, to Suez, a sea-port town near the head of the Gulf of Suez.

Africa is the second country in size. Its length and breadth are each about 5,000 miles.

The coast is unbroken by bays and inlets such as make secure harbors for vessels. In proportion to its size, it has the shortest coast-line.

There are many continental islands lying along the coast of Africa. Madagascar, the largest, is separated from the continent by a very shallow channel.

The interior of Africa is a plateau, which is highest in the south and south east. This, in most parts, is bordered by mountains, between which and the sea is a low and narrow strip of coast.

The average elevation of the high plateau is about 5,000 feet; and of the northern region, about 1,500 feet.

The principal mountain system extends along the eastern side of the continent. Mount Kenia, the highest peak, is about 20,000 feet above the level of the sea.

The Great Sahara Desert has an undulating surface, and is covered mostly with shifting sand and gravel. A small portion, south of Barca, is below the sea-level.

Oases, watered by springs and covered with groves of date-palm-trees, are met with in different parts of the desert.

Soudan, situated south of the Great Desert, is a region remarkable for its extreme heat and excessive rains and droughts.

Central Africa, or the region crossed by the Equator, is remarkable for its fertility; and, owing to its great height above the sea-level, its climate is mild and healthful. This region is drained by many large rivers.

Southern Africa is mountainous, but it contains many fertile valleys and plains well adapted to agriculture and stock-raising. The Kalahari Desert, though destitute of streams, is covered during a great part of the year with grass. The lakes of Africa are confined chiefly to the high, equatorial region, and are remarkable for their number and size. Lake Victoria is the largest lake in the world. Its outlet is the Nile river.

The River Nile flows through the most important part of Africa. Its lower course is in a region almost rainless, and for more than 1,500 miles it does not receive a single tributary. It is fed by the annual rains and the melting snows of the high mountains.

The water of the Nile is highest from May till September, when the lower valley is covered with a fine, rich soil, brought down by the flood; and the seeds which are scattered over the water, as it subsides, bring forth abundant crops of grain. Cotton, also, is an important product of the Nile Valley.

The Congo, first explored by Livingstone, and afterward by Stanley, drains the most fertile part of the continent. Its source is in the region of heavy rains.

The region of greatest heat is in the Egyptian Soudan. There the midday temperature during the summer months is often 140 deg. Fahr., while the nights are sometimes so cold that ice forms. In the desert, hot winds, known as simooms, are prevalent, and sand storms are often destructive. The coast, generally, is very unhealthy.

Southern Africa possesses a mild and genial climate. Here are the principal settlements formed by Europeans in Africa. This is the home of the Caffre.

Northern Africa yields grain, cotton, dates, almonds, and olive-oil. Rice is a leading product of the Guinea Coast. The date-palm flourishes along the shores of the Mediterranean and in the oases of the desert. The famous baobab-tree is found in Central Africa. It is famous for its great size and age. Groves of teak, mangrove, ebony, and India rubber abound on the western coast. Gum arabic, myrrh, cotton, coffee, sugar-cane, and spices are products of Eastern Africa. The islands produce tropical fruits, wine and amber.

Africa is noted for large and ferocious animals, and venomous serpents. The lion is found in all parts of the continent. The hippopotamus inhabits the upper Nile, while the marshes and streams of the low coast contain many crocodiles, lizards, and other reptiles.

The gorilla, the largest and fiercest of apes, and the chimpanzee, are met with in the west. The elephant, giraffe, and the two-horned rhinoceros, belong in Central and Southern Africa. There are many species of deer and antelope. The zebra and the gnu or horned horse, are numerous in the grassy plains of Southern Africa. The ostrich is hunted in various parts of the continent; but in Southern Africa, the rearing of those birds for their plumes is an important occupation.

The most useful animal in crossing desert regions is the camel. Travelers and merchants, with their camels carrying merchandise, cross the desert in companies, called caravans. For more than four thousand years camels have been almost the sole means employed to carry merchandise across the deserts. The camel will carry a load of four or five hundred pounds weight fifty miles a day for five or six days, although he may not be supplied with food or water during that time.

The coasts of Guinea and Senegambia have long been celebrated for gold. Copper, lead, salt, and saltpeter are obtained in some places.

Important diamond fields are in South Africa.

Africans comprise three races — the Caucasian, Negro, and Malay.

The Moors, Arabs, Berbers, Egyptians, and various tribes of the north are Caucasians; the tribes of Central and Southern Africa, and the east and west coasts, Negroes; and those of Madagascar, Malays.

Excepting the European colonists who have settled along the coast, nearly all the Caucasian inhabitants are Mohammedans, and are in a low state of civilization.

Most of the Negro tribes of Africa are savages, in a degraded condition. There are, however, several tribes which cultivate the soil, raise cattle, and observe laws.

The Barbary States, situated on the Mediterranean coast, extend from the Atlantic Ocean to Egypt.

The climate is mild and healthful. South of the Atlas Mountains, it is extremely hot and arid. There are two seasons, a rainy and a dry

The highlands are covered with forests of cedar, pine, cork-trees and other valuable timber. The lowlands are finely adapted to agriculture.

The most important productions are dates, oranges, bananas, pomegranates and figs.

The natives consist of Moors, Arabs, and Berbers. 'Although descended from a very enlightened people, they are extremely ignorant, degraded and treacherous. The foreigners are mainly French and Jewish colonists. Wherever they settled, agriculture, manufactures and commerce quickly followed.

Morocco is under the absolute government of a sultan, who is subject to Turkey. The country is sparsely settled. Cattle, sheep, and goats are reared extensively.

In tanning and dyeing leather the people exhibit great skill, and the leather manufactured there is exported to all parts of the world.

Morocco and Fez are the most important cities. The sultan holds court at one and the other, alternately.

Algeria is a French possession, and contains a large European population. It is one of the most prosperous of the Barbary States.

Several lines of railway are in operation, and caravans, trading in ivory, gums and ostrich feathers, penetrate the interior of Soudan.

Algiers is the capital and commercial center. It is connected with Marseilles by a submarine telegraph cable.

Tunis, also, is a French possession. It was formerly subject to Turkey. It is noted for its olive groves, date plantations, coral fisheries, and the manufacture of red caps, soap and leather.

Tunis, near the site of ancient Carthage, is the capital and sea-port. It is a very old city.

Tripoli, though nominally a Turkish province, is a despotic monarchy, governed by a bey.

It contains no rivers, and rain seldom falls; yet, on account of heavy dews, the soil is productive.

The leading exports are wool, hides, and ivory.

Tripoli is the capital and sea-port. Mourzouk, the capital of Fezzan, is the center of a large caravan trade,

The Nile Countries comprise Egypt proper, Nubia, and the Egyptian Soudan, or Kingdom of the Mahdi. They are governed by a hereditary monarch called the khedive, and are subject to Turkey.

The greater part of Egypt is a desert. Along the lower course of the Nile, only the narrow valley, which is annually inundated, is capable of producing crops.

Since the completion of the Suez canal rapid progress has been made in developing the agricultural and commercial interests of Egypt.

Railways have been built, and by means of irrigating canals extensive tracts of desert land have been made productive.

Most of the wealthier classes have been educated in Europe, and foreign customs are being introduced throughout the country. The laboring classes are greatly oppressed, and are practically in a state of slavery.

The principal products of Egypt are cotton, grain, sugar and rice. Gum arabic, ivory, indigo, and ostrich feathers are obtained in the Soudan. Manufactories have been established in the larger cities and towns.

Cairo, the capital of Egypt, is the largest city in Africa. Alexandria is the principal sea-port. Railways connect both cities with Suez, the southern sea-port of the Suez Canal. The northern, or Mediterranean, seaport of the canal is Port Said.

The other seaports of Egypt are Rosetta and Damietta.

Nubia and the Egyptian Soudan are inhabited by warlike tribes of Arab and Negro descent.

Khartoum, at the junction of the Blue and the White Nile, is the center of a large caravan trade.

Abyssinia is a high and rugged plateau, containing a number of fertile valleys. The climate, owing to the high altitude of the surface, is mild and healthful. The people, though of a dark, or swarthy complexion, belong to the Caucasian race, and consist, chiefly, of Copts and Berbers, who are ignorant and degraded.

Abyssinia consists of several independent states, having no general government.

Gondar is the capital. Massowah, an Egyptian possession, is the only sea-port.

South Africa comprises several prosperous colonies. Some of these belong to Great Britain, others are independent states founded by Dutch settlers, while others still are the homes of native tribes.

Cape Colony and Natal are British colonies. The surface of the land is high, undulating and well adapted to grazing.

The leading occupations are the raising of cattle and sheep, and the rearing of ostriches. Wool and ostrich feathers are among the most valuable exports.

Cape Town, the capital of Cape Colony, is the chief sea-port of South Africa.

Pietermaritzburg is the capital of Natal.

West Griqualand, also a possession of Great Britain, contains the most productive diamond mines in the world.

Kimberly, its capital, is situated in the diamond fields, and is the chief market for rough diamonds.

Caffraria and Zululand are inhabited by natives who are noted for their intelligence, fine physical appearance and great bravery. Both countries are governed by native chiefs, although subject to Great Britain.

The Orange Free State and the South African Republic (formerly Transvaal) are inhabited by Dutch farmers, called Boers. The Boers are noted for their bravery and love of independence.

Bloemfontein is the capital of the Orange Free State, and Pretoria of the South African Republic. Wool, cattle and grain are the exports.

Central Africa includes the regions comprised in Sahara, or the Great Desert, Soudan, the Congo Free State and the territory southward to the Boer republics.

Sahara contains about twenty oases, inhabited by wandering tribes, who live chiefly by plundering the caravans.

Soudan is inhabited by semi-barbarous tribes, each of which is governed by a chief, whose will is law.

Their occupation is herding cattle, but they are constantly at war with one another.

Timbuctoo, Sackatoo and Kouka are centers of a large caravan trade.

The Congo Free State embraces the basin of the Congo River. It is subject to the King of Belgium.

Zanzibar is a strip of coast nearly 1,000 miles long, including a number of small islands. It is an absolute monarchy, governed by a sultan.

Zanzibar, on an island of the same name, is the capital. It is the center of a large trade in ivory, gum copal and spices. Trade is almost exclusively in the hands of Hindoo and Arab merchants.

Mozambique includes a number of Portuguese colonies, extending from Zululand to Zanzibar. The city of Mozambique, the chief center of trade, is the residence of the Governor-General.

The West Coast is covered with forests of valuable timber. The highlands contain gold and silver.

Senegambia includes most of the basins of the Senegal and Gambia rivers. English and French traders have settled along the coast.

Sierra Leone is a prosperous English colony. It is inhabited by Negroes, many of whom were rescued from slave-ships. Freetown is the capital.

Liberia is a small republic, originally established as a colony for freed slaves from the United States. Monrovia is the capital.

Dahomey and Ashantee are absolute despotisms.

The natives are superstitious, warlike and ferocious. In Dahomey wholesale murders, or human sacrifices, form part of certain celebrations. Here the king has an army of women whose weapons are muskets, swords and clubs. Ashantee, also, is ruled by a native king, who is independent.

Madagascar, a kingdom, contains a civilized population, whose principal industries are agriculture and herding.

St. Helena belongs to Great Britain; the Canary Islands to Spain; the Madeira, the Azores and the Cape Verd Islands to Portugal.

NORTH AMERICA.

North America is the northern division of the western continent. It extends almost from the North Pole to the Equator.

The shape of North America is nearly that of a triangle, broad at the north and tapering almost to a point at the south. Its length is nearly 5,000 miles. Its area is equal to one-half that of Asia, or two and one-half times that of Europe. Its northern and eastern coasts are remarkable for numerous indentations and good harbors, while the western coast has but few.

The western part of the continent is a high plateau, on which are many nearly parallel ranges of mountains. The direction of these ranges is from north-west to south-east. They constitute the Rocky Mountain system, and form the main axis of the continent. The culminating ranges of this system inclose a large, oval-shaped plateau, called the Great Basin.

The Appalachian system, in the eastern part, is composed of several parallel ranges, extending from north-east to south-west. Their average height is about 3,000 feet, or about one-third that of the Western Highlands,

Volcanoes are numerous in the Western Highlands, and several of them are constantly active.

The highest peak of the Rocky Mountain system is Mt. St. Elias, 19,500 feet; and of the Appalachian system, Mt. Mitchell, 6,707 feet.

The great central plain, extending from Hudson Bay to the Gulf of Mexico, lies between the two mountain systems. The Height

of Land, an almost imperceptible divide, crosses the plain, separating the Arctic Slope from the Gulf Slope.

The lakes of North America are remarkable for their number and size. If a straight line were drawn from Chesapeake Bay to the mouth of the Mackenzie River, it would pass through nearly every large lake in North America.

The great lakes contain about one-half the fresh water on the globe. Lake Superior, the largest, however, is exceeded in size by Lake Victoria, in Africa.

Salt and alkaline lakes are numerous in the Pacific highlands. Great Salt Lake, in Utah, has an area twice that of Rhode Island. With the exception of the Caspian Sea, it is the largest salt lake on the globe.

The Mississippi basin is the largest basin in the world, excepting that of the Amazon river. Its chief stream, the Mississippi and Missouri, exceeds every other river in length.

The Yukon river, second in size, is, in many respects, unlike any other river on the continent. Its upper course is remarkable for falls and rapids. Its lower part contains many islands, and is often five and six miles wide.

The Columbia, Colorado, and many of their tributaries which rise in the interior of the continent, flow, in some places, through deep canons.

The soil is very productive. The Mississippi basin and the slopes of the Atlantic ocean and the Gulf of Mexico contain soil of great fertility. On the Pacific coast the climate is much milder than in corresponding latitudes on the Atlantic coast. The northern part of the continent is extremely cold; the central portion is characterized by hot summers and cold winters; the southern part, has a tropical climate. The rain-fall is greatest in the north-west and south-east. The rains of the Pacific Coast fall mostly in winter. In northern regions, vegetation is limited to mosses, lichens, and a few shrubs. A belt of cone–bearing and deciduous trees extends through the middle of the Temperate Zone. In the south, these are replaced by palms, tree-ferns, bananas, and agaves. Grasses are abundant throughout the Temperate Zone. Indian corn and tobacco are native to North America.

The fur seal, whale, walrus, polar bear, and musk-ox are the most important animals of the northern regions. The bison, deer, bear, wolf, and panther are common in the north central part. The grizzly bear is found in North America only. The monkey in the tropical regions.

Reptiles are numerous in the south. Nearly 500 species of birds are known. Fish are abundant; the cod, salmon, herring and mackerel are valuable as food.

The mineral resources of North America surpass those of any other continent. Iron and coal, minerals on which civilization and commerce so greatly depend, are abundant and widely distributed. Petroleum and natural illuminating gas are found in the Alleghany Mountains and the Coast Range. Gold, silver, and quick-silver are found chiefly in the Western Highlands; copper and lead, in the vicinity of the Great Lakes; and zinc, in the Eastern Highlands.

American Indians inhabited North America at the time of the explorations in the 15th and 16th centuries. A civilized people preceding these had disappeared from the region which now constitutes the United States, as the ruins of their habitations bear witness.

Civilized people were found by the Spanish explorers of Mexico. They were conquered by the Spaniards, and gradually disappeared.

The Esquimaux, who are found in the Arctic regions only, are thought by many to be of Mongolian origin. The Indians, also, are said to be of Mongolian descent, and to have come, originally, from Asia.

The white race, the ruling element of the population, are the descendants of Europeans. The inhabitants of Mexico and Central America are the descendants, in part, of Spaniards and native Indians.

The Negroes, originally brought to America as slaves, are fast becoming educated.

Industries.—The geographical distribution of the various industries is more noticeable in North America than in the other continents. Foreign commerce, manufactures, and fisheries are confined chiefly to the coasts and navigable streams.

Agriculture is carried on, principally, throughout the fertile prairies and river-valleys of the interior. Stock-raising is most profitable where there are mild winters and an abundance of grass.

Mining is a leading industry in the highlands.

North America includes Danish America, British America, the United States of America, Mexico, Central America and the West Indies.

Danish America belongs to the Kingdom of Denmark. It comprises Greenland, Iceland, and a few smaller islands.

Greenland extends farther north than any other country, or to within about 400 miles of the North Pole. Its area is nearly one third that of the United States.

The surface of Greenland is covered with ice and snow. The coasts are scored by enormous glaciers. The products are fish, oil, and reindeer skins.

The people comprise a few Danes and a number of Esquimau tribes.

Iceland, which is about half the size of Kansas, is noted for volcanoes, geysers, glaciers, and lava fields. Its southern part has a milder climate than its northern, and contains all the settlements.

The Icelanders are generally educated. Their trade is carried on with Copenhagen, the capital of Denmark. Their capital, Reikiavik, contains a college.

THE UNITED STATES.

A Republic, it is the middle division of North America. Alaska, a territory occupying the northwestern part of North America, is partly in the North Temperate Zone and partly in the North Frigid Zone. It was purchased from Russia by the United States. Extends from the Atlantic Ocean on the east to the Pacific Ocean on the west, from the Dominion of Canada on the north to the republic of Mexico and the Gulf of Mexico on the south. The distance across the United States from east to west through the center, is about 2,600 miles, and from north to south about 1,600 miles. The shortest distance between the Dominion of Canada and the Gulf of Mexico is about 800 miles.

The high mountains and plateaus of the United States are in the western part. There the mining of gold and silver, and the raising of cattle and sheep, constitute the leading occupations of the people.

The plains, prairies, slopes and lowlands extending from the great highland region eastward to the Atlantic Ocean, are remarkable for their fertile soil, which produces immense crops of grain, cotton, fruits and vegetables.

The valleys of the Pacific Slope are noted for their mild, genial climate and their great yield of wheat, fruits and vegetables.

Coal and iron are mined extensively in various parts of the United States.

The variety and importance of the products and industries of this country are due principally to its vast extent of territory and its great diversity of soil, elevation and climate.

Its increase in population, wealth and power is unsurpassed. A century ago there were but thirteen states, containing less than 4,000,000 inhabitants. Now there are thirty-eight states, ten territories, and the District of Columbia, with a total population of more than 60,000,000. A territory is under the control of the General Government of the United States, until it is admitted into the Union as a state by Congress. The original thirteen states were New Hampshire, Massachusetts, Rhode Island, Connecticut, New York, New Jersey, Pennsylvania, Delaware, Maryland, Virginia, North Carolina, South Carolina and Georgia. The first states admitted after them were Kentucky, Vermont, Tennessee, Ohio, Louisiana, Indiana and Mississippi.

The first colonies in the region now called the United States were established by the English, in Virginia, in 1607; by the Dutch, in New York, in 1613; and by the Pilgrims, in Massachusetts, in 1620.

All were subject to Great Britain from 1664 to 1776, when the thirteen colonies declared themselves free and independent states.

Each state has its own constitution, laws, legislature, and governor, while all the states are united under the constitution and laws of the United States. A state is entitled to be represented in the United States Senate by two senators, and in the House of Representatives by one member for every 154,325 inhabitants.

Every state is entitled to, at least, one member. A territory may send a delegate to the House but he has no vote, There are at present 76 senators and 325 members of the House of Representatives. The states which have the largest representation in the House are New York 34 members, Pennsylvania 28, Ohio 21, and Illinois 20. The states and territories of the United States have legislatures consisting of two houses similar to those of Congress, elected by the people. They are divided into counties, which are, in some cases, subdivided into townships. The divisions of Louisiana corresponding to counties are called parishes. The highest officials in a state are the Governor, Lieutenant-Governor, Secretary of State, Attorney-General, and Superintendent of Schools. Towns and villages are collections of houses and inhabitants. Cities have certain rights and privileges not possessed by towns and villages. The affairs of a city are usually controlled by its mayor and aldermen. A county seat is the chief town in which the official business of the county is conducted.

The general government comprises three departments, the legislative, the judicial and the executive. It has control of all matters pertaining to commerce and treaties with foreign countries, the army and navy, the declaration of war, the post-offices, and the coining of money.

The legislative power is vested in Congress, which consists of the Senate, (composed of two senators from each state, chosen by the state legislature, for six years. The Vice-president of the United States is the president of the Senate) and House of Representatives. Congress holds its sessions in Washington. The session of Congress begins on the first Monday in December of each year. A law cannot take effect unless passed by both the Senate and the House of Representatives, and approved by the President. If, however, he disapprove a measure which has been passed by both houses of Congress, it may become a law on being repassed by two-thirds of each house.

The judicial power is vested in the Supreme Court, which interprets the laws. The Supreme Court consists of a chief-justice and eight associate justices, all appointed for life by the president with the consent of the Senate.

The executive power is vested in the President, whose duty is to execute or enforce the laws. He is elected for four years. The President and Vice-President are elected by a number of electors, called the electoral college, chosen by the people of the states, or their legislatures. Each state is entitled to a number of electors, equal to the whole number of senators and representatives to which it is entitled in Congress. In case of a vacancy in the office of President, it shall be filled by the Vice-President. If there be no Vice-President, the law of 1886 vests the succession in those members of the cabinet who are constitutionally eligible, in the following order: Secretary of State, Secretary of the Treasury, Secretary of War, Attorney-General, Postmaster-General, Secretary of the Navy, and Secretary of the Interior.

MEXICO.

Mexico is a republic, composed of twenty-seven states, a federal district and the Territory of Lower California. It is situated in the North Temperate and the Torrid Zone, and is about one-fourth the size of the United States.

The surface is a high plateau, fringed by a belt of low, narrow coast. Several ranges of the Rocky Mountain System, of which the Sierra Madre is the highest, extend through the country from north-west to south-east.

A chain of volcanoes crosses the highest part of the plateau. The summits of several of these are above the limit of perpetual snow. Vol. Popocatepetl is the highest mountain in Mexico, and, next to Mt. St. Elias, the highest in North America.

The lakes are small and unimportant. Most of them are situated in the Valley of Mexico.

The rivers are short, and, excepting the Rio Colorado and Rio Grande, not navigable above tide-water.

The climate is hot and pestilential along the narrow coast, but mild and healthful in the high interior. In going from Vera Cruz to the city of Mexico, one may, within a few hours, experience nearly every gradation of climate, and find the productions peculiar to each zone. There are but two seasons; the rainy, and the dry.

The vegetable productions comprise mahogany, rose-wood, mesquite, various dye-woods, the agave, and cactus. Oranges, lemons, pine-apples, olives, and bananas are extensively cultivated. Tobacco, corn, sugar-cane, cocoa, beans, coffee, vanilla, and the indigo-plant are also grown.

The wild animals of Mexico comprise the grizzly bear, puma or Mexican lion, and coyote. Venomous reptiles and insects are numerous. Cattle, horses, and donkeys, in vast numbers, are the principal domestic animals.

The minerals include gold, silver, tin, quicksilver and marble.

The leading industries are agriculture, stock-raising, and mining. Coffee, sugar, cotton, cochineal, vanilla, metals, hides, and ornamental woods are exported. Great progress has been recently made in the building of railroads; but the unsettled condition of the government depresses every kind of industry.

The people consist chiefly of mixed races. About one-tenth are Creoles, or descendants of Spanish colonists. Spanish is the language of the country.

Mexico, the federal capital, is the metropolis. It is in the Valley of Mexico, elevation about 7,400 feet above sea-level.

Guadalaxara and Puebla are manufacturing centers.

Vera Cruz is the chief Atlantic sea-port.

Acapulco and Guaymas are the principal ports on the Pacific Coast of Mexico.

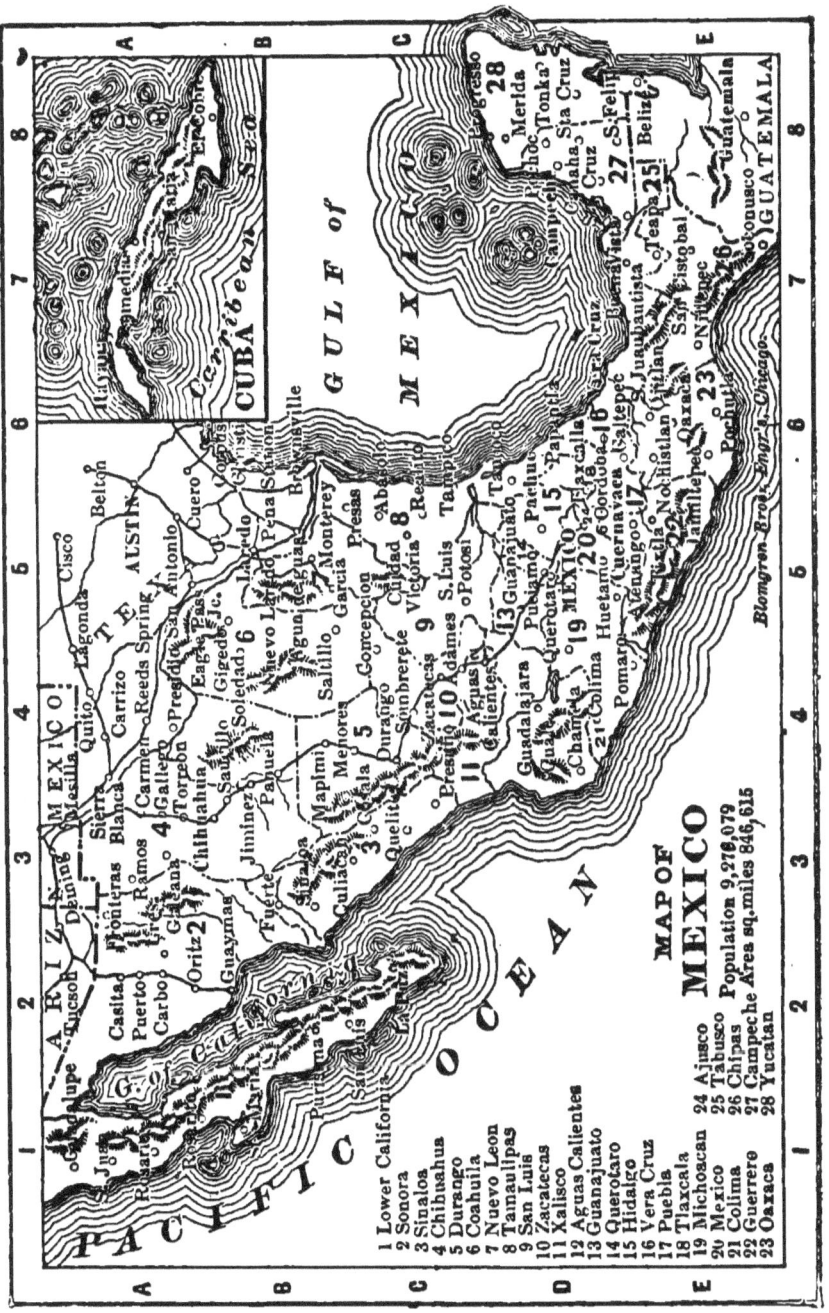

CENTRAL AMERICA.

Central America forms the most southern part of North America. It comprises five republics, and the British colony of Balize.

The surface resembles that of Mexico, being a high plateau situated between low coasts. The climate, however, is hotter and more moist, and its vegetation more luxuriant.

It contains several volcanoes. Destructive earthquakes are of frequent occurrence.

The principal products are coffee, dye-woods and sugar. Gold, silver, and coal are found in the highlands.

The inhabitants are chiefly meztizos and Indians. The white people are mainly of Spanish descent. There are many European merchants and planters in Balize and Costa Rica. The language of the country is Spanish.

Guatemala, the largest city of Central America, is the chief commercial port.

The West Indies comprise two chains of islands, extending southeast from the coast of North America.

The Bahama Islands, about 600 in number, are low, coral formations. Their climate is warm and healthful.

The sponge fisheries constitute the chief industry.

Oranges, lemons and pine-apples are the principal fruits. Salt is obtained from the lagoons of Turk's Island, by evaporation.

Nassau, the capital and commercial port, is situated on Providence Island.

The Greater Antilles comprise the islands of Cuba, Hayti, Jamaica, and Porto Rico. Their surface is mountainous; their climate and productions are those of tropical regions. The population is made up of Spaniards, Creoles and Negroes.

Cuba exports sugar, molasses, coffee, fruits, tobacco and cigars Its forests contain ebony, mahogany and rosewood.

Havana, the capital, is the center of a vast commerce. It is an important sugar market.

Matanzas also is an important city in Cuba.

The Island of Hayti comprises two independent republics, Hayti and Santo Domingo. The people and their rulers are Negroes.

Port au Prince is the capital of Hayti; and Santo Domingo of Santo Domingo.

Jamaica yields allspice, in addition to the products which are similar to those of the other islands. Rum is the principal export. Turtle-fishing is important.

Kingston is the capital.

Porto Rico contains many large and fertile plains.

The Lesser Antilles extend from Porto Rico to the mouth of the Orinoco River.

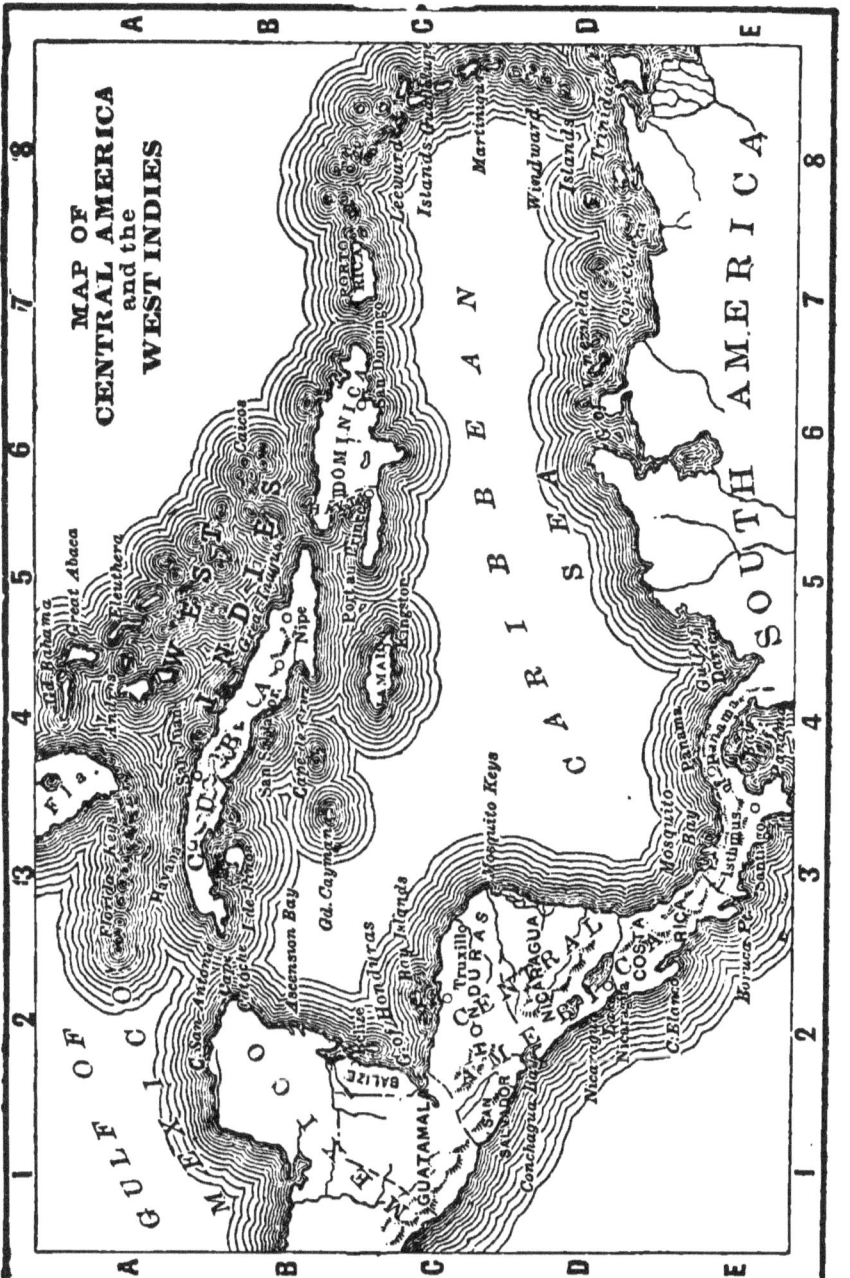

SOUTH AMERICA.

South America was discovered by Columbus in 1498, near the mouth of the Orinoco. The early Spanish discoverers found an Indian village near Lake Maracaybo, built over the water on piles. As it reminded them of Venice, they called it Venezuela, which means Little Venice.

Balboa, in 1513, crossed the Isthmus, and was the first man who saw the Pacific Ocean from the coast of the Western Continent; but, long years before this, the ancient Peruvians had lived there. They had built strong cities, fine temples, great aqueducts, and splendid roads and bridges, ruins of which still remain. Peru was invaded by the Spaniards, under Pizarro, who cruelly treated the natives, destroying their cities and plundering their temples.

South America was thus conquered and settled by Spaniards, except Brazil, which was settled by Portugese, and Guiana, which was settled by British, Dutch and French.

About 300 years afterward the people of the countries of South America (except Guiana) declared themselves independent of Spain and Portugal.

Simon Bolivar was the most distinguished general and patriot of South America. He was called the "Liberator," also the "Washington of South America."

South America is the Southern part of the Western Continent.

Its area is nearly twice that of the United States. In shape it is a triangle, which tapers to a point toward the south. The coast line has but few indentations.

Like North America it has mountain ranges in the west and east and a vast plain in the center.

The Andean Plateau, the main axis of the continent, extends along the entire western coast. It supports parallel ranges, which constitute the Andean System. Its high peaks are always covered with snow. The highest measured peak is Mount Aconcagua, which is about 24,000 feet in height. The most celebrated volcano is Cotapaxi.

The plains of South America cover about one-half its area. The llanos of the Orinoco are treeless plains. During the rainy season they become a vast inland sea. With the disappearance of the water comes a profusion of tropical vegetation, which quickly withers under the intense heat of the sun.

The largest lakes in South America are Maracaybo and Titicaca. The latter is 12,000 feet above the sea-level.

The Amazon is the largest and one of the longest rivers in the world. Its course is nearly along the Equator. Its highest source is within 70 miles of the Pacific Ocean. At its mouth the river is nearly 200 miles wide. Its current and the freshness of its water are perceptible 200 miles out at sea.

The soil is fertile in nearly all parts of the continent. The southern part, however, is barren, rocky and desolate.

The climate along the sea-coast is generally warm, except in the south. In the interior of the lowland plains, the heat is almost intolerable.

The banks of the Amazon produce a wonderful variety of ornamental woods, such as mahogany, rosewood, vegetable-ivory, and tortoise-shell wood. The India rubber, cacao, and cocoa-palm trees are abundant.

The lowlands abound in wild grasses, and on the mountain slopes are found the cinchona-tree and many kinds of medicinal plants.

The chief cultivated plants are coffee, sugar-cane, cotton, tobacco, indigo, manioc, and spices.

Minerals.—South America is rich in minerals. A large part of the silver now in use in the world was obtained from the Andes Mountains. Gold is mined in Colombia and Brazil.

Industries.—The chief industries of the inhabitants of South America are herding, agriculture, and mining.

BRAZIL.

The Empire of Brazil, the largest country of South America, is the only monarchy in the New World.

It comprises the eastern plateau and the basins of the Amazon and the La Plata. The northern and western parts are low, swampy, and, during the rainy season, completely inundated.

Near the coast, the valleys are rich and well cultivated.

The greater part of the country has a tropical climate.

Coffee, cotton, sugar, tobacco, rice, grain, tropical fruits, nuts, and spices are raised in abundance.

The leading industries are cattle-raising and agriculture.

The natives live in the interior. The ruling people are the Portuguese, or their descendants.

Rio Janeiro, the capital, is the largest city in South America. Its chief exports are coffee and India rubber.

Bahia is the center of the diamond trade.

The Andes Republics comprise the United States of Colombia, Ecuador, Peru, Bolivia, and Chili occupy the mountainous region along the coast of the Pacific Ocean.

The coast is very steep, affording few harbors.

The surface is rugged. The high plateaus are barren, but the mountain sides and the valleys afford pasturage, and yield grain and other products.

This region is subject to earthquakes, and it contains some of the most celebrated volcanoes in the world.

The governments are republican in form, modeled after our own; but they are subject to frequent revolutions.

Bogota, although within four and a half degrees of the Equator, has a climate of perpetual spring, due to its altitude of nearly 9,000 feet. Its wet seasons are our spring and autumn; its dry seasons, our summer and winter. It is warmest in February, and coldest in December. Grain is sown twice a year. Most of the houses are built but one story high, owing to the frequency of earthquakes. There are, however, many large, splendid buildings.

Panama, on the isthmus, is the largest and most important city.

It is connected by railroad with Colon, or Aspinwall. Its climate is tropical and unhealthy.

Quito, the capital of Ecuador, is situated on a very high plateau, surrounded by volcanoes.

Guayaquil is the chief commercial city.

Lima, a few miles from the coast, is the capital of Peru. Its port is Callao.

Arequipa was several times destroyed by earthquakes.

La Paz is the capital and largest city of Bolivia.

CHILI.

Chili is the most powerful and enterprising of the Spanish-American republics.

It is the same in extent from north to south as the United States from east to west — about 2,600 miles.

It is situated on the western slope of the Andes and extends from the Bay of Arica to Cape Horn.

Along the coast are numerous islands, which are rich in guano and niter.

Its climate is temperate and moist.

The people are chiefly of Spanish origin. They are active, industrious and intelligent.

Santiago is the capital. Valparaiso is the largest commercial city on the west coast of South America.

The Argentine Republic is a broad and level country, comprising most of the pampas.

The people are engaged in herding and in preparing dried beef, hides, tallow and horns, for export.

Buenos Ayres, the capital and largest city, has an extensive commerce.

Paraguay and Uruguay resemble the Argentine Republic in surface, products and the occupations of the people.

Montevideo, the capital of Uruguay, is an important commercial city.

Asuncion is the capital of Paraguay.

Venezuela lies almost entirely within the basin of the Orinoco. Its climate is tropical.

The people are engaged in cattle-raising and agriculture. Hides, meat, tallow, coffee, cocoa, cotton, sugar and dye-woods are exported.

Caracas is the capital. It has frequently suffered from earthquakes.

Guiana embraces three colonies—British, French and Dutch. Its products are like those of Venezuela.

Cayenne is the capital of French Guiana, Georgetown of British Guiana, and Paramaribo of Dutch Guiana.

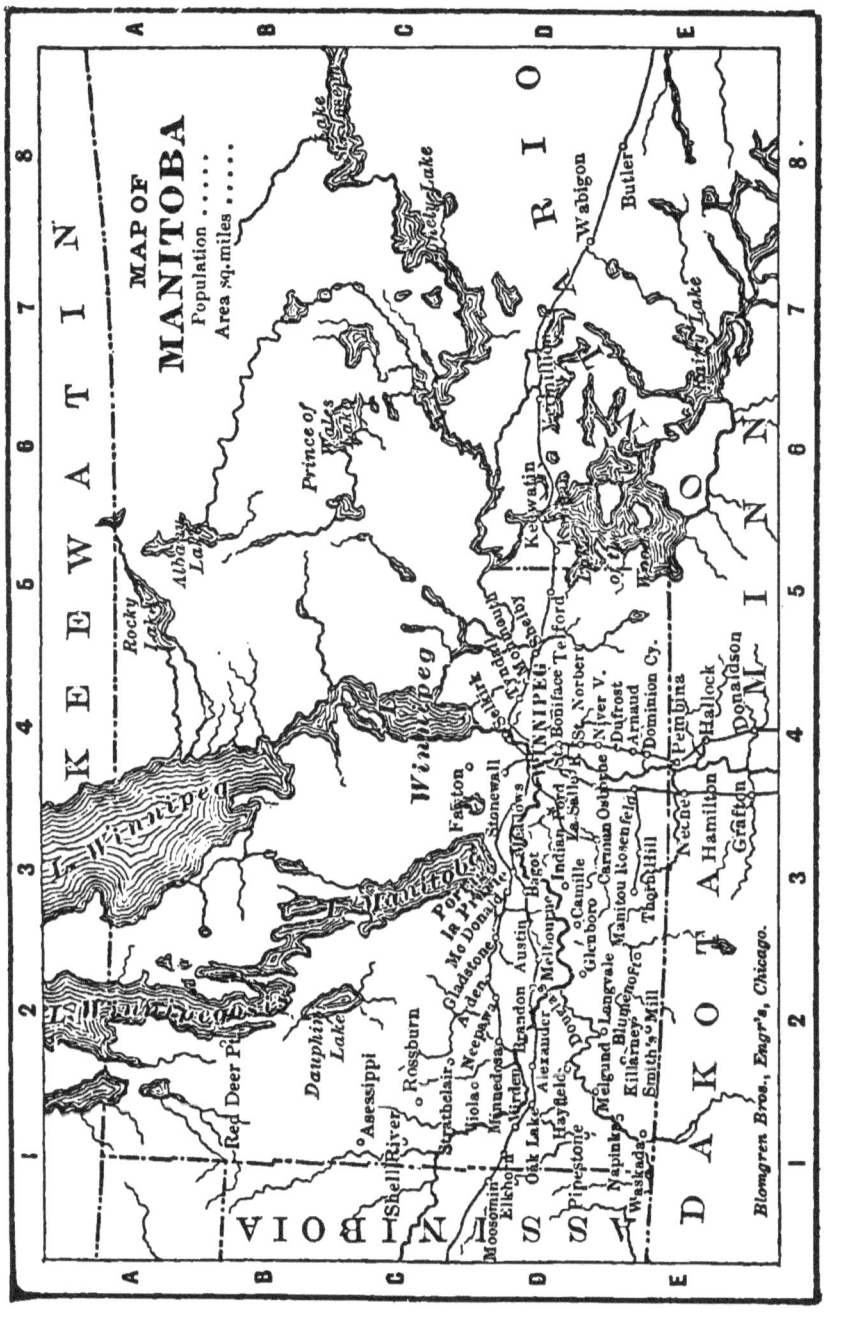

DOMINION OF CANADA.

The Dominion of Canada embraces the provinces of British Columbia, Manitoba, Ontario, Quebec, New Brunswick, Nova Scotia and Prince Edward Island, besides several territories and districts. Its area is about equal to that of the United States.

The surface is mostly a vast plain, bordered by a high plateau in the west, on which stand the Rocky mountains and the Cascade range.

A chain of lakes extends from the mouth of the Mackenzie river to the Great Lakes. The St. Lawrence, Nelson and Mackenzie rivers drain the principal basins.

The climate of the Pacific Slope is mild, but elsewhere the winters are of great severity. The summers are short and in the southern provinces hot.

A belt of timber, mostly pine, extends from the Rocky mountains to the Atlantic ocean. The Pacific Slope is covered with forests of fir, the valley of the St. Lawrence contains growths of maple, oak and elm.

The central prairie regions are covered with luxuriant crops of wild grasses, and, where cultivated, yield large crops of grain.

The wild animals comprise the bison, bear, moose, wolf, beaver, otter, ermine, mink and marten, most of which are hunted for their skins. The coast waters abound in seal, cod and salmon.

The minerals comprise gold, silver and coal, which are mined in the west. Copper and iron are found near Lake Superior. Coal is mined in Nova Scotia also.

The chief industries in the eastern provinces are lumbering and fishing. The central regions are agricultural. The uninhabited regions of the north yield valuable furs in great quantities.

Most of the inhabitants are of English descent. In the eastern provinces, however, there are many descendants of the early French settlers.

The government of the dominion is vested in the Governor-General and Parliament. The Governor-General is appointed by the sovereign of Great Britain. Parliament consists of a Senate and a House of Commons. The members of the Senate are appointed by the Governor-General. The members of the House are elected by the people. Each province has a Lieutenant-Governor and a legislature.

Ottawa is the capital of the Dominion of Canada. It contains magnificent public buildings.

British Columbia, including Vancouver and other islands, is the largest and most mountainous province of the dominion. Its mines of gold and coal are valuable. Lumber, fish, and wool are exported.

Victoria, on Vancouver Island, is the capital and metropolis.

Manitoba is noted for wheat and furs. Steamers ply on the Red River of the North, and on Manitoba and Winnipeg lakes.

Winnipeg, the capital, is the agricultural and commerical center.

Ontario, the most important province, contains nearly one-

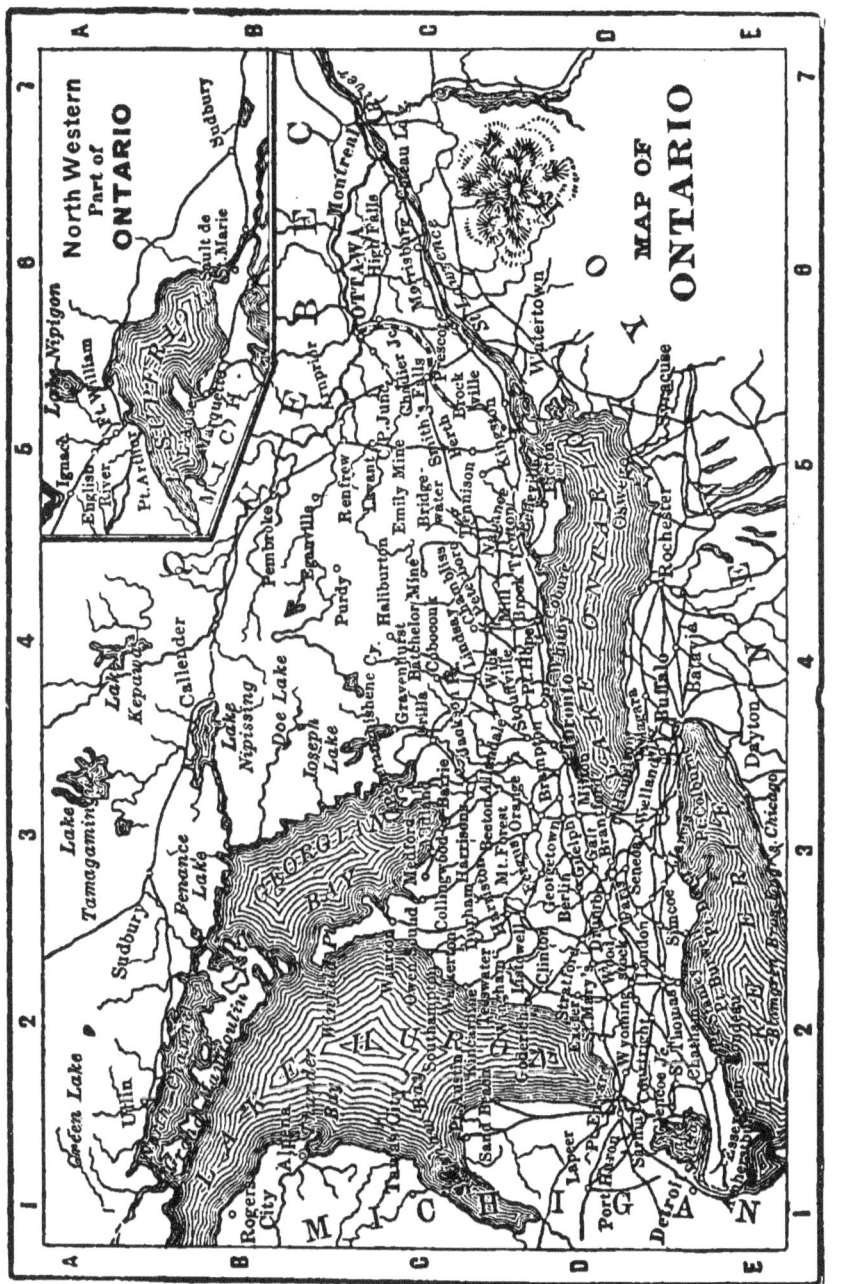

third the population of the dominion. Grain, fruit, and lumber are the principal products. Petroleum, copper, and iron are obtained near Lake Superior.

Toronto, the capital of the province, is noted for its manufactures and educational institutions. It is an important railway center and lake-port.

Hamilton, situated near the western extremity of Lake Ontario, is an important lake-port and manufacturing center.

Quebec is hilly. Its winters are extremely cold; its summers, warm, short, and foggy.

Its agricultural region is south of the St. Lawrence, and produces good crops of oats, potatoes, and hay. The most valuable export is lumber.

The people of this province are, chiefly, descendants of early French settlers.

Quebec, the capital, is the oldest city in the dominion. The heights, on which the upper portion of the city is built, are strongly fortified. The fortress of Quebec, next to that of Gibraltar, is considered the strongest in the world. It was, however, captured by General Wolfe during the French and Indian War. The principal business part of the city occupies the low ground.

Montreal, the metropolis, is noted for its magnificent cathedrals, and the tubular bridge across the St. Lawrence River.

New Brunswick is noted for lumber and ship-building.

Fredericton is the capital of New Brunswick.

St. John is the metropolis and largest port.

Nova Scotia has more sea-coast than any other province. Ship-building and the fisheries constitute the chief industries. Its coal-fields are extensive. Gold and gypsum are also mined.

Halifax, the capital, has an excellent harbor, and is the chief British naval station in North America.

Prince Edward Island, the smallest province, is the most densely populated. Agriculture and fishing are the chief occupations. Fish and eggs the principal exports.

Charlottetown is the capital.

Newfoundland is noted for its barren soil, cold climate and dense fogs.

The dense fogs which prevail in this latitude are due to the meeting of the cold Arctic Current with the warm waters of the Gulf Stream. During the spring and summer, icebergs and pack-ice are brought down by the Arctic Current, and drift about until melted. It is for this reason that the steam-ship route between America and Great Britain is one of the most dangerous in the world.

Its cod, salmon and seal fisheries give employment to about nine-tenths of the inhabitants.

St. John's, the capital, is the most easterly city in North America, south of Greenland.

The Territories were formerly owned by the Hudson Bay Company.

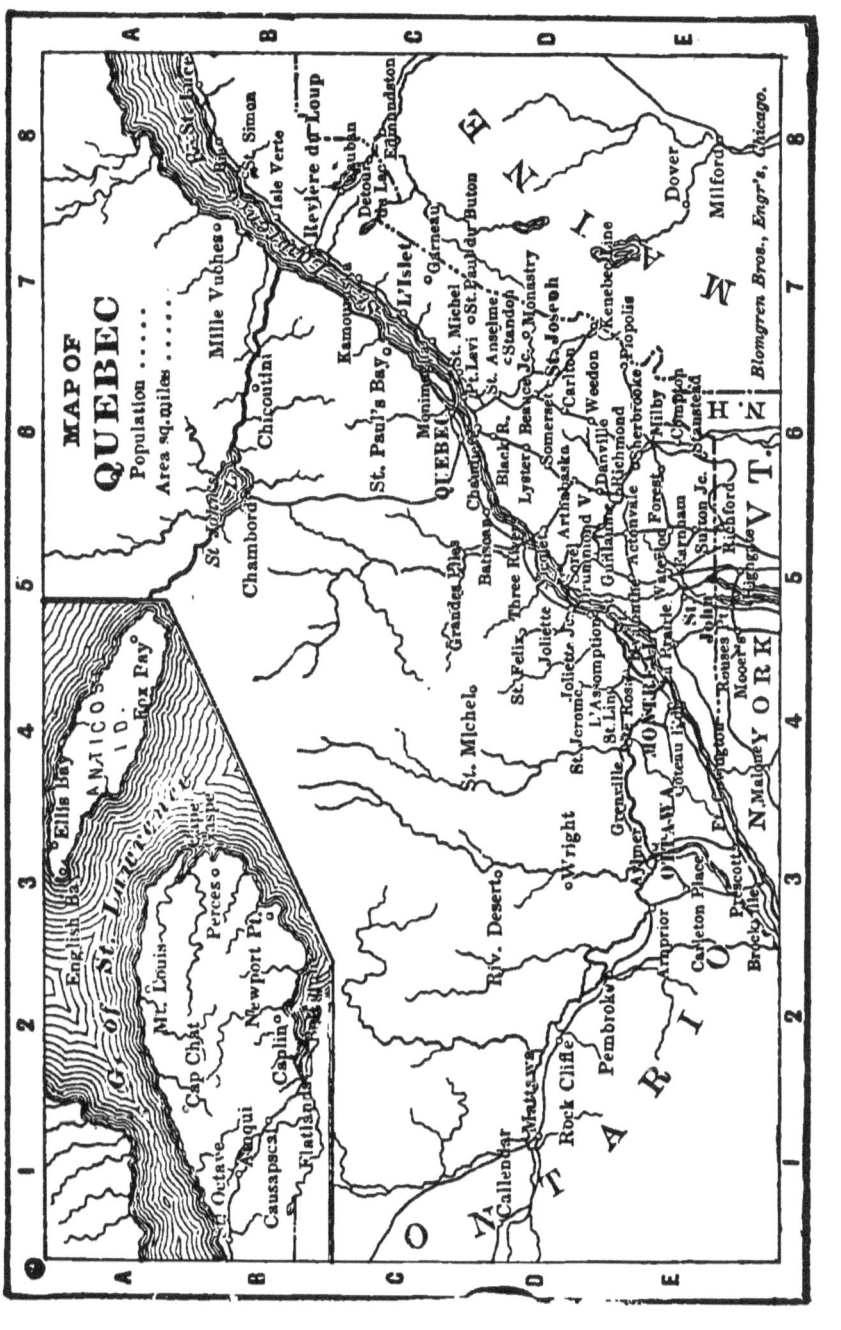

NEW HAMPSHIRE.

One of the thirteen original states. Named for Hampshir) county, England, called the "Granite State." Ratified United States Constitution June 21, 1788. Union soldiers 33,937. Number counties 10. Miles railroad 660. All elections Tuesday after first Monday in Nov., number senators 24, representatives 321, sessions of legislature biennial, in odd-numbered years, meeting first Wednesday in June. Terms of senators and representatives 2 years each. Number electoral votes 4, congressmen 2, number voters 105,138. Paupers excluded from voting. Dartmouth College, at Hanover, founded 1769. Compulsory education law, common schools excellent, school age 5-15. Legal interest 6 per cent., usury forteits 3 times the excess. Population 1880 346,991, male 178,526, female 176,465, native 300,697, white 346,229, colored 685, Indians 63. Extreme length N. and S. 181 miles, extreme width 92 miles, area 9,005 sq. miles—5,763,200 acres. Coast line 18 miles. Highest peak Mt. Washington. Largest lake, Winnipiseogee, 74 sq. miles. General elevation 1,200 feet. Isles of Shoals form part of state. The White Mountains occupy the northern portion of the state with unsurpassed scenery. Soil rocky, with small fertile districts. Hay best crop; corn, wheat, oats and ordinary vegetables do fairly with close cultivation. Forests largely exhausted, except at the north. Cleared lands average $16⅔ and woodland $25 per acre. Mica quarried at Grafton, soapstone at Haverhill, Keene and Francestown, granite at Plymouth, Troy, Roxbury, Concord. State ranks high in cotton manufacturing CLIMATE.—Winter average 24, summer 69 deg. Extremes great in White Mountains. Summer short and hot, with violent storms. Rainfall 41 inches. Frost late in spring and early in fall. Winter begins in Nov., cold till May. Snow lies two-thirds of year in mountains, elsewhere 70 to 130 days. Health good PRINCIPAL INDUSTRIES.—Agriculture, manufacture of cotton, woolens, lumber, leather, boots and shoes, etc. Quarrying mica, granite and soapstone. PRINCIPAL CITIES.—Manchester, pop. 32,630, Nashua 13,397, Concord (the capital) 13,843, Dover 11,687, Portsmouth (chief harbor) 969. The harbor of the latter place, Great Bay, never freezes over.

Salaries of State Officers.

Governor	$1,000
Secretary of State	$800 and fees
Treasurer	1,800
Attorney General	2,200
Superintendent Public Institutions	2,000
Three Railroad Commissioners	$2,000 to 2,500
Adjutant General	1,000
Secretary Board of Agriculture	1,000
Librarian	800
Chief Justice	2,900
Six Associate Justices	2,700

VERMONT.

First State to join original 13. Called the "Green Mountain State." Active in war of 1812. Union soldiers furnished, 33,288. Number counties 14. Miles railroad 944. First railroad built from Bellows Falls to Burlington 1849. State elections biennial, first Tuesday in Sept.; number senators 30, representatives 240. Sessions of legislature biennial, in even-numbered years, meeting first Wednesday in Oct. Terms of senators and representatives, 2 years each. Number electoral votes 4, congressmen 2. Number voters 95,651. Bribers excluded from voting. Colleges 2. School age 5-20. Legal interest rate 6%, usury forfeits excessive interest. Population, 1883, 332,286; male 166,888, female 165,399, native 291,327, foreign 40,959, white 331,218, colored 1,057. Length N. and S. 149 miles, width 34 to 52 miles, area 9,136 sq. miles, 5,847,040 acres. Highest Point (Green Mountains) about 4,600 ft. Green Mountains run N. and S. through the state and are 3,000 to 4,600 feet high. The surface is generally hilly. All east of mountains drained by the Connecticut, the only navigable river. Small streams abundant. Soil rocky but good in narrow strips on streams. Potatoes best crop. Corn, wheat, oats, hay, hops and bbckwheat yield moderately if well attended. Forests remain to considerable extent, but are cut over or culled. Cleared land averages $17.50 and forest land $18 per acre. Dairying profitable. Manganese, copper, iron, gold, black, white, red and variegated marble and slate are found, the marbles in great abundance. State ranks 1st in quarries, 4th in copper. Temperature ranges from 15 deg. below to 95 deg. above, but changes not sudden; winter averages 18 deg. to 33 deg. Summer averages 66 deg. to 75 deg. Summers short. Rainfall greatest at south and east where it averages 43 inches; in other sections the average is 35 inches. Snows heavy. Frosts early in fall and late in spring. Snow lies 80 to 140 days. Health excellent. Death rate very low, less than 1¾ in the 100. Industries very varied, numbering 2,900. Principal ones, agriculture, dairying, manufacture of flour, furniture, leather, tin, iron and copper ware, and lumber, mining, quarrying and finishing marbles and stones, and maple sugar making.

PRINCIPAL CITIES.—Burlington, pop., 1880, 11,365; Montpelier (capital), pop., 1880, 4,000; Rutland, pop., 1880, 12,149: Brattleboro and Bellows Falls are important and thriving towns and seats of large industries.

Salaries of State Officers.

Governor. $1,000; Lieutenant Governor, $6 a day; Secretary of State, $1,700; Treasurer, $1,700; Auditor, $2,000; Inspector of Finances, $500; Railroad Commissioner, $500; Adjutant General, $750; Superintendent of Public Instruction, $1,400; Chief Justice. $2,500; Six Associate Justices, $2,500; Senators and Representatives, $3 a day; District Judge, $3,500; Collector of Internal Revenue, $2,650; Collector of Customs, $1,000 and fees.

KENTUCKY.

Name Indian. Signifies dark and bloody ground, because the state was the hunting and battle ground of the tribes. Called "Corn Cracker State." Louisville founded 1780. Admitted as a State June 1, 1792. State furnished 7,000 troops in war of 1812, and 13,700 in Mexican war. Won great credit in latter. Neutral at beginning of civil war. State the scene of continuous cavalry raids during the war, and some sharp battles at Perryville, Richmond, etc. Put under martial law 1864. Civil government restored 1865. Union soldiers furnished, 75,760. Number counties 118. State elections biennial, first Monday in August, in odd-numbered years. Number senators 38, representatives 100, sessions of legislature biennial, in even-numbered years, meeting last day of December, holds 60 days. Term of senators 4 years, of representatives 2 years. Number electoral votes 13, number congressmen 11, number voters 376,221. Bribers, robbers and forgers excluded from voting. Number colleges 15, public school system framed 1838, good schools, school age 6-20 years. Legal interest 6%, by contract 10%, usury forfeits excess over 10%. Miles of railroad 1,887. Population, 1880, 1,648,690, male 832,590, female 816,100, native 1,589,173, foreign 59,517, white 1,377,179, colored 271,451, Chinese 10, Indians 50, slaves, 1860, 225,483. Extreme length E. and W. 350, width 179 miles, area 40,000 sq. miles, 25,600,000 acres. River frontage 832 miles, navigable water ways 4,120 miles. Soil fair, except in the famous "Bluegrass region," extending for 40 or 50 miles around Lexington, and one of the most beautiful sections on the globe. Natural wonder Mammoth Cave, greatest in the world. Kentucky ranks high as an agricultural and stock state. Staple crops, corn, wheat, tobacco, oats, barley, hemp, rye and vegetables, fruits do fairly. Famous for thoroughbred horses and cattle. Mules and hogs largely raised. At the east in the mountains are immense forests of virgin oak, poplar, ash, chestnut, elm, walnut, cucumber and other valuable timber trees. Coal, marbles, minerals, oil, stone, etc., also abound. Iron deposits of immense magnitude are known to exist. Cleared land averages $20 and woodland $5 per acre. The average of the former is raised materially by the high prices, often $100 or more per acre in the bluegrass section. Mountain lands rich in timber and minerals and not without agricultural value rate $2 to $5 per acre. The state ranks first in tobacco, and fourth in malt and distilled liquors. Climate variable, favorable to health and agriculture, healthfulness not surpassed. Thermometer ranges from 5 deg. below zero to 98 above, rarely greater extremes are known. Temperature averages, summer 75 deg., winter 38 deg., rainfall 50 inches. Snows fall, but disappear in a few days. Sleighing only for a day or so. Winters moderately long. Malaria very rare, except on the Ohio and Mississippi rivers. CHIEF CITIES.—Louisville, pop. 125,758. Frankfort (capital), pop. 6,958. Covington, 29,720. Lexington, former capital, founded 1776, pop. 16,656. Newport, connected with Covington by bridge, pop. 20,433. [Salaries of State Officers page 439.]

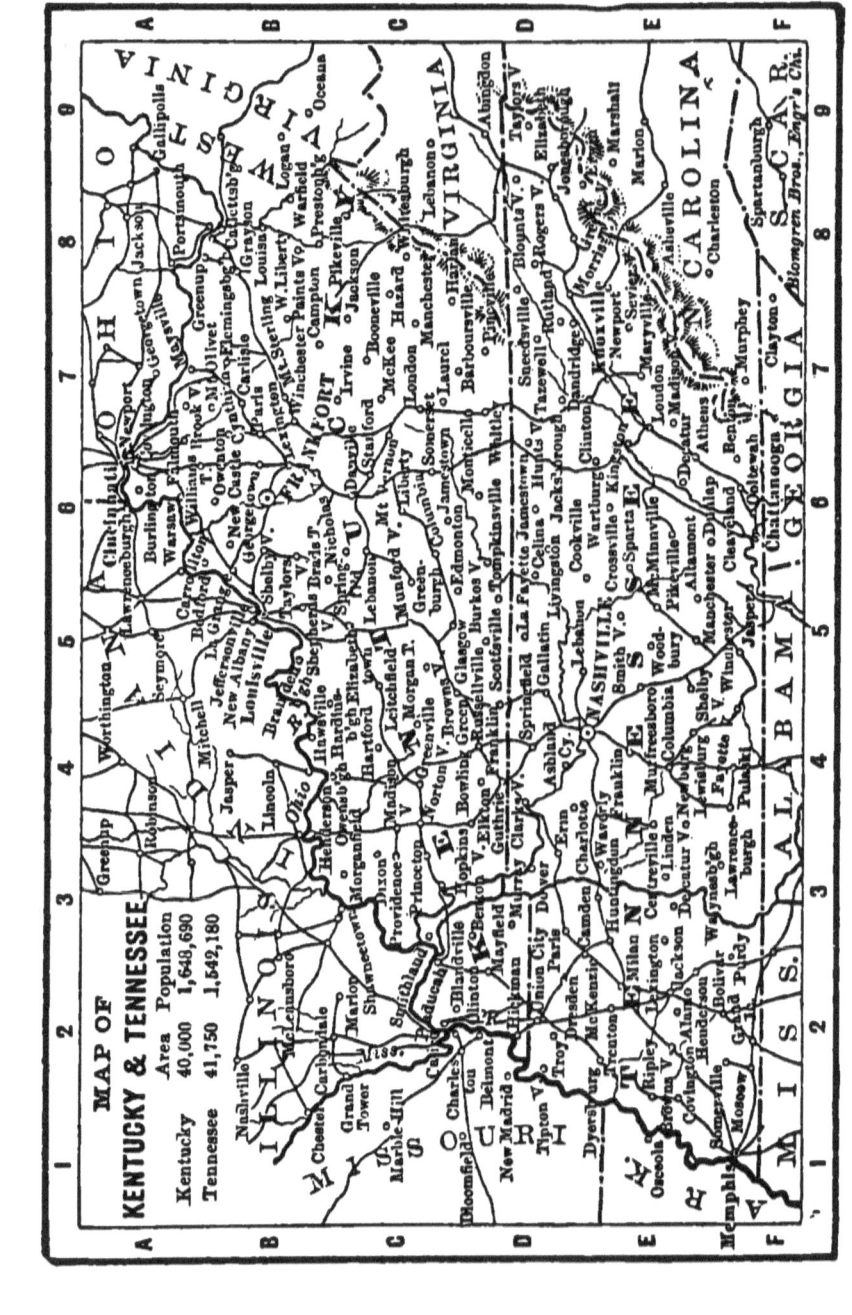

TENNESSEE.

"Big Bend State." First settled 1754. Became a part of North Carolina 1777. Organized as the State of Franklin 1785, but again became part of North Carolina 1788. Ceded to United States by North Carolina 1789. Admitted as state June 1, 1796. Capital, Nashville. First railroad part of N. & C., 1853, Nashville to Bridgeport. Seceded June 8, 1861. Re-entered Union 1866. Number counties 96. State, congressional and presidential elections, Tuesday after first Monday in November, number senators 33, representatives 99, sessions biennial, in odd-numbered years, meeting first Monday in January; holds 75 days. Terms of senators and representatives 2 years each. Number electoral votes 12, number congressmen 10, number voters 571,244, native white 240,939, foreign white 250,055, colored 80,250, non-payers of poll-tax excluded from voting. Legal interest 6 per cent., by contract any rate, usury forfeits excess of interest and $100 fine. Schools fair. Miles railroad 2,166. Population 1880 1,542,359, male 769,277, female 773,082, native 1,525,657, foreign 16,702, white 1,138,831, colored 403,151, Chinese 25, Indians 352. Slaves 1860 275,519. Extreme length E. and W. 430 miles, width 110 miles. Area 41,750 sq. miles, 26,720,000 acres. Mountainous at E. where Apalachians separate state from North Carolina. Soil fair, except in central basin, where it is very productive. State abounds in coal, iron, fine marbles and building stones, copper and other minerals. Possesses one of the finest areas of forest in the Union. Principal timbers, walnut, oak, poplar, ash, hickory, etc. Staple products, mules, hogs, peanuts, corn, wheat, cotton, vegetables of all kinds, potatoes, tobacco, hemp, flax, broomcorn, iron, copper, coal, marbles, etc. Ranks second in peanuts and third in mules. Resources but little developed, 5,000 sq. miles of coal field, with 3 to 7 workable veins. Cleared land everages $12.50, forest $5 per acre. Grape growing pays. Climate one of healthiest in world. Mild and pleasant, and owing to varying elevation very diverse. Snow light and lays briefly. Ice rarely more than a mere film in thickness. Average temperature winter 38 deg., summer 75 deg. Extremes seldom occur. Rainfall 45 to 47 inches. Air bracing. CHIEF CITIES.—Nashville capital, pop. 43,350. Memphis pop. 33,592, Chattanooga pop. 12,892, Jackson pop. 8,377, Knoxville pop. 9,693. Industries chiefly agricultural, mining, lumbering and iron making.

Salaries of State Officers.

Governor	$4,000
Secretary of State	$1,800 and fees
Treasurer	$2,750
Comptroller	2,750
Attorney General	3,000
Superintendent of Public Instruction	1,800
Adjutant General	1,200
Commissioner of Agriculture	3,000

NORTH CAROLINA.

One of the thirteen original states. Called "Old North State," "Fur State," and "State of Turpentine." Discovered by Lord Raleigh, 1584. Settled by English, 1650. State seceded May 21, 1861. Forts, etc., seized by state troops. Coast section scene of sharp fighting during civil war. State re-entered Union June, 1868. Number of counties, 96, miles of railroad, 1,366. All elections Tuesday after first Monday in Nov. Number of senators 56, representatives 120, sessions biennial, in odd-numbered years, meeting Wednesday after first Monday in January, hold 60 days. Terms of senators and representatives 2 years each. Number electoral votes 11, number congressmen 9. Convicts are excluded from voting. Public school system adopted, 1840, at present over 2,000 public schools in operation; school age 6-21; separate schools for whites and blacks. Legal interest rate 6 per cent., by contract 8, usury forfeits interest. Rate of tax less than 50c. on $100. POPULATION.— 1880, 1,399,750, male 687,908, female 711,842, native 1,396,008, colored 531,277, Indians, 1,230, slaves, 1860, 331,059. Greatest length E. and W. 453 miles; greatest width, 185 miles, area, 52,240 square miles, or 33,433,600 acres, less area water surface. Coast line 423 miles with many harbors. Much forest yet remains. Swamps extensive, most noted of them, the Great Dismal, north of Albemarle sound, contains 148,000 acres. Small streams abundant, water powers numerous; corn best crop, tobacco largest product, other staples are orchard products, sweet potatoes, rice, wheat, oats, peanuts, cotton, hay and vegetables in the order named. North Carolina ranks first in tar and turpentine, second in copper, third in peanuts and tobacco and fourth in rice. Has rich deposits of gold and the baser minerals. Stone, slate, coal, marble, mica. Excellent fisheries. Natural resources but slightly developed. Ample opportunities for homes, enterprise and capital. Cleared land averages $10 and woodland $5 per acre, and much of excellent quality in the market below this average. Stock thrives. Scenery varied, ordinary, picturesque and grand. Wheat harvested June. Corn ripe in Sept. Climate is varied, warm and moist in low sections; cool and dry in mountains, with all intermediate conditions. Average winter temperature, 49 deg., summer 78 deg. to 79 deg. Frosts light and seldom come till the end of fall. Rainfall, including some snow in mountains, 45 deg. Health good. CHIEF CITIES.—Wilmington, pop. 13,446; Raleigh, (capital), pop. 7,790; Charlotte contains assay office, pop. 4,473, New Berne, pop. 5,849. INDUSTRIES.—Agriculture principal occupation. Fishing, manufacture of turpentine and lumber, mining, etc. Number of diffrent industries, 3,800. Number boats engaged in fisheries, about 3,000. Copper mined, 1,640,000 lbs.

Salaries of State Officers.

Governor $3,000, Secretary of State $2,000, Treasurer $3,000, Auditor 1,500, Attorney General $2,000, Superintendent of Public Instruction $1,500, Adjutant General $600, Commissioner of Agriculture $1,200, State Librarian $750, Chief Justice $2,500.

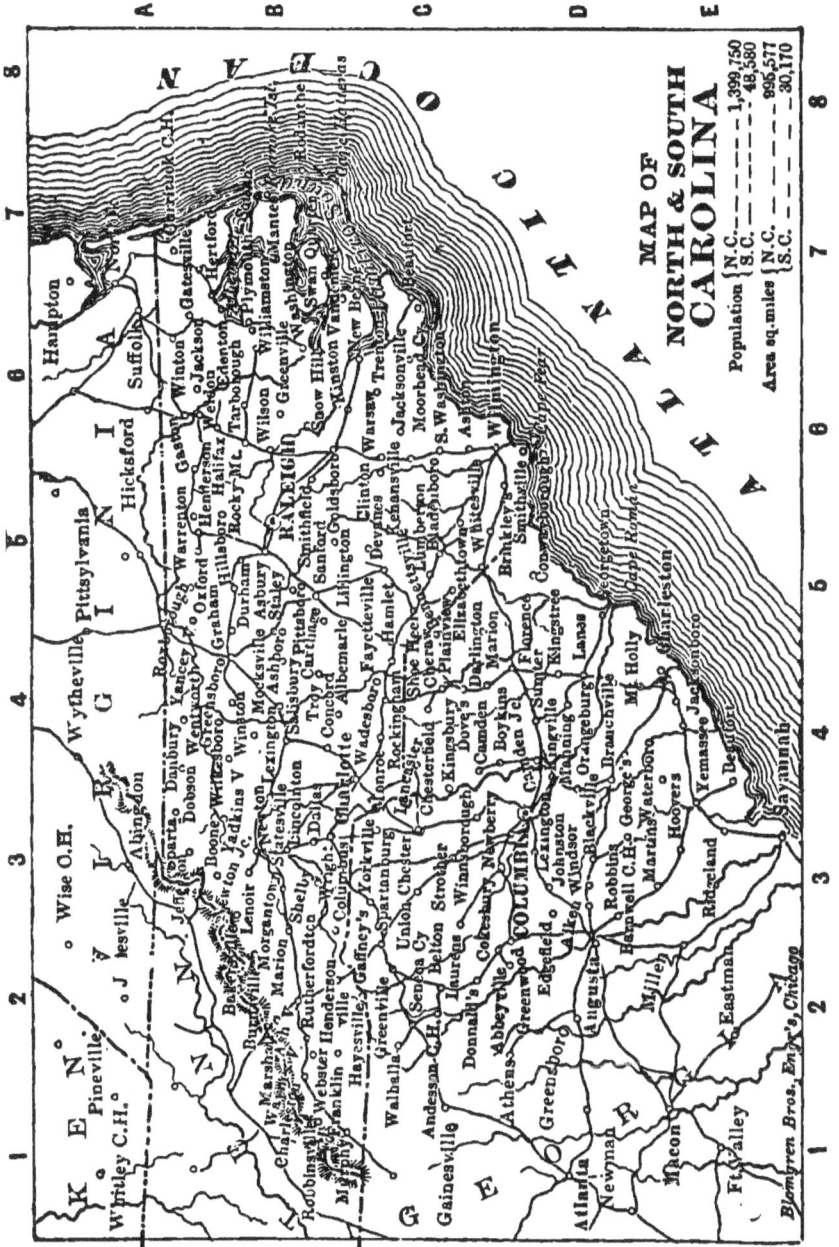

SOUTH CAROLINA.

One of the thirteen original states, "Palmetto state." Revolutionary record, brilliant. English seized the territory, but were thrashed at Cowpens and Eutah Springs and penned up in Charleston. First railroad in United States using American locomotive, 1830. First state to secede, Nov., 1860. Sumter bombarded April 12-13, 1861. Ordinance of secession repealed Sept., 1865, and slavery abolished. Re-entered the Union June, 1868. Number counties 34, miles of railroad 1,570. State, congressional and presidential elections, Tuesday after first Monday in November. State senators 35, representatives 124, sessions annual, meeting fourth Tuesday in November. Term of senators 4 years, of representatives 2 years. Number electoral votes 9, number congressmen 7. Insane, inmates of asylums, alms-houses and prisons, United States army and duelists excluded from voting. Number colleges 9, school age 6-16, school system fair. Legal interest 7%, by contract, any rate. Population, 1880, 995,577, male 490,408, female 505,169, native 987,891, white 391,105, Indians 131, slaves, 1860, 402,406. Greatest length 280 miles, greatest width 210 miles, area 30,170 square miles, or 19,308,800 acres, coast line 212 miles. Principal river Savannah, navigable 130 miles. Magnificent water power, undeveloped. Soil from medium to very rich. Forests extensive and valuable. Land, cleared or uncleared, averages $7 per acre. Rice and cotton, best crops. All other cereals as well as vegetables, fruits, grasses and fiber crops grow well. Phosphate beds enormous, gold, mica, marbles of all colors, building stones found in large quantities. Turpentine, tar, lumber and oysters largely produced. Stock thrives. Gold mines in Abbeville, Edgefield and Union counties, first mint deposits, $3,500, in 1827. White and variegated marbles found in Spartanburgh and Laurens counties. CLIMATE.—Temperature ranges 15° to 96 degrees F. Averages, summer 82 degrees, winter 51 degrees. Average rainfall 48 inches, decreasing to the south. Health good. Epidemics rare and confined to seaports. Resort for consumptives. Changes slight and infrequent, frosts rare. CHIEF CITIES.—Charleston, pop. 1880, 49,984, port of entry, seat of a Catholic bishop. United States customs districts at Beaufort, Charleston and Georgetown. Capital, Columbia. PRINCIPAL INDUSTRIES.—Agriculture, mining, fishing, quarrying, lumbering, turpentine and tar making, and phosphate digging.

Salaries of State Officers.

Governor $3,500, Lieutenant Governor $1,000, Secretary of State $2,100, Treasurer $2,100, Comptroller General $2,100, Attorney General $2,100, Superintendent of Public Instruction $2,100, Commissioner of Agriculture $2,100, Adjutant and Inspector General $1,500, Chief Justice $4,000, Associate Justices $3,500, Clerk of Supreme Court $1,000, Senators and Representatives $5 per day, mileage 10 cents; District Judge $3,500, Collector of Internal Revenue $3,250.

VIRGINIA.

One of the thirteen original states. Called the "Old Dominion," and "The Mother of Presidents." First English settlement in America, 1607. Active in Revolution and subsequent steps toward founding the Union, Virginia won the title of "First of the States." British burnt Norfolk 1779, and Richmond 1781. Yorktown surrendered Oct., 1781, practically vanquishing England. State seceded May 7, 1861, and capital of Confederacy moved to Richmond. Scene of gigantic energies of the war. Bull Run, the Wilderness, Cold Harbor, Fredericksburg, Port Republic and many other famous battles were fought on Virginia soil. Lee surrendered at Appomattox April 9, 1865, ending the war. State returned to the Union Jan. 26, 1870. Number of counties, 100. Sessions of legislature biennial, in odd-numbered years, meeting first Wednesday in December; holds 90 days. Term of senators 90 days, representatives 2 years. Number electoral votes 12, Congressmen 10. Lunatics, idiots, convicts, duelists, United States army and non-taxpayers of capitation tax excluded from voting. Number colleges 7, schools 4,502, school age 5-21, school system fair. Legal interest 6 per cent, by contract 3 per cent, usury forfeits all over 6 per cent. Miles of railroad, 2,894. ⁊ POPULATION— 1880, 1,512,565; male 745,589, female 766,976, native 1,497,869, white, 880,858, colored 631,616, Indians 85, slaves, 1860, 490,865. Greatest length east and west, 445 miles, greatest width, 190 miles, area 40,125 square miles, 25,680,000 acres. Coast line, 130 miles, tidal frontage, 1,556 miles. The state is rich in iron, gold, salt, coal, marble, slate, zinc, lead, stone, timber and other natural resources as yet little developed. Much good farming land is untilled. Cleared land averages $10 and woodland $6 to $7 per acre. The opportunities for homes and enterprise are inviting. All cereals, tobacco, peanuts (state ranks first in this crop and second in tobacco), fruits, grapes, and vegetables are extensively raised. Stock thrives. Climate varies, is genial and healthful, cool in mountains and warm in lowlands in summer. Winters are seldom severe. Winter averages 44, summer 78 degrees. Rainfall, including snow, averages 44 inches, being heaviest on the coast. CHIEF CITIES— Richmond (capital), pop. 63,600; pop. of Norfolk, 21,965, Petersburg, 21,656. Hampton Roads one of best harbors on coast. Seven ports of entry. INDUSTRIES—Half population engaged in agriculture, balance in quarrying, ship-building, lumbering, the trades, iron working, meat packing, tanning.

Salaries of State Officers.

Governor $5,000, Lieutenant Governor $900, Secretary of State $2,000, Treasurer $2,000, Auditor $3,000, Secretary Auditor $2,000, Attorney General $2,500, Superintendent of Public Instruction $2,500, Adjutant General $600, Commissioner of Agriculture $1,500, Superintendent of Land Office $1,300, President of Supreme Court $3,250, four Judges of Supreme Court $3,000, two District Judges $3,500, Senators and Representatives $540 per year.

WEST VIRGINIA.

Originally part of Virginia. Called "Pan Handle State." History up to 1861 same as that of Virginia. Refused to secede April 22, 1861. F. H. Pierrepont elected governor June 20, 1861. Admitted as state June 20, 1863, and Wheeling made the capital. Capital changed to Charleston, 1870. Moved again to Wheeling, 1875, and to Charleston again in 1884. Union soldiers furnished, 32,068. State advanced rapidly in wealth. Number counties 54, miles railroad 1,026. Governor and state officers elected quadriennially, and legislature every two years, on second Tuesday in October, number senators 26, representatives, 65. Sessions biennial, in odd-numbered years, holding 45 days. Terms of senators 4 years, of representatives 2 years. Number electoral votes 6, congressmen 4, number voters, 169,161, native white 123,569, colored 6,384. Insane, paupers, and convicts not voting. Flourishing free school system, school age 6-21. Legal interest 6 per cent, by contract 6, usury forfeits excess of interest. POPULATION.—1880, 618,457, male 314,495, female 303,962, native 600,192, white 592,537, colored 25,886, Indians, 29, increase in population 1870 to 1880, 38 per cent, number slaves, 1860, 18,371. TOPOGRAPHY, AREA, SOIL, PRODUCTS, ETC.—Length N. and S., 241 miles, greatest width 158 miles, area 24,645 sq. miles, 15,772,800 acres. Surface mountainous with fertile valleys, the Alleghenys principal range. Some high peaks. Scenery fine and much visited by tourists. Western part hilly, but gradually descends from 2,500 feet above the sea toward the Ohio river, where the elevation is 800 to 900 feet. Much of the state is virgin forest densely clothed with oak, walnut, poplar, ash, and other timber trees. Mineral springs abound. The soil, where not mountainous, is excellent. Mineral wealth, including coal, oil, iron, salt, is prodigal, Staple products include the minerals named, sheep, hogs, tobacco, wheat, corn, dairy products, fruit, wine, lumber. Petroleum extensively produced. The state ranks fifth in salt and coal, seventh in buckwheat, iron and steel. Cleared land averages $22.50. CLIMATE moderate, average temperature, winter 30 deg., summer, 70 deg. Elevation reduces heat which in the valleys averages 76 to 78 deg. Average rainfall 42 to 45 inches. Health is excellent. CHIEF CITIES.—Charleston, capital, Wheeling, pop. 30,727, Parkersburg, pop. 6,582, Martinsburg, pop. 6,335. CHIEF INDUSTRIES.—Sixty per cent. of laborers engaged in agriculture, balance in mining, iron making, lumbering, manufacturing, etc.

Salaries of State Officers.

Governor $2,700, Secretary of State $1,000 and fees, Treasurer $1,400, Auditor $2,000 and fees, Superintendent of Free Schools $1,500, Attorney General $1,000, Presiding Judge of Supreme Court $2,250, Associate Judges $2,250, Senators and Representatives $4 per day, mileage 10 cents; District Judge $3,500, two Collectors of Internal Revenue $2,875.

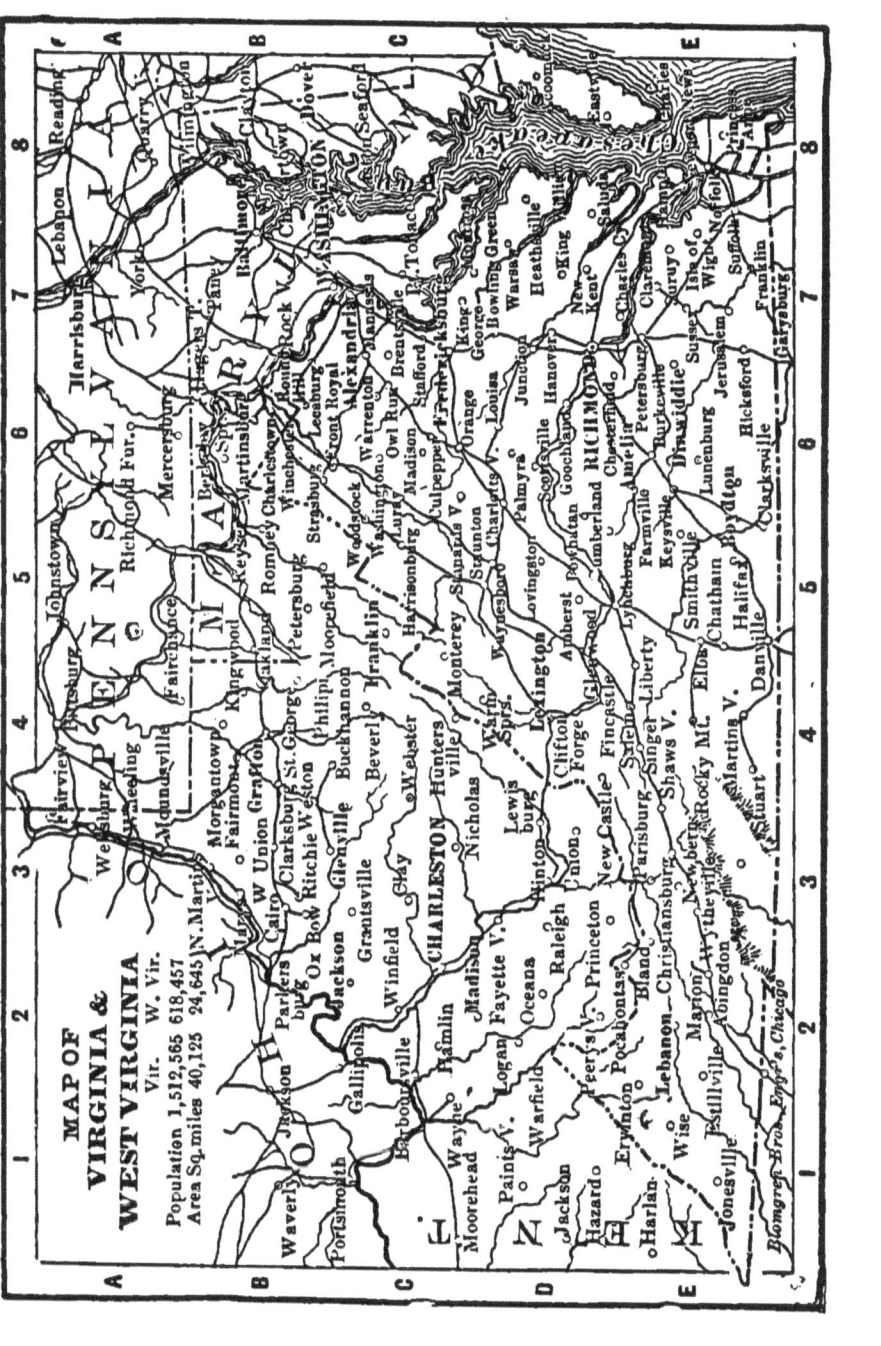

ALASKA.

Discovered by Vitus Behring 1741, and became Russian territory by right of discovery. Purchased by United States for $7,000,000, 1867, as a deed of gratitude to Russia for her course in civil war. Has paid five per cent. on investment ever since, and promises to become the source of enormous mineral, fur, agricultural and timber wealth. Governor appointed by the president of the United States.

POPULATION.—Whites, 2,000; Indians, estimated, Innuits 18,000, Aleutian 2,200, Ninneh 4,000, Thlinket 7,000, Hyda 800. Extreme length north and south 1,200 miles, width 800 miles, area (estimated) 531,409 sq. miles. Yukon, chief river, 80 miles wide at mouth, navigable 840 miles, length about 1,300 miles; coast line 5,000 miles. Fertile land. Good oats, barley and root crops are raised without difficulty. Rich grass land in the valley of Yukon. Timber abundant. Yellow cedar best, being of great value for boat-building. Berries plentiful. Fine quality of white marble is on Lynn Channel. Coal, amber and lignite on Aleutian Islands, the best coal being on Cook's Inlet. Gold, silver, copper, cinnabar and iron are found; sulphur abundant. Noted for fur-bearing animals, the chief of which are beaver, ermine, fox, marten, otter, squirrel and wolf. The main revenue is the fur seal, taking of which is regulated by law. The walrus is of value in furnishing ivory and oil. Whales, cod, herring and halibut and salmon are abundant.

CLIMATE.—Pacific coast modified by Pacific Gulf Stream and long summer days. Temperature at Sitka averages, winter about that of Washington, D. C. Rainfall copious and foggy weather common on coasts and islands. Sitka, one of the rainiest places in the world outside the tropics: annual precipitation 65 to 90 inches; rainy days 200 to 285 in year.

CHIEF CITIES.—Sitka, seat of Bishop of Greek church, and headquarters of governor, pop. 995, white 163, creole 219, Thlinket 613. Fort St. Nicholas, Cook's Inlet, Fort St. Michael and Norton's Sound are other main settlements. Harbors at Port Clarence, Michaelooski and Captain's Harbor.

INDUSTRIES.—Fishing, canning, trapping and mining.

Salaries of Territorial Officers.

Governor...$3,000
District Judge... 3,000
Clerk of District Court and ex-officio Secretary and Treasurer.. 2,500
District Attorney.. 2,500
Marshal and Surveyor General............................ 2,500
Collector of Customs............................$2,500 and fees
Three Deputy Collectors................................. 1,500
One Deputy Collector.................................... 1,200
Two Inspectors, per day.................................   3

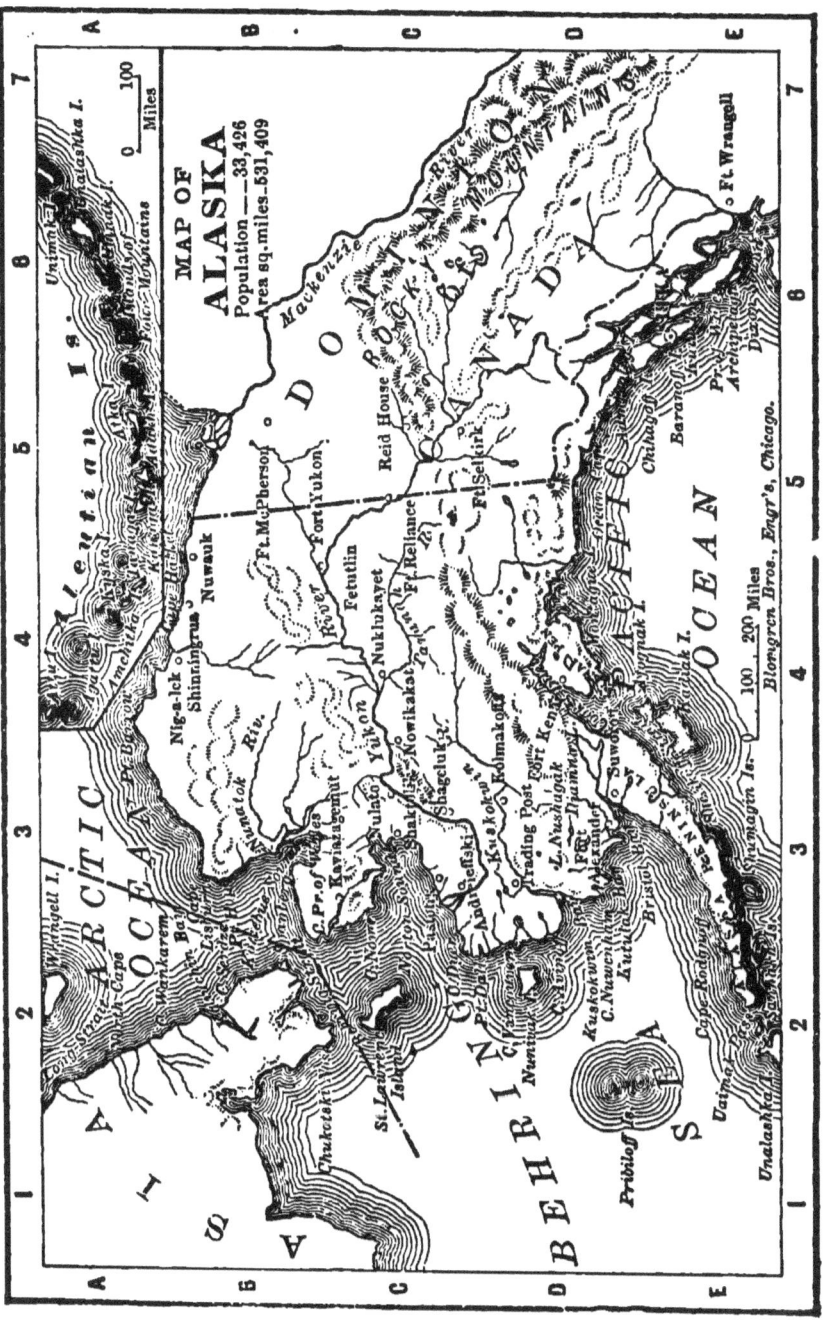

ALABAMA.

Name Indian, means "We rest here." Mobile founded by French 1702. Admitted to Union Dec. 14, 1819. Seceded Jan. 11, 1861. Montgomery made capital of Confederacy Feb. 4, 1861. Subsequently removed to Richmond, Va. State re-entered Union July 14. Number counties 66, miles of railroad 2,191. State elections biennial first Monday in Aug., number senators 33, representatives 100, sessions of legislature biennial in even-numbered years, meeting Tuesday after second Monday in Nov., and holding 50 days, term of senators 4 years, of representatives 2 years. Number of electoral votes 10, congressmen 8. Indians, idiots, convicts of crime excluded from voting. Number colleges 4, school age 7-21, schools good. Legal interest 8 per cent, usury forfeits entire interest. POPULATION.— 1880 1,262,505, male 622,629, female 639,876, native 1,252,771, white 662,185, colored 600,103, Indians 213, slaves, 1860, 435,080, estimated increase, 1885, 8 per cent. Length N. and S. 332 miles, width averages 155 miles, area 51,540 sq. miles, 32,985,600 acres. Surface at N. E. rugged, extending into Allegheny mountains, gradually descends, forming rolling prairies at center of state and flat low stretches at the south. Sea coast 68 miles. Mobile bay best harbor on the gulf, 1,600 miles of navigable waterways. Has fair soil and is enormously rich in coal, iron, lime and sandstone, timber and various minerals. Middle section soil fertile and varied. Coast region sandy, but by proper cultivation prolific. Vegetable farming near Mobile very successful. Cotton, mules, iron, coal, sugar, rice, tobacco, hay, oats, corn, staple products. Fruits are a good crop. Much forest remains. Cleared land averages $7, and woodland $4 per acre. State ranks fourth in cotton, fifth in mules and molasses, sixth in iron ore and sugar, seventh in rice. CLIMATE.—Temperature mild, cold at north, warm at south, average winter 47 deg., summer 81 deg., July hottest month, range of thermometer 20 to 95 deg., sometimes for a day reaching 102 deg. Rainfall 50 inches. Snow or ice very rare. Trees bloom in Feb. CHIEF CITIES.— Montgomery (capital) pop. 16,712, Huntsville pop. 4,977, Selma pop. 7,529, Mobile pop. 29,132. LEADING INDUSTRIES.— Agriculture and kindred pursuits, mining, iron making, lumbering, etc. Number industries 2,070.

Salaries of State Officers.

Governor	$3,000
Secretary of State	1,800
Treasurer	2,150
Auditor	1,800
Attorney General	1,500
Superintendent of Public Instruction	2,250
Librarian	1,500
Three Railroad Commissioners	$2,000 to 3,500
Chief Justice	3,000
Two Associate Justices	3,000

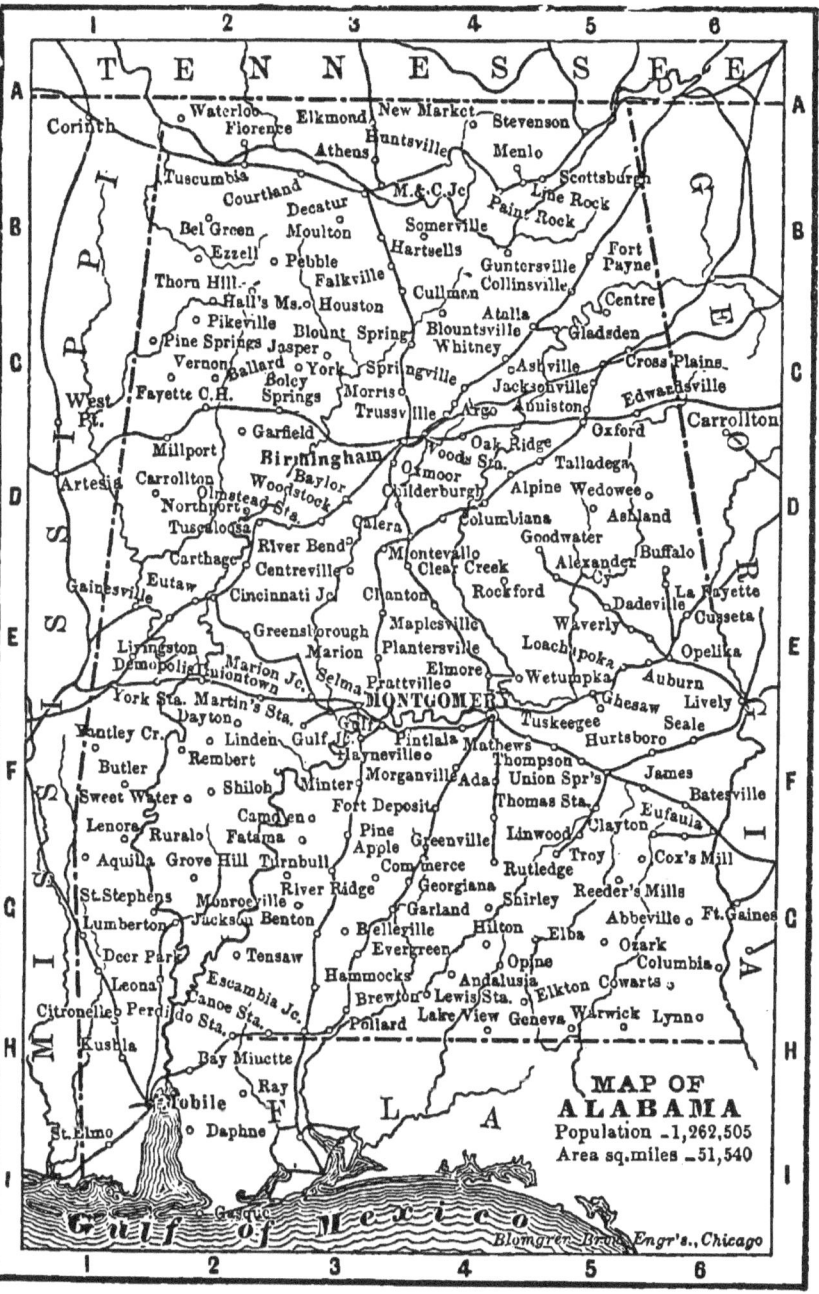

ARKANSAS.

"Bear State.", Settled 1685. Arkansas territory organized, 1819. Admitted as a state June 15, 1836. Slavery acknowledged. Seceded May 6. 1861. Considerable fighting during war, but no great battles. Re-entered Union 1868. Number counties 75. Miles railroad, 1,764. State elections biennial, in even-numbered years first Monday in Sept.; number senators 31, representatives 94, sessions of legislature biennial, in odd-numbered years, meeting second Monday in Jan., holding 60 days, term of senators 4 years, of representatives 2 years. Number electoral votes 7, congressmen 5, voters 182,977, native white, 129,675, foreign white 6,475, colored 46,827. Idiots, Indians, convicts not voting. Number colleges 5, school system progressive; school age 6-21. Legal interest rate 6 per cent, by contract 10 per cent, usury forfeits principal and interest.

POPULATION —1880, 802,525, male 410,729, female 386,246, native 792,175, foreign 10,350, white 591,531, colored 210,606.

Length N. and S. 240 miles, average breadth 212 miles, area 53,845 sq. miles, 44,460,800 acres. The scenery varied and charming. Hot Springs (temperature 140 deg.) great natural wonder and famous for medicinal properties. Soil varies, but greater portion exceptionally rich and suited to all crops, especially fruits, berries and gardening. State especially favorable to agriculture. Magnificently timbered. Pine, oak, cypress, cedar, hickory, walnut, linn. locust chief growths. Cleared land averages $10 and woodland, $3 per acre. Coal exists on the Ash river, iron in the Ozarks, salt near Ouachita. Oilstone near Hot Springs, kaolin in Pulaski county. Staple products, corn, wheat, cotton, tobacco, oats, sweet potatoes, mules, tar, tnrpentine, lumber, etc.

CLIMATE.—Genial. Temperature ranges 15 deg. to 95 deg., on rare occasions going to 100 deg. Averages winter, 45 deg.; summer 80 deg. Rainfall 44 inches, heaviest in S. E., lightest in N. W. Health unsurpassed, especially in N. W.

CHIEF CITIES.—Little Rock (cap.) pop., 13,138. Hot Springs.

INDUSTRIES.—2,100 in number. Chiefly agricultural.

Salaries of State Officers.

Governor...$3,500
Secretary of State... 1,800
Treasurer... 2,250
Auditor... 2,250
Attorney General... 1,500
Superintendent of Public Inst.. 1,600
Land Commissioner.. 1,800
Chief Justice.. 3,000
Two Associate Justices... 3,000
Senators and Representatives.......................................$6 a day.
Two District Judges.. 3,500
District Attorney..$200 and fees
Two Assistant District Attorneys.........................$1,200, 1,000

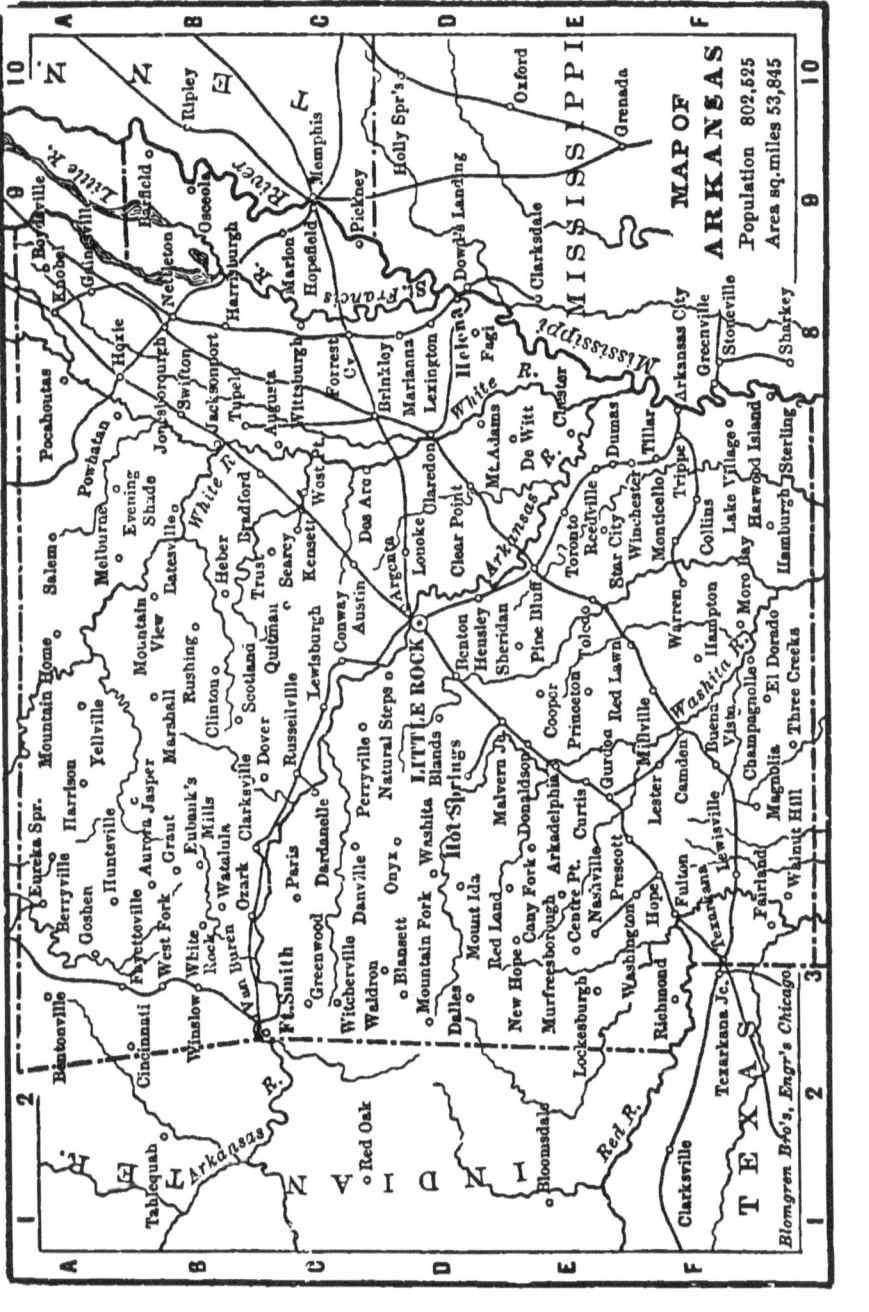

ARIZONA.

Explored 1526. Mineral wealth found, no important settlements effected because of hostile natives. Organized as territory, Feb. 24, 1863. Number counties, 11. Miles railroad, 906. All elections Tuesday after first Monday in Nov.; number senators, 12; representatives, 24; sessions of legislature biennial, in even-numbered years, meeting first Monday in Jan., holds 60 days; terms of senators and representatives, 2 years each; voters, 20,-398; native white, 9,790; foreign white, 8,256; colored, 2,352. School age, 6-21 years. Legal interest rate, 10 per cent., by contract, any rate; no penalty for usury. School endowment in lands reserved very large.

Population, 1880, 40,440; male, 28,202; female, 12,238; native, 24,391; foreign, 16,049; white, 35,160; colored, 155; Chinese, 1,630. Indians, 3,493. Estimated increase, 21 per cent. Extreme length north and south, 378 miles, width 339 miles, area, 113,929 sq. miles, 72,914,560 acres. Volcanic peaks reach an altitude of 10,500 feet. Southern portion a plain, dipping occasionally below sea level, and rising only to a very moderate elevation (200 to 600 feet usually), mountains numerous, highest point San Francisco, 11,056 feet. Colorado river navigable 620 miles. Flows between perpendicular walls cut in solid rock in places 7,000 feet high. Agriculture possible only in the valleys or where irrigation is practicable. Soil in valleys and bottoms very rich and prolific. Wheat, barley, potatoes, hay, corn, onions are staple field crops, corn follows wheat or barley, giving two crops yearly. Oranges and all semi-tropical fruits do well where water is obtainable. Cattle-raising extremely profitable. Desert tracts of considerable area are found. Timber grows on the mountains, foot-hills, and along the streams. The varieties include pine and cedar on mountains, cotton-wood, walnut and cherry on streams. Size of trees fair, and quantity large. Abundant mineral wealth exists, which can be developed with profit, owing to completion of railways. Nearly all mountain ranges contain gold, silver, copper and lead. Superior quality of lime found near Prescott and Tucson, beds of gypsum in San Pedro valley, remarkable deposits of pure, transparent salt near Callville. Territory ranks second in production of silver.

Climate exceptionally healthful, and generally mild, except in mountains, temperature averages 38 deg. winter, 73 deg. summer, much warmer at south, the thermometer reaching occasionally 115, and rarely falling below 35 deg. in winter. In central portion heat seldom exceeds 88 deg. to 90 deg., snow in mountains, but melts soon. Rainfall on Gila 6 inches, in foot-hills 28 inches. Heaviest in July and August.

CHIEF CITIES.—Tucson, pop. 7,007. Prescott, the capital, pop. 3,000.

LEADING INDUSTRIES.—Mining, grazing, agriculture, lumbering, smelting, etc.

[Salaries of State Officers page 439.]

CALIFORNIA.

"Golden State." First settled at San Diego, 1768. Gold discovered 1848. Rush of immigration set in 1849. State constitution, without the preliminary of a territorial organization, framed Sept. 1849. Admitted as a state Sept. 9, 1850. Number counties 52. Miles railroad 2,911. Governor and state officers elected quadrennially, and legislature every two years, number senators 40, representatives 80, sessions of legislature biennial, in odd-numbered years, meeting first Monday after Jan. 1, holds 60 days, term of senators 4 years, of representatives 2 years. Number electoral votes 8, congressmen 6, white voters 262,583. Idiots, Indians, convicts and Chinese excluded from voting. School system very fair, school age 5-17. Legal interest 7 per cent., by contract any rate.

Population 1880 864,694, male 518,176, female 346,518, native 571,820, foreign 292,874, white 767,181, colored 6,018, Chinese 75,132, Indians 16,277. Estimated increase 18 per cent.

Extreme length N. and S., 725 miles, width 330 miles, area 155,980 sq. miles, 99,827,200 acres. Coast line over 800 miles. San Francisco Bay (40 miles long, 9 wide) magnificent harbor. Yosemite in the Sierras, one of the greatest natural wonders of the world and the greatest marvel of the state, where scenery is always grand. Mt. Whitney 15,000, highest peak. Very rich agriculturally and in minerals. Soil warm, genial and rich. Two crops may be raised in season. Irrigation necessary in parts and almost always desirable. Wheat most valuable crop, all cereals, root crops and grasses do well, corn, barley, grapes, fruit, nuts, silk, hops and oats staples. Mineral deposits include gold, silver, iron, copper, mercury, coal, stones, salt, soda, etc. Ranks high as a fruit-growing state, fruits of temperate climates, sub-tropical fruits and nuts, grapes, north to 41 deg., olives, etc., grow to great perfection. Fine sheep-raising country. Ranks first in barley, grape culture, sheep, gold and quicksilver, third in hops, fifth in wheat and salt. Noble forests of redwood and other valuable growths. Land runs from $1.25 to several hundred dollars per acre. Improved land averages $30, unimproved $7.50 per acre. It is the paradise of the small farmer. Plenty of room for men with a little something to begin on.

Climate varies with elevation and latitude. Mild and pleasant on coast. Average temperature at San Francisco in summer 62 deg., winter 50 deg. Warmer in interior, reaching at times 100 deg. Rainfall variable, from 7 to 50 inches at San Francisco. Average at S. 10 inches. Melting snow from mountains replaces rainfall. Frosts rare.

CHIEF CITIES.—San Francisco port of entry, regular line of steamers to Australia, Panama, Mexico, China and Japan, pop. 233,959, Sacramento (capital) pop. 21,420, pop. Oakland 34,555, San Jose 12,567, Stockton 10,282, Los Angeles 11,183, U. S. navy yard at San Pablo Bay.

LEADING INDUSTRIES.—Agriculture, stock raising, fruit culture, mining, lumbering, etc. [Salaries of State Officers page 439.]

CONNECTICUT.

"Wooden Nutmeg State." One of the original 13 states explored by the Dutch settlers of Manhattan Island, 1615, by whom settlement was made, 1633, at Hartford. The state furnished a very large quota of men to the Revolutionary armies. Yale College founded 1701. Union soldiers furnished, 55,864. Number counties, 8. Miles railroad 994. State elections yearly on same date as presidential election. Elects 24 senators, 249 representatives, 4 congressmen and 6 presidential electors. State senators hold 2 and representatives 1 year. Legislature meets yearly on Wednesday after first Monday in January. Convicts and persons unable to read not permitted to vote. School system superior, includes 3 colleges with 160,000 books in libraries. School age 4 to 16 years. Legal interest 6 per cent. No penalty for usury. Population, 1880, 622,700, male 305,782, female 316,918, native 492,708, colored 11,547, Chinese 123, Indians 255. Area, 4,845 sq. miles, average length 86 miles, average breadth 55 miles; seacoast 110 miles. Surface less rugged than the other New England states. Mountain range terminates in this state in a series of hills. The coast is indented by numerous bays and harbors. Soil, except in valley, light and stony. Corn, oats, hay, wheat, tobacco and vegetables are the staple crops. Cleared land averages $40 and woodland $30 per acre. No valuable timber remains. Stone extensively quarried. Valuable iron mines exist. Climate moderate and healthy, average temperature, summer 72 deg. and winter 28 deg. Occasionally the thermometer sinks below zero, considerable snow falls, summers warm. Rain fall, including snow, about 47 inches. CHIEF INDUSTRIES.—Manufacture of hardware, clocks, silks, cotton, rubber, carpets, woolens, arms, sewing machines and attachments, dairying, quarrying, agriculture, etc. Total number of different industries, 4,488. PRINCIPAL CITIES.—Hartford, capital and noted for banking and insurance business, pop., 1880, 42,015. New Haven, "City of Elms," seat of Yale College, pop. 62,882. Bridgeport, noted for manufacture of fire-arms and sewing machines, pop. 27,643. Waterbury, important manufacturing city, pop. 17,806. Fairfield, Middletown, New Haven, New London and Stonington are ports of entry.

Salaries of State Officers.

Governor	$2,000
Lieutenant Governor	500
Secretary of State	1,500
Treasurer	1,500
Comptroller	1,500
Secretary State Board of Education	3,000
Adjutant General	1,200
Insurance Commissioner	3,500
Three Railroad Commissioners	3,000
Chief Justice	4,500
Four Associate Justices	4,0

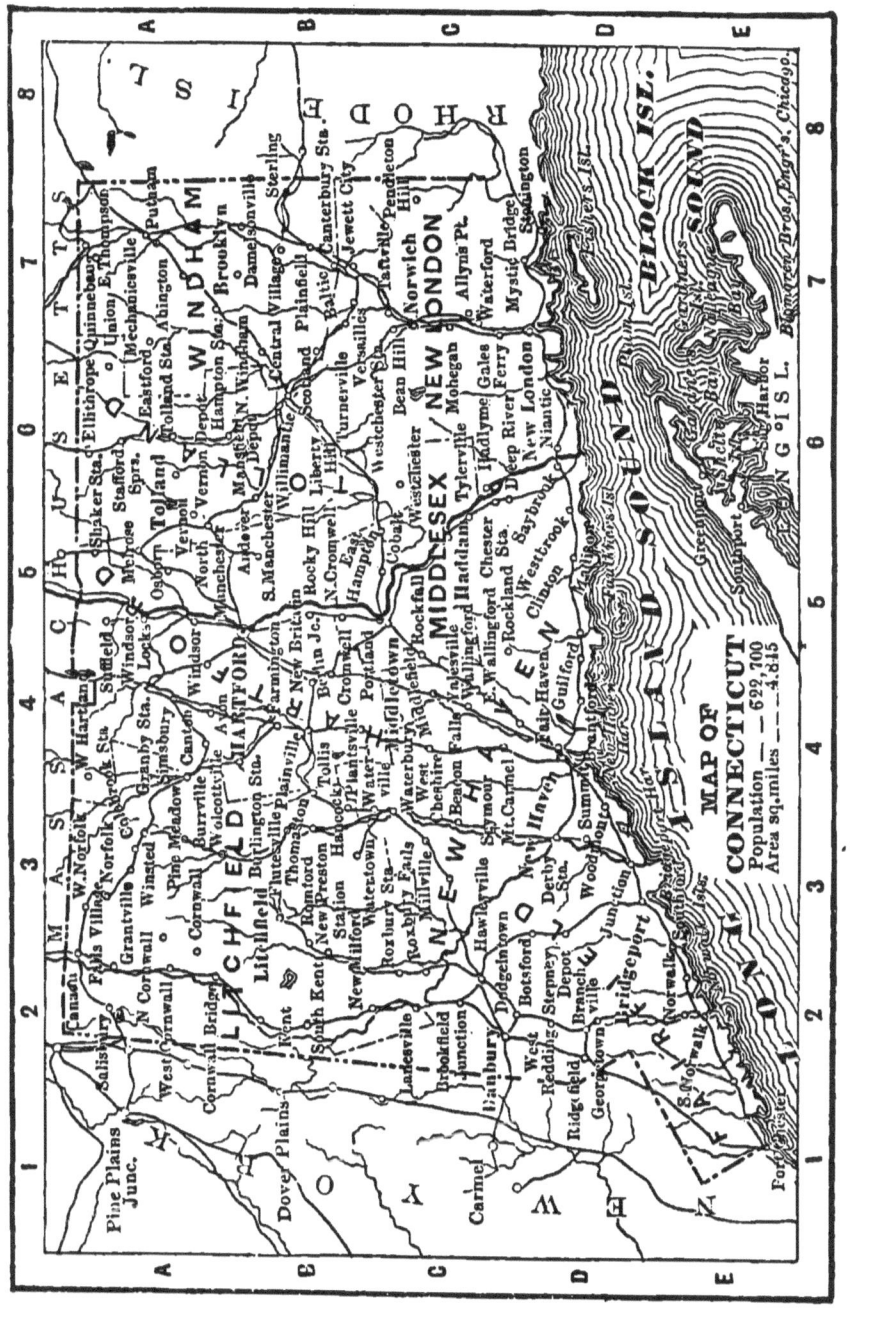

COLORADO.

"Centennial State." John C. Fremont, "The Pathfinder," crossed Rockies 1842-44. First American settlement near Denver, 1859. Mining begun. Organized as territory Feb. 1861. Indian troubles 1863-4. Union soldiers furnished 4,903. Admitted as a state Aug. 1, 1876. Number counties 39. No railroad in 1870. Mileage, 1885, 2,842. All elections Tuesday after first Monday in Nov., number senators 26, representatives 49, sessions biennial in odd-numbered years, meeting first Monday in Jan., limit of session 40 days, term of senators 4 years, of representatives 2 years. Number electoral votes 3, congressmen 1, voters 93,608, native white 65,215, foreign white 26,873, colored 1,520. Convicts excluded from voting. Number colleges 3, school system fair endowment, school age 6-21 years. Legal interest 10 per cent., by contract any rate.

POPULATION, 1880, 194,327; male 129,131, female 65,196, native 154,537, foreign 39,790, white 191,126, colored 2,435, Chinese 612, Indians 154. Estimated increase 12 per cent.

Length E. and W. 380 miles, width 280 miles, area 103,845 sq. miles, 66,460,800 acres, three-fifths unsurveyed. Rocky mountains traverse state N. and S. with 3 ranges having many peaks more than 13,000 feet high. Fine grazing grounds. Scenery grand beyond words. Much rich soil along streams and wherever irrigation is possible. Cereals do very well. Corn, wheat, oats, hay staple crops. Cattle, sheep and hog raising safe and profitable. Dairying pays, as does gardening. Timber resources moderate. Mountains fairly clothed with pine and other trees. Mineral wealth inexhaustible. State ranks first in silver, fourth in gold. Iron, soda, coal, copper, lead, stone, mica, etc., exist in large deposits.

CLIMATE.—Dry and range of temperature comparatively small. Winters mild, summers cool. Average temperature winter 31 deg., summer 73 deg. Rainfall, mainly in May, June and July, averages 18 inches. On mountains winters severe, accompanied by heavy snowfall; violent winds common; fogs unknown. Health unsurpassed.

CHIEF CITIES.—Denver, capital and metropolis, and contains assay office; pop. 35,650; Leadville, 14,820; Silver Cliffs, 5,040; Colorado Springs, 4,226. State University at Boulder; Agricultural College at Fort Collins; School of Mines at Golden City.

LEADING INDUSTRIES.—Mining, smelting ores, agriculture, grazing, e*-

Salaries of State Officers.

Governor	$5,000
Lieutenant Governor	1,000
Secretary of State	3,000
Treasurer	3,000
Auditor	2,500
Attorney General	2,000
Chief Justice	5,000

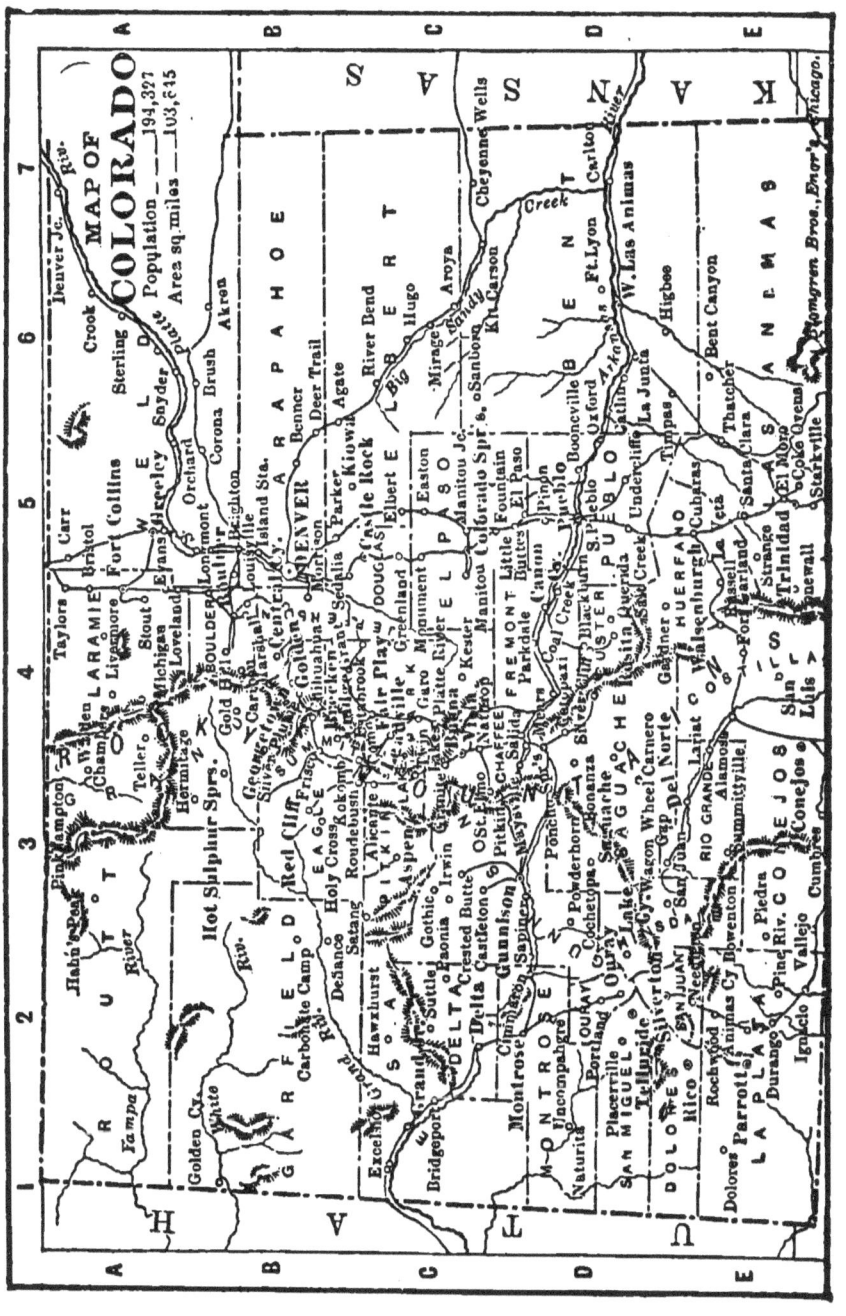

DAKOTA.

Named for Dakota Indians. First settled at Pembina 1812. Organized as territory March, 1861. First legislature met, 1862, at Yankton. Immigration became active 1866. Railroad building active and systems mammoth in their scale. Application for admission made. Number counties 129. All elections Tuesday after first Monday in Nov. Number senators 12, representatives 24, sessions biennial, in odd-numbered years, meeting second Tuesday in Jan. and holding 60 days. Terms of senators and representatives 2 years each. Legal interest rate 7%, by contract 12%, usury forfeits excess. School endowments, when the territory shall become a state, magnificent. Miles railroad 2,759.

Population, 1880, 135,177, male 82,296, native 83,382, white 133,147, Indians 27,550 (2,300 Sioux). Population, 1885, 413,759. Average length N. and S. 451 miles, width 348 miles, area 149,112 sq. miles, 95,431,680 acres. Indian reservations principally west of Missouri river, 42,000,000 acres, one-seventh good farming land. Surface high, level plain, 950 to 2,600 feet above the sea, traversed by ranges of lofty hills, which at the S. W. reach an elevation of 7,000 feet in the Black Hills. The Missouri river traverses the territory diagonally from N. W. to S. E., and is navigable. Lakes are numerous, especially in the north and east. Devil's Lake is semi-salt. Other large lakes. Soil is very rich and peculiarly suited to wheat, which is the staple crop. Corn, oats, grasses and potatoes do well. Fruit not a good crop. Cattle, and especially sheep-raising, favored and growing industries. Timber scarce, except along the streams and in some of the hills. Gold and silver extensively mined. Black Hills very rich in precious minerals. Ranks fourth in gold output. Good coal west of the Missouri. Not much developed as yet. Deposits of tin said to be of great value exist. Price of land $1.25 to $20 per acre (latter improved).

CLIMATE.—Temperature ranges from 32 deg. below zero to 100 deg. above. Averages, winter 4 to 20 deg., summer 65 to 75 deg. Winters at north severe, with heavy snow. Moderate at the south. Air clear, dry and free from malaria. Cold not so penetrating as in moister climates. Springs late and summers of medium length. Rainfall 19 in., chiefly in spring and summer.

CHIEF CITIES.—Fargo, northern metropolis; Bismarck (capital), Yankton and Sioux Falls important centers.

INDUSTRIES.—Almost entire laboring population engaged in agriculture and mining.

Salaries of State Officers.

Governor $2,600, Secretary of Territory $1,800, Treasurer $2,000, Auditor $1,000, Superintendent of Public Inst. $1,500, Chief Justice $3,000, five Associate Justices $3,000, Senators and Representatives $4 a day, mileage 20 cents; ten Indian Agents $1,000 to $2,200, Surveyor General $2,500, Chief Clerk $1,800, Chief Draftsman $1,500, Assistant $1,200, Collector of Internal Revenue $2,750, four Deputy Collectors $1,600.

MAP OF DAKOTA

Population — 1,591,750
Area sq. miles — 262,290

DELAWARE.

One of the thirteen original states. "The Diamond State." Settled by Swedes 1658, who bought from Indians. Took vigorous part in the revolution. Was a slave state. Slaves 1860, 2,000. Union soldiers furnished 12,284, the biggest percentage of any state. Contains three counties. Miles of railroad, 306. All elections Tuesday after first Monday in November, number senators 9, representatives 21, legislature meets in odd-numbered years first Tuesday in January, holds 21 days, term of senators 4 years, of representatives 2 years, number electoral votes 3, number congressmen 1, idiots, insane, paupers and criminals excluded from voting. Colleges at Newark and Wilmington, school age 6-21, schools fair, legal interest rate 6, usury forfeits the principal. Population 1880 146,608, male 74,108, female 72,500, native 137,140, white 120,160, colored 26,442. Length north and south nearly 100 miles, width 10 miles at north, 36 at south. Area 1,950 square miles, or 1,248,000 acres. Available area large. Northern portion rolling, but free from large hills. Scenery beautiful. Southern portion level and sandy, with frequent cypress marshes. Coast low and swampy with lagoons separated from sea by sand-beaches. Streams flow into Chesapeake and Delaware bays and are small. Tide reaches to Wilmington. The soil is good and the state of cultivation superior. Cleared land averages $45 per acre, and wood-land $40. Staple crops, corn, wheat, peaches, berries, garden vegetables, sweet potatoes. Iron is found, but is no longer worked. Climate mild. Tempered by sea breezes. Average temperature, winter, 32 deg. to 38 deg.; summer, 72 deg. to 78 deg. Rainfall 48 to 50 inches. At north health excellent. Some malaria on the low lands bordering the swamps at the south. CHIEF CITIES.—Wilmington, pop. 42,478. Dover, capital. Newcastle, 6,000. Breakwater protecting Delaware Bay at Cape Henlopen, greatest work of its kind in America, cost the United States $2,127,400, and was over 40 years in course of construction. INDUSTRIES.—Agriculture and kindred pursuits, manufacture of flour, lumber, cotton, iron, steel, leather, etc., shipbuilding, fishing, canning and preserving. Total number different industries, 750.

Salaries of State Officers.

Governor	$2,000
Secretary of State	1,000
Treasurer	1,450
Auditor	700
Adjutant General	200
Attorney General	2,000
Superintendent of Public Instruction	1,500
State Librarian	450
Chief Justice	2,500
Chancellor	2,500
Three Associate Justices	2,200
Senators and Representatives	$3 per day and mileage

FLORIDA.

Named for its flowers, "Peninsula State." Pensacola taken from England by Gen. Jackson during war of 1812. Entire province ceded to United States 1819. Organized as a territory 1822. Admitted as a state March 3, 1845. State seceded Jan. 10, 1861, re-entered Union July 4, 1868. Number counties 39, miles of railroad 1,324. All elections Tuesday after first Monday in November. Number senators 32, representatives 76. Sessions of legislature biennial, in odd-numbered years, meeting Tuesday after first Monday in January, holds 60 days. Term of senators 4, of representatives 2 years. Number electoral votes 4, congressmen 2. Idiots, insane, criminals, betters on elections and duelists excluded from voting. Schools fair, school age 4-21. Legal interest 8%, by contract any rate. Population, 1880, 269,493; male 136,444, female 133,039, native 259,584, white 142,005, Indians 180, slaves, 1860, 61,745. Estimated increase, 1885, 50%. Four-fifths of Florida is in the peninsula, which is about 350 miles N. and S. and 105 miles E. and W. Remainder is the narrow strip along the Gulf, 342 miles E. and W. and 10 to 50 miles N. and S. Area 59,268 sq. miles, 37,931,520 acres. 21st state in size. State surrounded by sea except on north. Coast line over 1,200 miles. Good harbors rare, mostly on Gulf. The northern section is a limestone formation, affording a fair soil. In the middle section are found tracts of great richness. At the south the soil, when dry or reclaimed, is inexhaustible. Shores very low, frequently not two feet above tide water. Coral growth at south continues. Surface dotted with lakes. The staple products are corn (most valuable crop), sugar, molasses, rice, cotton, oats, tobacco, vegetables of all kinds, peaches, oranges, and all tropical and semi-tropical fruits, cocoanuts, lumber, fish, oysters, etc. Poultry and stock raising are successful. Cleared land averages $12, woodland $3, swamp $1, and school land $1.25 per acre. Much forest remains. Timber chiefly pine, of moderate size, free from undergrowth. Game abounds. Climate superb. No snow. Frosts rare at north, unknown at south. Temperature ranges 30 deg. to 100 deg., rarely above 90. Winter averages 59 deg., summer 81 deg. Breezes blow across from gulf to Atlantic and vice versa, temper the heat and keep air dry and clear. Average rainfall 55 inches, chiefly in summer. CHIEF CITIES.—Key West, good harbor and naval station, pop. 9,890. Jacksonville, pop. 7,650. St. Augustine, oldest town in United States. Tallahassee, pop. 3,000, capital. Pensacola, pop. 6,845. PRINCIPAL INDUSTRIES.—Almost the entire laboring population is engaged in agriculture and fruit growing. Fishing for fish and oysters and lumbering largely followed.

Salaries of State Officers.

Governor $3,500, Lieutenant Governor $500, Secretary of State $2,000, Treasurer $2,000, Comptroller $2,000, Attorney General $2,000, Superintendent of Public Instruction $2,000, Adjutant General $2,000, Land Commissioner $1,200, Chief Justice $3,500.

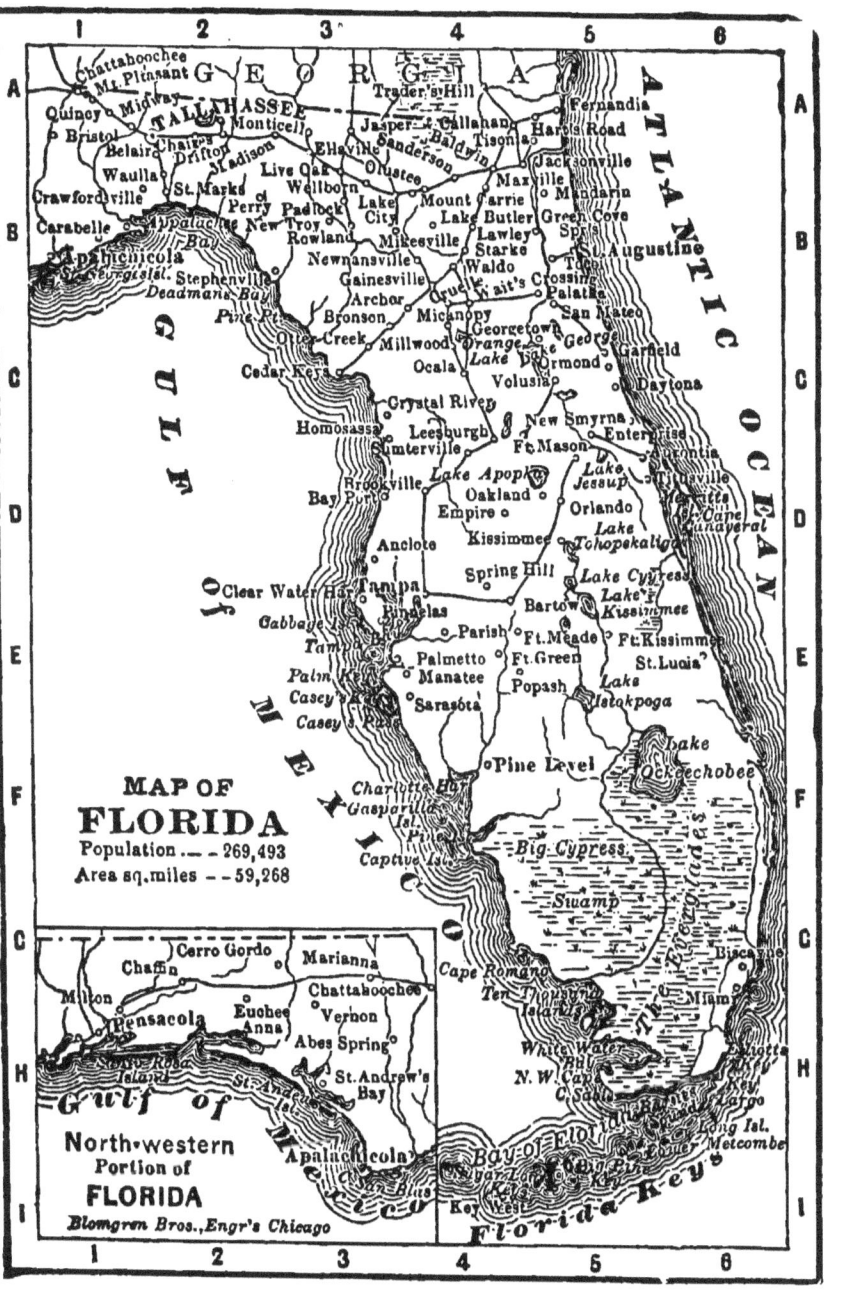

GEORGIA.

One of the thirteen original states, named for King George II. of England, called the "Empire State of the South." Originally a part of South Carolina and claimed by Spain. Active in the Revolution, suffering badly from devastation by English. Severe wars with Creeks and Cherokees settled by treaties 1790 and 1791. State seceded January 19, 1861. Many hard fought battles during civil war, including Atlanta, etc. Re-entered Union 1870. Number counties 137, miles of railroad 2,687, state elections first Wednesday in October, number senators 44, representatives 175, sessions biennial in even-numbered years, meeting first Wednesday in November, hold forty days. Terms of senators and representatives two years each. Number electoral votes 12, number congressmen 10. Idiots, insane, criminals and non-taxpayers excluded from voting. Number colleges 7, State University at Athens organized 1801, public schools excellent, school age 6-18. No state license law governing commercial travelers, but Atlanta, Athens, Augusta and Savannah exact a tax. Legal interest 7%, by contract 8%, usury forfeits excess of interest. Population, 1880, 1,542,180, male 762,981, female 779,199, native 1,531,616, white 816,906, Indians 124. Greatest length N. and S. 321 miles, greatest width 255 miles, area 58,980 square miles or 37,747,200 acres, exclusive of water area. Surface diversified. At the north are the Blue Ridge, Etowah and other mountains. In the southeast is the Okefinokee swamp, 150 miles in circumference. Coast irregular and indented, shore line about 500 miles, three sea-ports. Mountain streams are rapid with picturesque cataracts and immense basins. The chief falls are the Tallulah, in Habersham county, Toccoa, in the Tugalo, 180 feet high, Towaliga, in Monroe county, and the Amicolah, which descend 400 feet in a quarter mile. Corn, wheat, oats, cotton, rice, sweet potatoes, tobacco, sugar and melons, chief agricultural staples. Fruit, both temperate and semi-tropical, thrives. Stock flourishes. Wool-growing important. Gold is extensively mined. Coal, iron, marble exist. Cleared land averages $8 and woodland $5.50 per acre. One-fourth area heavily timbered with yellow pine of great value for lumber, turpentine, etc. CLIMATE.—At the north mild and extremely healthy, hot in the lowlands. Range of temperature 30 deg. to 105 deg. Average, winter 49 deg., summer 82 deg. Rainfall averages 55 inches. CHIEF CITIES.—Savannah, pop. 21,890, Brunswick, pop. 2,900, and St. Mary's, pop. 600, ports of entry. Columbus contains the largest cotton mill in the South, pop. 20,123. Atlanta, capital, pop. 37,409. PRINCIPAL INDUSTRIES.—Three-fourths population engaged in agriculture. Remainder in various pursuits. Manufacturing important. Raw materials becoming more abundant and cheap.

[Salaries State Officers, page 439.]

IDAHO.

Gold discovered, 1880, in Oro Fino creek. Organized as territory March, 1863. Number counties, 14. All elections, Tuesday after first Monday in Nov., number senators, 12, representatives, 24, sessions of legislature biennial, in even-numbered years, meeting second Monday in Dec., holds 60 days, terms of senators and representatives, 2 years each. Voters, 14,795, native white, 7,332, foreign white, 4,338, colored, 3,126. School age, 5-21 years. Legal interest rate 10 per cent., by contract, 18 per cent; usury forfeits three times excess of interest; miles railroad, 811.

Population, 1880, 32,610. Males, 21,818, females, 10,792, natives, 22,636, foreign, 9,974, white, 29,013, Indians, 165. Estimated increase, 16 per cent.

TOPOGRAPHY, AREA, SOIL, PRODUCTS, ETC —Length, 140 to 490 miles, width 45 to 286 miles. Area, 84,290 sq. miles, 53,944,600 acres. Surface table land and mountains. About one-twelfth is arable and one-tenth more grazing land. One-third barren, but may be reclaimed by irrigation. Many lakes are found, as well as numerous water powers. Forests estimated at 9,000,000 acres. The soil, where water can be had, is fertile. Wheat, oats, rye, barley, potatoes and hay are good crops, and dairying and stock-raising profitable. Gold is found in quartz veins in Idaho, Boise and Alturas counties, silver in Owyhee county. Some of the mines very rich. Wood river district on southern slope of Salmon River mountains, at headwaters of Wood or Malad river, gives promise of valuable mining operations, chiefly placers. Coal in vicinity of Boise City. Territory ranks sixth in gold and silver.

Climate severe, with heavy snows in mountains, on plains less severe, but cold and bracing. In the valleys it is milder, with moderate snowfall. Summers cool and pleasant. Temperature averages 20 deg. in winter, 70 deg. in summer. Rainfall small in the Rocky and Bitter Root mountains, and very light at the N. and W.

CHIEF CITES.—Boise City (capital), Florence, Silver City.

LEADING INDUSTRIES.—Mining, grazing, agriculture, smelting and lumbering.

Salaries of Territorial Officers.

Governor	$2,600
Secretary	1,800
Treasurer	1,000
Auditor	1,800
Librarian	250
Chief Justice	3,000
Two Associate Justices	3,000
Senators and Representatives	$4 a day and 20 cents mileage
Two District Attorneys	$250 and fees
Collector of Internal Revenue	2,250
Three Deputy Collectors	$1,400 to 1,600
Assayer	2,000

ILLINOIS.

Name derived from Illini tribe of Indians, meaning Superior Men. Called "Prairie State" and "Sucker State." Fort Dearborn (Chicago) massacre, 1812, by Pottawatomies. Admitted as State, 1818. Capital moved to Springfield, 1836. Soldiers in Mexican war, 5,000. Union soldiers, 259,092. Number counties, 102. All elections, Tuesday after first Monday in Nov.; number senators, 51; representatives, 153; sessions biennial, in odd-numbered years, meeting first Monday in Jan., term of senators, 4 years; representatives, 2 years. Number electoral votes, 22; congressmen, 20; number voters, 796,847; convicts excluded from voting. School system excellent; number colleges, 28; school age, 6-21. Legal interest, 6%; by contract, 8%; usury forfeits entire interest. Miles of railroad, 8,909. Population, 1880, 3,077,-871; male, 1,586,523; female, 1,491,348; native, 2,494,295; foreign, 583,576; white, 3,031,151; colored, 46,368; Indians, 140. Estimated increase 9%. Extreme length N. and S., 386 miles; extreme width, 218 miles. Average elevation, 482 feet; elevation at Cairo, 340 feet; highest point, 1,140 feet in northwest portion. Area, 56,000 sq. miles, 35,840,000 acres; miles of navigable waterways, 4,100. Frontage on Lake Michigan 110 miles. Among first agricultural states of Union. Staple crops, corn, wheat, oats, rye, barley, broomcorn, vegetables, hay, potatoes, etc. Fruits and grapes do well at south. Yield of all crops cultivated, large. Coal area, two-thirds state. First coal mined in America at Ottawa; quality moderately fair. Considerable forest of hardwoods at south on hills and in bottoms. Superior quality limestone on Fox and Desplaines rivers; lead, most important mineral; Galena in center of richest diggings in N. W. Rich salt wells in Saline and Gallatin counties, 75 gallons brine making 50 lbs. salt. State ranks first in corn, wheat, oats, meat packing, lumber traffic, malt and distilled liquors and miles railway; second in rye, coal, agricultural implements, soap and hogs; fourth in hay, potatoes, iron and steel, mules, milch cows and other cattle. Cleared land averages $28, and woodland or raw prairie, $18 per acre. Climate healthful as a rule; subject to sudden and violent changes at north. Temperature ranges from 30 deg. below zero to 101 deg. above. Average temperature at Springfield, 30 deg. winter; 78 deg. summer. At Chicago, 25 deg. winter; 72 deg. summer. At Cairo, 38 deg. winter; 80 deg. summer. Frost comes last of September. Vegetation begins in April. Rainfall 37 inches. CHIEF CITIES.—Chicago, pop. 503,185. Peoria, pop. 29,259. Quincy, pop. 27,268. Springfield (capital), pop. 19,743. INDUSTRIES.—Agriculture, mining, stock-raising, and manufacturing of all kinds.

Salaries of State Officers.

Governor $6,000, Secretary of State $3,500, Treasurer $3,500, Auditor $3,500, Attorney General $3,500, Chief Justice $5,000, Senators and Representatives $5 per day, mileage 10 cents and $50.

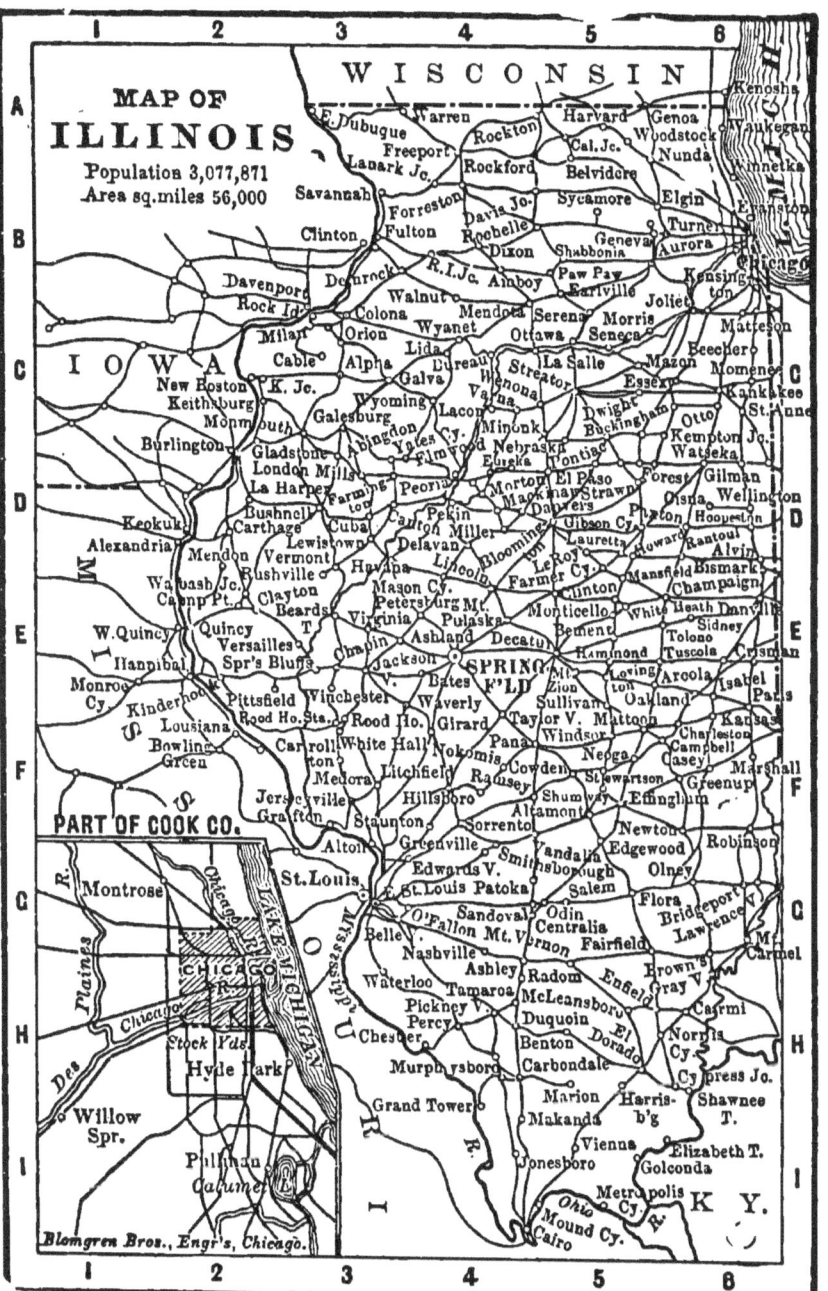

INDIANA.

"Hoosier State." Settled at Fort St. Vincents, now Vincennes, in 1702, by French-Canadian voyagers. Admitted as a state Dec. 11, 1816. Sixth state admitted. Soldiers furnished in Mexican war 5,000. Union soldiers 196,363. Number counties, 92. All elections Tuesday after first Monday in November; number senators, 50; representatives, 100; sessions of legislature biennial, in odd-numbered years, meet Thursday after first Monday, holds 60 days; term of senators 4 years, of representatives, 2 years; number electoral votes, 15; number congressman, 13; number voters 498,437. Fraudulent voters and bribers excluded from voting. Number colleges 15, State University at Bloomington; medical school at Indianapolis, university at Notre Dame, flourishing common-school system: school age, 6-21. Legal interest rate, 6 per cent, by contract 8 per cent, usury forfeits excess of interest. Miles of railroad, 5,534. POPULATION—1880, 1,978,301; male 1,978,301, female 967,940, native 1,834,123, foreign 144,178, white 1,938,798, colored 39,228, Chinese 29, Indians 246., Estimated increase 8 per cent. Extreme length N. and S. 275 miles, width averages 150 miles, area 35,910 sq. miles, 22,982,400 acres. Surface sometimes hilly. No mountains. Hills 200 to 400 feet above the surrounding country. Frontage on Lake Michigan 43 miles. River bottoms wide and unsurpassed in fertility, highlands when level, rich, black or sandy soil. All crops and fruits of the temperate zone do well both in yield and quality. State highly favored for agriculture and manufacturing. Ranks second in wheat, fourth in corn, hogs and agricultural implements, fifth in coal. Cattle, hogs, sheep, horses, etc., are most successfully raised. Corn, wheat, oats, staple crops. Timber still abundant at south, but in scattered tracts. Coal fields in southwestern portion of state over 7,000 sq. miles, on much of which are 3 workable veins. Kinds of coal, block, cannel and ordinary bituminous, cokes well, superior for gas. Building stones varied and of unsurpassed quality, including the famous Bedford stone. Supply unlimited. Land is cheap, cleared averaging $18, and woodland $14 per acre. In rich section to southwest cleared land $15, woodland $10 to $12. Chances for making homes, comfort and advantages considered, not excelled elsewhere. Iron ore is found.

CLIMATE changeable in winter, but seldom severe; winds from north and west; summers moderately long, and sometimes hot; temperature averages, winter, 34 deg., summer 78 deg. Trees blossom in March. Rainfall 40 inches. Health excellent. Malaria rapidly disappearing from bottoms before proper drainage. CHIEF CITIES.—Indianapolis (capital), contains deaf and dumb, blind and insane asylums, pop. 75,056, Terre Haute 26,042, Evansville 29,280, Fort Wayne 26,880. Michigan City lake port. INDUSTRIES.—Agriculture, mining and manufacturing.

[Salaries of State Officers, page 420.]

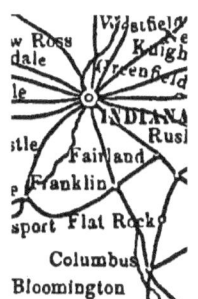

INDIAN TERRITOR..

Set apart for peaceful tribes. Organized 1834, no territorial government. Government in hands of tribes. Also contains Oklahoma and public land strip. Each tribe elects officers, legislatures and courts, and criminals are punished as in the states. No laws for collections of debt. All land held in common, and any Indian may cultivate as much as he wants, but one-quarter mile must intervene between farms. Whites can hold land only by marrying an Indian. Miles of railroad, 353. School system excellent, pupils educated and supported by the tribes, half entire revenue being set aside for the purpose. Three colleges, 200 schools.

Population, 80,000. Cherokees, 20,000, Choctaws, 16,500, Creeks, 14,500, Chickasaws, 7,000, Seminoles, 2,500, Osages, 2,400, Cheyennes, 3,298, Arapahoes, 2,676, Kiowas, 1,120, Pawnees, 1,438, Comanches, 1,475. Two-fifths of entire population can read. Extreme length east and west, 470 miles, average length, 320 miles, width, 210 miles, area, 69,991 miles, 44,154,240 acres. Surface vast rolling plain sloping eastward. Valleys timbered heavily w.th hard woods. South of Canadian river prairies very fertile, valleys rich and productive throughout territory, grass rich and heavy almost everywhere. Corn, cotton, rice, wheat, rye, potatoes are staples. Grazing interests large. Coal is found, but extent unknown. Fur-bearing animals numerous.

CLIMATE.—Mild in winter, warm in summer. Temperature averages 41 deg. winter, 80 deg. summer. Rainfall, at east, 50 inches, center, 36, far west, 22. Health as good as anywhere in Union.

CHIEF CITIES.—Tahlequah, capital of Cherokees, Tishomingo, capital of Chickasaws, Tushkahoma, of Choctaws, Muscogee, of Creeks, Pawhuska, of Osages, Seminole Agency, of Seminoles, Pawnee Agency, of Pawnees, Kiowa and Comanche Agency, of Kiowas and Comanches.

LEADING INDUSTRIES.—Agriculture and grazing.

INDIAN AGENCIES.

ARAPAHOE.		OSAGE.	
Agent	$ 900	Agent	$1,600
		Physician	1,200
CHEYENNE.		OTOE.	
Agent	2,200	Agent	1,500
Physician	1,200	Physician	1,000
KAW.		PAWNEE.	
Superintendent	1,600	Clerk	1,200
Physician	1,200	Physician	1,000
KIOWA AND COMANCHE.		PONCA.	
Agent	1,000	Superintendent	1,200
Physician	1,000	Clerk	720
OAKLAND.		QUAPAW.		SAC AND FOX.	
Supt	$1,000	Agent	$1,500	Agent	$1,200
3 Teachers	600	Physician	1,200	2 Physicians	1,000

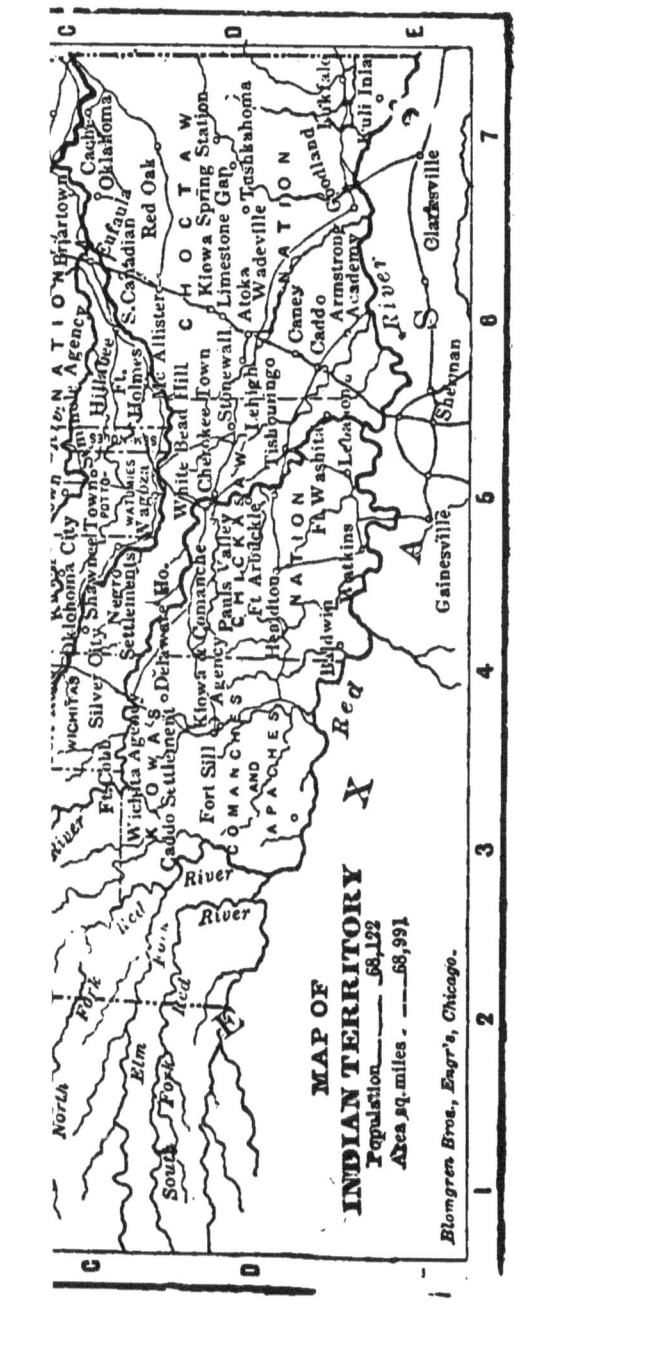

IOWA.

"Hawkeye State." Settled first by Dubuque, 1788, a French Canadian, for whom that city is named. First settlers miners of lead. Active immigration began 1833. Iowa territory organized July 4, 1838. Admitted as state 1846. Union soldiers furnished 76,242. Number counties 99, miles of railroad 7,510. State elections annual, Tuesday after second Monday in October, excepting years of presidential elections, when all elections occur together. Number senators 50, representatives 100, sessions of legislature biennial, in even-numbered years, meeting second Monday in January. Term of senators 4 years, of representatives 2 years. Number electoral votes 13, congressmen 11, number voters 416,658. Idiots, insane and criminals excluded from voting. Number colleges 19, school age 5-21. School system admirable, endowment liberal. Legal interest rate 6 per cent., by contract 10 per cent., usury forfeits 10 per cent. per year on amount. State has adopted prohibition.

Population, 1880, 1,624,615, male 848,136, female 776,479, native 1,362,965, foreign 261,650, white 1,614,600, colored 9,516, Chinese 33, Indians 466. Estimated increase, 15 per cent.

Extreme length E. and W. 208 miles, width 208 miles, area 55,470 sq. miles, 35,500,800 acres. Surface almost an unbroken prairie, without mountains and with very few low hills. Natural meadows everywhere and water abundant. Many small lakes at north. Highest point, Spirit Lake, 1,600 feet above the sea. Soil superior. Corn, wheat, oats, potatoes, hay, barley, sorghum, rye, staples. Apples unsurpassed in United States: pears, plums, cherries, grapes and berries are excellent crops. Cattle and other stock interests large and thrifty. Dairying attractive. Forest area small—scarcely equal to home requirements. Coal area fair. Other minerals unimportant. Manufacturing active. Improved land averages $20; unimproved, including railroad and government domains, $12.50. State ranks first in hogs, second in milch cows, oxen and other cattle, corn, hay and oats; third in horses: fifth in barley and miles of railway.

Climate subject to extremes. Winter severe, with sharp north and west winds; summers pleasant. Temperature averages, summer 72 deg., winter 23 deg.; ranges from 10 deg. below to 99 deg. above zero. Rainfall 42 inches. Wheat harvest in August.

CHIEF CITIES.—DesMoines, metropolis and capital, pop. 22,408. Pop. of Dubuque 22,254; of Davenport 21,831; of Burlington 19,450; of Council Bluffs 18,063. Keokuk, Burlington and Dubuque are United States ports of delivery.

LEADING INDUSTRIES.—Agriculture, stock-raising and manufacturing.

[Salaries of State Officers, page 439.]

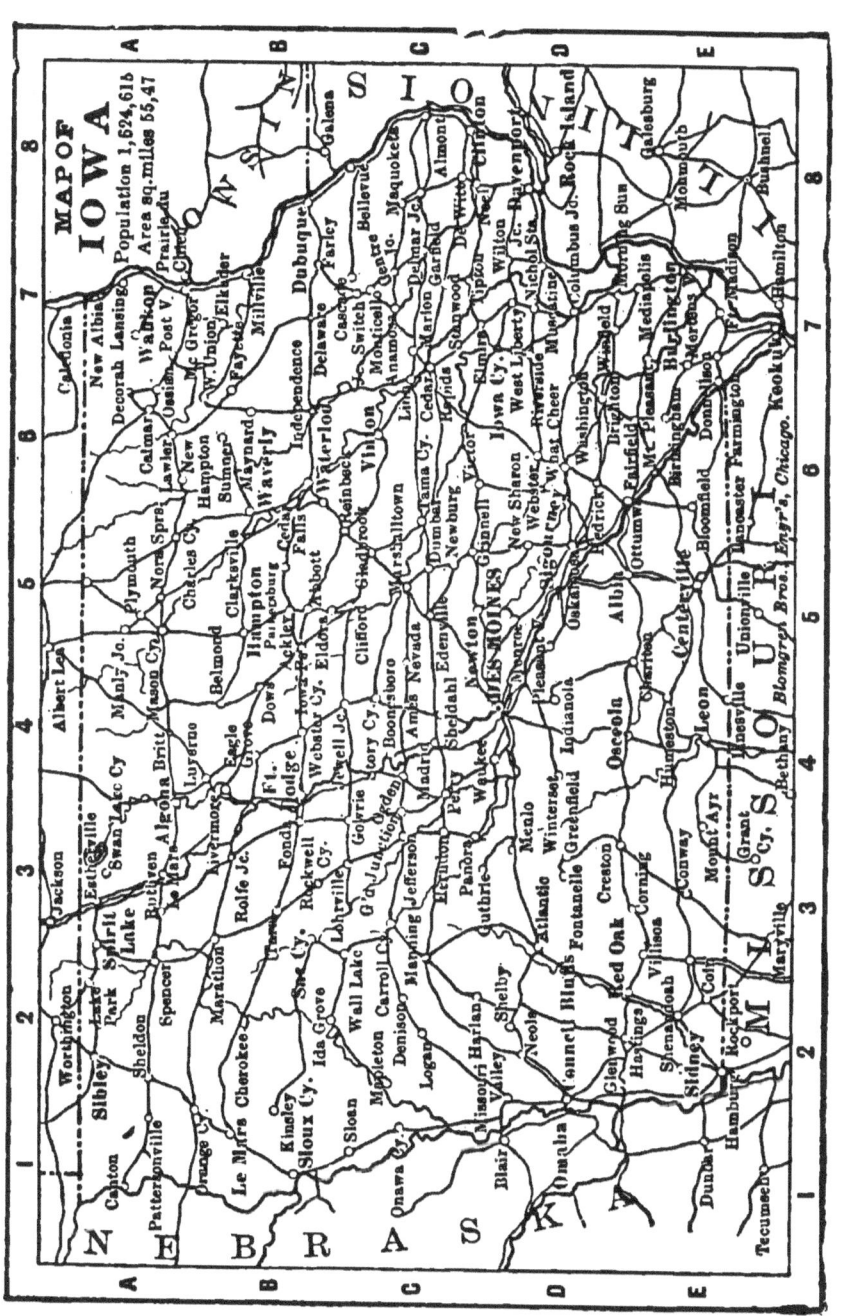

KANSAS.

Name Indian, means "Smoky water." Called the "Garden State." Kansas Territory organized May, 1854. Law known as "Missouri Compromise," forbidding slavery in states formed out of Louisiana purchase north of latitude 36 deg. 30 min. repealed, and question of slavery left to the territory. At first it was decided for slavery. Constitution prohibiting slavery adopted July, 1859. Admitted as a state, 1861. Union soldiers furnished, 20,149, number counties 95, miles railroad 4,205, first railroad built 1864 40 miles long. All elections Tuesday after first Monday in Nov.; senators 40, representatives 125, sessions biennial, meeting second Tuesday in Jan. in odd-numbered years, limit of session 50 days; term of senators 4 years, of representatives, 2 years. Number electoral votes 9, congressmen 7, voters 295,714. Idiots, insane, convicts and rebels excluded from voting. Number colleges, 8, number schoolhouses over 8,000, school age 5-21 years; school system magnificent. Endowment immense. Legal interest 7 per cent, by contract 12 per cent, usury forfeits excess of interest.

POPULATION.—1880, 996,096, male 536,667, female 459,429, native 886,010, foreign 110,086, white 952,155, colored 43,107, Chinese 19, Indians 815. Estimated increase 16 per cent.

Extreme length E. and W., 410 miles, breadth 210 miles, area 81,700 sq. miles, 52,288,000 acres. No mountains. There is little navigable water. Water powers of fair proportion, irrigation necessary in large sections. Coal area of moderate extent; veins usually thin; quality fair. Soil fine. Corn, wheat, oats, hemp, flax and rye, staples. Castor beans and cotton grown successfully. Soil of prairies deep loam of dark color; bottoms sandy loam. Peculiarly favorable to stock-raising. Prairie rich in grasses. Dairying favored. Fruits successful. Forests small. Limestone and colored chalk furnish building materials. Value improved land averages $12 per acre, woodland $15. Manufacturing growing. State ranks fifth in cattle, corn and rye. CLIMATE.—Salubrious; winters mild, summers warm, air pure and clear. Temperature averages winter 31 deg., summer 78 deg., ranges 8 deg. below to 101 deg. above zero; such extremes exceptional. Rainfall averages 45 inches at east, 33 inches at west.

CHIEF CITIES.—Leavenworth, pop. 15,546, Topeka (capital), pop. 15,542; State University at Lawrence, state asylums for insane and feeble-minded at Topeka and Ossawattomie: institution for education of the blind at Wyandotte; for deaf mutes, Olathe.

INDUSTRIES.—Agriculture, stock-raising, manufacturing, etc.

Salaries of State Officers.

Governor $3,000, Secretary of State $2,000, Treasurer $2,500, Auditor $2,000, Attorney General $1,500, Superintendent of Public Inst. $2,000, Secretary Board of Agriculture $2,000, Insurance Commissioner $2,500, three Railroad Commissioners $3,000, State Librarian $1,500, Chief Justice $3,000, two Associate Justices $3,000, Senators and Representatives $3 per day, mileage 15 cents; District Judge $3,500, Pension Agent $4,000.

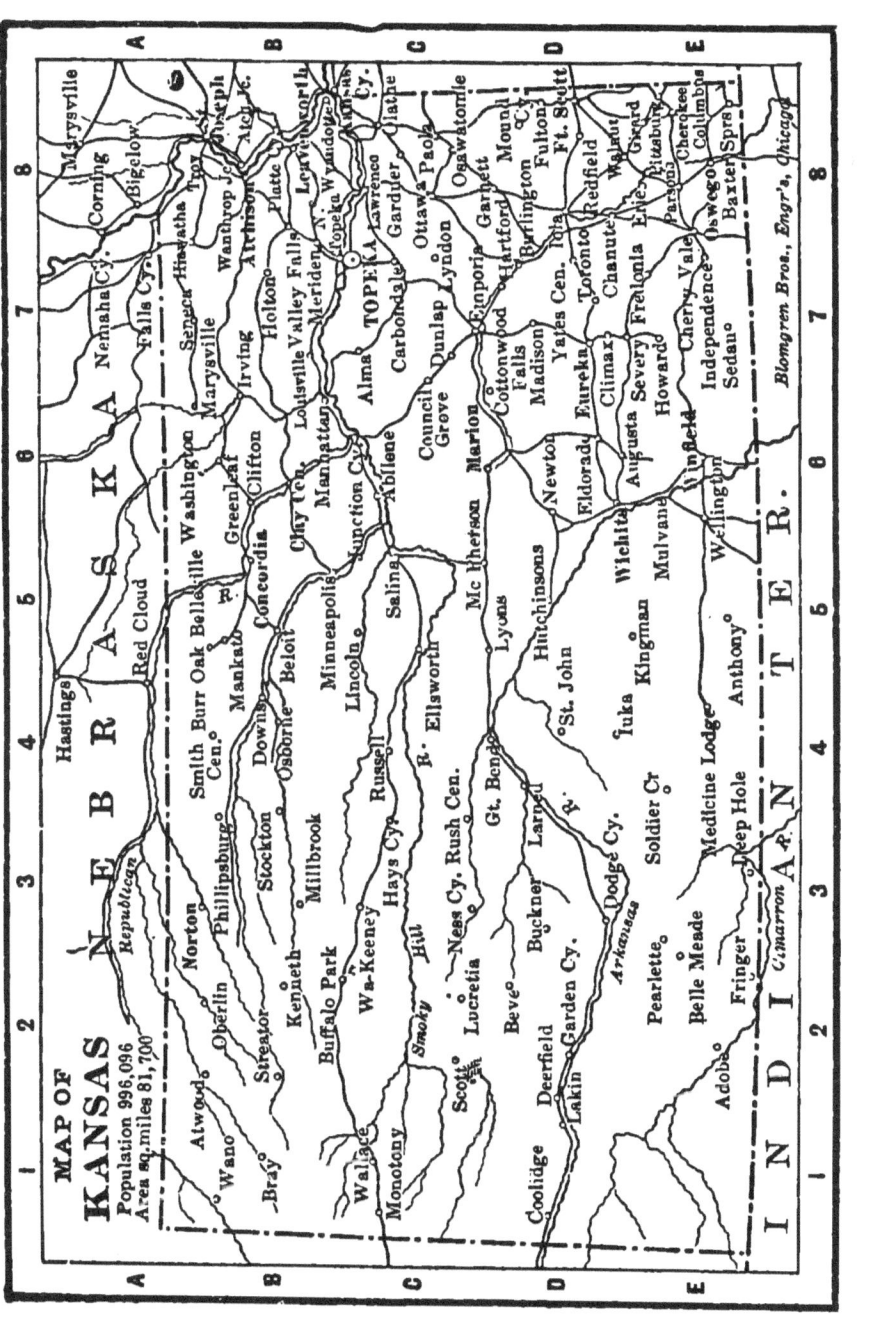

LOUISIANA.

Named for Louis XIV of France Called the "Pelican State" and the "Creole State." First sugar cane cultivated in United States near New Orleans 1751. First sugar mill 1758. First shipment of cotton abroad 1784. Purchased by United States, 1803, for $15,000,000. Louisiana admitted as a state under present name April 8, 1812. In the war with England immediately following, the state made a glorious record, and at the battle of New Orleans, Jan. 8, 1815, humiliated the British and ended the war. Seceded Jan. 26, 1861. Some fighting on the river between boats and forts. New Orleans captured May 1, 1862. 1868, in June, state reentered Union. Capital, Baton Rouge. Number of parishes or counties 58, miles railroad 1,316. Legislature and state officers elected quadrennially, members congress biennially, state elections Tuesday after third Monday in April, number senators 36, representatives 98, sessions biennial, in even-numbered years, meeting second Monday in May, holds 60 days, terms of senators and representatives 4 years each. Number electoral votes 8, congressmen 6, voters 216,787, colored 107,977, native white 81,777, foreign white 27,033. Idiots, insane and criminals excluded from voting. Legal interest 5 per cent., by contract 8 per cent.; usury forfeits entire interest. Educational facilities average. POPULATION, 1880, 939,946, male 468,754, female 471,192, native 885,800, foreign 54,146, white 454,954, colored 483,655, Chinese 489, Indians 848, slaves, 1860, 331,726. Extreme length E. and W. 294 miles, breadth 248 miles, area 45,420 sq. miles, 29,068,800 acres. Coast line 1,276 miles, very irregular navigable rivers 2,700 miles. Mississippi flows in or on the borders of the state. Bays numerous on coast but harbors indifferent. Many small islands in Gulf. Staple products, sweet potatoes, sugar, molasses, rice, corn, cotton, grasses, oats, etc. All fruits of the semi-tropical climate thrive. State ranks first in sugar and molasses and third in rice. Forests almost inexhaustible. Timber superior in kind and quality, lumbering important industry. Salt produced on a large scale. Iron discovered. Cleared land averages $12.50, woodland $3 to $4 per acre. Reclamation of marshes very profitable and beginning to be done on a large scale. Moss-gathering profitable and invites more attention. CLIMATE.—Temperature ranges from 44 to 100 deg., average summer 81 deg., winter 55 deg. Rainfall 57 inches, chiefly in spring and summer. Summers long and occasionally hot. Health average. Actual death rate lower than in many northern sections. Occasional yellow fever in the cities. CHIEF CITIES.— New Orleans port of entry and largest cotton market in the world pop. 216,090, Baton Rouge (capital) pop. 7,197, Shreveport pop. 8,009, Morgan City port of entry. State institution for insane at Jackson, for deaf mutes and blind Baton Rouge. INDUSTRIES.—Three-fifths of laboring population engaged in agriculture. Average income of rural population among highest in Union. Number industries 1,600.

[Salaries of State Officers, page 439.]

MAINE.

Called the "Pine Tree State," or "Lumber State"; originally included New Hampshire; settled by English 1607, by French in 1613. Number counties, 16; Union soldiers, 70,107; miles of railroad, 1,142. State elections second Monday in Sept.; number senators, 31; representatives, 151; sessions biennial in odd-numbered years, meeting first Wednesday in Jan.; terms of senators and representatives, two years each. Number electoral votes, 6; congressmen, 4; number voters, 187,323; paupers and Indians not taxed excluded from voting. Number colleges, 3; system of common, high and normal schools excellent; school age, 4-21 years. Legal rate interest 6, by contract, any rate. POPULATION, 1880, 648,936, male 324,058, female 324,878, native 590,053, foreign 58,883, white 646,852, colored 1,451, Chinese 8, Indians—Penobscots 625, Passamaquoddies 502. Extreme length north and south 298 miles, width 210 miles, shore line about 2,480 miles, area 33,056 sq. miles, land 29,385 sq. miles, 21,155,840 acres, 37th of states and territories in size. Surface hilly, mountainous toward center. Highest point, Katahdin 5,400 feet; largest island, Mount Desert, 92 square miles. Area of lakes and streams, one-thirteenth entire state. The soil is medium only, except on some of the streams, where it is rich. Hay the best crop. Wheat, oats, corn, hops, potatoes, buckwheat and the ordinary vegetables grow. Cattle do fairly, dairying pays. Half the state is forest of excellent timber. Cleared land averages $15 and forest land $14 per acre. Slate, copper, granite are found in large quantities. Winter average 29 deg., summer 67 deg., rainfall 45 inches; snow lies 80 to 130 days. Climate excellent, except for pulmonary troubles. Death rate low. Chief industries—Agriculture and kindred pursuits, lumbering, fisheries, $3,620,000 yearly, quarrying, ship-building (380 establishments). Principal cities—Portland (seaport) population 31,413, Lewiston 19,083, Bangor, port of entry, 16,856, Biddeford 12,651, and Augusta, the capital, 8,665.

Salaries of State Officers.

Governor	$2,000
Secretary of State	1,200
Treasurer	1,600
Attorney General	1,000
Adjutant General	900
Superintendent Common Schools	1,000
Secretary Board of Agriculture	600
State Librarian	600
Chief Justice	3,000
Seven Associate Justices	3,000
Senators and representatives	$150; mileage 20 cents.
District Judge	3,500
Collector Internal Revenue	2,500
Collector Customs	6,000
Surveyor Customs	4,500
Pension Agent	4,000

MARYLAND.

One of the thirteen original states. Baltimore laid 1730. Federal congress met at Annapolis 1783, when Washington resigned command of army. Federal constitution ratified April 28, 1778. Fredericktown and other places burned in war of 1812, and Fort McHenry bombarded. First blood of civil war shed at Baltimore April 19, 1861. Legislature opposed war April 26, 1861, but passed resolutions favoring the South. Battle of Antietam Sept. 16 and 17, 1862. Slavery abolished 1864. Union soldiers furnished, 46,-638. No. counties, 23. Miles railroad, 1,082. All elections Tuesday after first Monday in Nov., number senators 26, representatives 91, sessions biennial in even-numbered years, meet first Wednesday in Jan. and hold 90 days, term of senators 4 years, of representatives 2 years. Number of electoral votes 8, congressmen 6. Insane, convicts and bribers excluded from voting. Number colleges 11, school age 5-20, school system fair. Legal interest 6 per cent, usury forfeits excess of interest. POPULATION.—1880 939,943, male 462,187, female 472,756, native 852,137, colored 210,-230. Slaves, 1860, 87,189. TOPOGRAPHY, AREA, SOIL, PRODUCTS, ETC.—Length east and west 196 miles, width 8 to 122 miles. Area, 9,860 sq. miles. Acreage of state 6,310,400, water surface large. Western and northern sections mountainous and broken. Chesapeake bay almost divides the state. Tide-water coast nearly 500 miles. Chief navigable rivers, Potomac, Susquehanna, Patuxent, Patapsco, empty into the bay. At the west is the Youghiogheny. Soil varies from very poor to very good. Cleared land averages $22.50, and woodland $14 per acre. The average value of latter lowered by mountain sections. Considerable good timber remains. Enormous coal fields west. Copper is found in Frederick and Carroll counties, iron ore in Allegany, Anne Arundel, Carroll, Baltimore, Frederick and Prince George's counties. Great oyster, fish, fruit and vegetable producing state. Oyster beds most valuable in Union. Wheat, corn, oats, buckwheat and tobacco staple crops. Opportunities for capital are yet excellent. CLIMATE.—Mild, agreeable and healthful, some little malaria in lowlands. Temperature softened by ocean. Winter averages 37 deg., summer 78 deg. Rainfall, 42 inches. CHIEF CITIES.—Baltimore, port of entry, pop. 332,313. Annapolis, capital, contains United States Naval Academy, pop. 5,744. Cumberland, pop., 10,693. CHIEF INDUSTRIES.—Agriculture and fruit growing, oyster and other fishing, canning, coal, iron and copper mining, manufacturers of cotton goods, etc.

Salaries of State Officers.

Governor $4,500, Secretary of State $2,000, Treasurer $2,500, Comptroller $2,500, Attorney General $3,000, Chief Justice $3,500, Seven Associate Justices $3,500, District Judge $4,000, Senators and Representatives $5 per day and mileage, Two Collectors Internal Revenue $2,625 to $4,500, Collector of Customs $7,000, Two Collectors $250 and $1,200 fees, Auditor $2,500, Naval Officer $5,000, Surveyor $4,500.

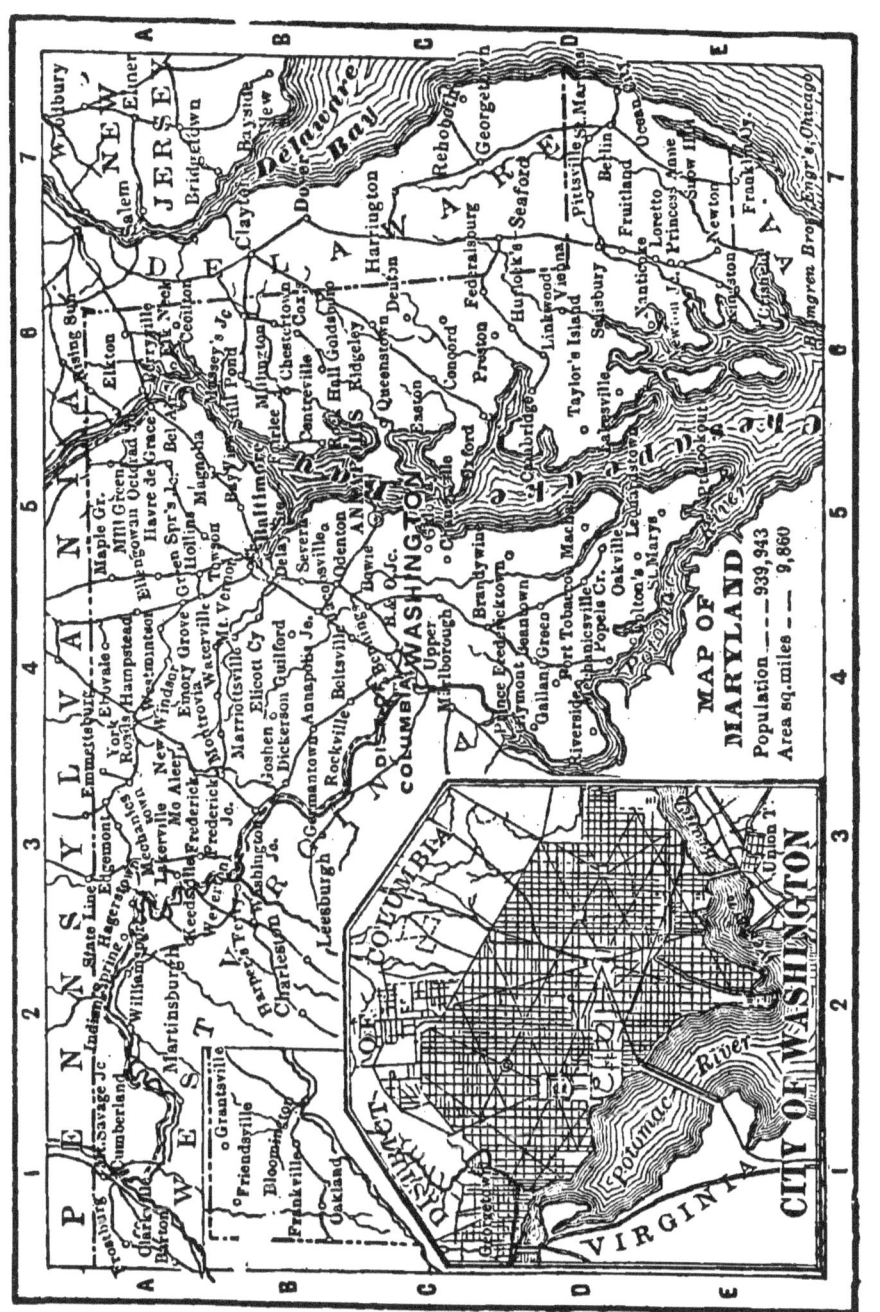

MASSACHUSETTS.

"Old Bay State." One of the 13 original states. First settlement 1602, abandoned the same year. Explored 1614 by Captain John Smith. First permanent settlement 1620. Pilgrims landed on Plymonth Rock Dec. 22. Boston settled 1630. First American newspaper Boston, 1690. Massachusetts was active in bringing on Revolution. Boston massacre March 5, 1770. Destruction of tea Dec. 16, 1773. Boston port bill passed March, 1774. Battle of Lexington first blood of Revolution. Ratified U. S. constitutfon Feb. 6, 1788. Union soldiers, 146,730, besides sailors. Number counties 14. Miles railroad, 2,399. All elections Tuesday after first Monday in Nov. Number senators, 40; representatives, 240; meeting first Wednesday in Jan.; yearly terms of senators and representatives, 1 year. Number electoral votes, 14; congressmen, 12. Number voters, 502,648. Paupers, persons under guardians, non-taxpayers, and men unable to read and write, excluded from voting. School system excellent; attendance compulsory; age 5-15 years. Seven colleges, including Harvard. Legal interest, 6 per cent.; by contract, any rate. POPULATION—1880, 1,783,085. Females outnumber males. Indians 369. Length, N. E. to S. W., 162 miles; breadth, 47 miles in western and 100 in eastern part; area of 8,040 square miles, 5,145,600 acres. Coast extensive and irregular, with numerous good harbors. The Merrimac only large stream entering sea within the state. The Taconic and Hoosac ridges traverse the state at the west. Saddle mountain, 3,600 feet, the highest peak. The east and northeast divisions are hilly and broken, and the southeast low and sandy. Scenery very beautiful, especially in Berkshire hills; soil generally light; hay best crop; wheat, oats, corn and vegetables grown. Forests practically exhausted. Cleared land averages $80 and woodland $45 per acre. Stone is found. No minerals mined. Elizabeth Islands, Martha's Vineyard, Nantucket and smaller islands to the south belong to the state. Winters severe and protracted, summers short and warm, thermometer ranges from 10 deg. below to 100 deg.; averages summer, 73 deg., winter 24 deg. Snow falls October to April. Rainfall, including snow, 44 inches. CHIEF INDUSTRIES.—Agriculture and kindred callings. Fishing for cod and mackerel (half the fishing vessels of the Union owned here.) Manufacture of cotton, woolen, worsted, silk, iron and steel goods, soap and implements, quarrying. PRINCIPAL Cities.—Boston, 362,830. Lowell, pop. 59,475. Lawrence and Fall River, famous for cotton manufactures, pop. 39,151 and 48,961. Worcester, railroad and manufacturing center, pop. 58,201. Cambridge, seat of Harvard Coliege, pop. 52,669. Lynn, famous for manufacture of boots and shoes, pop. 38,274. New Bedford, greatest whaling port in the world, pop. 26,845. Springfield contains greatest arsenal in the United States, pop. 33,340. Ports of entry, 9.

[Salaries State Officers, page 439.]

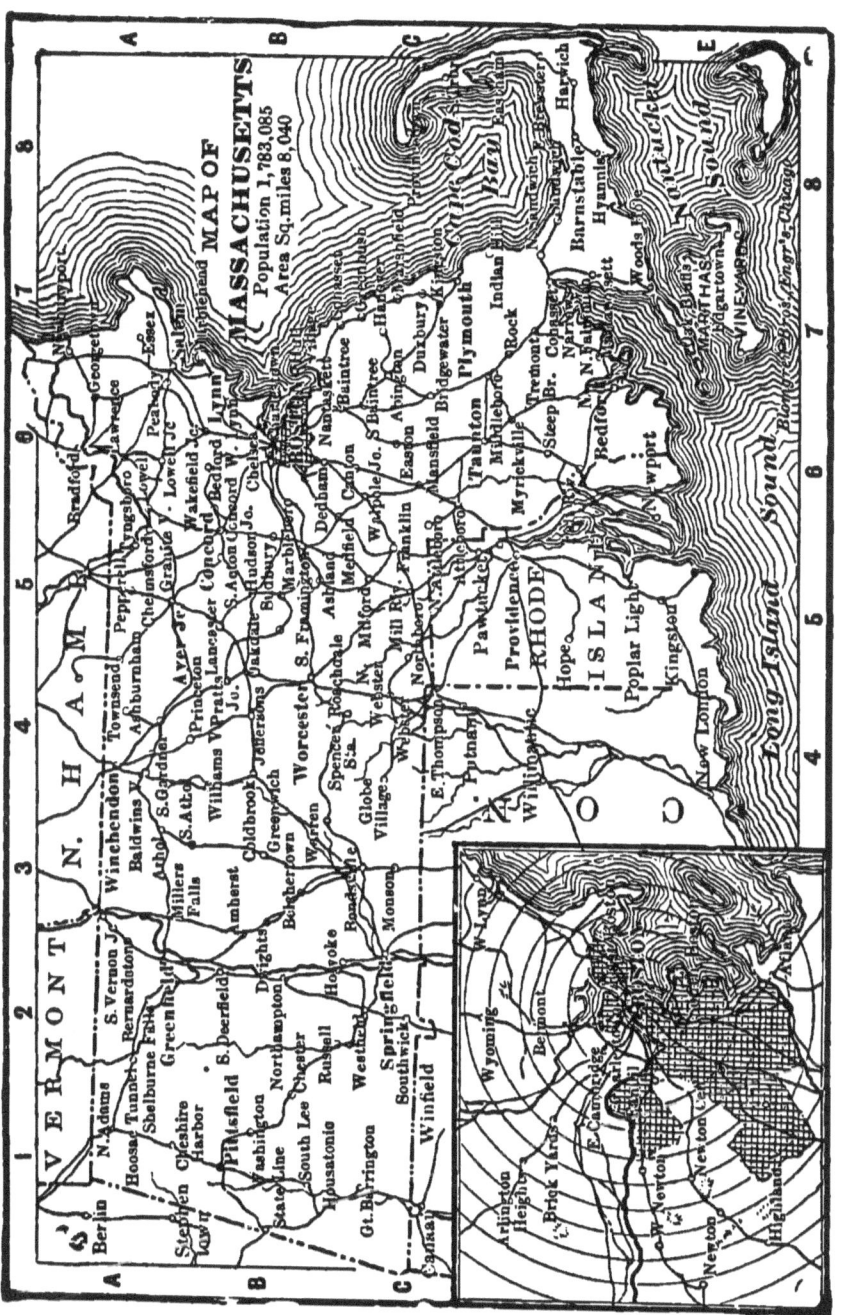

MICHIGAN.

Called "Wolverine State." First settlement by Father Marquette, 1668, at Sault Ste. Marie. Admitted as state Jan. 26, 1837. Thirteenth state to enter Union. Received upper peninsula as compensation for disputed territory same year. Capital, Lansing. Union soldiers furnished 87,364. Number counties 79. Miles railroad 5,233. All elections Tuesday after first Monday in November. Number senators 32, representatives 100, sessions of legislature biennial, in odd-numbered years, meeting first Wednesday in January; terms of senators and representatives 2 years each, number electoral votes 13, number congressmen 11. Number voters 467,687. Duelists excluded from voting. Number colleges 9, efficient public schools, school-age 5-20 years. Legal interest 7 per cent., by contract 10 per cent, usury forfeits excess of interest. POPULATION, 1880, 1,636,937; male 862,355, female 774,582, native 1,248,429, foreign 388,508, white 1,614,560, colored 15,100, Indians 7,249. Estimated increase 11 per cent. Extreme length lower peninsula north and south 278 miles, breadth 260 miles. Extreme length upper peninsula east and west 320 miles, width 24 to 165 miles, area 57,430 sq. miles, or 36,755,200 acres. Length shore line 2,000 miles. Lower peninsula consists of plains and table lands, heavily timbered with pine and hardwoods and small prairies. Soil generally good, but patches of sand occur. Fruit raising, especially apples, peaches and grapes, very successful. All cereals make good crops, except corn at north. Staples, wheat, corn, oats, buckwheat, potatoes, barley, etc. Upper peninsula broken, rocky and almost mountainous, rising at west to 2,000 feet above sea. Western portion mining region, eastern portion favorable to agriculture. Rivers, inlets and small lakes numerous. Water good and well distributed. Copper, valuable iron, coal and salt abundant. Timber yet in immense tracts of virgin pine and hardwoods. State ranks first in copper, lumber and salt, second in iron ore, third in buckwheat, fifth in sheep, hops and potatoes. Cleared land averages $20 per acre, forest $10. CLIMATE.—Temperature averages at Detroit winter 30 deg., summer 70 deg., at Sault Ste. Marie, winter 23 deg., summer 65 deg. Rainfall at Detroit 30 inches, at Sault Ste. Marie 24 inches. Health excellent. Temperature at Marquette averages about 3 deg. lower than at Sault Ste. Marie.

CHIEF CITIES.—Detroit, pop. 116,340; Grand Rapids, pop. 32,016; Lansing (capital) pop. 8,310; Bay City, pop. 20,693; East Saginaw, 19,016; Jackson, 16,105; Muskegon, 11,262; Saginaw, 10,525. Detroit, Marquette, Port Huron, Grand Haven ports of entry.

CHIEF INDUSTRIES.— Lumbering, mining, farming, fruit raising, manufacturing, fishing, etc.

[Salaries State Officers, page 439.]

MINNESOTA.

"Gopher state." Explored by Fathers Hennepin and LaSalle, 1680, via Mississippi river to Falls St. Anthony. Admitted as state, 1858. Foreign immigration immense. Number Union soldiers furnished, 25,052. Number counties, 80. Miles railroad, 4,193. All elections Tuesday after first Monday in November; number senators, 47; representatives, 103; sessions of legislature, biennial, in odd-numbered years, meeting Tuesday after first Monday in January; holding 60 days; term of senators, 4 years; representatives, 2 years. Number electoral votes, 7; congressmen, 5; voters, 213,485; idiots, insane and convicts not voting. Number colleges, 5; school age, 5-21; school system, first-class. Legal interest rate, 70; by contract, 10%; usury forfeits excess over 10%.

Population, 1880, 780,773; male, 419,149; female, 361,624; native, 513,097; foreign, 267,676; white, 776,884; colored, 1,564; Indians, 2,300. Estimated increase, 20%. Length N. and S., 378 miles, average width, 261 miles, area 79,205 sq. miles, 50,691,200 acres. Surface rolling plain 1,000 feet above sea level, except at N. E., where are a series of sand hills called "Heights of Land," 1,600 feet high. It is the state of small lakes, including over 7,000, varying from a few rods to 32 miles across. In one of these, Itasca, the Mississippi rises and flows 800 miles through the state. The other principal rivers are the Minnesota, Red River of the North, and the St. Louis. Small streams and lakes make water plentiful. The scenery is picturesque and beautiful. The soil is splendid, as a rule, and the accessibility to market and general attractions render the state especially favored by agriculturists. The forests of the state are small (2,000,000 acres), but in parts are rich in fine timbers. Two-thirds of the state is unoccupied. Cleared land averages $12.50 per acre and woodland $8. Wheat is the great crop. Corn, oats, barley, hay and dairy products are also staples. State ranks fourth in wheat.

CLIMATE.—Healthful. Air pure and dry, summers warm, averaging 68-70 deg.; winters cold, averaging 9-24 deg. Rainfall 36 inches, chiefly in summer. Snowfall medium. The dryness mitigates the cold in winter.

CHIEF CITIES.—Pembina, port of entry on Red river. St. Paul, capital, pop. 41,473. Minneapolis, pop. 46,887.

CHIEF INDUSTRIES.—Agriculture, dairying, milling, etc.

Salaries of State Officers.

Governor	$3,800
Lieutenant Governor	600
Secretary of State	1,800
Treasurer	3,500
Auditor	3,000
Attorney General	2,500
Superintendent of Public Instruction	2,500
Adjutant General	1,500
Public Examiner	3,000
Insurance Commissioner	2,000

MISSISSIPPI.

Indian name meaning Father of Waters. "Bayou State." Visited by De Soto 1542, by LaSalle 1682. Settled Biloxi, 1699, by M. de Iberville. Formed a part of the territory of Louisiana, and belonged to France. Admitted as a state Dec. 10, 1817. Seventh state admitted. Capital fixed at Jackson, 1822. State active in war of 1814 and with Mexico. Seceded 1861. Shiloh the most notable battle of the rebellion in the state. State re-entered Union 1870. Number counties 74, number miles of railroad 1,844. State officers elected quadrennially, and legislature every two years, all elections Tuesday after first Monday in Nov., sessions of legislature biennial, in even-numbered years, meeting Tuesday after first Monday in Jan., number senators 37, representatives 120, term of senators 4 years, of representatives 2 years, number electoral votes 9, congressmen 7, voters 238,532, colored 130,278, foreign white 5,674. Idiots, insane and criminals excluded from voting. Number colleges 3, school age 5-21, school system fair. Legal interest 6 per cent., by contract 10 per cent., usury forfeits excess of interest. Miles railroad 1844, 26. Population 1880 1,131,597, male 567,177, female 564,420, native 1,122,388, foreign 9,209, white 479,-398, colored 650,291, Chinese 51, Indians 1,857, slaves 1860, 436,631. Estimated increase 1885, 9 per cent. Greatest length N. and S. 364 miles, average width 143 miles, area 46,340 sq. miles, 29,657,600 acres. Coast line, including islands, 512 miles. Harbors, Biloxi, Mississippi City, Pascagoula and Shieldsburg. Surface undulating with a gradual slope from elevation of 700 feet at N. E., W. and S. to the Mississippi and Gulf. Some hills reach 200 feet above surrounding country. From Tenn. line S. to Vicksburg, Mississippi bottoms wide, flat, with more or less swamp, and covered with cypress and oak. Soil an inexhaustible alluvium. Soil light but productive, at south sandy with pine growth. Cotton prolific. Staple crops, cotton, rice, sugar, molasses, tobacco, corn, sweet potatoes, grapes for wine. Fruits and vegetables are splendid crops, but are neglected. Forest area large, pine, oak, chestnut walnut and magnolia grow on uplands and bluffs, long-leafed pine on islands and in sand. Lumbering important industry, mules raised with great success. State ranks second in cotton, fifth in rice. Oyster and other fisheries valuable. Cleared land averages $7.50 per acre, woodland $3. Climate mild, snow and ice unknown. Summers long and warm, July and August hottest months. Temperature averages summer 80 deg., winter 50 deg. Rainfall 46 in. at north, 58 in. at south. Highlands very healthy. Malaria in bottoms. CHIEF CITIES.—Jackson (capital), pop. 5,204. Natchez, pop. 7,058. Vicksburg, pop., 11,814. LEADING INDUSTRIES.—Agriculture, lumbering, fishing and canning.

Salaries of State Officers.

Governor $4,000, Lieutenant Governor $800, Secretary of State $2,500, Treasurer $2,500, Auditor $2,500, Attorney General $2,500, Superintendent of Public Education $2,000, Commissioner of Agriculture $1,000, Land Commissioner $1,000.

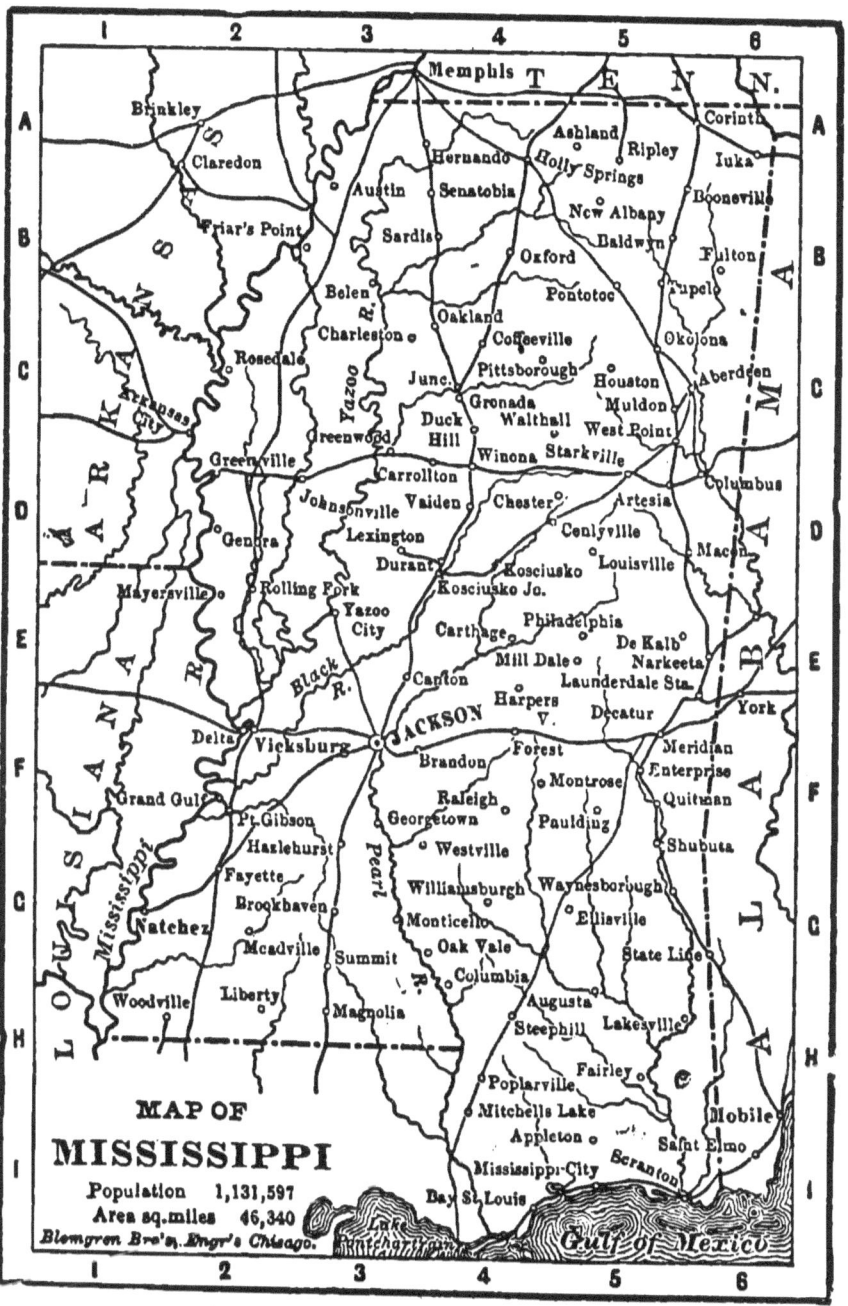

MISSOURI.

Name Indian, means "Muddy River. Settled first at St. Genevieve. Organized as territory under present name 1812, included Arkansas, Indian Territory, etc. Admitted March, 1821. Eleventh state admitted. Admission aroused much discussion. "Missour Compromise" effected and state permitted to retain slavery. State divided on secession and was scene of perpetual internal warfare. Martial law declared Aug. 1862. Union soldiers furnished, 109,111. Number counties, 115. Miles railroad, 4,710. State officers elected quadrennially, and legislature every two years. All elections Tuesday after first Monday in November, number senators 34, representatives 141, sessions of legislature biennial in odd-numbered years, meeting Wednesday after January 1, holds 70 days, term of senators 4 years, representatives 2 years. Number electoral votes 16, congressmen 14, number voters 541,207. United States army and inmates of asylums, poorhouses and prisons excluded from voting. Number colleges 17, school age 6–20, school system good, endowments large. Legal interest rate 6 per cent., by contract 10 per cent., usury forfeits entire interest.

Population 1880, 2,168,380, male 1,127,187, female 1,041,193, native 1,956,802, foreign 211,578, white 2,022,826, colored 145,350, Chinese 91, Indians 113. Estimated increase 12½ per cent.

Length N. and S. 575 miles. Average width 246 miles. Area 68,735 sq. miles, 43,990,400 acres. Soil generally good. South the surface is broken with hills, sometimes 1,000 feet high. The most noted, Iron Mountain and the Ozarks. West of Ozarks is a prairie region with wide, deep, fertile valleys. Entire area well watered by small streams, springs, etc. Chief crops, corn, wheat, oats, potatoes, tobacco. Fruits do splendidly. Peaches especially fine. Vegetable gardening successful. Improved land averages $12, unimproved, $7 per acre. Coal, iron, marble, granite, limestone, lead and copper found in enormous deposits. Lead area 5,000 sq. miles. Forests magnificent. Growth walnut, poplar, oak and the hardwoods, grazing a leading business both in extent and profit. Stock of all kinds raised with success. State ranks first in mules, third in oxen, hogs, corn and copper, fifth in iron ore.

Climate variable, with sudden changes, but generally pleasant and healthy. Summers are long and warm, but not enervating. Winters moderate, with occasional severe days. Average temperature, summer 76 deg., winter 39 deg. Rainfall greatest in May, averages 34 inches.

CHIEF CITIES,—St. Louis, largest city west of the Mississippi, port of entry and great commercial and manufacturing point, pop. 350,518. Capital, Jefferson City, pop. 55,785. Pop. St. Joseph 32,431, Kansas City 55,787.

LEADING INDUSTRIES.—Agriculture, mining, manufacturing, quarrying, grazing, fruit and vegetable growing, lumbering, etc.

[Salaries of State Officers, page 439.]

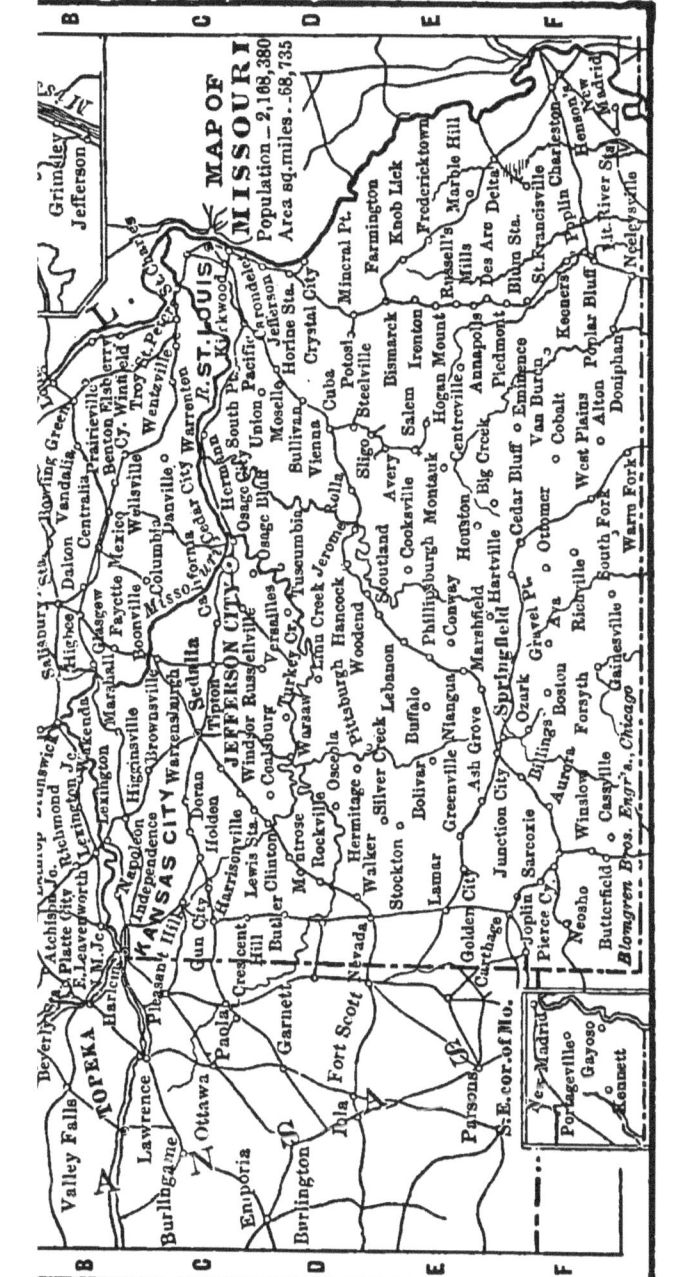

MONTANA.

Gold discovered 1860. Formed part of Idaho, organized 1863. Organized as territory May, 1864. Custer massacre June 25, 1876, 350 men of the 7th United States Cavalry annihilated by Sioux under Sitting Bull, on the Little Big Horn river. Number counties 14. Miles of railroad 1,046. All elections Tuesday after first Monday in Nov. Number senators 12, representatives 24. Sessions of legislature biennial, in odd-numbered years, meeting second Monday in Jan., holds 60 days, terms of senators and representatives 2 years each. Voters 21,544, native white 12,162, foreign white 7,474, colored 1,908. School age 4-21 years, graded schools in Deer Lodge City, Virginia City and Helena. School lands reserved for sale when territory becomes state valuable and extensive. Legal interest 10 per cent, by contract any rate.

POPULATION.—1880, 39,136, male 28,177, female 10,982, native 27,638, foreign 11,521, white 35,385, colored 346, Chinese 1,765, Indians 1,663, Indians on reservations 19,791. Estimated increase, 24 per cent. Extreme length E. and W. 540 miles, average width 274 miles, area 145,310 sq. miles, 92,998,400 acres, two-fifths good farm land, of which about 4,000 acres is cultivated. Three-fifths of territory rolling plains, rest mountainous. Surface fairly supplied with small streams. Timber supply ample. Soil good. Immense area of arable land. Wheat best crop, oats, potatoes, hay, also staples. Too cold for corn. Area grazing land, over two-thirds territory. Grazing interests great. Splendid grazing grounds yet untaken. Mineral wealth great. Ranks fifth in silver and in gold. Climate dry. Rainfall about 12 inches. Warmer than same latitude farther east. Snows heavy in mountains, light in valleys and on plains. Temperature averages summer 62 deg., winter 18 deg. Colder in mountains. Health excellent.

CHIEF CITIES.—Three United States districts, court held twice a year at Helena, twice at Virginia City, pop. 2,000, and three times at Deer Lodge, pop. 1,500. Helena pop. 4,000, capital and most important town.

LEADING INDUSTRIES.—Mining, lumbering, grazing, agriculture, smelting, etc.

Salaries of Territorial Officers.

Governor	$2,600
Secretary	1,800
Treasurer	1,500
Auditor	1,500
Superintendent of Public Instruction	1,200
Chief Justice	3,000
Two Associate Justices	3,000
Senators and Representatives	$4 per day and 20 cents mileage
Surveyor General	2,500
Chief Clerk	1,800
Chief Draftsman	1,600
Collector of Internal Revenue	2,500

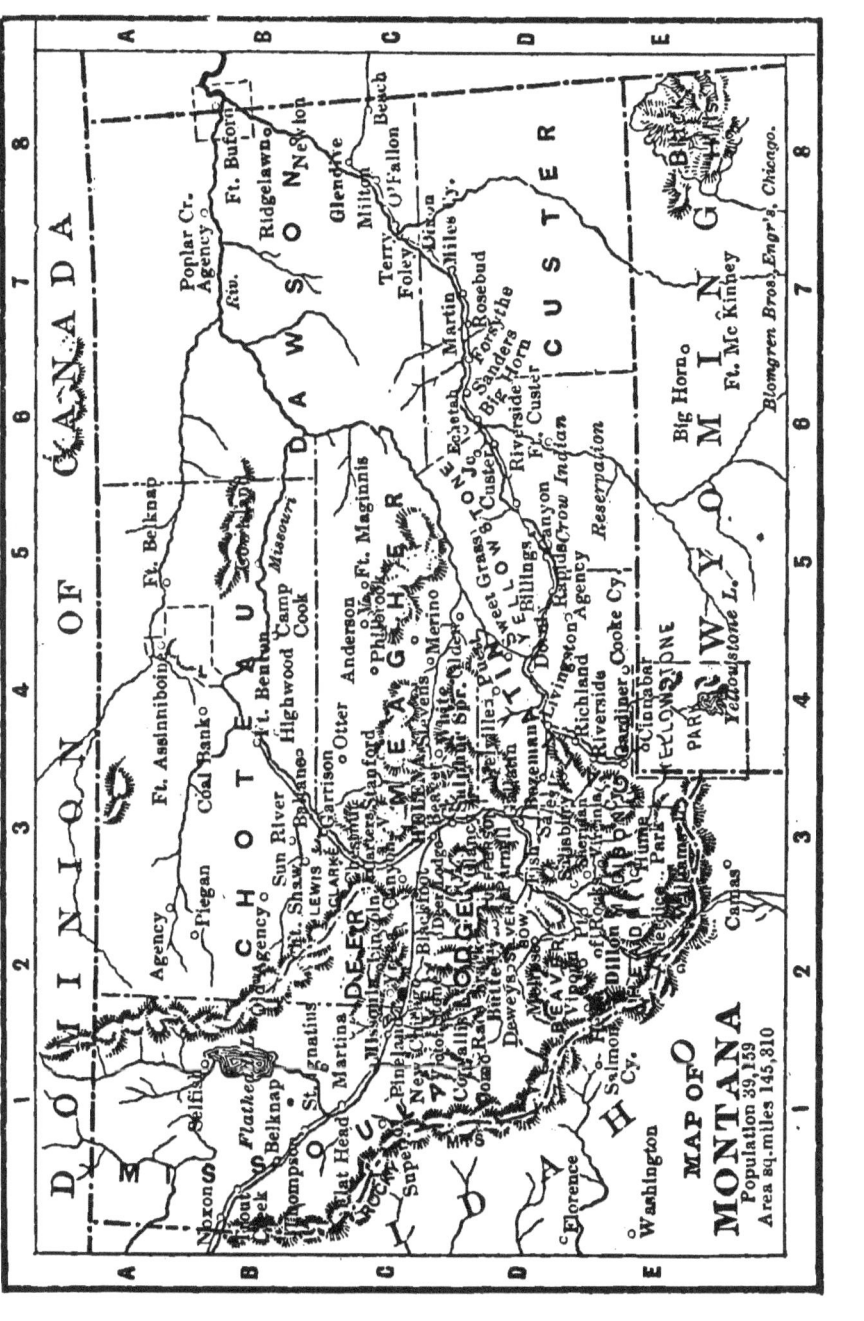

NEBRASKA.

Name Indian, means "Shallow Water." Nebraska Territory organized May, 1854. Few settlements till 1864. Idaho cut off March, 1863, and present boundaries fixed. Bill to admit July, 1866, unsigned by President Johnson, and another Jan. 1867, vetoed. Bill passed over veto Feb. 1867. Admitted that year. Lincoln capital. Union soldiers furnished, 3,157. Number counties 74. Miles of railroad 1865 172, 1885 2,794. All elections Tuesday after first Monday in Nov., number senators 33, representatives 100, sessions biennial, in odd-numbered years, meeting first Tuesday in Jan., holding 40 days, terms of senators and representatives 2 years each, number electoral votes 5, number congressmen 3, number voters 129,042. U. S. army, idiots and convicts excluded from voting. Number colleges 9, school age 5-21, school system superior, school endowments liberal. Legal interest 7 per cent., by contract 10 per cent., usury forfeits interest and cost.

Population 1880 452,402, male 249,241, female 203,161, native 854,988, foreign, 97,414, white 499,764, colored 2,385, Chinese 18, Indians 235. Estimated increase 25 per cent.

TOPOGRAPY, AREA, SOIL, PRODUCTS, ETC.—Extreme length E. and W. 424 miles, width 210 miles, area 76,185 sq. miles, 48,755,000 acres. Surface a vast plain, undulating gently, and principally prairie with a few low hills. At extreme northwest are spurs of the Rocky mountains, and Black Hill country begins, general slope from W. to E., Missouri, Platte, Niobrara, Republican and Blue, principal rivers, and are fed by numerous smaller streams. Southern portion of state peculiarly favorable to all kinds of crops, western half magnificent series of pastures and best suited to grazing. Whole eastern two-fifths a great natural garden. Corn the great crop; wheat, oats, hay, rye, buckwheat, barley, flax, hemp, apples, plums, grapes, berries, staples and flourish. Cattle raising of vast importance and magnitude. Good herd laws. No important minerals. Manufacturing growing wonderfully. Improved land averages $9, unimproved $5, and woodland $18 per acre.

Climate dry, salubrious and free from malaria. Temperature averages, summer, 73 deg., winter 20 deg. Rainfall east of 100th meridian, including snow, 25 inches, heaviest in May. At west, precipitation falls to 17 inches. Rainfall gradually increasing.

CHIEF CITIES.—Omaha, U. S. port of delivery, commercial center, pop. 30,518, Lincoln contains State University, pop. 13,003, Plattsmouth, pop. 4,175, Nebraska City 4,183.

LEADING INDUSTRIES.—Agriculture, cattle-raising, dairying, manufacturing, etc.

Salaries of State Officers.

Governor $2,500, Lieutenant Governor $6 a day, Secretary of State $2,000, Treasurer $2,500, Auditor of Public Accounts $2,500, Attorney General $2,000, Superintendent of Public Ins. $2,000.

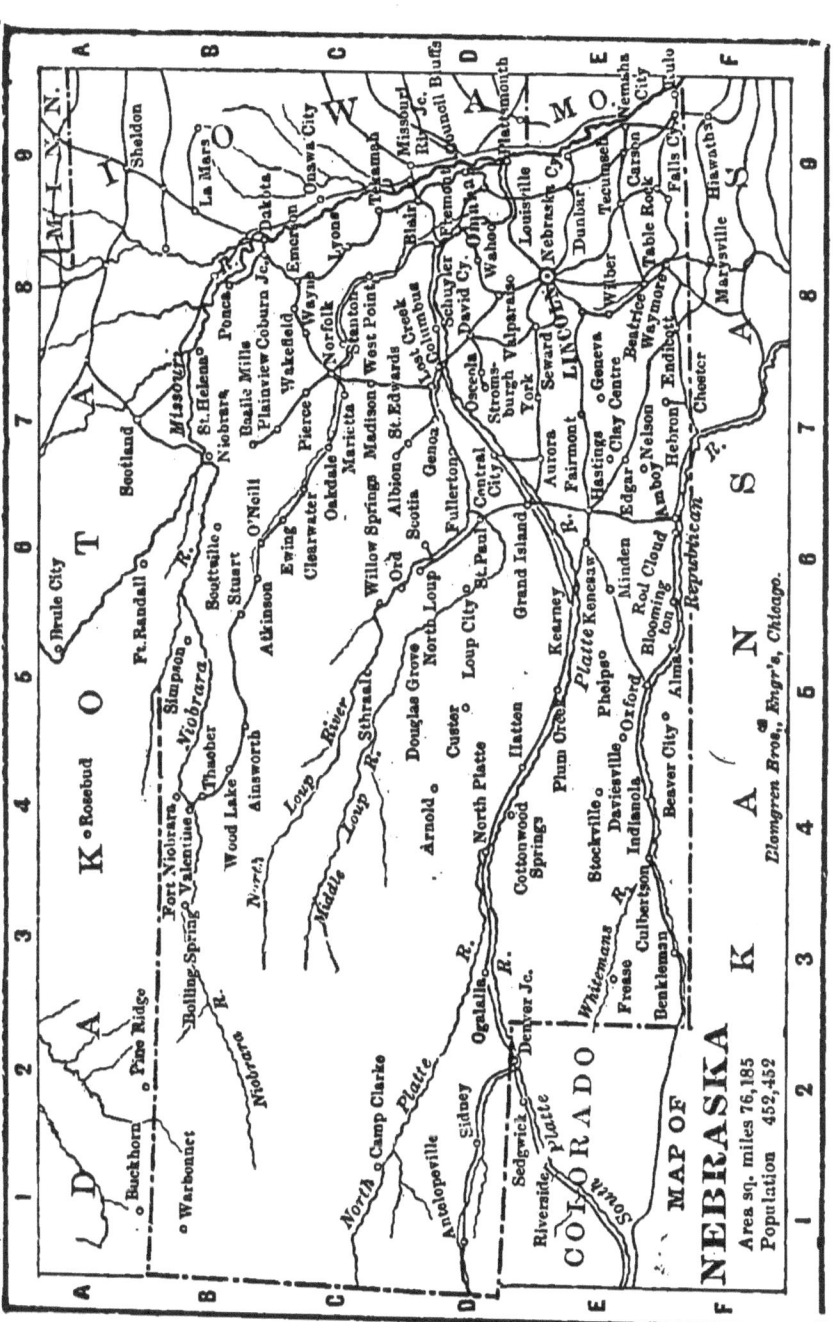

NEVADA.

"Sage Hen State." First settlements in Washoe and Carson valleys 1848. Gold discovered 1849, silver 1859. Territory organized March, 1861. Admitted as state Oct., 1864. Number counties 15. Miles railroad 948. Governor and state officials elected quadrennially, and legislature every 2 years, on Tuesday after first Monday in Nov.; number senators 20, representatives 40, sessions of legislature biennial, in odd-numbered years, meeting first Monday in Jan., holding 60 days. Term of senators 4 years, of representatives 2 years. Voting population 31,255, native white 11,442, foreign white 14,191, colored 5,622. Idiots, insane and convicts excluded from voting. School age 6-18 years. Legal interest rate 10 per cent., by contract any rate.

Population, 1880, 62,266, male 42,019, female 20,247, native 36,613, foreign 25,653, white 53,556, colored 488, Chinese 5,416, Indians 2,803.

Extreme length N. and S. 485 miles, width 320 miles, area 109,740 sq. miles, 70,223,000 acres. Lake Tahoe, 1,500 feet deep, 10x22 miles in area and 9,000 feet above sea, temperature year round 57 deg. Many mineral springs, warm and cold. Great part of surface unavailable for cultivation. Considerable areas of grazing land; many valleys, rich, easily worked and prolific soil. Corn, wheat, potatoes, oats and barley, staple crops; horses, mules, cattle, hogs and sheep do well. Forests valuable. Mineral resources enormous. Comstock lode supposed to be richest silver mine in the world; Eureka one of the most productive. Rich in lead and copper; zinc, platinum, tin and nickel, plumbago, manganese, cobalt, cinnebar, etc., found. Extensive deposits of borax. Coal and iron. Ranks second in gold, fourth in silver. Kaolin, building stones, slate, soda and salt are obtained. Little land improved.

Climate mild in valleys; little snow except on mountains. At north mercury sometimes falls to 15 deg. below zero; air bracing, health good. Extremes of cold unknown. Summer heat occasionally reaches above 100 deg. Temperature averages, summer 71 deg., winter 36 deg. Rainfall slight, chiefly in spring.

CHIEF CITIES.—Virginia City, chief commercial center, pop. 10,917. Carson City (capital), and contains a branch mint, pop. 4,229.

LEADING INDUSTRIES.—Mining, reducing ores, lumbering, agriculture, etc.

Salaries of State Officers.

Governor	$5,000
Lieutenant Governor	3,000
Secretary of State	3,000
Treasurer	3,000
Comptroller	3,000
Attorney General	3,000
Superintendent of Public Inst.	2,400

NEW JERSEY.

One of the thirteen original states. Battles of Trenton, Princeton, Monmouth and others fought within its borders during the Revolution. State Constitution adopted 1776, revised 1844, and amended in the present decade. United States Constitution unanimously adopted Dec., 1787. Capital established at Trenton 1790. A slave state till 1860, when but eighteen slaves remained, and it was counted a free state. Union soldiers furnished, 75,814. State contains 21 counties, and has 1,890 miles railroad. State elections annual, same date as congressional and presidential. Number of senators 21, representatives 60, meeting of legislature 2d Tuesday in January. Term of senators 3 years, representatives 1 year. Number of electoral votes 9, congressmen 7. Paupers, idiots, insane and convicts excluded from voting. Number colleges 4, schools good, school age 5-18. Legal interest 6%, usury forfeits entire interest. Population, 1880, 1,131,116, male 559,922, female 571,194, native 909,416, foreign 221,700, white 1,092,017, colored 38,853, Chinese 170, Indians 74. Length north and south 158 miles, width 38 to 70 miles, area 7,455 square miles, or 4,771,200 acres. Forty-third state in size. Atlantic coast 128 miles, Delaware Bay coast 118 miles. The famous Palisades of the Hudson at the northeast are 600 feet high. Toward center state slopes to a rolling plain, and at south becomes flat and low. Hudson river forms the eastern border. Delaware Water Gap and Falls of Passaic are the natural wonders of the state. Cleared land averages $80 and woodland $60 per acre. Hay the best crop. Other staple crops are potatoes, wheat, corn, rye, buckwheat, cranberries, fruit and garden produce. Little woodland valuable for timber remains. Iron and fertilizing marls are abundant. Climate variable; temperature averages, summer 68 deg. to 75 deg., winter 31 deg. to 38 deg. Range of temperature from about zero to 100 deg. Rainfall, including snow, 46 inches, reaching 50 inches in the highlands, and falling to 40 inches at the south. Highlands and seashore healthy. Ague and malarial fevers in the lowlands. PRINCIPAL CITIES.—Newark, Perth, Amboy, Great Egg Harbor, Tuckerton, Bridgeton and Lumberton are ports of entry. Newark pop. 136,508, Jersey City 120,722, Trenton (capital) 29,910, Paterson 51,031, Elizabeth 28,229, Hoboken 30,999, Camden 41,659. CHIEF INDUSTRIES.—Manufacture of fabrics, jewelry, clay wares and brick, flour, crystals, fishing, oyster fishing, gardening, agriculture, marl and iron ore digging, etc.

Salaries of State Officers.

Governor $5,000, Secretary of State $6,000, Treasurer $4,000, Comptroller $4,000, Attorney General $7,000, Superintendent of Public Instruction $3,000, Adjutant General $1,200, Librarian 1,500, Chief Justice 7,500, Eight Associate Justices $7,000, Chancellor $10,000, Senators and Representatives $500 a year, District Judge $3,500, Superintendent of Life Saving Service $1,800, Thirty-nine Keepers $700.

NEW MEXICO.

Name supposed to be of Aztec god. Settled earlier than any other part U. S. Permanent settlement, 1596. Santa Fe, then an Indian town, chosen as a seat of Spanish government. The natives were enslaved and forced to work in the fields and mines. Organized as Territory, 1850. Santa Fe captured by Confederates, 1862, but soon abandoned. Number counties, 13. All elections, Tuesday after first Monday in Nov. Number senators 12, representatives 24, sessions of legislature biennial, in even numbered years, meeting first Monday in Jan., hold 60 days. Terms of senators and representatives, 2 years. Voters 34,076, native white 26,423, foreign white 4,558, colored, 3,095. School age, 7-18 years. Legal interest rate, 6 per cent., by contract 12 per cent. Miles railroad, 1878 to 1885, 1,191.

Population, 1880, 119,565. Male 64,496, native 111,514, white 108,721, Indians 9,772. Estimated increase, 1885, 21 per cent. Average length N. and S., 368 miles, width 335 miles. Area 122,000 sq. miles, 78,400,200 acres. Elevation, 3,000 to 4,000 feet. Mountain peaks, 12,000 feet. The Staked Plain, an elevated region, unwatered and without wood, extends into the southeastern part of the territory. No streams are navigable in the territory. Timber scarce, except in few sections. The mountains are clothed with pine, spruce and fir. Cedar grows in foot-hills, and cottonwood and sycamore in valleys. Soil rich where water can be had for irrigation or on streams. Corn, wheat, oats, alfalfa, grapes, vegetables, especially onions and root crops and semi-tropical fruits are prolific. Sheep raising very profitable. Grazing interests extensive. Gold found in Grant, Lincoln, Colfax and Bernalillo counties, rich copper mines in Bernalillo county, and in the Pinos Altos region. Zinc, quicksilver, lead, manganese and large deposits of coal have been found. Irrigable surface, 7,000 sq. miles.

Climate varies with different elevations. Temperature averages, summer, 70 deg., winter, 33 deg. Range of temperature, 4 deg. below zero to 90 deg. above. It is much warmer than the average in the lower altitudes, and colder in the higher. Air dry, rarefied and pure. Rainfall, 9 to 11 inches.

CHIEF CITIES.—Santa Fe, capital, pop. 6,635. Las Vegas, Silver City and Albuquerque.

LEADING INDUSTRIES.—Mining, stock-raising and agriculture.

Salaries of Territorial Officers.

Governor	$2,600
Secretary	1,800
Treasurer	1,000
Auditor	1,000
Commissioner of Immigration	900
Librarian	600
Chief Justice	3,000
Two Associate Justices	3,000

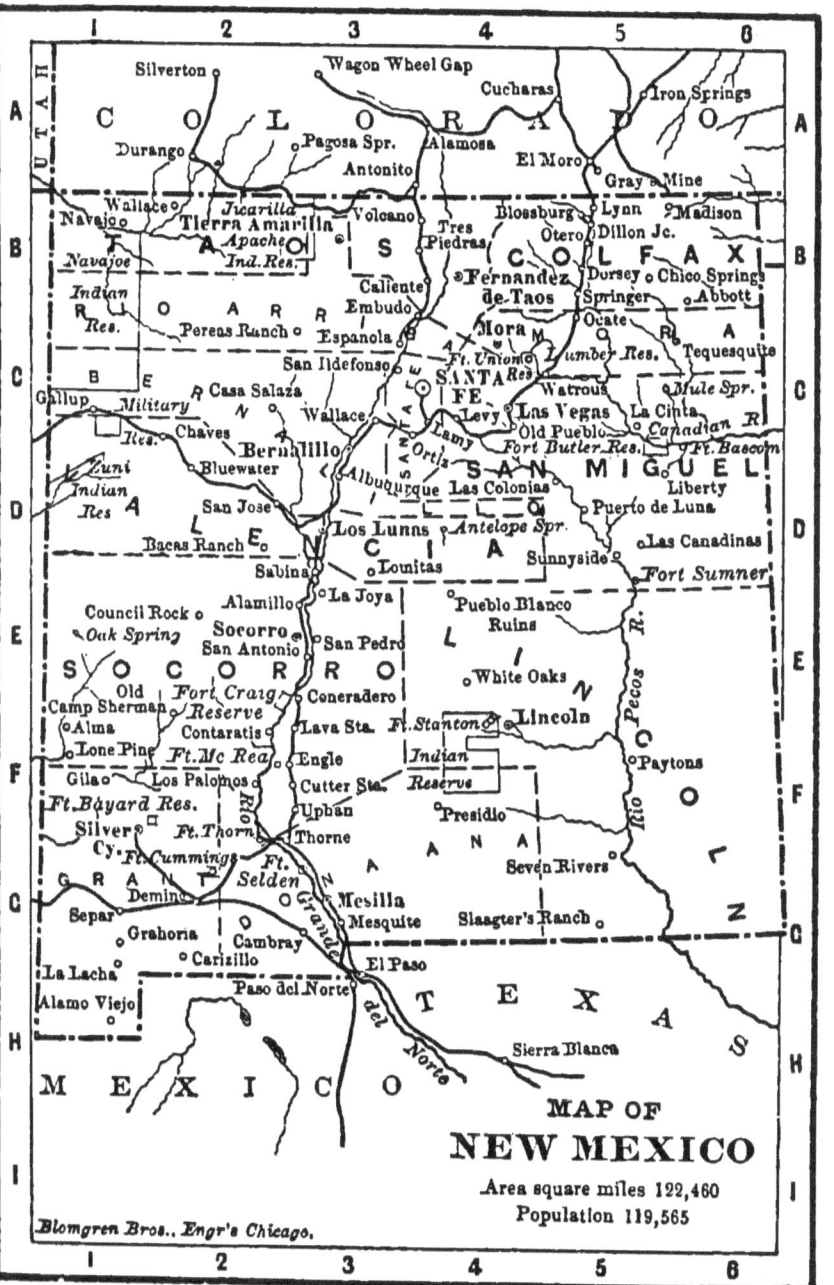

NEW YORK.

One of the thirteen original states, "Empire State." Explored by Henry Hudson, Sept., 1609. Samuel de Champlain discovered and named Lake Champlain. olland owned the territory. The Dutch settled on Manhattan Island, 1614. Country called "New Netherlands." Manhattan Island purchased from Indians for $24, 1626. Indian troubles 1640-45. Swedish settlements on the Delaware incorporated with the New Netherlands, 1655. England claimed the country as part of Virginia, captured Manhattan) New Amsterdam) Aug., 1664, and named it New York. New Yrok the battle-field of the French-English war 1754, was prominent in the Revolution. West Point fortified 1777-78. New York city capital 1784 to 1797. Slavery abolished 1817. Union soldiers furnished, 448,850; number counties 60, custom districts 10, first railroad Albany to Schenectady 1831, miles of railroad 7,812, miles canal 900. State officers elected every 4 and senators (32 in number) every 2 years, representatives (125 in number) yearly, on same day as presidential election. Legislature meets first Tuesday in Feb. yearly, congressmen 34, presidential electors 36. Election betters and bribers and convicts excluded from voting. School system superior, includes 28 colleges. School age 5 to 21 years. Legal interest 6 per cent, usury forfeits principal and interest. Population 1880, 5,082,871, male 2,505,322, female 2,577,549, native 3,871,492, Indians 819, white 5,016,042, Chinese 907. Extreme length E. and W. 410 miles, extreme width 311 miles, area 47,620 sq. miles, 30,476,800 acres, water frontage 900 miles, surface varied. The Hudson, rising in the Adirondacks, and flowing south over 300 miles to New York bay, is the chief stream. The Allegheny and its tributaries drain the S. W., and the Susquehanna the southern central division. The Mohawk is the chief affluent of the Hudson. The state is noted for the beauty of its lakes. Long, Manhattan and Staten Islands form important divisions of the state. The soil is also varied, and agriculturally the state is very rich. Cleared land averages $60 and wooded $40 per acre Considerable forests yet remain. The production of corn, wheat and dairy products is very large. The state ranks first in value of manufactures, soap, printing and publishing, hops, hay, potatoes, buckwheat and milch cows, second in salt, silk goods, malt and distilled liquors, miles railway and barley, third in agricultural implements, iron ore, iron and steel, oats and rye. Climate diverse, mean annual temperature for the state 47 deg. In the Adirondacks the annual mean is 39 deg., in the extreme south it is 50 deg., average rainfall 43 in. including snow, the fall being greatest in the lower Hudson valley, and smallest (32 in.) in the St. Lawrence valley. Range of temperature 10 deg. below to 100 above zero. PRINCIPAL CITIES.— New York City pop. 1,206,299, Brooklyn pop. 566,633, Buffalo "Queen City of the Lakes" pop. 155,134, Rochester pop. 89,366, Syracuse pop. 51,792, Albany (capital) pop. 90,758. LEADING INDUSTRIES.—Manufacturing of all kinds, agriculture, dairying, the trades, etc. [Salaries State Officers, page 439.]

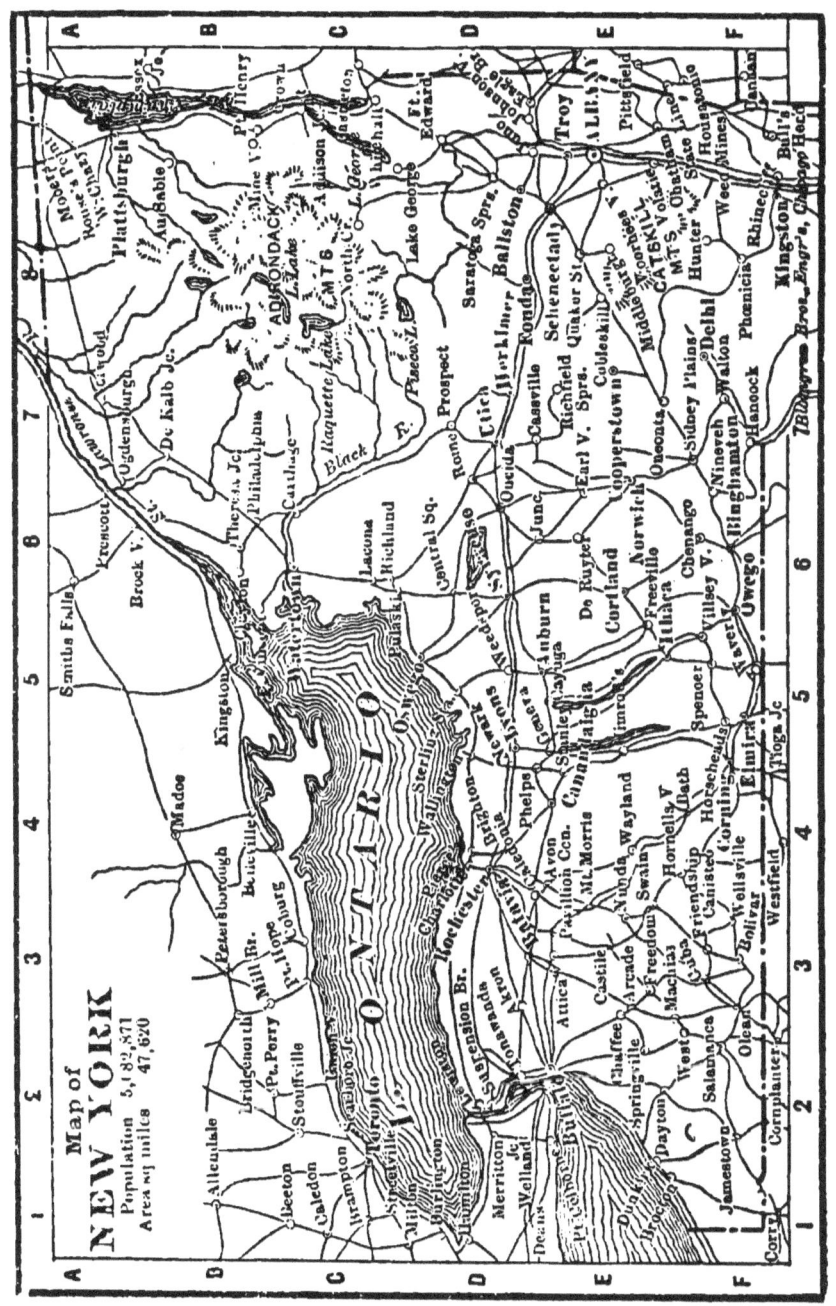

OHIO.

"Buckeye State." Explored by LaSalle 1679. Ohio Territory organized May 7, 1800. Admitted as a state April 30, 1802. Number Union soldiers furnished 313,180. Number counties 88. State and congressional elections second Tuesday in October. Number senators 33, representatives 105, sessions biennial, but "adjourned sessions" practically amount to annual meetings; assembles first Monday in January. Terms of senators and representatives 2 years each. Number electoral votes 23. Number congressmen 21. Number voters 826,577. Insane and idiots excluded from voting. Number colleges 35, school age 6-21, school system first-class. Legal interest rate 6%, by contract 8%, usury forfeits excess. Miles of railroad 7,276. Population, 1880, 3,198,062, male 1,613,-931, female 1,584,126, native 2,803,119, foreign 394,943, white 3,117,920, colored 79,900, Chinese 109, Indians 130. Extreme length E. and W. 225 miles, breadth 200 miles, area 40,760 sq. miles, 25,686,-400 acres. Includes Kelley's and Bass islands in Lake Erie. Lake frontage 230 miles, Ohio River frontage 432 miles. Entire state well watered. Valleys extremely productive. Uplands fertile as a rule. Ohio ranks first in agricultural implements and wool, second in dairy products, petroleum, iron and steel, third in wheat, sheep, coal, malt and distilled liquors, fourth in printing and publishing, salt, miles railway and soap, fifth in milch cows, hogs, horses, hay, tobacco and iron ore. Coal, building stones, iron ore and salt are found in vast quantities. Staple crops, wheat, corn, oats, potatoes, tobacco, buckwheat, etc., vegetables, apples, and the hardier fruits. Cleared land averages $45, woodland $40 per acre. Little forest valuable for lumber remains, except in small reserves. Climate as healthful as any in the United States. Warmest on Ohio River. Temperature for state averages, winter 35 deg., summer 77 deg., range of temperature 16 deg. below zero to 101 deg. above. Snowfall considerable. Average rainfall, including snow, 42 inches; decreases to 37 inches at north and increases to 47 inches at south. CHIEF CITIES.—Cincinnati, "Queen City of the West," pop. 255,139. Cleveland, pop. 160,146, Columbus, capital, pop. 51,647. Chillicothe, Zanesville, Toledo, Sandusky, Cleveland and Cincinnati ports of entry. LEADING INDUSTRIES.—Agriculture, dairying, mining, quarrying, iron making, pork packing, manufacturing.

Salaries of State Officers.

Governor	$4,000
Secretary of State	3,000
Treasurer	3,000
Auditor	3,000
Attorney General	2,000
School Commissioner	2,000
Superintendent of Ins. Department	1,800
Railroad Commissioner	2,000
Secretary Board of Agriculture	1,800

OREGON.

Name means "Wild Thyme." Oregon territory organized August, 1848. Indian troubles, 1844, '47 and '54. Oregon admitted as a state 1859. Number counties 25, miles railroad 1,165. State officers elected quadrennially, and legislature every two years; number of senators 30, representatives 60, sessions of legislature biennial in odd-numbered years, meeting first Monday in Jan., holds 40 days, term of senators 4 years, representatives 2 years. Number electoral votes 3, congressmen 1, voters 59,629, including women. United States army, idiots, insane, convicts and Chinese not voting. Number of colleges 7, school age 4-20, school system good. Legal interest rate 8 per cent, by contract 10 per cent, usury forfeits principal and interest.

POPULATION, 1880, 174,768; male 103,381, native 144,265, white 163,075, Chinese 9,510, Indians 1,694. Estimated increase 11 per cent.

Average length E. and W. 362 miles, average width 260 miles, area 94,560 sq. miles, 60,518,400 acres. Two-thirds entire state mountainous, with wide rich valleys. Columbia river 1,300 miles long, navigable 175 miles, full of cascades and runs through entrancing scenery. Soil generally superior. Wheat the best crop, superior in yield and quality; other crops do well, as do also fruits and vegetables, etc. Extremely favorable to cattle and sheep. Rich in minerals, gold in Jackson, Josephine, Baker and Grant counties, copper in Josephine, Douglas and Jackson, iron ore throughout the state, coal along coast range. Timber resources enormous, and but little touched. Salmon fisheries among best in world. Improved land averages $17.50, unimproved $4. Area arable two-fifths state, forest one-sixth state.

CLIMATE.—In western Oregon moist, equable, rainfall 59 inches. In eastern Oregon dry. Both pleasant and healthful, though subject to occasional extremes at east. Crops in east do not suffer, however, from drouth. At west snow and ice unknown, except on peaks, where it is perpetual. Frosts on high lands. Average temperature summer 65 deg., winter 45 deg.

CHIEF CITIES.— Portland, Astoria and Coos Bay ports of entry, Rosenburgh, Portland pop. 17,577, Salem capital.

LEADING INDUSTRIES.—Agriculture, grazing, mining, fishing, lumbering, fruit growing, canning, etc.

Salaries of State Officers.

Governor $1,500
Secretary of State, Auditor and Comptroller 1,500
Treasurer 800
Superintendent of Public Instruction 1,500
State Librarian 500
Chief Justice 2,000
Two Associate Justices 2,000
Senators and Representatives ...... $3 a day and 15 cents per mile
District Judge 3,500

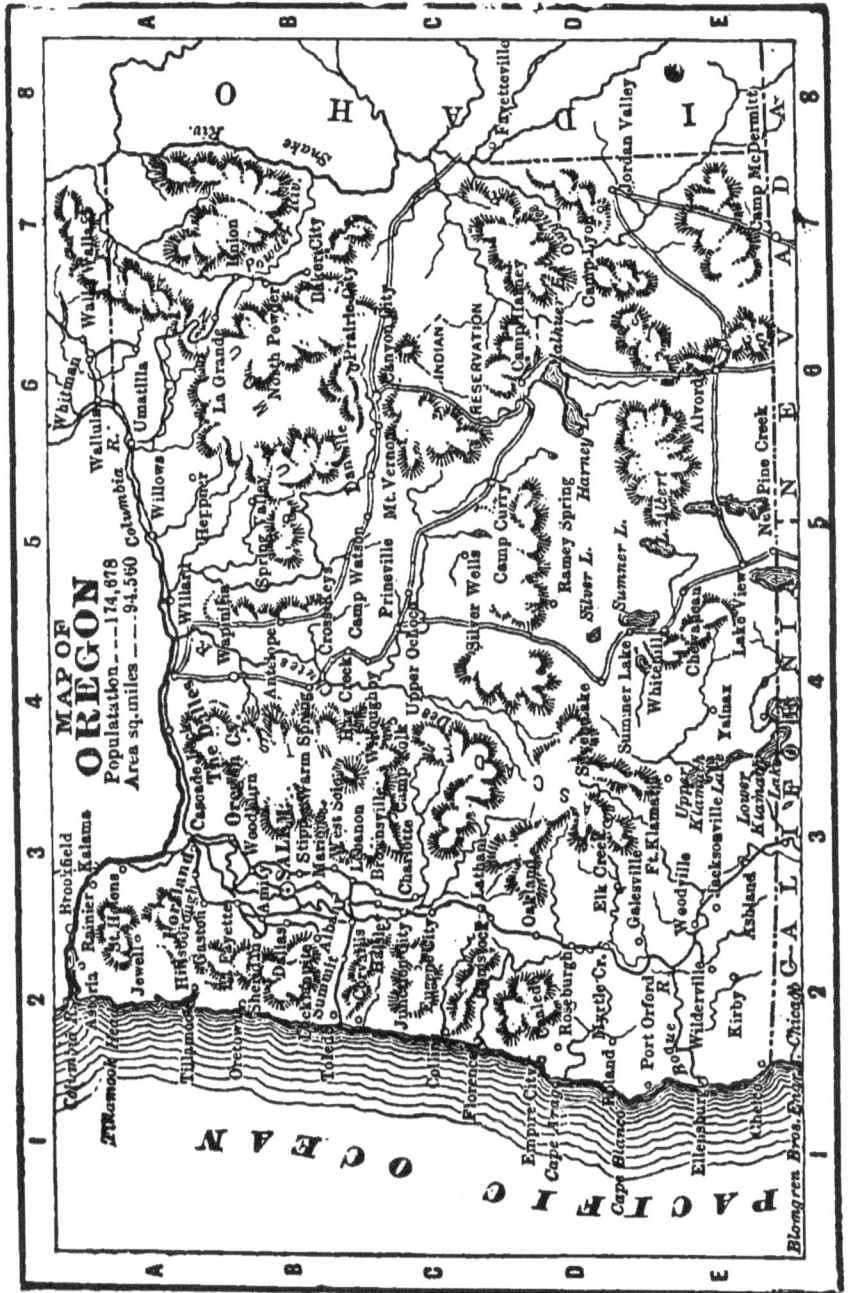

PENNSYLVANIA.

One of the thirteen original states, named for Wm. Penn, the "Keystone State." State invaded three times by confederates, 1862, 1863, when battle of Gettysburgh was fought, and 1864, when Chambersburg was destroyed. Union soldiers furnished, 337,930. Number counties 67, miles railroad 7,546. State elections annual, same date as presidential. Number senators 50, representatives 201, sessions biennial, meeting first Tuesday in Jan., hold 150 days, term of senators 4 years, representatives 2 years, number electoral votes 30, congressmen 28. Non-taxpayers and bribers excluded from voting. Number colleges 26, school age 6-21, school system good. Legal interest 6%. Usury forfeits excess of interest. POPULATION.—1880, 4,282,891, male, 2,136,655 female, 2,146,236, native 3,695,062, colored 85,535, Chinese 464, Indians 184. TOPOGRAPHY, AREA, SOIL, PRODUCTS, ETC.—Length east and west 300 miles, width 176 miles, area 44,985 sq. miles, 28,790,400 acres. Surface very diverse. Level at the southeast, hilly and mountainous toward the center, and rolling and broken at the west and southwest. Soil varies from barren hills to sections of great fertility. Many superb farms. Cleared land averages $45, woodland $30 per acre. Much good timber remains. Farms average 100 acres. Oil, coal (anthracite at east, bituminous at west), iron, copper, kaolin, building stones, salt abound. Rye, corn, wheat, buckwheat, potatoes, vegetables, hay, oats, tobacco are staple crops. Dairying and stock flourish. Climate in mountains severe in winter, with much snow, summers pleasant. Summers hot on the Delaware, reaching 100 deg. Summers long in Susquehanna valley. West of mountains summers hot and of moderate length, winters cold. Average winter temperature 34 deg., summer 74 deg., rainfall, including snow, averages 42 inches. Climate healthy. CHIEF CITIES.—Philadelphia, second city in United States, contains mint and navy yard, pop. 846,984. Pittsburg, extensive manufacturing city, pop. 156,389. Harrisburg, capital, pop. 30,762. Philadelphia, Pittsburg and Erie are ports of entry. INDUSTRIES —Pennsylvania is the great iron, oil and coal state. The other industries include agriculture and kindred pursuits, lumbering, manufacture of paper, woolens, liquors, implements, machinery, etc.

Salaries of State Officers.

Governor...$10,000
Lieutenant Governor... 3,000
Secretary of State.. 4,000
Treasurer.. 5,000
Auditor General... 3,000
Attorney General.. 3,500
Chief Justice.. 8,500
Six Associate Justices.. 8,000
Senators and Representatives, $1,000 for 100 days; $10 per day; mileage 5 cents.

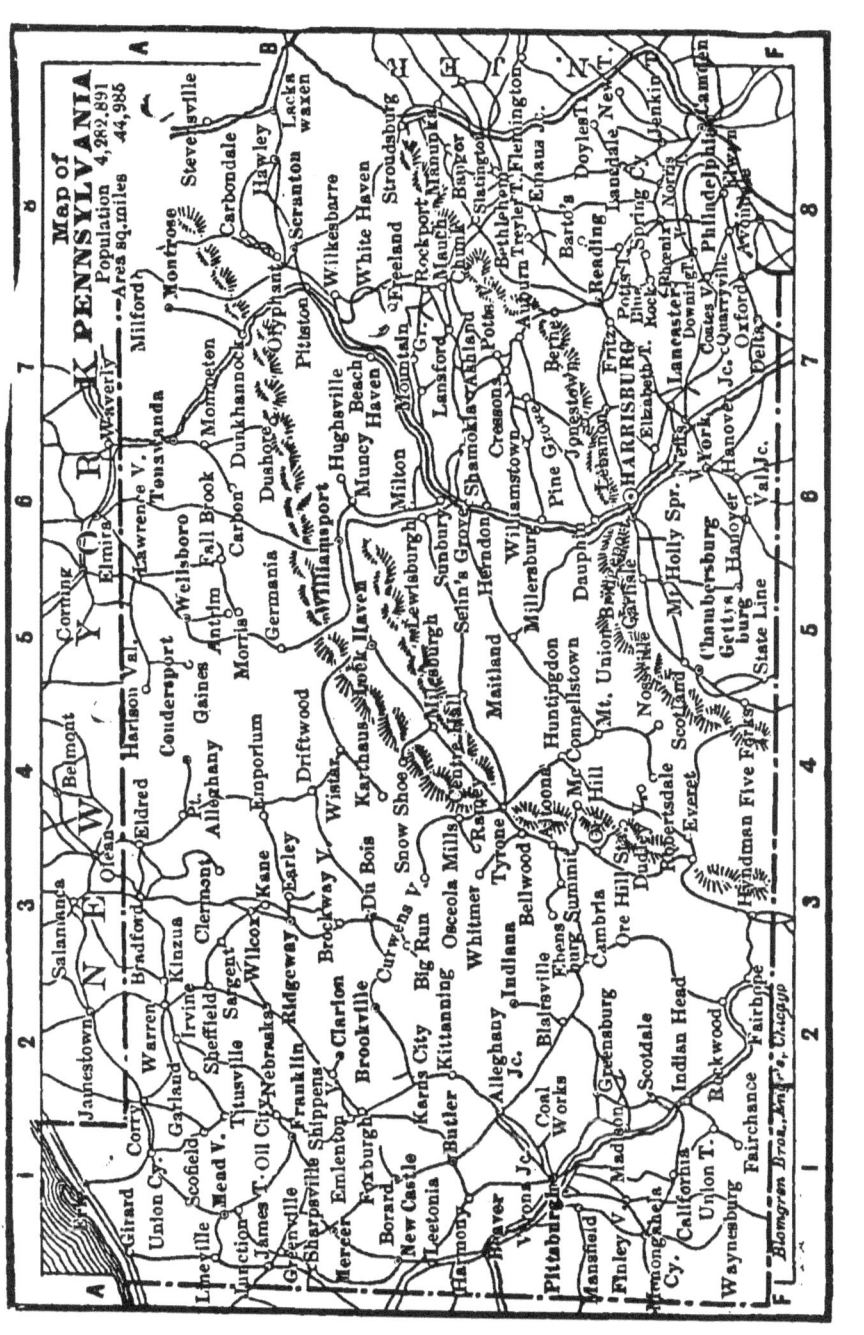

RHODE ISLAND.

One of the 13 original states. Called "Little Rhody." First settled at Providence, 1636, by Roger Williams. Island of Aquidneck (Rhode Island) bought from Indians, 1638, and Newport and Portsmouth founded. Lands of Narragansett Indians acquired by pnrchase, 1709. R. I. seamen distinguish themselves in the Anglo-French wars, 1750 to 1763, and in the Revolution. Union soldiers furnished, 23,236. Number counties, 5. Miles railroad, 147. State elections first Wednesday in April. Elects 72 representatives, 34 senators, 3 congressmen and 4 presidential electors. Legislature meets annually on last Tuesday in May, at Newport, and holds adjourned session annually at Providence. Terms of senators and representatives one year. Persons without property to the value of $134 excluded from voting. Brown's University at Providence founded 1764. Common school system excellent. School age 5-15. Legal interest rate 6 per cent., by contract any rate. Population, 1885, 297,531, three-fourths native, females predominate, Indians 74. Area 1,088 sq. miles, or 696,320 acres. Length N. and S. 46 miles, width 40 miles. Narragansett bay divides the state unequally, the western and larger part extending N. from the ocean some 27 miles. The bay is 3 to 12 miles wide, and contains several islands, of which Acquidneck, Canonicut and Prudence are largest. Block Island, at the western entrance of the bay, also belongs to this state. Surface of state broken and hilly. Small rivers unfit for navigation are numerous, and afford valuable water powers. Chief rivers: Pawtucket and Pawtuxet, entering Narragansett Bay, and Pawcatuck, falling into Long Island Sound. The state contains numerous small lakes, some of great beauty. Scenery varied and pretty. Soil middling quality. Hay best crop. Potatoes, corn and oats are the next most important prodncts. No forests. Dairying profitable. Land highpriced. No minerals mined. Climate, owing to nearness to sea, moderate. Average temperature—winter 24 to 42 deg., summer 44 to 74 deg. Rainfall 43 inches. Snow lies 60 to 100 days, Health good. CHIEF INDUSTRIES.— Manufacture of fabrics of cotton, flax, linen, wool, boots and shoes, rubber goods, metals, jewelry, etc., agriculture, dairying. Rhode Island, in proportion to size, is the largest manufacturing state in Union, PRINCIPAL CITIES.— Providence, capital and seaport, pop., 1880, 104,857. Newport, capital, seaport finest in the world, and great pleasure resort, pop. 15,693. Bristol, seaport. Warren, seaport. Lincoln, pop. 13,765. Pawtucket, pop, 19,030. Woonsocket, pop. 16,050.

Salaries of State Officers.

Governor, $1,000; Lieutenant Governor, $500; Secretary of State, $2,500; General Treasurer, $2,500; State Auditor, Insurance Commissioner, $2,500; Railroad Commissioner, $500; Attorney General, $2,500; Adjutant General, $600; Commissioner Public Schools, $2,500; Chief Justice, 4,500; Four Associate Justices, $4,000; Senators and Representatives, $1 per day, mileage 8 cents; District Judge, $3,500; Appraiser of Customs, $3,000.

TEXAS.

"Lone Star State." Settled first by French under LaSalle 1685, was a part of Old Mexico. Independence declared Dec. 20, 1835. Houston inaugurated as president Oct., 1836. Independence of the republic recognized by United States March, 1837, by European powers 1839 and '40. Continued wars with Mexico, embarrassed finances. Proposition for union with United States 1845, and admitted as a state Dec. 29. State paid $10,000,000 by United States for all lands outside present limits 1850. Seceded Feb. 1861. Houston, who refused to secede, deposed. Military operations small. Last battle of the war near Rio Grande May 13, 1865. Re-entered Union 1870. Number counties 228, miles of railroad 6,198. All elections Tuesday after first Monday in Nov., number senators 31, representatives 106, sessions of legislature biennial in odd-numbered years, meeting second Tuesday in Jan., holds 60 days, term of senators 4 years, of representatives 2 yeas.r Number electoral votes 13, congressmen 11, voters 380,376. Unitde States army, lunatics, idiots, paupers and convicts excluded from voting. Number colleges 10, school age 8-14. School endowment enormous, includes 23,470,377 acres yet unsold. Legal interest 8 per cent., by contract 12 per cent, usury forfeits entire interest. POPULATION, 1880, 1,591,749, male 837,840, female 753,909, native 1,477,133, foreign 114,616, white 1,197,237, colored 393,384, Chinese 136, Indians 992. Estimated increase 25 per cent. TOPOGRAPHY, AREA, SOIL, PRODUCTS, ETC.— Extreme length E. and W. 830 miles, extreme width 750 miles, area 167,865,600 acres, largest of the states and territories. Coast line 412 miles, Galveston bay largest, has 13 feet of water, 35 miles inland. Rio Grande (navigable 440 miles). Lands extremely fertile, except in the N. W., where water is scarce. Lands on Rio Grande and at south require irrigation for good results, although crops will grow to some extent without. Entire state covered with rich grasses, affording pasture the year round. All cereals, root crops, vegetables, fruit and stocks flourish. Cotton best crop. Other staples-sugar, molasses, sweet potatoes, corn, wheat, grapes and fruits. Dairying extensive. Cattle, sheep, goat and hog raising on mammoth scale. Cotton picking July to Dec., corn planting middle of Feb., grain harvest May, corn harvest July. Ranks first in cattle and cotton, second in sugar, sheep, mules and horses. Coal area 6,000 sq. miles, quality good. Iron ore and salt deposits extensive. Other minerals found, but extent unknown. Improved land averages $8, and unimproved $3 to $4 per acre. Uncultivated and timber land seven-eighths of area, timber area one-fourth. CLIMATE varies, temperate at North, semi-tropical at south. Health everywhere most excellent. Thermometer ranges from 35 to 98 deg., but seldom rises to the latter temperature. At Austin averages winter 56 deg., summer 80 deg. Rainfall averages at Austin 35 inches, increases on coast and to the south, decreases to 13 inches in N. W.

[Salaries State Officers, page 439.]

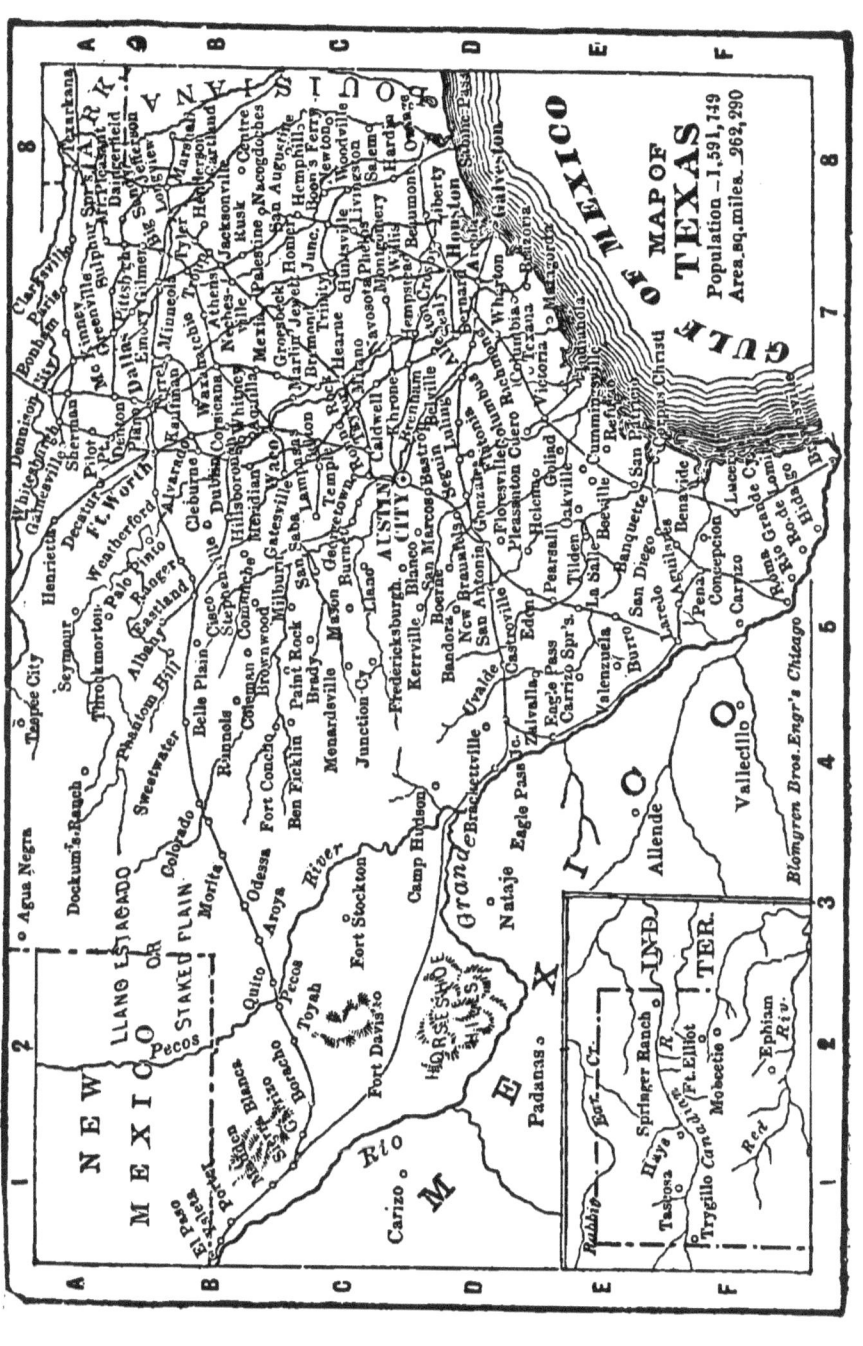

UTAH.

Settled 1848 at Salt Lake by Mormons from Illinois. March, 1849, state of "Deseret" organized. Congress refused to receive constitution adopted. Utah territory organized Sept., 1850. Troubles with government till 1858. Federal officers driven from territory 1856. Number counties 24, miles railroad 1,134. Territorial elections annual, first Monday in Aug. Number senators 12, representatives 24, sessions of legislature biennial, in odd-numbered years, meeting second Monday in Jan., holds 60 days. Terms of senators and representatives 2 years each. Voting pop. 32,773, native white 15,795, foreign white 18,283, colored 695. School system fair, school age 6-18 years, number colleges 1. Legal interest 10 per cent., by contract any rate.

Population, 1880, 143,963, male 74,509, female 69,454, native 99,969, foreign 43,994, white 142,423, colored 232, Chinese 501, Indians 807. Estimated increase 10 per cent.

Average length 350 miles, width 260 miles, area 82,190 miles, 52,601,600 acres. Surface rugged and broken, with some rich valleys. Traversed by Wahsatch, Uintah, Roan, Little, Sierra Lasal, Sierra Abajo, San Juan, Sierra Panoches and Tushar mountains. Southeast portion elevated plateaux, western portion disconnected ridges. Great Salt Lake is 130 sq. miles in area. In N. W. a large area of desert land. Soil in valleys very productive. Yield fine crops of cereals and vegetables. Wheat best crop. Fruits successful. Grazing important interest. Dairying profitable and interest is growing rapidly. Forests sufficient for home purposes. Gold, copper and silver in Wahsatch mountains. Silver predominates, Coal in valley of Weber river. Salt found in large deposits and the lake supply inexhaustible. Territory ranks third in silver.

Climate mild and healthy. Warmer W. of Wahsatch mountains. Summers dry and hot in S. W. Rainfall averages 16 inches at S. and 17 at N., chiefly in Oct. and April. Spring opens in April. Cold weather begins late in Nov. In mountains winters severe and snows heavy. Temperature at Salt Lake averages, winter 35 deg., summer 75 deg.

CHIEF CITIES.—Salt Lake City, capital, pop. 20,768. Ogden, pop. 6,069.

LEADING INDUSTRIES.—Mining, stock-raising and agriculture.

Salaries of Territorial Officers.

Governor $2,600
Secretary 1,800
Treasurer 600
Auditor 1,500
Superintendent of Public Ins 1,500
Librarian 250
Chief Justice 3,000
Two Associate Justices 3,000
Senators and Representatives .... $4 a day, mileage 20 cents.

WASHINGTON

Named for George Washington. First settlement 1845, preceded, however, by Hudson Bay Co.'s trading posts. Organized as territory 1853. First legislature assembled at Olympia February, 1854. Indian wars 1855 and 1858. Gold discovered 1855. Island San Juan in dispute between United States and England 1859. Rights of the Hudson Bay and Puget Sound Co.'s purchased. Number counties 33. Miles railroad 675. All elections Tuesday after first Monday in Nov. Number senators 12, representatives 24, sessions of legislature biennial in odd-numbered years, meeting first Monday in October. Terms of senators and representatives 2 years each. Voting population 27,670, native white 15,858, foreign white 8,393, colored 3,419. Number colleges 2, school age 4–21 years, school endowment reserved large. Legal interest 10 per cent., by contract any rate.

POPULATION, 1880, 75,116; male 45,973, female 29,143, native 59,313, foreign 15,803, white 67,199, Chinese 3,186, Indians 4,405. Estimated increase 14 per cent.

TOPOGRAPHY, AREA, SOIL, PRODUCTS, ETC.—Extreme length E. and W. 341 miles, width 242 miles, area 66,880 square miles, 42,803,000 acres. Coast line 200 miles. Columbia river navigable 175 miles. Excellent harbors in Puget Sound, Admiralty Inlet and Hood's canal. Scenery, especially on Columbia, grand. Columbia river current overcomes tide at the mouth, and water in the bar drinkable. Cereals flourish but corn not successful, Wheat, oats, hops, fruit of temperate climates, except peaches, are staple. Grazing region entire section east of Cascades, coveren with inexhaustible supply of bunch grass. Stock raising and dairying growing industries. Lumber resources unsurpassed. Coal on Bellingham bay and at Seattle, area of coal-bearing strata 20,000 sq. miles. Gold-bearing quartz and silver lodes in Cascade and Coast ranges. Copper, cinnabar, lead and other minerals are found.

CLIMATE.—On coast dry season April to November, rest of year rainy. Rainfall averages at north 96 inches, for entire section 54 inches. Winters mild, little snow or ice. Summers cool with sea breezes. Temperature averages winter 39 deg., summer 61 deg., ranges 30 deg. to 90 deg. Eastern section dry, rainfall 10 inches.

CHIEF CITIES.—Olympia capital, Walla Walla, pop. 4,000; Seattle, pop. 4,000.

LEADING INDUSTRIES.—Agriculture, lumbering, grazing, mining, etc.

Salaries of Territorial Officers.

Governor $2,600, Secretary $1,800, Treasurer $1,200, Auditor $1,200, Superintendent of Public Instruction $1,000, Librarian $400, Chief Justice $3,000, three Associate Justices $3,000, Senators and Representatives $4 a day and 20 cents mileage, Surveyor General $2,500, Chief Clerk $1,800, Chief Draftsman $1,700.

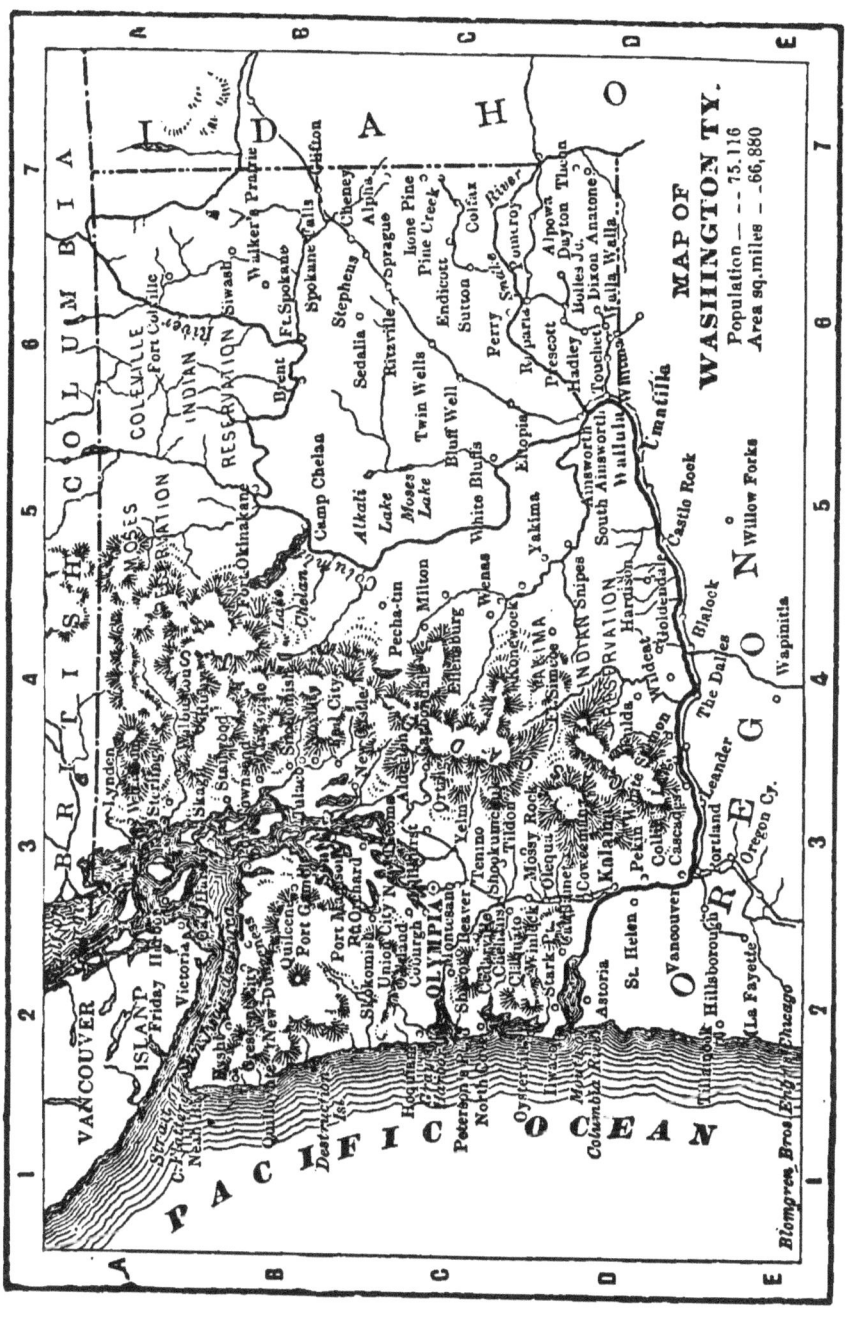

WISCONSIN.

"Badger State." Settled first by French at Green Bay, 1669. Formed part of Northwest territory. Included in Indiana territory, 1800. Became part of Michigan territory, 1805. Wisconsin territory organized 1836. Present boundaries fixed, 1838. Madison made capital, 1838. Admitted as state, May, 1848. Seventeenth state to join Union. Number Union soldiers furnished, 91,327. Number counties, 66; miles railroad, 4,289. All elections Tuesday after first Monday in Nov.; number senators 33, representatives 100, sessions biennial, in odd-numbered years, meeting second Wednesday in Jan., term of senators 4 years, of representatives 2 years. Number electoral votes 11, number congressmen 9, number voters 340,482; insane, idiots, convicts, bribers, betters and duellists excluded from voting. Number colleges 7, number public schools 6,588, school age 4–20 years. Legal interest 7 per cent., by contract 10 per cent., usury forfeits entire interest.

POPULATION, 1880, 1,315,497; male 680,069, female 635,428, native 910,072, foreign 405,425, white 1,309,618, colored 2,702, Chinese 16, Indians 3,161. Estimated increase 12 per cent.

TOPOGRAPHY, AREA, SOIL, PRODUCTS, ETC.—Extreme length N. and S. 298 miles, width 260 miles, area 54,450 sq. miles, 34,848,000 acres. Besides the great lakes Michigan and Superior the state contains Green Bay, Winnebago, Geneva, Devil's lake and innumerable other lakes in the central and northern sections of the state, of unsurpassed beauty, making the state a favorite place of summer resort. Much of state prairie, but enormous stretches of magnificent pine and hardwood timbers remain untouched. Soil excellent and adapted to farming, dairying and stock raising. Fruits grow and berries are a fine crop. Cranberries largely raised. Wheat the best crop, flax, buckwheat, hay, corn, oats staples. Extensive lead mines in Grant, Lafayette and Iowa counties, native copper in the north, in Crawford and Iowa counties. Iron ores in Dodge, Sauk, Jackson and Ashland counties. Ranks second in hops, third in barley and potatoes, fourth in rye and buckwheat, fifth in oats and agricultural implements. Improved land averages $18 and unimproved $10 per acre. Much government and railroad land yet untaken.

CLIMATE.—Temperature averages winter 20 deg., summer 71 deg., ranges from 32 deg. below zero to 95 deg. Rainfall 31 inches, including snow. Snows heavy, especially at north; spring late, summers short, falls pleasant. Milwaukee river frozen over an average of 105 days in year.

CHIEF CITIES.—Milwaukee, port of entry, great pork-packing and beer-brewing center, grain and wheat market; pop. 125,000 Madison (capital), pop. 12,063. Eau Claire, pop. 21,653; Fond du Lac, pop. 13,094; Oshkosh, 21,947; La Crosse, 21,212.

LEADING INDUSTRIES.— Lumbering, farming, mining, manufacturing, brewing, pork-packing, dairying, etc.

[For salaries of state officers, see page 439.]

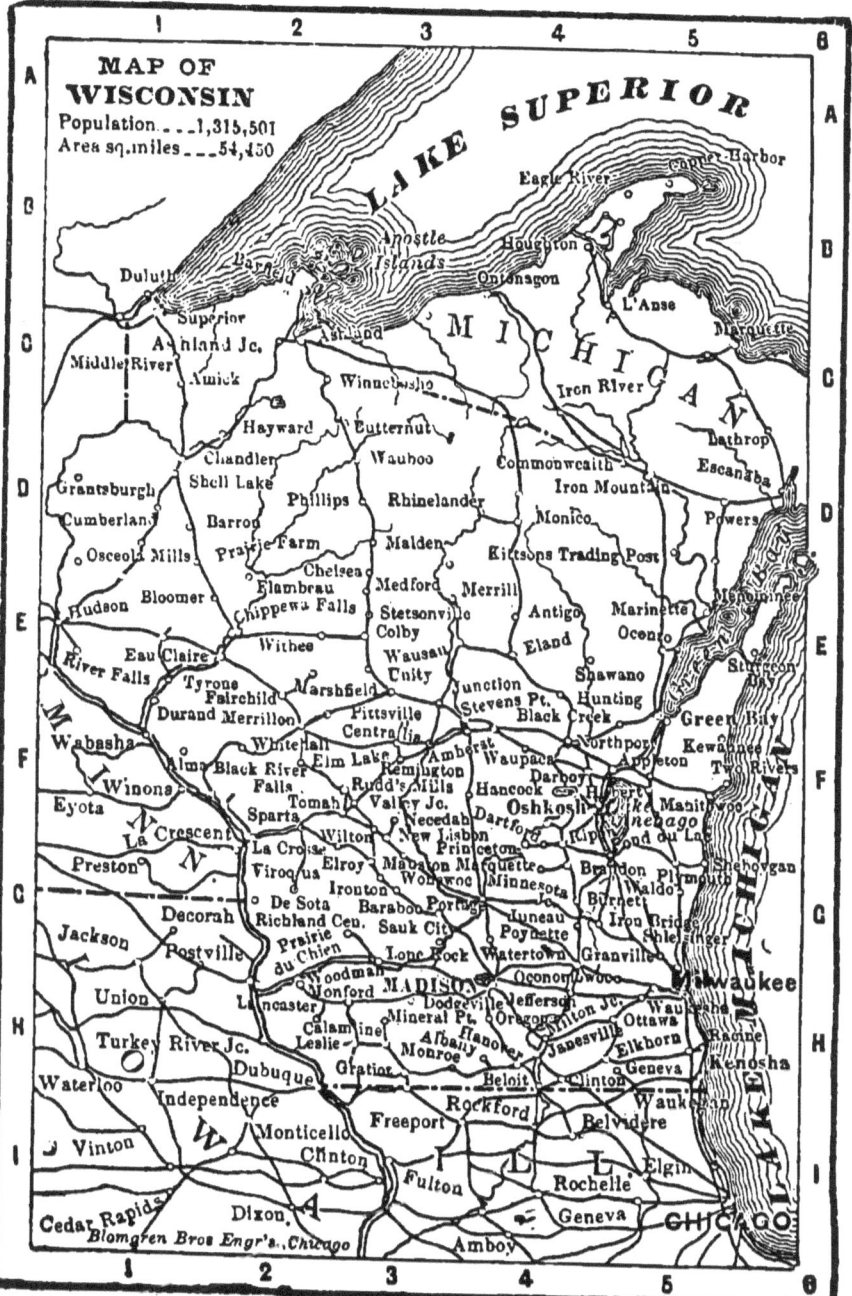

WYOMING.

First settlement Ft. Laramie, 1867. Organized as a territory from 1868. Number counties 9, all elections Tuesday after first Monday in Nov., number senators 12, representatives 24, sessions biennial, in even-numbered years, meeting second Tuesday in Jan., hold 60 days, terms of senators and representatives 2 years each; voters 10,180, native white 6,042, foreign white 3,199, colored 939. Good school system started, school age 7-21. Legal interest rate 12 per cent., by contract any rate. Miles of railroad 616.

POPULATION.—1880, 20,789, male 14,152, female 6,637, native 14,939, foreign 5,850, white 19,437, colored 298, Chinese 914, Indians 2,400. Estimated increase 29 per cent.

Length 350 miles, width 275 miles, area 97,575 sq. miles, 62,438,-000 acres. Surface traversed by Rocky Mountains, forming the continental divide, and is high and mountainous, varying in elevation from 4,800 to 12,000 feet. At the N. W. is the Yellowstone National Park, 3,600 sq. miles in area, and one of the greatest natural wonders of the continent. It varies from 6,000 to over 12,000 feet in elevation, and its scenery is one vast panorama. Along the streams and in the valleys are tracts of arable lands which may be made to produce prolifically with irrigation. Mountains, covered with forests of considerable extent, contain precious and base minerals in great deposits. Soil, where water can be had, is good, soil chiefly suited to grazing. Half the territory grazing land. Wheat, rye, oats and barley flourish, frost too frequent for corn. Water plentiful, game and fur-bearing animals numerous, iron ore abundant, mainly red hematite. Copper, lead, plumbago and petroleum found, gold in the Sweetwater country and near Laramie City, valuable deposits of soda in valley of the Sweetwater. Coal abundant and of good quality at Evanston, Carbon, Rock Springs and other points. Climate cold, severe in mountains, milder in valleys. Healthful, air pure, dry and bracing. Rainfall, 15 inches. Temperature averages, summer 66 deg., winter 18 deg., ranges from 31 deg. below to 80 deg. above. July warmest month, January coldest, latter averages 10 deg.

CHIEF CITIES.—Cheyenne (capital), pop. 4,500, Laramie City, pop. 3,800.

CHIEF INDUSTRIES.—Grazing, mining and agriculture, but little is done in manufacturing.

Salaries of Territorial Officers.

Governor...$2,600
Secretary.. 1,800
Treasurer..$800 and com.
Auditor.. 1,000
Superintendent of Public Inst........................... 400
Librarian... 400
Chief Justice... 3,000
Two Associate Justices.................................. 3,000
Senators and Representatives......$4 a day and 20 cents mileage

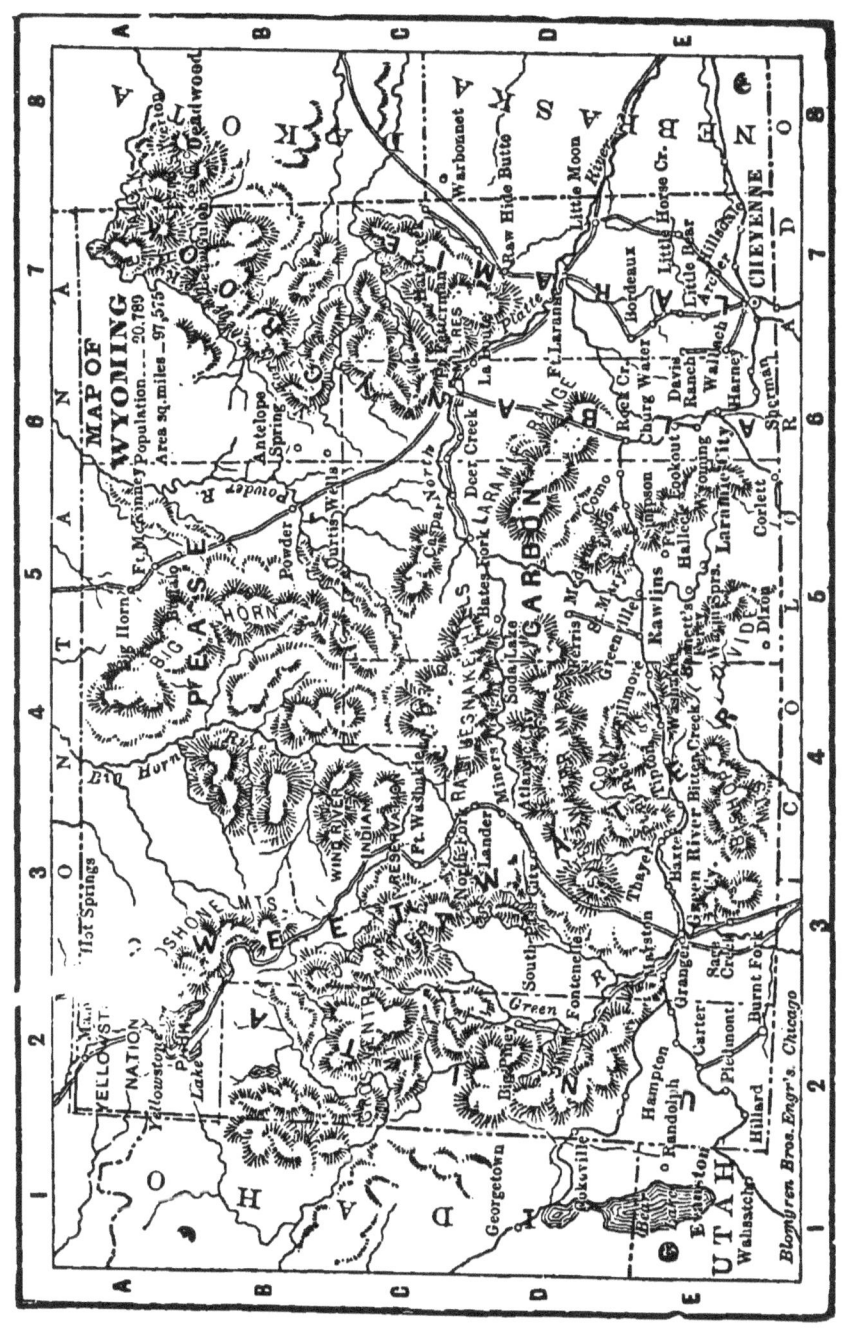

DISTRICT OF COLUMBIA.

Named for Columbus. Fixed as seat of U. S. government 1790 by act of Congress. Formed out of Washington Co., Md. (64 sq. miles). Government removed to District 1800. Captured by British 1814, and capitol, executive mansion and congressional library burned. Governed by Congress till 1871, when a legislative body of 33 (11 appointed by the president and 22 elected) was created. Executive officers still appointed by president. Officers appointed are paid by the United States, those elected by the District. Citizens of District have no vote for national officers. Schools superior. Legal interest 6 per cent., by contract 10, more forfeits entire interest. Population, 1880, 177,638. Miles railroad, 18. Surface made up of flats and hills. Similar in all features and products to Southern Maryland. Cities.—Washington (capital U.S.), pop. 147,307, Georgetown, pop. 12,576.

THE WHITE HOUSE AT WASHINGTON, D. C.

The White House, at Washington, D. C., is 170 feet long by 86 feet wide. The largest apartment, known as the east room, is 80 by 40 feet in dimension and 22 feet high. The adjoining blue room, finished in blue and gold, is devoted to receptions, diplomatic and social. The green and red rooms, so called from their finishing, are each 30 by 20 feet. The rooms on the second floor are occupied by the executive office and the apartments of the President's family.

THE WASHINGTON MONUMENT.

The corner-stone was laid by President Polk, July 4th, 1848, and December 6, 1884, the cap-stone was set in position. The foundations are 126½ feet square and 36 feet 8 inches deep. The base of the monument is 55 feet 1½ inches square, and the walls 15 feet ¼ inch thick. At the 500 foot mark, where the pyramidal top begins, the shaft is 34 feet 5½ inches square and the walls are 18 inches thick. The monument is made of blocks of marble 2 feet thick, and it is said there are over 18,000 of them. The height above the ground is 555 feet. The pyramidal top terminates in an aluminum tip, which is 9 inches high and weighs 100 ounces. The mean pressure of the monument is 5 tons per square foot, and the total weight, foundation and all, is nearly 81,000 tons. The door at the base, facing the capitol, is 8 feet wide and 16 feet high, and enters a room 25 feet square. An immense iron framework supports the machinery of the elevator, which is hoisted with steel wire ropes two inches thick. At one side begin the stairs, of which there are fifty flights, containing eighteen steps each. Five hundred and twenty feet from the base there are eight windows, 18x24 inches, two on each face. The area at the base of the pyramidal top is 1,187¼ feet, space enough for a six-room house, each room to be 12x16 feet. The Cologne Cathedral is 525 feet high; the pyramid of Cheops, 486; Strasburg Cathedral, 474; St. Peter's, at Rome, 448; the capitol at Washington, 306, and Bunker Hill monument, 221 feet. The Washington, monument is the highest structure in the world; total cost, $1,500,000.

Additional List Salaries of State Officers.

[For States not given in this list see Atlas Descriptive Matter.]

Arizona.—Governor $2,600, Secretary $1,800, Treasurer $1,000, Auditor $1,000, Superintendent of Public Instruction $2,000, Librarian $600, Chief Justice $3,000, Two Associate Justices $3,000, Senators and Representatives $4 per day and 20 cents mileage, Three District Judges $3,000, Collector of Internal Revenue $2,250, Two Deputy Collectors $1,600 to $1,700, Clerk $1,100, Surveyor General $2,500, Chief Clerk $2,400, Land Clerk $1,600, Land Copyist $1,200, Spanish Translator $2,500.

California.—Governor $6,000, Secretary of State $3,000, Treasurer $3,000, Comptroller $3,000, Superintendent of Public Instruction $3,000, Attorney General $3,000, Surveyor Gen. $3,000, State Librarian $3,000, District Judge $5,000, Senators and Representatives $8 per day, mileage 10c., and $25, Two Collectors Internal Revenue $3,125 to $4,500, Collector of Customs, San Francisco, $7,000, Pension Agent $4,000, Superintendent of Mint $4,500, Assayer $3,000, Melter and Refiner $3,000.

Georgia.—Governor $3,000, Secretary of State $2,000, Treasurer $2,000, Comptroller General $2,000, Attorney General $2,000, Commissioner Agriculture $2,500, Chief Justice $2,500, Associate Justices $2,500, Senators and Representatives $4 a day and mileage, 3 District Judges $3,500, District Superintendent Railway Service $2,500, Collector of Internal Revenue $2,500 to $3,125, 24 Deputy Collectors $300 to $1,700, Customs Surveyor $1,000 and fees.

Indiana.—Governor $5,000, Lieutenant Governor $8 a day, Secretary of State $2,000, Treasurer 3,000, Auditor $1,500, Attorney General $2,500, Superintendent of Public Instruction $2,500, Secretary Board of Agriculture $1,200, Librarian $1,200, Five Judges $4,000, Senators and Representatives $6 a day and 20 cents per mile, District Judge $3,500, Pension Agent $4,000, Six Collectors Internal Revenue $2,375 to $4,500, Surveyor Customs $1,000 and fees.

Iowa.—Governor $3,000, Lieutenant Governor $1,100, Secretary of State $2,200, Treasurer $2,200, Attorney General $1,500 and $5 a day, Superintendent of Public Instruction $2,200, Three Railway Commissioners $3,000, Librarian $1,500, Chief Justice $4,000 Four Associate Justices $4,000, Senators and Representatives $550 per year, Two District Judges $3,500, Pension Agent $4,000, 4 Collectors of Internal Revenue $2,500 to $4,500, Auditor $2,200.

Kentucky.—Governor $5,000, Secretary of State, $1,500, Treasurer $2,400, Auditor $2,500, Attorney General $500 and fees, Register Land Office $2,400, Commissioner of Agriculture $2,000, Insurance Commissioner $4,000, Three Railway Commissioners, $2,000, Chief Justice $5,000, Three Associate Justices, $5,000, Senators and Representatives $5 a day mileage 15 cents, District Judge $3,500, Pension Agent $4,000, Six Collectors Internal Revenue $4,500, 60 Deputy Collectors $300 to $2,000.

Louisiana.—Governor, $4,000, Lieutenant Governor $8 per day, Treasurer $2,000, Secretary of State $1,800, Auditor $2,500,

Attorney General $3,000, Adjutant General $2,000, Superintendent of Public Instruction $2,000, Commissioner of Agriculture and Immigration $2,000, Chief Justice $5,000, Four Associate Justices $5,000, Senators and Representatives $4 per day and mileage, Two District Judges $3,500 to $4,500, Collector of Customs New Orleans, $7,000.

Massachusetts.—Governor $5,000, Lieutenant Governor $2,000 Secretary of State $3,000, Treasurer $4,000, Auditor $2,500, Attorney General $4,000, Chief Justice $6,500, Six Associate Justices $6,000, District Judge $4,000, Senators and Representatives $650 per year, Pension Agent $4,000, Three Collectors of Internal Revenue $3,000 to $4,500, Collector of Customs, Boston, $8,000, Naval Officer $5,000.

Michigan.—Governor $1,000, Lieutenant Governor $3 a day, Secretary of State $800, Treasurer $1,000, Auditor General $2,000, Superintendent of Public Instruction $1,000, Adjutant General $1,000, Secretary Board of Agriculture $1,500, Insurance Commissioner $2,000, Railway Commissioner $2,500, Immigration Commissioner $2,000, Chief Justice $4,000, Senators and Representatives $3 a day and 10c. per mile, 2 District Judges $3,500, Pension Agent $4,000, Four Cols. Int. Rev. $3,875 to $2,625.

Missouri.—Governor $5,000, Secretary of State $3,000, Treasurer $3,000, Auditor $3,000, Attorney General $3,000, Adjutant General $2,000, Superintendent of Public Schools $3,000, Register of Lands $3,000, Three Railroad Commissioners $3,000, Supt. Insurance Department $4,000, Chief Justice $4,500, Senators and Representatives, $5 a day and mileage and $30, Two District Judges $3,500, Five Collectors of Internal Revenue $2,250, to $4,500, Surveyor of Customs, St. Louis, $5,000.

New York.—Governor $10,000 and house, Lieutenant Governor $5,000, Secretary of State $5,000, Treasurer $5,000, Comptroller $6,000, Attorney General $5,000, Chief Justice $7,500, Senators and Representatives $1,500, mileage 10 cents, Three District Judges $4,000, Postage Stamp Agent $2,500, Dep. Superintendent Railway Service $2,500, 12 Collectors Internal Revenue $2,750 to $4,500, Collector Customs, New York, $12,000, Superintendent Assay Office $4,500, Pension Agent $4,000.

Texas.—Governor $4,000, Lieutenant Governor $5 a day, Secretary of Sate $2,000, Treasurer $2,500, Attorney General $2,000, Adjutant General $2,000, Land Commissioners $2,500, Railroad Commissioners $3,000, Chief Justice $3,500, 2 Associate Justices $3,500, Senators and Representatives $5 a day and mileage, Three District Judge $3,500, Collectors of Internal Revenue $2,500 to $2,750, 17 Deputy Collectors $300 to $1,850.

Wisconsin.—Governor $5,000, Secretary of State $5,000, Treasurer $5,000, Attorney General $3,000, Railroad Commissioner $3,000. Chief Justice $5,000, Four Associate Justices $5,000, Two District Judges $3,500, Senators and Representatives $500 per year and 10c. mileage, Pension Agent $4,000, Indian Agent $1,500, Four Collectors Internal Revenue $4,500 to $2,750, 23 Deputy Collectors $1,800 to $300, Collector of Customs $1,000 and fees.

www.ingramcontent.com/pod-product-compliance
Lightning Source LLC
Chambersburg PA
CBHW020525300426
44111CB00008B/547